IMPORTANT!

HERE IS YOUR REGISTRATION CODE TO A[...]

YOUR PREMIUM McGRAW-HILL ONLINE R[...]

D0163732

For key premium online resources you need THIS CODE to gain access. Once the code is entered, you will be able to use the Web resources for the length of your course.

If your course is using **WebCT** or **Blackboard**, you'll be able to use this code to access the McGraw-Hill content within your lecturer's online course.

Access is provided if you have purchased a new book. If the registration code is missing from this book, the registration screen on our Website, and within your WebCT or Blackboard course, will tell you how to obtain your new code.

Registering for McGraw-Hill Online Resources

TO gain access to your McGraw-Hill web resources simply follow the steps below:

1. USE YOUR WEB BROWSER TO GO TO: **http://www.mhhe.com/pang2e**

2. CLICK ON **FIRST TIME USER**.

3. ENTER THE REGISTRATION CODE* PRINTED ON THE TEAR-OFF BOOKMARK ON THE RIGHT.

4. AFTER YOU HAVE ENTERED YOUR REGISTRATION CODE, CLICK **REGISTER**.

5. FOLLOW THE INSTRUCTIONS TO SET-UP YOUR PERSONAL UserID AND PASSWORD.

6. WRITE YOUR UserID AND PASSWORD DOWN FOR FUTURE REFERENCE. KEEP IT IN A SAFE PLACE.

TO GAIN ACCESS to the McGraw-Hill content in your lecturer's **WebCT** or **Blackboard** course simply log in to the course with the UserID and Password provided by your lecturer. Enter the registration code exactly as it appears in the box to the right when prompted by the system. You will only need to use the code the first time you click on McGraw-Hill content.

Thank you, and welcome to your McGraw-Hill online Resources!

0-07-308070-5 T/A PANG: MULTICULTURAL EDUCATION 2/E

REGISTRATION CODE

T6AW-GIML-G5WT-Z46X-0O5P

SECOND EDITION

Multicultural Education

A Caring-Centered, Reflective Approach

VALERIE OOKA PANG
San Diego State University

Boston   Burr Ridge, IL   Dubuque, IA   Madison, WI   New York   San Francisco   St. Louis
Bangkok   Bogotá   Caracas   Kuala Lumpur   Lisbon   London   Madrid   Mexico City
Milan   Montreal   New Delhi   Santiago   Seoul   Singapore   Sydney   Taipei   Toronto

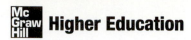

The McGraw-Hill Companies

Higher Education

MULTICULTURAL EDUCATION: A CARING-CENTERED, REFLECTIVE APPROACH

Published by McGraw-Hill, a business unit of The McGraw-Hill Companies, Inc., 1221 Avenue of the Americas, New York, NY, 10020. Copyright © 2005, 2001, by The McGraw-Hill Companies, Inc. All rights reserved. No part of this publication may be reproduced or distributed in any form or by any means, or stored in a database or retrieval system, without the prior written consent of The McGraw-Hill Companies, Inc., including, but not limited to, in any network or other electronic storage or transmission, or broadcast for distance learning.

Some ancillaries, including electronic and print components, may not be available to customers outside the United States.
This book is printed on acid-free paper.
1 2 3 4 5 6 7 8 9 0 DOC/DOC 0 9 8 7 6 5 4
ISBN 0 07 282788 2
Publisher: *Emily Barosse*
Sponsoring editor: *Allison McNamara*
Senior developmental editor: *Cara Harvey*
Developmental editor: *Beth Kaufman*
Senior marketing manager: *Pamela S. Cooper*
Project manager: *Ruth Smith*
Production supervisor: *Janean Utley*
Design coordinator: *George Kokkonas*
Interior and cover design: *Kay Fulton*
Cover image: *Alamy photos*
Media project manager: *Kathleen Boylan*
Permissions coordinator: *Karyn Morrison*
Typeface: *10.5/12 Sabon*
Compositor: *Carlisle Communications, Ltd.*
Printer: *R. R. Donnelley and Sons Inc.*

Library of Congress Cataloging-in-Publication Data
Pang, Valerie Ooka,
    Multicultural education : a caring-centered, reflective approach/Valerie Ooka Pang.—
2nd ed.
        p. cm.
    Includes bibliographical references and index.
    ISBN 0-07-282788-2 (softcover : alk. paper)
    1. Multicultural education—United States. 2. Curriculum planning—United States. 3.
Prejudices—Study and teaching—United States. I. Title.
LC1099.3.P35 2005
370.117—dc22

                                                    2004044829

www.mhhe.com

Photos: courtesy of the author

Dedication

This work is dedicated to Jenn, Matt, Gerry, Debbie, Kathy, Cheryl, Karen, Trish, Naomi, Kyle, Andy, Ariana, Cameron, Mirei, Connor, Nicole, and Sophie.

Special Dedication

To Carl Masami Ooka and Marie Horiuchi Ooka

Brief Contents

Contents

CHAPTER 5   Aren't Mary and Michael Too Young to Be Prejudiced?   146

CHAPTER 6   How Can I Look beneath the Surface for Prejudice in Schools?   176

About the Author

VALERIE OOKA PANG is a professor in the School of Teacher Education at San Diego State University. She was a first- and second-grade teacher in rural and urban schools.

This is a revision of her book on Multicultural Education. In addition, Dr. Pang was senior editor of a text called *Struggling to Be Heard: The Unmet Needs of Asian Pacific American Children,* published by State University of New York Press. It is the only multidisciplinary text on Asian Pacific American children and was awarded honorable mention by the Gustavus Myers Center for the Study of Bigotry and Human Rights at Boston University.

Due to her work in Multicultural Education, social studies education, and teacher education, Dr. Pang has been a consultant for corporations such as Sesame Street, Fox Children's Network, Family Communications (producer of *Mr. Roger's Neighborhood*), McGraw-Hill, and Scott Foresman.

Dr. Pang has published in a variety of journals, including *Harvard Educational Review, The Kappan, Journal of Teacher Education, Action in Teacher Education, Educational Forum, Theory and Research in Social Education, Social Education, Equity and Excellence, and Multicultural Education.*

She was a senior fellow at the Annenberg Institute for School Reform at Brown University. She was honored with the 1997 Distinguished Scholar Award from the American Educational Research Association's (AERA) Standing Committee on the Role and Status of Minorities in Education. Dr. Pang has also received the Outstanding Teaching Award in the Liberal Studies Program at San Diego State University. In addition, she founded the Multicultural Education Infusion Center at San Diego State University, which provided professional development for university professors in teacher education.

Her own children are pursuing careers in immunology, engineering, and law.

 # Preface

Schools can be places of great hope, mediocrity, or severe oppression. I wrote this book with the hope of providing insights for current and future educators about the importance of creating caring and equitable educational environments.

Students that I know thrive in classrooms where teachers care and believe in them. They also learn more effectively when teachers build upon their cultural and experiential knowledge. This book is founded upon three foundational theories that emphasize democracy, diversity, culture, and community: care theory (ethic of care), education for democracy (progressive education), and the sociocultural theory of learning.

The Goals and Foundations of This Book

In this book, I encourage readers to explore and think about how they can make changes in their current and future classrooms—changes that are based on strong philosophical orientations, a clear understanding of schools as social systems, and the importance of compassion and social justice in that endeavor. The book is also written to encourage current and future teachers to build communities of care with other educators, students, parents, and community members.

People utilize a variety of "lenses" when looking at issues. For example, Martin Luther King, Jr.'s, orientation was heavily based upon civil rights and his religious beliefs. A primary lens utilized within this book is *ethic of care*—a moral commitment to care for and teach all students. In my work with children, I have found that most seek and respond to caring human connection. Older students also value trusting relationships with teachers who believe in them. The relationships that teachers and students create are critical in the learning process because these relationships form the context and motivation for growth.

Additional lenses that form my belief system include *culture, community, and social justice*. Culture is critical because each student develops within a complex cultural context. In addition, learning occurs within a social environment in which there are continuous interactions with others. These interactions can serve to extend or clarify a person's thinking. When students and teachers form a community based on social justice and compassion, they develop a unity devoted to building an equitable society (Gibson 1999).

Finally, I am committed to creating a society built on social justice. We are members of a democracy, and, as such, all of us—teachers and students—need to develop higher-order thinking skills that will allow us to address complex social and personal issues. Today more than ever, we must challenge oppression with compassion, collaboration, and courage—whether in schools or the community in general.

Text Approach and Organization

I wrote this book *in a personal style* that encourages current and future educators to *reflect* on their educational practices and philosophy. Because of its personal, reader-friendly style and caring-centered framework, this book is unique within the Multicultural Education field. The text also utilizes *an applied, real-life approach.* It conveys many course-related concepts through the use of personal stories, case studies, comic strips, photographs, and teacher voices. Modeling is one of the most powerful tools that teachers have, and the book tries to present many real examples of what occurs in effective, culturally meaningful classrooms.

In terms of text organization, the book is divided into five sections:

Part One: A Culturally Relevant and Caring Teacher.

Part Two: Confronting Prejudice in Ourselves and Our Schools: The Challenge of Change.

Part Three: Multicultural Education: Framework and Principles.

Part Four: Creating a Caring and Culturally Meaningful Classroom.

Part Five: Personal Professional Development.

Each of the five sections contains one or more chapters that use questions as their titles. Questions are used to focus reader attention on key concerns. For example, the title of Chapter 2 is "Why Is Culture Important?" This question encourages the reader to reflect on a vital issue (culture) that affects curriculum and instruction.

Text Content New to the Second Edition

I would like to highlight some specific examples of important new and unique text content that can be found within the second edition:

Part One

Chapters 1 and 2 in Part One lay the foundation for the rest of the text. **Chapter 1** is entitled "Why Multicultural Education?" This chapter explains the circumstances that prompted me to seek out principles of Multicultural Education in my own teaching. In addition, I explain the theoretical framework that guides Caring-Centered Multicultural Education. This framework is not only dedicated to good teaching, but it is also committed to an educational philosophy that utilizes *care theory,* also known as the *ethic of care,* as its foundation. The framework calls for change on an individual, school, and societal level. This chapter is designed to motivate the reader to think about the purposes of schools and how to provide the best education for students. It extends the discussion of Caring-Centered Multicultural Education that was initially presented in the first edition of the book. This chapter includes the important work of Dr. Vanessa Siddle Walker, who studied the Caswell County Training School, a segregated school founded on beliefs in caring, social justice, and culture.

Chapter 2 of the book (also found within Part One) discusses the impact of culture. Culture is all around us, but people do not often recognize it. In order for teachers to reach every student, they must consider the influence of culture in teaching and learning. The description of culture is presented early in the book to initiate reflection from the reader about its complex nature. People's worldviews evolve from the values, behaviors, beliefs, history, and many other aspects of their culture(s). Often, culture and its components are invisible to one who lives within its daily workings. As educator and author Jack Nelson shared with me, "Cultures define us and we define culture. We come to know and absorb our own culture's values and behaviors, and we recognize differences from others through education. It is the 'multi' part of multicultural that makes multicultural education so important" (Nelson 2000). These first two chapters describe the power of culture and how it is created, transmitted, and sustained.

One of the highlights of Chapter 2 is a new section written by a teacher about working with Somali refugee students in Ohio. Educator Merry Merryfield presents critical examples of how conflicts and cultural issues arose when many new students from Somalia began to attend school in the United States. The cultural expectations of Somali students and their teachers in school often clashed.

Part Two

Part Two of the book presents four chapters (**Chapters 3–6**) that describe individual and social oppression such as racism, gender bias, classism, and homophobia. One of the most difficult challenges that many of us face is confronting our own racism, biases, and participation in institutional oppression. It is usually easier to identify one's own biased remarks toward others than to identify accepted school practices that harm students. It may be difficult to see how some educational practices are damaging to students because these practices have been seen as legitimate and rational for many years. For example, Gibson (1998) provides data that demonstrate how standards are "veiled literacy tests" because from standards come tests. The tests that measure student knowledge of standards then become even more powerful than the standards because the understanding of students will be seen as measured by these tests. Secondly, students who have middle-class and ethnic backgrounds similar to the individuals who wrote the standards are more likely to do well on the standardized examinations. The standards and their tests are extremely influential, although, like the *National History Standards* (National Center for History in Schools 1994), they represent a "common legacy" and are nationalistic and elitist in their orientation (Gibson 1998).

Part Two of the book also covers how people and children develop prejudice and bias toward others. Research is presented to describe how prejudice and social oppression can impact the development of one's racial identity and sense of affiliations. How did the concept of race arise? Is race an accurate biological concept or a sociopolitical one? These are questions addressed in **Chapter 3.** In addition, there are many social issues that people may not have had the opportunity to think about. For example, classism is an issue that is difficult for some to understand. In Chapter 3, the author describes many who fall into a group referred to as the working poor. The people in this situation work full time, but are paid only minimum wage and cannot financially sustain themselves because their incomes are too low.

Often, individuals do not see their own prejudices because the prejudices are viewpoints held by many others in the community. A good example of this is White privilege. This dynamic is thoroughly discussed in **Chapter 4.** Moving to identity development, **Chapter 5** discusses how children learn prejudice and develop racial identity. Current and future teachers will benefit from using the antibias strategies explained in this chapter. **Chapter 6** provides examples of prejudice and discrimination in schools. The chapter explains the concept of the culture of power—a hegemonic culture that attempts to choke off the divergent ethnic cultures of students, or convey negative messages about various social differences due to gender, racial differences, class, religious beliefs, and sexual orientation. Several real case studies from schools are included in this chapter. One of the issues covered is Native American mascots. The extensive description of Native American mascots gives several viewpoints within the framework of a culturally and caring community. Because one of the major goals of this book is teacher reflection within a democracy, the reader is asked to "Take a Stand" on the issue. (See the section "New Pedagogical Features" for a detailed description of the new text feature entitled "Take a Stand.")

Part Three

Part Three of the book presents an in-depth and expanded discussion of Caring-Centered Multicultural Education. I present examples of four types of teachers that I see in schools: the assimilationist, the human relations, the social action, and the caring-centered. These teachers have different goals, although some of their actions may be similar. The comparison of the four types of teachers is described in **Chapter 7.** Because an issues-centered approach to education is a component of the text's framework, **Chapter 8** includes discussion of several hot topics. These topics present controversial issues such as the national uses of racial categories in U.S. data collection processes. It is critical that all teachers consider these social issues and think about how the issues may affect their classrooms. One such teacher who has spent a lifetime examining issues of oppression and compassion is Linda Christiansen. As a caring-centered English teacher in Oregon, Christiansen is an excellent role model who provides important insights into how to actually create a classroom in which culture is affirmed and students thrive and are successful.

Part Four

Part Four (**Chapters 9–11**) is devoted to discussing culturally relevant teaching. How can teachers create a curriculum that reflects and resonates with their students who may come from a multitude of cultural communities? How can relevance and meaning become the core of the teacher's pedagogy? A number of research projects carefully describe how ethnic, family, and neighborhood contexts can be integrated into the teaching strategies utilized and curriculum content presented in schools. The work of Luis Moll and his colleagues' project Funds of Knowledge is an example of how the lives of bilingual students can form the basis for a meaningful and successful academic curriculum.

As Moll's research has demonstrated, one of the vital areas of culture is language. Teachers need to understand how a second language like English is learned. A brand new **Chapter 9** centers on English language learners and how they acquire language. The chapter includes two case studies written by teachers who work with bilingual students. The first case study by Kathee Christiansen presents the needs of a young deaf child who was faced with the huge task of learning Spanish, English, and American Sign Language in order to communicate in his family and school settings. In the other case study, Evangelina Bustamente Jones discusses strategies she used in teaching writing to Spanish-speaking college students. She provides both attitudinal and concrete suggestions.

In **Chapters 10 and 11,** there are many curriculum strategies that are recommended and can be used in K–12 classrooms. I suggest the natural integration of the following: personal experiences of students, role models of students, culturally grounded stories and songs, cultural expressions, multiple perspectives, include cultural knowledge in subject area content, and community issues. Several issues-centered units are also included within these chapters. All students can benefit from a culturally meaningful classroom.

Part Five and End-of-Text Epilogue

Finally, Part Five is devoted to personal and professional development. In order for all educators to continue to grow, they must continue to reflect upon their practices and examine practices in light of their belief systems. If they have chosen social justice and caring as core values, do their instructional practices mirror these beliefs? Teachers must also work to increase their knowledge base of content area disciplines and examine their assessment tools. In **Chapter 12,** the author provides a rubric that teachers can use to examine the effectiveness and meaningfulness of their teaching. An important addition is a discussion of crucial educational principles developed by Dr. James Banks and his colleagues. In addition, this chapter presents six components of a caring-centered school that integrate the importance of caring, culture, and community throughout the entire school structure.

The **Epilogue** is designed for additional personal reflection. Reflection refers to the importance of teachers continually reevaluating their teaching. These efforts toward change can produce new levels of understanding of teaching and learning and overall reform in school policies and structures.

New Pedagogical Features

Many colleagues reviewed the first edition of this text and provided excellent suggestions for improvement. Based on their recommendations, *I have tried to make this second edition a more effective learning tool for students taking the Multicultural Education course.* The text now contains a useful and comprehensive pedagogical structure. In each chapter, students will find the following new text features that encourage mastery of course content and personal reflection:

- **Chapter Main Ideas outlines** can be found at the beginning of each chapter, and serve as an outline of the key topics that will be covered within the chapter.

- **Chapter Overview** paragraphs, located at the beginning of each chapter, provide a quick narrative summary of the chapter's main themes.

- Helpful **Marginal Notes** found throughout each chapter reinforce key points within the chapter narrative.

- **Case Studies** spotlight a real educational figure, institution, or situation. These case studies illustrate key themes within the chapter using real-life experiences related to multicultural education.

- **New Photos and Cartoons** enliven the text and help students apply course concepts in a fun and visual way.

- **OLC Connection boxes**—Within the text, Online Learning Center Connection boxes describe useful Web resources related to chapter content, such as Web links or Web-based readings. Students and instructors can go directly to the text's OLC and connect to these Web-based resources from there. Please visit the text Online Learning Center to check out all the great resources included for each chapter.

- **Take a Stand boxes** present a hot or controversial educational issue and encourage readers to comprehensively examine their own biases and consider multiple perspectives before making a decision. These boxes are also great tools for starting class discussion.

- **Chapter Summaries** reiterate the key themes and findings within each chapter and allow students to check their understanding of key chapter concepts.

- **Reflection Activities,** located at the end of each chapter, make excellent class assignments, homework assignments, journaling activities, or portfolio activities. More Reflection Activities and an electronic template for their submission to the instructor can be found on the text's Online Learning Center (www.mhhe.com/pang2e).

- **Key Terms lists** can be found at the end of each chapter with their accompanying page numbers from the text.

- An **OLC Chapter Review** at the end of each chapter reminds students to visit the text's Online Learning Center (www.mhhe.com/pang2e) to utilize its numerous study tools and resources. Each chapter includes quizzing features, Web-based resources that accompany each chapter, interactive reflection activities, student study tools, and much more.

Supplements Package

The second edition of *Multicultural Education* is accompanied by expanded ancillary materials:

- The second edition of *Multicultural Education and the Internet* by Paul Gorski accompanies each copy of the text. This brief text provides practical guidance for using the Internet as a tool for teaching in a multicultural manner.

- **OLC** **Student and Instructor Online Learning Centers at www.mhhe.com/ pang2e** contain a wealth of resources for taking and teaching the course. This website includes many special features that extend the content and goals of the text.

- An **Instructor's Resource CD-ROM with Instructor's Manual, Test Bank,** and **Computerized Test Bank** is available to adopters of the text.

- *Folio***Live** is an online portfolio tool that you can use to create an electronic portfolio in three easy steps. (1) Use a template to create a homepage; (2) choose to create a custom framework or framework to structure your portfolio, and (3) add the artifacts to build your portfolio by uploading existing files (from Word to PowerPoint to Video), linking to artifacts posted elsewhere on the Web, or creating an artifact through *Folio*Live embedded forms. Go to www.foliolive.com to learn more about this product or to purchase a one-year account.

Conclusion

The value of this text is what the reader does after thinking about the issues raised in the book. I hope that all teachers continue to seek more effective ways to reach all their students. This book is one of hope—the hope that teachers, along with their students and parents, will work together to form bonds of trust that lead to the creation of exceptional schools. Bonds of humanity and caring propelled the civil rights movement in the 1960s. Today, these same bonds can propel us toward definitive actions that will address the damaging social practices of inequities due to race, class, ethnicity, gender, and other differences in schools and society.

Acknowledgements

I would like to thank the following friends and colleagues for all their help, inspiration, and support:

Ramón Valle, Jack Nelson, Gwen Nelson, Pat Larke, Geneva Gay, Merry Merryfield, Wayne Ross, Mary McCabe, Evangelina Bustamente Jones, Joyce King, Hassimi Maigi, Angela Camozzi, Jaime Lujan, Cynthia Park, Myluong Tran, Russell Young,

David Strom, Eveline Takahashi, Karen Toyohara, Cathy Pohan, Kathee Christiansen, Jenni Pang, Matthew Pang, Gerry Pang, Joe Newsome, Sylvia Hernandez, Anne Graves, James Banks, Olga Welch, Carole Hahn, Jackie Jordan Irvine, Judith Singer, Alan Singer, Kevin Pang, Dennice Rousey, Larry Frase, Lionel "Skip" Meno, Jessica Gordon Nembhard, Rich Gibson, Amber Goslee, Francisco Rios, Elizabeth Amezcua, Ernest Anderson, Julie Chun, Tamara Coffin, Amanda Erhardt, Brandon Fuentes, Patrick Funk, Vanessa Geno, Luis Granada, Illian Guzman, Rosa Hernandez, Lisa Kessler, Peter Madden, Romero Octavio, Angela Wright, James Anaya, Cheri Barlow, Amanda Jones, Kelly Kohl, Julia Kulla-Mader, Betany Porter, Charles Scholl, Jenny Silva, Colleen Francke, Ariana Erwood, Cameron Erwood, Connor Howard, Nicole Howard, Sophie Hofman, Kristen Cartwright, Katrina Perez, Andrea Houston, Catherine Ray, Dawn Davis, Ana R. Kissed, Gerry Pang, Marc Pruyn, David Hursh, Kevin Vinson, Steve Fluery, Neal Fogelhut, Ann Porter, Bernie Porter, Karen Swisher, Valerie Grayson, Rick Stewart, Jackie Brunner, Juan Rivera, Muriel Green, Ron Torretto, Lucille Hee, Anna Perliss, Nancy Michalowski, Gene Sommers, Neil Kooiman, Maria Marshall, Suzanne Negoro, Lisa Dillman, Renee de la Torre, Heidi Mellander, Cameron Erwood, Matthew Heibel, Connor Howard, Nicole Marie Howard, Anthony Evans, Michael Small, Christina Lovaas, Jennifer Adams, Jennifer Covell, Leslie Warren, Ronie Daniels, Jennifer Stahl, Arturo Salazar, Krystal Rodriguez, Hindeliza Flores, Margie Gallego, and John Goodlad.

Many others also shared their thoughts and beliefs with me. I appreciate the contributions of my students, colleagues, and teachers who have inspired me such as Dennis Martinen, who was my high school math teacher. In addition, I would like to thank Beth Kaufman, editor at McGraw-Hill, to whom I am extremely indebted for nourishing the completion of the original book and the second edition. It was her belief in my work that encouraged me to write the initial book using the ethic of care as a foundational theory. She was also the only editor with whom I talked who supported my use of comic strips. I believe the comic strips are very useful because they can provide powerful messages for teachers and students to consider while using humor. I am also extremely grateful to Cara Harvey who saw this edition to its completion.

Three other invaluable people who have guided my work are Geneva Gay, Jack Nelson, and Ray Valle. They continue to challenge me to more clearly articulate my ideas. Their advice and mentoring have been key to my continued growth. Another person who has been instrumental in my professional growth is Stan Sue. As a graduate student many, many, many years ago, he introduced me to the importance of mental health. Although my area is not psychology, his work provided unique insights and led me to realize the importance of the classroom environment and development of self-esteem in students. In addition, this book would not have been possible without the extensive assistance of Ruth Smith, who guided the production of this second edition.

Many people have shared their insights with me. Some read over initial drafts of chapters. Others provided suggestions and new ideas. I am very grateful to many people who have supported my work for many years. I would also like to thank the following people who have reviewed the manuscript throughout its creation:

Michael O. Afolayan, *Carroll College*

Wendy W. Brandon, *Rollins College*

Terry J. Burant, *Marquette University*

Karen Carrier, *Northern Illinois University*

Richard Gordon, *California State University, Dominguez Hills*

Charles Hancock, *Ohio State University*

Samuel Hinton, *Eastern Kentucky University*

Heather M. Pleasants, *University of Delware*

Denise St. Patrick-Bell, *Broward Community College*

Dale Brent Warby, *Community College of Southern Nevada*

References

Gibson, Rich. 1998. History on trial in the heart of darkness. *Theory and Research in Social Education* 26, no. 4: 549–64.

———. 1999. Pay no attention to that man behind the curtain. *Theory and Research in Social Education* 27, no. 4: 541–601.

National Center for History in the Schools. 1994. *National standards for world history: Exploring paths to the present.* Los Angeles, Calif.: Author.

Nelson, Jack. 2000. Private interview. San Diego, March 17.

A Culturally Relevant and Caring Teacher

Why Multicultural Education?

CHAPTER MAIN IDEAS

- *How Did I Become Interested in Multicultural Education?*
- *Who Are We? Diversity in Our Nation and Schools*
- *What Does It Mean to Be a Culturally Relevant Teacher?*
- *Culturally Relevant Teaching: Connecting to Student Knowledge*
- *Caring-Centered Multicultural Education*
- *Care Theory: The Power of a Caring-Centered Teacher*

- *The Sociocultural Theory of Learning: What's Culture Got to Do with Schooling?*
- *Education for Democracy: Schools as Laboratories of Democracy and Community*
- *Testing in a Caring, Socially Responsible School*
- *The Power of One Caring Teacher: The Story of John Leguizamo*

CHAPTER OVERVIEW

The purpose of this chapter is to encourage the reader to begin thinking about the importance of multicultural education and how students arrive at school from many cultures. In addition, the chapter introduces the framework for Caring-Centered Multicultural Education based on the work of scholars such as Vygotsky, Dewey, Gay, Siddle Walker, Noddings, Nussbaum, and others.

How Did I Become Interested in Multicultural Education?

My interest in Multicultural Education began many years ago when I was 20 years old. My first position was at a predominantly Black-neighborhood elementary school in a large urban district. It was March and I had just received my bachelor's degree in education from a small private university. I felt I was ready to tackle the problems of the world. My first teaching assignment was in a school of 300 children; 93 percent of the students were Black, 3 percent were Asian and Native American, and 4 percent of the youngsters were European American. All my students were either on reduced-cost or free lunch.

Of the 14 teachers at the school, only three had more than six years of teaching experience, seventy-five percent of us were women, and many of us had been teaching for fewer than three years. The upper-grade teachers fought an underlying atmosphere of frustration and hopelessness.

Most of the staff didn't think that I, a relatively quiet, young, and barely five-foot-tall Asian American woman, would make it at this tough neighborhood school. The week after I took the job, the principal mentioned to me, "We had a knifing in the parking lot last year, so be sure to lock your car." I was definitely a greenhorn.

Right away, I realized that I knew little about the lives of the students in my first-grade class. Although my apartment was only five miles from the school, it was as if I lived in another city. The good news was that I finished the year and taught another full year at this school. The bad news was that *I wasn't prepared* to teach in a culturally diverse school. Fortunately, the students were patient and forgiving, although I made many mistakes. In those 16 months, I learned more from the children than they learned from me.

Even though I wanted to assist children in becoming the best they could be, I was unprepared to teach in a school where the life experiences of children were different from my own. I taught the way I had been taught and socialized. For example, the district had chosen reading materials that weren't suited for most of the children in my class. The students spoke Ebonics (Black English vernacular), but the district mandated the use of a highly phonetic commercial reading series for the primary grades. The basal reader was built upon the phonemes and semantic structure of standard English. The methods used at that time were mechanical and did not encourage students to make their own meaning out of the text. The stories in the texts were about a boy named Sam who carried around a ham and had little to do with the lives of my students. The reading selections used word families, but the stories did not make much sense.

Upon reflection, I realized that I was teaching students how to decode without teaching them comprehension skills. I was also asking the children to learn a new dialect of English while simultaneously trying to teach them to read standard English. The problems were my approach and the textbooks, not the kids. I had never thought about *myself* as being culturally disadvantaged. At that time, it was a common practice in education to label low-income, culturally diverse children as culturally disadvantaged. Now I know that *schools* that operated on these beliefs were culturally disadvantaged institutions because many teachers did not understand the life experiences or background of students. The deficiency was not in the students; rather the educational system was based on a mainstream way of life and teachers often saw students of color as being deficient. No one questioned the way schools were organized or the knowledge that was taught. However, thinking about the negative beliefs that were embedded in schools, I came to understand that children are children. They come to school with a rich knowledge of their cultures and neighborhoods. They have hard-working parents. At the time, I didn't understand or value the students' shared life experiences and I didn't know how to make school meaningful.

After teaching for several months, I recognized I had little knowledge about my students or the community. I began to search out various African American community groups and read about African American and Native American history. I also knew it was important for me to earn the respect of parents and students. I hadn't grown up in the school neighborhood and the parents didn't know if they could trust me, so I visited many students at home and regularly called parents in order to get to know them. Out of 20 children in my classroom, I had three Native American students, one European American child, and 16 African American youngsters. All of the children, regardless of their ethnic backgrounds, spoke Ebonics and were bright and eager to learn. I began to understand that I held misconceptions about the community and didn't know what the critical issues were in the neighborhood. Parents slowly began to trust me because I cared and was honest. I made mistakes, but the parents were very open-hearted because they knew that I was a new teacher. In fact, they were extremely accessible. Jimmy's mom told me to call her in the morning because she worked in the late afternoon. I called Lisa's mother at work at the telephone company in the evening to give her an update on Lisa's reading progress. Cecilia's grandma came in regularly to read to small groups of children in the classroom.

I wish I had been a more effective teacher. I didn't know where to begin. What did I need to learn? What changes did I need to make to be a better teacher? My early experiences taught me that I needed to understand the role culture played in learning. It was clear that I needed to learn about Multicultural Education because knowledge gained from this field would help me become a more effective teacher. I knew that a good teacher would be able to reach all students. This is how my interest in Multicultural Education began.

 ## Case Study

DID WE FAIL ROSEMARY?: YEARS LATER

Many years later my commitment to Multicultural Education was dramatically affirmed. I was an adjunct professor at a university in the same large urban city where I landed my first job as a first-grade teacher. I often took teachers on field trips. On one trip, we went to a public high school, one of only two public institutions in the nation devoted to the schooling of Native American students. As the vice principal led my class through the buildings, I noticed a female student, obviously pregnant, walking toward us. There was something familiar in her eyes.

As she passed by, I realized the student was Rosemary. I remembered her as a scrawny little six-year-old in my first-grade class 14 years ago. I asked the counselor about her. Rosemary was 20 years old and trying to earn her high school diploma. She had a toddler who attended the high school day care and another child on the way. I remembered her as a spunky, curious, loving six-year-old, and although I didn't know what had happened during the past 14 years, I could see that life had not been easy on her. The energy and sparkle in her eyes were no longer there. The counselor was concerned because he didn't think that Rosemary would finish her high school degree before her 21st birthday. Public funding for her education would cease on that day.

I kept asking myself, "What happened to Rosemary? In first grade, she was an excited learner who looked forward to school. Did I fail Rosemary? Did schools fail Rosemary? Did society fail Rosemary? Did her parents fail Rosemary?" However, Rosemary still had the drive to get an education and that's why I saw her after so many years at that high school. She hadn't given up.

Seeing Rosemary reminded me how important our job is. I felt as if we as a community may have lost some of Rosemary's dreams and enthusiasm that I saw 14 years earlier. She was trying hard to get an education, and I believe Multicultural Education staff development for teachers could have assisted her educators in creating a more effective learning environment.

Culture was important to Rosemary, as shown by the choices she made. Rosemary was enrolled in the urban district's only high school that focused on the needs of Native Americans. She had her daughter in the Little Eaglet Daycare at the school. Rosemary obviously felt a kinship with and connection to the school community. Maybe if there had been teachers along the way who could have integrated more about Native American culture such as history, community guest speakers, and literature into the school curriculum, Rosemary would have finished her studies when she was younger. I wished I had done a better job in affirming her cultural identity and infusing the cultural knowledge she valued into the curriculum so that schooling had been more meaningful to her.

We, as a society, struggle today with providing all students with an effective and successful education. Probably a multiplicity of events that Rosemary grappled with led to her dropping out of school several times. She was not only a young Native American female, but she was also a member of a family with few financial resources. However, I think there are many other students like Rosemary who would benefit from an education that integrates culture into the curriculum and instruction.

Multicultural Education as a field rose out of the Civil Rights Movement of the 1960s when citizens pointed to the lack of consistency between our ideals of equal educational opportunity and the reality of a severe achievement gap between students from oppressed groups and mainstream communities. Multicultural Education as a field calls for total school reform to address these inequities (Banks 2002; Grant and Sleeter 1998; Gay 2000), and many beliefs are based on the work of John Dewey, the educational philosopher.

When Rosemary was a student in schools, many teachers did not believe culture was important; however, today many districts all over the country are integrating Multicultural and Bilingual Education into their schools because of the great diversity of our national student population. The next section describes our country's diversity. ❀

Who Are We? Diversity in Our Nation and Schools

The culturally diverse population in our schools represents a long reality of diversity in what is now known as the continental United States, even before European explorers reached the Americas. For example, in 1492 when Columbus landed in San Salvador, an island in the Bahamas, there were more than 500 Native American tribes. Today, our population is growing and is increasingly diverse, as you can see in Table 1.1 (Social Science Data Analysis Network 2001). Over 281 million people now live in the United States.[1]

If you have ever worked for or volunteered for the U.S. Census Bureau, you know that the process of counting all individuals in the United States is a complicated one. One of the reasons for this is that our nation covers a lot of territory. For example, some villages in Alaska are remote and surrounded by snow and ice year-round and these places are not easy to reach. The Census Bureau must hire pilots and two-seater airplanes to take census workers to count people in these areas. Another aspect that makes the census a complex undertaking is that in the 2000 count an Hispanic person could identify with any race because both race and Hispanic ethnicity were asked as different questions (Social Science Data Analysis Network 2001). Individuals see themselves in many ways, so ethnic identification can be a complex process. Therefore, it is often difficult to figure out how to ask people how they identify themselves because the census may include numerous categories. In addition, categories change as people alter the way they identify themselves. For example, Native Hawaiians and Other Pacific Islanders were not counted separately until the 2000 census; therefore, persons in this category in 1990 were counted as Asians (Social Science Data Analysis Network 2001).

TABLE 1.1   U.S. Population by Racial Group

Growth Rate	2000 Population	Past 10-Year Growth Rate (%)
Total U.S. Population	281,421,906	13.15
Total Hispanics	35,305,818	57.94
White (non-Hispanic only)	194,552,774	3.41
Black	33,947,837	16.19
American Indian and Eskimo	2,068,883	15.34
Asian	10,123,169	45.27
Hawaiian and Pacific Islander	353,509	—
Other	467,770	87.79

Source: Census 2000 analyzed by the Social Science Data Analysis Network (SSDAN). http://www.censusscope.org/.

[1]In the Appendix on page A-1 there is a chart that shows the rapid growth of U.S. population from 1960 to 2000.

Which ethnic populations are increasing in the United States? From Table 1.1 you can see that most categories have seen growth in the past 20 years. The Hispanic and Asian communities have experienced some of the largest gains. In the past 10 years the Hispanic community grew at a rate of 58 percent, while the Asian community grew by 45 percent. The Black population grew by 16 percent, while the Native American population grew by a little over 15 percent. The White population increased by only 3.4 percent. In fact, Dr. Steve Murdock, a demographer for the state of Texas said at an urban education conference at Texas A&M, "Our future is tied to non-Anglo populations. Our nation's future rests on how well diverse students do in school and the employment they secure" (Murdock 2002).

As our country becomes more diverse, the number of multiracial/multiethnic students also is rising dramatically.[2] About 6.8 million people (2.4 percent) in the United States marked two or more races in the 2000 census. Table A.3 in the chapter appendix shows the actual population figures. More multiracial citizens live in Hawaii and Alaska (Social Science Data Analysis Network 2001).

National Enrollment in U.S. Public Schools and Two Examples, Dallas and Boston

As the diversity of our country continues to grow, so do the number of students of color. Statistics about all public elementary and secondary schools in 1999 show that almost 38 percent of the students came from communities of color. The number of White students fell from 70.4 percent to 62.1 percent of the total number of students from 1986 to 1999. Tables 1.2 and 1.3 show these changes. Student diversity in our schools also continues to increase due to interracial marriages and immigration. We are a nation of many peoples.

If you have visited schools in a major school district, you may have noticed the diversity of students. Table 1.3 provides the totals across the nation, but does not tell the reality of the largest districts in the country. In school districts such as Chicago, Los Angeles, St. Louis, New Orleans, Houston, Baltimore, and Seattle, the majority of students are from communities of color. There are regional differences in the

TABLE 1.2   U.S. Public School Population (Fall 1999)

Race/Ethnicity of Student	Percentage of Population (Fall 1999)
White (non-Hispanic)	62.1
Students of Color	37.9

National Center for Education Statistics, *Mini-Digest of Educational Statistics* ©2001, Charlene Hoffman, U.S. Department of Education, Office of Education Research and Improvement NCES 2002-026, 13.

[2]Although the U.S. Census Bureau uses race as a category, the author of this book sees race as a sociopolitical construct and not as a biological one. Read more about race in Chapter 3.

TABLE 1.3   U.S. Public School Population by Background (Fall 1999)

Race/Ethnicity of Student	*Percentage of School Population
Black (non-Hispanic)	17.2
Hispanic	15.6
Asian/Pacific Islander	4.0
American Indian/Alaskan Native	1.2

*Numbers may not sum to totals due to rounding. *Mini-Digest of Educational Statistics*, 2001.

TABLE 1.4   Boston Public Schools Enrollment (October 2001)

	Black	Latino	White	Asian	Native American	Total
Total (Students)	30,113	17,836	9,005	5,640	264	62,858
Total (Percentages)	48	28	15	9	<1	100

Source: Facts and Figures, Boston Public Schools, Enrollment, http://boston.k12.ma.us/bps/enrollment.asp.

TABLE 1.5   Dallas Independent Public School District Enrollment (October 2001)

	Hispanic	African American	White	Asian	American Indian	Total
Total (Students)	93,065	56,220	11,766	2,131	581	163,763
Total (Percentages)	56.8	34.3	7.2	1.3	0.4	100

Source: http://www.dallasisd.or/inside_disd/facts_stats/students.htm.

ethnic enrollments of students in each district. For example, in Boston Public Schools in October 2001, a total of 85 percent of the students were non-White. In this district 48 percent of the students were Black and the next largest group were Latinos, who represented 28 percent of the population. In comparison, at Dallas Public Schools during the same time period, the largest group was Hispanic, followed by African Americans. See Tables 1.4 and 1.5 for the enrollment information for these districts. The group labels used in these charts are the same as those noted in each district; therefore, in one chart a population is called Black, while in another city the students are identified as African American. It is apparent from the demographics that our students come from diverse cultural and linguistic communities. Teachers will need to understand how to build on students' strengths and address their needs.

What Does It Mean to Be a Culturally Relevant Teacher?

Approximately 86 percent of teachers in K–12 schools are from mainstream, middle-class backgrounds. Many newer teachers will most likely find positions in urban districts that have great cultural and linguistic diversity like Boston or Dallas. Students will bring various cultural experiences and knowledge about life to the classroom. Teachers will also bring new ideas and perspectives to the school. Although the following example refers to ethnic cultural values, people adopt values from many cultures, such as family, nation-state, and religious groupings.

Let's consider, for example, a new teacher named Mrs. Andrews. In her junior high classrooms she has a student named Christine, an Asian immigrant student from the Philippines. Christine believes teachers should be respected and therefore not questioned. Mrs. Andrews's class also includes Amy, a Chinese American student who also believes teachers should be respected, yet she does not believe it is disrespectful to ask questions in class. Therefore, Amy asks questions in order to gain a clearer understanding of the concepts that Mrs. Andrews teaches. Amy was raised within a middle-class orientation, so her views are more similar to those of Mrs. Andrews in the classroom. She is more comfortable in school because her expectations and behaviors are in line with what she has learned from her family.

Mrs. Andrews is comfortable with both students, but she believes students should be active learners, so she encourages Christine to ask questions first in a one-on-one discussion during lunch recess. Mrs. Andrews understands that Christine's experiences are different from hers in many ways and so the student's behavior is not what she expects. Mrs. Andrews becomes somewhat frustrated because Christine smiles but says little in class; however, she understands that it will take time for Christine to understand the expectations of her new school. Mrs. Andrews hopes that Christine will become more comfortable raising questions in discussions later in the year after she is coached and observes the modeling of other students in the class. As a culturally relevant teacher, Mrs. Andrews learned that at home Christine was taught to be more reticent and not aggressively verbal. Therefore, she will provide opportunities for her to work in small groups where Christine can develop her verbal skills among peers and not in front of the whole class. Later, when Christine is more confident and has developed public speaking skills, she will provide many opportunities for her to contribute to class discussions. One way the teacher encourages her is by writing comments on her papers praising her for the verbal contributions she does make in class. A **culturally responsive or relevant teacher** like Mrs. Andrews is culturally affirming to her students, understands the cultures of her students who are making adjustments in the classroom, and encourages students to become self-directed thinkers.

> ✍ A culturally relevant teacher is affirming to her or his students, builds on what students bring to school, and encourages students to become self-directed thinkers within a caring and democratic society.

Caring, culturally diverse teachers

Culturally Relevant Teaching: Connecting to Student Knowledge

Culturally relevant teachers are responsive to and affirm the many cultural backgrounds students bring to school (Ladson-Billings 1995; Larke and Carter 2002). They know how to connect the students' prior knowledge with the academic content being taught. Culturally relevant teachers understand their students' value systems and act as **cultural mediators** in situations where the behaviors and values of children conflict with mainstream expectations. Let's take two examples. In schools every day, students are given assignments to do at their desks. Gay (2000) explained that many African American and Latino students who come from traditional cultural backgrounds may be sensitive to the cultural context of the classroom, especially in doing their seatwork. So students engage in stage-setting or "getting ready" behaviors. Have you ever had a student who needed to sharpen his pencil, stretch his arms, and push his chair backward into a more comfortable position before beginning his assignment? It may have seemed as if it took forever for him to start working. Gay believes behaviors like these can be explained as "preparation before performance" or ways of centering one's attention or "setting the tone" to begin working. A culturally responsive teacher will understand these behaviors as part of some students' learning process.

Another example appears in the comic strip *Zits* on page 11. Jeremy's dad, who is a dentist, has a new patient. This patient is unhappy about needing braces because he thinks he will not look "cool." Although the dentist may or may not agree with piercing, he tells the young man not to think of the wires as braces, but as getting his "smile pierced." Piercing is an important aspect of this young person's identity, and

the young man now sees his situation in a new way. This wise dentist has become a cultural mediator. He understood that piercing was a valuable practice to the young man and created a motivating link between braces and youth culture.

Culturally relevant teaching can be a powerful force in learning. I wish I had been able to use culture in teaching Rosemary and her first-grade classmates. As I mentioned at the beginning of this chapter, the children in the class taught me that I did not make the cultural connections I should have in my teaching. I wasn't as wise as the dentist in the comic strip. I didn't know how to be a cultural mediator and make bridges in teaching new skills and information. In Chapters 3, 4, 9 and 10, I will provide more information about culturally relevant teaching.

As you have read in this chapter, culture is a critical component in my philosophy about teaching. This is one of the reasons that I believe Multicultural Education is an important field. The next section of the chapter provides the core of how I conceptualize Multicultural Education. It summarizes the beliefs that I think Multicultural Education is built on, and since one of the most important building blocks is caring, I call it Caring-Centered Multicultural Education.

Caring–Centered Multicultural Education

It is important for educators to have a strong philosophy that guides their work. I have chosen three theories that form an educational framework called Caring-Centered Multicultural Education. A **framework** is an overarching belief system that can include theories, beliefs, and attitudes. The Caring-Centered Multicultural Education framework combines the concepts of caring, culture, and community in schools. The three theories used to build the framework are as follows:

- Care theory (Noddings 1984, 2002a, 2002b; Walker 1995), of which personal integrity is a component (Palmer 1998).
- Sociocultural theory of learning (Vygotsky 1978; Moll 1990).
- Education for democracy (Dewey 1916; Nussbaum 1997).

> ☯ Caring-Centered Multicultural Education integrates three major theories: care theory, sociocultural theory of learning, and education for democracy.

Since I am introducing my thoughts about education, I provide a limited description of the educational philosophy that guides this book. I want you to begin to think about how the Caring-Centered Multicultural Education paradigm is different from other viewpoints. This section of the chapter is an introduction to the framework. More comprehensive discussions of the framework can be found in Chapters 7 and 8. The first component is the care theory.

Care Theory: The Power of a Caring-Centered Teacher

Caring in this framework is not "touchy feely stuff." It doesn't mean a teacher goes around hugging every child all the time. Noddings (2002a) tells her readers that care theory "is relation-centered rather than agent-centered, and it is more concerned with caring relation than with caring as a virtue" (Noddings 2002a, 2). Care theory is one of the cornerstones of the Caring-Centered Multicultural Education framework. It directs teachers to understand that relationships are at the heart of teaching. The theory also considers ethical principles as the foundation for education (Noddings 2002a). It is important to note that Noddings (2002a) has indicated that the ethic of care can be seen like the "ethics of duty and right" and therefore implies an obligation. However, in contrast, Noddings views care theory not as a duty, but as relationship-centered in which one is moved to care for others arising out of one's felt connections with others. Noddings wrote,

> Because we (lucky ones) have been immersed in relations of care since birth, we often naturally respond as carers to others. When we need to draw on ethical caring, we turn to an ethical ideal constituted from memories of caring and being cared for. Thus the ethic of care may be regarded as a form of pragmatic naturalism. It does not posit a source of moral life beyond actual human interaction. It does not depend on gods, or eternal verities, or on essential human nature, or postulated underlying structures of human consciousness (2002a, 15).

Research has also shown that teachers who study aspects of the care theory have more positive interactions with their students because teachers move toward a more student-centered pedagogy (McAllister and Irvine 2002).

One caution that has been raised about care theory is that women have generally been seen as nurturers in society. It is important for individuals to understand it is not an oppressive belief system in which the carer gives her or his all to the cared for. Caring does not refer to a domination of another's needs over the carer. Care theory as defined by Noddings is clearly reciprocal. The cared for responds to the carer and in this way the carer is able to evaluate her or his effectiveness (Noddings 2002b). Caring can come from women and men. A moral, caring teacher brings trust, respect, and compassion into the classroom. Her or his moral commitment to teach arises out of her or his commitment to the community. The teacher is dedicated to contributing to the betterment of the community by guiding each student toward excellence. This teacher listens and talks with and not to her or his students. The teacher does not model a monologue orientation; rather, he or she encourages dialogue.

Another caution given by Thompson (1998) is that the care theory as described by Noddings was created within the context of a mainstream, patriarchal orientation. Although care theorists like Noddings have referred to natural caring, this has not always been historically seen. The treatment of many people from communities of color throughout U.S. history has demonstrated that caring for others who are seen as different is not automatic or natural. Therefore, it is important to reflect upon care theory along with issues of culture and oppression such as racism. Ladson-Billings (1994), Walker (1996), and Irvine (2002) broadened the discussion of the theory through their research with African American teachers. A caring teacher models the building of **kinship** and community by encouraging her or his students to work with each other through genuine listening, support, and collaboration (Walker 1996). These researchers consistently found successful African American teachers whose belief in the power of caring extended beyond the classroom and were partially defined within the context of the community. The teachers studied viewed caring as arising from the African American community notion of *helping*: The teachers were ethically committed to and believed in each student (Walker 1996). Caring for their students, in part, was an act of liberation. In addition, African American parents trusted African American teachers to care for their children. African Americans who believe that they have been called to teach have a sense of wholeness or being about teaching as a profession; they have a spiritual purpose (Irvine 2002). Therefore, a caring teacher makes an ethical commitment to reach his or her students. Within this context, a caring school is made up of students, parents, teachers, and community people who share the goal of developing ethical and self-fulfilled citizens who contribute to a just and compassionate community.

In a caring school, issues of bias must be examined and addressed. For example, teachers and their students tackle racism, ethnocentrism, gender bias, and homophobia because they understand how these biases serve to undermine integrity and respect in the school (Irvine 2002; Starratt 1994). As Starratt reminds us, "When these underside issues dominate an exchange, they block any possibility of open and trusting communica-

> ☙ "*Teaching is caring . . . Students said teachers cared when they laughed with them, trusted and respected them . . . Students defined caring teachers as those who set limits, provided structure, had high expectations, and pushed them to achieve.*"
> —JACQUELINE JORDAN IRVINE 2002, 141

tion. Mistrust, manipulation, aggressive and controlling actions or language on the part of an administrator, teacher or student can lead to relationships that are hypocritical, dishonest, disloyal and dehumanizing" (1994, 83). Starratt poses that an ethical school builds more than "contractual" associations between teachers and students. In an ethical and caring school, faculty see students as unique and valued individuals who are part of a community where more than academic content is stressed (Walker 1996).

Like Starratt, Noddings (2002a, 2002b) believes we, as teachers, must be ethical in our behavior in schools and must teach children how to make prudent judgments. Her work is greatly influenced by the teachings of the educational philosopher, John Dewey. Noddings writes:

> Dewey encourages educators to provide a social environment in which it is possible for children to be good and in which they will learn to exercise sound judgment so that the larger society to which they belong will become better through their wise participation (Noddings 2002a, 80).

Since our traditional public school curriculum is oriented towards disseminating more and more knowledge and not always expanding our students' critical thinking skills, there are disciplines in schools in which a teacher might wonder how discussions of moral ideas have a place. For example, a teacher might ask, "What can we teach in mathematics about moral issues? That is not our area." Noddings (2002a) responds with the following:

> In mathematics classes, teachers can share with students the great interest of many mathematicians in theological questions: Descartes's attempt to prove God's existence, Pascal's famous wager, Newton's expressed feeling that theology is more important than mathematics, . . . the contemporary fascination of mathematicians with the infinite, mathematical arguments for a pluralistic society and possible forms of polytheism, the Platonic positioning of mathematical forms just beneath the supreme good. Beyond all this, mathematics teachers should share relevant literature (including science fiction), poetry, games, history, and biography (125).

As Noddings has shown, even mathematicians deal with issues of ethics and beliefs about life and the importance of an educator with a strong sense of integrity.

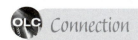 *Connection*

If you are interested in reading several pieces by Nel Nodding, go to
http://www.mhhe.com/mayfieldpub/lawhead/chapter5/nel_noddings.htm

Care Theory: Integration of Integrity and Identity

Competent teachers whose lives arise from care theory know who they are and how culture and ethnicity shape their beliefs (Irvine 2002). For educators to be effective, teachers must have deep personal integrity to connect with students in genuine and sincere ways (Palmer 1998). Palmer wrote, "Good teaching cannot be reduced to technique; good teaching comes from the identity and integrity of the teacher" (1996, 10). This can be challenging because, as Palmer explained, this includes the ability of educators to identify the discrepancies between their beliefs about heartfelt and connected teaching with their actual actions. They do not want to be members of schools that do nothing but blame schools as organizations. They understand

their own responsibilities to act to change
schools for the better. Care theory is built
upon that sense of personal integrity. Although people have the capacity to care for
others, this capacity must be developed and
cultivated. These teachers also know that
caring for the whole child involves a clear un-

> *"[G]ood teaching cannot be reduced to technique;*
> *good teaching comes from the identity and integrity*
> *of the teacher."*
> —PALMER 1996, 10

derstanding of culture. The next section is a case that describes a school where caring was at its heart.

Case Study

CASWELL COUNTY TRAINING SCHOOL, A SEGREGATED
BLACK SCHOOL: AN EXAMPLE OF THE CARE THEORY

What do caring schools look like? What kind of education do you think a
Black segregated school in the South provided? Vanessa Siddle Walker (1996)
studied a segregated Black school that exemplified principles of the care theory. The school provided excellent education within a strong community partnership. This school in North Carolina, called the Caswell County Training
School, was segregated from 1934 until 1969. Legalized segregation was the
norm and demonstrated deep social inequities in the United States. Segregated
practices were built on socially accepted beliefs about the inherent inferiority
of Black students. These schools were part of a legalized system of inequalities and oppression. Segregated schools were not dismantled until the Civil
Rights Act of 1964 (Walker 1996). In fact school segregation in the town
where the Caswell County Training School existed did not end until 1970.

The funding for Caswell County Training School was not at the same level
of funding as schools for White students. However, this school provided excellent education because of the dedication of parents, faculty, and administrators who worked collaboratively as a community to provide their children
with the best-quality education. The parents understood racism and resulting
inequalities for their community. However, this did not limit their efforts to advocate and build strong segregated Black schools (Walker 1996). The school
served as the center for the community where parents got together for both social and business affairs. The PTA sponsored many programs where children
could show their talents. Principal Dillard also participated in many school
programs, telling stories and jokes "reminiscent of the Brer Rabbit tales traditionally valued in the African American community" (Walker 1996, 67). The
rabbit was able to triumph over more powerful enemies using his creativity
and his wit. These stories were often used to teach the importance of challenging inequalities. Jokes were part of a common cultural preaching style
found in many Black churches and was a way of linking the school to community norms (Walker 1996). Cultural elements were naturally integrated into
all aspects of schooling. At other times, the PTA held business meetings that

focused on supplying needs of students. For example, parents were asked to raise money for a bus that could take students to sporting and music events in other local schools.

Walker found through her many data sources of interviews, PTA documents, and historical records that what stood out was that teaching was seen as much more than imparting information. Teaching was about caring for the whole child and "giving personally of oneself" (Walker 1996, 201). This included not only teaching so that each child lived up to his or her "highest potential," but also "preparing their children to deal successfully in the 'white man's world' " and with the racism that the teachers knew existed. A former student of the school remembered that Principal Dillard told her, "The best equipment may be across the way [at the White high school], but the best minds are here in this school."

Caring was an integral part of the school climate and philosophy; it was a way of being and permeated all aspects of school (Irvine 2002). The school arose out of a sense of community and their mission to provide equitable education to students. Caring for students was a foundational value:

> *More than any particular pedagogical style or curricular content, this sense that they [students] were cared about is the component of school relationships most explicitly linked to their motivation to excel. They [students] did not want to let the teachers and principal down* (Walker 1996, 202).

Students appreciated the work of their parents and teachers. They knew Principal Dillard and his faculty believed in them and expected many to attend college. What were the characteristics of this caring school? Walker presented the following attributes:

1. Faculty worked collaboratively with parents. Teachers were encouraged to attend church functions and to seek out parents through home visits.
2. Parents were advocates for their children and raised money for their school buildings and resources. They also made numerous requests to the White school board and state representatives on behalf of the school. These were self-empowered parents.
3. Teachers and principal held the highest expectations for all students. They also cared about young people and worked with them outside the classroom.
4. Teachers and principal took time to talk with students individually and in small groups. In this way they got to know the social, academic, and personal needs of each young person.
5. The overarching school message was that all students could be what they dreamed of if they worked at it.
6. Teachers and principal were concerned with development of the whole student.

Teachers and principal in this school saw themselves as professionals who were part of a larger community dedicated to the education of young people. The educators made a moral commitment to do all they could to ensure that each student was successful. These educators understood their critical role in supporting and building a strong community. Schooling was integrally tied to the culture of the students and their community. The next section describes the second theory of Caring-Centered Multicultural Education, the sociocultural theory of learning. ✸

The Sociocultural Theory of Learning: What's Culture Got to Do with Schooling?

Culture is one of the most important components of who we are, how we define our-selves, and how we see the world. We are socialized into a group of people, usually our nuclear and/or extended families. Our cultural background arises from what the people who are close to us teach through the use of language and nonverbal com-munications. New ideas are interpreted in relationship to prior knowledge, how we identify ourselves, and our perspectives. The sociocultural theory of learning was developed by Vygotsky to explain how learning is socially mediated. He believed that people learn through social interactions and these interactions occur within mul-tiple cultural contexts.

Scholars like Vygotsky believe language and social interactions are major cul-tural tools needed to develop brainpower, our cognition. Nussbaum, a humanist, writes: "We each have a language (in some cases more than one) in which we are at home, which we have usually known from infancy. We naturally feel a special af-fection for this language. It defines our possibilities of communication and expres-sion. The works of literature that move us most deeply are those that exploit well the resources of that language" (1997, 61–62). Language is used to communicate im-portant aspects of a culture such as values, beliefs, thoughts, norms, so it is a cul-tural tool. Thoughts and language are both needed in developing intelligence; they are reciprocal (Wink and Putney 2002). Research has indicated that there are cul-tural differences in the way people think. For example Nisbett (2003) found that Westerners have been trained to use categorization in their thinking processes "which helps them to know what rules to apply to the objects in question, and for-mal logic plays a role in problem solving" (xvi). In contrast, Asians view problems in a broad context, knowing that the situation is often complex, needing the consid-eration of a range of elements. "Formal logic plays little role in problem solving [for Asians]" and "the person who is too concerned with logic may be considered im-mature" (Nisbett 2003, xvi). In other words people around the world do not think in the same ways. Cultural belief systems differ because the way people understand the world and interpret what they see can be different.

How do language and social interactions shape what you think? As children we learned about what was acceptable and valued in our culture from members of our family. If your parents read to you every night before bedtime, their behavior showed you that they thought reading was important. Maybe your grandmother also told oth-ers, "She's always got her nose in a book." These behaviors reinforced the impor-tance of reading. In addition, if the books your parents read held messages about the importance of family, working together, and fighting for social justice, your parents taught you to value helping others and being fair. Another excellent example comes from a study of a Mexican American elementary-grade teacher as she taught mathematics (Gutstein, Lipman, Hernandez, and de los Reyes 1997). Although the researchers found few references to Mexican history, Mexican cultural artifacts, and other aspects of Mexican culture, they found that the teacher saw her classroom relationships as extending a sense of family. In other words, the teacher saw culture in a holistic way and to her learning in schools was an extension of learning in a family atmosphere at school. Here is what the teacher, Ms. Herrera, said about teaching in a bilingual-Spanish classroom:

> I try a whole lot to connect to them, to try to understand . . . I come in here thinking from the first day, they are already a part of me, already a part of my family. That makes me want so hard to help all of them. They're part of me, my family, my culture, little bits and pieces of me . . . I know they're going to go through the same things I went through, I want to see them go beyond what's expected of them . . . it's so hard to see how a lot of Hispanics are being treated . . . I want them to stand out, be special in their own way . . . (Gutstein, Lipman, Hernandez, and de los Reyes 1997, 729).

This is another good example of how caring and culture can be intimately connected depending on the teacher's belief system.

Let's take an example from another family. What if values weren't taught by reading books, but through the oral tradition. What values might you have learned through this process? First, you might have been indirectly taught to respect and honor older members of the community. Second, you would have been taught how to listen and remember. In addition, the content of your grandparents' stories would also have taught you specific family and cultural values. Interactions in this family taught that the valuable members of the community were elders and that it was extremely important to know how to listen.

 Case Study

A STORY TO LIVE BY: TEACHING THROUGH ORAL TRADITION

One of the teachers in my class, Pia Parrish, a member of the Blackfoot community, shared how important the stories of her grandparents and other elders in the community were to her. As a child, she would sit and listen to stories from the elders in the evenings. This was their way of sharing cultural values. She learned as a little tyke that their stories were the foundation for her life. These stories help to guide her beliefs today. Stories are important to many Native peoples. Since many cultural traditions developed without written languages, stories are an integral way of communicating cultural values. These social interactional patterns often differed from Pia's school culture.

Here is a short sample of one of the stories she heard about change and how two people who love you may not always get along. The story may be about divorce, siblings, and/or community relationships. The story emphasizes the importance of mutual respect. Through the social interactions Pia had with her grandparents and the carefully chosen words they used, Pia understood the lessons they were teaching.

The Moon and the Sun

Long ago, the Moon and the Sun lived in a small house. They had a little girl named Earth. They were happy. But then they started to fight.

The Moon said, "You are too hot!"

The Sun said, "You are too cold!"

"Okay," said the Moon, "Let's live apart. But the Earth will live with me."

"No, she will get too cold without me," said the Sun.

They went to wise old Thunder. Thunder listened to the fight. Then he said, "Let the sun watch the Earth in the day. Let the Moon watch the Earth in the night."

That is why the sun shines in the day, and the moon shines at night. When the Moon is busy, the stars shine on the Earth.

Using the oral tradition of the Blackfoot culture, Pia's elders taught her ways to look at conflicts in relationships. The story can be used to explain how children in a divorced family need both their parents to take care of them, even though they may not live in the same house. There is much symbolism in the story. The segment of the story that says "When the Moon is busy, the stars shine on the Earth" is interpreted by some Native people to symbolize the roles of aunts and uncles. Aunts and uncles can also play important roles in child-rearing. As an adult, Pia reflects back to the cultural values she was given as a child. These stories guide her life today. ✳

Like all of us, Pia learned about life within cultural contexts. The socialcultural setting of sitting in the evening and listening to her elders and the use of the oral tradition taught her much about what her family values in life. This was a familiar cultural practice. Her grandfather and other elders used language and social interaction practices as means of communicating ideas with Pia. Vygotsky, the Russian psychologist, believed that language stimulates thought and is a tool for learning (Wink and Putney 2002). His work led to the development of the sociocultural theory of learning. This theory emphasizes the importance of language and social interactions. Let's take Pia's experiences. She learned specific cultural practices, and language was the tool that stimulated and conveyed her grandfather's ideas and beliefs. The social situation was meaningful and relevant to Pia because her grandfather was a valued person in her family and she had been taught by her parents and culture that he had important lessons to teach. Her grandfather became a facilitator or teacher in her learning. Pia's grandfather did not explicitly say, "This story is about divorce"; rather, he allowed her to become active in the learning process and she made sense of his stories. In this way her grandfather stimulated her thoughts by teaching her how to interpret the many stories she heard from him and other members of the Blackfoot community.

In a sociocultural orientation, the teacher takes on a role similar to Pia's grandfather's role as storyteller; the teacher is a mentor and facilitator who guides students. The teacher is sensitive to her students' cultural backgrounds, knowing what her children value and always looking for ways to connect to what her students already know. To do this, the teacher needs to have a comprehensive understanding of the cultural backgrounds of her students. The teacher sees the wholeness of culture, knowing that culture is not only composed of separate elements like food, dress, and customs, but also there are connections between the elements. Pia learned how to approach life; she also learned what to do around others, what to say, and how to respond. Culture, which is a whole system of thinking, believing, and acting, is another important component of the sociocultural theory of learning. This teacher knows that there are many cultural orientations and that these orientations differ due to aspects of society like social class, gender, sexual orientation, religion, and ethnicity. She has seen in her classroom how different students bring different perspectives to class about many issues they discuss, from students' favorite foods to our nation's immigration policy. She knows that these perspectives have arisen from the diversity in factors like family histories, immigration experiences, weekend activities, religious beliefs, languages, careers, labor history, and childrearing practices, just to name a few (Villegas and Lucas 2002). She also understands that since language is a vehicle for culture, a person's identity is highly tied to her or his language. Therefore, the teacher builds on her students' different languages. She affirms all the languages students bring to school by encouraging them to continue to develop their home- and second-language skills (Villegas and Lucas 2002). One way to accomplish this is by providing students with an environment where they can complete assignments in both languages. For example, a child may be planning and designing a science project that includes a poster board. The board could include definitions of terms in both English and Spanish. The student could use science resource books and dictionaries written in both Spanish and English.

As Pia's experiences have shown, the creation of a strong, collaborative, and trusting community can form the foundation for lifelong learning. The next section discusses why Dewey's education for democracy and the creation of a democratic community are critical components in schools.

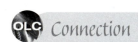 *Connection*

To read more about Vygotsky, the Russian psychologist, his work, and his impact on education go to **http://www.psy.pdx.edu/PsiCafe/KeyTheorists/Vygotsky.htm**

Education for Democracy: Schools as Laboratories of Democracy and Community

The third component of Caring-Centered Multicultural Education is education for democracy. John Dewey, an educational philosopher of the 20th century, was one of the most influential scholars who saw schools as laboratories of democracy and community building. Many practices that you may take for granted in schools came from Dewey's work. For example, Dewey believed in aspects of schools such as service learning, individualized instruction, and project-based activities that are used today (Tanner 1997). These approaches are founded upon inquiry education. Inquiry learning is often difficult to include in one's curriculum today when standardized testing seems to be at the center of public schooling. Dewey did not believe in testing that emphasized rote memory of isolated and fragmented information or testing outside of a relevant context. Dewey's philosophy centered around the creation of an educated democratic citizenry.

As a firm advocate of democracy, Dewey believed that schools should be major institutions to mentor children to become active citizens who make just decisions based on the common good. Dewey proposed that schools should be laboratories of democracy where students developed communication and collaboration skills that enabled them to work with others as responsible citizens (Cremin 1988). Dewey saw democracy as a way of life and not only a form of government (Dewey 1916). In addition, he also thought that through collaborative living, racial and class bias could be broken down. Since students would be in classrooms with students of many different cultural backgrounds, they would be enriched by the many viewpoints and belief systems that they shared with each other. Dewey viewed schools not only as places where children could develop their minds and their abilities to read, write, and do mathematics, but also as places where students could learn about society and different ways of looking at the world through discussions and subject areas related to the arts, nature, and ethics (Cremin 1988).

 Connection

The John Dewey Society is an organization dedicated to expanding the ideas of liberal education.

The following is a statement from their website at **http://cuip.uchicago.edu/jds/** explaining the goal of the institution.

> In the February 1936 issue of *The Social Frontier,* the name choice was explained: The new society was named for John Dewey, not because the founders wished to devote themselves to an exposition of the teachings of America's greatest educator and thinker, but rather because they felt that in his life and work he represents the soundest and most hopeful approach to the study of the problems of education. For more than a generation he has proclaimed the social nature of the educative process and emphasized the close interdependence of school and society. Presumably, without being bound by his philosophy, the John Dewey Society will work out of the tradition which John Dewey has done more than any other person to create. Such an organization is badly needed in America today.

Citizens of a Global Society

Extending Dewey's work, Nussbaum (1997) and Merryfield (2001) believed that it is important for all of us to think and act beyond national or ethnic boundaries. They considered it crucial for all citizens to make ethical decisions based on understanding the perspectives of people from other countries, ethnic communities, and organizations. How easy will considering multiple perspectives be? Merryfield (2001) recommended that we move away from the basic assumptions of some traditional global education programs whose aim is to educate students to continue to exert the cultural ways and political role of the United States in the world. Globalization does not mean Westernization. For example, teachers should not teach the attitude that *our* way is the best or the only way to address global problems. An important challenge for our students and ourselves is to reconsider U.S. imperialism and global control in the marketplace and on political issues. Questions that we, as educators, can ask ourselves are as follows: Will our students be able to understand the perspectives of people from Third World countries who may have different values than those found in the United States? Will students be able to work within cross-cultural situations in other countries?

In addition, as Nussbaum has argued, we should see ourselves as citizens of humanity, instead of considering only the views of a local group like an ethnic community or only our country's needs. How easy is it to really understand another's view, especially if it conflicts with our own? It can be extremely difficult to do so because placing oneself in someone else's shoes may mean giving up for a moment one's own beliefs. In addition, we may also have difficulty understanding other people's perspectives because of lack of knowledge of another group who we see as different and/or because of unconscious prejudices. However, as Socrates explained, education must be cross-cultural; we learn from others and our understanding of the world and of ourselves can be greatly expanded through exposure to diverse people, cultures, and ideas (Nussbaum 1997). This is even more important today, given our close relationships to other countries in the area of economics, politics, education, and environment. Estela Matriano, an international education specialist, also encourages educators to create a culture of peace that is more than the lack of war. Matriano wrote, "It is positive peace rooted in mutual understanding, tolerance, economic and social development, democracy and freedom. It should be a responsibility that each of us has towards our fellow human beings" (2000, 92).

> ᓯ *Globalization does not mean Westernization.*

Building a Trusting Community in the Classroom

Dewey believed in the importance of building a strong community by teaching students roles and responsibilities within a democratic classroom (Tanner 1997). Each child must share in the power of directing the classroom and/or school. We see teachers who foster democratic education through the use of classroom meetings in which students develop common goals and then take on various roles to address community goals (Nussbaum 1997). In these schools students are encouraged to face difficult issues. For instance, many young people face homophobia and harassment based in social class. Teachers can guide students to address prejudice. In a caring, democratic community, every person has the responsibility to treat others with respect and to act justly. For example, in many schools across the nation, high school students say, "Our homework is gay." These students mean that they consider the homework to be "bad" or not desirable, and they don't want to do it. Similarly, grade school students can often be heard taunting another child who is usually male with a label like, "John is gay; John is gay." Another common example is one child calling another child "retard" to hurt him. In caring-centered schools, teachers and students discuss the issue together and adopt strategies to eliminate prejudice and name-calling. Students, teachers, and parents know that because prejudice and harassment act as barriers to learning and to building a trusting community, issues like homophobia must be addressed and not ignored or shoved under the rug. Students may create posters that are a take-off on announcements created by the Anti-Defamation League of B'nai B'rith. Their posters say, "If you really believe in America, prejudice is foul play." Students may create new posters with pictures of students in solidarity at the school with a phrase such as "If you really believe in our country, name-calling is foul play" to convey the message to students in the entire school. In addition, teachers should periodically remind students about how hurtful name-calling is to others. In high school, students might decide to say to those who use inappropriate labels, "That's not cool. We don't talk that way to each other." These are strategies students and teachers can build together.

The Ethic of Critique

Many educators like Dewey, Nussbaum, and Merryfield believe schools should teach children critical thinking skills. Nussbaum (1997) wrote about the importance of students questioning authority in the tradition of Socrates. This Greek philosopher also believed that a strong democracy is one in which the common good is a foundational aspect of society. In order to develop a sense of the common good, we must develop citizens who examine their beliefs and question their actions in light of the needs of the community as a whole. This takes priority over individual needs. Since it is also important for teachers to examine the status quo and power relationships in society and schools, I think the ethic of critique (Starratt 1994) should be an essential component of schooling. One of its major goals is to develop students' critical thinking skills so that students become ethical individuals and active participants in our democracy. Starratt has drawn the ethic of critique from the work of neo-Marxists who developed what is known as critical theory or critical pedagogy. Students will need to make difficult choices in life. Their education should prepare them by encouraging them to wrestle with questions like:

Who decides what is most important to teach?

Who makes the choices in our school?

Why are those choices made?

Who benefits from those choices?

How is the status quo reinforced?

Who will lose if changes in schools are made?

Take a Stand

SUBJECT AREA CONTENT: WHO DECIDES? WHAT SHOULD BE TAUGHT?

In this chapter, education for democracy as developed by the educational philosopher, John Dewey, strongly advocates teaching students higher-order thinking skills. A key issue that high school students and teachers should consider is who chooses what is taught in schools. Standards and testing are powerful forces in education today; however, people often do not have the opportunity to consider who chooses the content taught in schools. The following are several questions that can be used as the starting point in the development of an issues-centered unit on the content of school curriculum:

Who decides on what is taught in the public schools?

Who should decide?

What criteria should be used to decide on what is taught in schools?

Many of these questions reflect a **critical theory** orientation (Starratt 1994). Critical theory directs scholars to look at the structure of schools and/or other social institutions to see who benefits from its organization and policies. This perspective is aimed at getting individuals and groups of people to examine organizations for inequalities due to categories of class, race, language, disabilities, sexual orientation, and gender. Schools have something called the hidden curriculum. The hidden curriculum is the implicit set of values that exists but may be found mostly by looking at behaviors and unstated practices and content. They are hidden and informal policies, but still powerful forces that reinforce what knowledge and values are taught. For example, values about a group can be taught by not teaching about them. This is often the case with Asian Americans in schools. How many heroes from the Asian American community can you identify? I don't think a teacher has said that Asian Americans are not important; however, students may interpret the lack of information about Asian American leaders in textbooks to mean that their community is not significant or they haven't made many contributions to our country. These are examples of implicit or hidden messages that can be conveyed to students.

Organizational change is more likely when groups of people work collaboratively to examine the hidden curriculum. Teachers, along with their students, can address the hidden curriculum they have been exposed to by analyzing the validity of knowledge they have been taught about various groups of people. Students need critical thinking skills in order for them to examine, to think rationally, and to question the status quo and what they have been taught. There was a comic in the newspaper that showed a young girl named April, who had heard the presentation of a Native elder, Mr. Crow. April made personal connections with the values Mr. Crow talked about such as family, respect for the earth, and respect for each other. When she went home, she asked her grandfather why folks called Natives "savages." April did not believe the stereotypes she had seen in society. Students can learn a great deal from their social interactions with others.

Education for democracy is built on the belief in our mutual humanity and the worth of each individual. A democracy becomes stronger when mutual respect forms the basis for society. Starratt has warned that a socially just society cannot be built primarily on laws. Laws do not create true equality. He placed emphasis on building trusting relationships and the use of an ethical foundation. As Nussbaum (1997, 64) explained, if you are truly living an examined life as envisioned by Socrates, you will love others "from the heart" and you will feel joy when you work for the good of the community and not because of a sense of duty. An examined life is one that is purposeful, connected to others, and one in which a rational person chooses beliefs and values that guide her or his existence (Nussbaum 1997). Oftentimes trusting relationships must be built outside of mainstream organizations when ethnic groups have been excluded. The next case presents members of ethnic collaboratives as good examples of democratic and compassionate communities who fought oppression by pooling their social and financial resources.

Case Study

ETHNIC COLLABORATIVES FIGHTING OPPRESSION

Members of ethnic communities have for hundreds of years, in what is now known as the United States, created strong communities in which financial, artistic, cultural, and social resources were shared and preserved. As Pia revealed about her family and members of the Blackfoot community, people worked together in order to survive, especially within a larger society that tried in many ways to destroy Native ways of living.

John Blassingame (1979) researched the life of African American enslaved people and found that a strong camaraderie and community arose from the oppression people encountered. The people from Africa brought their own cultures to the plantations and from diverse countries developed their own unique culture as a collaborative community. When the practice of slavery began in the South, most Africans retained their languages and did not learn English because their contact with Whites was minimal. In addition, for many enslaved Africans, not learning English was a way to resist the oppression they were forced to endure. The use of folk tales was a cultural element that Africans retained. African tales often were about animals like lions, elephants, and monkeys and later they were transferred into tales about rabbits. As the number of enslaved Blacks grew, Black culture in the South evolved to include folktales that showed how weaker animals could outwit larger ones, spirituals of hope and freedom, and a strong religious faith; the slave community fought their oppression through uniting. In fact, though Southern plantation owners tried to assimilate enslaved Blacks, Southerners adopted words such as Mandingo, Hausa, and Ibo from African languages. The following vocabulary words now used in English originated in African languages: "cooter (turtle), cola, okra, goober and pinder (peanut), yam, gumbo, mumbo-jumbo, juju [a magic charm], buckra (White man), banjo, bamboula, hoodoo [voodoo], okay, and tote" (Blassingame 1979, 99). The life of Blacks in the South during enslaved times demonstrated the courage and ability of Africans to fight against oppression and build their worldview. Blassingame wrote, "The socialization process, shared expectations, ideals, and enclosed status system of the slave's culture promoted group identification and a positive self-concept . . . Recreational activities led to cooperation, social cohesion, tighter communal bonds, and brought all classes of slaves together in common pursuits" (1979, 106).

Oppression toward African Americans was legalized and socially structured for decades. Although Asian immigrants were not enslaved, they found themselves in a hostile society often taxed because of their Asian ancestry or excluded from participating fully in society. One difficulty that Asians had was borrowing money to build businesses or purchase land. In order to support each other, Korean Americans developed a *kae,* which was a rotating-credit system in which an individual could borrow from a Korean collaborative fund (Takaki 1989, 275). Individuals paid into the fund and then took turns borrowing the resources. The borrower repaid the loan with interest. This system was also a common practice in Chinese American and Japanese American communities. For example, members of a Chinese family formed a *woi,* a resource cooperative that was like a "loan-of-the month club" (Takaki 1989, 241). Members placed a small amount of money every month into the collective fund, and through this process many Chinese Americans were able to establish businesses.

The history of many ethnic communities in the United States provides ample examples of how people worked collaboratively to support each other. Though members of many ethnic communities were often excluded from participating in mainstream society, through their persistence and strong identity as a community, they created successful ways to help each other, to establish themselves, and to fight social and cultural oppression. These communities are important role models of community and democracy. ✻

> ↺ Successful ethnic communities are important examples of caring cooperatives that individuals created to support each other within an oppressive host society.

The next section takes the issue of standardized testing and examines it using the caring-centered framework. As Nussbaum carefully describes, social issues must be examined within the context of the common good and along with a commitment to cultivating humanity.

Testing in a Caring, Socially Responsible School

How can Caring-Centered Multicultural Education assist a teacher in examining the standardized testing movement? Today, testing has become one of the most powerful forces in schools because individuals are calling for teacher accountability. However,

A learning community of students and teachers

various districts around the country are questioning the value of using standardized instruments such as the Stanford 9 Achievement Test, because many of their students are
not Anglo or middle class. In 2002 school boards in Los Angeles and San Francisco
school districts proposed looking for alternative testing measures. One reason was the
diversity of student language proficiency. Many educators do not believe that a test given
in English can provide the most accurate assessment of students who are learning English. In California more than 25 percent of the students arrive at school speaking a home
language other than English. Although this doesn't necessarily mean that children do not
have excellent English skills, many of them are English language learners. Darder (1991)
pointed out that standardized testing has been a tool often used to reinforce a social hierarchy in which students of color find themselves labeled as underachievers. She has
documented that these instruments have been used to legitimize the placement of underrepresented students in lower-level classes—an educational caste system.

   In addition, some parents and educators argue that the goal of testing is to assist students to learn more effectively, rather than to use one score as a measure of
student knowledge. Standardized testing today often implies that the tests are permanent and all-knowing evaluation measures of student abilities; however, many
educators and parents know that tests are feeble attempts to measure student
knowledge. These tests can often become tools of oppression and methods of power

and control of what is taught, rather than constructive methods for educators to use in teaching (Mathison 1997).

Schools receiving federal funding for "disadvantaged" students are required to test their students yearly as mandated by the No Child Left Behind legislation (Reauthorization of the Elementary and Secondary Education Act) that was signed in January 2002. The rationale behind this requirement is to assess the effectiveness of school programs that are directed towards immigrant and low-income students. The tests are thought to measure areas needing attention by first providing a base-line level of student performance. Later, districts administer post-tests to see if students have improved after being in federally funded programs for the school year.

Some educators have argued that it is not fair to use these standardized measures with students who do not have comprehensive English skills. However, others argue that not using standardized tests would suggest that teachers have lower expectations for low-income students. Some educators point to inner-city schools, whose populations are primarily ethnically diverse students from lower-income families, where youngsters perform well on standardized instruments (*Los Angeles Times,* 2002).

Educators who use the caring-centered framework believe it is important to continually measure the academic growth of their students because effective testing provides a way to help reach students. They also understand that the measures they use to monitor that growth must be accurate and appropriate for their students. In addition, educators understand that not all children wear size 5 shoes, so there is no single measure that is accurate for all students. Some teachers are concerned that there is little concern with other aspects of the development of their students. For example, they know these assessments cannot measure how collaborative, how compassionate, or how respectful students are and these are also important elements in a school and society whose purpose is to educate citizens for a diverse democracy.

Case Study

LAUREN FAILS HIGH-STAKES TESTS

One of the connecting themes in Caring-Centered Multicultural Education is focusing on the education of the whole child. Educators know that one test cannot measure the multitude of student abilities. A student is a complex whole. For example, Lauren, who speaks English, Spanish, and Russian, is able to solve a physics problem, can sew a seam on a sewing machine, changes the oil in her car, shoots a basketball from 10 feet away, is Jewish, edits the high school paper, and works at the local YMCA with middle-school students after school. From looking at a short description of Lauren and observing her in class, you can see that she is community oriented, motivated, creative, and hardworking. Can a standardized test measure these aspects of her abilities? Are these characteristics important?

When Lauren was in the third grade, she moved to the United States from Russia. Although she could understand only an elementary level of English,

she was a fluent Russian and Spanish speaker. Her parents spoke both languages. When Lauren first enrolled in the third grade, she was given many tests, and since she wasn't feeling confident, she did not do well. Not only was she scared of making conversational errors in English, but she was not comfortable in her new school. Lauren developed test anxiety, especially because many of the tests were timed. Even as a senior in high school, her hands became clammy when standardized tests were handed out. As she worked feverishly through the Scholastic Aptitude Test (SAT), she was concerned that her test scores would be too low to earn her financial aid for college. This added to her anxiety. As immigrants, her parents had to start their careers over in the United States and therefore did not have much money to help her pay for college. She also wanted to earn her own scholarships, so that college would not be a financial burden to her family. The comic above shows Jeremy, a character in the comic, who also is concerned about his performance on the SAT.

Lauren's high school math teacher was Juan Hernandez. As a caring-centered multicultural educator, he continually assesses his students' level of knowledge, and he doesn't believe in **high-stakes testing** (isolated tests used to decide life-affecting decisions of student tracking, placement, admissions, etc.). Since he believes it is important to have curriculum guidelines for teachers, he does not object to his district holding him accountable for effective teaching. However, Mr. Hernandez believes that many standardized tests emphasize the importance of one correct answer and should not be used to assess the effectiveness of teachers. In his state, the use of tests is becoming extremely rigid and regulatory. He is more concerned with how Lauren thinks through a problem and chooses her answer than he is with which answer she selects (Kohn 1999). He also wants Lauren to become engaged with issues and topics in school that motivate her to discover ideas herself and to see relationships between concepts and thoughts. Mr. Hernandez sees that many questions on standardized tests are examples of unrelated facts and believes that the instrument often does not evaluate his students within a cohesive context like the contexts his students might face in life. However, since he understands it is unlikely that tests like the SAT will be eliminated, he makes sure that he teaches test-taking skills so that Lauren and other students will know what to expect and know how to respond to the format.

Since he knows that Lauren suffers from test anxiety, he realizes that a measure primarily consisting of questions of isolated knowledge does not give Lauren the opportunity to demonstrate her ability to perform logical analysis in the way that a test with open-ended questions would. As a caring-centered teacher, Mr. Hernandez is an advocate for his students, so he invites teachers and parents from his school who are also concerned about the issue to a meeting.

The group creates an ad hoc committee and sets up several objectives:

1. Research various standardized tests.
2. Research student performance-based assessment measures.
3. Examine what other districts are doing to address accountability.
4. Research a broad range of authentic assessment measures.

In this process, teachers are less concerned with students' providing a right answer than on the thinking and analysis processes students use to formulate their answers (Mathison 1997). In authentic assessments, students would be involved in addressing a real issue in life (Mathison 1997). This type of assessment is more localized and could be action oriented. For example, if students are concerned with racism in the school, they could take an aspect of the racism they see in school, develop a plan, and implement it. After much discussion the entire group came together and decided on performance-based measures. Several parents and teachers testified at school board meetings and proposed that a two-year moratorium on the use of standardized tests be instituted so that the issue could be studied. However, the committee knew that the **No Child Left Behind Act of 2001** requires schools to show that students are making yearly progress in math and reading. Later, there will also be requirements for measuring student achievement in science. Measures used to determine the yearly progress of students are decided by each state.

Much discussion resulted from the proposal. Some parents were concerned that students were not learning and believed standardized tests were the most efficient form of assessment. Some students were upset because universities required SAT scores to qualify them to apply for admissions and financial aid. The superintendent worried that the federal government might stop sending funding to the district. This was a complex issue. The school board decided to work together with representatives from the high school to study the issue in depth for the year.

Mr. Hernandez exemplifies the components of a caring-centered teacher. He built trusting relationships with his students and saw the anxiety and self-destruction the tests caused them. In addition, he believed in continually monitoring his students' progress and he wanted to institute the most effective measures to do this. He knew that his students, like Lauren, were extremely knowledgeable, strong thinkers; they had displayed their abilities in his classroom as peer tutors and on individual projects. He also had read a piece written about the SATs that concerned him. The National Center for Fair and Open Testing found that in 2003 "boys now average 43 points higher than girls.

Whites outscore African Americans on average by 206 points . . . [and] [t]he White-Mexican American gap is 158 points on the SAT scale" (Shaeffer 2003). He realized the importance of more research on standardized testing.

Because Mr. Hernandez was committed to a collaborative community, he initiated several discussions with his students and together they instituted a portfolio assessment project. They developed a rubric of skills collaboratively to measure student progress. Each student kept a portfolio of her or his performance-based measures and examples of her or his work. The problem that Mr. Hernandez and Lauren faced was not an isolated issue, and Mr. Hernandez felt it best to organize a community of learners to address the problem. ✻

Assessment and accountability are important aspects of teaching. Going back to the questions posed by Starrat in his ethic of critique approach, consider the following:

Who decides that students should be given standardized tests every year?

Why was that decision made?

Do children do better when they are tested every year?

Who benefits from the testing?

What impact are these tests having on children? On teachers? On schools? On districts as a whole?

All of these questions and more need to be addressed. The standardized test issue is not a simple one, especially since the federal government mandated that schools receiving federal funds must test their students. Some educators contend that large testing corporations make a lot of money by supplying these tests. Is this true? One of my concerns is that teachers do not get the results of each student's performance, so they can't really make any adjustments in their teaching at the end of the year. Are the tests really used to make instruction more effective? A community that believes in democratic values and that is concerned about the lives of children will address these complex questions. Many teachers like Mr. Hernandez want to comply with federal regulations; however, they feel that the law does not provide teachers with viable options, and his school does not want to lose its federal funds. This is an ethical issue that each teacher must decide on his or her own.

The Power of One Caring Teacher: The Story of John Leguizamo

Many of us teach because we believe in students and hope to be a part of their learning and growing. Just think: Maybe Oprah Winfrey's sixth-grade teacher listened to her dreams and this helped her keep them alive. What if you had been Stephen Spielberg's third-grade teacher? You might have encouraged him to write down his daydreams and stories. Maybe you were Cesar Chavez's teacher and you supported his quiet but firm leadership.

Teachers, we can and do make differences in our students. In Marlo Thomas's new book, *Right Words at the Right Time,* there is a chapter written by John Leguizamo,

OLC *Connection*

For more information about testing see the following websites:

*   The National Center for Fair and Open Testing at **www.fairtest.org**
*   The PBS website where James Popham, a leader in educational testing, is interviewed and provides important background about how tests should be developed. **www.pbs.org/wgbh/pages/frontline/shows/schools/interviews/popham.html.**

If you are interested in finding out more about fair testing, go to the National Center for Fair and Open Testing at **www.FairTest.org.** This organization argues that standardized tests are imperfect and schools often place too much emphasis on one or few scores to identify student competence. On their website they report, "Students from low-income and minority-group backgrounds are more likely to be retained in grade, placed in lower track, or put in special or remedial education programs when it is not necessary. They are more likely to be given a watered-down or "dummied-down" curriculum, based heavily on rote drill and test practice. This only ensures that they will fall further and further behind their peers." **www.fairtest.org/facts/howharm.htm**

> ☺ *We are interdependent beings and caring for others forms the foundation for principles of social justice.*

an actor and comedian. You may have seen him in movies or on Broadway. He brings laughter and enjoyment to many people. However, in junior high he hung out with students who cut class and smoked marijuana. He was an angry kid who didn't have much money. It wasn't as if he didn't have skills. In fact, one day he organized a strike and many students walked out of school in the middle of the day. He was always cracking jokes in class and students and teachers would laugh out loud.

Not everyone thought Leguizamo was doing the right thing. He explained what happened:

> Anyway, one day during my junior year, I was walking down the hallway, making jokes as usual, when Mr. Zufa, my math teacher, pulled me aside. I got collared by the teachers all the time, so I didn't think much about it . . . "Listen," he says, "instead of being so obnoxious all the time—instead of wasting all that energy in class—why don't you rechannel your hostility and humor into something productive? Have you ever thought about being a comedian?" . . . The big change didn't happen overnight. Eventually, I got into New York University, where I did student films. One of the movies won a Spielberg Focus Award . . . I've run into Mr. Zufa a bunch of times . . . and told him how his advice turned my life around. Here's a guy who was able to look beneath all the stuff I pulled in class and find some kind of merit in it, something worth pursuing. How cool is that?" (Leguizamo 2002).

Leguizamo was fortunate that a teacher cared enough to tell him to do something with his talents. Caring teachers support their students and (gently and sometimes a little more forcefully) push them to see their own potential. Teaching may not be the easiest career in the world, but for many of us it is the most meaningful!

Chapter Summary

Working Hard May Not Be Working Smart: Using the Caring-Centered Framework

Why Multicultural Education? At the beginning of this chapter, I discussed how my lack of knowledge about my students motivated me to become a better teacher. It was difficult to teach children whose lives were quite different from mine. They all spoke Ebonics and I did not. They were from the school neighborhood and I was not. They knew Black culture and I had little knowledge of the behaviors and history of African Americans.

One of the students was Rosemary, a student whose background included multiple cultures. I think I could have been a much better teacher for Rosemary if I had known about her Black American neighborhood and Native American cultures. However, I hadn't even thought about it when I first arrived at the school. **Culture** was the farthest topic from my mind. I was so concerned about learning to teach the reading method that all the other teachers were using. Of course, reading pedagogy was important, but what I really lacked was knowledge of Rosemary, her life, her goals, her family, and cultures. I don't remember ever meeting or talking to Rosemary's mom or dad. I don't think anyone came to her parent-teacher conference.

I enjoyed Rosemary and made an ethical commitment to reach her as presented in the **care theory.** I worked hard, but working hard doesn't mean working smart. I didn't include aspects of her life and cultural background into the curriculum. I didn't use what she knew as a bridge in teaching her new concepts. I could have benefited from these principles if I had known about Vygotsky's **sociocultural theory of learning.** Rosemary did respond to me and we had positive interactions. However, I didn't develop a partnership with her parents or with other members of her family. I still remember skinny Rosemary hunched over her desk trying to figure out why Sam had a pan and a fan. The story in her reader didn't make sense. It wasn't very meaningful but did present a word family (pan, fan, man, tan, ran). Yes, she knew the man in the story had a frying pan, but what was he doing with it? He just seemed to be waving it around like a fan. The story lacked cultural context and content and it never occurred to me that this would be an obstacle to Rosemary's learning to read.

I was able to create some sense of a learning community in the classroom. The students and I did talk to each other about personal responsibility, and I tried to be democratic; but for the most part I was probably more authoritarian than I should have been. **Education for democracy** wasn't really one of my goals then. I believed that I had to be the person in control, and unfortunately, I gave students few opportunities to develop self-discipline. I was so busy teaching the alphabet, word families, how to add, and how to print that I wasn't teaching the whole child or the skills the students would need. I did not realize that the children would soon leave me and part of my job was to prepare them to make sound and rational decisions in life and to work well with others after they left my classroom.

I don't think I was a bad teacher, but I know now I could have been a better one. The caring-centered framework would have helped to guide me. Carefully choose your theoretical framework because that will serve as your rudder on your journey with many wonderful and enriching students and parents. As Socrates has advised, an examined life is one in which we continually look at our personal values and actions in hopes of creating a better world for humanity.

Chapter Review

Go to the Online Learning Center at **www.mhhe.com/pang2e** to review important content from the chapter, practice with key terms, take a chapter quiz, and find the Web links listed in this chapter.

Key Terms

culturally responsive or relevant teacher, *9*

cultural mediators, *10*

framework, *11*

kinship, *13*

critical theory, *24*

high-stakes testing, *29*

No Child Left Behind Act of 2001, *30*

culture, *33*

care theory, *33*

sociocultural theory of learning, *33*

education for democracy, *33*

Reflection Activities

I suggest that you create or buy a journal to keep track of your responses to chapter questions and to provide a place for you to write other reflections about topics and issues raised in this text. The questions are designed to assist you in reflecting upon your own perspectives and to think about some of the issues presented in Chapter 1.

1. How do you care for your students now? If you are not a teacher in the classroom, what caring practices have you seen other teachers implement? How would you describe a caring teacher?

2. Observe several students and try to identify their cultural backgrounds. Can you provide characteristics of their family cultures, neighborhood cultures, or youth culture? How do these multiple cultures intersect within the student? In some students religion is easily seen. Maybe a young woman wears a veil because she is Muslim and this is a sign of modesty. How do other students respond to her cultural behaviors and values?

3. Developing students for a democracy is a critical goal. What are skills that students in the grade you are teaching or observing should have? What citizenship skills do the students think are the most important for them to develop? How are your ideas and theirs different? Why are they different? Have students prioritized their skills? Now develop a plan to teach them at least three skills that they practice throughout the year.

Skills may include the following: ability to identify the main issue or theme; ability to identify causes, limitations, economic, and social elements that have influenced the issue; ability to design a plan to collect data about an issue and analyze the information. Have students make a decision about what should be done and have them create a plan of action to solve the issue.

4. Begin thinking about choosing an educational framework. What goals do you have for yourself as a teacher? What goals do you hold for your students? What is your overarching philosophy about teaching? As you read through this book, you will get ideas. I encourage you to read the work of John Dewey, James Banks, Jackie Irvine, Martha Nussbaum, Merry Merryfield, Pat Larke, Pauline Lipman, Joyce King, Asa Hilliard, Geneva Gay, Nel Noddings, Jessica Gordon Nembhard, Luis Moll, Alan Singer, and many others. Their work will provide many more critical thoughts for you to consider. Have fun reading their works!

5. What do you know about Multicultural Education? List at least five components of the field. Have you learned anything new from the discussion in this chapter? If so, list new insights and why you think they are important. Do you have other ideas that were not included? You can also write about what you would add to your philosophy.

Why Is Culture Important? The Power of Culture

CHAPTER MAIN IDEAS

- *Why Is Culture Important?*
- *What Is Culture?*
- *How Do Children Learn Culture?*
- *What Is U.S. American Culture?*
- *Schools Transmit U.S. American Culture*
- *Culture Shapes Our Values and Behaviors That Arise from Those Values*
- *Culture: Connections between Deep and Surface Levels*
- *Cultural Values in Conflict*

- *Walking the Tightrope between Stereotypes and Cultural Generalizations*
- *How Can We Find Cultural Keys to Help Us Reach Others?*
- *How Culture Can Be Distorted in Schools*
- *Understanding Culture: Influencing the Success of Your Instruction*
- *Bilingualism and Multilingualism*

CHAPTER OVERVIEW

Teachers need to understand how they themselves learned culture and how their students acquired culture. This chapter reviews not only how we are socialized into various cultures, but also how to walk the tightrope between stereotypes and generalizations. One of the most important components of culture is language. Multilingualism is extremely beneficial for students. Teachers need to be aware of possible cultural clashes refugee students may face in schools.

Why Is Culture Important?

In the past decade, numerous books have been written about multicultural education. Some cover the history of various groups and discuss the importance of social justice. Others direct teachers to integrate art techniques or customs from various ethnic communities into their lessons. Still others present social categories such as race, class, gender, sexual orientation, religion, disability, and ethnicity as separate groupings. However, few Multicultural Education books describe the elements of culture and how they can impact the learning and teaching process. One of the key differences between this text and many other Multicultural Education tests is its attention to culture.

Children come to school with differing cultural backgrounds. Each child is a complex mixture of many cultural subgroups. In fact, Gibson (2000) believes that subgroup cultures are a far more accurate description of a person or group than a larger generalization like the label African American culture. He gives the example that there are African American industrial-working-class, African American labor-union, African American Southern-landowner, and bourgeois African American cultures. Gibson believes that although members of each of these groups may hold, as a collective, common elements of language, music, symbols, values, and history, their cultures are primarily taken from contexts that are shaped by specific social class and labor values. In addition, children may be influenced by a multitude of other social forces such as neighborhood, gender, sexual orientation, age, religion, language, disability/ability, and ethnicity. For example, a child may be a Mexican American female from a middle-class rural community in California's Imperial county and have parents who are Presbyterian. On the other hand, a child may be a Swedish male from a working-class family in St. Paul, Minnesota, and live in a large neighborhood that is predominantly Hmong.

Culture Is All around Us

Culture is like air; it is always there, but people who live in it and follow its ways may have difficulty seeing it. One of the best descriptions of how culture is taught from a multitude of sources comes from the novel *Ishmael* by Daniel Quinn (1992). As an ecologist, Quinn has created a powerful novel about cultural perspective. His story is about a teacher and a student. The teacher, Ishmael, is a gorilla and the student is a human. Quinn describes how their different cultural perspectives and backgrounds give both Ishmael and his student contrasting views about why the world was created. The male student thinks the world was created for humans. Ishmael asks the man how he learned that belief. The man isn't sure. The following is what Ishmael tells his pupil about culture:

> Mother Culture, whose voice has been in your ear since the day of your birth, has given you an explanation of how things came *to be this way.* You know it well; everyone in your culture knows it well. But this explanation wasn't given to you all at once. No one ever sat you down and said, "Here is how things came to be this way, beginning ten or fifteen billion years ago right up to the present." Rather, you

assembled this explanation like a mosaic: from a million bits of information presented to you in various ways by others who share that explanation. You assembled it from the table talk of your parents, from cartoons you watched on television, from Sunday School lessons, from your textbooks and teachers, from news broadcasts, from movies, novels, sermons, plays, newspapers, and all the rest (Quinn 1990, 40).

We are products of what Ishmael would call a cultural view because the culture that surrounds us teaches us how to look at and respond to our life experiences. He attempted to teach his student how to transcend the cultural boundaries and to view life from the perspective of other living beings. It can be difficult for a person to understand another's cultural viewpoint.

> ⑤ *Culture is like the air we breathe in. It is all around us.*

Just as Ishmael taught, culture is a complex set of elements that we almost breathe in. It is that blanket that has warmed us or taught us what to do in life. We transmit culture from one generation to the next (Brislin 1993); it is dynamic and ever-changing. As I explained in Chapter 1, to teach the whole child, educators must understand the cultural views of their students. Children may bring to the classroom differing cultural expectations and values, and there may be miscommunications between teachers and students or among students.

What Is Culture?

The story of Ishmael demonstrates the complexity of culture, so there are various definitions given. However, culture is generally defined as a social system of rules, language, customs, rituals, arts, government, expectations, norms, values, and ideals that people share. In actuality culture is much more because it includes behaviors, assumptions, ways of doing things, ways of seeing things, methods of learning, methods of interacting, choices made, expectations, and communication styles. Culture shapes much of who we are and what we think. The answers to the following questions may help you to more fully understand cultural knowledge.

Who am I? How do I define myself?

What is expected of me? What is my purpose in life?

What are my ideals?

What choices do I make and what does that say about my values?

How am I motivated?

How do I relate to others?

What methods do I think are best to teach children?

How do I care for myself? For others?

It was difficult for me to understand another viewpoint about the complexity of culture until I read a book by Gregory Cajete, a Tewa from New Mexico, called *Look to the Mountain.* He explained more in-depth about the wholeness of culture:

> When teachers examine culture, they need to look at the affective elements—the subjective experience and observations, the communal relationships, the artistic and mythical dimensions, the ritual and ceremony, the sacred ecology, the psychological and spiritual orientations—that have characterized and formed Indigenous education since time immortal (Cajete, 1994, 20).

Cajete reminds us that culture is a large holistic sense of who one is, what one believes, and how one acts. It includes meanings, values, actions, and decision making shared by and within a social group. As children we eat culture, we live culture, we breathe it, we see it at work every day, and we don't even realize it. We learn to understand even subtle nuances of culture. I went to a photography exhibit and admired the work of Carl Mydans who was a *Life* magazine photojournalist. One of his most famous works was the photo of General MacArthur during World War II landing on Luzon in the Philippines as he walked in the water onto shore. The photo sent messages of strength and determination needed to win a war. MacArthur's confident stride and the look on his face, in part, conveyed that strength. As a photographer, Mydans was a careful observer of people. He said:

> I am fascinated by human behavior. By the time I used a camera seriously, I had become an obsessive people-watcher, observing mannerisms and body postures, the slants and curves of mouths, the falseness of smiles, the directness or evasion of eyes. When I learned to understand these signals and interpret them, I had found a source of stories as wide and varied and as captivating as the human race (Mydans 1997).

What guided Mydans in his work was that he was a careful student of culture.

Just like Mydans, teachers should be careful observers of culture. Turning to your classroom, what do you know about the cultures your students bring to school? Do you see particular behaviors that differ from expectations in mainstream schools? Do you notice certain symbols students use that you aren't familiar with? The **explicit culture** is made up of tangible or outward symbols of culture that an outsider may see or experience (Valle 1997), such as food, ceremonies, music, dance, dress, history, and nonverbal behaviors. What do you know about the **implicit culture,** or the hidden culture of your students? This includes the underlying meanings and beliefs of a culture that can be seen in gender role orientations, philosophies valued, expected interactional behaviors, and understood cultural values. Unfortunately, when teachers primarily present elements of the explicit culture, children begin to see those tangible articles as culture.

Help children to understand that:

Tacos and frybread are *not* cultures.

Origami, paper folding, is *not* culture.

Kwanzaa is *not* culture.

Rather,

Tacos and frybread are specific elements within various cultures.

Origami is a specific art form within a culture.

Kwanzaa is a specific celebration within a culture.

Later in the chapter, information about how to guide students in learning the underlying significance and meaning of expressions of culture will be discussed. For example, why is Kwanzaa important to the lives of some people? What is the history of origami? What values does origami have within its original cultural context?

The next section is a discussion of Valle's model of culture. This model will assist you in understanding how the various layers of culture intersect with each other to form what we see as culture.

Culture: Understanding the Three Major Layers

Brislin (1993) sees culture as elements of life widely shared by people and transmitted from one generation to the next over time. He believes culture is not often discussed because there is a mutual acceptance of it. This makes the concept of culture difficult to explain. Valle (1997) provides a multidimensional model to explain culture. Culture is defined by Valle (1997) as having three layers:

Language, symbols, and artifacts.

Customs, practices, and interactional patterns.

Shared values, norms, beliefs, and expectations.

Culture is made up of many elements and together they make an integrated whole. Separating culture into distinct elements tends to fragment it. However, I believe Valle's typology helps teachers to understand how many different elements contribute to culture. Looking at culture through Valle's three layers makes it easier for teachers to see that culture represents a complex system of thinking, behaving, and valuing.

Breaking down the three layers further, I find it helpful to think of them in the following way:

Layer 1: Language, Symbols, and Artifacts (means of communication)— language, dialects preferred, proverbs, signs, sayings, jokes, stories, myths, analogies, folklore, art forms, heroes, dances, rituals, children's games, currency, holidays, history (family, national, and global).

Layer 2: Customs, Practices, and Interactional Patterns (means of interaction)— verbal (tone of voice, phrases used) and nonverbal (eye contact, proximity of stance, gestures) communication patterns, family behaviors, governmental and

Learning cultural elements at home

social institutions, conversational styles (formal-business, casual, ritualized), friendship patterns, community roles, gender roles.

Layer 3: Shared Values, Beliefs, Norms, and Expectations (values driving people, groups)—attitudes, cultural values, religious and spiritual beliefs, fears, laws, standards, norms, levels of political participation, and expectations.

Valle believes that these three layers of culture shape a collective social environment. The most difficult aspects of a culture to understand are the underlying values. The cartoon on page 41 displays a collection of sayings people may know. The interactional pattern, or layer 2 of Valle's model, associated with the sayings may be a child, parent, or adult using the mottos in conversation. The person uses the sayings to make a point or to teach a lesson about life. For example, a teacher may tell her students that "The early bird catches the worm." Using this motto, she may be trying to tell her students that the prepared students will be the ones most successful in school. The teacher holds this underlying value and she is conveying it to her students. The underlying value is layer 3 of Valle's culture model. Many sayings and values that a student knows spring from her or his cultural background.

Language shapes how we communicate with others including objects, images, and ideas from our shared experiences. The preceding comic was about proverbs or truisms. Another example of the power of culture is one I learned from a colleague, named Kyoung-Hye Seo, who studies math education. In a conversation I had with her, she explained that students in Korea and Japan do not have many problems understanding the concept of place value because the structure of Korean and Japanese languages teaches the base-10 concept. For example, in Japanese students learn to count 1, 2, 3, and so forth. When they get to the number 11, they learn that this number is 10 and 1. Following this pattern, 21 is two 10s and 1. So in these particular languages, the concept of place value is taught by the way these languages are structured. Unfortunately, a common problem for students in the fourth grade is to understand place value. Teachers in the United States must take much more time to explain the concept.

Language also impacts other aspects of our worldview. The comic on page 42 shows how expressions sometimes shape our expectations and beliefs about everyday life. The literal meanings of common sayings may not always be applicable for everyone. The young woman in the comic realizes that she has just said something that seems natural for her, but not for her friend. She didn't mean to hurt her friend's feelings. She used a casual phrase, intending its culturally accepted meaning (to stretch, to take a break, to refresh) without first considering the phrase's literal meaning. The next section discusses how culture also impacts those with whom we identify and the groupings we feel we belong to in our lives.

Cultural Identity

The purpose of this portion of the chapter is to assist you in reflecting on how culture shapes who you are and also who your students are. Culture is a large part of how we identify and understand our lives. Identity is a core component of who we

LUANN reprinted by permission of United Feature Syndicate, Inc.

are. A person may identify herself as a mother, a Puerto Rican, a second-generation American, a middle-class person, and a teacher. These categories may symbolize for her the various cultural groupings of which she is a member. For this person ethnicity is an important element. **Ethnicity** refers to common aspects such as cultural beliefs, customs, and communication styles, along with a sense of belonging that comes with a shared history (Cushner, McClelland, and Safford 2003). Therefore, for the woman in the previous example, Puerto Rican ethnicity is an important facet of her cultural background. She also values her national identity as an American.

Today, people may not identify with an ethnic group, but see nationality as a key characteristic of who they are. For example, some people may not identify themselves as Irish Americans or German Americans or even European Americans, but rather "Americans," which means a member of the U.S. society. For these individuals, nationality is important; they feel connections with a shared concept that includes territory, history, government, language, culture, symbols, and common allegiances (Ragin and Hein 1993).

In addition, ethnic identity of people may change as their identification with the established or host cultural group increases. For instance, immigrants may initially arrive in the United States with strong ethnic ties to their ancestral country. However, as they become acculturated or take on attitudes and beliefs of U.S. culture, they may become more assimilated. Cultural assimilation means that people discard their original ethnic practices and values and take on the cultural beliefs of the host group. For example, children may not continue to speak Cambodian or Spanish and may gravitate toward skateboarding and going to the mall rather than attending large family celebrations. U.S. mainstream culture can become a powerful force in the way people identify themselves.

The Cultural Identity Continuum: Traditional, Bicultural, and Assimilationist

Do people from the same cultural group disagree about an issue? Let's say that a predominately Mexican American community is going to be cut in two by a new freeway. On one side of the debate, people are concerned about fragmenting the community, but because a priest of the local Catholic church assured them that the city was hearing their concerns, they decided not to openly fight the city. This part of the community chose several male members to work with city transportation officials. Those who

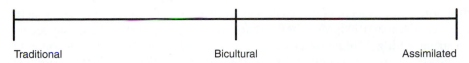

Figure 2.1   *Cultural Identity Continuum*

decided to work with the governmental officials held more traditional values about authority in working with religious leaders and trusting elected officials. However, another group of people from the same community is extremely unhappy. They write letters to the newspaper and to city officials demanding a meeting. They operate from a more bicultural perspective. Those who use more mainstream techniques such as picketing, holding news conferences, and testifying at city council meetings may be part of a bicultural group. They are able to function in both the ethnic community and mainstream society. When the two factions come together in a community meeting, the traditionalists and biculturalists cannot agree on a collaborative strategy.

The two groups fall on different places on the cultural identity continuum (see Figure 2.1). Members of one group are **traditional** and follow the ways, beliefs, and patterns of the cultural group much of the time and continue to speak the native language. **Bicultural** members retain cultural values, customs, and ways of seeing life, yet they may have adopted practices and beliefs of the host culture. A third group is a segment of the community made up of individuals who have culturally **assimilated** into society and do not identify with the ethnic group. They highly identify with mainstream society and take on a mainstream view that the new freeway benefits many other people, so it isn't as important if one neighborhood is cut in half. Although cultural identity and cultural patterns are more complicated than a linear model, the model does provide an understanding of how individuals within the same community may adopt different levels of cultural assimilation (Valle 1997).

One of the key aspects of culture is language. Many traditionalists in a culture can speak the native language of the group. According to Gillian McNamee, "Language, both spoken and written, embodies the ties that people have with one another, their culture, and their own thinking" (McNamee 1990, 288). Language is the vehicle of culture and shapes the way people receive information, think, and process information. It transfers much of the images, beliefs, assumptions, norms, and cognitive concepts of a cultural group. Today there is much discussion about language instruction.

How Do Children Learn Culture?

You may have learned the phrase "stretching one's legs" (see comic, page 42) by hearing it from someone in your family. Children often learn culture from their families. Families are holders and *teachers* of culture (Bruner 1990). Your parents were some of your most important teachers. They taught you how they expected you to act and how to talk to and work with others. When you were young, you learned from your parents, siblings, friends, and neighbors. You learned in a family context; it was not in a formal setting like school. In Caring-Centered Multicultural Education, children are believed to learn in a social and cultural context; sometimes others tell children how to act or think, but they also learn from talking, playing, and watching others (Bruner 1990; Moll 1990; Tharp and Gallimore 1988). Learning occurs in a social setting. Children watch their peers and adults in their world learning to pay attention to selected cultural stimuli. They perceive other stimuli as background noise and filter it out. Parents and significant others train children how to succeed in the community by teaching the cultural worldview. Culture identifies what is important to the community—the values, beliefs, interpretations, skills, and selected ways of solving problems. Adults teach children particular sequencing in the learning process, and children, when confronted with new situations, look for that sequence in order to figure out how to solve problems.

The next section describes how the work of Shirley Brice Heath (1983) helped teachers to understand how different cultural family environments taught diverse values. As an educational anthropologist, Heath studied how parents interacted with their children from two communities: Trackton and Roadville. Although both communities believed in schooling, Heath found basic cultural differences.

Cultural Sequencing in Learning: How Babies Are Taught to Respond in Trackton

Trackton is primarily a Black working-class community with roots in farming. In Trackton, when a newborn is brought home from the hospital, the baby is carried continuously for the first year of life by many different family members. The child is constantly surrounded by verbal and nonverbal communication, although it is usually not directed at the baby. During the first year of life, adults talk about how much the child eats or how they just finished changing the diaper; yet the child is not engaged in a great deal of interaction (Heath 1983). Also during that first year, the child observes how people talk to each other. He or she observes how people posture, hears how the pace of speaking changes, and observes how the context of a situation shapes the way one responds in a social setting.

This community guides boys as young as 12 to 14 months old to begin to participate in public oral communication in the form of teasing, bossing, scolding, and defying. In fact, Heath (1983, 79) writes, " 'The measure of a man is his mouth,' so males are prepared early by public language input and modeling for stage performances." Young males learn at an early age how important it is to be verbally competent and also to use the appropriate tone and nonverbal facial expressions. Girls also learn in the same way. They are held constantly and they observe the talking of adults, but are not encouraged to participate in conversations until 22 months old.

Children learn how to deal with various situations and, when it is appropriate, to use "a particular word, phrase, or set of actions" after being asked, "Now what are you gonna do?" (Heath 1983, 84). For example, adults often tease children, pretending to take away their candy or bottle. Since children do not have physical power, they must learn skills in dealing with others by outwitting, outtalking, or outacting their aggressors (Heath 1983). This is all part of the cultural sequencing children learn from their interactions with adults. Children learn about the type of situations they will need to be able to cope with; they learn acceptable behavior and favorable verbal responses.

What are the cultural cues that children learn in their families? To what type of social situations are children expected to be able to respond? How are they expected to respond? The answers to these questions help teachers understand how adults shape the cultural context of learning.

Cultural Sequencing in Learning: How Babies Are Taught to Respond in Roadville

Roadville is a White working-class, textile mill community in the Piedmont area of the Carolinas. Many of the families were originally from the Appalachian Mountains and moved to the Piedmont in the early 1900s. In this community, the arrival of babies is an important social and familial event.

For the first three months of their lives, babies are placed on feeding and sleeping schedules to encourage them to learn the routine. Relatives and close friends visit the mother and her new baby and offer assistance and advice. Heath (1983) found that new mothers had regular visits from older women with experience with children. These women would talk with the baby, calling her or him by name and asking questions using a sing-song intonation. This way both baby and new mother would learn about how they should be behaving and responding to each other.

Mothers are encouraged to respond to their babies, but not to "spoil" them by carrying them all the time. Relatives encourage mothers to let their babies explore, talk baby talk, and make noises. When children begin talking, parents, siblings, and others teach children the names of pets, people, objects, and events. They are taught to "pay attention, listen, and behave" and how to talk appropriately through their communications with adults (Heath 1983, 127).

Comparing Trackton and Roadville: Differences in the Socialization of Children

Heath (1983) found that the communities of Trackton and Roadville are different in their socialization of children. This section describes several of her major findings. First, children in Roadville are primarily brought up by their own parents, while children in Trackton are tended to by many members of the community, including parents, older siblings, children in the neighborhood, relatives, and other adults. Second, verbal interactions and skills are especially coveted in the Trackton community. Children are expected to show their abilities to perform creatively when verbally challenged. They are also taught to be spontaneous and to develop keen role-playing skills. In Roadville, children are expected to develop adult-like speech and engage in adult-like activities such as fishing, cooking, and taking care of younger siblings. For example, parents teach their children to tell stories and to report exact dialogue (Health 1983).

Both communities have strong oral traditions; however, the way they structure their stories differs. In Roadville, stories are primarily factual, deviate little from actual events, and affirm the values of the community. In Trackton, people creatively describe real-life events and demonstrate their storytelling abilities. Finally, oral tradition is highly valued in the Trackton community. Children are taught stories and are expected to tell those stories as young as the age of two. They learn to use gestures and embellish actual events in order to be entertaining. Though children in Roadville are also encouraged to tell stories, they must tell the stories as accurately as possible. Parents also read to their children and ask them questions about the stories. Many of the books contain nursery rhymes or are simplified stories from the Bible (Heath 1983).

Trackton and Roadville communities differ in the way they teach and view the use of language. Though the two social groups believe schooling is important, most members do not see how schooling could be linked to the future of their children because many find their occupations through friends, family, or accidentally.

Young people are socialized in many ways by family. The next portion is a story of how a Chinese American young person was taught many cultural values through interactions with his aunt and other family members.

Case Study

CULTURAL SOCIALIZATION THROUGH FAMILY INTERACTIONS

When Gerry was 10 years old, he went to his grandmother's 80th birthday party in Hawaii. The family had the party at a Chinese restaurant. Everyone was smiling and talking. Gerry sat next to his Auntie Sara at a round table with nine other people. Because this was a big birthday celebration, the family honored their grandmother with a nine-course dinner.

Many years ago, Gerry's grandmother traveled to Hawaii from Canton, China, by ship when she was only 15 years old. She was betrothed to his grandfather, who at that time was about 25 years old. The couple eventually had eight children. His grandfather died when Gerry was four years old and left his grandmother as matriarch of the family.

In honor of the grandmother, the family had golden peach pins for everyone. Because peaches symbolize long life, every family member was given not only pins, but also vases with peaches painted on the front panel.

As each course of food was brought out to the table and served, Gerry became more full. He wanted to rest his stomach, so he stuck his chopsticks into his bowl of rice. The chopsticks stuck straight up. His Auntie Sara placed her hand on his shoulder and whispered, "Gerry, don't do that because it means death."

Gerry quickly took the chopsticks from his bowl of rice and placed them on his white dinner plate; his face was slightly red because he was embarrassed. He knew children were not supposed to do anything to bring disgrace to their family. Children were supposed to act properly, just as they did in school.

One of the nine courses was a noodle dish. Noodles are served at birthday parties in many Chinese and Chinese American families because noodles are long and therefore represent a long life. When the large blue platter of noodles was pushed in front of Gerry on the table's lazy susan, he took the large spoon and began to put noodles on his plate. However, some noodles were falling off the serving plate so he cut them with the spoon. His Auntie Sara frowned and leaned down toward Gerry, gently whispering in his ear. This time she said, "Gerry, don't cut your noodles or you will be cutting the life of your grandmother short."

The young man quickly scooped the noodles onto his plate and pushed the lazy susan toward the next diner.

In the course of the meal, each person was also given a small packet of dried coconut and fruit that had a sugar coating. The sweetness of the dessert represented more sweetness in life for his grandmother.

Gerry learned much about the importance of long life and symbols of longevity within a cultural family context. He understood more clearly the explicit aspects of culture, and he also knew that he had to obey elder members of his family like his auntie. Children are educated not only by parents, but also grandparents, aunts, uncles, and other important family friends.

Like most children, Gerry learned values and beliefs besides other cultural elements like traditions and customs through social interactions with family members. The example demonstrated that Gerry grew up in a supportive, extended family context. His learning came not only from direct statements from his auntie, but also from other elements like tone of voice and nonverbal behaviors of other family members. The birthday party gave a powerful cultural context for learning. Gerry learned in more detail which behaviors were expected and accepted, while learning cultural values that emphasized longevity, respect for grandparents, and the importance of obedience.

Gerry was socialized into the cultural values and practices of his family. **Socialization** refers to the process in which an adult or child is taught the ways, norms, and beliefs of a group so that he or she will identify with and behave like others in the group. ❊

What Is U.S. American Culture?

I believe there is something that can be called U.S. American culture. (The term *U.S. American* is used throughout this book, because the concept of American is not exclusively used in the United States. For example, people in South America and Latin America also use the term *American*.) This culture is, for the most part, U.S. American middle-class Caucasian culture (Brislin 1993), although it does include elements from other ethnic groups. In the U.S. American culture, holidays like the Fourth of July, Thanksgiving, Easter, and Christmas are observed; however, not everyone celebrates those days, and some U.S. Americans may celebrate other holidays like Rosh Hashanah, Ramadan, and Kwanzaa. Our nation has a strong Judeo-Christian orientation, so many of the holidays come from that tradition; however, Buddhists, Muslim, agnostics, and atheists are members of society, too.

There are also less obvious elements of U.S. culture that impact us every day and that we may take for granted: for example, our currency. Take paper money from your wallet, purse, or pocket and lay the money flat on a table with the portraits facing up. Whom do you see on the $1 bill? Five-dollar bill? Ten-dollar bill? Twenty-dollar bill? Fifty-dollar bill? Culture is composed of many everyday elements (Valle 1997). One of those elements is our currency or money. We use it to buy groceries, clothes, gas, services, and many other things.

Whom did you discover pictured on our paper money? Below is a chart listing the person who is portrayed on each note.

Images Found on U.S. Currency: Paper Money

Amount of Note	Portrait	Picture on Opposite Side of Note
$1 note	George Washington	Great Seal of the United States
$2 note	Thomas Jefferson	Signing of Declaration of Independence
$5 note	Abraham Lincoln	Lincoln Memorial
$10 note	Alexander Hamilton	U.S. Treasury Building
$20 note	Andrew Jackson	The White House
$50 note	Ulysses S. Grant	U.S. Capitol
$100 note	Benjamin Franklin	Independence Hall

Each bill has the face of a U.S. statesperson. Our money reinforces the contributions of European American males. This is a powerful statement, considering how often we use money. Therefore, our beliefs about who are our notable leaders indicate a belief system that is based on cultural background and gender. Gould, the paleontologist, wrote that he believed the United States has "a truly sexist past that regarded males as standards for humanity" and ignored women (1996, 20). The messages conveyed in much of our culture are hidden and yet dominant. Many European American men did contribute to the building of the United States from its beginning; however, others, such as Native American women and men, were original inhabitants who also played roles in the development of this country. Why then don't we have women and people from underrepresented groups on our paper money? The comic on page 49 depicts one person's view of how our paper money could be changed in order to show the diversity of our nation. Although I don't agree with the part of the comic strip that accuses Cuco, the artist, of creating counterfeit money, I do like the idea of adding other folks to U.S. currency. The cartoonist has a different cultural understanding of what it means to add color. He thinks the United States should consider adding "color" by including the portraits of leaders such as Dolores Huerta, Geronimo, Malcolm X, Martin Luther King, Jr., and Cesar Chavez. Have you ever considered how culture is conveyed by small details of life?

Another important aspect of culture is our government. U.S. currency also depicts many important governmental locations such as the White House, the U.S. Treasury Building, and the Lincoln Memorial. These landmarks are often seen as symbols of our government. Indirectly, these landmarks may represent the values of democracy, equality, and justice to some folks (Valle 1997). In addition, because we have a representative government, an important interactional pattern in our culture is the voting process. We vote for others to act on our behalf because our country is a democratic republic.

LA CUCARACHA   **BY LALO ALCARAZ**

Another aspect of what I will loosely call U.S. American culture is economic status. Many people in this country who are wealthy also have more political, economic, and social power than those who have fewer financial resources. Capitalism is an influential force in our society and how much money a person has is often seen as an important measure of her or his status. Bill Gates has been on the cover of many of our nation's magazines such as *Time* and *Newsweek,* not only because he built Microsoft, but because he is the richest ($60 billion at this time) person in the United States. The high social class of Gates also includes a level of prestige and influence that is usually not available to people with few financial resources. In contrast, in a country like Tibet, one of the most important figures is the Dalai Lama. Although he was exiled in 1959 when the Chinese Communists took the country, he still remains a precious symbol of strength and empathy. He believes in owning only one set of clothes, and as a Buddhist monk he has few possessions; however, he is seen by many Tibetans and others in the world as someone who holds priceless riches of spirituality and compassion for others.

History is another important element of culture. Through history we can see how our values and beliefs have changed as a collective. For example, in the past, some laws barred women and people of color from voting and becoming citizens. They did not have the same freedoms that White males had. These discriminatory beliefs were held for years by many people, including lawmakers and other community leaders. Although our belief system as a nation has moved away from those limiting ideas, citizens still disagree about how to create a just and fair society. For example, in the 1970s and the 1980s, affirmative action programs were instituted and praised as encouraging integration and providing more equal opportunities to those from underrepresented groups who had been treated unfairly due to race, class, or gender. Today, affirmative action programs have, for the most part, been eliminated. People in the United States may believe it is important to support equality for all; however, the strategies people implement to accomplish goals may change.

Schools Transmit U.S. American Culture

Schools are an important part of U.S. culture. We teach U.S. American culture throughout the years children attend schools. The next case described how some aspects of gender roles can be taught and/or reinforced by a common nursery rhyme.

 Case Study

PETER, PETER PUMPKIN EATER

Young children are often taught nursery rhymes. In fact, some districts mandate that their teachers teach specific nursery rhymes. One common nursery rhyme taught in U.S. schools is "Peter, Peter Pumpkin Eater." When my friend's son John was in kindergarten, he had to learn this rhyme. The teacher first introduced the poem to the whole class and then later she had different learning centers where various activities could be chosen by her students. "Peter, Peter Pumpkin Eater" was one of them. The poem was written for the students on a half-sheet of paper.

Peter, Peter Pumpkin Eater

Peter, Peter, Pumpkin Eater
Had a wife and couldn't keep her.
Kept her in a Pumpkin shell.
And there he kept her very well.

At the nursery rhyme center, John cut two identical pumpkin shapes out of orange paper to act as the front and back covers. He then stapled the stems together and pasted a copy of the rhyme inside, making a book. Then the teacher told all the students to cut out a magazine picture of a woman and glue it inside the pumpkin on the other side of the rhyme. John was so proud of his pumpkin that he took it home and showed his mother, his face beaming. "Look, Mom. I did a good job of cutting and pasting," he said. John had cut out a picture of a woman in a bathing suit and pasted it inside his pumpkin. His mother was mortified. How could *her* son place such a gender-biased picture of a woman inside his pumpkin? Of course, his answer was, "Mom, why don't you like my pumpkin. It is just a picture of a lady." John was only five years old and he was learning social messages about women from curriculum in the school culture. It was not only difficult for John's mother to understand his choice of a picture of a woman in a bathing suit, but she was not sure why the teacher asked children to place a woman in the pumpkin. The teacher told her later that it was to reinforce sequence of events in the poem.

This poem was part of the district-mandated curriculum for teachers. However, the use of the poem "Peter, Peter, Pumpkin Eater" seemed to suggest distinct values about women and men that should be reflected upon. First, the husband couldn't keep his wife, so he had to put her in the pumpkin. Does that mean he was not a loving person and so she wanted to run away? Why would a woman need to be put in a pumpkin shell? Couldn't she take care of herself? Other messages could be consciously or unconsciously conveyed by the rhyme, too. The poem teaches negative messages about both women and men. In addition, it has a strong traditional gender role message. Unfortunately, neither John's teacher nor her kindergartners talked about gender roles; rather the children were intently involved in cutting, pasting, and coloring. Cultural ideas about women were being implicitly taught by this activity. The teacher did not realize what subtle messages the children could be learning. This is an example of why it is critical for teachers to reflect upon the questions presented in Chapter 1:

Who decides what is most important to teach?

Who makes the choices in our school?

Why are those choices made?

Who benefits from those choices?

How is the status quo reinforced?

Who will lose if changes in schools are made?

Let's apply the Valle's model of culture to the "Peter, Peter Pumpkin Eater" example. The nursery rhyme situation can be used to reveal various cultural elements.

Layer 1: Artifact, Symbol, Name, Poem—Children's nursery rhyme; "Peter, Peter Pumpkin Eater"

Layer 2: Interactional Patterns—Teachers, parents, and others read, model, and teach the rhyme to children. Children recite the poem from memory and make art projects.

Layer 3: Values, Beliefs, Norms—Possible underlying messages or beliefs: Women need to be taken care of; men may not be able to hold on to their wives; men may need to put their wives in a pumpkin; reinforced traditional gender roles.

These are strong messages. Are they the beliefs that you as a teacher would like to teach your students? Why do you think the nursery rhyme was taught year after year? ❁

Older students also learn about U.S. American culture in schools. In high school, the "smarter" young people are placed in advanced placement (AP) classes and others are placed in regular classes. Advanced placement classes are college-level courses taught in high school. How do we measure who is smart? This is a cultural question. As I sat at my daughter's high school graduation, I noticed that several students who were good at auto mechanics and could fix any

> ⑤ *Schools transfer values, beliefs, expectations, norms, behaviors, symbols, heroes, and other elements of mainstream culture to students.*

car were not given much recognition, but students who scored in the top 1 percent of the Preliminary Scholastic Achievement Test (PSAT) received a special national merit award and were recognized in front of all the parents. Whom do we value more—the young person who scores well on the national test or the youth who has the talent and knowledge to fix one of the most relied-on machines in our society today? Maybe we should honor both students for their diverse accomplishments and abilities. What message do our culture and schools give out about who is more valued?

Case Study

HISTORICAL PERSPECTIVES: TEACHING POWERFUL CULTURAL VALUES

In schools a powerful subject area that teaches a great deal about U.S. American culture is history, history that focuses upon the revolution and evolution of the 13 colonies from Britain. Little information is provided about Native Americans who lived on the land before the colonists migrated to the continent. In addition, our children learn that colonists from England fought for freedom and democracy. The colonists are portrayed as the founders and thinkers of a civilized society in this country. This is a powerful filter used in history.

Children study historical events like the Boston Tea Party, the Battle of Bunker Hill, and Paul Revere's ride as examples of bravery and belief in independence and fairness. Children may learn that people such as Benjamin Franklin, George Washington, and Thomas Jefferson founded our country with courage and great leadership. Like most of us, those presented had their strengths and weaknesses. However, many textbooks provide a one-dimensional understanding of our leaders. For example, texts may not discuss that both George Washington and Thomas Jefferson owned slaves. Why isn't this mentioned? Because the mythology being taught about our nation is that the United States stands for democracy, freedom, and equality. Some historians believe that it is only reasonable and fair to view these men within the context of the times; their behaviors as slave owners should not be seen negatively because many men owned slaves. The implicit layer of our culture is a powerful one.

The history taught in schools contains a strong theme of **hero-making** (Loewen 1995). We have many stories about famous people such as Betsy Ross and Woodrow Wilson. However, few students know that Ross had nothing to do with the making of the first flag and Wilson was extremely racist (Loewen 1995). Why aren't students taught this information? As Loewen wisely explains, we, like many other nations, teach ideals. Through our national **mythology,** which includes heroes, we teach our students the values of courage, independence, and hard work. In addition, because underrepresented groups have often pointed out the paradox between reality and our ideals, schools have been reluctant to provide a comprehensive view of history by including the perspectives of African Americans, Latinos, Asian Americans, or Native Americans who may challenge and question our national mythology. As is the case in most countries, history is usually written from the perspective of the victors or those in powerful positions. In Chapters 8 and 9, I discuss how culture can be integrated into our school culture. School faculty, curriculum, policies, and materials convey influential messages to our students about race, class, and gender. Mythology transmits the message that society is working for the best interest of all citizens, and this myth is conveyed over and over through the media, newspapers, schools, businesses, and government (Sherman and Wood 1989). One of the most powerful ideological myths of U.S. American culture is that "your dreams will come true if you work hard." Does it matter if people are rich or poor, Black or White, female or male (Sherman and Wood 1989)? The mythology of our culture glosses over the inequities in our country. The mythology also assumes that social biases such as racism, sexism, homophobia, and classism do not exist, or if they do exist, they are found primarily in extremely prejudiced people and not in our institutions such as schools.

One question I ask teachers is "Does everyone have the same chance to succeed in life if he or she works hard no matter what his or her background?" Most teachers say, "Of course." Then I probe deeper. "So you are saying that if a Latina worked hard, went to the best schools, she would be able to rise to any level in society?" All of sudden I can hear a few gasps of air as if some teachers are rethinking this idea. Several teachers say, "Yes." Then I ask, "How many women and Latinos have we had as president?" The teachers begin to reevaluate their perception. I continue with, "How many presidents have been Black, Asian, or Native American males, not even women?" Educators are beginning to see that although we do hold ideals of equality, there are still psychological, social, and political barriers to full equality for all citizens. Our mythology often teaches that leaders are primarily men, not women and also projects the belief that our leaders are usually White men and not generally women and/or people of color. This mythology combined with the cultural belief in hard work forms the cultural model of **meritocracy** (Lipman 1998). In other words, people who succeed are those who are smarter and work harder. However, as you can see with the example of who has been president, bias is still at work.

Sometimes teachers are aware of the mythology they were taught as children. However, it does take time and effort to research issues and learn other perspectives of an issue. In one of my classes a tall White male novice teacher came up to me and said, "When are we going to learn about Thanksgiving?" He was training to be an elementary teacher and was taking a class in Multicultural Education pedagogy. I asked him what exactly he wanted to know. He replied, "I want to know about the history of the Wampanoags and how they actually saved the Pilgrims from starving to death. I would like to have a more comprehensive understanding about the contributions of many groups to our national history." I was happy that he thought about the importance of delving into issues from other cultural viewpoints.

How would you define U.S. American culture? What do you value or do in your life that is part of American culture? What are some of the ideals of U.S. American culture? What are some of the important social institutions in U.S. American culture? A great deal of the U.S. American culture that I am involved in has to do with my children. Our daughter is an adult now, but when she was little, my husband and I took her to ballet lessons, guitar lessons, and Girl Scout meetings. When she was older, she was involved in cross-country running and was editor of the high school newspaper. We took our son to soccer practice, tennis lessons, and to Little League games. Now he is a college student. All these activities are what I perceive as elements of U.S. American culture. People in other countries may also have similar elements in their culture, including higher education, music lessons, and sport lessons. ❋

 Case Study

CULTURAL KNOWLEDGE: STUDENTS AND TEACHERS MAY DIFFER

Students and teachers may have different popular cultural knowledge, even though they live in the same country. They may have different experiences in life due to aspects such as age, religion, and hobbies. The following is an example that demonstrates how a teacher's knowledge of an aspect of popular culture differed from her student's and how cultural elements are often found within a cultural context.

A teacher named Lucille told me this story about one of her students. She explained that there was a cultural generation gap between herself and a youngster named Jacob. In class, she said in an enthusiastic voice, "Yahoo, that is a great job, Jacob!"

Jacob gave her a puzzled look. He said, "Mrs. Wong, Yahoo is a search engine. What are you talking about?!"

Mrs. Wong laughed and laughed. She had forgotten that Yahoo was a website on the Internet, where many of her students looked up various information from maps to recipes.

Jacob then went on to explain, "Yoohoo is also a chocolate milk drink. I don't know what you mean. I buy it at the grocery store."

After Mrs. Wong recognized the misunderstanding, she said, "We hold different meanings of the same word. When I say 'Yahoo' in an enthusiastic way, I mean hurray or good. I guess we are learning new vocabulary together."

Then Jacob smiled. "I'll think of some more examples that you won't know tomorrow."

Jacob and his teacher laughed. ❋

In my experience, teachers vary in their knowledge of children's culture and children also come to school with different levels of cultural knowledge. Children take on elements of multiple cultures that may be ethnic, family, neighborhood, and/or popular in nature. The next section gives examples of how culture shapes the way we think through the images created and conveyed in the community. These images and beliefs shape the way people look at life. Teachers can begin to utilize these culturally familiar models if they are aware of or understand them.

Culture Shapes Our Values and Behaviors That Arise from Those Values

Culture shapes how we see the world and interpret the world. Sometimes children come to school with different perceptions and values because they have diverse cultural orientations. Children of color may experience cultural clashes when what they are taught at home is in conflict with what they are learning at school.

Case Study

LEARNING A DIFFERENT PERSPECTIVE FROM PRESCHOOLERS

In order for teachers to better understand the difference people have in their worldviews, I ask my students, who are teachers, to volunteer time with a community that is culturally different from their own. This has given an excellent opportunity for teachers to go beyond the surface aspects of culture and to understand more about their values; this can happen when people develop personal relationships with others from other cultures. For example, a teacher volunteered at a local YMCA in an African American and Latino low-income neighborhood. She chose this site because she realized that she had little knowledge of the life of a student from another neighborhood, a neighborhood that was not only African American, but what she perceived as violent. She described herself as a "23-year-old White, blond, green-eyed woman from a conservative White city doing volunteer work in the community of City Central. What a mismatch!"

Her first instinct when she got out of her car at the YMCA was, "Oh, my gosh, what am I doing in this part of the city!" She wrote in her paper, "I wanted to get back in my car and find another place to go, a place without so many problems. Looking around all that I saw was a rundown YMCA in a horrible area of town with police raiding a house across the street. I won't be able to relate to these kids."

She stayed at the YMCA and learned that aspects of life look different through someone else's cultural glasses. She wrote, "The children are surrounded daily by a world that is uncaring and unkind. Their parents care, but they were busy supporting their family." During one of their games with preschool children, she learned a valuable lesson about how her worldview was different from that of some of the young people in the neighborhood.

In a game called "Guess That Sound," she played a variety of sounds and the children had to guess them. The children were having lots of fun until she played the sound of a siren. When the children heard the siren, about four of them began to cry and others screamed, "It's the police! Hide! Hide!" The children became anxious and worried. She was flabbergasted to learn that three- and four-year-olds believed that the police were not there to protect them. Some of the children were scared of the police in that neighborhood. She did not make any judgments about their views, but she realized that not all the children thought in the same way she did. She began to understand how the issues of race and class were intimately linked and did impact children and how they grew up, saw the world, and responded to others.

To the children who hid under the tables, the sound of police sirens had strong underlying values associated with it, so the symbol of sirens in this neighborhood was threatening. The next section discusses how culture has surface and deep levels. ❋

Culture: Connections between Deep and Surface Levels

Culture has both surface and deep elements. Many of the things I mentioned in a previous section on U.S. American culture were surface elements like holidays, soccer games, and famous Americans. However, I also pointed to values like freedom, equality, and democracy, which are a part of the deep structure of culture.

Let's look at examples of explicit expressions of U.S. American culture: symbols such as the U.S. flag, the scroll to represent the U.S. Constitution, the dollar sign meaning money ($), and the White House; institutions such as schools, universities, police departments, fire departments, and hospitals; and businesses such as McDonald's, Sears, Microsoft, Kleenex, Purex, and Kellogg. The editorial cartoon

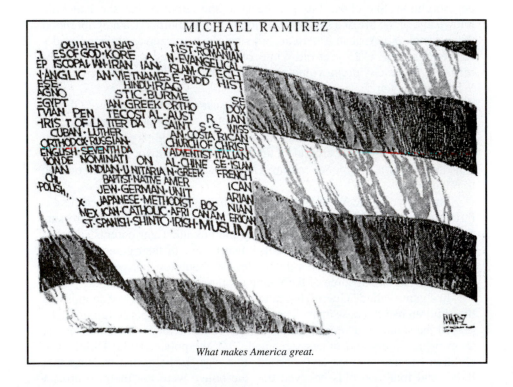

What makes America great.

on page 56 not only uses the flag as a symbol of the United States, but also conveys the underlying belief in diversity in the United States.

What are some of the underlying values of another symbol? The dollar sign ($) not only represents money, but may also suggest capitalism. Capitalism is an important system of economics in the United States. A major aspect of capitalism is the belief in individualism and that being an entrepreneur is an acceptable and valued career. This quest of a personal goal is often seen positively within the national value that each person has the right to pursue happiness. Our social culture also includes large corporations such as Burger King, Wal-Mart, Barnes & Noble, and Tiffany's department store. Many people support capitalism.

The U.S. Constitution represents the belief that we are a nation committed to the values of freedom, justice, and equality, and that those values are at the foundation of who we are as a society. Civil rights is an important theme in our history. English immigrants fought to establish a new country where they would have religious freedom. African Americans, Asian Pacific Americans, Latinos, Native Americans, women, gays, lesbians, people with disabilities, Jews, and others have fought for equal rights and continue to do so.

The implicit cultural values of a person are often difficult to see. However, it is easier for others to recognize the explicit or surface elements of culture, such as the type of clothing a person wears or the language an individual speaks or what Valle called layer 1 in his cultural model. It is much more difficult to learn about underlying cultural beliefs, such as what motivates a child or what her or his values happen to be. Valle told me, "Kids don't come with a list that says these are my values. Teachers are going to have to watch kids. They will learn by talking with young people. It will take a while before teachers may develop a real understanding of the values of their students." This is an awesome task. Table 2.1 presents several examples about how tangible elements may represent much deeper, implicit cultural values. Teachers must be cultural translators or mediators, people who understand the implicit culture, in order to make schooling most meaningful and effective. They must understand underlying values and beliefs that may motivate or give a sense of purpose to students.

TABLE 2.1   Cultural Elements: Examples of Surface and Deep Culture

	Language, Symbols, and Artifacts	Customs, Practices, and Interactional Patterns	Shared Values, Beliefs, Norms, and Expectations
Example 1	First Amendment	a. Stand up and speak out about one's views. b. Organize group and community meetings. c. Worship as one chooses.	a. Value an individual's or group's right to speak out, assemble, and worship. b. Safeguard the right of an individual or group to speak out, meet, or worship.

continued

TABLE 2.1   Cultural Elements: Examples of Surface and Deep Culture *(continued)*

	Language, Symbols, and Artifacts	Customs, Practices, and Interactional Patterns	Shared Values, Beliefs, Norms, and Expectations
Example 2	Community action of Malcolm X	a. Spoke to many people in community. b. Taught about the importance of freedom, humanity, education, religion, and justice. c. Built community organizations.	a. Valued equality. b. Valued freedom. c. Valued education. d. Believed in social change. e. Believed in community unity. f. Held Islamic beliefs. g. Believed in African American determination.
Example 3	Eighteen-year-old male in a Cuban American family gives opinion during a family dinner	a. Parents and grandparents encouraged children to express themselves. b. Son (and grandson) spoke respectfully to family members. c. Son waited his turn to talk in the conversation.	a. Family believed in respectful and loving family relationships. b. Family valued a strong cultural community. c. Family wanted son to develop confidently and competently. d. Son lived at home until after college because he chose to be close to his family.
Example 4	Origami—Japanese paper folding crane	a. Child watches another child or adult fold paper. b. Child folds paper one section at a time modeling the "teacher." c. "Teacher" waits patiently and shows folds several times as needed. d. Child and teacher treat each other with respect.	a. Develops sense of patience. b. Reinforces a sense of community. c. Teaches respect for the teacher or someone with a skill. d. Cranes represent good luck and long life in Japanese life. e. Reflects value of simplicity and beauty.
Example 5	The Wampanoags and Thanksgiving	a. Wampanoags lived in the area now known as Massachusetts. b. Massasoit, leader of the Wampanoags, welcomed Pilgrims and invited them to settle in Plymouth.	a. Wampanoags, like many Native Americans, gave thanks yearly for the fall harvest. b. Wampanoags cared for other humans and for the land.

TABLE 2.1   Cultural Elements: Examples of Surface and Deep Culture *(concluded)*

Language, Symbols, and Artifacts	Customs, Practices, and Interactional Patterns	Shared Values, Beliefs, Norms, and Expectations
	c. Wampanoags invited Pilgrims to join them in their celebration. d. Pilgrims and other Europeans brought new diseases like cholera, typhus, tuberculosis, small pox, bubonic plague, and diphtheria to Native Americans who had no immunity (Loewen 1995). e. Wampanoags and Pilgrims helped each other and built strong community relationships (Loewen 1995).	c. Though few Wampanoags live today, Thanksgiving represents to many of them a sad chapter in their history because most Wampanoags were killed within 50 years of the settlement of the Pilgrims due to disease or wars (Loewen 1995).

 Case Study

ORIGAMI: SISTER TEACHING BROTHER CULTURAL VALUES
THROUGH CULTURAL ART

Let's take one example from the table. Origami is often used by teachers to teach about Japanese American or Japanese culture. Usually teachers teach students how to make a crane or ball. What do you think students are learning about the culture of the Japanese? They may see origami as clever and/or beautiful. Students may also sharpen their spatial relationship skills. However, what underlying values of the culture are communicated?

When our daughter was only five years old, we went to the wedding of one of my friends. A beautiful exhibit of a thousand paper cranes hung above the head table at the reception. Our daughter enjoyed the many strands of beautiful colored origami cranes. She went up to the head table and asked the bride why she had so many of them at her wedding. The bride told her that the thousand cranes symbolized good luck. In addition, since cranes live a long time, the cranes represented a long and wonderful marriage.

That day our daughter became very interested in making cranes. I took a napkin from the table and taught her how to make a crane. The first crane she and I made together was from a cloth napkin! It took a little time. Our daughter folded the napkin carefully by observing what I did. Since that was the limit to my expertise in origami, she bought several short how-to books and taught herself to create beautiful flowers, geometric paper boxes, and many-sided hanging balls by following the pictures. When her brother was small, he often watched her fold paper into birds, elephants, and flowers. It was too difficult for him and he did not have the patience to learn until he was about six years old. Then he asked his sister to sit down with him and teach him the crane. From then on, he became very interested in origami. They began making things together and sharing their paper. They would carry small sheets about 3 inches square in their pockets in the car and make things during the drives to the doctor or supermarket. One of their favorite activities was to go to China-town in Seattle and buy new origami paper at Uwajimaya's, a Japanese food and variety store. Uwajimaya's carried many different colors of paper; some were gold, silver, and traditional Japanese patterns.

To our children, origami represents not only an ancient Japanese art form, but also family and a special brother-sister bond. It also exemplifies a personal art form. It takes much patience and accuracy to create a successful piece. To-day, both of our children still share origami ideas with each other and make various shaped boxes, kangaroos, and five-pointed stars. This example also demonstrates how culture is often transferred through family interactions and modeling. ❀

Historically, origami is an art form that is over a thousand years old. *Ori* means folded and *kami* refers to paper in the Japanese language. When the two parts are put together, the word is *origami*. This art form was an activity of the imperial court.

Origami, as Valle explains, represents not only the tangible product, but also in-teractional cultural patterns and underlying values. To provide students with a more complete understanding of culture, teachers must share with them not only the how-to sequence of folding, but also explain that it is an art form that reinforces the im-portance of observation skills, working with others, and patience and that it represents simple beauty. In order to create a beautiful piece of art one must be pa-tient. Using a single piece of paper, a person can create a myriad of objects and artis-tic expressions. There were various levels of cultural significance.

Read through the other examples in Table 2.1 and notice the connections be-tween the tangible outward behaviors and symbols, the interactions between people, and the underlying values that the implicit culture refers to within the specific cul-tural context. What does culture have to do with teaching? Oftentimes you as a teacher might act as a **cultural translator** or **mediator** who understands the lay-ers of culture (Bustamante-Jones 1998). Cleary and Peacock (1998) give numerous illustrations of how majority and Native American cultures may hold different ex-pectations. For example, many Native American young people grow up in families where children are expected to listen rather than speak. Young people learn to watch others before they do something that might make them look like fools. Children are also advised not to show off. Therefore, some students have difficulty participating in class and may choose to withdraw instead of showing up for school, knowing that they must speak out or act aggressively. Other times, Native American youngsters may choose not to participate because they do not trust or feel comfortable with

Teacher as cultural mediator

teachers. Some teachers may feel that this lack of participation shows disinterest in learning, though this is not accurate. Cleary and Peacock (1998) also note that if the young adult chooses to participate, he or she may have to take on a different cultural role. This role may be uncomfortable because the student must discard cultural behaviors and beliefs. For example, the student might need to learn how to interrupt in order to be heard in a Socratic social studies discussion. This can be extremely uncomfortable for someone who was taught that this behavior is disrespectful. However, in many discussions, if a person does not interrupt, she or he may not have the opportunity to participate and be heard, and school culture rewards aggressive verbal behavior. The school often mirrors the cultural values of mainstream society.

> ⑤ Caring–Centered Multicultural Education teachers are cultural mediators. They learn, understand, and build upon the cultures of their students.

Sometimes older students have cultural values that do not fall right in line with what is understood as acceptable in mainstream schools. The work of Thomas Kochman provides a view into the differences that African American students may find in schools.

Cultural Values in Conflict

Understanding the sociocultural background of your students can be extremely eye-opening. Maybe some of the friction you see in your classroom is not showing a conflict but rather an example of how people express or communicate themselves differently. As Heath's research has shown, people grow up with different values and ways of interpreting other people's actions. One of the best resources describing how the communication styles of African Americans and European Americans may differ is Kochman's book, *Black and White Styles in Conflict.*

Kochman (1981) provides many situations about how people with different styles misinterpret the actions of others. For example, Kochman describes how Blacks often engage in posturing. This pattern of behavior sends the message of courage and fearlessness to one's opponent (Kochman 1981). It is a way to settle an argument before physical fighting begins by asserting one's dominance. There is also a sense of drama that plays into this pattern. The posturing behavior often is a sign that the person does not intend to get into a physical fight. Posturing is a talking strategy to resolve a disagreement.

In contrast, Kochman (1981) believes that in the White community verbal threats show that aggressive physical actions will follow. Whites perceive heated verbal exchanges as most likely ending in fighting; verbal fighting will lead to physical fighting. In addition Whites believe that heated discussions are already indications that a fight is in progress.

How will these cultural differences impact the classroom? Kochman illustrates his point by telling a story about a White female teacher who had begun teaching in a Black high school in Louisville (1985, 44). Two Black students were loudly arguing at the beginning of class about who was going to sit in a particular seat. Each looked at the other defiantly and took confrontational stands; however, no physical fighting took place. The teacher sent the students to the principal's office for fighting. After class several Black students asked the teacher why she sent the two students to the office, because they weren't going to do anything. The teacher told them that she disagreed. She said the two students were "fighting" because of their loud arguing. The teacher was sure that the young men were going to throw punches at each other. She wanted to keep the situation from escalating. The students told her the others weren't really "fighting"; they were setting up boundaries with their words.

In this situation, it is clear that the teacher and her Black students had different understandings of what was a fight, when it had begun, and whether violence was going to arise. The teacher was sure the two students were fighting because of the anger that they expressed. However, the students saw their behaviors as setting the stage for a possible confrontation, and words and actions were very different (Kochman 1981). The students and teacher grew up in different cultural contexts where styles of interacting varied. If the teacher had had a better understanding of this, she may have been able to diffuse it quickly and quietly. In this case, knowing the cultural values of students in her class would have assisted her in her classroom management.

The next section discusses the difference between stereotyping and seeing tendencies in a cultural group.

Walking the Tightrope between Stereotypes and Cultural Generalizations

One of the questions I am often asked is, "What is the difference between a stereotype and a cultural generalization?" The person may go on and say, "People naturally develop categories in their mind in order to sort through the vast amount of information we are confronted with every day. I don't want to stereotype someone, but lots of Black folks speak Black vernacular. Is that a stereotype? Or lots of Mexican Americans eat rice and beans. Is that a stereotype?"

As Milton Bennett explained, "Stereotypes arise when we act as if all members of a culture or group share the same characteristics . . . Stereotypes . . . are problematic in intercultural communication for several obvious reasons. One is that they may give us a false sense of understanding of our communication partners . . . Additionally, stereotypes may become self-fulfilling prophecies, where we observe others in selective ways that confirm our prejudice" (1998, 6). As Bennett observed, many stereotypes are negative. One of the most difficult skills a teacher must develop is to refrain from stereotypically using cultural patterns to identify each student from a particular culture.

Bennett believed that people can make cultural generalizations about others that indicate a preference, but this preference does not identify everyone in a cultural group. Usually preferences are founded on the basis of a large number of people. For example, if we did a survey and found that a large sample of people in the United States eat hamburgers and hotdogs, we might understand that this is a general preference even though you and I may eat them once every 10 years.

Valle and Brason (2002) explained cultural generalizations in a slightly different way. They believe that people in cultures pass down, from one generation to another, ideas about what is considered acceptable. There are unique cultural elements within groups and sometimes the ways the elements are used are distinctive. Although there is variability within a group, there are also norms about aspects of life such as how to interact with others, what language to use, and what is expected from a person who is a member. He and his colleague used the normal curve as a theoretical concept to describe the **variation** of people within a group who follow the cultural worldview (Valle 2001; Valle and Brason 2002). The normal curve in Figure 2.2 shows that many people within a cultural group may follow or agree with many aspects of a cultural community (Valle and Brason 2002). The left end of the curve demonstrates that there are people who do not hold many cultural elements at all and these individuals probably will not hold a high level of cultural identity. However, people on the right side of the curve are those who have adopted many elements of the culture and identify themselves as a member of the cultural group. The chart also reinforces the following ideas:

1. There is great within-group diversity.
2. No individual represents all of a culture's values, practices, or beliefs.

Figure 2.3 shows two unique cultures and their overlap in cultural ideas and values. Valle and Brason (2002) believe most cultures have overlapping areas. For

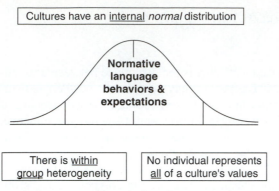

Figure 2.2   *Intragroup Cultural Heterogeneity*
Valle © 1997

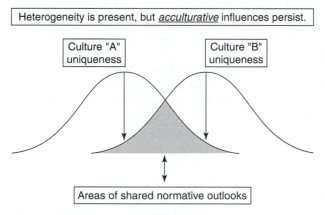

Figure 2.3   *Intragroup and Intergroup Cultural Heterogeneity: Overlapped Cultural Contact. In a multicultural society cultures can overlap to share outlooks and expectations.*
Valle © 1997

example, two cultural groups may have similar beliefs about family and education. The shaded area represents those areas that we have in common with people who are raised in other cultures. Maybe individuals in culture A and culture B believe in having high expectations for their young people. Therefore, both people from both cultures encourage their students to go to school and do well. However, maybe culture A and culture B also have differences. Let's say they do not believe in the same discipline methods. People in culture A prefer a strict approach, while members of culture B use a more permissive and self-disciplined approach.

Many cultural differences are also situation specific. Understanding culture is extremely complicated. I know that as a young person, Eugene, a student I had in my class, spoke Black vernacular exclusively at home and with his peers. However, around teachers and other adults he always used "school" or more formal English.

Although Eugene's life may be described as African American, he is bicultural and is comfortable with both environments, African American and mainstream U.S. society.

How Can We Find Cultural Keys to Help Us Reach Others?

Case Study

A CULTURAL SOLUTION TO HEALTH

Why is it important for teachers and others to consider culture in their work? Sometimes teachers may have a difficult time reaching or understanding students. There are many reasons why students do not respond to materials found in their textbooks and other materials. Maybe students do not have much of a reference point. For example, if the story is about life on the farm, but a student has never been to the country, she or he may need a cultural bridge to help her or him to understand the context. Sometimes materials that are more meaningful to students are also more motivating. If a Filipino American student discovers that yo-yos were made popular by a Filipino American businessperson named Pedro Flores and that the word *yo-yo* means "come back" in Tagalog, she or he may be more interested in what the teacher is presenting. Culture can provide keys for many issues. The following discussion explains how cultural knowledge was used to solve an important health problem.

An excellent example of how researchers used their knowledge of culture to reach a large number of people can be found in the health field (Smith 1999). In Mexico malnutrition is a grave problem because many people live in deep poverty. People cannot afford to eat much protein or fresh vegetables. Numerous children do not have normal energy and are underweight because they do not have a healthy diet. Children also get sick more often, which impacts their ability to learn.

Health researchers from Mexico's Health Ministry and National Nutrition Institute and the United Nations Children's Fund searched for a cultural element in the diet of the people. The key was the tortilla! The tortilla is a corn-based food that has been a traditional staple for thousands of years in what we now know today as Mexico.

When researchers found that most families received more than two-thirds of their nutrition from tortillas, they realized that tortillas could be used as a vehicle to enrich the diet of many families. Officials asked major cornmeal manufacturers to add six vitamins and numerous minerals to cornmeal that they sold. The addition was not that costly. This change has had a major positive impact on the health of many Mexicans, children and adults. People have more energy and students are doing much better in school because they are more nourished.

Researchers are also studying ways in which protein can be added to the tortillas. They would like to fortify tortillas with protein-rich soy. Health officials say that the addition of soy will help increase the height, birth weight, and physical and mental ability of children (Smith 1999). Because researchers knew the population and understood their cultural lifestyles, it was possible for them to find something that was common in the lives of many Mexicans. The tortilla is becoming an important nutritional tool because of the combination of scientific research and culture. ✺

Case Study

FOOD MEANS MORE THAN NUTRITION

Sometimes food is also important not only because of its nutritional value, but also because it symbolizes various values and contexts important in a culture. Do you have a favorite dish that you like to eat that may have important cultural roots? As you will read later in the book, using food to represent culture can be stereotypical; however, I don't want to give the impression that food isn't important to most of us. Many of us really enjoy food! We like food for a variety of reasons. We may have dishes we like because we think they are especially delicious. Maybe food reminds of us of special times with our families or special celebrations. Food can also have important religious meanings.

Food can be an important manifestation of cultural values in the lives your students. Do universities take culture seriously? The following is an example of how cultural elements such as food and religion are important to administrators, staff, students, and community individuals at the California Institute of Technology. This university is also known as Caltech.

The administrators at Caltech wanted to attract students, staff, and faculty to their school and found that food was a concern because there were *no* kosher restaurants or markets in the area (Hong 2002). Therefore, the university built a kosher kitchen and employed a full-time chef to prepare kosher meals. *Kosher* in relation to food means "proper for eating." Kosher practices are explained in the Book of Leviticus in the Bible and there are careful rules regarding the suffering of animals. The slaughtering process must be carefully conducted so that animals die quickly. In addition, for kosher meals, there is a "strict separation of dairy ingredients from meat" (Hong 2002, B16).

Caltech was also sensitive to the needs of Muslim students and realized there was little to eat on campus for members of the Islamic community. Therefore, the university also created a menu of halal meals[1] for Muslims and vegetarian food for others (Hong 2002). Both Jews and Muslims do not eat pork so there are some similarities in their religious practices. However, although kosher meals can use wine, halal meals cannot contain any alcohol. Muslims

---

[1] Muslim children in schools are having difficulty eating school lunches. Most lunches do not comply with Islamic practices. Parents in Dearborn, Michigan, are requesting that schools prepare halal meals. Muslims also believe that animals eaten should be killed in such a way that the animal suffers as little as possible. When children see their school breakfasts and lunches, they throw out much of the food and eat unhealthy snacks instead. http://www.islamfortoday.com/michiganhalal.htm

adhere to teachings found in the Koran that also call for minimizing the suffering of animals when they are killed.

The food service department at Caltech has been successful in preparing meals for diverse cultural groups on campus. Others who work in the Caltech neighborhood also dine at the university. The new meals have encouraged more faculty lunch meetings, because the dining hall has meals for many different diners. The university continues to work toward accommodating the needs of faculty, staff, and students. In fact, the food service "is trying to find a way to accommodate Muslim students with stricter requirements, such as those who believe their meat must be slaughtered by a Muslim. Such meat would not be kosher and thus could not be prepared with the same pots and utensils used for the kosher food" (Hong 2002, B16).

These are excellent examples of how understanding culture not only assisted in providing better nutrition, but also improved the quality of life for people.[2] Many of us hold important beliefs about why we choose the food we eat. It is part of who we are and how we live our lives. Think carefully about the lives of your students and how what they know and value can be integrated into your curriculum. ❈

How Culture Can Be Distorted in Schools

When a teacher uses separate elements of culture, such as holidays in isolation to teach about a culture, then the teacher is dividing culture into small pieces and fragmenting it from its important underlying values and interactional patterns. That is why I caution teachers about using food fairs as an activity to teach the culture of other ethnic groups, because foods are only one aspect of a culture. Isolated and non-contextualized information about food by itself may serve to stereotype. If students learn only a small fragment about a group of people, this information may create overgeneralized images about individuals from a group based upon superficial knowledge.

Students may not understand that the food eaten may be an example of how people responded to their environment. Many years ago in what is now Guatemala, the Mayans developed a culture in which maize was a key element. In fact, the people honored a goddess of maize called Centeotl (Cornelius 1999). People had a special ceremony to give thanks for the corn and were careful to make sure to harvest all the corn to avoid wasting any of the precious life that was shared with them. Social studies textbooks may indicate that corn was important, but they may not explain how the culture of several ethnic communities centered on corn. The diet of communities revealed powerful philosophical and religious beliefs about the role and origin of corn in people's lives (Cornelius 1999).

Other implicit cultural values may also come from family experiences. For 15-year-old Gabriella, corn tortillas that her mom makes are her favorite food. When she comes home from school and sees her mother making tortillas, Gabriella smiles.

---

[2]Other universities are also opening dining halls that offer kosher and halal meals. One of these dining halls is at Mount Holyoke College in Massachusetts.

She and her brothers help mix and roll out the dough. Her mom places the flattened dough on the grill. The house is filled with the wonderful smell of tortillas. Gabriella knows that corn is an important part of her family's diet, but to her, making tortillas reminds her of good dinners with her family. Her teachers usually did not emphasize the community and family aspects of food, so for Gabriella, corn tortillas trigger in her a special warm feeling about family and her mom. In addition, many Guatemalans were and continue to be grateful for the role corn has played in the physical survival of families (Cornelius 1999).

When people enjoy food from another ethnic group, dress in traditional clothing of another community, and sing songs in another language, they may still have little knowledge of another cultural viewpoint regarding gender roles, the meaning of life, childrearing practices, and other important issues. Students may feel an aesthetic connection with the music or dance that they are participating in; however, usually it takes a knowledgeable teacher to explain the underlying interpretations and meanings of the cultural elements to students so that they can understand the historical, social, and belief systems that the components represent. External manifestations can provide stepping stones for further comprehension and investigation into another culture, but they usually cannot represent the "culture" as understood by insiders.

When deciding upon presenting cultural information, use the examples in Table 2.1 to help you clearly identify the implicit values that you are presenting about a cultural group in your classroom lessons. The table demonstrates how a more holistic view of culture can be presented. How would you feel if a teacher in Russia taught his students that U.S. American culture dealt with eating hot dogs, going to baseball games, and wearing Levis? What would you want Russian teachers to teach about Americans (U.S. citizens)? Teachers in my classes have said they would want Russian educators to focus upon our commitment to equity, justice, and freedom, and our heroes, local and national, who have worked to bring the dream of equality to all Americans. Teachers could also explain that, although those are our ideals, we have many families living in poverty and that we are struggling as a nation to do something about the gap between our ideals and realities of society.

Teaching about culture is most difficult in a classroom where many of the children are from mainstream culture. It is often difficult for students to see that they have a culture. It can be puzzling for them to identify elements of culture because they are seeped in a cultural orientation, as Ishmael has explained. It is usually easier to teach about culture when you have several different cultures in the classroom. Often, cultural conflicts or differences will naturally arise; then the teacher can discuss culture as an integrated part of the curriculum. Sometimes teachers find it easier to bring various dishes into the classroom, rather than discussing various beliefs and values. It takes much time for teachers to learn about the cultural value system of another cultural community and become a cultural mediator.

In some of our classrooms, children bring 20 different languages and cultures to school. It is also a great challenge to act as a cultural mediator when students come from quite different ethnic communities like Somali or Hmong, where some

Take a Stand

CULTURE: ARE SCHOOLS CULTURALLY NEUTRAL?

This chapter presents an in-depth discussion of culture. The United States is a multicultural society and students who come to school are from many different cultural communities. For example, students may speak a home language other than English.

Many teachers believe that schools are culturally neutral institutions because they teach basic knowledge that everyone needs to know. It is critical for teachers to consider these questions:

Are schools culturally neutral? If so, how? If not, what evidence can one present to demonstrate that schools are not culturally neutral? What is basic knowledge? Whose knowledge does it represent?

Teacher teamwork

value orientations are extremely different from majority culture. If you are a European American, you probably will be more like the child who is an immigrant from an English-speaking province of Canada, not only because of the language, but also because of the religious and political similarities of Canada and the United States. If you have little cultural knowledge of some of the students in your classes, find social workers, school liaisons, or community counselors who are willing to speak with you or members of your faculty to help initiate the process of understanding some of the cultural conflicts children face in school. You may also find cultural conflicts with children who were born in the United States, when the students come from strongly traditional Mexican American, African American, Native American, or Chinese American families. Again, cultural mediators can help you identify the roots of the conflicts.

Understanding Culture: Influencing the Success of Your Instruction

Many of us may not understand how culture really can influence the success of a lesson. Let me give you an example of what several teachers in my class found. One group of teachers worked in an African American community. They excitedly prepared a lesson on static electricity for their students in middle school. The teachers were team teaching a lesson and got together the materials they would need for their experiments. They brought filled balloons, cereal, a large poster board, combs, picks, and pieces of wool fabric.

The teachers first demonstrated how static electricity could be created by rubbing a balloon on each other's head. The rubbing caused an imbalance of electrons when electrons moved from one surface (hair) to another (the balloon), so when the teachers put the balloon next to a tray of cereal, the cereal danced. The electrons rebalanced themselves and this caused the cereal to move. It was fun for the children to see the hair on their teachers' heads standing straight up.

When the teachers rubbed balloons on their heads again, plastic forks held by string moved when placed near the balloons. The teachers had discussed how to create static electricity and now they wanted students to conduct the experiment themselves.

Each student chose a partner and received a balloon. The students worked hard at rubbing the balloons on each other's heads. Everyone was engaged, but after the balloon rubbing the students held the balloons over the cereal and not much happened. The cereal did not jump as it did when their teachers performed the experiment. It was a little damp outside, so that could have had something to do with the lack of creating static electricity.

What was going wrong? The teachers finally realized that their students liked hairstyles of braids, cornrows, and dreadlocks. Many used hair products that were primarily made with oil. The oil acted as a barrier so static electricity could not be built up. If the teachers had understood a little about the lifestyle of their students, they would have given the students pieces of wool instead of first asking them to use their hair. Of course, the lesson could now extend to teaching how oil creates a wall to the buildup of static electricity, so all was not lost. However, there was a small glitch in the lesson and the teachers and students initially became frustrated with the experiment. They both tried to rub the balloon over and over on the students' heads with little success. The teachers finally realized that they themselves did not use the same type of hair products as their students. It was as if they responded to life in particular ways and thought that everyone else did the same. This was quite an eye-opener for them. An understanding of culture could have made a difference in their instruction.

This science experiment is a good example of why teachers need to be cultural mediators. Teachers may not be able to integrate ethnic cultural content knowledge into every lesson; however, cultural aspects may influence the effectiveness of their instruction. The next example discusses the impact of social class on student learning.

Teachers in another class were surprised with cultural differences related to social class. Every semester novice teachers in my classes create a learning fair at a neighborhood apartment complex. The complex is located in an African American and Latino community and is made up of about 100 apartments; my college department has built a relationship with many residents in the complex.

To create the learning fair, preservice teachers formed groups of four or five people to create a learning booth. One set of teachers developed a lesson on waves and the influence of the moon. They brought pictures of the moon and an ocean and painted large posters that showed various science principles. Since they were working to build on the students' experiences, they began their lesson with two questions, "Have you been to the beach? Did you like it?" What surprised the teachers was that so many of the children had never been to the beach. They lived only about 25 minutes from several beaches, but the elementary grade students had not been there. When the teachers asked the children why they hadn't gone to the beach, many said because "my parents don't have a car to take us." The teachers were surprised because in Southern California one cannot get around easily without a car. The teachers had created the lesson using their own experiences as the point of reference; they had not thought that their students may not have the same knowledge base. Although the teachers were going to a public university, they did not understand that there are many families and individuals who may not have the same financial resources as they had. Many of the families in this complex could not afford to maintain a car, and students often took the bus.

At the same complex, another group of teachers had created a fun hands-on learning booth. Since this particular learning fair was held the day before Halloween, the group had created a "Creepy Boxes" booth. They had five boxes covered with orange paper with a hole in the front where students reached in to feel "eye balls" and "spider webs." Children enjoyed hypothesizing, using their sense of touch, about what was in the boxes. The teachers had used peeled grapes for eye balls, red jello for cold blood, and noodles for spider webs. Children described in detail what they felt and then hypothesized about what the items were in the boxes.

At the end of the two-hour fair when the teachers were cleaning up the parking lot where the fair had been held, a mother and her three children came running over. The mother said, "Where's the candy? Where are all the booths? We didn't know the fair was going on." Then the mother saw the plates of grapes, jello, and old noodles. She asked if she could have them because her children were hungry. The teachers who created the Creepy Box booth felt uncomfortable. They didn't want to give the mother the used food. They did find a little candy for the mother and then referred her to the volunteer activity coordinator at the apartment complex.

From this experience, the teachers realized that they should use food more carefully in their teaching. Some children go hungry at night because they do not have enough to eat at home. The teachers concluded that it was important to consider the viewpoint of children in their schools who may also come from families with limited financial resources. Many of the teachers in this class decided that they would not use food as toys. In addition, if food was to be used in a lesson, the teachers would then allow the students to divide and eat the food if they wanted. For example, after a lesson on fractions using cookies, students were able to choose a cookie to eat with their lunch.

Social class did have an impact on this lesson because there were students who did not want to tell the teacher that they were hungry. To the teachers who used the Creepy Boxes, the food was not that important. The food added to the hands-on, fun nature of the lesson. However, to the mother and her children, the food meant survival.

Though many preservice teachers thought of themselves as persons with little money, they realized there was a big difference between themselves and this family. The students also found that many parents in the complex spoke only Spanish, so they used Spanish to make connections with them. They did not realize how their knowledge of Spanish might also help them in their teaching and developing partnerships with parents. The next section discusses the importance of bilingualism and multilingualism.

> ⑤ Teacher knowledge of student cultures can influence the success of instruction.

Bilingualism and Multilingualism

The United States is not only a culturally diverse nation, but it is also a multilingual society. The issue of bilingualism is an important one. In the United States approximately one-third of all students come to school with a language other than English (Ovando and Collier 1998, 7). Unfortunately, in many schools, students are encouraged to learn English, and other languages are regarded as secondary to English. Every student needs to learn English, but it is also important for teachers to value the languages children bring to school because their language is like a cultural blanket. Students have grown up with their language and language is the most important means of communicating. Through language children relate to family, community members, and other important individuals. Language is also an important part of who students are and how they define themselves.

According to Bruner (1977), children learn language through their interactions with adults. Much of what youngsters learn deals with social context. The adults in their lives provide various patterns of expression, a scaffolding of interactions (Minami and Ovando 1995). For example, a mother might say to her daughter, "Can you say 'Mommy'? Say 'Mommy.' " Then the child responds. The mother has used a simplified form of language. This form may be considered good, while in another community like the Kaluli of Papua New Guinea, youngsters are expected to speak as adults (Minami and Ovando 1995) and so are not encouraged to speak in "baby talk." Children from various communities learn social rules. In addition, young people learn grammar, vocabulary, emotional emphasis, and meanings placed on words through their interactions with adults.

Language is one of the lenses that one receives as a child. We use language to categorize and understand the world, so it shapes our perceptions; however, language also reflects the cultural views of a community. For example, in the cold lands of Canada and Alaska, Innuit communities have more than 200 words to describe snow (Christiansen 1997). Since snow is a powerful element in their lives, their cultures have developed many specific terms and phrases to identify diverse weather conditions. Languages construct the way people categorize and perceive the many different types of snow. For example, snow can be hard, soft, wet, powdery, or icy.

Do people in southern Florida use various words for snow? No, because snow is not an important aspect of the environment. However, in Florida, there are numerous terms for humidity, such as clammy, damp, humid, soggy, and wet.

When teachers understand the cultural and linguistic context that students bring to school, educators can provide more examples and links between the home and school knowledge. Native language can be effectively used to learn English. Regardless of whether students speak Farsi, Hindi, Somali, or Russian, a native language can act as a linguistic bridge to learning English.

Bilingualism and multilingualism should be encouraged in schools, especially with our shrinking world and the need for U.S. Americans to be able to communicate with people from many other countries. Individuals who can speak and write in several languages are more prepared to participate in a global community because of their linguistic abilities. Today many issues we must address are not local or even national; they are global. These issues may involve our environmental, political, and economic survival. We live in a world where a car may be assembled in Mexico, but the parts come from the United States, Korea, and Germany. The car is a global product. We live in a time when nations from around the world are part of a global system of economics. When the yen and dollar are down in value, people around the world are impacted, too. When the dollar is strong, companies in the United States are not able to sell as many goods to other countries because the goods cost more. Our national economy ties into our international relationships with other countries. In addition, with the creation of nuclear weapons, countries can target distant countries. However, a nuclear fallout would affect everyone who lives on the planet. Therefore, cross-national communications are extremely critical today and teaching languages in schools is desirable.

In fact, there are corporations that also believe language is an important aspect of life. Blockbuster Video, a national business that rents films and video games, provides Spanish-language videos to more than 1,000 of its stores (Soto 2002). Because Latinos, one of the fastest-growing ethnic populations in the United States, have a purchasing power of $600 billion, Blockbuster began providing bilingual and Spanish-language movies. The videos include dubbed or subtitled films, and many are for children. One reason that Blockbuster decided to stock these items is that they found that Latinos watch 7 hours of every 10 hours of television in Spanish. The corporation also sells Latino-favorite snacks like Tostitos, *chicharrones,* and peanuts *con chile y limón* (Soto 2002, C3).

Valuing Native Languages

In the United States, we have a history of teaching academic subjects in languages other than English. Ovando and Collier (1985) describe how bilingual instruction in the 1800s was used in many schools around the country. They wrote, "During the second half of the nineteenth century, bilingual or non-English-language instruction was provided in some form in some public schools as follows: German in Pennsylvania, Maryland, Ohio, Indiana, Illinois, Missouri, Nebraska, Colorado, Oregon; Swedish, Norwegian, and Danish in Wisconsin, Illinois, Minnesota, Iowa, North and South Dakota, Nebraska, Washington; Dutch in Michigan; Polish and Italian in

Wisconsin; Czech in Texas; French in Louisiana; and Spanish in the Southwest (Ovando and Collier 1985, 24). When nationalism became much more of an issue and the importance of cultural assimilation dominated the nation, society began to see schools as places of "Americanizing" students, especially new immigrants, into the (U.S.) American way (Ovando and Collier 1985). This signaled a new direction away from encouraging and maintaining home languages.

Today, there is a definite bias in many schools about language. Why do schools offer foreign-language classes for students in German, Russian, Italian, and French but do not encourage students who bring Vietnamese or Spanish into the school community to use it? In Chapter 3, Hindeliza Flores, who is now an elementary school teacher, describes how she and others were forbidden to speak Spanish in school. In fact, her teacher would not use the name her parents had given her. The teacher gave her a different name because she said she couldn't remember Hindeliza's name. Ms. Flores felt humiliated because so many aspects of who she was were taken away from her. Teachers in her school gave her negative messages about her family and culture by how they tried to eliminate her home language. This was extremely harmful to her developing cultural and linguistic identity. It wasn't until she was an adult that Hindeliza chose to be called by her given name.

Many schools emphasize the teaching of languages from European countries, but do not offer languages like Japanese, Arabic, Tagalog, and Mandarin. However, our continued success as an economic and political power rests on our ability to communicate with dignitaries and individuals from other countries. The need for multilingual citizens in the United States has become an important priority in businesses and corporations because not only will multilingual individuals be able to communicate to people across the globe, but they will also understand cultural motivations and ways of living in various markets (Moran and Hakuta 1995). The comic, above, shows that Hector and Jeremy both understand the importance of knowing languages other than English, but that it also takes work to develop those skills. In our country, many languages are spoken and preserved because many people who live here are immigrants. The next section presents information about two sisters from Iraq and the cultural conflicts they encountered.

Case Study

TWO SISTERS: FROM IRAQ TO NEBRASKA

Our country is a global one. All of us are either immigrants ourselves or descendants of immigrants, unless we are members of indigenous families. Today, many individuals and families are requesting refuge in the United States. Many come from countries where governments persecute them for their religious or political beliefs. Others come because they are starving in their home nations from lack of employment and food. To get a sense of the difficulty and change in the lives of refugees, Pipher (2002) has written a book called *The Middle of Everywhere: The World's Refugees Come to Our Town.* One of the stories is about Shireen and Meena, Kurdish sisters from Iraq. Read about the sisters and think about what adjustments you would have made as their teacher. Their surface and deep elements of culture differed in many ways from U.S. American culture.

Shireen and Meena could speak six languages including Kurdish, Arabic, and English. Their family was middle-class and lived in Baghdad, Iraq; however, after their father opposed Saddam Hussein, their world was turned upside down. The family escaped to Iran and lived in a refugee camp that was a collection of tents with little food. The conditions were horrible, so they walked all the way to Pakistan with only salty water.

Their father and brothers left their sisters and mother because of the terrible stress and the inability to care for the family. The women found themselves in a small town called Quetta where single women could not leave their home alone. Men would follow and harass them, so only their mother went out alone to find food. One night men with guns came to their home and took the little jewelry and money they owned. The police only laughed at them when they reported what had happened. The family moved to Islamabad in Pakistan. It took 10 years for their family—mother, five other sisters, and themselves—to get permission to go to the United States. After taking numerous air flights, they arrived in Lincoln, Nebraska.

Shireen and Meena thought Lincoln looked beautiful with the sparkling night lights and clean air, unlike the towns where they had lived in Pakistan. However, there were also problems in Nebraska. Their family had little money and they both needed work on their teeth. Although they could speak English, they had thick accents and some of their high school peers made fun of them. In fact, Pipher shares the following incident about Shireen being ridiculed by one of her classmates. Pipher explained:

> One boy had accosted her in the hall and asked her, "Do you suck dick?" She hadn't even known what he meant, but she'd asked her teacher to translate. The teacher had encouraged her to report the harassment and she did. "I am through suffering," Shireen said. "If this happens again, I will slap him." I was struck with the resilience of these sisters. In all the awful places they had been, they'd found ways to survive and even joke about their troubles (2002, 29).

Pipher met with the sisters' mother, Zeenat, who had been through much. Now in the United States, Zeenat was a single parent, could not speak English, had various medical problems, and suffered from severe depression. She had no friends and missed her family and country. Nevertheless, she smiled and was still strong minded. The girls also suffered from post-traumatic stress and often had difficulty sleeping. They had nightmares about being trapped or chased and not being able to escape.

In addition to this family, Pipher interviewed other refugee family members. One of the big cultural conflicts that arises has to do with sexuality. Families from the Middle East, where religious cultures require women to wear clothing that covers their bodies, are disturbed by the more casual culture of U.S. women. Since many women wear shorts, sleeveless tops, and sandals, women sometimes seem to have minimal modesty. Pipher wrote:

> *There are two common refugee beliefs about America—one is that it is sin city; the other is that it is paradise. I met a Cuban mother whose sixteen-year-old daughter got pregnant in Nebraska. She blamed herself for bringing the girl to our sinful town, weeping as she told me the story . . . A Mexican father told me that his oldest son was in a gang. He talked about American movies and the violent television, music, and video games . . . He said, "My son wears a black T-shirt he bought at a concert. It has dripping red letters that read, 'More Fucking Blood.'" He looked at me quizzically. "America is the best country in the world, the richest and the freest. Why do you make things like this for children?" (2002, 61–62).*

So as you can see, mainstream U.S. Americans may see the world differently than others do. Children and parents may come to school not only behaving differently, but also holding different beliefs about what is expected and accepted by others. In addition, many suffer from severe depression from the violence and war they have witnessed as children. A teacher may not know what a student is feeling or thinking without establishing trust and then engaging in conversation and sharing. A teacher may learn a great deal about his or her students by having lunch with or meeting one-on-one with young people after school. ✳

Chapter Summary

Caring-Centered Multicultural Education is a student-centered orientation to teaching and learning that is founded on trusting relationships, affirmation of students, and the importance of community. This chapter provides information about the power of culture and how it shapes our worldview, how we act, what we think, what we expect, and what we value. Cultures have warmed, taught, and affirmed people.

Remember Ishmael? As the teacher who was a gorilla, Ishmael strongly suggests that we break out of our own cultural boxes in order to see other perspectives about life. What does this mean in schools? Teachers will be able to make more meaningful connections with students when they are able to see life from their students' viewpoints. As cultural mediators, people who understand the deep and surface layer of culture, teachers can create bridges between students' families and/or cultural perspectives and what they are learning in schools. Students benefit from maintaining their home cultures so that they can continue to communicate with those in their families and ethnic communities, but they also can learn multiple worldviews of people from other cultural groups. This will assist them in developing respectful and caring relationships with many others.

This chapter also emphasized that culture is made up of multiple layers. As defined by Valle (1997), the three layers are language, symbols, and artifacts; customs, practices, and interactional patterns; and shared values, norms, beliefs, and expectations. It is important for teachers to understand the culture of children from a holistic orientation. In addition, one of the most important components of culture is language. Language shapes our identity, how we process information, how we interpret experiences, and how we relate to others. It is the vehicle of culture.

Our students come from many countries around the world. Unfortunately, some young people have been driven from their countries because of civil and political strife. Their beliefs may be in great contrast to what they find here in the United States.

The United States is a multilingual and multicultural society. It is imperative that teachers understand not only the importance and power of culture, but also how to make schooling meaningful to all their students, including those who come to school with a native language other than English.

Chapter Review

Go to the Online Learning Center at **www.mhhe.com/pang2e** to review important content from the chapter, practice with key terms, take a chapter quiz, and find the Web links listed in this chapter.

Key Terms

explicit culture, *38*
implicit culture, *38*
ethnicity, *42*
traditional, *43*

bicultural, *43*
assimilated, *43*
socialization, *47*
hero-making, *52*

mythology, *52*
meritocracy, *53*
cultural translator or mediator, *60*
variation, *63*

Reflection Activities

Journaling can be extremely helpful to you in reflecting upon issues like culture, inequalities, and culturally relevant teaching. Much of this chapter is devoted to helping you become more articulate about what your culture is. Although the activities may ask you about specific aspects of culture, cultural elements do not occur in isolation. Cultural elements are used in a social context and many are integrated with several aspects. Culture represents the integration of diverse components like symbols, customs, gender roles, educational expectations, economic values, and religious beliefs.

The following questions are designed to assist you in thinking about your own cultural background. Please write your answers in your journal.

1. **Unpacking Layers of Culture** How would you describe yourself in cultural terms? The following sections ask questions about various aspects of culture. Reflect on each section and then describe yourself not only in terms of ethnic or cultural groups that you identify with, but also discuss your most important values and ideals.

Communication

When do you use formal language patterns? When do you use slang? Do you use words that have different meanings from what your students understand?

What analogies do you use in your teaching?

What jokes do you tell?

What is your interactional style (aggressive, formal, warm, quiet, talkative)?

History

What is your family history?

Where in this country or in what other country did your ancestors first live? What is the immigration history of your family?

What kind of careers are important in your family?

Gender Roles

What do you believe is the role of women in society?

What role do you believe men should have in society?

Who has the most power at your workplace? Who has the least? Is it gender related?

Who was the disciplinarian in your family?

Traditions

Were there certain holidays that your family celebrated?

How did your family prepare for the beginning of the school year?

Value Orientations

What kind of behavior do you expect from your students? When they do not behave in the manner that you expected, who do you believe is at fault?

What do you believe the role of parents should be in student achievement?

2. Have you seen cultural conflicts between people in your lives? Between students in your classroom? Among your peers? With supervisors? What do they look like? Describe the situations and how you could act as a cultural mediator.

3. List some ways that you could begin to learn about a child's culture without asking the child to become the expert. Students enjoy being the expert about some aspects of their lives such as teaching you phrases like "good morning" in Tagalog or Spanish; however, a teacher can overwhelm a student by asking too many questions if the student is not prepared to volunteer that much information about herself, her family, or her culture.

4. Case study: a teacher naturally integrating culture into the curriculum. Do you know a teacher who naturally integrates culture into the classroom without stereotyping? Describe that person to us. What does she or he do that is different from the methods of other teachers? How does the teacher infuse culture effectively and meaningfully into the curriculum?

5. Do you know any children or parents who were refugees or immigrants? If you have the opportunity, interview someone. Compile a set of questions such as, What was your happiest day in the United States? Why did you choose this day? What was one of your most desperate days? Why? What should teachers know and do when they get new students from other countries?

Confronting Prejudice in Ourselves and Our Schools: The Challenge of Change

CHAPTER 3

What Are Our Hidden Hurdles?

CHAPTER MAIN IDEAS

- *Hidden Biases*
- *The Biggest Hurdle*
- *Eliminating the Roots of Prejudice*
- *Signs of Hidden Prejudice*
- *Why Is It Sometimes Difficult to See Prejudice?*
- *Can Prejudice Be Positive?*
- *Stereotypes: Forms of Bias*
- *Understanding Race: A Sociopolitical Construct*
- *Origins of a Racial Taxonomy*

- *Defining Ethnicity*
- *Various Forms of Racism*
- *Classism and Sexism: Other Oppressive Social Practices*
- *Classism and Sexism Impact Our Students*
- *Sexism or Gender Bias: Implications in Schools*
- *Old-Fashioned and Modern Racism and Sexism*
- *Park's Theory of Race Relations*

CHAPTER OVERVIEW

The purpose of this chapter is to assist the reader in her or his investigation and understanding of personal prejudice, social exclusion, and institutional discrimination. Race is a political construct and teachers need to understand what impact this human-made concept has on intercultural relationships. Just as with racism, there are other types of oppression such as gender bias and classism. This chapter covers the research about classism and the state of Title IX in the 21st century.

"We have met the enemy and they are us."
—Walt Kelly, Pogo

"Can we talk of integration until there is integration of hearts and minds? Unless
you have this, you have only a physical presence, and the walls between us are as
high as the mountain range."
—Chief Dan George

Hidden hurdles exist in all of us. We may have biases about financial status, languages, accents, gender, sexual orientation, disabilities, body shapes, height, and many other aspects of life. Our beliefs may act as barriers to making connections with other people. Do your beliefs influence the way you interact or see others? As the character in the following cartoon reminds us, the enemy is not someone else; the enemy is we ourselves. Our own biases may act as barriers to our caring for others. Looking at ourselves can be difficult, but it is part of caring for our own development and of creating more authentic and trusting relationships with others.

JUMP START reprinted by permission of United Feature Syndicate, Inc.

This chapter examines possible hurdles we may hold about others. One of the key principles of Caring-Centered Multicultural Education is to continually examine oneself for social biases. If, as you begin to "unpack" your own biases, guilt creeps in, move it aside; guilt is not an effective motivator. Rather, I believe most of us need a chance to think about our own biases in order to purge them from our minds. Caring teachers work hard at being open-minded and refrain from labeling others. As one teacher said, "Labeling is disabling." We are all connected and when one of us succeeds, then we all succeed. The opposite is also true: When a person is treated unfairly, we are all hurt because the act and intention to exclude one person jeopardizes the building of compassion, respect, and equality in our community. The field of Multicultural Education holds the long-term aim of creating a caring society that affirms cultural diversity and emphasizes our common values of democracy, justice, equality, and freedom. As Martin Luther King, Jr., wisely wrote in his Letter from a Birmingham Jail:

Injustice anywhere is a threat to justice everywhere.

We are caught in an inescapable network of morality, tied in a single garment of destiny.

What affects one directly, affects all indirectly.

Hidden Biases

Do you think Multicultural Education is mainly learning about other cultures? Most teachers want me to tell them everything they need to know about African American, Vietnamese, or Hopi cultures. In a discussion in one of my classes, I asked teachers, "What do you hope to gain from taking a Multicultural Education class?"

These are some of the most common responses:

"I hope to gain a better understanding and awareness of other cultures."

"I want to better understand different ethnic groups, because basically, I feel, it's the child who is 'different' who usually has low self-esteem."

"I would like to learn ways to get culturally diverse kids to feel comfortable with each other."

"I hope to learn different strategies for teaching."

Did you have some of the same thoughts? Are you expecting a lot of information about other cultures? In this book, I do provide some information about various cultural groups, but first I think it is necessary for you to begin to examine your personal biases. Are there any hidden hurdles in you that may prevent you from helping each child do her or his best?

The Biggest Hurdle

If you are like many teachers, you probably think your most important task in Multicultural Education is to learn more about the cultural customs, holidays, and history of your diverse students. Yes, educators need cultural knowledge. However, I believe the biggest hurdle we face is to challenge and rid ourselves of personal biases and prejudices and to view others with new eyes. This can be a *painful and lifelong* process, and it is helpful when we support each other through this undertaking.

As you recall, when I asked teachers in my classes what they hoped to learn in a multicultural class, most wanted cultural knowledge. A few acknowledged the need to look at their own attitudes. Two teachers wrote thoughtful responses about themselves:

"How can I go into a classroom and not just give my narrow-minded White perspective on subjects?"

"I want to limit my prejudices and biases."

We all have **hidden hurdles** in our minds, prejudices we are not conscious of. I, too, have been conditioned by society for many years to see others as either "we" or "they." These hurdles have acted as obstacles to my seeing the ability of some students. It has taken me many years to understand how my own biases have acted as powerful filters that shaped the information I gathered about others every day. I did not want to think that I was a prejudiced person.

Most of us have been influenced by messages we received as young people growing up, from friends, parents, siblings, aunts, uncles, grandparents, family friends, and others. Besides people in our family and neighborhood, another influential force today is the media, especially television. If you were a child who watched a lot of television, by the time you entered school, you probably watched as many hours of television as it takes to get a four-year college degree. The messages you saw on television were continual, visual, and **uncensored.** Some of the messages were helpful, while others should have been talked about. On the computer, we can easily use the delete key and, in less than a second, those thoughts and ideas are gone. Unfortunately, it isn't as easy to delete beliefs and attitudes from our minds as it is to erase words from a computer document.

You may believe that you are not a prejudiced person because you are fair and have strong morals. I agree. You probably didn't go into teaching to make money because most people know that teachers do not make megabucks. Rather, you are committed to making a difference in young people's minds. As a society, we need you. Yet, since ethnic and cultural prejudices are often carefully hidden in the nooks and crannies of our minds, you may hold some attitudes that may limit how you view your students. Many teachers take multicultural education classes believing that they do not need any instruction because they are not biased.

Eliminating the Roots of Prejudice

Prejudice and bias often have deep roots like weeds. If you cut off the top portion of the weed and leave several tiny roots, there's a possibility that the weed will sprout again. We have all been socialized by society and have heard stereotypical comments or have seen stereotypical images. We took in stereotypical beliefs about others. In our society there are many examples of stereotypes. African American males are often seen as being athletic and therefore expected to be great basketball players. Children from European American families who have little money are labeled "poor trash," and some people assume they can't read well and aren't motivated. Businesspeople with a great deal of money are viewed as greedy and selfish. Asian Pacific American and Mexican American women are often seen as weak and subservient, rather than competent leaders. Native Americans are stereotyped as people who live on reservations, although most Native Americans live in cities. Women are sometimes portrayed as emotional rather than logical, and men are seen as macho instead of gentle. I believe there are few of us who did not learn prejudicial views about others, but most of us continually need to work at eliminating our biases throughout our lives. Teachers remark that once they begin to see how prejudices are so much a part of life, they cannot go back to sweeping them under the rug.

Signs of Hidden Prejudice

On a television news program, reporters sent out two men, one African American and one European American, into the community. Both had comparable bachelor's degrees in business. In fact, they were college buddies. First, the men went out to buy a car. Although both men showed interest in the same car, the African American man was quoted a price several thousand dollars higher than his White friend. The two were sure that this was just an isolated incident of prejudice, so they found an ad for an apartment and called on its owner. The African American male went first and was told that all the apartments were already rented. Several minutes later, the European American male approached the same apartment manager about an apartment and was shown one. The manager told the European American that an apartment was available and could be rented on the spot. A television camera filmed each incident. When the experiences of the two were compared, it was sadly obvious that the Black male faced a great deal of discrimination. The two friends were shocked by their experiences because the year was 1990—more than 25 years since the Civil Rights Acts of 1964 had been passed.

Why Is It Sometimes Difficult to See Prejudice?

Prejudice may be hard to see unless it is directed *at you.* In the previous example, the European American male was shocked when he viewed the videos showing high levels of prejudice aimed at his friend. The African American male knew that racial discrimination still occurs, but he was also surprised at how much he encountered in a short time. The people who would not rent to the African American male had no apparent reason to reject him. He had the same qualifications as his friend. They were reacting to his physical and perceived racial differences.

Gordon Allport, a sociologist who has done much research, uses the *New English Dictionary* definition of **prejudice:**

> a feeling, favorable or unfavorable, toward a person or thing, prior to, or not based on, actual experience (Allport 1954, 7).

Allport believes that most ethnic prejudice is primarily negative. Why? When people use overgeneralizations in looking at others, they do not see the real person. For example, let's say that someone meets you for the first time at a school board meeting. During the course of the meeting, you provide excellent reasons why a new math series should be adopted. You answer questions professionally and effectively. Unfortunately, by the end of the meeting, that person maintains that since you are a female and a kindergarten teacher, he or she is unsure of your professional judgment. A prejudiced person will use selective memory in her or his judgment and continue to hold on to overgeneralizations about members of a group (Stephan 1999). Prejudice can act as a filter that prejudges people and can cause us to hear or see only the information that reinforces what we already believe about others in a category.

Our minds automatically use categories to sort the millions of pieces of information that we take in every day. Allport helps us to understand what prejudice is. Allport believes that you can prejudge a person without being prejudiced when you are open to new information about a group or person. However, ethnic and cultural prejudices are often difficult to get rid of and can contribute to the inequitable treatment of people. Allport defines **ethnic prejudice** as:

> an antipathy based upon a faulty and inflexible generalization. It may be felt or expressed. It may be directed toward a group as a whole, or toward an individual because he is a member of that group (Allport 1954, 10).

Can Prejudice Be Positive?

The comic on page 86 brings up the issue of positive stereotypes. Some people have argued that they believe ethnic stereotypes can be positive. Consider for a moment an Asian Pacific American student.

John is a Chinese American student in a fifth-grade classroom. The teacher believes he is a bright kid. He works hard and is fairly well behaved in class. The only weakness John seems to have is that he doesn't do well in math.

One day the teacher has a chat with John and says, "What's going on with your math? I know that you can do better. Your older sister was a math whiz kid. I think that you aren't working hard enough."

John looks down at the floor and says, "But, teacher, I do work at it. I don't think math likes me."

With a big sigh, John continues, "You sound just like my parents. They tell me I must not be working as hard as my sister."

The teacher doesn't want to believe John because she thinks he is not working hard enough. As the days go by, the teacher watches John work on his math homework. She begins to see that John is on task and struggles with the unit on fractions.

The teacher then asks herself, "Why did I think math should be easy for John? Why did I think that because his sister was good in math, John should also be great at it? Was it because he is Chinese American and I assumed he would be good in math and science? Why didn't I stop and really look at John's strengths and weaknesses?"

In this example, the teacher let her own biases creep into her expectations about this Asian Pacific American student. It limited the way she helped John. Many teachers believe Asian Pacific American students are good in math and that comes from a positive belief system about Asian Pacific Americans. However, there are Asian Pacific American students who are *not* good at mathematics, but their teachers expect them to excel. Some students, like those in any social group, catch on quickly to math concepts, but there are others who may struggle with simple computations. Many Asian Pacific American children are often pushed by parents, teachers, and even themselves toward math, science, and computer careers. Yet they may be more

Take a Stand

INSTITUTIONAL AND PERSONAL PREJUDICE IN SCHOOLS

Prejudice and bias can be difficult issues to address in schools. People prejudge others because of various groupings such as ethnicity, culture, age, gender, language, religion, disability, or social class. In order to begin to eradicate inequalities in school, it may take an organized effort on the part of the entire school to address discrimination. The effort should include students, staff, faculty, and parents. Although there may be several types of prejudice that are consistently found in the behavior of folks in the school, the school community may want to begin addressing biased attitudes with one particular aspect.

- What is the most pervasive prejudice that is found in the school?
- What long- and short-term strategies can be designed to address this bias?

JUMP START reprinted by permission of United Feature Syndicate, Inc.

interested in careers in drama, politics, or law enforcement. Sometimes students feel the burden of fitting the stereotype of Asian Pacific Americans (Pang 1995).

You can help all your students by encouraging them to develop their interests and talents in many areas like drama, creative writing, political science, or physical education. Help your students see themselves in many different settings and occupations. After looking at your perceptions of others, you may realize how important it is not only to encourage your students to expand their dreams of who they can be, but you may need to stretch your beliefs about what students from culturally diverse groups can do and accomplish.

Stereotypes: Forms of Bias

Like most people, you probably realize that stereotypes are harmful, but you may find it difficult to catch your own stereotypical thoughts. As a teacher educator, I often am in schools supervising student teachers and I drive on the freeway to see them. The freeways are usually busy during the day. One day a driver in a large blue sedan entered the freeway, merged into the slow lane, and then cut over three lanes to the fast lane on the far left. I saw this car moving over without regard for the busy traffic. As the car cut in front of me, I noticed that the driver was a woman. Instantly the thought appeared in my mind, "Those terrible women drivers!" I was shocked by my own bias. I had to tell myself, "Wait a minute. I am a woman and I don't drive like that. In fact, both male and female drivers have cut in front of you on the freeway." In my anger, it was easier for me to fall back into old patterns of thinking. I was labeling all women as bad drivers. Allport would say that I had "a fixed idea." He defines **stereotypes** as:

> a favorable or unfavorable exaggerated belief associated with a category whose function is to justify our conduct as it relates to the category (Allport 1954, 187).

A stereotype is an untrue, fixed picture in your mind that has a value judgment attached to it. For example, the woman-driver stereotype promotes the belief that women are incompetent drivers who can't be expected to drive carefully and correctly. Stereotypes are used as a screening measure in accepting or rejecting a person or group. Many stereotypes are based on a fear of the group, a lack of knowledge of the group, differences in beliefs and practices, and/or misconceptions.

Stereotypes are destructive because these **overgeneralized images** act as filters about how we view others. Most of us belong to various groups that may hold stereotypes about other groups. We all need to continue to challenge our perceptions of others throughout life.

Understanding Race: A Sociopolitical Construct

Now let's get down to several complex issues. Maybe you are beginning to settle into your easy chair and feel confident that racism, sexism, classism, and homophobia are not problems in the way you live your life. You believe everyone is equal and you work toward a just society for everyone.

Remember the analogy of the weeds in a garden? Prejudice is like the weeds in our garden. They are there to remind us that the garden needs to be attended to constantly. New research on prejudice has shown how old-fashioned racism and sexism have sprouted up into modern racism and sexism like weeds in a garden. Before looking at how prejudice appears today, I would like to share thoughts about the terms *race, ethnicity, personal racism, cultural racism, institutional racism, classism,* and *sexism.*

Race is an extremely complicated social and **political concept** that humans have created. It is not a biological one (Gould 1996; Olson 2002). Omi and Winant view race as a "concept which signifies and symbolizes social conflicts and interests by referring to different type[s] of human bodies" (1994, 55). In traditional sociology, scholars for the most part equated biological characteristics of race with hair texture and color, skin color, head shape, and other body features, although this is a powerful myth that people learn. In addition, race is often equated with levels of intelligence and intimately tied to power and political relationships. The following example was used by Omi and Winant to demonstrate how political the term *race* is in our society.

A Louisiana woman, Susie Guillory Phipps, wanted to change her racial classification from Black to White. She thought of herself as White, but found that records with the Louisiana Bureau of Vital Records listed her as being Black. She sued the agency but lost. The state contended that because Phipps was a descendant of an 18th-century White planter and a Black slave, she had been listed as Black on her birth certificate because of a 1970 state law, which stated that anyone with at least 1/32nd of Negro blood was Black. Why did she lose her case? The court ruled that the state had the right to classify and identify racial identity. During the trial, a Tulane University professor found that most of the Whites in Louisiana were at least 1/20th Negro (Omi and Winant 1994, 53–54). Race is often used to place people into a large social category that does not consider individual differences, as in the Phipps example. Racial categories have been used to discriminate against others. Our history has many examples of how "race" has been used to oppress members of specific groups. African American slaves were prohibited from learning to read during much of the 1800s. In some cases African Americans were killed because of their knowledge of books. Chinese immigrants became the first group to be identified by racial group and excluded from entrance into the United States with the Chinese Exclusion Act of 1882. Another example is Executive Order 9066, signed in 1942. Through this order, the U.S. government placed 120,000 Japanese Americans in concentration camps during World War II. Racial identification is an extremely political construct in the United States and other countries. Often it is about power, relationships, and oppression. However, race is not an accurate biological construct. Most biologists do not see humans in terms of race; rather, they use the term *phenotype,* which refers to physical characteristics. The next section discusses how the social and political construct of race evolved.

Origins of a Racial Taxonomy

Race is often used not only as a political construct, but as if it is a *proven* biological concept based on physical differences. The taxonomy of racial classification was originally created by Carolus Linnaeus, a Swedish naturalist (Gould 1996). Originally, Linnaeus developed the classification system that is used by biologists today to categorize plants and animals. In his system, he placed humans in the order of primates; the genus given was Homo, or man, and the species name was sapiens, which means wise. Therefore, the term *Homo sapiens* means "wise man." Linnaeus gave human beings their classification of Homo sapiens. In his quest to further categorize humans, Linnaeus extended his classification to include a four-race system that was primarily based on geography and three characteristics of people: physical color, disposition, and posture (Gould 1996). In order, as Linnaeus discussed them, were these four categories: *Americanus, Europeus, Asiaticus,* and *Afer* (or African). See Table 3.1 to understand how Linnaeus classified the four groups.

Read through the chart carefully and see if you note which category or group seems to be characterized most positively. Would you rather be described as optimistic or angry? Muscular or stiff? There appear to be more positive traits used to describe those in the European category. In addition, Gould noted that Linnaeus's categorization followed the four regions of the world: Africa, the Americas, Asia, and Europe.

Later his student, J. F. Blumenbach, a German naturalist, added a fifth category, Malay, and moved from a geographically linked ranking to a hierarchical one. As Gould (1996) explained, it was unfortunate that Blumenbach developed the human taxonomy that many use today, because in contrast with his peers during the Enlightenment period, he was more egalitarian than other writers about human diver-

TABLE 3.1   Linnaeus's Racial Classification and Identified Racial Characteristics

	Americanus	*Europeus*	*Asiaticus*	*Afer*
Physical color	red	white	pale yellow	black
Disposition	angry	optimistic	melancholy	apathetic
Posture	upright	muscular	stiff	relaxed

sity. In fact, Blumenbach did not believe that Black Africans were inferior to others because he believed in the unity of the human race. He saw physical differences resulting from the migration of individuals to parts of the world where there were climate and environmental differences. However, Blumenbach lived in a society in which progress and European superiority were intimately tied. Scientists are human, and like others, they may not be free from racist ideas that are often pervasive in their community (Gould 1996). Blumenbach identified the people who lived near Mount Caucasus as the ideal in physical beauty. Blumenbach also thought it was probable that humans originated in this area. He named this group of people Caucasian. Blumenbach had a powerful influence on the myth of race with his five-category classification of Caucasians, Mongolians, Ethiopians, Americans, and Malays that was published in his 1776 book, *On the Natural Varieties of Mankind* (Fredrickson 2002). Blumenbach's work impacts the way some people have been taught to see race today.

Unfortunately, Blumenbach's ideas are a powerful force. Science has been used to legitimate race and oppression (Hilliard 2002). In a speech at the American Educational Research Association meeting, Asa Hilliard III reminded his audience of the following: "Racism is real; race is not." He argued that science was used to create social practices and ideas that justified the domination of Europeans over Africans and other groups. Hilliard believed scientists, like others, are influenced by social attitudes about race.

> ⑤ *"Racism is real; race is not."*
> —ASA HILLIARD

The Human Genome Project

Today scientists from all over the world are collaboratively working on one of the most important scientific studies of the last 20 years, the **Human Genome Project.** This study is not the African Genome Project or the American Indian Genome Project or the Asian Genome Project or the European or the Latino Genome Project; rather it is known as the *Human* Genome Project, because humans are basically similar in their biological makeup. Researchers in labs in over 18 countries are working to identify the approximately 30,000 genes in our human DNA (Ridley 1999). The research is designed to map out the traits found on each human chromosome, such as diseases a person might inherit or characteristics such as the ability to curl one's tongue (Siegfried 2001). If you are interested in learning more about this research, I suggest that you go to the National Institutes of Health's website for the Human Genome Project at http://www.genome.gov/page.cfm?pageID=10001167. The U.S. Department of Energy also has a website that you can access at http://www.ornl.gov/hgmis/. Both give the history and goals of the Human Genome Project. I found the second website to be more user-friendly and suggest that you read through the question and answer section. Why would the Department of Energy partner with the National Institutes of Health? The website explains that after the United States dropped the first atomic bomb on a civilian population, Congress requested that the Department of Energy research the impact of radiation on the genome and genetic mutations.

The Bell Curve: Biological Determinism

Do people still believe in innate racial differences in intelligence? As Blumenbach's taxonomy was adopted by scholars, underlying beliefs about various racial groups also took hold. **Biological determinism** became a pervasive concept and many people believed that there was scientific evidence to support the belief that certain groups were intellectually inferior. In fact, a book published by Hernstein and Murray in 1994, called *The Bell Curve,* brought back theories that posited that human intelligence was related to racial and environmental differences in people. This book was on the *New York Times* bestseller list for 10 weeks (Hilliard 2002) Their book presented two claims: First, social Darwinism, "a general term for any evolutionary argument about the biological basis of human differences" (Gould 1996, 368), was used as the foundation for their arguments. Hernstein and Murray argued that it was possible to identify a person's intelligence with a single number, and this number could then be used to rank a person's intellectual capabilities (Gould 1996). Do you think your intelligence is fixed for life? As you know, on some days you may do well on an intelligence test and on another day, you may not be as successful. Have you taken tests that included information that you had not been exposed to or been taught? When you didn't know the information, did that mean you weren't as intelligent as your friend who answered the question correctly? Many factors impact performance on intelligence measures. As many psychologists have warned, tests measure **performance** at that moment, but not necessarily one's **competence.** Some researchers have found that junior-high school students who believed that test scores could change did better on their tests (Henderson and Dweck 1990; Kohn 1999). However, elementary-grade students who felt that intelligence was fixed did not do as well on their tests in junior high. They also demonstrated higher levels of academic anxiety and thought that their lower scores were a reflection of their ability rather than their level of effort.

Second, when individuals from lower incomes were consistently found to do less well than others on IQ measures, some researchers believed this showed that low-income individuals were permanently and genetically inferior. In addition, Hernstein and Murray (1994) used the documented 15-point-lower IQ scores between Blacks and Whites as evidence that Blacks are biologically inferior. However, Hernstein and Murray did not examine or consider the IQ score increases of Black American students from middle- and high-income families in their analysis (Gould 1996). Rather, Hernstein and Murray used only that part of the testing data that promoted the idea that social inequalities arise from inherent biological factors and not from social practices. Unfortunately, some individuals have attempted to use the information they presented in their book to eliminate programs like Head Start, Title I, and other educational projects, arguing that the programs are useless because of the inherent biological inferiority of the participants who are members of communities of color or who are European American from lower-income families.

Can you see how biological determinism may have impacted the way some teachers view culturally diverse students? Without even being aware of it, teachers may have been taught biological determinism and may have internalized, consciously or unconsciously, lower academic expectations for students who come from less financially resourced families and/or communities of color (Hilliard 2002). Teachers may spend less time with students from underrepresented groups because they believe the youth are biologically inferior and teachers can only have minimal impact on the students (Pang and Sablan 1998). An accompanying and equally powerful belief system that exists in the minds of some teachers is deficit theory (Hilliard 2002; King 1994). This theory is based on beliefs that students do not do well in school because of their home experiences and cultures. Together, biological determinism and deficit theory produce a double whammy of inbuilt stereotypes and negative attitudes that interfere with teaching effectiveness. However determined teachers are to do a good job, the unexamined acceptance of biological determinism and deficit theory block positive outcomes and a powerful reason why stereotypes are difficult to eliminate from people's minds (Stephan 1999).

However, as Stephen Jay Gould (1996, 377) wrote: "We must fight the doctrine of *The Bell Curve* both because it is wrong and because it will, if activated, cut off all possibility of proper nurturance for everyone's intelligence."

Gould counsels his readers to be aware of possible personal and professional prejudices. He asks us all to examine our actions and the underlying beliefs that we may hold about others that are not true.

> 🖋 *"We must fight the doctrine of The Bell Curve both because it is wrong and because it will, if activated, cut off all possibility of proper nurturance for everyone's intelligence."*
> —STEPHEN JAY GOULD, *THE MISMEASURE OF MAN*, 377

I encourage you to read more about the evolution of the construct of racism in Stephen Jay Gould's text, *The Mismeasure of Man,* and George Fredrickson's book, *Racism: A Short History,* because both texts provide a more comprehensive understanding of how racist and prejudicial beliefs are formed and maintained over generations. Chapter 8 provides more discussion about science and the concept of race.

Defining Ethnicity

The previous section discussed how the concept of race evolved and became pervasive from one generation to another. Many people believe that race is an accurate and exact **biological concept,** although it is not. Another concept that is often confused with race is ethnicity.

Ethnicity is a concept that some scholars use to move away from the biological orientation of race to a discussion of culture and group consciousness. Ethnicity is a complex social construct that extends beyond discussions of culture and identity. In this book, ethnicity is seen as a group category that deals with culture, ancestry (Omi and Winant 1994; Valle 1997), and sense of oneness (Kleg 1993). Some characteristics often identified with ethnicity are culture, geographical origin, language, religion, shared traditions, common political interests, moral orientation, and sense of kinship. Not all groups emphasize the same characteristics. For example, although African Americans are descendants from many different nations in Africa, because of their common historical experiences of slavery, segregation, discrimination, and victimization, many African Americans have developed a strong ethnic identity (Kleg 1993). Ethnicity and culture are intimately tied and the terms are used almost synonymously because ethnic groups are defined by cultural characteristics (Valle 1998). Many ethnic groups are defined by the following: shared language, which includes other aspects of communication like artwork and music; shared interactional patterns that often focus on marital, familial, and social relationships; and shared values and standards (Valle 1998). In Chapter 8 you can read more about ethnicity as it relates to the concept of culture. This section of the text centered upon issues of racism, and the next portion of the chapter discusses various forms racism takes and the role they play in how people think and treat each other.

Various Forms of Racism

As you have read in the previous section, the biological construct of race is a myth; however, people often believe and act as if there are different human racial categories. The result often is an "us" and "them" orientation or in-group and out-group perspectives. Just as Blumenbach explained, some people believe one racial group is more beautiful than another. There also exists the belief that one group of people may be smarter than another. Within this context, racism is a complex construct. It involves a system of beliefs that ranks and values people from various groups differently. Most often racism involves treating or perceiving people differently and therefore involves issues of power and control. **Racism** can be both overt and covert, and personal, institutional, and cultural (Bennett 1995). Racism is the belief that one's race is superior and others are inferior. Nieto (1992) uses the definition of Meyer Weinberg, who defines racism as "a system of privilege and penalty" based on the belief that groups of people are inherently inferior. This belief is used to justify the unequal distribution of opportunities, goods, and services. **Personal racism,** which is the belief that one's race is superior to another, perceives racism on an individual basis rather than as a reflection of cultural, social, and institutional oppression.

Cultural racism is the belief that the culture of a group is inferior or that the group does not have a culture (Nieto 1992). For example, I have been in classrooms where teachers tell their children that music by Bach is an example of high culture and highly valued, whereas the blues are a form of low culture and not as well developed.

Institutional racism is a system of legalized practices designed to keep the dominant group in power (McIntosh 1992). There are institutional laws, policies, and rules that serve to discriminate against certain groups of people. Underrepresented groups are marginalized by the society; they are placed at the borders of society, and they have little power to make large-scale changes. Let's take one of today's most pervasive issues in schools, high-stakes testing. Have you ever wondered what impact high-stakes testing could have on African American and Latino students? High-stakes tests are those tests in which how well a student does on the measures determines whether she or he is retained, promoted, placed into a desired program, and/or graduated (Brennan, Kim, Wenz-Gross, and Siperstein 2001). A study looked at the performance of eighth graders in Massachusetts. In 1998 Massachusetts adopted the practice of using the Massachusetts Comprehensive Assessment

System (MCAS) to determine how well the standards were being taught. Children in 4th, 8th, and 10th grades were tested. Students must pass the 10th grade examination in mathematics and English in order to graduate from high school. Brennan, Kim, Wenz-Gross, and Siperstein (2001) found that "MCAS hurts the average competitive position of African American students in math . . . the MCAS may also have a differential impact on Latinos/Latinas in math (206). What do they mean? The measures used in Massachusetts are probably not an accurate assessment of student competence. Why? Tests do not assess everything you know about a discipline. Tests can only include chosen items in isolation. Tests also cannot measure a student's passion or interests in certain topics within a discipline. Tests cannot measure one's creativity. Tests do not measure a student's sense of responsibility or ability to work with others. Tests like the MCAS are often used as gatekeepers. A **gatekeeper** is a practice or policy that keeps many individuals in a specific group from opportunities available to others. In the case of students in Massachusetts, the MCAS can act as a gatekeeper and keep some students from graduating, even though they have earned passing grades from their teachers and completed the required number of courses. The next section discusses other social issues that are pervasive within our nation, classism, and sexism.

Classism and Sexism: Other Oppressive Social Practices

Closely related to racism is classism. **Classism** is prejudice or discrimination based on one's financial or economic status. Oftentimes classism and racism are intimately connected. For example, when Latinos or Pacific Islanders faces continual societal prejudice, they may find it difficult to find employment or housing. In this way their opportunities to find economic success are limited, and they find themselves scrambling to survive economically. Then, as they attempt to find additional opportunities, others may discriminate against them not only because of their racial membership, but also because they are from lower-income communities.

Case Study
NICKEL AND DIMED: CLASSISM

A book that describes the impact of classism is *Nickel and Dimed: On (Not) Getting By in America* by Barbara Ehrenreich. The author of the book is a professional writer interested in looking at the impact of welfare reform on individuals in our society. She found out what it meant to live on meager wages. She also noted that as a White woman who was a native speaker of English, she had advantages because she was more likely to be hired than others who were from underrepresented groups and spoke with a Spanish accent. As a service worker, Ehrenreich was forced to work at least two jobs and an average of 11 hours a day in order to earn enough money to pay for food and housing. In addition, there was never the possibility of getting benefits like health, dental, or vision insurance, so medical bills could push a person into homelessness. Ehrenreich met many people who are often labeled "the working poor," not because they did not work hard, but because they worked full-time and did not make enough money to rent safe, clean housing and were not able to buy enough to eat.

Ehrenreich worked as a Wal-Mart clerk, nursing home aide, house cleaner, hotel maid, and waitress. One of her jobs as a waitress paid her $2.43 an hour and tips. She did note in her book that the Fair Labor Standards Act requires employers to pay a restaurant server at least $5.15 if the server has not made up the difference in tips. However, Ehrenreich explained that neither employer at two restaurants ever informed her of this law (Ehrenreich 2001, 16). Later most of her jobs paid $6 to $7 an hour, but even with this increase she could barely afford nutritious food. The most difficult aspect of living was finding affordable, safe housing. Most service workers do not make enough money to save first and last month's rent, so they end up renting hotel rooms by the week or living in their cars. When people live in hotels with no kitchen facilities, they usually end up eating fast food such as hot dogs or hamburgers.

Is there something wrong with a country where folks who work hard for at least eight hours a day cannot make enough to live?

When Ehrenreich began her journey into the life of service workers, she wondered why they did not just move to another job when they were mistreated. She thought, Why didn't they just quit? However, the reality of the lives of many she met was sobering. Many did not own a car so they could not just change from one job to another. They needed to be close enough to ride a bike, walk, or catch a bus. Also, the workers knew the problems of one place, but a new job would have a whole new set of issues to cope with. It was sometimes easier to stick with what one knew even if it wasn't the best situation.

One of the most difficult aspects of the lives of service workers is the humiliation and disrespect they often are subjected to at their jobs. Ehrenreich said that the boss could search her purse at any time looking for stolen food or salt shakers. In addition, many jobs required a drug test even though some people see this as a violation of the Fourth Amendment freedom from unreasonable search (209). Sometimes a service worker must urinate in a cup while a technician is watching.

From reading Ehrenreich's book, one can see that service professions do not pay enough. A person who works an 11- to 12-hour a day job at $6 an hour will only be able to minimally survive. This is even more complicated for the millions of single mothers with young children who need day care in order to go to work. Ehrenreich calls for business reform in a country where some folks make hundreds of millions of dollars a year as chairpersons of corporations while others barely make $15,000 working full-time jobs. She calls for higher wages for service workers so that they can adequately provide for themselves and their families. They need a living wage. Enrenreich explained how service workers work to make the lives of many of us much richer and easier:

The "working poor," as they are approvingly termed, are in fact the major philanthropists of society. They neglect their own children so that the children of others will be cared for; they live in substandard housing so that other homes will be shiny and perfect; they endure privation so that inflation will be low and stock prices high. To be a member of the working poor is to be an anonymous donor, a nameless benefactor, to everyone else. As Gail, one of my restaurant coworkers put it, "[Y]ou give and you give" (2001, 221).

Ehrenreich discovered that a social hierarchy was in place. If one had a position deemed a job rather than as a profession, some folks considered those who held those positions as inferior, not only in regards to financial resources but also intellectually. Many waitresses and other clerks are subjected to humiliation and belittling because others believe less of them. The hierarchical system is based on the belief that a service position such as secretary, waitress, security guard, or gardener, is not as desirable as a professional position. **Meritocracy** is affirmed. In other words, those who hold lower-paying positions do not work hard or are not as smart; therefore, they do not merit higher-paying positions or careers.

The United States is a democracy and it is important for us to raise questions about issues of equity. When we are a fully functioning community in which we care for others, we are more likely to examine severe inequities, as pointed out by Ehrenreich. When we feel connections with and care for others, we cultivate humanity through an inclusive society (Noddings 2002; Nussbaum 1997). It is a community built on ethics where we acknowledge the contribution of all constituent groups (Noddings 2002; Nussbaum 1997), and this includes service workers and other full-time people who cannot make a decent living, but who contribute to the wealth and stability of our nation. The issue of social class is a major obstacle to our creation and maintenance of a just society.

As Socrates suggested, an examined life is one worth living. Sometimes we may not understand the lives of others. I hope that this information helps teachers understand that there are many parents who may not come to class picnics, class assemblies, and other school activities, not because they don't want to be there, but because they literally can't afford to take the time off from their jobs because they would lose valuable income. In addition, in our country, power and money are intimately intertwined. Wealthy individuals may have more political and social power because they have the time and resources to be active in local or national politics. We see this even in our schools. *Savage Inequalities,* a book written by Jonathan Kozol, documents how poor, ethnically diverse communities often had schools in which the textbooks were outdated and buildings were crumbling and dangerous to students. More discussion of his work is found later in Chapter 6. ❀

 *Case Study*

FOOD INSECURITY

You may find yourself teaching in a school where almost every student qualifies for reduced-cost or free lunch. The federal government calls those who are not able to provide healthy and nutritious food in safe and socially acceptable ways for themselves and their families as food insecure.[1] Hunger is defined as the condition in which a person does not have enough food and this need causes bodily discomfort and pain. After a period of time, this can result in malnutrition. In the year 2000 almost 20 percent of all children under 18 years of age were food insecure. This means that nearly 13 million youths were consistently hungry (Nord, Kabbani, Tiehen, Andres, Bickel, and Carlson 2002). Unfortunately, Black and Hispanic households had hunger rates three times those of Whites in the United States (Nord, Kabbani, Tiehen, Andres, Bickel, and Carlson 2002). If you have students coming to class hungry, they may exhibit a variety of symptoms, such as falling asleep at their desks, daydreaming more, having trouble concentrating, being angry and frustrated, and/or showing other learning problems.

What have some communities done to assist families with child hunger? America's Second Harvest, a nonprofit organization dedicated to eliminating hunger, has created a program called Kids Café. It began in 1989 when two brothers broke into a kitchen in a housing community because they were hungry. Now there are about 100 Kids Cafés across the nation where kids can go after school to eat a healthy meal. The cafés are also safe places where young people can do their homework. Many cafés are housed in boys' and girls' clubs (Center on Hunger and Poverty 2002). Find out what is available in your city for students in your classrooms. ❈

Classism and Sexism Impact Our Students

Have you noticed how important financial resources are in our society and schools today? Whether we consider the designer clothes students wear in class or the kind of car a person drives to school, individuals often label others by the trappings that money can buy. Some schools now require students to wear uniforms, not only to prevent gang-color affiliation, but also because of the discrimination that some youths have been subjected to when they cannot afford to wear designer clothing or choose not to wear them.

Case Study

KRISTEN ISN'T ATTENDING SCHOOL

As mentioned previously, some teachers may believe that there is a relationship between low income and lower intelligence. The beliefs teachers hold about the financial resources a child has can influence their expectations of what the child can do in school. In addition, sometimes teachers may not understand how lack of money can affect the life of a child. I remember wondering why one of my

---

[1]To read more definitions regarding food insecurity and hunger, go to the following website: http://www.ers.usda.gov/briefingFoodSecurity/.

students, a young second-grade girl, Kristen, was not attending school. I thought maybe her parents didn't care about school or perhaps she didn't care about school. Unfortunately, after I did some checking, I found I was the one who had a problem. I held prejudicial misconceptions. When Kristin arrived at school, I curtly began asking her why she didn't come to school.

Kristin said, "I was too embarrassed to come."

Since I wasn't sure what she meant, I said, "You must not care about learning because you didn't come to school."

Finally, Kristin looked up into my eyes and said, "I didn't come to school because I lost my socks and I was too embarrassed and cold to come to school with shoes and no socks."

I thought about the snowy playground and felt about two inches tall. I had doubted Kristin without really listening to her. I had assumed many things that weren't true.

"My mom had to wait until she got paid on the 15th before I could get another pair of socks," Kristin said quietly.

Although I had thoroughly embarrassed her, I had embarrassed myself, too. Later in the year, I also found out that Bill missed school because he didn't have a pair of underwear that fit.

After numerous situations like the ones Kristin and Bill found themselves in, parents in our school began a small clothing bank for students. I know of a clothing bank in a high school that is just as important for older students. They can purchase a pair of pants or a blouse for a dollar or less.

Lipman (1998, 236–37) also discovered the impact of not having enough money on parent involvement in two schools she studied. Teachers wanted parents to get involved. Many of the students were African Americans from working-class families. At first the educators thought parents weren't involved because they didn't care about education; then the teachers found out that many parents worked during the day and couldn't take off from their jobs without reprisal. Also because most did not have cars, they didn't have transportation to attend meetings at night. Unfortunately, these parents were not able to advocate for their children as other middle-class parents in the school could. So many ethnically diverse students from low-income families often found themselves at the margins of the school concentrated in remedial or nonacademic classes (Lipman 1998). ❈

Sexism or Gender Bias: Implications in Schools

Another common form of social discrimination is sexism, also known as gender bias. **Sexism** is "the belief that females and males have distinctive characteristics and that one gender has the right to more power and resources than the other; it is policies and practices based on those beliefs" (Schniedewind and Davidson 1998, 8). Sadker and Sadker also think sexism includes the belief that "one sex is superior to the other" (2000, 568). Sexism has powerful implications in our schools. Let's begin with the history of women in public schools in this country.

Did you think women and men always went to school together? In fact, girls were prohibited from going to school. For example, Sadker and Sadker (2000, 437) found that in 1687 the town council of Farmington, Connecticut, wrote that all children would learn to read and write, but that the phrase "all children" meant males only. Coeducation did not became a reality until the early 19th century (Tyack and Hansot 1990). As Tyack and Hansot wrote:

> Gender is a basic organizing principle in society, but the importance of gender distinctions may vary between societies . . . We see gender as a social construct, a set of cultural meanings attached to the biological division of the sexes (1990, 2).

Shortly after the American Revolution, there were discussions about the possibility of creating a public grammar school for girls in Massachusetts. Civic leaders and business owners wanted their daughters to have the opportunity to read, write, and compute. However, there were many men who objected. They argued that females' minds were inferior to those of males and if women went to school, the relationships between men and women would be undermined (Tyack and Hansot 1990). Some also argued that girls would ignore their work and write love letters instead. These examples certainly provide some indication of underlying beliefs people held about the role and abilities of women in society. Those who did believe in educating women thought that schooling would make women more efficient wives and mothers; they did not believe that women would challenge the authority of men (Tyack and Hansot 1990). Remember, at this time women could not vote, but they were seen as important in raising children to become good citizens.

There were women who worked for womens' right to an education during the mid-18th century. For example, Judith Sargent Murray believed women should get a good education. She fought those who said that women were not as intellectually able as men. She believed that women should develop skills for a profession and that education should not just be oriented toward duties in the family. Some private schools for women were established. However, many schools did not provide the same level of education for females as was provided males in public schools. Like the history of

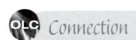 Connection

The NARA (United States National Archives Research and Records Administration) website (**http://www.archives.gov/digital_classroom/lessonswoman_suffrage/woman_suffrage.html**) provides information and a lesson plan about the struggle toward women's suffrage. Please visit Chapter 3 of the book website to link directly to NARA.

NARA is an independent federal agency whose goal it is to record and manage federal records. It is a public trust that not only takes care of critical documents like the original copy of The U.S. Constitution, but also documents policy making and how policies are carried out.

racism, there is a long history showing that women have been excluded from important aspects of society such as schooling and voting. I suggest that you read the book *Learning Together* by David Tyack and Elisabeth Hansot so that you will more fully understand the changes we have made as a society in regards to gender roles.

The next section is about **Title IX.** Although this law was passed over 30 years ago, there are some individuals who would like to make changes in it. Read through the piece carefully. What would you want for your daughters and sons?

Case Study

TITLE IX: WRESTLING WITH GENDER EQUITY

As a nation, one of our most cherished values is equality. But what does equality mean? In 2002, during the 30th anniversary year of the passage of Title IX of 1972, the College Sports Council, an organization of coaches "representing nonrevenue men's sports" sued "the Department of Education over Title IX, alleging that it amounts to a discriminatory quota system. As evidence, the coalition cites the elimination of 170 men's wrestling programs in the past 20 years, a cutback caused by schools seeking to get closer to compliance with Title IX" (Sullivan 2002, C6). Let's look more specifically about what the law says.

In 1972, the federal government passed Title IX of the Education Amendments, which stated that women and men could not be "excluded from participation in, or denied benefits of, or be subjected to discrimination under any educational program or activity receiving federal aid" (Preamble to Title IX of the Education Amendments of 1972). This law protected the rights of women and men, from grade school through graduate school, from inequities in areas such as sports, scholarships and financial aid, employment, counseling, health benefits, and admissions. In sports, in order to be in compliance with Title IX, schools need to have roughly the same percentage of female athletes and male athletes as their percentage enrollment in the institution (Ziegler 2003). Nationally, colleges are comprised of about 55 percent women and 45 percent men, so a college with 55 percent female students should have an athletic participation of 55 percent women and 45 percent men. What happened in schools because of Title IX? In middle schools, gender-separated physical education was eliminated. In the past some schools allowed boys to engage in basketball skills, while women were taught dancing steps. Having both genders in the same class is thought to discourage the difference in physical education curriculum.

Complaints continually arise about women sports and the proportion of funding that schools and colleges must provide to women's athletics. Today, many men's wrestling and gymnastic coaches contend that the Title IX compliance structure of proportionality is like a quota system that is unfair to male students (Ziegler 2003). They are concerned that many men's sports programs have been eliminated and that this has been unreasonable to male athletes. They believe

that although not as many women are interested in participating in school sports, many schools have done away with some men's programs like wrestling.

If you have little knowledge of this issue, I suggest that you go to the following website from the Department of Education, http://www.ed.gov/offices/OCRregs/34cfr106.html. At this website you can read the regulations that serve as guidelines for Title IX. Here is a list of questions for you to consider when thinking about Title IX.

- Do women and men have the same opportunity to participate in sports?
- Do the sports offered accommodate the interests and abilities of women and men?
- Are scholarships for women and men athletes proportional?
- Do women and men athletes use comparable locker rooms?
- Are women and men athletes provided with comparable housing facilities?
- Are women and men athletes provided with comparable tutoring services?
- Are women and men athletes provided with comparable advertising?
- Are women and men receiving comparable travel and per diem allowances?
- Are coaches for women and men receiving comparable compensation?

There are three ways that the federal government assesses whether an institution is in compliance with Title IX:

1. Substantial proportionality—Are the opportunities for women and men to participate in sports "substantially proportionate" to their enrollments?
2. History and continuing progress—Have the interests and abilities of the underrepresented gender, usually women, been addressed by the institution?
3. Effectively accommodating interests and abilities—In institutions where the number of women is disproportionate to the number men, are the interests and abilities of females being addressed?

In 1997 a report, "Title IX: 25 Years of Progress," was published a by the Department of Education and Office for Civil Rights (Riley and Cantú 1997). This document reports the strides made by women toward equality since Title IX was passed. Table 3.2 summarizes their findings:

TABLE 3.2   College and Graduate Degrees since Title IX

	1994	1973
Percent of high school women graduates enrolled in college	63 percent	43 percent

	1994	1971
Percentage of women and percentage of men college graduates	27 percent—women and men	18 percent—women; 26 percent—men

	1994	1972
Percent of medical degrees awarded to women	38	9

	1994	1972
Percent of law degrees awarded to women	43	7

From the preceding table, you can see that in 1994, 63 percent of women high school graduates aged 16 to 24 were enrolled in college compared to 43 percent in 1973. There was also an increase in the number of women who had earned a bachelor's degree from 1971 to 1994. The percentage of women earning a college degree jumped from 18 percent in 1971 to 27 percent in 1994. There was also a large increase of professional degrees earned by women. In 1972 only 9 percent of medical degrees and 7 percent of law degrees were earned by women. The percentages in 1994 jumped to 38 percent of medical degrees and 43 percent of law degrees being earned by women. These large increases show the dramatic change in women and the educational opportunities they participated in. Just as career and college opportunities have changed for women, the participation of women in sports has also increased. (See Table 3.3 for the data.)

Athletic participation also has drastically increased since the passage of Title IX. In 1995, more than 129,000 women participated in intercollegiate sports. Their participation increased more than 400 percent from the number of those participating in 1972. These numbers were reflected in the 37 percent of all athletes in 1995 as compared to only 15 percent of all athletes in 1972. The changes were also seen in high school sports. In 1996, the number was 2.4 million high school girls or 39 percent of all high school athletes compared to only 300,000 women or 7.5 percent of athletes in 1971.

Another important aspect of Title IX is the protection of women and men against sexual harassment. This includes harassment against gay and lesbian students. Sexual harassment still continues to be an issue in schools and colleges. The federal government takes the position that instances of

TABLE 3.3   Athletic Participation since Title IX

	1995	1982
Women in collegiate sports*	129,376	91,986
Men in collegiate sports*	222,077	230,047
	1995	1972
Percent of college athletes who were women	37	15
	1996	1971
Percent of high school athletes who were women	39	7.5

*Figures derived from NAIA and NCAA Annual Reports, enrollment data from the U.S. Department of Education, National Center for Education Statistics, Fall Enrollment in Colleges and Universities surveys and Integrated Postsecondary Education Data System (IPEDS) surveys, August 1994.

sexual harassment serve as obstacles to the freedom to learn in a nonthreatening environment.

In July of 2003, the Bush administration sent a letter to colleges and high schools that reaffirmed the basic provisions of Title IX (Litksy 2003). However, the letter signed by the assistant secretary of education for civil rights, Gerald Reynolds, also stressed that men's teams should not be eliminated in order to ensure equality. There are three ways that universities, colleges, and high schools could comply with Title IX:

1. The percentage of female students should be in line with the percentage of females athletes.
2. Expand the number of women's teams and/or rosters.
3. Provide women's sports that are most popular in that area (Litsky 2003).

Marcia Greenberger, the copresident of the National Women's Law Center indicated that their organization was pleased with the decision made, and she also noted that serving women still lags behind men. For example, there is $50 million less in athletic scholarships awarded to women in comparison to men (Litsky 2003). In contrast, Eric Pearson, chair of the College Sports Council, an organization that represents coaches and sports groups, was concerned that opportunities for men will lessen in order to comply with Title IX (Litsky 2003). This is a complex issue.

Going back to the initial issue presented by coaches regarding the loss of wrestling programs in colleges for the past 20 years, what do we find regarding the status of athletic programs in schools? Here are some examples of the status of women in college sports:

1. In 1997 in high schools, there were 24,000 more male varsity teams than female varsity teams (Riley and Cantú 1997).
2. In 1997 in colleges, women received only one-third of all athletic scholarships (Riley and Cantú 1997).

3. In women's college sports from 1992 to 1997, expenditures for athletic programs grew only 89 percent while men's programs grew by 139 percent (Riley and Cantú 1997).
4. In 2002 men's football and basketball accounted for 72 percent of athletic budgets in college (Sullivan 2002).

Does revenue make a difference in identifying which sports are cut? Sports such as wrestling, swimming, tennis, and track and field are more likely to be eliminated from college offerings because they usually do not generate additional funding for an institution. Those who feel wrestlers have been treated unfairly have sued various universities because the sport has been dropped from the sports programs. For example, unsuccessful suits have been filed against California

Take a Stand

WHAT ACTION SHOULD BE TAKEN ABOUT TITLE IX?

Eliminate Title IX	Continue Title IX
Title IX was passed in 1972 and the evidence shows that it has done its job and is no longer needed.	Title IX has assisted in providing equal educational opportunities for women; however, statistics show that parity has not been fully achieved.
Gender-separate physical education classes no longer exist. Therefore, both women and men are now receiving the same instruction, and this has stopped discrimination in the physical education curriculum.	There are still many other areas that need to be addressed, such as equality in financial resources for women's and men's sports. Men's sports still receive proportionately more funding; football is a good example.
Title IX is unlawful because it is like a quota system. So many men's sports have been eliminated because of this law. Men are being legally discriminated against. In fact, the number of men who participated in collegiate sports dropped from 1982 to 1995.	There has been a dramatic increase in the number of women who participate in collegiate sports. From 1982 to 1995, there has been an increase of about 43 percent.
There are typically more men who participate in sports and therefore it is not realistic to use a system in which there must be exactly the same percentage of men and women athletes.	Women still do not make up 50 percent of participants in high school sports. In 1996, women accounted for 39 percent of all high school athletes.
Smaller sports such as men's wrestling have suffered drastically from the enactment of Title IX. Many collegiate wrestling teams have been eliminated and although these men have participated in the sports as high school students, because of Title IX they are not able to continue their interest in college due to cuts in men's sports.	Women's sports still are not as equally funded as men's sports, when we view sports as a whole. For example, in 1997 women received only one-third of the athletic collegiate scholarships.

State University at Bakersfield, Illinois State University, and the University of North Dakota (Suggs 2002). Wrestlers and others believe that their sport is being short-changed because colleges must provide open spots on teams even when women are not interested. They often cite the example of women rowing, in Midwest colleges where women can "walk on" and fill spaces where men face limits in the number of positions available to them (Suggs 2002).

People cannot seem to agree on solutions to the issue. Many argue that since a sport like football usually makes money and provides resources for both women's and men's sports, football should be exempt from Title IX requirements. Others say that 85 scholarships for male football and basketball teams are proportionately too many and therefore result in a minimum of scholarships for women athletes.

What should be done about inequities in sports? There are few easy solutions to these issues when college sports is an important business that can generate dollars that an institution needs. Sporting events can be a critical aspect of building loyal alumni and a college presence in the community. But underlying all of the arguments, many believe schools and universities are there to provide equal educational opportunities for students. One avenue for individuals to fund their college education is through athletic scholarship. In the United States, where democracy is one of our basic values, we as educators must provide all students, women and men, the opportunity to develop physical skills within a team situation. Participation in sports not only suggests the importance of a physically fit person, but a person who is self-disciplined, sets goals, and can work collaboratively with others in a community.

Many people feel that they have moved away from sexism and racism. However, in the following section, I will share with you some new research on how people's perceptions of racism and sexism still exist but are more hidden than in the past. The work of Swim, Aikin, Hall, and Hunter (1995) found that negative attitudes about women and people of color are more subtle than in the past and that there is continual denial that discrimination is a force in society. ❊

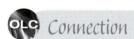 *Connection*

Please visit Chapter 3 of the book website to link to the American Association of University Women (AAUW) website **http://www.aauw.org/takeaction/policyissues/index.cfm** for more information about Title IX and other issues regarding equity for women.

The organization offers pieces on Title IX, equal pay, managed care, civil rights, family and medical leave, and other issues.

Racism and sexism take on new forms as we change as people and as a society. The next section describes how we may change somewhat in the way we view others, but those views may still be somewhat rooted in prejudicial beliefs.

Before I describe the work of Swim and her colleagues, ask yourselves the following questions. Write down the responses that come to your mind right away. Don't censor your responses. Write them down as quickly as you think of them.

- Whom would you prefer as a boss, a woman or a man?

- Whom would you prefer to have as your representative in Congress, an African American or European American?

- Whose responsibility is it to care for the children in a family?

- How do you feel about interracial marriage? If you fell in love with someone from another ethnic group, would you marry that person? How would you feel if your child dated someone from another group?

- How would you describe the progress African Americans have made in securing equal rights?

What were your responses to the questions? Were you surprised by your thoughts?

Swim and her colleagues found that people's views of women and people of color, specifically African Americans, exhibited both old-fashioned racism and sexism and modern racism and sexism.

Old-Fashioned and Modern Racism and Sexism

In the old-fashioned type of racism and sexism, the statements used were strong and blatantly prejudicial. Most of us would cringe if we heard these things today. For example, statements like the following show powerful biases:

"Women are generally not as smart as men."

"Black people are generally not as smart as Whites."

"It is a bad idea for Blacks and Whites to marry one another."

"It is more important to encourage boys than to encourage girls to participate in athletics."

Swim, Aikin, Hall, and Hunter (1995) wanted to know if people had moved from narrow views of others. In order to examine modern racism and sexism, they used the following statements in their research:

"Discrimination against women is no longer a problem in the United States."

"It is rare to see women treated in a sexist manner on television."

"Blacks have more influence on school desegregation plans than they ought to have."

"Blacks are getting too demanding in their push for equal rights."

TABLE 3.4   Reviewing Racism: The Old-Fashioned and the Modern

	Old Beliefs	Modern Beliefs
Racism	Generally speaking, I favor full racial integration.	Discrimination is no longer a problem in the United States.
	I am opposed to open housing.	There is little need for federal programs focusing upon equity.
	Interracial marriage is not a good idea.	
	The United States Supreme Court should not have outlawed segregation in 1954.	People who do not work and who live off welfare are to blame for their own problems.
Resentment Toward African Americans	Blacks are not as smart as Whites.	Discrimination is no longer a problem in the United States.
	Blacks are not to be trusted.	There is little need for federal programs focusing upon equity.
	Blacks do not work hard, so often they are not able to keep a job.	People who do not work and who live off welfare are to blame for their own problems.
	In the United States, we have no reason to complain.	The United States is built upon a belief in equity and anyone can make it who works hard.
		Blacks are getting too demanding about equal rights.
		Blacks should not be as influential as they are in the issue of desegregation.
		Blacks have gotten more economically than they merit.
		In the past few years, the news media and the federal government have shown more respect toward Blacks than they deserve.

Read through Tables 3.4 and 3.5. Many of these statements place blame on underrepresented people and women for the lack of movement toward equality. The statements were used to distinguish between old-fashioned and modern sexism and racism.

In their research (see Tables 3.4 and 3.5), Swim and her colleagues found that men held higher levels of old-fashioned and modern sexist beliefs than women. They also found that those who were more individualistic and not egalitarian were more likely to show old-fashioned and modern prejudices. Swim and her colleagues

TABLE 3.5   Examining Sexism: The Old-Fashioned and the Modern

	Old Beliefs	Modern Beliefs
Sexism	Women are generally not as smart as men.	Discrimination against women is no longer a problem in the United States.
	Women are more emotional and men are more logical.	Women are rarely treated in a sexist manner on television.
	It is easier to work for a male boss than a female boss.	Men and women are treated equally in society.
	Boys should be encouraged more than girls to participate in sports.	Women have the same opportunities to succeed as men in the United States.
	Women should be the primary caregiver in a family.	
Resentment toward Women		In the past years, the federal government and the news media have shown more concern about the treatment of women than is warranted by their actual experiences.

felt that strong individualism and inequitable values correlated with racism and sexism. Individualistic values focus upon individual merit, effort, and achievement. Many people who support racism and sexism and who believe in individualism believe that inequalities in society are due to deficiencies in women and people of color. Look back at the work of Barbara Ehrenreich and think about how hard the people she met worked. They were not slackers, but the jobs they held may be stereotypically viewed by others. Why do people believe that many waiters, waitresses, maids, house cleaners, and clerks deserve to be in those positions?

Swim and her colleagues also found that people who hold egalitarian values think everyone should have equal access to opportunities. They recognize that in today's society some people have special privileges and entitlements because of their economic, gender, or racial status. They are more likely to read Ehrenreich's book to understand how classism and racism are intertwined in society. People who hold social justice as one of their prime values believe that until equal opportunity is a reality, society must develop ways to address these inequalities.

One of the most powerful findings in the Swim research is that many Americans do not believe that discrimination is a current problem in the United States. They believe that racism and sexism are patterns of the past and that the Civil Rights Movement of the 1960s and subsequent legislation healed our nation. However, evidence points to the contrary. The 1990 Gallup poll found that 54 percent of the female respondents and 43 percent of the male respondents preferred a man as a boss, in comparison to 12 percent of women and 15 percent of men who preferred a woman boss a social problem is differential salary levels. Catalyst, a research organization, reported that in 1997 women of color made only 57 cents for every dollar a White male

earns. Even though women of color make up 10 percent of the workforce in the United States, only 5 percent of the women of color held management positions (Jackson 1997). The opportunities of women from Asian American, Black, and Latino communities in management were even more limited than those for White women; White women represent 86 percent of the female managers, Asian Americans represent 2.5 percent, Blacks make up 7 percent, and Latinas make up 5 percent of the management force (Jackson 1997). This situation is happening today in our nation, right now. It impacts all of us because it limits the opportunities of our mothers, sisters, friends, aunts, grandmothers, and ourselves, if we are women. It also limits the possible impact they could have on organizations. The statistics show how gender and race are intimately tied. An example appears in the comic above about a glass ceiling for women. Although there are many more women in the workforce today, they still fight prejudice about their intellectual ability and emotional stability.

Individuals who hold gender-biased beliefs also may hold other types of prejudices. The next section discusses how, in a country like the United States, racism and the concept of race are powerful, culturally assimilating forces.

Park's Theory of Race Relations

As Swim and her colleagues have found, people hold various prejudices about others based on perceived race and gender. Robert Park, a sociologist, believed there are influential beliefs about race that push some people into cultural assimilation or taking on the values, behaviors, and belief system of the majority society. The dominant culture holds specific beliefs about race that are usually based on generalized physical characteristics. As I discussed in a previous section about **racial taxonomy,** race is a political construct used often to exclude or treat others differently. Park found that people saw differences, whether those differences were real or not. For example, in the United States, African Americans may be culturally mainstream, but are sometimes treated as outsiders because of physical differences. **Park's theory** of race relations is helpful for teachers to understand because he explains, in part, how powerful the forces of assimilation are in society (Sherman and Wood 1989).

First, Park theorized that when cultural groups come into **contact,** they may conflict with each other over goods like jobs, housing, or cultural values. For example, when the Irish immigrated to the United States, some Anglo-Saxons became threatened when the Irish moved into their neighborhoods. Second, Park believed that, as groups lived with each other, they learned how to cooperate and then entered a period of accommodation. The Irish and Anglo-Saxons learned to live more harmoniously. Then the Irish entered into a period of assimilation in which they, as the minority community, took on the culture of the dominant group. This happened to many communities such as the Irish, Russian, Japanese, and others.

When people become assimilated in the United States, they **adopt** values of the dominant society, such as competition, individualism, upward mobility, and an orientation to the nuclear family rather than the extended family (Sherman and Wood 1989). The final stage of Park's theory is amalgamation, in which individuals from different groups marry and become more unified. This stage is in contrast to some practices in schools that are designed, consciously or unconsciously, to rid people of cultural traits that differ from the majority culture. For example, if teachers tell children they must not speak Black English or Vietnamese or Spanish in school because only English is acceptable, then children will tend to give up their home language and assimilate into mainstream society.

Although many culturally diverse individuals may give up much of their culture, they may still be seen as **outsiders.** Park's theory does not take into consideration what Gordon (1964) calls structural assimilation. People may take on the values of the dominant or mainstream culture, but that does not mean individuals are accepted into all aspects of the group. Although people may have given up their home language and learned English and have mainstream behaviors, they may still be excluded from the more primary relationships found in society's social structure (Sherman and Wood 1989). For example, individuals may or may not be allowed to join specific clubs, live in certain neighborhoods, or attend elite universities. Therefore, even though people may have been able to culturally assimilate, they have still not been able to be accepted into all realms of society.

Here again, perceived differences are powerful forces in society because people use those differences to exclude, isolate, or segregate others. Whether those differences are seen to be due to physical characteristics, language, dialect, cultural values, gender, political power, and financial resources, they dictate how people treat others; and many of those who are from underrepresented groups are excluded from higher-level positions in society. The following section continues the discussion, focusing on what happened in Los Angeles during the early 1990s and what happens when people feel continually excluded from participating fully and equally in society.

Do Race, Class, and Gender Matter Today?

Do you remember the 1992 upheaval in Los Angeles? Maybe you viewed it as a race and class riot. Cornel West (1993), a philosopher and theologian, believed strongly that it was not a race riot; rather, it was a powerful demonstration of social rage. People were tired of being poor and treated as nonhuman (West 1993). Both liberals and conservatives have placed the blame for the racial, class, and gender problems on people of color and women. Our inability as a nation to act with ethics, compassion, and justice is at the root of many of our social problems. Some people felt a rage far beyond frustration. Even though West primarily examined the problems of justice and equity from the perspective of the Black community, he provided a clear picture of how discrimination and prejudice continue to destroy our nation's fulfillment of its promise of a truly just society.

How can we solve such deeply embedded problems? West has hope and believes in our ability to rally as a community. He writes:

> First, we must admit that the most valuable sources for help, hope, and power consist of ourselves and our common history . . . Second we must focus our attention on the public square—the common good that undergirds our national and global destinies. The vitality of any public square ultimately depends on how much we *care* about the quality of our lives together. The neglect of our public infrastructure, for example—our water and sewage systems, bridges, tunnels, highways, subways, and streets—reflects not only our myopic economic policies, which impede productivity, but also the low priority we place on our common life.
>
> The tragic plight of our children clearly reveals our deep disregard for public well-being. About one out of every five children in this country lives in poverty, including one out of every two black children and two out of every five Hispanic children. Most of our children—neglected by overburdened parents and bombarded by the market values of profit-hungry corporations—are ill-equipped to live lives of spiritual and cultural quality. Faced with these facts, how do we expect ever to constitute a vibrant society (West 1993, 6–7)?

West adamantly believes the problems of Blacks and other people of color stem from a social system that has a long history of inequities and cultural stereotypes. Our nation has demanded that people of color fit into the system and act worthy of inclusion, rather than understanding the human connectedness of all people in society. Why does this occur? Does the phrase "We the People" include all the people? If not, what does the phrase "We the People" mean in today's nation? Although West is focusing upon the issue of race, his viewpoint could also be used in looking at issues of gender, class, religion, sexual orientation, and other issues dealing with equity.

Chapter Summary

This chapter was designed to help you to examine your personal biases. One of the key points in this chapter emphasizes how our individual prejudices are part of a larger social system of racism and sexism that include institutions like schools. We must be attentive in our struggle to eliminate our hidden biases. Getting rid of our stereotypes and prejudices is not easy. Many teachers in my classes have argued that they are not racist. I agree that they are not consciously racist, but they may have a difficult time examining their views. Many are excellent teachers who work extremely hard every day for all kids.

There are various types of prejudice and social oppression. This chapter defines racism, sexism, and classism. It is important for you to reflect on how the construct of race developed and how it is still used today as an obstacle to a society in which all people are valued and treated equally. In Gould's text, *The Mismeasure of Man,* the paleontologist carefully outlined how scientific data have been used to create racist categories. These categories were part of a prejudicial belief system that questioned the human dignity, beauty, and intelligence of groups of people based on perceived physical differences. More discussion about the evolution of humans will be presented in a succeeding chapter.

As a society, we have many other social issues of oppression to deal with. Previously adopted laws like Title IX are coming under attack because some people feel we have dealt with the issue of sexism and so sexism is not of major importance. Ask your daughters, sisters, mothers, aunts, and friends about experiences they have in present-day society. Are they still impacted by gender-bias beliefs and practices? If so, what are they and how do they limit their opportunities or quality of life?

Research by Swim and her colleagues found that people had moved from old-fashioned racism and sexism to a more modern version of biases in which many feel that discrimination has been eradicated and so they do not need to consider it any longer. Even though a decision by the Bush administration in 2003 reaffirmed the tenets of Title IX, there are still many unanswered issues about gender equity that continue to arise. When people bury their heads in the sand, they will not feel responsibility to make changes. Some teachers learn that they need to seek out and listen to other teachers' viewpoints, especially teachers of color. In this way both mainstream and teachers of color can examine the institutional barriers that teachers face in schools. To deny the reality of each other limits compassion and the spirit of inclusion. In one case a White teacher, Judy, cared about what happened to her colleagues and students. She was willing to take a painful look at herself because she was concerned that maybe there had been a time when her biases kept her from really listening to the comments of teachers of color. She knew she had to listen, but she, in addition, wanted to make changes in how she taught and what she taught. To do this she needed to build relationships of trust with other colleagues, parents, and students. Judy knew that it requires hard work to care, but the rewards she would gain as a person and teacher were great.

Most of us have internalized negative views about others and they creep into our lives like weeds. Sometimes we do not know they are part of our garden because they blend so well with other plants.

The next two chapters deal with how children learn prejudice and how we, as teachers, may be perpetuating racism, sexism, and classism intentionally and unintentionally in schools.

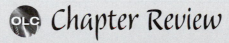

Chapter Review

Go to the Online Learning Center at **www.mhhe.com/pang2e** to review important content from the chapter, practice with key terms, take a chapter quiz, and find the Web links listed in this chapter.

Key Terms

hidden hurdles, *82*
uncensored, *83*
prejudice, *84*
ethnic prejudice, *84*
stereotypes, *86*
overgeneralized images, *87*
race, *87*
political concept, *87*
Human Genome Project, *89*
performance, *90*

competence, *90*
biological determinism, *90*
biological concept, *91*
ethnicity, *91*
racism, *92*
personal racism, *92*
cultural racism, *92*
institutional racism, *92*
gatekeeper, *93*
classism, *93*

meritocracy, *95*
sexism, *97*
Title IX, *99–104*
racial taxonomy, *108*
Park's theory, *108*
contact , *108*
adopt, *109*
outsiders, *109*

Reflection Activities

Answer the following questions in your journal:

1. I find dialogue to be most helpful in carefully thinking through many issues about equity. Find another person with whom to discuss these issues. Do you have a colleague or friend who is willing to talk about issues of equity? If you are unable to do this, dialogue with yourself in a journal. Take time to look at several sides of each issue. Ask yourself these questions:

   • Do racism, sexism, and classism exist today? If so, what do they look like?

   • Is discrimination part of American society? How do I know?

   • Am I biased? What am I doing to eliminate inequities that I see in my personal and professional life?

   • Have I thought about how the concept of race has been created? What do I really believe about people who are physically darker than I? What does this mean to me as a teacher?

2. Write about a time when you were discriminated against or describe a situation you witnessed in which someone was hurt by prejudice. Would you do something differently about it today? If so, what?

   Journal writing can assist you in better understanding yourself and can also help you see your growth. In addition, use your journal to write down great ideas like fun instructional strategies that you may see someone try or an insight that you came up with about the impact of culture and the classroom.

3. How would you describe the differences between what Swim and her colleagues considered old-fashioned racism and new racism? Old-fashioned sexism and new sexism?

   Write a response in your journal. It is important for all of us to look at the subtle meanings hidden in the messages found under new racism and new sexism. If a person holds the beliefs in Tables 2.2 and 2.3, the individual may not be willing to examine how schools have practices that are detrimental to some children more than to others.

4. Go to the website for the Center on Hunger and Poverty at **http://www.centeronhunger.org/ programs.html.** Read through their goals and the statistics they present on hunger and food insecurity. Then read through their section called "Feeding Children Better." In this website you will find that one out of every four people in line at a food bank may be a child. Are there ways that your school can assist families who are not food secure? How can a school develop programs so that children who benefit from such programs are not treated with contempt or pity? How can we share in a caring manner? Is this possible?

5. Title IX continues to be a controversial issue for some folks. Take time to do some research on the history of the legislation. Also gather facts about its impact on both women and men. Then have a discussion in class or with peers. See the Take a Stand Box on page 103 within the chapter for more information.

How Does It Feel to Be Discriminated Against?

CHAPTER OVERVIEW

This chapter encourages readers to look at their own experiences with discrimination. How does it feel when someone discriminates against her or him? What impact does it have on the individual? This happens to students in schools too frequently. Since our society is racially stratified, students and teachers often develop a "racial" identity. This chapter describes the processes that people go through. In addition, because it is important for teachers to develop intercultural sensitivity skills, the chapter presents a model that will help educators better understand the skills they need in order to become intercultural specialists and cultural mediators.

Have you ever been discriminated against? How does it feel? Most of us have felt the hurt, frustration, embarrassment, humiliation, and anger, whether we are Irish, Muckleshoot, African American, Filipino American, Cuban American, or Swedish. Discrimination hurts. After the terrorist attack of New York City on September 11, 2001, an increase of hate crimes were directed toward Arab Americans and other Middle Eastern Americans. Many people and students were called "rag heads" or "dot heads." Clergy at mosques received threatening telephone calls and messages. Prejudice doesn't contribute to a compassionate and equitable community.

Teachers from many diverse communities have written powerful papers about being hurt by prejudicial comments or discriminatory actions. I feel it is important that educators and other service providers understand the pain and destructive nature of discrimination. Before we can truly understand how difficult it is for children to cope with discrimination, we must look at how prejudice hurts students, teachers, others, and ourselves. Prejudice can severely harm the spirit and self-image of any person. It is especially important for teachers to examine the force of prejudice and discrimination because these influences can limit our ability to create caring relationships in classrooms and schools. When teachers discuss their experiences in small groups, they begin to understand each other better and, through dialogue, build bridges with each other. These discussions often help to establish compassion among participants. Sharing experiences with each other provides opportunities to clarify the impact of prejudice and discrimination for all. European American teachers gain a better understanding of how personal, institutional, and cultural prejudice can be consistent and frustrating elements in someone else's life. These discussions also assist teachers from underrepresented groups because they often do not know that European Americans also have been targets of personal prejudice. As the discussions progress, teachers begin to realize the negative impact prejudice can have on the self-esteem and aspirations of their students. They gain more understanding of how the commitment to care for children includes knowing how prejudice and discrimination develop and become part of our everyday lives. The bonds of the community are strengthened through this sharing, and teachers learn how destructive discrimination is to all of us.

Teacher Voices about Discrimination

Since this book is for educators, the following are several selections from teachers who have written about the discrimination they felt and the impact the bias had on them.

Hindeliza Flores, Mexican American Female

I translated for my mom since I was the oldest of my sisters at that school. We registered my younger brother and my three younger sisters and everything went fine. (The names of my sisters are easy to say and pronounce.) But when it came to filling out my papers the secretary had a hard time. She typed it wrong and I let her know. (By this time I was used to people pronouncing my name wrong, so I'd write it down for everyone.) Anyway, she finally finished and she showed us where our rooms were located. She turned to me and said, "From now on your new name will be Lisa. [Her name is Hindeliza.] Because your name is too hard to say." That's how she introduced me to my new teacher. I used to get in trouble because I wouldn't respond to that name. I wasn't used to it. Also because it wasn't my name. But I eventually got accustomed to it.

For many years I thought of that secretary. She didn't realize what she stole from me. I lost a big part of me when she took my name away. As an 11-year-old child, that was a big part of ME. My name and my language were part of my culture. When that was taken away, I had nothing. I could only be myself at home. Later when other Spanish-speaking children came to the school, we were not allowed to speak Spanish to each other. We were punished for speaking Spanish. Years have passed and I still think about this incident. I wonder if my life would have been different if this hadn't happened. Would I still have wanted to be a bilingual teacher and help other Mexican children?

Suzanne Akemi Negoro, Japanese American Female

In my junior high history class, I remember sitting in the rigid single desk, resting my feet on the bookrack of the desk in front of me. I always used to sink low in my seat, and on one particular day I was sinking even lower than normal as our teacher announced that it was Pearl Harbor Day. Usually anything that is given its own day is something that's good; there's Valentine's Day, Martin Luther King, Jr. Day, President's Day, Labor Day, and Independence Day. But Pearl Harbor Day is one of the few dark-designated days, left in the same camp with D-Day. This day not only marks the day that Japan bombed the United States; it also marks that day that my family and other Japanese-Americans officially became suspected traitors. Sitting in my junior high history class, this day also marked me. I can still picture the student in the row next to me, leaning towards me and whispering, "So why'd you bomb us anyway?" Four generations and forty years, and not much had changed.

The biggest problem I had in dealing with this student's comment was my own inability to reconcile my cultural identity, both Japanese and American. I remember words from my childhood: being praised, "You speak so well," "Your English is so good"; being questioned, "What are you anyway?" "No, what are you *really?*"; and being criticized, "You don't speak Japanese? Why not?" "How sad that you've lost your language," "How sad that you've lost your culture." I remember being about three feet tall with the voice of a mouse, trying to talk as loud as possible so that people could hear how well I spoke, i.e., without an accent. I remember my years of adolescent female fun that always ended up matching me with the other Asian boy in my class—and I remember always wanting to be matched with every other boy but him. I wanted to prove to people that I was American, and to me that meant proving that I was White.

I was not, however, simply just trying to prove that I was White. I was simultaneously trying to prove that I was still "Japanese-enough." As a child, the most difficult part was figuring what was enough.

Krystal Rodriguez, Latina

There have been many times in which I have felt discrimination . . . People would verbally tell me such things as, "Are you sure you're in the right place? You look like you don't belong here." But the words and the looks did not hurt as much as my fourth grade teacher did . . .

In the fourth grade, my teacher was Mrs. McGeorge (pseudonym). I will never forget her name. The very first day I started to notice things about her that I never noticed about other teachers. I started to notice that she spoke to the White students with a softer tone and with more passion. She spoke to the rest of us in a voice that was more stern.

The first day she also put the class into reading groups. There were three reading groups: The robins, the blue jays, and the black birds. Everyone wanted to be in the robin group because we all knew that they were the group that could read the best and that the black birds were the "dumb" group. As Mrs. McGeorge was placing people into the groups, I remember thinking that my third grade teacher said I read very well for a third grader so I knew that I was at least going to go into the blue jays. But I was wrong. I was placed into the black birds.

The next day it was reading time so the class had to separate into their reading groups. As I was in my reading group I remember looking around at all three reading groups. That is when I noticed something else. The robins were all White. The blue jays had two minorities and the rest were White. And the black birds were all minorities.

Even though I noticed many things that year, I just thought that that was the way it was supposed to be. I never questioned the teacher or told anyone about the things I noticed . . .

It was time again, in the fifth grade, to get put into our reading groups. Most of the same students that were in my fourth grade class were now in my fifth grade class so the teacher just had us go into the same groups . . . The teacher heard me read. After we were finished the teacher came up to several students in our group, including myself, and told us that she did not know why we were put in the lower group. We read very well. I was then moved up to the robins.

Ronie Daniels, African American Female

I am a woman, Black, short in stature, thick in build, with kinky hair. I began my life in a small diverse California city, but as I neared the age of eleven, my family and I migrated to a small town in the Mojave desert . . . There are people of a variety of ethnicities such as Hispanic, African American, and Asian, but they are still in the minority. I attended both private and public schools during my years in the desert and I was often the only or one of the few African Americans in my classes. By this point in my life, race was a well known factor to me and I also knew that I was considered to be a minority . . . I was never taught to be anyone other than myself, which in a large sense is Black.

About two weeks ago, my friend, K, and I were sitting in the living room with a mutual friend. During our conversation, she told me that I was not "Black." I was not majorly affected by it because it came from a friend, but what did she mean by saying that I'm not Black? She told me that I was not really Black. I suppose she meant to say that I was not "ghetto" or like the "other Black" people she sees on campus because I express my Blackness and my culture to her quite often.

How did she discriminate against me if she was not truly harsh? She discriminated against me because she put Blackness in a small little category and she excluded me from it. By doing this she is claiming that I do not know my culture, that I do not accept my culture, or that I have no part of my culture. Could this be true? No. I believe that she made this judgment based on clothing, hairstyles, and other outward appearances. She knows that I grew up with horses and off-road vehicles, which in California is typically termed as White.

Due to the color of my skin I was separated. I had to read the words "GO BACK TO AFRICA NIGGERS" spray painted on the walls of my high school cafeteria one morning. In addition, I had to endure racial jokes at our local public pool, and I had to realize as I grew up that no one looked quite like me in many of my classrooms . . .

As I mentioned before, my home life was very Afro-centric . . . It is sad that I am considered to be non-Black because of my interests and hobbies.

Jennifer Stahl, Irish American Female

Instances of discrimination against me occurred when I first began attending preschool. I was an intelligent, motivated, confident red-headed child. I was very compliant with figures of authority, and would do anything to gain their acceptance. I wanted to be a grown up, as I perceived them, as soon as possible. I was absolutely silent during classroom lectures . . . I worked diligently towards perfection and I always raised my hand before talking.

But my attempt at adult perceptions superseded those attempts of my peers. When Rob Gibbs, an obese African American was told by other kids, "Quit drinking so much chocolate in your milk and you won't be so brown and fat," I was quick to tell them that they were being prejudiced and shouldn't judge people by the color of their skin. When they called Carl Feazel "Feazel the weasel" to mock his intelligence, I'd defend him by telling them they should spend the time they spent teasing studying instead, and they wouldn't be so jealous.

Naturally, their antics were directed at me as well. They called me "Horsey-Stahl, Frances the Talking Mule, Mr. Ed, and Chest-NUT" to mock my affinity for horses. Carrot-top came next, naturally followed by the most grotesque of all, "Red on the head like a _____ of a dog." I used to wonder what in the world the other kids' parents were teaching them when mine were telling me to treat everyone with kindness and equality and to right the unjust wrongs around myself. This wasn't the worst of it. Because my behavior was non-conforming to peer pressure and because of my academic achievement, my instructors always, and I do mean always, stuck me in between three or four of the most disruptive students. They did more than talk without raising their hands. They threatened to poke my eyes out with pencils poised inches from my face if I didn't pass a note for them. They threatened to beat-me-up on the walk home from school if I told on them . . . When I complained to my parents about it they'd visit with my teachers. The teachers would tell them, and in turn, my parents told me the reasons why I was put between them . . . So while everyone on the other side of the room bonded and gained social skills by sharing their favorite colors, drawing pictures for each other, and assisting one-another in their studies, I was overcoming continual verbal and physical abuse and sat surrounded by boys only.

Arturo Salazar, Latino, Mexican

When I was a freshman in high school, I was enrolled in a freshman algebra class with a teacher that regularly called on students for their participation. One day, this teacher called on me for the answer to an extremely easy equation, an equation that had the answer of ten . . . I knew very well the answer was ten but could not get my vocal cords to say it because of my stuttering. Noting that the teacher knew this was an extremely easy equation, he continued to call on me until I was able to give him the answer. In the meantime, he began to laugh in a sarcastic manner, indicating that he thought I was dumb. This implication was evident and increasingly humiliating because the teacher turned to the class and continuously pointed at me, implying that I was dumb for not knowing the answer . . . These types of experiences influenced the level of shyness that I exhibited throughout my preparatory schooling. Stuttering in this forum (my high school algebra class) would have been especially detrimental to my self-concept that was already weak.

Following this class period, I was so humiliated that I never returned to class. I went immediately to my counselor and practically begged him to take me out of that class and to place me with a different teacher. Although I had told the counselor that I stuttered and felt embarrassed when I was not able to answer this question even though I knew the answer very well, he refused to place me with another teacher . . . Feeling uncomfortable with this teacher, I was truant for this class period for the remainder of the semester.

The feeling that I was discriminated against continued into my sophomore year. My counselor decided to place me into remedial English and math courses, even though I consistently scored in the 90th percentile on the yearly Standardized Achievement Tests on all parts. I viewed this as discrimination against people that stuttered, because it was assuming that I was dumb because I had a speech impediment. I complained to my counselor but he did not change my classes.

Teachers from all cultural groups write powerful papers. They demonstrate through different experiences that prejudice is extremely hurtful. There are many different reasons why people discriminate against each other. Many of the examples I have included show how discrimination can be found in a school. I have found that discrimination can be destructive to a 10-year-old fifth grader or a 70-year-old grandfather, because they may question themselves. Thoughts like "What's wrong with me?" and "Why don't people like me?" may surface. Yet discrimination says more about the oppressor than the victim. One of my friends has always reminded me, "When a person points a finger at you, she has more fingers pointing back at herself." People may not realize that discrimination says more about the oppressor than about the victim. In many cases the oppressor wants to maintain a separation or boundary from others based on a belief of superiority (Daniels and Kitano 1970).

Why Do We Discriminate?

Although we may feel the hurt of discrimination, we also may discriminate against another consciously or unintentionally. When people discriminate against others, their actions say more about them than about those who are poorly treated. Allport has defined **discrimination** as the act that "comes about only when we deny to individuals or groups of people equality of treatment which they may wish" (1954, 50). When this happens, discrimination is usually based on social categories or groupings and not individual characteristics. For example, there are numerous situations in which people are being excluded from living in specific neighborhoods, going to certain schools, or receiving promotions because of categories like race, class, or gender and not due to people's abilities.

We may treat others unfairly for one or more of the following reasons. First, we may have been taught that those from another group are not as capable or as good as those in "our" group. There is an in-group affiliation and sense of belonging. As members of specific in-groups, we may learn that to be part of this group, we are expected to think of other groups unfavorably. People who are members of the out-group are often seen as being less desirable.

When people feel insecure about themselves and who they are, they may want to believe that their way of doing something is the one right way. Believing that others are not as "smart" or "virtuous" may make one feel "better," but it is often a hollow feeling. You know when you are putting others down without reason.

Another example of discrimination is **scapegoating.** This involves shifting the blame of a problem to a victim. When we **blame the victim,** we shift the fault of a problem to a victim or targeted party. I have heard comments such as, "All those Mexicans are taking our jobs" or "Our economy is so bad here in the United States because those Japanese are flooding the market with cheap cars." Historically there have been numerous examples of scapegoating. Prior to and during World War II, the Nazis continually condemned the Jewish community. The Jews were used as scapegoats for the economic and political problems in Germany. Another group that has been used as a scapegoat in the United States is Native Americans. Many people have grown up believing Native Americans were obstacles to progress during the early years of this nation. People do not see that Native Americans were victims of our nation's belief in manifest destiny; their land was taken away and their way of life was destroyed as settlers moved westward. Also manifest destiny was a movement that advanced the interests of the elite, especially large land speculators and owners. This was in contrast to common settlers who wanted to coexist with Native Americans.

Blaming the victim is a societal strategy that has been commonly used against people of color, women, poor Americans, and other disenfranchised groups (Ryan 1976). Children who come from poor or low-income families have often been blamed for mediocre achievement in schools. Educators can be heard saying, "Those [poor] parents don't care about their kids. I know they don't care because they never come to parent-teacher conferences. I call parents and they are never home. Heaven knows where they are while their kids are roaming the streets. Those kids come to school speaking Spanish or Black dialect and they don't have any manners. I think it is horrible that we have to put up with these kids." Comments like this show that this teacher has strong underlying prejudicial attitudes against children who do not speak standard English or who may live in a household with little financial resources. When we blame the victim, we are engaging in a complex psychological system of beliefs (Ryan 1976). Prejudice represents a complicated social and personal phenomenon because it includes personal and group values. Ryan thinks many prejudiced people hold conflicting beliefs. They may blame others because of group membership, but also want to make a difference in the lives of their students. These teachers know that racism and poverty are barriers in the lives of many students. They also realize that race, class, and gender have been used to discriminate against or exclude African Americans, Asian Pacific Americans, Native Americans, Latinos, women, and those living in poverty. These liberal teachers may find themselves with a dilemma.

> In the words of an old Yiddish proverb, they are trying to dance at two weddings. They are old friends of both brides and fond of both kinds of dancing, and they want to accept both invitations. They cannot bring themselves to challenge the system that has been so good to them, but they want so badly to be helpful to the victims of racism and economic injustice (Ryan 1976, 27).

Ryan discusses how the inclusion of those who have been excluded may threaten our way of thinking. These issues of equity are difficult ethical ones and are not easily solved.

White Teacher

Did you know that while increasing numbers of students who attend school are from communities of color and from families with incomes at the poverty level, our teaching force continues to come from White middle-class communities? By the year 2000, it was projected that 96 percent of all teachers in the United States will be European American and about 40 percent of the student population will come from culturally diverse groups. What does this mean in the classroom? Children and teachers may find that they come to school with different views of life. I suggest that you read the book *White Teacher* by Vivian Gussin Paley (1979). She describes her own prejudices, biases, and different perceptions of culturally diverse children.

Paley writes her thoughts about race and social class as a kindergarten teacher. In the book, Paley shares her reactions in the classroom toward children of color. She invites us into her mind and heart as she wrestles with her own prejudices. Paley feels a bond with her students and is committed to addressing her biases. In addition, she lets us see how she began to question her prejudices and strove to behave in a more equitable and compassionate manner. One of the great lessons in the book is that Paley does not see herself as a martyr or missionary for children of color. Paley understands her role is to teach and guide children toward developing new beliefs about themselves and others. She challenges children to work through their own contradictions, misconceptions, and self-defeating ways. She shows the reader how she learns from her children because she is willing to listen and watch children teach her about her own misconceptions. In the foreword of the book, James Comer and Alvin Poussaint describe one of Paley's most important insights—that she, as a White teacher, does not slip into the role of "overaccepting do-gooder."

Some important questions you might ask yourself are: Why are you committed to teaching culturally diverse children? Do you feel that you can save them from their "horrible" surroundings? Do you feel that you have the answers? One of the most difficult issues for some teachers to understand is that they are not in schools to "save" students. You can guide and work to support others, but as a teacher, you will not have the answer for all your students.

Many of your children may come from families who live in poverty and have difficult home lives. If you begin to think that you know what is best for children and that their parents are the problem, ask yourself what you really know about their lives. One of the comments that may come from some parents is, "What makes that teacher think she knows better than I do about what is best for my kid?"

Miscommunications often occur when people do not have the same expectations or ways of behaving. This is more likely to happen when teachers and parents do not have open lines of communication. For example, a teacher in an inner-city high school tells his students that every one of them should go to college. The teacher hopes that all of his students develop high-level white-collar skills. He sees that high-paying factory jobs are becoming sparse and that a college degree rather than a high school diploma will become an expected requirement for jobs. A parent who has worked for General Dynamics for many years and who has a high school diploma may want his or her child to go to college, but may not have the finances to send her or him. In fact, the family may be dependent upon the child to find a job right after high school to help support the family. Since this parent has done well without a college degree, he or she may not believe it is an absolute necessity. This parent may comment, "Why do you put these notions into my kid's mind when he will never be able to afford college? He's got to work now. He can't put it off. We need the money."

Paley's book also helps readers to understand that European American teachers and children of color do have differences. These differences do not have to be obstacles in developing a sense of community. These differences in beliefs also do not mean that one group is better than another, but these differences must be discussed openly. Dialogue can assist people in eliminating misconceptions and help folks come to some common understandings. European American teachers should not be intimidated or scared to talk about ethnic, racial, gender, or social class differences. Children know that we are different in many ways. Paley wrote,

> Each child wants to know immediately if he is a worthy person in your eyes. You cannot pretend, because the child knows all the things about himself that worry him. If you act as if you like him, but ignore the things he is anxious about, it doesn't count. The child is glad you are nice to him, but down deep he figures if you really knew what he was like, you'd hate him (1979, 30).

Paley realized that many of her children were not sure about their racial identity as African Americans, and they wanted her to acknowledge their racial difference in a positive manner to help validate their self-esteem. She realized that if she ignored that aspect of her African American students, she was indirectly saying she did not respect an important part of who they were. In addition, Paley found initially that she automatically grouped children by racial similarities. As their teacher, she was not seeing the individuality of each child. But in a balanced perception, Paley also realized that group membership can be an important part of how the child identifies him- or herself. If the teacher ignores differences children know they have, children may feel that the differences are something negative, negative enough for the teacher to overlook.

Being Part of the Majority

If you feel a little defensive as you read this book, you may say to yourself, "Wait a minute. I'm not one of those bigots. I'm different. I'm not prejudiced." During my many years of teaching, I have found this to be a common reaction when members of the class discuss issues dealing with racial prejudice. In addition, when teachers read new information about U.S. history that has not been included in most social studies textbooks, teachers feel a range of emotions about race, class, and gender that will be discussed later in this section.

History provides a lens through which people may interpret and judge present-day experiences. According to Valle's model of culture, discussed in Chapter 2, historical experiences and information may represent more than just facts; the history a group has experienced may result in the development of strong values. For example, if a community such as that of the Sioux has historically been pushed from the land, Sioux values about the westward movement may be shaped by their group history. Therefore, in order for teachers to begin to understand the viewpoint of another group such as Mexican Americans or African Americans, studying the history of the group can be extremely informative. Teachers in my classes have chosen to read texts such as Howard Zinn's book, *A People's History of the United States, Lies My Teacher Told Me* by James Loewen, or Ronald Takaki's *A Different Mirror.* Many teachers are surprised by their lack of understanding of the complexities of many issues in U.S. history. They often have been taught only a majority perspective, a viewpoint that represents the power structure of our country. Most history texts do not raise important perennial issues that are important for students to grapple with in their social studies classes in order for them to become thoughtful citizens (Loewen 1995). In fact, much history is presented as being truth, although it was shaped within a specific context that included social values of racism, sexism, and classism (Nelson and Pang 2000; Zinn 1990).

Let's look at several examples of how these texts can provide a different perspective on events and people in history. Zinn (1980) discusses Andrew Jackson's land speculation, prejudices toward Native Americans, and how his values shaped much of what he did as president. President Jackson had positional power, and his actions were more destructive than those of others because he legitimized them using his presidency and the national orientation toward manifest destiny. Jackson is often hailed as the great leader; however, as Zinn points out, Jackson even ignored Chief Justice Marshall's ruling in favor of the Cherokees. Jackson did not believe he had to follow the judge's decision. In fact, Loewen quotes Jackson as saying, "John Marshall has made his decision; now let him enforce it!" (Loewen 1995, 126).

Loewen (1995), in *Lies My Teacher Told Me,* shares his analysis of 12 textbooks of American history. These books were written for junior and senior high American history courses. Chapter 5 in his book is titled " 'Gone with the Wind': The Invisibility of Racism in American History Textbooks." Loewen believes that racism is the most important issue of history, and yet he did not find any of the 12 textbooks connecting "history and racism" (1995, 145). He believes that because textbooks gloss over or do not address racism in U.S. society, students do not get the opportunity to look at the beliefs and events that contributed to racism, or learn how racism can be addressed today in order to limit it tomorrow.

Living in the Southwest, I have learned a great deal about the history of Mexican Americans. History in this part of the country could be told, not from the East to the West, but from the South to the North and then to the East and West. After the Mexican War, the United States, as a victor, took much of what was known as Mexico and later became states like California, New Mexico, Texas, and Arizona. Although the Treaty of Guadalupe Hidalgo of 1848 assured that the Mexican people retained their property and civil rights, this did not happen. Many Mexicans were treated as a conquered people (Knowlton 1972) and became foreigners in their native land (Takaki 1993). In many instances land was taken away from Mexican ranchers by U.S. citizens because of changes in the law, taxation, and lack of accurate boundary descriptions (Takaki 1993). Mexicans were often left without their homes.

Do you have a sense of how history can impact the way your students feel about race relations? In many ethnic communities adults pass on from generation to generation historical information about the experiences of past family members. These experiences may be the same or conflict with what students are learning in school. If a student's family history includes the taking of the family land after the Treaty of Guadalupe Hidalgo, then this person may view history through a different cultural lens, as Valle (1997) has pointed out.

The books I suggest that teachers read may be difficult for some teachers to contemplate because they provide a different view of inequities in our history and how these inequities are, in some cases, continually perpetuated. The books may help you understand how those in dominant positions shape the teaching of history so that it serves to forward the beliefs of a (U.S.) American ideology of equality within a self-righteous orientation of objectivity and fairness.

Teachers, especially those who are European American, may experience a variety of emotions when reading these books or dealing with issues of equity. I find that teachers experience a range of emotions from anger, defensiveness, guilt, disbelief, benevolence, helplessness, solidarity, and advocacy, and sometimes several of these feelings arise simultaneously (Pang and Nieto 1995). I can't say to teachers, "Don't feel that way," because these are honest emotions. Rather, I ask teachers to try to look at experiences and issues from other people's viewpoints and reevaluate their beliefs and attitudes. Where do these feelings come from? How can you work through them and move toward solidarity, advocacy, and social action?

Emotions are an integral part of prejudice. We may know intellectually that stereotypes are harmful, but our feelings are not as easy to change. These feelings can get in the way of real communication and personal change. I believe that achieving lasting change is difficult for everyone, and it is only natural to feel somewhat threatened when we are asked to rethink our views of the world. It takes courage to change and a strong commitment to care for others and for oneself in order to address these complex beliefs. In addition, I believe that sometimes people feel uncertain when they are asked to build bridges with new people and examine different ideas. In order to encourage a broader view of U.S. society, I ask teachers to review their knowledge of history.

As already discussed in this chapter, books by Zinn and Loewen provide numerous examples of inequities in U.S. history. Sometimes I felt defensive learning about unfair situations; however, I know that feeling defensive usually isn't constructive. If you are like I am, when I feel attacked, I do not clearly hear the message another person is conveying. Feeling defensive probably won't benefit anyone because it may cause one to shut down. None of us today has anything to do with the forced removal of Cherokees from their land almost 200 years ago, but I ask myself, "What responsibilities do I have today when similar issues arise?" The next section describes research about White racial identity formation. Racism impacts not only people of color, but also White folks who are members of the majority. Prejudice is difficult to get rid of because it includes not only a set of beliefs about others, but also our emotional reactions, which can include feelings of goodness, morality, and ethics (Brislin 1993, 179–80). The next section describes stages that European Americans may find themselves going through as they become more aware of racism.

Racial Identity Formation for European Americans

What process do many European Americans go through in their awareness of their own racial identity? In the past three decades some individuals have become more open about discussing issues of race. Within that context, many European Americans have become more aware that they are members of a racial group and sometimes referred to as White. Just as people from underrepresented groups deal with racial identity, European Americans also pass through different states of awareness and development about who they are. I like the definition of racial identity given by Beverly Tatum, a psychologist at Mount Holyoke College. Tatum says that racial identity formation "refers to a process of defining for oneself the personal significance and social meaning of belonging to a particular racial group" (1997, 16). She (Tatum 1992; 1997) has studied the development of racial identification and believes her students pass through the stages of White racial identity described by Janet Helms. These stages are contact, disintegration, reintegration, pseudo-independence, immersion/emersion, and autonomy (Helms 1990). From my experiences with many European American teachers, I know that White teachers go through a process of understanding who they are and must struggle with racial identity. Table 4.1 is an adaptation of the work of Helms and Tatum.

There are five major stages European Americans may pass through in developing their racial identity. The following is an explanation of the stages given in Table 4.1:

1. **Acceptance of Status Quo.** In this stage, European Americans are unaware of societal racism. Individuals in this stage have thought little about culture and racism. Although people in this stage may intellectually understand that racism is a problem in society, they do not see institutional racism. They may consider racism to be individual acts of discrimination and not a system of legitimized practices. People in this stage also do not understand that as members of the majority, they benefit from White privilege (McIntosh 1992).

   Another response may be disbelief. The person may not want to listen to another person's point of view, especially one that criticizes the United States. People may say something such as, "He's giving such a distorted view of history." However, perhaps that person has a different perspective about an issue or event.

   European Americans may be scared of people of color because they have internalized social stereotypes. These images shape the way people see others, especially when individuals have little knowledge of nonmajority communities. When individuals from the majority come into contact with people of color and begin to see acts of racism, they may find themselves in the next stage.

2. **It's Not My Fault: Uncomfortable.** In this stage, European Americans may feel guilty, ashamed, or angry because they become aware of racism and the underlying belief of White superiority in society (Helms 1990). Sometimes European Americans in this stage blame victims for oppression (Tatum 1992; 1997). Others in this stage may try to convince their close friends and family that racism is a powerful problem. For example, when someone tells a racist joke, persons in this stage will challenge the person who told the joke. However, those in this stage may return to accepting the status quo because they want to remain

TABLE 4.1   White Racial Identity Formation

Stages	
1. Acceptance of Status Quo	Little knowledge of culture and racism, individual and institutional. Does not see cultural differences in students or other people. Accepts dominant culture as standard. Does not question learned stereotypes of others. "I'm just normal" (Tatum 1997, 95).
2. It's Not My Fault: Uncomfortable	Feels guilty and defensive. Avoids discussion of racism. Wants acceptance of peers. Sees some inconsistencies in society and a little of one's own racism.
3. Denial: I'm an Individual	Begins to look at inequalities in society. Angry and upset toward those who question racial inequities. Believes strongly in individual merit and White privilege reflects that merit. "I don't feel I have any advantage because I am White."
4. Clarification of Whiteness	Examines racial self-identity. Seeks information about others. Rejects White superiority. Seeks historical information. Begins to understand how White privilege is perpetuated in society. People feel ashamed for being White and not sure what to do (Tatum 1997).
5. Acceptance of Self and Group	Accepts membership in White collective. Realizes being White does not mean a person is racist. Accepts positive and negative aspects of own group. Studies White antiracist role models.
6. White Anti-racism: Change Agents	Sees role of European Americans in fighting racism. Forms alliances with people of color. Dedicated to changing society.

accepted by their majority peers. They may avoid discussion of racial issues or have little interaction with people of color.

People in this stage may be unwilling to examine issues from the view of victims and issues of racism. Guilt and defensiveness may manifest as feelings of anger and resentment toward people of color. A person in this stage may feel attacked and say, "It's not my fault that there's prejudice in the world. What do you expect me to do? I can't help being White."

Sometimes feelings of guilt arise because the person may have family members who are extremely racist or biased.

3. **Denial: I'm an Individual** (Tatum 1997). In this stage, a person is struggling with being a member of the White collective. Although this person understands there is racism in society, he does not want to be identified with the racism and so rejects his membership in the community by saying, "I'm an individual. I am not like those other people. Judge me for myself and not the group." People feel uncomfortable with others judging them based on their group membership. They may feel extremely frustrated in this stage. Persons do not understand how, as members of the dominant culture, they have privileges non-White people do not have. There is still a strong value in individual merit and a belief that the system rewards individual merit equally.

4. **Clarification of Whiteness.** As European Americans explore their racial identity, they challenge themselves to delve into the question of what it means to be White. A person in this stage may distance herself from others in the majority who are extremely racist. The individual in this stage may have mixed feelings about the White collective, so she may seek information about her history and culture that can assist her in working through the myths and stereotypes about her group that may include issues of superiority or missionary zeal (Tatum 1992; 1997). In addition, biographies of White Americans who have been instrumental in fighting racism provide role models for those who believe in activism.

   Others in this stage may initiate conversations with colleagues of color to find out more information about culturally diverse communities. They want to better understand how the system of privileges is supported and how culturally diverse peoples are systematically denied access to the opportunities in various aspects of society. People begin to understand that there is institutional racism and they have an ethical responsibility to work toward equity in society.

   One of the issues that may arise is the feeling of benevolence. This orientation can fuel a "savior" or "missionary" orientation. A person in this stage, although well intentioned, may not understand how her actions can also be oppressive if they are patronizing. One possible message that the person does not mean is "I can solve your problems. Although you cannot help yourself, I can help you." There is an undercurrent of superiority that can reinforce the separation between different communities. Folks in this stage may need more communication and dialogue with others in order to arrive at collaborative solutions.

5. **Acceptance of Self.** In this stage, European Americans understand the importance of challenging racism and social oppression in everyday life. People accept themselves as members of the White collective and as interdependent with others. They see that feelings of guilt and anger do not change society, but their energy should be channeled into actions aimed at equality. There is a truer view of oneself in this stage. People see that being White does not mean someone is racist, but that racism is part of society and that Whites benefit from the way society has been set up. Therefore, it is imperative that European Americans be active against racism. They may also feel a strong connection and solidarity with others. They develop a commitment to all people and understand that what they do also affects others who may have different cultural and ethnic

backgrounds from theirs. The richness and gifts of diversity are exciting and expand their understandings of life.

6. **White Antiracism: Change Agents.** In this stage, European Americans confront racism on both individual and institutional levels. They have a healthy understanding of themselves and their racial identity. People in this stage are committed to learning more about racism and to making alliances with people from diverse communities to eradicate oppression; they may find out about civil rights activists like Viola Liuzzo, James Reeb, or Michael Schwerner (Tatum 1992; 1997). They know that White Americans have a moral obligation to examine their privileged status and must choose to act to rid our social system of inequities (McLaren 1997). Those in this stage seek new ways of thinking and solving our social problems. People in this stage are realistic about society and work against racism in their everyday lives. They work with other culturally diverse people on community issues such as homelessness, voter registration, and lack of health services.

In this model of White racial identity development, the key is openness and an ethical commitment to care for others by getting to know oneself better, to understand one's own personal shortcomings and strengths.

In order for teachers to change, they must understand that racism has impacted their lives. It is not something only for people of color to deal with and eradicate. Racism and other forms of social oppression are not easy to get rid of in our society. One of the most difficult issues for folks who are members of the majority to understand is White privilege.

White Privilege

A complex issue for European Americans to understand is that they are members of a collective often referred to as White, White American, Caucasian, European American, or Euro-American. Although they may not identify with being European American or White, others may place them into those categories because race is a powerful **sociopolitical** construct in society. In the next chapter, I will discuss in detail how the biological construct of race is a myth; however, in a social and political context, our society operates as if race were an accurate depiction.

Many majority teachers have found it difficult to understand the issue of White privilege. As part of the majority, they usually are not confronted with their racial membership: "I am an individual," as a teacher remarked. However, Peggy McIntosh (1992) believes that European Americans are members of a community that has advantages, although many Caucasians do not understand that it is a privilege to be able to see their lives as morally neutral, normative, average, and ideal—lives that others should adopt.

McIntosh wrote an important piece about **White privilege,** defining it as "an invisible package of unearned assets" that can be cashed "in each day, but . . . was 'meant' to remain oblivious. White privilege is like an invisible weightless knapsack of special provisions, maps, passports, codebooks, visas, clothes, tools, and blank checks" (McIntosh 1992, 33). Through accepted social practices, White privilege has shaped elements of our culture such as our government's legalizing slavery and

Jim Crow legislation (Scheurich 2002) and educational practices (Sleeter 1994; Manglitz 2003). For example, during the 20th century there were numerous examples of the U.S. government, through the Bureau of Indian Affairs, taking Native American children from their homes and sending students to boarding schools in order to assimilate them into mainstream society. These practices demonstrated a deep belief in the inherent inferiority of Native cultures and languages and, in contrast, the superiority of the values of the White mainstream society. One of the privileges that White teachers have is the ability to take on the **color-blind** approach (Johnson 2002). Many do not have to address race because they are part of the majority community and are not continually discriminated against or profiled by race. This sense of color blindness is almost like a freedom that many people of color do not have. In McIntosh's article "Unpacking the Invisible Knapsack: White Privilege" (1992), she describes some of the privileges that she and her peers have as members of the European community. The following are several that she identified for White Americans to consider:

> "I can, if I wish, arrange to be in the company of people of my race most of the time."

> "I can turn on the television or open to the front page of the paper and see people of my race widely represented."

> "I can be sure that my children will be given curricular materials that testify to the existence of their race."

> "Whether I use checks, credit cards, or cash, I can count on my skin color not to work against the appearance of financial reliability."

> "I can speak in public to a powerful male group without putting my race on trial."

> "I am never asked to speak for all the people of my racial group."

> "I can criticize our government and talk about how much I fear its policies and behavior without being seen as a cultural outsider" (McIntosh 1992, 34).

To continue the discussion about White privilege, I asked teachers the question, "What does it mean to be White?" This was challenging for many teachers because they are rarely asked about their group membership. Some felt defensive. However, after several class sessions discussing this issue, many European American teachers began to realize that they had privileges that others did not; yet they did not feel privileged.

Here are a few of the comments the teachers shared:

Val: What does it mean to be White? How do Whites view racism?

Tammi (European American): I never thought about what it means to be White until today.

Dawn (European American): I never thought much about being White either. It just wasn't an issue I thought about. I didn't have to think about being White because I am part of the majority.

Take a Stand

WHITE PRIVILEGE

White privilege is a difficult issue for members of mainstream society to understand. Peggy McIntosh describes White privilege as "an invisible package of unearned assets" that can be cashed "in each day, but . . . was 'meant' to remain oblivious. White privilege is like an invisible knapsack of special provisions, maps, passports, codebooks, visas, clothes, tools, and blank checks" (McIntosh 1992, 33). The following questions can assist teachers in examining this issue:

- Do you believe White privilege is real? Why or why not?
- What if it is real, how can we, as teachers, address it in schools?

Sally (European American): I think White people should start looking at their ancestors. White is so vague. I don't know much about my family and maybe if we did we would be more understanding.

Bruce (African American): We are being so nice. Yet Whites have little information about African Americans. They gave us the shortest month [February] to celebrate Black history. We aren't all the same. People say we are but we aren't. Why can't I feel good about myself? I've taken White history. How many classes in African American or Latino history have you taken?

Michael (European American): None.

Bruce: I go into a store and a cashier follows me around. My White roommates are beginning to see it when they come with me. They are shocked how I am treated.

Kathy (Japanese/European American): There's also a lot of racism between groups of color, too.

Tammi: I didn't realize how deep-rooted racism is. I have taken for granted my privileges. I only think of racism in its extreme forms like the Ku Klux Klan. But many of us are, "innocently" racist because we are ignorant of the racism within our institutions.

Joe (European American): White racism does exist and it is completely intertwined within our society. I think most of us in the White society do not want to jeopardize our "position" so we don't talk about racism.

Tim (European American): I agree. We don't want to discuss racism because we don't want to give up our lifestyle, privileges, and resources that we took from others. Basically I believe I must stop pointing fingers and look at myself first.

Joyce (European American): I know that we are racist, but I don't think it is right to overgeneralize about White racism. I don't think we stick together about issues of race. I have a Black brother-in-law and though it took a while for my family to accept him, we have. So people can move ahead.

Victoria (Vietnamese American): I don't see White people as a race, I sort of see past them. But I think they can contribute greatly to the discussion of racism.

Kristen (Mexican American): Whites don't openly talk about racism. Other races talk about it more openly. Whites are more likely to discuss cultural differences than racism or Whiteness.

Elizabeth (European American): I never realized that racism was institutionalized, not just individual. I think we tend to surround ourselves with Whites with similar views in order to legitimize our ideas. I don't think most people are conscious of their racism.

Joe: White people don't take racism personally because they don't think it will affect them. Therefore, people tend to be inactive when it comes to fighting racism.

The teachers carefully began to examine the issue of White racism. Although it was a challenging topic, there was more discussion in small groups. Caring teachers take on tough topics like this. They will not push issues of prejudice and control under the rug but listen to other viewpoints. Many European American teachers find these discussions hard, yet they feel that they learn more about themselves and how others see them. In this way teachers develop a deeper understanding of how we are all part of a society that has built-in systems of privileges that favor majority people. Sleeter has written that White racism is "the system of rules, procedures, and tacit beliefs that results in Whites collectively maintaining control over the wealth and power of the nation and the world. For at least 500 years, Europeans and their descendants have taken huge amounts of land, wealth, labor, and other resources from peoples of color around the world . . . We seem to have agreed tacitly to continue to reap the benefits of the past, and not to talk about it, except largely in ways that render present race relations legitimate" (1994, 6). Although this can be a tough topic for many people who are part of the majority and other teachers, too, I believe it is important for us to talk cooperatively about institutional racism. If we do not, then we will never be able to make the changes needed to create truly equitable schools or society.

> ⑤ White racism "is the system of rules, procedures, and tacit beliefs that results in Whites collectively maintaining control over the wealth and power of the nation and the world."
> —CHRISTINE SLEETER

Tim Wise (2000) wrote an essay called "Membership Has Its Privileges: Thoughts on Acknowledging and Challenging Whiteness." Here is what he wrote about White privilege and what people should consider doing:

We're used to talking about race as a Black issue, or Latino, Asian, or Indian problem. We're used to books written about "them," but few that analyze what it means to be white in this culture. Statistics tell of the disadvantages of "blackness" or "brownness" but few examine the flipside: namely, the advantages whites receive as a result.

When we hear about things like racial profiling, we think of it in terms of what people of color go through, never contemplating what it means for whites and what we don't have to put up with. We might know that a book like *The Bell Curve* denigrates the intellect of blacks, but we ignore the fact that in so doing, it elevates the same in whites, much to our advantage in the job market and schools, where those in authority will likely view us as more competent than persons of color.

That which keeps people of color off-balance in a racist society is that which keeps whites in control: a truism that must be discussed if whites are to understand our responsibility to work for change . . .

If we recognize our privileges, yet fail to challenge them, what good is our insight? If we intuit discrimination, yet fail to speak against it, what have we done to rectify the injustice? And that's the hard part: because privilege tastes good and we're loath to relinquish it. Or even if willing, we often wonder how to resist: how to attack unfairness and make a difference.

Wise then discusses the importance of people taking a stand against racial profiling or attending local school board meetings and testifying against racial tracking in schools. Parents can lobby school board members, principals, and teachers to ensure that all students have equal access to and successfully acquire knowledge and skills being taught in schools. As Kyrstal Rodriguez wrote in one of the teacher stories at the beginning of this chapter, she was placed in a reading group that was working at a lower level than her ability. Krystal felt that she was discriminated against and had been tracked in her reading instruction. **Tracking** refers to the sorting of students by achievement levels.

Caring teachers who hold equity and justice as core values believe academic tracking in schools is unethical because schools are public institutions that should provide all students with comparable opportunities for learning. Since it has been shown that students who are found in upper educational tracks usually come from middle-class and higher-class families, there is controversy regarding the criteria that is used to sort students (Oakes 1985). Researchers believe the criteria used by many schools in the sorting process are an indication of social class and not intellectual ability (Hilliard 2002; Oakes 1985). Sadker and Sadker report that some teachers of lower-track classes have lower expectations for their students, are less demanding on their pupils, and give less feedback (Sadker and Sadker 2000).

Krystal is like other teachers who work to institute detracking: In contrast to students being placed in classes that are tracked, they are placed in mixed-ability groups. All students then have access to a core or foundational curriculum.

After reading these pieces and participating in discussions, I asked teachers to draw their views of White privilege on large poster papers. Here is a sample of two of the images that teachers have created over the years.

Why do you think the teachers created these images? What messages do you think the teachers are sending? They represent the difference in social and economic power.

The White House visual was created by five White teachers. They saw the social hierarchy and how it impacts our country. The person looking over the gate is a person of color and he or she is excluded. In U.S. history, all of our presidents have been European American and all have been male. Most have also been from wealthy families. The five teachers in this cooperative group felt that the White

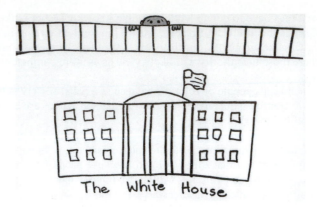

White Privilege: The White House

House epitomized White privilege in the United States. How close do you think we are as a nation to electing a president who is not European in ancestry or not a male? Our country is over 225 years old and our pattern has not changed. Do you agree with the five teachers that there is a social hierarchy in place? If so, how do you know? If not, what evidence can you provide?

Racial Identity Formation in Culturally Diverse Young People

Just as White teachers go through a process of understanding their racial identity, your students of color go through a process of racial identity formation because society has created categories based on physical characteristics; although genetically we are 99.9 percent the same. The following comic shows how parents of a child are concerned that their baby may encounter prejudice as she grows up.

Both children and teachers of color often must deal with the social stigmas of being physically different. In addition, people of color are often members of groups that have less political, financial, personal, institutional, and social capital than majority ethnic communities (Gordon 1999). As you read through the next section, notice the similarities between the theoretical work of Helms and Tatum to Cross. William Cross (1991) has developed a typology that can be used to explain the confusing and difficult process that African American adolescents, in particular, pass through. Although this typology was developed for African Americans, it can also be applied to people from other racially and ethnically different individuals.

Cross (1991) identified five stages in his **racial identity formation** model: pre-encounter, encounter, immersion/emersion, internalization, and internalization/commitment. In many ways the process is similar to the one White Americans pass through in order to clarify their own identity.

1. **Pre-encounter.** Children learn about majority culture from the media, school, their friends, textbooks, and other ways. In this stage, African American children learn about the superiority of White Americans and learn that the standard for success is a European one. A child in this stage has not thought much about her

JUMP START reprinted by permission of United Feature Syndicate, Inc.

own racial identity. At this point, a child learns a Eurocentric view of the world and takes in information from schools, media, and many other avenues without understanding the impact on her self-esteem or possible identity confusion.

2. **Encounter.** In this stage, the child has had contact with someone who either called her a name or excluded her from the group. This emphasizes the issue of race and the child will begin to question what happened and why the conflict arose. Cross believes that this often occurs when the child is in middle school. As part of adolescence, a student may be questioning much about herself. Physical appearance becomes an increasingly important characteristic of a young person.

   Similarly, I never realized I was part of a group known as Japanese American. I thought I was Val and that I was like everyone else. I found out when I went to school that other children saw me as someone who was different because I looked different. I was not an American or even Japanese American; I learned I was labeled that "Oriental" kid.

   Tatum (1997) found in her own research that African American students in this age group began asking parents and friends questions about their ethnic and racial identity. She found that dating became an extremely important issue at this stage of life, and students became anxious about interracial dating, in particular. In addition, Tatum found African American males to be more aware of the negative role models they saw on the media, like African American men handcuffed or shown as violent.

Unfortunately, Tatum (1997) discovered that some African American students developed an identity that confronted the White idea of success. Since Black students felt alienated from the majority society, they turned their backs on academic performance because they saw it as acceptance of European values and identity.

3. **Immersion/Emersion.** A young person in this stage explores and learns about her racial or ethnic community. Oftentimes the student may not only want to read about the history of her group, but also associate with others from the same racial community (Tatum 1997). The youngster enjoys learning about her group and becoming involved in ethnic or racially oriented community organizations. A high school student, who in the past had no interest in the Black student union, may now begin attending meetings at school and taking an active role in the activities. She may seek out a sense of safety and comfort that she finds in a same-race organization.

4. **Internalization.** In this stage, the young person becomes more secure with who she is and has self-identified her own feelings about racial membership. There is less anger toward Whites because the person feels comfortable with who she is (Tatum 1997). The student may now belong not only to the Black student union, but also to the human relations group on campus. She is active in both and works to develop coalitions between members of different communities.

5. **Internalization/Commitment.** In this stage, the student is secure in her identity as an African American person and has friends in both African American and other communities (Tatum 1997). The young person is committed to making life better in the African American community and works toward a more just society for all people.

This model shows the process a junior high/middle school student may begin. The journey can continue on to young adulthood or an older age. This developmental continuum can also describe the process an adult individual of color might pass through. The person may not have moved beyond the pre-encounter or encounter stage until she or he is an adult.

When Students from Ethnic Groups Challenge White Teachers

Just as you may find yourself with an array of feelings about ethnic and cultural groups, your students may also have developed strong perceptions of others based on cultural background. If you are European American, you may encounter children who first behave toward you as a member of the White collective. They may be hostile and not very trusting. Do not take this personally. They may have encountered many incidents of prejudice and group people into prejudged categories. Even if students have encountered only one European American teacher who is prejudiced, they had to sit through an entire year of discriminatory treatment, no matter how covert. Initially, students may see you, not as an individual, but as a representative of a larger group. As in any human relationship, you may need to prove to children that you believe in them and that you are fair. Don't feel guilty or worry about being European American. Instead, take that energy and be fair, respectful, and caring and treat each child as an important person. Most children will respond to you in the same respectful manner. You can set the tone of respect or animosity; it is your choice. Students want to believe that you are pulling for each one of them. Students have prejudices, too. You may even be called racist or gender-biased by a student. Will you know how to respond?

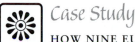 *Case Study*

HOW NINE EUROPEAN AMERICAN TEACHERS DEALT WITH CHARGES OF RACISM

Linda Valli has written a helpful article about the dilemmas teachers find themselves in when dealing with the issues of race. She placed nine European American preservice teachers in high schools that had a majority of African American or other underrepresented students (Valli 1995). Several teachers were anxious and worried about teaching in an inner-city school because they had visions of violent students and out-of-control classrooms.

Initially, Valli found her teachers to be conscious of color. Race did matter to them. The teachers were worried and expected hostility from their students. They also felt that they stood out physically in the school because they were White. As time went by, the teachers did not ignore the issue of race. And race did not continue to become an obstacle to reaching students, because teachers had a better understanding of their own feelings and the beliefs of their students.

It was not uncommon for students to accuse teachers of being racist. Teachers from majority and underrepresented groups have been challenged or tested. Students know that this can be a hot button, or threat, for all teachers. However, children also accuse their teachers because they are trying to better understand who they are and the parameters of race in society. Valli (1995) found that when students accused the teachers in her program of racism, the teachers had to deal with color. They could no longer ignore it. Let's look at the experience of a teacher named Matt:

> *If I told him to sit down, he would stand up. Whatever I did, he totally did the opposite. And every comment was, "Well, you're just pickin' on me because I'm Black." Or "You're doing this because I'm Black." And I was like "No, it's because you're talking." By muttering things under his breath like "He's just trying to make me White," Kahlil gave Matt the impression that his reactions were part of a broader resistance to White and White-imposed education* (Valli 1995, 123). ❉

What would you have said to Kahlil? Matt was being tested and he could have lost the entire class based on what he said to this one student. Before reading on, think about how you would respond. If you became defensive, what would the students say?

I believe one of the most effective strategies is to use humor because it often defuses the situation. Defensiveness most likely will escalate the issue. If you are consistently fair, use the same rules for everyone, and then use humor, students will know that you heard them, but that in this class it is their effort and ability that count, not their skin color. Matt could have replied with "Come on, Kahlil. You know that

I believe in equity. I remind all my students who talk when they aren't supposed to. You know you're not that special." If Matt had spoken to Kahlil with humor, yet still indirectly said that he was not racist just because he was European American, Kahlil would most likely have dropped the issue. Valli found that those teachers who dealt with the issue of race immediately and did not let it slide were much more successful in their teaching.

What did Valli's preservice teachers learn? They learned that race is a school issue. Although initially her European American teachers had not thought a great deal about race, they found that it was an integral part of U.S. society. The European American teachers also realized that their skin color was neither neutral nor privileged. They had a race and the students forced them to address their racial membership. Valli wrote about what her teachers learned: "Their students were engaged in the act of constructing Whiteness, an act in which they were the objects. Roles were reversed. Skin color had functioned as an interpretive lens in their own interactions with students. Now that lens was focused on them. But they, like most Whites were unaccustomed to this gaze" (1995, 124). To the students at the school, White was a color and their teachers were members of this collective. The students in the school continued to remind teachers that racism is an active issue in society. An important model that can be explained to students is one that fosters intercultural sensitivity. The next section presents an excellent model developed by Bennett.

Development of Intercultural Sensitivity

One of my major goals in writing this book is to help teachers move away from racism and toward **cross-cultural understanding** and intercultural perceptions. The existence of race is a myth; however, there are numerous cultures and cultural communities in the world. As discussed in Chapter 2, cultures can differ in language, behavior patterns, beliefs, symbols, and many other aspects. Bennett (1998) further explained the difference between culture with a capital *C* and culture with a small *c*. The concept of Culture (with the capital *C*) is the objective culture dealing with social, political, and linguistic systems and may include a class on the history of a community like the history of African Americans similar to Valle's discussion of the surface level of culture in Chapter 2. However, little *c* culture has more to do with the shared worldview and thinking patterns of a community. Bennett wrote, "A good working definition of **subjective culture** is the learned and shared patterns of beliefs, behaviors, and values of groups of interacting people" (3). This worldview shapes and supports the continuation of the social structure of the cultural group. Bennett saw international education and multicultural education as fields that center upon the objective or capital *C* culture. The small *c* culture refers to Valle's third layer of culture that he saw as values, norms, beliefs, and expectations. In other words, why we do and think the way we do arise from the deep level of culture. Bennett's writings centered on the subjective mode of culture, so he gave the example of **interculturalists** as being more interested in how language is used in human relationships, rather than their linguistic structure. Although Bennett's model has some elements that are similar to the racial identification work of Helms, Cross, and Tatum, Bennett's goal is different. Bennett developed a developmental model for cross-cultural understanding. His work goes beyond describing stages of identity to suggesting strategies to eliminate prejudice and discrimination.

Since culturally relevant teaching is a core component of Caring-Centered Multicultural Education, it is so important for educators to understand the worldview of their students. To build upon the cultural knowledge of their students, teachers must develop an "insider" viewpoint. In other words, educators must be able to take on the frame of reference of students who may be culturally different from themselves. This is a complex process, as Bennett has described.

Bennett explained that intercultural understanding and sensitivity are not necessarily natural. In fact, he believed that

> Ⓢ Intercultural sensitivity teaches people to move from ethnocentrism toward viewing behaviors from the cultural frames of reference of others.

many intercultural exchanges have led to massacres or other forms of oppression. So the question, we might ask is, How can professional development be organized in order to teach intercultural communication skills? Bennett has developed a model in which individuals move on a continuum from denial of other viewpoints and cultures towards integration, a stage where a person reflects upon diverse cultural realities.

Bennett's model is founded on several basic assumptions. They are as follows:

1. People from different cultures may respond *differently* to the same events and/or conditions.
2. People *move from* seeing reality *ethnocentrically.* They understand that there is no universal response to what happens in life and can see the situation from various cultural views.
3. *Ethical choices* are important in intercultural sensitivity and the belief that there are various ethical choices that can be made. There are no universal or absolute principles.

See Table 4.2 for Bennett's Developmental Model of Intercultural Sensitivity.

TABLE 4.2   Bennett's Developmental Model of Intercultural Sensitivity

The Ethnocentric Stages	The Ethnorelative Stages
I. Denial	IV. Acceptance
II. Defense	V. Adaptation
III. Minimization	VI. Integration

What is Bennett's model of intercultural sensitivity about? Bennett has created a complex and dynamic model to describe how individuals can developmentally move from ethnocentrism towards reflection and understanding of various worldviews. He also noted that people from oppressed cultural groups may find their way through the model differently. Their experiences are "controlled by a dominant cultural group . . . [that] demands conformity or segregation, which forces minorities who desire both inclusion and unique identity into fight or flight" (Bennett 1993, 28).

The first set of stages is called ethnocentric because the stages describe a worldview in which individuals see their reality as central to all experiences. In other words, individuals in these stages believe others see reality the way they do. Racism and outsider/insider positions come from this ethnocentric perspective (Bennett 1993).

Ethnocentric Stages

I. Denial   In this stage ethnocentric individuals do not see that there are other cultural viewpoints in their society and community. One reason for this ethnocentric viewpoint may be **physical isolation.** Maybe there are three African American students in the local high school; however, the population at the school seems to be homogeneous. There is no move to try to see issues from the view of culturally diverse people.

One of the examples Bennett used was the cultural differences between Japanese and Chinese Americans. When a float celebrating the sister city of a U.S. city had both Japanese American and Chinese American women, a high-ranking Japanese official was concerned. However, the parade coordinator said, "Chinese, Japanese . . . close enough" (Bennett 1993, 31). This person did not know there are distinct differences in the cultural backgrounds of Chinese and Japanese communities.

Another reason for ethnocentrism may be **separation.** This refers to the conscious creation of social barriers to maintain a distance and denial of unique realities. Today's cities experience separation by way of inner-city, barrio, and ghetto communities. These are ways people are isolated from mainstream populations. People who are in this stage do see some differences and that is why they want to separate themselves from others.

Unfortunately, through isolation and separation, prejudice may be fostered and reinforced through the teaching of stereotypes. When people do not have the opportunity to get to know each other on a personal level, it is possible to portray outsiders as less than human. Bennett did not believe that people of color experience the stage of denial because the differences being ignored are theirs.

II. Defense   The second stage is characterized by defensiveness. Individuals in this stage are threatened by another's reality and cultural differences are seen in a negative light. Members who are in the defense stage may try to protect their social privileges and not want others to have similar opportunities (Bennett, 1998). The most common defense is through **denigration.** Broad, negative stereotyping based on social categories such as race, cultural group, age, gender, religion, and other characteristics is used to discredit others. This can be seen in comments of hostility toward a group. One of the most powerful examples of this was the stereotypical, untrue, and extreme comments made by Nazis about the Jewish community in Germany and other European countries.

Bennett believed that the root of denigration is ethnocentrism and not ignorance or lack of knowledge. Another form of defensiveness is the teaching of **superiority** of one's group. An example of this is extreme nationalism. Another less obvious example is the policy of our nation toward some countries. For example, when the United States Agency for International Development uses the view of assisting "developing countries," this position sends the message that these countries are moving toward a culture similar to that of the United States (Bennett 1993). The viewpoint can be interpreted as our way of life is better, rather than seeing differences are just that, different. Both superiority and denigration are interrelated. One way to move away from this defensiveness is to have students study abroad and clarify the positive aspects of being American. During this period, students will be able to identify differences between American culture and the host culture they are studying. This experience can help individuals realize how understanding cultures and their differences can move people toward cultural sensitivity.

Another consequence to this stage is that people may choose to look down on their own cultures and see the new culture as superior; this is described as **reversal** by Bennett. For example, a Westerner who studies Eastern values and religion may "embrace the superiority of Eastern over Western cultural values" (Bennett 1993, 39.) Individuals in this stage may have studied the new cultural community and so they are not reacting defensively. However, if they denigrate their own cultures, they are not moving toward real understanding of their own and other cultures.

Bennett suggested that one of the best avenues to move people beyond being defensive is to have them discover the commonalities people have as humans.

III. Minimization   In this stage of development, people tend to treat cultural differences as if they do not matter. In other words, folks in this stage minimize differences and focus on our shared humanity. Although this seems to be a good position, Bennett cautions that people can continue to hold ethnocentric beliefs and not deal with cultural differences. For example, when people feel there are universal values that all share, those values usually come from their own cultures. Bennett cautions that people of color may be somewhat wary of the "assumption of common humanity. Too often, the assumption has meant 'be like me' " (1993, 42).

In this stage people often cite the basic needs of humans as being common shared characteristics that support the feeling that all individuals can understand each other. Cultural differences are marginalized. Bennett saw this viewpoint as **physical universalism;** however, he felt this position ignored the social context of communities. Bennett suggested that students study cross-cultural work in various fields such as anthropology, psychology, sociology, and communications in order to move beyond the idea of basic human needs.

Another form of minimization is **transcendent universalism.** Bennett cited a religious example of this: "The statement, 'We are all God's children' " (1993, 43). Another example of this form "include[s] the Marxist notion of historical imperative, wherein all people are subject to the same historical forces; [and] economic and political laws that are thought to affect all people in the same way, such as the capitalist concept of individual achievement" (Bennett 1993, 43). People in this stage may see cultural differences and yet believe that others will find the way to a transcendental truth. Persons in this stage are ethnocentric because they believe that others with diverse cultural views will arrive at the same worldview that they hold.

Ethnorelative Stages

The second half of Bennett's model moves to **ethnorelativism.** What is it? Bennett saw the ethnorelativism stages as movement toward an understanding of behaviors based upon the cultural context in which they are used. That the behaviors may be different is neither "good" nor "bad." The cultures that one holds are not better or more desirable than those of others; they are just different. How is this phase of development different from the ethnocentric stages? People do not feel threatened or become defensive. Instead, people see cultural differences as new ways of thinking and acting, and they are not trying to continue to maintain their own.

Bennett provided an excellent example of the contrast between the two phases. He reported on the study-abroad experiences of two students who had lived in France:

> One student stated, "My homestay mother was always yelling at me in French, which I didn't understand well. I felt like I was always doing something wrong. It was a bad situation, and I was happy when I got changed to a different home where the mother spoke some English." The second student reported a similar situation but a different reaction: "My homestay mother would burst into my room in the morning, throw open the window, and yell things in French I didn't understand. It was just wonderful—so French!" (Bennett 1993, 50).

The first example showed a person who saw the mother's behavior as threatening, but the second student saw the mother's behavior as cultural and exciting.

IV. Acceptance   People see and respect cultural differences in this stage. This is the beginning of moving from ethnocentrism towards ethnorelativism.

One of the forms of acceptance is **respect for behavioral difference.** Individuals may begin to understand that unfamiliar behaviors may arise from cultural differences. One of the cultural differences that can easily be identified is language. In addition, people from various cultures may show diverse verbal and nonverbal communication styles and use different customs, tones, and nonverbal gestures.

The next form of acceptance is **respect for value difference.** In this stage people see that their worldviews are culturally bound. They also understand that others have cultural contexts, too, and individuals have been part of a process in which they have learned what "goodness" and "rightness" are from living within a structured organization (Bennett 1993). Those who are in this stage see that people from diverse cultural contexts go through different processes in which they learn values. They understand that people may have gone through different cultural processes, but they do not necessarily agree with their beliefs. One example that Bennett provided was that some cultural groups value men more than women. People may revert from an acceptance stage to defense stage if they feel superior. Individuals who are able to continue in their intercultural development will see this value as one that arose from the community's worldview, although they may not agree with this value.

IV. Adaptation   Bennett clearly articulated that in this stage people do not assimilate into the new culture. In other words, ethnorelative individuals do not take on the new culture and abandon their own. Rather people develop new skills and add them to their knowledge base. *Culture is understood as a process and not an object.* "One does not have culture; one engages in it" (Bennett 1993, 52). In this stage, persons move from their own "cultural frame of reference" to that of others and their knowledge of perspectives expands.

The first step of this stage is **empathy.** In order for people to develop intercultural sensitivity, it is critical for them to take on the views of others. Some people refer to this as border crossing. What does that really mean? There is a clear shift to another's cultural context and worldview and there is respect for the cultural differences of others while one moves toward the new worldview. Empathy differs from sympathy. With sympathy, one continues to hold his or her ethnocentric viewpoint as the frame of reference. An example of empathy is a Westerner going to Japan and taking to her host a gift of a ceramic teapot with four teacups. Although being given four is seen as unlucky in Japan, the Japanese host accepts the gift graciously because she sees the gift within the cultural values of the Westerner. The visiting person placed no value on the number four. The number of teacups was a Western practice.

The next form of acceptance, **pluralism,** represents not only that there are diverse values, norms, and ways of life, but that differences must be seen within their cultural contexts or frames of references. People in this stage are able to participate more fully in another culture than those who act only from empathy.

VI. Integration   The last stage of the ethnorelative phase is **integration.** When people understand diverse worldviews, they engage in a process of clarifying who they are. Through this process of self-identification, individuals no longer identify with any one culture (Bennett 1998). They see themselves as multiculturalists or interculturalists and are able to use a variety of worldviews in their lives. A good example of this individual is the mythologist, Joseph Campbell. His work took him around the world, where he studied the frames of references of numerous cultural communities. His ethics arose from an integration of many cultural belief systems that he studied.

Bennett developed a model of intercultural sensitivity that guides people from engaging in an ethnocentric orientation toward interculturalism. Interculturalists or multiculturalists are able to view interactions within the cultural contexts of the others. They are able to examine behavior, issues, and policy from the frame of reference of other cultures. Bennett's model encouraged individuals to move away from a black-and-white view of ethics and reality. He suggested that experience is a key aspect of this model because when one lives in another culture, one is more apt to see cultural differences and the reality or cultural context of others. It is crucial for teachers to work on their intercultural sensitivity in order to understand and address the needs of a culturally diverse student population.

 Connection

Please visit Chapter 4 of the book website to link to the Intercultural Communication Institute (**www.intercultural.org/**).

↺ *"One does not have culture; one engages in it."*
—MILTON J. BENNETT

Chapter Summary

People from many groups have felt discrimination. The experience can be emotionally disturbing, especially if one has to deal with it continually. Discrimination can have a severe impact on the feelings of self-worth, identity of children and adults, and learning. This chapter included stories from many teachers who have experienced discrimination. They have not forgotten it, even though the event may have occurred decades in the past. There are many kinds of discrimination. Some occur because of individual bias, others occur because of social beliefs, and still many instances arise from institutional prejudice.

One of the most pervasive types of oppression is racism. The discussion in this chapter explained the process that African Americans and White Americans pass through in developing their racial identity. The research of Janet Helms and Beverly Tatum found that White students go through a process that can be described as the following: acceptance of status quo, feeling uncomfortable with discussion of race, denial of inequities in society, seeking clarifi-cation of own racial identity, acceptance of self and group, and becoming a change agent. William Cross discovered a similar process for African Americans. He found that African American students first learn about how society views the African American community. Then, as children, when young people encounter racism, they may begin to question their racial identity. In the next stage, young people begin to explore aspects of the community. Following this stage, people begin to become more secure with who they are and work toward making society a more just place.

White privilege is one of the most difficult aspects of racism to understand. Peggy McIntosh gives many insights into how people benefit from being members of the majority community without understanding how their membership provides opportunities that others may not have. In fact, she believes European Americans do not understand that it is a privilege that they see their lives as morally neutral, normative, and the standard for others.

Prejudice and discrimination are powerful forces in society. They can impact the way teachers act and react to their students, and vice versa. It is important to understand the process that people go through in order to understand who they are in a racially conscious society like the United States.

Bennett provided teachers with an intercultural sensitivity model of development by which people can engage in a process that encourages movement from ethnocentrism toward interculturalism. In this state, people have clarified who they are and their values through the examination of and experience in various cultural contexts. They do not identify with one culture over another or see that one culture is good and others are bad. Persons who are truly interculturalists or multiculturalists see their identities "existing within a collection of various cultural and personal frames of reference" (Bennett 1993, 60). What impact can this intercultural sensitivity have on teachers? When teachers are able to examine student and parent behaviors from diverse frames of reference, cross-cultural

understanding is more likely. They do not operate from stereotypical beliefs. When teachers give up their own ethnocentric orientation, they then will be more capable to address the conflicts and needs of culturally diverse students. In this way relationships can be strengthened.

Several chapters about culturally relevant teaching appear later in the book. To assist teachers in understanding the cultural frames of reference of students who have different worldviews, Bennett's model can facilitate personal growth in intercultural knowledge. It will be more difficult for teachers to integrate culturally relevant teaching strategies if they do not develop intercultural sensitivity. As the book has explained, the process of becoming Caring-Centered Multicultural Education teachers is a complex one in which teachers challenge their own biases, develop cultural understandings of others, and are able to build a curriculum that arises out of their experiences. Pedagogy, when culturally sensitive and relative, is built upon the knowledge base of students.

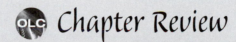

Chapter Review

Go to the Online Learning Center at **www.mhhe.com/pang2e** to review important content from the chapter, practice with key terms, take a chapter quiz, and find the Web links listed in this chapter.

Key Terms

discrimination, *118*
scapegoating, *118*
blame the victim, *118–119*
sociopolitical, *127*
White privilege, *127*
color-blind, *128*
tracking, *131*
racial identity formation, *132*
cross-cultural understanding, *136*

subjective culture, *136*
interculturalists, *136*
physical isolation, *138*
separation, *138*
denigration, *138*
superiority, *139*
reversal, *139*
physical universalism, *139*
transcendent universalism, *140*

ethnorelativism, *140*
respect for behavioral difference, *140*
respect for value difference, *140*
empathy, *141*
pluralism, *141*
integration, *141*

Reflection Activities

Answer the following questions in your journal. Reflect on how your understanding of prejudice and discrimination is deepening as you think about the experiences and dialogue you have with others.

1. When you were discriminated against, how did it feel? What emotions did you have? How did the discrimination impact you and your ideas?

2. List the ways that prejudice and discrimination can be hurtful to others. Include situations in which students have felt the sting and pain of prejudice and discrimination. Do you see why prejudice can cause trouble in the classroom?

3. If you are European American, read through the chart on White racial identity and find the stage that best describes you. If you are a person from an ethnic minority group, use William Cross's discussion of racial identity and find which stage describes where you would place yourself. Go back to the chart as you read through this book. Have you changed or are you staying in the same place? Why or why not?

4. Milton Bennett has provided a comprehensive model for cross-cultural understandings. How could a move from ethnocentrism assist you, as a teacher in the classroom, in becoming a more effective teacher? How have you looked at cultural differences? Bennett believed that when a person does not deal with differences and emphasizes a human universal orientation, she or he is not dealing with cultural differences. Do you agree? Why or why not?

5. Reading major scholars in the field can help teachers to better understand White privilege. I encourage you to read Christine Clark and James O'Donnell's book *Becoming and Unbecoming White: Owning and Disowning a Racial Identity* and/or James Schuerich's text, *Anti-racist Scholarship: An Advocacy*. Both are excellent resources that will provide you with new perspectives about racism. The authors are antiracists and are dedicated to eliminating racism not only in schools but also in society in general. Their passion and thought-provoking ideas challenge all of us to rethink many of our beliefs about social justice.

6. The Arab-American Anti-Discrimination Committee has a website that provides information from an Arab American viewpoint. Its website address is **http://www.adc.org/index.php?id=119**. It provides legal information about issues dealing with Arab Americans. If you seek information on Islam, the Council on Islamic Education has another website that provides free materials on the teaching of religion at **http://www.cie.org/teachers/TeachersGuideToReligionInThePublicSchools.asp**.

7. Teaching for Change, a wonderful organization that provides many materials for teachers, has an informative website with lessons about how to teach the issue of 9/11. The website is at **http://www.teachingforchange.org/Sept11.htm**.

8. **Positive and Fun Activity** I want you to think about how you can involve your students in fun and collaborative activities that encourage people to think about what they can do to stop social oppression. I have seen high school groups create posters called "One Hundred Ways to Stop Racism" or "One Hundred Ways to Stop Sexism" or "One Hundred Ways to Stop Homophobia." I adapted the idea from the National Association of Social Workers, which has a poster called "100 Ways You Can Stop Violence . . . " I have used many of their ideas in my example. Have your students help you create the poster. I find young people have exceptional imaginations and will extend the activity beyond my original vision. Add another 50 ways to complete a 100 ways list.

Twenty-Five Ways You Can Stop Racism, Sexism, Classism, and Homophobia

1. Smile at 10 new people from other groups.
2. Make someone else laugh.
3. Learn about another's group history.
4. Say positive things about other people.
5. Write a positive letter to someone.
6. Object to an ethnic or gender-biased or homophobic joke.
7. Read children's books with positive role models of women and people of color to your students.
8. Appreciate differences.

9. Learn a new language.
10. Watch movies like *Sarafina, Picture Bride, Soul Food, Zoot Suit, Mi Familia, Secrets and Lies, Amistad, Shall We Dance, Whale Rider,* and *Rabbit Proof Fence.*
11. Be fair with your students.
12. Teach children how to talk out a conflict.
13. Be respectful of your students and colleagues.
14. Invite students to lunch.
15. Teach children an integrated U.S. history.
16. Help children see African American history as U.S. history.
17. Help children see women's history as U.S. history.
18. Help children see Asian Pacific American history as U.S. history.
19. Help children see Native American history as U.S. history.
20. Help children see Latino history as U.S. history.
21. Invite guest speakers from different communities to the classroom.
22. Call parents every Friday, congratulating their children for excellent work.
23. Put on a play about Angela Davis or Malcolm X, or César Chavez.
24. Invite a class from another school to lunch.
25. Invite parents to school for lunch.

For more of these, please visit the website for Chapter 4.

CHAPTER 5

Aren't Mary and Michael Too Young to Be Prejudiced?

CHAPTER MAIN IDEAS

- *Who Am I and Whom Should I Be Like?*

- *Stages of Prejudice and Identity Development*

- *An Antibias Curriculum*

- *Teaching about Discrimination and Stereotypes in the Classroom Curriculum: Vocabulary*

- *Curriculum That May Reinforce Stereotypes: Christmas around the World*

- *Using Antiracist Role Models: An Accurate Portrayal of Rosa Parks*

- *White Antiracist Role Models*

- *Homophobia: Sexual Orientation and Student Identity*

CHAPTER OVERVIEW

The purpose of this chapter is to explain how prejudice is taught. Children learn negative attitudes about others from those they interact with in their lives. Teachers can integrate a curriculum that assists students in understanding how prejudice is learned and taught in many ways. One of the most difficult aspects of teaching about prejudice, discrimination, and stereotypes is defining the concepts for young children. This chapter focuses on racism and homophobia. Students can learn from role models who fight racism, classism, gender bias, homophobia, and other kinds of oppression in society.

I believe most of us learn prejudice about others while growing up. One of the articles that helped me get a clearer picture of how children are taught values and beliefs without really consciously taking in the ideas was an interview with Robert Coles, child psychiatrist. Coles has written more than 50 books on children and remarked that he found that many children were aware of racial differences as young as two or three years old. In interviews with first- and second-grade children, Coles also discovered that children were extremely aware of class differences. Although adults may believe children do not know much about social class, gender, and race, children have learned that these things should not be talked about because they are embarrassing matters (Teaching Tolerance 1992). Coles discovered that children were very savvy about how people are treated differentially because of race and class.

A teacher relayed a story about his young neighbor. He was in the yard talking with a White mother and her child, who was almost three years old. An African American child who lived several houses away asked to play with the younger child. The mother politely said, "She needs to take her nap now, so she won't be able to play." When the mother took her daughter inside to the porch, her tone changed dramatically. She said harshly, "I don't want you playing with any of those ugly children. Don't let me catch you with them." The young daughter's eyes opened wide as she carefully listened to her mother. The little girl didn't say anything. The teacher, who overheard the conversation, was shocked by the comments of his neighbor. He couldn't believe what he had heard. He knew that this young person could grow up thinking negatively about African Americans.

Another teacher from one of my classes gave a similar example. Her daughter had a close friend who was Japanese American. The Japanese American young woman was seeing a Latino. Her parents never said anything directly to oppose the young man; however, one summer her parents suggested that she go to cultural activities at the Buddhist church. The young woman asked, "Why do you want me to go with you?" Her father said, "I want you to learn about Buddhism and Japanese history. It will be a wonderful experience." He paused, then said, "You might find another boyfriend too, one who is more like you." Prejudice can be taught by people whom we trust and care for; some may be members of our family.

> ⑤ *Children learn prejudice from people they trust and care for.*

Who Am I and Whom Should I Be Like?

Children begin to make sense of the world by understanding themselves first. They know their names and who are members of their family. Later they begin to distinguish that those who are uncles, aunts, and cousins are relatives, while neighbors and others are friends. Children also show fear of strangers at about six months of age (Allport 1954). These strangers may wear different colors or talk to children in an unfamiliar way. As children grow, they develop a sense of who they are while they are learning prejudicial attitudes from their environment.

As children come into contact with others, they learn about people and make generalizations about life. Allport (1954) believes that children adopt the prejudices of others and develop prejudices as part of life experiences. When children adopt prejudices, they accept and take in the attitudes and stereotypes of important people in their lives. Allport believes that children who grow up in a highly authoritarian and disciplined family are sensitive to the approval and disapproval of their parents. Oftentimes, they are taught that authority and power rather than trust and care are key aspects of interpersonal relationships. Allport believes that children who are brought up in authoritarian families are more likely to be fearful or suspicious of others. If children are criticized a great deal, they will develop personalities that are more critical of others (Sleeter and Grant 1987). On the other hand, children who grow up in families where love is unconditionally given are more likely to acquire higher levels of self-esteem and confidence. They are also more likely to accept others because their parents have accepted them.

Stages of Prejudice and Identity Development

Children learn who they are as they learn who they are not. *Prejudice and identity formation are integrally linked.* The prejudice children learn may be due to physical characteristics, ethnicity, culture, class, gender, language, and other social categories (Byrnes 1988). As you read through this section, remember that there are many layers of identity. Although this section deals primarily with a social category defined by many as racial identity, this may primarily deal with physical attributes and not with an accurate biological construct. Many children develop other ideas of who they are, and this involves the integration of a cultural or ethnic identity, religious identity, national identity, and family identity. These are complex constructs, yet they are often developing simultaneously. Children try to figure out where they fit in with their families, as persons with particular physical characteristics, as members of a family that has ties with an ancestral country other than the United States, and as members of a nation/country called the United States.

Stage One: Curious of Others

Allport has identified four **stages of prejudice** that children experience as they mature, these are listed in Figure 5.1. In the first stage, children as young as two years old are **curious** about differences they see in others (Allport 1954). They may notice that someone's skin color, hair texture, or name is different from their own (Goodman 1964); the differences are not negative ones. At this time, children begin to sort out distinctive characteristics of people and place them into categories like race, language, gender, and physical abilities (Derman-Sparks, Higa, and Sparks 1980). Simultaneously children see that their differences have social categories. Have you ever heard a child ask a parent or sibling, "What am I?" One mother told the story about how her four-year-old daughter, Helen, began developing a sense of self and how it involved a discussion of others.

> "You're an American, and so am I, and so's your father." At nursery school the other day, she asked the teacher, "What are you?" Mrs. X said, "I'm an American," and Helen drew herself up very proud and said, "I'm an American too" . . . And then a little while back Mary said she'd rather play with David than Helen. Mary said, "He's white and you're colored." But she wasn't takin' that. She came right back with, "Oh no I'm not. I'm a tantalizin' brown!" (Derman-Sparks et al. 1980, 7).

How Do Children Learn Prejudice?

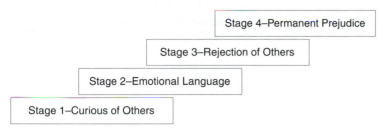

Figure 5.1   *An Adaptation of Allport's Stages of Prejudice: How Do Children Learn Prejudice?*

In this conversation, Mary, another four-year-old, had already developed a belief about racial categories, skin colors, and national identity as an American (U.S. citizen). Yet Helen, with the help of her parents, had created her own racial identity and she was not hurt by what Mary said. Three- and four-year-olds are sorting out characteristics by saying things such as, "I'm no girl—I'm a boy," or "I got curly yellow hair." (Derman-Sparks et al. 1980, 8).

Young children learn to categorize people based on identifiable physical characteristics because our country has strong political and social orientations toward race. Young children, three to five years old, are interested in their physical differences and those of others. Skin color is usually one of the attributes children focus on. "A frequently reported question asked by White children about Black children [is]: 'Will the color come off in the bathtub?' " (Derman-Sparks et al. 1980).

At this age children are not only attempting to identify who they are, but they are beginning to understand the concept of group. I believe that these young children are not "color blind," but that many grow up in an environment that continually reinforces the belief that racial and other differences have positive and negative values attached to them. These beliefs come from their environment and the experiences children have with adults and other children.

Like Goodman, Derman-Sparks and her colleagues found preschool and elementary grade students to be "color conscious" (Derman-Sparks et al. 1980). They discovered that young children were not color blind; rather, they were extremely aware of racial differences. The children asked questions such as:

"Why are there Black people?

Is Mexican my color?

Why am I called Black if my skin is brown?

If I'm Black and White, and Tim is Black and White, how come he is darker than me?

Do Indians always run around wearing feathers?

Why is my skin called yellow? It's not yellow, it's tan." (Derman-Sparks, et al. 1980, 8).

Young children, especially preschoolers, are struggling with their own identity as they learn about social categories. From the questions that the youngsters posed, their perceptions were primarily about physical characteristics or dress. They are being taught at a very young age that bodily attributes symbolize important beliefs about themselves and others.

Children also learn about gender differences. Sometimes that knowledge is biased knowledge. Young children may come to school with definite perceptions about the roles of women and men. The comic, above, shows that Zoe and Hammie were surprised that their new doctor was a female. This is an example of how positive role models can generate powerful new learning in students.

Stage Two: Emotional Language

Although children do not always see differences as negative, how do children learn that differences have values attached to them? Allport believes that children in the second stage begin to notice that the words people use to describe others have strong **emotional connotations** attached to them. These words are sometimes used to hurt another and, by the age of four, many children have learned that the differences have values attached to them. Derman-Sparks and her colleagues (1980) found that one of the most important developmental tasks young children of color must deal with is to build positive racial and ethnic identities. This can be difficult, especially within the context of a White society, where labels and images from the media and from others may be negative.

Stereotypical images of people are found in many places. The media often reinforce biased views (Byrnes 1988). Asians are often portrayed as karate-fighting mobsters who are so devoted to their cause that they will even commit suicide because of fanatical loyalty. African Americans are usually the drug smugglers or dope addicts. Heroes are usually physically attractive and many villains still wear black. The image of beauty usually involves a thin, tall, blond, shapely woman. These beliefs are often reinforced through the hundreds of hours of television children watch every year.

During this stage of identity formation, children are also trying to understand how national identity as an American (in this context I am referring to a U.S. citizen, native or naturalized) and ethnic identity can be related. I believe it may take many years, even into adulthood, before a person of color understands her- or himself.

Although the person is an American—whether American-born or naturalized—if she or he has not been accepted by the majority culture, then the person may not feel like a full-fledged partner in the process. Prejudice can cause people to question themselves and can tear away at their self-esteem.

National and ethnic identity can be an extremely complicated aspects of some children's lives. In San Diego are many new immigrant families from all over the world whose children go to public school. Children have migrated from countries like Somalia, Korea, Russia, Iran, Mexico, and Vietnam. Many of these children must begin to build a sense of who they are within this new cultural and political context. I believe that as the children grow up in their new home, the United States, they develop a complicated self-concept, which is a combination of new American values and behaviors mixed with home-country culture. Many times this adjustment is extremely difficult, especially when prejudice and discrimination are directed toward them because of differences due to language, accent, behaviors, clothing, and traditions.

Stage Three: Rejection of Others

In the third stage of prejudice, children begin to reject the people their parents, friends, and important role models also do not like. This occurs at about 7 to 11 years of age. They accept their parents' values without question. Allport wrote about a child who ran home and asked her mother, "What was the name of the child I was supposed to hate?" (Allport 1954, 292). Since the young child wanted to please her mother, she had a sense of labels that people used to call each other as being "bad" and wanted to make sure that she did what her mother wanted her to do. During this stage, children may totally reject those in a group. They may not want to play with someone who is from another race, or they may choose children who are only from their group.

Children of color and majority children need the support of their parents and teachers when they deal with issues of prejudice and discrimination. Parents, teachers, and other adults can help children develop in positive ways through their modeling. Children of color whose parents teach a strong sense of family and cultural pride often are more able to deal with prejudice because they know their roots. For example, a child who has been called "Jap" at school probably will be hurt; however, if her parents have taught her to be proud that her family has a long legacy of culture and commitment to civil rights, the child knows that her family is strong and has triumphed over prejudice in the past.

My husband and I knew that our daughter and son would encounter racism in their lives, and we tried to prepare them as best we could. When they were babies, we would say things like, "I love your beautiful black hair and skin," or "You have beautiful brown eyes." And as they grew old enough to go to school, we were careful to tell them that they should not allow other kids to call them names.

As any mother, I was concerned that they someday would have to deal with the name-calling and exclusion that racism can bring. Our daughter is somewhat quiet. She is not shy, but she is not an aggressive person and I worried about her ability to deal with bullies and name-callers. I thought she would ignore any name-calling. One day when she was in the fifth grade, she came home somewhat upset. I asked her what happened. She said that several children on the playground had taunted her with the sing-song rhyme, "Ching Chong Chinaman." As she walked around with her friends at recess, my daughter turned around, looked directly at them, and said, "Cut it out." Even though she is a caring individual, she is also a strong person and would not allow others to tear her down. Fortunately, she had supportive friends and they also told the kids to stop their taunting. They quit. I told her I was proud of her because she had the courage to stand up for herself. She beamed. Children need feedback from their parents, teachers, and other adults to help them filter through the thousands of messages they receive every day about race, class, and gender.

Stage Four: Prejudice Becomes Permanent

By stage four prejudicial attitudes become more fixed or permanent when children become teenagers. During this part of their lives, children have developed cultural categories dealing with characteristics such as sexual orientation, race, ethnicity, class, and gender. In addition, young people do not usually reject everyone from a group and are not as prone to overgeneralizations. Allport believes that this is a stage of differentiation. Teens make exceptions for individuals. They may say, "I'm not prejudiced. My best friend is Black." Interestingly, Allport reminds his readers that while children are learning prejudice, people are also talking about democracy and equality (1954, 295). Children learn about the complexities of prejudice within a society where equality is valued, and although underrepresented groups may have positive qualities, their negative ones justify exclusion.

I believe that children learn from infancy the values of race, class, and gender. These values are part of their everyday lives. They learn who they are and whom they should be like. They also learn whom they should not like. They take on the values of the people they trust and who are their role models.

 Case Study

HOW PREJUDICE AND STEREOTYPES ARE LINKED

When I began teaching first grade, I didn't realize children's views of race affected their impressions of others. The following story describes the color-conscious values of a six-year-old. He seemed to be between stage two and stage three. He did not outrightly reject someone who was different, but he did seem to hold strong values about those differences.

During the first several days of first grade, I had small groups of four children and their parents visit school for an hour. This was done to help first graders make the adjustment to a full day of school. I noticed one child standing outside the classroom not wanting to enter (Pang 1988). I asked his mother what was wrong. She said, "My son Rodney doesn't want to come in." I began to worry. What was I going to do? Finally, I asked, "Is he scared?" "No," she said. "Rodney says he doesn't want to come in because he can't speak Chinese!" At first I couldn't understand the problem, because I am Japanese

American not Chinese American. It did not occur to me that this six-year-old had looked into the classroom and decided that since I looked Asian I wasn't an American (U.S. citizen) and therefore couldn't speak English. He thought I could only speak Chinese. I was surprised by Rodney's matter-of-fact belief that I must be a foreigner, because I did not look European American.

Many children such as Rodney, who enter school, are aware of many messages that society holds about group membership. Five- to eight-year-olds realize they are members of different social groups. Children develop categories about other children and may exclude them because of their skin color, accent, physical attributes, neighborhood, and language. Prejudicial attitudes also include **stereotypes.** These overgeneralizations are used to justify how we behave (Allport 1954). Unfortunately, children at this age also can be acutely aware of racist, gender-biased, and classist attitudes of others and may take on prejudicial attitudes of parents, friends, and neighborhoods. Name-calling is common at this age and children understand that these names are used to hurt others. At this age children struggle with gathering accurate information about others, but children of color also must struggle with racial self-identity in a society where the ideal models presented are oftentimes tall and thin, with fair complexion and blond or brown hair. Teachers need to be aware of how prejudice impacts people of all ages. ✳

An Antibias Curriculum

An important component of Multicultural Education is reducing prejudice and discrimination in students. If you teach preschool or the primary grades, I suggest that you read the book *Anti-Bias Curriculum: Tools for Empowering Young Children* by Derman-Sparks and her colleagues (1989). It is an excellent resource because it may answer your questions about how to guide children away from prejudicial attitudes and discriminatory behavior. The book covers issues of race and gender and also has a chapter aimed at helping youngsters develop antibias attitudes toward children with learning and developmental differences. A continual thread throughout the book is that children need to learn to accept each other in a safe and respectful environment. This setting must also provide children with new ways of interacting with each other. Just placing children together does not necessarily build bridges of communication among students.

Derman-Sparks and her colleagues have identified several important goals for learning about culture that will help all children develop a positive sense of self while learning to foster healthy social interactions. I believe that these goals can help you create a classroom that cultivates equity and cultural diversity. The following is an adaptation of their goals:

1. A teacher affirms and fosters children's knowledge and pride, not superiority, in their cultural identity.
2. A teacher fosters children's curiosity, enjoyment, and empathetic awareness of cultural differences and similarities.

"Why are kings higher than
queens? Aren't men and women
s'posed to be equal?"

3. A teacher expands children's concept of fairness and feeling of empathy for others.
4. A teacher helps children change uncomfortable and inappropriate responses to differences into respectful and comfortable interactions.
5. A teacher helps children think critically about stereotyping.
6. A teacher helps children develop the tools and self-confidence to stand up for themselves and others against prejudice and discriminatory behavior.

✆ Children can be taught to question actions and words that are not fair or caring.

When students are encouraged to think and question, they often raise interesting questions on their own. In the comic, above, Dolly has come up with an important question. The teacher could turn her question into a teachable moment about gender bias.

Dealing with Biases in Children

How can you help children become aware of racist, gender-biased, or classist behavior? As a teacher, you can help children see that when their behavior excludes others, they are discriminating against someone. Students may be treating others in an uncaring way. For example, when name-calling occurs, teachers should talk with their students right away. It is important that children realize that racist, gender-biased, and classist terms are unacceptable. Like adults, children need to understand that when someone is called a name, it threatens justice for all of us. Help children understand the "we" of a community. Even though they may not be the perpetrator or victim of a particular situation, when the dignity of one person is threatened, our communal values of justice and equality are also being questioned. Relating prejudice to children's notions of fairness helps young students realize they can eliminate prejudice. The following excerpt shows how a young child can question his or her own perceptions.

> When D. was about seven he began dancing one day to a record of Navajo music we have. All of a sudden he stopped himself, looked at us and said, "You know, I don't know how they dance. I'm just making it up." Another day, he told us, after seeing a movie, "I know one way that movie was racist. It only had white people in it." (Derman-Sparks et al. 1980, 7).

We can help children learn to respect each other's cultural ways and understand how powerful messages about cultural differences are given in society all the time.

Suzanne, a principal in Laramie, Wyoming, shared with a group of teachers a public way she dealt with name-calling on the playground. She witnessed some serious name-calling one morning when several first graders used a racial slur at a peer. At first, she was stunned to see and hear the interchange. Then she walked up to the small group of children, looked at the child who had been treated disrespectfully and said, "I am sorry this happened to you at our school. We will work harder to make sure this doesn't happen again to you or anyone else." Suzanne was providing a powerful message for all the children. She as an administrator was not taking the situation lightly and it was the responsibility of all members of the school to eliminate prejudice and discrimination. Suzanne is not only a competent administrator who directs the school, but she is also a good institutional role model, showing her students the ownership they can take in the fight against racism.

Name-calling and other bullying behaviors may relate to race, but may also relate to sexual orientation, gender, size, religion, and disability.

Lourdes, a teacher in North Miami, Florida, shared another important strategy to deal with conflict (Teaching Tolerance 1999). As a kindergarten grade teacher, she believes that peace and caring should be at the core of her classroom. As a teacher involved in the Peace Education Foundation, she adopted the "I Care Rules." These rules are as follows:

1. We listen to each other.
2. Hands are for helping, not hurting.
3. We use "I care" language.
4. We care about each other's feelings.
5. We are responsible for what we say and do (Teaching Tolerance 1999, 143).

In addition to these general guidelines, Lourdes has instituted an important place in the classroom. When children have conflicts with each other, she has "The Peace Table," a place where children feel safe and accepted. Lourdes helps her children role-play various situations that might arise during the year and teaches how to focus on a solution.

The Peace Table has the following guidelines for the children to use:

1. Identify the problem.
2. Focus on the problem.

3. Attack the problem, not the person.
4. Listen with an open mind.
5. Treat a person's feelings with respect.
6. Take responsibility for your actions.

🌀 *The Peace Table is a safe place to solve problems together.*

Students in this classroom are learning how to solve their own problems. They do not ignore them. The classroom becomes a place where children want to be because they know their feelings and perspectives will be respected.

Helping Older Students Deal with Prejudice

Many students have told me how much it hurts when someone throws a racial slur at them. It is almost as if the hurt goes down to their souls. Their sense of self can be seriously damaged, especially in the adolescent years. For some very young children, the impact may not be as hurtful to their self-esteem because they are not as oriented toward their peers, and oftentimes they make up quickly after a conflict. However, for older students the role of prejudice may be much more disturbing and long lasting.

As students grow older, they may find that they must deal with more severe aspects of prejudice. The comments may be more cutting and the actions of peers may be more deliberate. When students feel like their "arms have been tied behind their back" due to an act of prejudice, then that feeling can lead to further feelings of helplessness. Students also may feel that they cannot be themselves; for example, they may not feel comfortable speaking Spanish or identifying as Mexican American. The prejudice may be even more destructive because students feel victimized. In addition, when prejudice is felt at this age, the experiences may tend to reinforce stereotypes they were forming about members of a particular group. For example, although Mary intellectually knows that it was only "three (name of an ethnic group) girls" who pushed and terrorized her in the bathroom, she may transfer this image to all young women in the group and not feel comfortable making friends or talking with other students in her classes from the same ethnic community as the perpetrators.

Encouraging students not to generalize is an important aspect of dealing with prejudice. As with the example of Mary, it would be helpful if her friends, teachers, parents, and others suggested that she remember other people she has worked with from the ethnic community who have been positive, encouraging, and collaborative. Looking at other role models in that community can help a young person understand that several individuals do not represent an entire community.

Teachers can be important role models for students and employ long-term strategies that help young people deal more effectively with prejudice when it is directed at them.

1. Affirm the self-esteem of the students. When this is done consistently, students will have the self-confidence to respond to the event from a position of personal centeredness rather than one of defense.

2. Affirm the ethnic/bicultural self-esteem of students. When students are knowledgeable about the strengths and weaknesses of their cultural orientations, they may develop a more honest identity. This ethnic identity is not built on feelings of superiority or inferiority in comparison to other groups. This is especially important for students from underrepresented groups that have been historically oppressed.

3. Teach students about the diversity found in society. Knowing the history, culture, and beliefs of other ethnic communities can assist them in understanding another perspective and to see that prejudice may arise from historical viewpoints. For example, there are many nation-state conflicts that students bring to the United States from other countries. These conflicts may have risen from long-standing wars of the past.

4. Reflect on your own biases, stereotypes, and prejudices. All of us have misconceptions of others that we have learned.

5. Teach students the process of how people become prejudiced and racist, sexist, and homophobic. When students understand the process, they are more likely to stop themselves from developing biases.

6. Oppose messages given out by society that are prejudiced. Students need to think about how society presents the value of equality and justice; however, many institutional practices give privilege to members of the dominant group. Silence does not make for change.

7. Encourage students to establish a diversity club. The purpose of this organization could be to create a safe and comfortable place for all students. One of the goals could be to choose social justice issues that the members feel should be addressed in the school.

8. Create a schoolwide drive for antiracist and culturally diverse books for the library.

Short-term strategies also can be taught to students when name-calling or an incident occurs and must be dealt with immediately.

1. Support students without saving them. Students must be encouraged to work through the event without teachers protecting them so much that they do not learn how to deal with opposition and conflict.

2. Suggest to students that they not personalize the comments. They do not know what motivated the perpetrators. The causes may stem from the perpetrator's own experiences and have little to do with the victim.

3. Explain to students that "It's not about them; it's about the person who is prejudiced." Students may not realize that discrimination is about the perpetrator and not the victim.

4. Help students understand that messages given by families may contradict student judgment or what is expected at school. Students must make their own decisions about how to deal with the situation. This can be difficult because some families recommend that their members fight back, while school officials may discourage this. Other students may want to fight back, but their parents tell them not to. However, in some settings, it is important to set boundaries of respect for oneself.

5. Build trusting relationships with people from many different cultural groups. This not only helps students create networks of support, but also gives them the opportunity to find others to help them to debrief the situation in a cross-cultural setting/discussion.

6. Students must not feel disempowered. One of the most destructive aspects of prejudice and discrimination is that it makes the victim feel powerless. It is important that students feel that they are acting—and acting in a way that they felt was most appropriate—even if it meant walking away. They must look at the event as learning something or demonstrating that they made a specific rational choice.

Teaching about Discrimination and Stereotypes in the Classroom Curriculum: Vocabulary

Many of the teachers in my classes have addressed issues of prejudice in their classrooms. They have discussions with their students about how it can hurt others. Oftentimes, teachers may use picture books like *The Lotus Seed, Tar Beach,* or *A Day's Work* to begin discussion of exclusion, classism, racism, immigration, discrimination, prejudice, and stereotypes. High school students might read the novel, *Farewell to Manzanar.*

Regardless of their grade level, students need to know the definitions of words so that there is a common understanding of the concepts that you are discussing. In a high school classroom, teachers can ask students to define terms such as *stereotype, prejudice,* and/or *discrimination.*

Merriam-Webster's Collegiate Dictionary, 11th edition, defines these terms as follows:

- **Prejudice**—"**a** (1) : preconceived judgment or opinion (2) : an adverse opinion or leaning formed without just grounds or before sufficient knowledge **b** : an instance of such judgment or opinion **c** : an irrational attitude of hostility directed against an individual, a group, a race, or their supposed characteristics."

- **Stereotype**—"something conforming to a fixed or general pattern; *especially* : a standardized mental picture that is held in common by members of a group and that represents an oversimplified opinion, prejudiced attitude, or uncritical judgment."

The definitions I used from Gordon Allport (1954) in Chapter 3 are as follows:

- **Prejudice**—"A feeling, favorable or unfavorable, toward a person or thing, prior to, or not based on, actual experience" (7).

- **Stereotype**—"A favorable or unfavorable exaggerated belief associated with a category whose function is to justify our conduct as it relates to the category (187).

(Consider looking up other words by going to the *Merriam-Webster Dictionary* website at http://www.m-w.com/cgi-bin/dictionary.)

When students review the two sets of definitions, it is important for them to identify the common elements of the definition. For example, for the word *stereotype* there is the belief of a category or grouping and an overgeneralized and fixed idea. High school students can understand these definitions and find examples in a novel such as *Farewell to Manzanar.* Many people held stereotypes about Japanese Americans even though they did not know any of them personally. Their knowledge came from films, radio, and friends. Many perpetuated prejudice and added to high levels of racism. The novel can be used to teach many issues such as institutional racism and racial profiling. Before these issues should be discussed, it is important for students to understand the definitions of core terms. High school teachers were able to easily cover these definitions.

However, elementary grade teachers found it much harder to explain the definitions. Although students could easily think of examples of stereotypes such as "All girls like dolls and all boys like basketball," they had a difficult time defining terms. Vocabulary development is extremely important so that students will understand the content they are learning and reading. It is often difficult to explain terms like prejudice and stereotype because their definitions are dense. In other words, the definitions from the dictionary contain several abstract ideas all tied together.

Teachers in one of my classes developed the following matrix of definitions for prejudice and stereotype. It is important for teachers *before* they teach a lesson on prejudice and stereotypes to have carefully identified definitions for the concepts. This knowledge will enhance their ability to teach the terms. The definitions will also assist English-language learners. Students who are learning the language may have difficulty learning the abstract ideas along with the subjective contexts or connotations that accompany the terms. Although most educators, when they think of antiracist or multicultural curriculum, focus upon the affective component of prejudice, they can also extend the understanding of important concepts through vocabulary development.

The following table is only an initial attempt to identify definitions for two terms, prejudice and stereotype. Teachers learned that many of the concepts were far more complex than they had anticipated. They learned that it was not always easy to think of definitions on the spot as they were teaching. Many realized they would prefer to have a definition prepared—a definition they could use and reinforce the entire year with the class. Reading through the table, you can see that some definitions are better than others.

Another way to have students develop a comprehensive understanding of concepts such as prejudice and stereotypes is to have them list similes. A simile shows a comparison between two different things using the words *as* or *like.* Oftentimes this activity can provide students with more examples. The following table lists similes teachers have suggested. Some examples are better than others.

Can you come up with definitions for the younger grades that are more accurate and easier to understand than what are listed in the two tables?

TABLE 5.1 Possible Definitions

Term	Prejudice	Stereotype
Grades K–3	• Not liking something different just because it's different from what you're used to. • Having bad feelings about someone based on what you've been told by others. • Disliking someone without knowing him or her.	a group. • A wrong idea of a person based on what a person thinks of a whole group. • A negative picture based on one bad experience.
Grades 4–6	• To think people are a certain way before you know them. • To treat others unfairly because of their appearance or beliefs.	• False image of someone not based on experience with the person. • An overgeneralization.
Middle School	• A feeling about someone or something before you know anything about him or her or it. • To prejudge a person, place, or thing.	• Categorization of people based on appearance. • Labeling a person based on a generalization.
High School	• A preconceived judgment without prior knowledge of the person or thing. • An unfounded belief about someone before any actual experience with him or her. • Untrue picture of someone or	• Overgeneralized opinion held about another person, group, or its values. • Oversimplified, standardized image held about a person or a group.

TABLE 5.2 Similes

Prejudice	Stereotyping, Stereotypes
• Prejudice is like a filter that prejudges people. • Prejudice is like having tunnel vision. • Prejudice is like judging a book by its cover.	• A stereotype is like a trap. • A stereotype is like a straight jacket. • Stereotyping is like finding one rotten apple and assuming the whole bushel is rotten.

Connection

Please visit Chapter 5 of the book website **http://www.partnersagainsthate.org/ publications/pahprgguide302.pdf** to link to Partners against Hate. For teachers of high school teachers, you might want to go to the MTV website **http://www.mtv.com/onair/ ffyr/discrimination/** that is entitled "Take a Stand against Discrimination." At this site there is information about Arab Americans and civil liberties.

Curriculum That May Reinforce Stereotypes: Christmas around the World

Do you know about well-intentioned teachers who include a "Christmas around the World" theme for first graders? Children like coloring pictures of other children in traditional clothing and eating rice crackers, tacos, and anise cookies. They also may make colorful masks, paint beautiful eggs, and learn traditional dances. However, what do children really learn? Do you think these activities help to develop respect and a deep knowledge of others? Do they build a sense of fairness in children about others? Do these activities help children understand the values of others?

I know many teachers and students who really enjoy the activities centered around "Christmas around the World," yet I also realize that many countries do not have a Christian worldview. As a result, countries in the Middle and Far East are not studied. This unit often centers on European countries. The messages can be simplistic and reinforce stereotypes about those who seem foreign or strange. Many times the traditions and outward manifestations of culture are seen; however, the values that lie beneath them are not understood. Stereotypes may be created and reinforced when students lack understanding of the values of a group. Let's look at an example of someone who comes to the United States.

What if Mei Lee, a tourist from China, arrived in Seattle, Washington, to visit the United States at the beginning of July. During her stay in Seattle, she often ate at Burger King and Wendy's. Because Mei Lee wanted to take souvenirs to her family, she went downtown shopping and bought tee shirts. In the evening, Mei Lee went to a musical called "Tommy." On her last day in the United States, Mei Lee went to a Fourth of July picnic and ate potato salad, barbecue chicken, and jello salad. Her friends invited her to a neighborhood tug of war and they laughed and laughed. At night she watched beautiful fireworks. The next day Mei Lee boarded the airplane and left for home. What did Mei Lee learn about what is important to us in the United States?

I think Mei Lee probably had a fun time and may have really enjoyed the food she ate, but I hope that she could return to learn more about our values as a community.

For example, in Seattle there is a strong sense of social justice; numerous programs exist to house homeless and low-income families. King County has a federal job-training program in west Seattle, which places unemployed adults into positions where they can become self-sufficient. I hope that we try to help our students gain a balanced view of others. Unfortunately, much of what we cover about cultural groups deals with food, customs, and holidays. I have seen fifth-grade teachers also use "Christmas around the World" as a theme. Oftentimes a teacher focuses on the superficial elements of a cultural group; however, some teachers do delve into more substantial issues like gender roles, family relationships, and religious beliefs.

When young children do not have the experience of living in another country or neighborhood, quick units such as "Christmas around the World," become a travel brochure study of others (Nakagawa 1992). Little is discussed about the values and beliefs of a people. Unfortunately, many teachers believe that "Christmas around the World" or a similar unit will help children better understand other groups. Many times this travel brochure to other cultures and countries reinforces stereotypes because culture is presented in isolated pieces. It is easier to focus on the **explicit culture** of a group, what can be seen on the surface, than on the **implicit culture** including underlying beliefs and values.

Instead of having students travel around the world eating and dancing, have your students learn about the communities that surround the school, city, or area. In this way, children have the chance to make connections with their peers in class. Children can share many aspects of their family cultures with each other. I know teachers who encourage students to bring in an important person from their family or a special toy, or to share several words from a home language other than English and other precious gifts. When teachers ground discussion of culture to the lives of children, students are less likely to overgeneralize because they see how culture is dynamic and ever-changing. Using relevant and personal cultural knowledge, children are encouraged to build connections with others. When they share things from home that are important to them, they not only develop a stronger sense of self, but also help other children to understand other cultural ways and beliefs, thus creating a flexible and open atmosphere. We need to be attentive to and understand the values of people from other cultures. Cultural differences do not separate us; rather, our *response* to differences creates gaps between people.

Some teachers are able to incorporate the use of arts experiences, such as singing and dancing, into their curriculum. With proper sensitivity and attention to the cultural context, music and dancing can convey cultural beliefs, traditions, values, and customs in more effective ways than just telling students or having people read about these aspects of culture. The aesthetic quality of the artistic experiences can unify and connect people of various cultures. Teachers who have a deep respect for and understanding of a cultural community can provide these experiences for their students. For example, the teacher who taught her students the song,"De Colores," which can be found on page 379, wove the words of the piece with the history of civil rights and her personal experiences as a child with her mother.

Derman-Sparks and her colleagues (1989) suggest that an alternative to a December holidays unit can be a unit on the struggles of communities for freedom, justice, and peace. They suggest honoring community people who have worked hard for civil rights. The unit can be called "Community Heroes."

The work of these community heroes can be tied to the children's experience with fairness. Often I hear children tell their teachers, "But that's not fair." By teachers' using dolls or puppets who represent various people, children can learn about how individuals contributed to making our society more just. Bring in community people who can tell stories about how they changed unfair practices or instituted collaborative programs. This unit can be tied in with Martin Luther King, Jr.'s birthday in January and/or a discussion of César Chavez.

Using Antiracist Role Models: An Accurate Portrayal of Rosa Parks

Students in upper-elementary school should be asked to examine social structures for institutional bias. A unit on community heroes should include information about how these heroes changed society. They not only worked to make life better for themselves, but they were committed to challenging social practices that were unfair to all people.

One of the most important pieces I ask teachers to read is "The Myth of 'Rosa Parks the Tired': Teaching about Rosa Parks and the Montgomery Bus Boycott" by Herbert Kohl (1993). The article is powerful because Kohl explains how children can become change agents for civil rights and justice.

Kohl was in the audience of a fourth-grade play about Rosa Parks and the Montgomery bus boycott. In the play Parks was portrayed as a tired person who would not move from a seat at the front of the bus to a seat in the back. Next, a mixed crowd of African American and European American students carried signs that said "Don't Ride the Buses," "We Shall Overcome," and "Blacks and Whites Together." A child playing Martin Luther King, Jr., then spoke to the crowd and told them that African Americans and European Americans boycotted riding buses in Montgomery because Rosa Parks had been arrested. Students gave the audience the message that it was through the cooperative efforts of Blacks and Whites that justice prevailed.

Unfortunately, Kohl found that the children did not really understand the meaning of the Parks story and the boycott. First, the Montgomery bus boycott was organized and carried out by African Americans; European Americans were not involved in boycotting buses (Kohl 1993). Kohl felt it was crucial for students to know that the people who are oppressed have the power to confront their oppressors. Second, when Rosa Parks was presented as a person who was too tired to move, children got the impression that she was just tired and stubborn that day. In reality, Parks was a long-time community activist who was committed to fighting segregation. Third, the boycott had been planned by E. D. Nixon and other African Americans in Montgomery. Martin Luther King, Jr., was at first reluctant to join the others, but later he did become an important force in the boycott. Finally, the community was already organized to support a bus boycott. Rosa Parks knew what she was doing when she refused to move from her seat, and her friends knew that she had the courage to be strong. As soon as Parks was arrested, the boycott began and lasted for 381 days.

The most important aspect of teaching about Rosa Parks and the Montgomery bus boycott is the issue of racism. Kohl found that children did not really understand what were the underlying reasons for the boycott. Yes, they did know that Black people could sit only in the back of the bus; however, they did not really tackle the social issue of racism. Teachers need to ask their students, "Why were African Americans not treated as equals? Why were there laws that wouldn't let African Americans use the same facilities as European Americans? Why did they have to sit in the back of the bus? Why couldn't they use the same toilets, swimming pools, and schools?" (See Chapter 11 for additional ideas in teaching a unit about the contributions of Rosa Parks.)

Children need to talk about how racism today and in the past hurts all of us. Children need to know that racism is part of our social structure. Another question children can think about is "Why do some groups live in this part of town and others live in that part of town?" Children need to understand that prejudice can be deep seated in society and that it is called racism. People are treated in a negative way, not because of what they have done, but because there are preconceived notions of who they are based on their group membership, whether it is race, ethnicity, or skin color.

Older students, intermediate grades and higher, can examine other issues of oppression such as institutional racism and sexism that have impacted society. Historical issues to study might include: What impact did the Revolutionary War have on the Iroquois League? Why were Japanese Americans placed in internment camps? What were the goals of manifest destiny? How has the institution of slavery affected the African American community today? Why did the United States have a quota system of immigration? Why haven't we elected a woman president? Why hasn't the Equal Rights Amendment passed? These questions will help students examine how prejudice impacts society. These are complicated issues, but as teachers we must help children to develop the mind-set of openness and action. In addition, it is crucial that children understand that no one has to stand by and allow discrimination to repeat itself. We all have the reponsibility to make sure equity is not only an ideal but a reality in society. Caring teachers are advocates for their children, and they are important role models who show their students that talking about oppression is not enough. We all must be active citizens, trying to make our nation and world more caring, equitable, and free for all. As a result, I hope children will learn that racism, sexism, classism, handicappism, and homophobia should not be accepted and that we must be active participants against those who treat others unfairly and without respect.

White Antiracist Role Models

When I ask teachers to name people who have been important in our fight against racism, they offer names like Martin Luther King, Jr., Harriet Tubman, and César Chavez. However, when I ask teachers to think about racism in a different way and ask the following questions, they seem to struggle with their answers. James Scheurich believed that many White folks are aware of racism; however, they do not see or understand institutional racism. In fact, he wrote, "There is a hierarchy of positions, with upper-class white men at the top and lower-class men and women at the bottom. Resources and power—economic, intellectual, and emotional—are largely distributed according to this hierarchy" (Scheurich 2002, 29). Scheurich wrote with passion about the importance of addressing White racism as a White person because he felt "compelled—spiritually, morally, ethically, and democratically to work to remove it [White racism]" (3).

Who Are Our White Antiracist Models?

There will be a long silence; then someone may suggest Abraham Lincoln. Then another person says, "Well, I am not sure if he is a good model." There will be more silence. Role models are extremely important in teaching people what can be possible in life. A role model exemplifies not only a set of beliefs, but a person who has acted on those beliefs and made a difference in society. This is one of the most powerful ways to get teachers and students to explore the issue of racism.

When this question is posed, teachers and students must decide in their minds the criteria for an antiracist, and that includes what kinds of actions that person would take. In schools we often discuss the issue of racism but not of antiracists, especially those who are White.

Since many of our students are White, having White role models who stand out is extremely powerful. Otherwise, what I find is that students do not have a real vision of how a white person who is antiracist would act in life. Students begin to realize that an antiracist isn't just a person who does not like prejudice or someone who is against racism, but it is a person who takes action and those actions take courage and great commitment. Their actions are usually directed at institutional practices of prejudice because they know that unless power relationships are changed, people from underrepresented groups will continually find themselves in oppressed positions.

It is also important for students from underrepresented groups to know about White folks who see their responsibility in eliminating racism and who act on their values. Students may then see the importance of creating cross-cultural coalitions that include Whites. Change will not occur if people only from ethnic minority communities fight racism. It will take members from all groups to make any substantial changes in institutions like schools, businesses, and government because racism is so pervasive.

Take a Stand

WHITE ANTIRACIST ROLE MODELS

It is important that students have a variety of civil rights role models. Although students often know about Martin Luther King, Jr., or Rosa Parks, they may not know about White antiracist role models. Movement toward civil rights would not have come about without folks from various communities. Students from both mainstream and nonmainstream groups will benefit from knowing individuals who have fought for equity for all of us. The following questions are important for teachers to grapple with:

- Whom would you teach as a White antiracist role model? What criteria would you use to choose a role model?

Whom can you name as **White antiracist** role models? Here are a few individuals that teachers in my classes have suggested:

Eleanor Roosevelt—civil rights activist, women's rights activist.

Levi Coffin—abolitionist.

Lillian Smith—abolitionist.

Elizabeth Cady Stanton—suffragist, abolitionist.

Lucretia Coffin Mott—suffragist, abolitionist, Quaker minister.

Lloyd Garrison—abolitionist.

John Brown—abolitionist.

Lyndon Johnson—president who signed Civil Rights Act of 1964.

Henry David Thoreau—philosopher and writer.

Lucy Stone—suffragist, abolitionist.

Harriet Beecher Stowe—writer.

Morris Dees—lawyer, founder of Southern Poverty Law Center.

Peter Irons—lawyer, civil rights activist.

Howard Zinn—teacher, writer, civil rights activist.

Jane Addams—social activist.

Linda Christiansen—teacher and writer.

Burke Marshall—lawyer, civil rights policy maker, crafter of the Civil Rights Act of 1964.

Tim Wise—columnist.

Some of these names you may agree with and others you may not. What criteria would you use to decide whether they were appropriate role models for students? This is an important aspect of teaching about racism. Students must know that there are people who worked hard to get rid of prejudice and discrimination in society. It is critical that students, all students, understand that name-calling and discriminatory actions do not need to paralyze them, but that they can do something about the discrimination. Then students will feel less impacted by the oppression. Role models help them to understand that they can act positively against prejudice.

> ✺ *Who are your White antiracist role models?*

Case Study

LEONARD COVELLO: AN ANTIRACIST AND INTERCULTURALIST

One day I found myself in a book store off Harvard Square after an educational conference. I saw a title that caught my eye: *Teacher with a Heart*. It was a book by Vito Perrone about Leonard Covello, a principal and teacher for 45 years in New York City schools. The book was the first in a series of books designed by one of my favorite educators, Herbert Kohl.

Leonard Covello was a White educator who dedicated his life to children and to fighting racism. Covello was a teacher and principal at Benjamin Franklin Community High School in East Harlem for 22 years (Perrone 1998). He devoted himself to the community of the school. Perrone describes Covello's philosophy as one that focused on the students; he had a firm belief in their ability and future. He wrote that teachers like Covello who "are fully engaged with their work see possibilities, not liabilities. They lose the language of pathology, the language of stigmatization" (Perrone 1998, 25).

One of Covello's core beliefs was to see life from the perspective of his students and parents. For example, when he understood the problems of new immigrants, he could help them work through their struggles. Covello did not see his students as victims because the students did not see themselves as victims (Perrone 1998).

When Covello began his career, many of his students were Italian Americans or new Italian immigrants. He was able to use his own cultural knowledge to better understand the perspectives of his students. Since he spoke Italian, Leonard could communicate effectively with parents and students. He organized English classes and academic tutoring programs in the neighborhood East Harlem branch of the YMCA. One of the clubs he organized was the Young Men's Lincoln Club of Little Italy to assist young people in developing a positive bicultural identity, bridging home and society. Later Covello organized several Latino organizations for the community, too. He felt that cultural studies were important to young people and could not understand why schools would not make them a central component to schooling (Perrone 1998). The curriculum of schools needed to be relevant to students, and to be relevant, schools had to facilitate students in solving social problems.

As the population of the community changed, Covello found more Puerto Rican immigrants and African American families moving to the neighborhood. He had a great compassion for the new families because, like the Italians, they faced similar struggles. He honored the cultures and languages of the community. For example, a Puerto Rican mother visited the school with her son. He spoke to her and her son in Spanish. He wrote, "The only language of education is the language which people can understand—no matter where it originates. To this simple Puerto Rican woman I have become more than the principal of an English-speaking high school. I am a human being who understands and is trying to help her. In the eyes of the boy I have given respect and status to his parent. The process of education has been translated into human terms" (Covello, quoted in Perrone 1998, 37, 38).

At Benjamin Franklin High School, Covello was extremely aware of the need for intercultural education. By 1938, intercultural issues were woven throughout the curriculum and in teacher discussions. In fact, one of the committees in the school was the Racial Committee, whose purpose was to direct the school in integrating culture through the curriculum and to sponsor forums revolving around issues of race (Perrone 1998). The school also sponsored several major conferences on race and ethnic relationships.

One of the major goals of Covello was to include issues from the community in an integrated school curriculum to develop in students the skills and knowledge that they could use in addressing social problems. The English teachers had students read traditional writers such as Shakespeare and Milton, but they also had young people study Upton Sinclair and Ida Tarbell, who discussed relevant social issues. The social studies teachers had students look at various aspects of the community. The art teachers led students in mapping the community. In East Harlem the students found 41 churches/missions, 22 political clubs, 9 labor organizations, 506 stores that sold candy, 26 junk stores, 378 restaurants, 74 dentists, 297 doctors, and 262 barber shops (Perrone 1998). The young people also discovered that the area housed 28 liquor stores and 256 bars. Students were concerned because in comparison to the 284 bars and liquor stores, there were only three public halls, a couple of playgrounds for kids, and no neighborhood newspaper. From this project students chose various social issues to research and to develop plans of action. Students developed not only knowledge of the community, but also a sense of community responsibility, and they became active in neighborhood change.

One of the projects students from the high school chose to tackle was affordable housing and the threat of speculators purchasing land on the river that would drive up the price of apartments in the area (Perrone 1998). Students researched various configurations of city dwellings, built a variety of models, and had a public showing of their work. They were able to rally the community and gather signatures on petitions. The land on the river was saved for new low-income housing. This was an important community victory.

Because Covello wanted to learn as much as he could about his students, he went to Puerto Rico (Perrone 1998). He visited the extended families of many of his students in New York City. In this way, he came to know the culture of his students through a comprehensive lived experience, meeting people, listening to the music, viewing the physical scenery, and learning about the roles of various people in the family.

Covello believed that the high school was to be the center of the community. He welcomed parents and other members of the neighborhood into the school. Covello had a community advisory board made up of individuals from civic groups, religious organizations, businesses, and social services. Initially, many of the members argued against becoming involved in the school; however, Covello conveyed to them that they were responsible for the success of students, along with teachers in the school. The school also became a center for after-school community activities. For example, the high school housed adult education classes in English, preparing adults for citizenship, cultural studies, art, and dance (Perrone 1998). Covello was a teacher with a heart and a valuable role model for all of us. Through his leadership, the school community fought social oppression with a curriculum that addressed issues of racism and democracy. The next section of the chapter moves from racism to another type of social oppression, homophobia, and how another school community addressed the issue. ✿

Homophobia: Sexual Orientation and Student Identity

Along with racism, other types of oppression can be commonly found in schools. Beth Reis, Mona Mendoza, and Frieda Takamura were concerned community people who wrote an article about prejudice in schools. They discovered that in the Seattle school district 43 percent of the students reported being victims of an "offensive racial comment" or attack either at or on the way to or from school in a 1995 study. Students heard comments such as "You can't sit with us because you are White" and "The only good Indian is a dead Indian." This surprised many teachers and parents because the district is culturally diverse and many had thought the community had worked hard to eliminate prejudice. Teachers had training in addressing racial harassment. However, the statistics demonstrated how difficult it was to eliminate racism in schools. The authors were also concerned with **homophobia,** a fear of or bias against gay and lesbian people. In a 1999 study in the same school district, 34 percent of high schoolers reported experiencing gender-based verbal or physical attacks. Students encountered comments such as "dyke," "faggot," "sissy," and "queer."

Coretta Scott King, the wife of Martin Luther King, Jr., believed homophobia must be addressed and challenged in society. She said, "Homophobia is like racism and anti-Semitism and other forms of bigotry in that it seeks to dehumanize a large group of people, to deny their humanity, their dignity and personhood . . . This sets the stage for further repression and violence that spread all too easily to victimize the next minority group" (Hatecrime.org 2002, 2)

Why are teachers reluctant to address issues of homophobia? Pohan and Aguilar (1998) found that both new and seasoned teachers hold serious misconceptions and fears about sexual orientation. Here are some of the comments teachers gave in a study they conducted (Pohan and Aguilar 1998, 2):

> "I believe homosexuality is a sin and should not be modeled for children as acceptable."

> "I am not homophobic. I do not hate gay or lesbian people, but I do believe that the practice of homosexuality is sinful in God's eyes and I cannot condone it."

> "All societies who have accepted gay/lesbian lifestyles in the past were wiped out within two generations."

When teachers bring attitudes such as these to school, it is difficult to create a caring and socially just school. Even when teachers ban name-calling, this strategy will probably not eliminate biased attitudes because deep-seated prejudices are not being addressed. It is important that teachers and students receive accurate information about homosexuality, so that people can develop a comprehensive and accurate understanding of the issue (Prince 1996). Allport's model of prejudice demonstrated that biased views become permanent in adolescence. In order to guide older students and teachers to change attitudes, they need to carefully examine their beliefs for inconsistencies and inaccuracies. In this process people should reflect on biased views in light of values of caring and social justice. In a multicultural education course for teachers, educators reflected upon their personal views about homosexuality, read literature on gay and lesbian youth, interviewed gay and lesbian professionals, and talked with parents of gay and lesbian children (Pohan and Aguilar 1998). Teachers began to learn about gay and lesbian cultures and to see their own misunderstandings. Some educators were still uncertain about issues of sexual orientation, but they did feel that as teachers it was important for them to provide a supportive environment for students who are struggling with their identity and sexuality.

Often teachers do not realize that accepted school curriculum practices give out clear messages about sexual orientation. In grade school when your teachers had you make Valentine's Day cards for classmates, did they give explicit messages about what was expected and accepted? I remember teachers distinctly asking me which male student I was making a card for. They assumed that I was heterosexual and that I would be coloring a card for a male classmate. How has this message been changed today? Now many teachers understand that they do not want to make sexual orientation choices for young people, so students are often asked to make friendship cards for every child in the class. Another example is Mother's Day or Father's Day. A child may not have a mom or a dad. A child may have two dads and a grandmother. Teachers are important role models, and students learn many implicit beliefs from what they say and how they conduct their classrooms.

Many teachers may not have had the opportunity to examine their values about sexual orientation. The following questions were created by Mathison for teachers to ponder honestly and personally. These questions can help teachers to review their beliefs about sexual orientation:

Do I assume that all my teacher education students and colleagues are heterosexual?

Do I believe that it is appropriate for gay men and lesbians to become teachers?

As I discuss historians, philosophers, theorists, and practitioners with teacher education students, do I ever identify individuals as homosexual in the same manner that I might mention ethnicity, gender, or other cultural attributes?

Do the examples I use in class assume that everyone is heterosexual?

If someone were to look at my course syllabi or any other aspect of my teaching activities, would that person see any evidence that preparing teachers to serve gay and lesbian students was important to me? (Mathison 1998, 153–54).

For Better or For Worse®   **by Lynn Johnston**

© *Lynn Johnston Productions, Inc. Distributed by United Feature Syndicate, Inc.*

The questions that Mathison has posed provide a starting point for teachers to examine their feelings and beliefs about gay and lesbian students. The comic strip, above, below shows how difficult it is for a young man's best friend to accept that he is gay. It is also distressful for the fellow who is gay because the underlying message that he is getting from his friend is that he is confused. The next section presents the experiences of a young lesbian and how a Catholic high school district addressed the issue of homophobia that arose in the community.

 Case Study

HEIDI'S STORY: A POWERFUL FORCE IN A CATHOLIC ARCHDIOCESE SCHOOL DISTRICT: A DISTRICT WORKS TO ELIMINATE HOMOPHOBIA

Making lasting and effective changes in schools often takes an entire community working collaboratively. A high school district of the archdiocese of St. Paul and Minneapolis took on the challenge of providing a safe climate for gay and lesbian students. The faculty at one of the schools had asked students in an interdisciplinary honors class to share their experiences on gender. A female student walked to the front of the class and then explained how she had been beaten and kicked by her parents and later thrown out of her home at the age of 14. She had lived from place to place for three years. She was always treated like an outcast in the three high schools she had attended. Why was she beaten and thrown out of her home? Heidi told her parents she was a lesbian.

Is Heidi's story out of the ordinary? No, a study by the Hetrick-Martin Institute found that half of gay and lesbian students are rejected by their parents (Gevelinger and Zimmerman 1997). This can be psychologically and sociologically damaging to the development of young people because parents are core role models and the family is a basic social unit of protection, acceptance, and love.

Heidi learned that she was a "throwaway" kid and not important. She became an abandoned child. Unfortunately, scholars believe, the isolation, harassment, and confusion that gay and lesbian students often feel and experience contribute to high levels of suicide (Gevelinger and Zimmerman 1997). It is believed that gay and lesbian youth make up almost a third of all adolescent suicides.

Because Heidi's story was not an isolated one, the archdiocese of St. Paul and Minneapolis established a study group on pastoral care and sexual identity. The group gathered many documents. For example, they looked at the church's directives about homosexuality. They also studied the history of gays and lesbians, gay and lesbian culture, and literature about safe school communities.

Representatives from 11 high schools were members of the committee. They developed the following four goals:

1. *Hold a workshop for all teachers, administrators, and counselors on the topic of sexual identity.*
2. *Train faculty members in each school to function as "safe staff."*
3. *Teach students and teachers that homophobic behavior is inappropriate and unacceptable.*
4. *Form an interschool support group for students* (Gevelinger and Zimmerman 1997, 67).

As part of the training for teachers and students, issues of homosexuality were integrated into the school curriculum. Teachers discussed various issues such as the social oppression of homosexuals and their struggle for acceptance. A student support group was established. A parent support group was also founded to provide parents of gay and lesbian students who also might feel isolated with others to talk with. Through this process, lesbian and gay faculty felt supported although many had remained closeted because they were afraid of losing their teaching positions (Gevelinger and Zimmerman 1997).

Heidi's courage in sharing her life story pushed others to consider the devastating power of homophobia on young people. The faculty, students, and parents of the archdiocese came together because of their belief in the human dignity and worth of each student and their commitment to a socially just community. ❁

Chapter Summary

This chapter describes how and why children learn prejudicial attitudes that later turn into discriminatory actions. Although people think that young children do not learn prejudice early in their lives, research by Allport, Helms, and Tatum demonstrates that children adopt and accept the biased views of parents, friends, and other people whom they see as important. Racism is reinforced through comments and actions of significant others. In addi-

tion, children who grow up in loving families where criticism is minimal are more likely to grow up as confident adults and develop a healthy view of life.

Much of this chapter deals with self-identity. As young people grow up, they are trying to figure out who they are and where they fit in society. Young children want to feel accepted at school, with peers, and in their families. Their identity is integrated with group memberships such as race, ethnicity, culture, religion, and gender. This sense of identity is often tied to their physical characteristics. The United States is not a color-blind society. The physical characteristics of various groups have positive and negative meanings that society attaches to them. Young people are taught that those physical characteristics have deep social meanings. Race becomes a powerful sociopolitical construct in life. It is often most difficult for children from communities of color because they must sort through those connotations.

As they come in contact with people, children note that certain words are used to describe differences in others. These words often have strong negative feelings attached to them. Older students may reject those who are different because of the negative messages they have learned from others. For teenagers, the prejudice becomes more permanent, and their categories based on social characteristics such as race, class, sexual orientation, or gender are more firmly set.

Teachers should work daily at reducing prejudice and discrimination in students. This can be done first by providing an affirming classroom and then by teaching students how to interact with respect and compassion. This way students begin to build bonds of trust, and when conflicts like name-calling arise, the teacher has already set a foundation of working things through. Teachers can also present White antiracist role models like Leonard Covello, an educator in New York City. It takes the efforts of all citizens to make a difference in society. The Civil Rights Act of 1964 would probably not have passed without the tireless work of African Americans who organized and led many marches and sit-ins. But the laws also might not have changed without the efforts of European Americans such as Burke Marshall, who was a key strategist for the civil rights legislation.

Stereotypes are overgeneralized images based on inflexible social categories; it is important for teachers to carefully review their curriculum for materials and lessons that may reinforce these images. Unfor-

tunately, schools, in their concern to present cultural information about people from underrepresented communities, have not clearly identified strong educational objectives. This can result in the "Christmas around the World" travelogue curriculum. Unfortunately, many teachers focus on elements such as food or dance without giving students the opportunity to learn about the underlying values of a group. This oftentimes reinforces the exotic or strange stereotypes of people who come from diverse communities. An alternative may be to present community heroes who have helped to build our city of many people. This study can highlight those who have led the struggle for freedom, justice, and peace. Students can look at the lives of people such as Leonard Covello and find important role models.

People have prejudices about others based on many social categories. This chapter discusses not only racism, but also homophobia. The issue of sexual orientation is a challenging one for schools because people have less knowledge about the issue and individuals may hold more misconceptions. The story about Heidi motivated a large Catholic high school district to take action and to make changes in their schools to address the issue of sexual orientation. The district worked on making institutional and structural changes. Within this process, the district community found it important to assist students in understanding the issues of identity and abandonment. A learning community will not exist if members feel threatened and/or abandoned. As this district demonstrated, it is important for every school to examine their climate, curriculum, and policies for homophobia to ensure that harassment and misconceptions of gays and lesbians are challenged.

Children learn prejudice from us adults. We must do all we can to teach accurate information about folks from many different communities and assist students in addressing their own biases and to develop action plans to eliminate them.

⊙ᴸᴳ *Chapter Review*

Go to the Online Learning Center at **www.mhhe.com/pang2e** to review important content from the chapter, practice with key terms, take a chapter quiz, and find the Web links listed in this chapter.

Key Terms

stages of prejudice, *148*

curious, *148*

emotional connotations, *150*

explicit culture, *162*

implicit culture, *162*

stereotypes, *153, 158*

anti-bias curriculum, *153*

prejudice, *158*

White antiracist, *166*

homophobia, *169*

Reflection Activities

Continue writing in your journal. These questions will help you reflect on the issues presented in the chapter.

1. Read the passage from Vivian Paley's book, *White Teacher,* on pages 45–46. (If you cannot find the book at the library, I have summarized the situation for you at the end of the question.) Write answers to these questions in your journal:

   How important is race to this situation? Why do you think that?

   Why would Barbara use a racial term?

   Do you agree with Janet's decision and comments to Barbara and Ellen? Why or why not?

   How would you have dealt with this situation?

   How would Ellen feel? What impact does this situation have on both children?

   What are possible alternative actions? What consequences or impacts does each have?

   White Teacher (summary of pages 45–46):

   Paley talks about a situation in which a White child excludes a Black child. This happened when Paley had a student teacher named Janet. As an African American, Paley wondered how Janet would deal with this incident in particular, because it dealt with race.

   When the students were getting ready to take a walk to a neighborhood pond, a White child named Barbara loudly proclaimed, "I don't want Ellen again. She always wants to be my partner. I want someone White" (Paley 1979, 45).

   The student teacher was extremely calm and naturally said to the kindergarten African American child, "Ellen, Barbara feels like walking with someone who looks like her. Sometimes people get that feeling. Can I help you find another partner for this time?" (Paley 1979, 46). Ellen then found a different White child to be her partner and they went to the pond.

   When Paley asked Janet why she handled the situation in the way she did, Janet carefully explained that she did not believe that using guilt was a positive manner in resolving the issue even though it was hard to step away from the situation and not feel somewhat beaten.

2. Another excellent book that discusses a program that addresses prejudice and discrimination in schools is *Waging Peace in Our Schools* by Linda Lantieri and Janet Patti. The program for peace that the authors suggest is also built on caring, democratic schools where children work collaboratively with each other to eliminate violence in schools. As violence in schools escalates, an increasing number of examples of student violence tie in with their feelings about diversity and conflict. One of the most important aspects of the book is discussion of the authors' conflict resolution model. Lantieri and Patti identify four strategies that their students are taught:

   a. Talk; discuss feelings.

   b. Hear the other person's point of view.

   c. Agree to disagree and therefore there is no attacking of another.

   d. Problem solve together and identify a collaborative solution.

   Think of a situation in the classroom that you did not know how to handle. Read through their book and write down new ways to address the event. Maybe you realize now that it would have helped to see the issue as "a problem to be solved rather than a contest to be won" (87).

The authors provide numerous strategies that will be helpful in school when conflicts arise.

3. Have you ever thought about White folks who are antiracist? Who are your role models? Identify someone and research their goals and life works. What have they done? Do people know about them? If not, why not?

Students need to know not only about people of color but about people from the mainstream who have also fought racism. Can you add to student knowledge of folks who work against racism? Can you name others whom you have learned and gained from? What contributions have they made?

4. Another important advocacy group whose goal is to fight social oppression is Teaching Tolerance. I suggest that you visit their website at **www.tolerance.org**, where there are numerous resources for parents, teachers, and students. The Southern Poverty Law Center, which established Teaching Tolerance, also keeps statistics on hate crimes. Their website is at **www.splcenter.org**.

5. An organization dedicated to ending antigay bias in schools is GLSEN. As a national group, they provide information on what students, faculty, and parents have done to address homophobia. Review their website at **www.GLSEN.org.**

CHAPTER 6

How Can I Look Beneath the Surface for Prejudice in Schools?

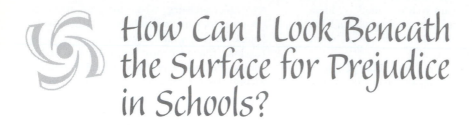

CHAPTER MAIN IDEAS

- *Allport's Five Levels of Prejudice*
- *Hidden Prejudice in Schools*
- *Examples of the Five Levels of Prejudice Found in Schools*

- *How Prejudice Can Influence Teacher Confidence: Need for Self-Regulation of Bias*

CHAPTER OVERVIEW

This chapter is dedicated to providing the reader with information about various forms of prejudice found in institutional organizations such as schools and government. Practices accepted by the general public may convey unconsciously, or without meaning to, prejudice or a limited view of people from nonmajority ethnic communities. One of the examples discussed is Martin Luther King, Jr., whose contributions are oftentimes minimized when teachers do not provide students with an understanding of the societal context in which he lived and provided leadership.

Schools are busy places, where much is going on that we often do not see or have time to reflect on. I hope this chapter will give you a chance to think about the inequities in schools. They are part of the systemic inequities that flourish in society. I thought that most schools were fairly democratic and just places; but as I think more clearly about what happens in schools, I am reminded that schools are products of our society, its successes and its weaknesses.

Are our schools fairly democratic? Don't you think that we provide a fairly equitable place for learning? Let's begin by looking beneath the surface.

Allport's Five Levels of Prejudice

When I first began thinking about bias, I didn't realize how damaging prejudice and discrimination could be. Prejudicial attitudes and beliefs filter and shape the information we receive. Allport's (1954) model of five levels of prejudice can help teachers understand how prejudice escalates from casual remarks to exclusionary practices. The levels are antilocution, avoidance, discrimination, physical attack, and genocide. As you read through the levels of prejudice, see how one level becomes more damaging than the next.

Level One: Antilocution

Has anyone ever told you an ethnic joke in private? About the Irish? About the Polish? Or about African Americans? Maybe you laughed at a joke someone told about women, men, or Muslims. You were participating in **antilocution.** It is Allport's first stage of prejudice where negative things are said in the privacy of close friends. People use labels to describe others in gossiplike conversations. Oftentimes this type of conversation is a way people reinforce their own beliefs because others laugh or agree. It is also a way to say, "I am like you because I think like you. I don't like those people either." It supports the idea that "we" are different from "those people" and "our group" is better. This reinforces an "our group" orientation. Name-calling is part of this level. Antilocution can lead to the next level of prejudice, avoidance.

Level Two: Avoidance

If a person avoids a specific group of people because of a social category and does not know the individuals, then the person is engaging in Allport's second level of prejudice. I have heard parents tell their children not to talk with "those kids bused in from the ghetto" because they are dangerous. Some parents can be heard telling their children, "Be careful of those kids because they will mess with your head." Individuals may choose not to talk with or get to know someone because they have been taught to avoid all people in "those" groups. This is considered **avoidance.**

Level Three: Discrimination

People may not always act on their prejudices, but when they treat someone unfairly or inequitably, they are engaging in **discrimination.** For example, although many of the laws dealing with redlining in housing—enacted because of social biases or membership clauses in country clubs that discriminated against people of color— have been eliminated, exclusion of people still exists.

Several culturally diverse teachers have described in class how they would call for information on an advertisement for apartment vacancies. Often they are told to come immediately to see the apartments because there are vacancies. Yet when the students arrived within an hour, the apartments were mysteriously no longer available. One of my teachers was a light-skinned African American female who had a very dark-skinned husband. One year, the couple encountered so much discrimination that they finally developed the following strategy.

The wife would first look at the apartment by herself and she would place a deposit on the apartment. She would fill out most of the paperwork. Later, her husband would go with her to finish signing the lease. The couple found that since housing near the university was difficult to get and that many apartment managers did not want African Americans living in their complexes, the managers were visually screening renters. Because the wife had fair complexion, many apartment managers did not think she was African American.

Level Four: Physical Attack

You can probably guess what this level of prejudice is. People's strong, emotional feelings can lead to aggressive behavior. Organized groups such as the Ku Klux Klan and Aryan Nation actively lobby, write, and organize events that are aimed at people of color. People who have strong prejudices have bombed stores that belonged to Jews, Mexican Americans, Korean Americans, and many others. During the Persian Gulf War, a grocery store owned by an Iranian American family was looted and set on fire because of prejudice. There are Black gangs and Mexican American gangs who fight for territory. These are examples of how prejudice can escalate into violence and **physical attack.**

Level Five: Genocide

The most extreme form of prejudice is **genocide,** extermination. The history of the United States is filled with many instances of lynchings of African Americans. If you are unaware of this part of U.S. history, read John Hope Franklin's excellent book, *From Slavery to Freedom.* Slavery was an institution that was widely accepted in the colonies and later the states. Because of our country's dependence on the labor of slaves, prejudice and extreme forms of discrimination against African Americans were an integral part of U.S. economics. Allport explains that when these attitudes were combined with poor law enforcement during those early days of this nation, lynchings occurred. Even when killers were apprehended, most were never prosecuted because a social norm of acceptance existed. Do you think that we have genocide today?

Genocide is a global problem. Recently we have seen the massacre of millions of people in many countries. For example, people have been killed in Kosovo, Indonesia, Tibet, and Rwanda. This is part of our contemporary history, not about the past. Students and teachers need to be aware of and review their values about issues such as ethnic cleansing and genocide.

Teachers and students may have some knowledge of the Holocaust when many Jews were tortured and killed. Do they realize that another six million people, who included gays, lesbians, mentally ill, and Gypsies, were also killed during the same time under Hitler? The "our group" mentality became so pervasive that people who belonged to the "other group" were seen as less than human. Do people realize what

1-20-99 THE PHILADELPHIA INQUIRER. UNIVERSAL PRESS SYNDICATE.

it means in human terms that six million Jews died? It is easy to read things in a book and not really take in the human meaning of these actions. I use the following activity in class to help teachers more fully understand what these numbers mean in human life (Frelick 1985).

Approximately six million Jews were killed in concentration camps during World War II. I ask, "How many people were killed in a year?" A student will raise his hand and say, "One million people per year were killed." Then I ask, "How many people were killed every month?" Usually someone in the class has a calculator and tells us that 83,333.3 human beings were killed every month. Then I ask, "How many human beings were killed every day?" The larger figure is divided by 30 days in a month and this means about 2,777.78 people were killed every day. The class then finds out that 115.74 people were killed every hour and that almost two Jews were killed every minute for six years. I usually have about 30 students in each class section, and I tell them, "In 15 minutes from the time we entered the classroom door, all of us would be gone. Since there are approximately 28,000 college students at our university, it would take only 10 days before everyone on our campus was eliminated."

Although this begins to give a sense of reality to historical numbers that people often gloss over when reading history, I continue with a discussion about local communities. I ask the teachers to give me the names of cities in this area and their populations. In some areas of the United States, an entire state may not have a population as large as six million. The teachers add up the population of cities and towns where they live. This allows them to put these large numbers in context. In some communities, the discussion will show that no one would be left living in several states. This gives teachers an everyday example that they can use with their students in order to help them to conceptualize the depth of the genocide. In addition, students can look at present-day examples of genocide in other nations such as Bosnia, El Salvador, and Cambodia.

There are also several hundred thousand children in the United States who are homeless every night, with nowhere to sleep. Although this is not an example of organized aggression against a group, students need to understand that when we lack a connection to others, it is easy not to do anything when someone else is being hurt or oppressed. The next section discusses how the five levels of prejudice exist in schools.

Hidden Prejudice in Schools

I do not believe most teachers consciously discriminate against children; however, oppression based on race, class, and gender can also be found in our social institutions such as schools. In the past, schools were segregated, with children of color going to one school while European American students attended another school. Although this is no longer the case, there are still many instances in which schools that serve large numbers of students of color have less funds than other schools (Kozol 1991). Another example of how many students have been excluded from schooling deals with the issue of disabilities. Not until 1975 when schools were mandated by the Education for Handicapped Children legislation to provide students with physical and psychological disabilities with the "least restrictive" education, did the needs of students with disabilities begin to be addressed. The fact that many children had been excluded from participating in schools is an example of societal biases.

The purpose of this chapter is to identify how prejudice and discrimination appear in schools. Schools are institutions of society and mirror social values. Many school practices are antithetical to equity and caring. For example, some schools begin sorting children as early as kindergarten when they place children in classes by ability groupings. Many students of color are placed in lower-tracked groups and sometimes are unable to move into higher-ability groups throughout their education. Students of color are often disciplined in disproportionately higher numbers than majority pupils, and the curriculum may not include the life experiences of students from low-income or culturally diverse communities and therefore may have little connection with their lives (Nieto 1990; Oakes 1985). These practices demonstrate how inequities are a structural part of schools.

Unconscious prejudice may surface and enter into the workplace. I have gathered a list of various examples of how prejudice looks in schools. I believe that teachers rarely have the opportunity to examine how prejudice impacts teaching and the school's environment. I don't believe teachers intentionally engage in these behaviors; but like many behaviors, they become part of the way we act because no one has challenged us to really think about the effect our actions may have. Read each level of prejudice and ask yourself the following questions:

Have you ever found yourself thinking or doing these things?

Do you think there is anything wrong with being this way?

How can you move away from being prejudiced?

Do you find some of this in your school?

Can you bring it up during a staff meeting?

Examples of the Five Levels of Prejudice Found in Schools

Sometimes it is difficult for us to understand how theory is translated into practice. Teachers have helped me gather examples of how the five levels of prejudice may look in schools. Many times teachers are unaware of how lower levels of discrimination can develop into more serious and pervasive actions. Examples are provided to help you understand how easily we may fall into the trap of being discriminatory. These examples are not to be used to implicate anyone; however I believe that how we think has been shaped by social biases. We must all work toward eliminating them from our minds. These are only examples and should not be considered behaviors in which all teachers engage.

Level One: Antilocution

Teachers can be talkative people. Unfortunately, antilocution, although often done in private, may limit the way other teachers see children from diverse racial, ethnic, language, and socioethnic classes, and limit views of females. The following are a sample of examples my teachers reported:

- Teachers talk about children in the teachers' lounge, by saying, "My Black students always . . ."
- Teachers name children by social class, with comments such as, "Those kids from the projects are troublemakers. They'll never make it. I don't want to waste my time with them."
- A teacher tells a parent aide, "Those migrant kids are always moving from one school to another, so there is no sense doing much for them. They will soon be gone. Besides, this is America and those kids should be speaking English, not Spanish. This isn't Mexico. I don't think it is our responsibility to teach them if they can't even speak English."
- A new child moves to the neighborhood. The coach calls the student on the phone to let him know about the first football practice. During the conversation, the coach asks, "Are you Black?" The student replied and the coach said, "Oh, that's good."
- A sixth-grade teacher describes his female students in the following ways: "beautiful," "playboy-centerfold material," and "developing rather nicely." This teacher also made this comment to his class about the teaching assistant: "Isn't Miss Smith sexy?"

Level Two: Avoidance

At this level, prejudice is more intense and individuals begin to act on their prejudice. People do not just talk about their feelings, but they begin to discriminate against another person or children. The following are examples of avoidance in school:

- Teachers avoid discussing incidents in which children call each other names that refer to race, class, gender, physical differences, and religion. Teachers may not know how to talk about these incidents, but avoiding open discussion when children know the teacher heard the name-calling suggests that the teacher does not object to the use of those terms. It is passive acceptance of the discrimination.

- Teachers may avoid calling upon culturally diverse students or females. Numerous studies show that teachers call on males more often than females and that this is an unconscious rather than a conscious form of discrimination.

- Teachers place students in group activities or in seating arrangements that segregate students by race, gender, or class.

- Teachers avoid home visits to students who are bused in from the ghetto or inner city but may visit students who live in suburban communities.

- Teachers avoid calling parents from inner-city communities because they feel that the parents do not care.

Level Three: Discrimination

In this level of prejudice, discrimination becomes more overt. These examples demonstrate how prejudice escalates in schools:

- Teachers may get frustrated trying to understand students whose English is not fluent and may not call on them because it takes these students longer to explain their points of view.

- Teachers may give more individual attention or feedback to students who come from families with professional parents and those who live in more affluent neighborhoods.

- Teachers may give more challenging work to students who are from majority middle- and upper-class families in comparison to students from African American and Latino lower-class communities.

- Teachers divide physical education into boys' sports and girls' sports within the same class. Boys engage in wrestling while girls learn to dance.

- Teachers may isolate children who wear baggy pants because they fear these students are members of gangs, yet their parents may like baggy pants because they can be handed down and fit several children of different sizes.

- Out of 10 junior high students to interview a famous astronaut, seven males and only three females were included.

- A male high school student was called a "girl" by his peers and the teacher assumed that the student was gay.

- Several sixth-grade girls ask their teacher if they can be included in the baseball game. The teacher says laughingly, "Girls can't play baseball. Go back to the kickball game."

- A fourth-grade student moves to a small town. The teacher introduces the child by saying, "Michele, our new student, is from Hollywood where all the movie stars and rich people live." Students in class call her "a Hollywood snob" or "rich brat."

- Many more children of color are bused from their neighborhoods than majority children.

- A teacher gives an Asian American high school student a B when his grades totaled 92 percent, even though White students with 88 percent were given an A. The student was told that, since he was Asian, he was expected to score higher than other students to receive an A.

- In a preschool class, the teacher asks his young students to sit in a circle. A child finds a place and sits down. A boy screamed, "Nigger, get out of my spot."

- A high school chemistry teacher says to a blond female student, "Wow, I'm impressed. I thought you were just one of those blond airheads."

- A teacher places students with limited or no English skills in special education classes instead of newcomer programs, sheltered English classes, bilingual education, or tutored situations.

- The curriculum systematically excludes the contribution of culturally diverse individuals/communities in the United States in most subject areas.

- The curriculum and instruction of most schools stem from a European American worldview. A few units and guest speakers about culturally diverse groups may be added, but are not integral to the curriculum.

- Two captains are appointed by the teacher for two teams in kickball. Tall and physically large boys are chosen first. Shorter boys are picked next.

- A Latina enrolls in a high school biology class. When the teacher reads the roll, she calls her name and asks, "Is Jorge Rodriguez your brother?" When the student says yes, the teacher says, "You'd better leave my class because I am going to fail you, because I hate your brother and I hate Mexicans." The student transferred from this class.

Level Four: Physical Attack

In this stage, prejudice leads to acts of violence or the heightened use of physical strength. The following are examples found in schools:

- A teacher is more physical in breaking up a fight between two African American students than he is with two White students.

- A teacher loses her temper and pushes a Latino male and yells at him, saying he needs to get himself under control.

Level Five: Genocide

Gordon Allport considers prejudice to be at its most extreme in this stage. Although I don't believe that teachers attempt to physically exterminate children, I do believe that if we do not question school practices that give some students fewer opportunities, we are contributing to this level of prejudice. Students' opportunities in life may also be restrained or eliminated because they are not encouraged to develop their capabilities. The following are examples teachers have found in their schools:

- Culturally diverse students often find themselves in lower academic and vocational tracks even though they aspire to a college education.

- Teachers assume students whose first language is other than English should develop their talents in math and science classes rather than creative writing, advanced history, and drama.

- Schools in some inner cities do not have the same financial resources necessary to properly equip a classroom and to hire enough teachers for smaller classes. (Read Jonathan Kozol's book, *Savage Inequalities.* Kozol documents that in the same area of a state, per-pupil spending can range from $5,585 to $11,371.)

- Teachers expect all children to respond to the same learning modes and do not provide for diverse learning styles, ways of behaving, and worldviews.

- A Black high school baseball player is an important player for the school to win the state championship. Teachers let him slide academically and coaches do not encourage him to study. Because of his grades, he has no chance for a collegiate athletic scholarship.

- Disproportionately more students of color and male students are suspended or expelled from school than other students.

- Classes for gifted and accelerated students have disproportionately more White students than any other group.

- High dropout rates of students of color jeopardize the economic, political, and educational health of communities.

Prejudice and discrimination usually go hand in hand. We all have attitudes about other groups that may result in our excluding or treating others unequally. I believe that if teachers realized that these kinds of things were happening, they would take proactive steps to examine their own actions and the structures of schools in order to move away from biased and damaging practices. Prejudices easily can creep back into your attitudes and actions like weeds in a garden. Prejudices can be hurdles to our being the best teachers we can be. These hurdles in our mind can be eliminated, but their removal requires effort and courage.

Take a Stand

DROPOUTS

Are dropouts a problem in schools today? In many of the largest school districts and in smaller rural districts, students from nonmainstream ethnic and low-income communities may drop out proportionately more often than other students. Teachers should consider the reasons behind the increasing numbers of students who drop out. For example, do teachers have lower expectations for students from some communities than from others. Here are some questions that may be considered:

- What are the dropout rates of students based on ethnicity and gender in the school or district?
- What accounts for the differences in group dropout rates?
- What new policies or strategies can be implemented to address dropout rates?

Case Study

PREJUDICE LEVEL THREE—DISCRIMINATION
A HIGH SCHOOL ENGLISH CLASS: EXAMPLES OF RACISM
AND SEXISM IN A VOCABULARY ASSIGNMENT

People have difficulty visualizing how racism and sexism can be a part of the curriculum. Districts have worked hard to select textbooks that are bias free. They have provided staff development for their teachers so that they can include culture in their instructional day. As research has shown, teacher quality is the most important component of school achievement in students. When teachers do not understand how to examine their own biases, the curriculum the educators create can be outstanding and relevant, but it can also present prejudicial attitudes.

A teacher shared some examples of what Allport would describe in his model as discrimination. He found the information in his son's homework. He was surprised to see that in 2000 these kinds of things were still part of the high school curriculum. The homework materials were developed by a high school teacher who had been using these examples for several years. Not one student, parent, or colleague had ever suggested that she review them for bias.

Here is a sample of the materials that were shared with me. Ask yourself the following questions:

What messages are given in the materials?

Are these messages true?

What impact could these messages have on students?

Whose viewpoint do the materials support?

Vocabulary Lesson

Students were asked to memorize the definitions and companion sentences.

1. Abolish—to retard, to do away with.
   One of Lincoln's goals as president was to abolish slavery.

2. Ambush—to lie in wait or hiding for an attack.
   The Indians tried to ambush the settlers as they went by.
3. Impromptu—unplanned, done on the spur of the moment.
   She was so happy that she did a little impromptu dance on the table top.
4. Rapture—ecstasy, thrills, keen delight, supreme joy.
   She was filled with rapture when he kissed her.

The teacher has positional power in a school. When she presents information as if it is true, students tend to believe what she teaches. Although this was a sophomore English class, the messages were about different groups in society. The attitudes in these examples seemed to say that women, or at least some women, find that dancing on table tops is acceptable and that women want the attention of men. In addition, the rapture example seemed to indicate that women are the receivers, not the actors, in a relationship, and that men are the people in charge of female-male relationships. What underlying views and hidden messages are the sentences in the English lesson communicating to young women and men?

I felt the examples about Indians and Lincoln gave inaccurate information. The sentence about Indians (Native Americans) was extremely offensive. Basically the teacher conveyed to students that Indians ambushed settlers, thus indirectly reinforcing the stereotypical view of Native people as warring, primitive, and cowardly people. The sentence about Lincoln is also problematic because many historians debate whether Lincoln wanted to abolish slavery.

Abraham Lincoln struggled with the issue of slavery continuously through his life (Bennett 1984; Loewen 1995). Loewen, a historian, explained that Lincoln's racism was like that of any average person. He wrote, "If textbooks recognized Lincoln's racism, students would learn that racism not only affects Ku Klux Klan extremists but has been 'normal' throughout our history. And as they watched Lincoln struggle with himself to apply America's democratic principles across the color line, students would see how ideas can develop and a person can grow" (Loewen 1995, 179). Lincoln began the desegregation of the White House by inviting Blacks to serve in the White House, a practice that continued until Woodrow Wilson became president. However, Lincoln also had his staff explore the possibility of sending or "colonizing" African Americans to Africa or Latin America (Loewen 1995). Loewen believes that Lincoln knew that slavery was morally wrong and, within the context of the times, Lincoln's *Gettysburg Address* richly explained his views against slavery.

Other historians like Bennett (1984) questioned Lincoln's attitudes about slavery. Referencing the materials of Frederick Douglass, he presents the view that Lincoln did not provide strong leadership against the entrenched institution of slavery. After Lincoln had his advisors explore the possibility of sending African Americans to other countries in 1862, members of the Black community strongly protested. Lincoln's position was that there were differences between Black and White folks, and both groups were suffering from a country that combined the two communities. Douglass was extremely unhappy with

Lincoln's comments and said, "No, Mr. President, it is not the innocent horse that makes the horse thief, nor the traveler's purse that makes the highway robber, and it is not the presence of the Negro that causes this foul and unnatural war, but the cruel and brutal cupidity of those who wish to possess horses, money and Negroes by means of theft, robbery, and rebellion" (Bennett 1984, 193).

Another historian, Howard Zinn, presents a similar view. Zinn writes in his book that Lincoln did not believe in slavery, but "could not see slaves as equals, so a constant theme in his approach was to free the slaves and to send them back to Africa" (Zinn 1980, 183). Zinn also provides further information about slavery in northern states. Although many teachers may believe that most citizens in the North opposed slavery during the 1850s, this is not generally true. In fact, a free African American in New York was not able to vote unless he owned at least $250 in property, even though this was not a requirement for White voters (Zinn 1980). When the Emancipation Proclamation was put into effect, only slaves living in "areas still fighting against the Union" were freed (Zinn 1980, 187). Zinn presents a great deal of information about the United States after the Civil War in his chapter, "Slavery without Submission, Emancipation without Freedom."

The sentence the English teacher presented gave her viewpoint about Lincoln and his position about slavery. As the foregoing materials discuss, there are varying views of Lincoln's attitudes about racism and his actions to eradicate it. Like much prejudice found in school, it is not necessarily vicious in nature, but it can have a far-reaching impact on students. ❄

Case Study

PREJUDICE LEVEL TWO—AVOIDANCE: AN EXAMPLE IN SCHOOLS: THE LIFE OF MARTIN LUTHER KING, JR. AVOIDING A DISCUSSION OF INSTITUTIONAL AND SOCIETAL PREJUDICE

Sometimes we, as teachers, may avoid discussing how racism is presented and the role it plays in shaping the way we think. We also may not have a comprehensive understanding of prejudice on societal and institutional levels. It is easier to understand how a person can discriminate against another individual than to understand how prejudice is perpetuated on a larger scale. Of course, slavery was a powerful example of how racism was accepted in society in the United States for many years. Let's take another example. In the last section, you may have learned that African American males could vote in the North during the mid 1860s; however they had to own a minimum of $250 of property. White male voters did not have this requirement. This is an example of how racism was reinforced through a social institution, our government. This section of the chapter focuses upon the life of Martin Luther King, Jr., and how the presentation of his life often ignores the institutional and societal racism that he fought. The way we teach about his life also avoids discussion of how pervasive and insidious racism has been in our country.

Who was Martin Luther King, Jr.? Most teachers have come to class believing they are knowledgeable about his life and what he stood for. When I asked them about this U.S. figure, all knew he fought for civil rights and what he looked like. However, when I asked them more specifically about his life and what he went through, few teachers really knew about his struggles or his written work. They also did not understand how violent and destructive racism had been and that racism was condoned by many respected leaders.

How did I come to the realization that most teachers had only a surface knowledge of Martin Luther King, Jr., and the social context of his times? When I taught an education class one January, I reminded teachers of our national celebration of Martin Luther King, Jr.'s birthday. When I asked them the date of his birthday, only two teachers out of 65 knew the answer, January 15th, and no one knew that he was born in 1929. One reason why they did not know his birthdate is that we, as a country, do not always celebrate on his birthdate. The date of the holiday is a floating one. As a nation, we honor him on the third Monday of every January. I think that in some way it is a holiday of convenience in that we have a three-day weekend every year. I guess that is positive, but there are consequences. Something is lost, but then how important is that date?

Not knowing his birthdate did not concern me as much as the discussion in two classes about Martin Luther King, Jr. As an introduction, I asked the teachers to describe him and what he represented. One teacher said, "When I think of him, I think of his 'I Have A Dream' speech and believe that through his work, we are now a more equitable nation. He was admired by everyone."

Another teacher said, "Martin Luther King, Jr., is a legend to me. He was a reverend who led a band of people for civil rights. He is a national hero who opened the doors of communication between Whites and Blacks."

I felt that the teachers had some idea of who he was, but really did not understand the pervasive nature of racism in society and personal commitment of Martin Luther King, Jr., to fight it. I presented a time line that gave a sense of his life from his birth on January 15, 1929, to Alberta King, a school teacher, and Michael Luther King, a Baptist minister. As an adult, Martin Luther King Jr., was the first president of an organization called the Southern Christian Leadership Conference, which fought for freedom and equality. In a typical year of travel, King made 208 speeches and covered 780,000 miles. He admired Mohandas K. Gandhi and adopted his nonviolent methods. In 1965, Martin Luther King, Jr., was honored with the Nobel Peace Prize. Later in his life he also demonstrated against the Vietnam War because he opposed the presence of the United States in Vietnam. He was assassinated on April 4, 1968, by James Earl Ray.

> ⑤ "The ultimate measure of a man is not where he stands in moments of comfort and convenience, but where he stands at times of challenge and controversy."
> —MARTIN LUTHER KING, JR.

To get a more in-depth understanding of Martin Luther King, Jr., I asked the teachers to read one of his powerful written pieces, "Letter from a Birmingham Jail" (April 16, 1963). The teachers used various search engines and found his piece on the Internet.

The letter was a response to a written statement published on April 12, 1963, by eight clergy from Alabama (Christian and Jewish). The group urged Martin Luther King, Jr., to be patient about the racial conflict in Alabama and to adhere to court rulings. They believed that public demonstrations increased racial tensions between Blacks and Whites.

The teachers learned a great deal about Martin Luther King, Jr.'s passionate commitment to equity and freedom, and they also began to more fully understand the context of the times. He fought individual prejudice, but most of his efforts were aimed at societal and institutional racism and oppression. Many people did not agree with his methods of protest. Dr. King fought a governmental system that did not treat African Americans equally as White folks. His legacy is one of fighting for equality, but he also wanted to eliminate **institutional racism.** Our laws have changed. The behaviors and beliefs of many individuals in society have also changed because of his leadership and the work of thousands of other protestors. It is important for teachers to talk about the historical context of Martin Luther King, Jr.'s life rather than to avoid discussing the hostile and prejudicial attitudes he faced throughout his life.

Teachers learned that the **national mythology,** or the ideal way our country portrays itself, over the years has changed the way Martin Luther King, Jr., is presented. Here are some of the comments that teachers shared about how his image in the 1960s and today is different:

- "Well, among mainstream Americans his image has changed tremendously. Once considered a racist and hated by many Whites and Southerners, jailed, and even assassinated for his leadership, now nationally celebrated even to the point of having a day for his remembrance." (White female, 23)
- "Today MLK is seen as a hero which was not the case in 1963. He was seen as a 'Black man' who was uneducated and had goals that were unrealistic." (White female, 23)
- "MLK is seen as an important leader and a noble humanitarian. He is seen as the father of civil rights in this country, and also a martyr. In 1963, he was seen possibly as a terrorist. Because of his assassination, his peaceful demonstrations, and his unquenching need for justice, he is seen today as the former. I believe that slowly his words began to penetrate the people who were 'moral' and he himself shaped his perception today." (White male, 28)
- "MLK's image has definitely been watered down. He was so passionate in his fight for rights and now I feel he is more marginalized and so is his struggle." (White female, 25)
- "I suspect that he is considered a lot less revolutionary now. His image has been co-opted by the powerful class. And it is they who have reshaped his image to control his impact on the status quo." (White male, 48)

- "I think MLK has been sanitized and secularized. His name is a buzz word for liberals and the 'holiday' is more of a token gesture that 'gets us off the hook' for our racist past and present. I doubt highly that many people have actually read MLK's words and that they actually know and study what he stood for." (White male, 23)
- "In the 50's and 60's MLK's image was one of a radical and extremist. A civil rights extremist who caused trouble and created tension. Today, with civil rights advocacy, MLK is viewed as a holy figure, a saint, someone who was not controversial but inherently right on his beliefs. I think White Americans shaped his image. If he is continued to be viewed as controversial, older Whites would be continually showing how wrong they were." (White male, 23)

So what caused the change in Martin Luther King Jr.'s image? This is a complex question. As the last three teachers wrote, society takes their heroes and uses them to promote the image they want their children, their members, and people from other countries to see them. I agree that the image change from Martin Luther King, Jr., as a radical to a hero and saint reinforces the mythology that the United States is a country that highly values freedom and equality. Unfortunately, in many cases people tend to avoid serious discussion of racism. Avoidance is the second level of prejudice that Allport identified in his work. Through our national mythology, in many ways we avoid addressing oppression because King was adopted as a hero. We need to encourage our students to research the impact of racism on our relationships, social practices, and laws. We also must guide students in talking with each other about these issues, especially since they are often emotional and difficult to discuss. Avoiding discussions can lead to suspicion and misunderstandings between folks and groups.

What will you teach your students about Martin Luther King, Jr.? Do you think it is important to teach them?

Let's say we are having our students examine the life of Martin Luther King, Jr., and his work.

Who was Martin Luther King, Jr.?

What impact did he have on the history of the United States? How do you know?

What do students and U.S. citizens need to know about him today?

To help you think about these questions, I suggest you use techniques developed at Central Park East Secondary School in Harlem (Wood 1993). The faculty at this school believe that caring and social justice are at the core of good education and that it is critical that students are taught how to think and make decisions about serious problems in society and their lives. As a part of the ethic of critique (Starratt 1994), teachers encourage students to ask crucial questions. Therefore, on the walls of classrooms in Central Park East Secondary School, where approximately 95 percent of the students go on to college, teachers have posted the following questions to use when examining an issue:

- *Evidence. How do we know what we know? What kind of evidence do we consider "good" enough?*
- *Viewpoint. What viewpoint are we hearing, seeing, reading? Who is the author, where is she standing, what are her intentions?*
- *Connection. How are things connected to each other? How does "it" fit in? Where have we heard or seen this before?*
- *Conjecture. What if? Supposing that? Can we imagine alternatives?*
- *Relevance. What difference does it make? Who cares?* (George Wood, *Schools That Work*)

I would ask one more set of questions: Who benefits from the perspective? Practices? Decision? Chosen solution?

These questions can help students to comprehensively examine the life and work of Martin Luther King, Jr. They may accept or challenge ideas that are being taught about him.

In order to eradicate social oppression, we must teach our students to question and to see the consequences of our actions. For example, although Martin Luther King, Jr., is seen as a hero today in comparison to how he was viewed in the 1950s, are there negative consequences to this image? Unfortunately, as many teachers have indicated, his image has been shaped in a way that led teachers away from explaining how he as a Black man stood up against a White authority system. This system included institutions like the courts and other governmental bodies. Race did matter in his time period and, unfortunately, racism still exists today. Although it has taken on different faces, social oppression based on perceived racial group membership is still an obstacle to equality and freedom today.

I wonder what Reverend King would say to us today. How far do you think he would believe we have gotten in the fight for civil rights in our country and the world? ❋

Case Study

PREJUDICE LEVEL THREE AND FOUR—DISCRIMINATION AND PHYSICAL ATTACK IN SCHOOLS: THE LEMON GROVE INCIDENT, 1931, AND A CHALLENGE TO SCHOOL SEGREGATION

Many years before the 1954 legal case of *Brown* v. *Board of Education*, Roberto Alvarez, a 12-year-old student, was the main plaintiff in the first legal challenge to school segregation (Espinosa 1986). This case is known as the Lemon Grove Incident. Alvarez was a student in school in Lemon Grove, California, a small city in San Diego County.[1]

---

[1]One of the best sources for information about the Lemon Grove court case is a one-hour video called "The Lemon Grove Incident." It was produced by Paul Espinosa, a writer and producer from the San Diego television station, KPBS. I recommend that you watch this film to better understand not only the impact of a young Latino child on your life, but also how the Mexican American community fought against inequality and for the rights of their children to have access to equal education.

⑤ *Roberto Alvarez v. The Lemon Grove School District, 1931 was the first successful court challenge to school segregation.*

Roberto Alvarez was born in California and was therefore a U.S. citizen. He was part of a class-action suit that represented 75 Mexican American families who fought the **segregation** of their children in public schools. Parents believed that their children would not receive quality education in a separate building that was a converted barn.

The case came at a time when many mainstream residents were concerned with immigration from Mexico and Mexican Americans. Some individuals blamed Mexican immigrants for economic problems that the area was experiencing. The arguments are similar to ones that are present today. There was a deep divide in the community about the importance of Americanizing all students through the schools. Some parents believed it was important that there be a transitional school where students would be culturally assimilated and then they would become part of mainstream society.

Anglo members of the community requested during a Lemon Grove School Board meeting that Mexican American children be separated from Anglo students because they brought various diseases and could not speak English. Prejudicial attitudes existed. The school board decided the best alternative was to create a school for Mexican American students on Olive Street. The school was a converted barn. Mexican American parents argued that they paid taxes like their Anglo neighbors, and so they wanted the same quality of education for their students. They wanted their children to continue to attend the neighborhood school. One morning when they were directed by their grammar school principal to go to the barn, the Mexican American children went home. Their parents continued to keep them home because they did not want their children to participate in segregation. The parents created a social action association.

Mexican American parents formed the Neighborhood Association of Lemon Grove. The association approached the Mexican consulate, which provided a lawyer. With the help of the lawyer, the parents sued the school district and won their suit. The judge agreed that although segregation laws allowed for the separation of Anglo students from Black, American Indian, and Asian Americans, Mexicans were considered to be Caucasians and so they could not be segregated from other Anglo students. The Mexican American children went back to Lemon Grove Grammar School.

There are many other examples of Mexican Americans who have fought school segregation (San Miguel 2001). In 1947, the *Mendez* v. *Westminster School District* ended segregation of Mexican Americans in schools in California. Sylvia was only eight years old when she, along with her aunt and brothers, attempted to register for school in Westminster, a city in Orange County, California. She and her brothers were turned away by school officials because of her dark skin and Mexican last name. At the time when Sylvia tried to register for school, Orange County had many segregated theaters, stores, and restaurants. Her parents, Gonzalo and Felicitas Mendez, fought inequality by organizing a group of parents who filed the position that their children were being discriminated against based on national origin, an action that violated the U.S. Constitution. Briefs were also filed in support of the Mendez family by the NAACP, ACLU, Japanese American Citizens League, and the American Jewish Congress. The Ninth Circuit Court of Appeals ruled in their favor and outlawed the segregation of Mexican American children in schools in California. Thurgood Marshall, the lead lawyer in the *Brown.* v. *Board of Education* in the 1954 segregation case, utilized the Mendez decision in his arguments. I use the two examples to demonstrate not only discrimination but also physical attack because the children were physically removed from attending their neighborhood schools. I believe that the two cases demonstrated more than simple discrimination; they were cases of physical and intellectual exclusion. Social institutions were used to discriminate against children.

> ⑤ *Physical segregation in schools creates intellectual segregation.*

In 1954 the Supreme Court ruled in *Brown* v. *Board of Education* that separate schools were "inherently unequal." This decision has guided school policies for many years. However, does segregation continue to plague U.S. schools today? Unfortunately, we are seeing a trend toward the resegregation of students. Today, segregation in schools is often a result of housing and other institutional policies (Frankenberg, Lee, and Orfield 2003). **Resegregation** is the reverting back to patterns of segregation.

In a recent report called *A Multiracial Society with Segregated Schools: Are We Losing the Dream?* authors Frankenberg, Lee, and Orfield (2003) relate that our schools are becoming more segregated. In fact, segregation is reaching the levels of the 1960s in some regions of the country. The following highlight some of their key findings:

- In 2000 and 2001, the most segregated group were White students; they attended schools with a student population of 80 percent or more other White youth.
- Desegregation for Blacks was increasing until the late 1980s; however, since the end of that decade, Black students are finding themselves in segregated schools. Some scholars have identified these conditions as apartheid-like conditions.
- In 1967 many suburban school districts were primarily White; now many resegregated schools are found in suburban schools. Therefore, the issue of resegregation involves both urban and suburban schools.
- The largest growth in student population is among Latinos. In the past 10 years, Latinos have shown a growth of 45 percent—22.4 million to 32.4 million students. They are the most segregated group and show signs of being segregated by language, too. They have the high dropout rates.
- The fastest move toward segregation is happening for Black students in the South, where they attend increasingly segregated schools.[2]

[2]The following states are considered in the regions marked South and West: South—Alabama, Arkansas, Florida, Georgia, Louisiana, Mississippi, North Carolina, South Carolina, Tennessee, Texas, and Virginia. West—Arizona, California, Colorado, Montana, Nevada, New Mexico, Oregon, Utah, Washington, and Wyoming.

Frankenberg, Lee, and Orfield (2003) believe that we as a nation must move to support efforts toward desegregation as in the past. These efforts should focus on integrated housing patterns and encouraging schools to continue their desegregation plans.

Does their report demonstrate discriminatory practices, as defined by Allport? The courts have already ruled various times that segregated schools fail to provide equal protection to all students under the law. Frankenberg, Lee, and Orfield referenced one of the speeches of Martin Luther King, Jr., (Washington, 1991) that described some of the negative effects of segregation. King addressed a large crowd of 20,000 students who were protesting segregation (Frankenberg, Lee, and Orfield 2003, 7).

It [segregation] injures one spiritually. It scars the soul and distorts the personality. It inflicts the segregator with a false sense of superiority while inflicting the segregated with a false sense of inferiority.[3]

Unfortunately, there continue to be many examples of discrimination in schools. I have listed only a few. The question is not Is there resegregation? but rather What are we as educators doing to eliminate resegregation? We will need a multipronged solution such as allowing students to transfer from metropolitan school districts to suburban ones. As a country we need to examine our housing and employment patterns. What we are seeing in schools is a reflection of what is happening in our society. Simple answers will not solve this complex issue of resegregation. ✹

 Resegregation is becoming the rule and not the exception in many U.S. school districts.

 Connection

Please visit Chapter 6 of the book website to link to the Civil Rights Project at Harvard University. It is one of the best websites **http://www.civilrightsproject.harvard.edu/** for information about issues of equity in schools. The personnel at the Center have published an excellent paper on resegregation.

Case Study

PREJUDICE LEVELS TWO, THREE, AND FOUR: NATIVE AMERICAN MASCOTS AND LOGOS: AN ISSUE OF RESPECT AND JUSTICE

I believe that the use of Native Americans as mascots is an issue that straddles various levels of Allport's model of prejudice. First, the issue can be seen as

---

[3]Frankenberg, Lee, and Orfield on page 7 of their document referenced *A Testament of Hope: The Essential Writings and Speeches of Martin Luther King, Jr.,* edited by James B. Washington. San Francisco: Harper San Francisco, 21.

an example of avoidance. Many people do not want to address the use of a long-time mascot, and so they ignore the request of others who believe the issue warrants serious study. Second, avoidance may also be a sign of the invisibility of Native Americans as a political group. Often, because there are few Native students in a school, they may not have a political presence within the school. In addition, the mascot issue may be discriminatory, if the school mascot presents biased and inaccurate information about an ethnic community. And if the mascot also encourages **physical violence,** then the mascot issue may be considered as contributing to level four where physical violence occurs. As Bennett has described in his intercultural sensitivity model, in order to develop interculturalism, one must be able to understand the cultural frame of reference of another.

Have you ever thought about the issue of using Native Americans as mascots, logos, or symbols for school and professional sports teams?

If your team in high school was the Anytown Panthers, the issue may never have arisen. Let's say the professional football team you root for is the San Diego Chargers and their mascot is an electrical bolt. However, in some areas of the country where Native Americans are used as mascots, the issue is a sensitive one.

Professional sports organizations have mascots of Indians, chiefs, braves, or redskins. Have you heard of the following professional sports organizations?

Kansas City Chiefs (football).

Atlanta Braves (baseball).

Washington Redskins (football).

Cleveland Indians (baseball).

When I first began researching this issue, I thought that there might be a few middle or high schools sprinkled throughout the United States where this was the case. Unfortunately, I found that there are thousands of elementary, middle, and high schools that have adopted Native American mascots. The American Indian Cultural Support website (www.aics.org) has identified many of the schools. For example, in Ohio there are over 200 schools that have a Native American mascot. The mascots chosen vary; here is a partial list:

Apache

Braves

Camanches

Comanches

Chieftains

Chiefs

Indians

Kiowas

Papooses

Red Raiders

Redskins

Tomahawks

Totems

Warriors

Yeguas

Many mascots and logos have been chosen by and for students.

Many communities, whether small towns or large cities, often take great pride in their mascots, because they are associated with long-time traditions. For example, at Atlanta Brave baseball games fans enthusiastically engage in what is now known as the tomahawk chop. Fans raise a large Styrofoam red spongy object that looks like a large tomahawk and make chopping motions. This tradition represents chopping or getting rid of baseball players on opposing teams. Many people in the stands can be seen supporting the Atlanta Brave players by engaging in this act. The team feels supported, and the fans feel like a united community. For many Atlanta Brave fans, symbols of the tomahawk and the tomahawk chop are important elements of team spirit.

The Atlanta Braves is a professional sports team and therefore the team is a large private corporation. I believe the portrayal of Native Americans on this national level should be carefully examined because of the mixed messages about Native Americans that are often given out. However, the issue takes on more urgency in schools. An educator who speaks out against the use of Native American mascots is Barbara Munson, a member of the Oneida nation. She believes mascots present racist and stereotypical images of Native Americans. These stereotypes often show Native Americans as primitive and extinct people. These images marginalize Native people. This issue is even more important to address in schools because schools are public institutions that are directed to teach young people national values of respect, human dignity, citizenship, and community.

Munson (nondated) explained:

The logos, along with other societal abuses and stereotypes separate, marginalize, confuse, intimidate and harm Native American children and create barriers to their learning throughout their school experience. Additionally, the logos teach non-Indian children that it's all right to participate in culturally abusive behavior. Children spend a great deal of their time in school, and schools have a very significant impact on their emotional, spiritual, physical and intellectual development. As long as such logos remain, both Native American and non-Indian children are learning to tolerate racism in our schools.

Schools are one of the most important places for cross-cultural discussion and collaboration to occur. Many individuals and organizations have fought to

Take a Stand

WHAT SHOULD SCHOOLS DO ABOUT THEIR INDIAN MASCOTS?

Keep the Mascot	Adopt a New Mascot
The mascot represents long-standing traditional honor and pride of the high school. Many alumni and students identify with the most positive characteristics of their Indian mascots. They see themselves as courageous and strong people. Mascots were not chosen to ridicule Native Americans.	In a multicultural and global world, it is important that students learn about and respect the cultural values of people from other cultural frames of reference. Mascots act to dehumanize rather than to honor people.
The issue can be used to teach students, parents, and community people about the history and culture of or the Indian community. This can be an opportunity for folks to learn about Native Americans. People can engage in honest dialogue about the issue.	The use of nicknames, derogatory images, and stereotypes does not honor Native Americans. In fact, it results in marginalizing and degrading Native people as objects to use in sporting events. This also impacts the ethnic identity and self-esteem of Native students. Mascots result in Native students' feeling excluded, intimidated, and/or humiliated.
The mascot can be changed or modified to be a more accurate representative of the Native American tribe. This is an excellent compromise and a way to honor the traditions of Indian tribes.	Schools should be places of respect and compassion. They should be social institutions where students work together to create caring and just communities.
The First Amendment guarantees the freedom of speech and in this situation the school community has the right to honor the group that they see as the best representative for their team. This is a First Admendment issue and should be respected.	When stereotypical images of Native Americans are in schools, students also are taught that racism is tolerated by the community and teachers. All students should be treated equitably.
It will be extremely expensive for schools to replace all of their band, football, and other uniforms if a new mascot is chosen. The school cannot afford to revise logos and mascots because only a small segment of the community is offended.	The issue of the mascot represents deep-seated racism that goes beyond the treatment of Native Americans as a lucky charm. Native Americans are often invisible with little political and financial resources. They have been subjected to severe genocide and cultural extermination.

make schools places where students from all communities regardless of gender, ethnicity, disabilities, and religion come together to work and learn in an atmosphere of mutual respect and collaboration. The nondiscrimination policies that schools have instituted after the Civil Rights Act of 1964 demonstrate our move as a society toward creating compassionate schools where cultural perspectives are shared and stereotypes and prejudices are barred. Students must learn not only through their academic studies, but also through their social interactions with each other about issues of equity. Schools should be places where students address public issues in collaboration in a respectful atmosphere. If young people from all over this country grapple with the complex and emotional issue of human mascots, maybe members of the business world will follow the role model of young people and address the issue, too.

In schools teachers often teach respect and fairness. However, have you identified hidden practices that we accept every day that may be hindering or even hurting students? I, like many other teachers, did not think about this issue. I was extremely busy as a public school teacher and it was difficult just keeping up. However, there are things I should have addressed as a member of the school community. One of those issues was Native American mascots in the district I taught in. Since I believe in caring for others and social justice, I should have raised the issue in my district.

Schools give out messages about race and groups of people through their hidden curriculum. Although a Native American mascot may not be hidden, there are hidden values behind the use of the mascots that may not have been reviewed by the school community. Schools, as John Dewey recommended, can be places where democracy is practiced and where young people develop democratic skills. Addressing social issues in schools encourages students to develop critical thinking and social communication skills within a meaningful context (Noddings 1984; Hilliard 2000; Pewewardy nondated). Students also use their skills of comprehension, interviewing, and research and learn to prioritize their values and make difficult decisions. They must synthesize, analyze, and evaluate the information they are discovering. Through dialogue and research, students can see how understanding multiple perspectives can assist them in understanding the complexities of public issues such as the use of Native Americans as mascots. After these discussions students may want to address the use of other humans as mascots, such as pirates and Vikings.

The issue of Native American and human mascots is important for teachers to include in the curriculum of government, civics, history, social studies, English, journalism, and physical education classes. This issue relates to various curriculum standards. For example, the Wyoming Social Studies Content Standard Peformance Proficiency for grade 11 states, "All people have a stake in examining civic ideals and practices across time and in diverse societies as well as at home, and in determining how to close the gap between present practices and the ideals upon which our democratic republic is based." In addition, Standard 6 in Wyoming addresses the ability of students to "access, organize, synthesize, evaluate, and interpret information using appropriate resources and technology to . . . make decisions, solve problems." It is conceivable that teachers could use this issue to address this standard because it relates to making decisions based on civil ideals in a democratic republic.

To introduce the unit, students can be asked to consider a question such as "Should anything be done about the Native American mascot in schools? Why or why not?" These are complex questions and students should comprehensively investigate them in order to come to a decision of action. Students can take pro or con positions and find evidence to support their viewpoints.

Faculty may also pose the following key questions, in light of the model described in the Martin Luther King, Jr., section, about evidence, viewpoint, connection, conjecture, and relevance:

Are Native American mascots and logos appropriate for public schools? Why or why not? What do you think schools that have adopted Native Americans as their mascots should do?

In examining this issue, students need to research other questions in order to make a decision about what they think should be done. Here is a sample of questions that could guide them in their inquiry unit:

What is the mascot? What is a definition of a mascot?

Why are mascots chosen?

Why were Native American mascots chosen? When were the mascots chosen? Who made the choice of the mascot?

What impact do the mascots have on various student groups?

How do students, parents, and community people feel about the chosen mascot? What do Native students think? What do Black students think? What do Latino, disabled, younger, older, parents, alumni think?

What is the history of the mascot at the school?

Whose beliefs does the mascot reinforce? Why? Whose don't they agree with? Why?

Several strategies that can be employed to explore an issue are as follows:

- Explore various viewpoints on the issue.
- Gather data that supports various perspectives on the issue.
- Identify your own values.
- List various possible solutions and the consequences of each solution.

The following is a compilation of some of the evidence that students gathered about the issue.

TABLE 6.1 Native American Mascots

Pros	Cons
Honoring of Native Americans.	Stereotypes and misconceptions are conveyed.
Team pride.	Culture is about spiritual values and not about sporting events.
Local pride of the community.	Harassment and marginalization of Native Americans are not solid foundations of pride. Self-esteem of Native American students can be influenced by stereotypes.

continued

TABLE 6.1 Native American Mascots (Continued)

Pros	Cons
Use of accurate depictions of Native Americans.	Lack of understanding of philosophical and religious value systems.
Freedom of expression issue.	Civil rights issue.

Since it is important for students to look at the issue from various viewpoints, the next table was used to identify various mascot names in use and then to come up with parallel names. In this way students began to see how they had become accustomed to some labels and therefore did not look at them from the perspective of a Native American who was offended. Many students did not object to the term *Redskins* because it is commonly used. However, when the name was changed to *Whiteskins,* they did not like the label. Students began to see how difficult it is to place oneself in the shoes of another. To take on the cultural frame of reference of another often takes much compassion and effort. When I asked, "Would you ever use the term *Blackskins* instead of *Redskins,* there was an immediate response of no. They understood how denigrating and negative this term was, especially within the historical context of slavery of Black folks and the genocide of Black culture. Students would never adopt the term *Blackskins;* however, they initially felt comfortable with the term *Redskins.* They realized that much of the issue deals with power and authority and that the Native American community does not have great political power or a strong voice in society and schools. The students also noted that they had covered some history of Black Americans and less history about Native American communities and, therefore, they were not as sensitive or knowledgeable about the viewpoints of Native Americans.

TABLE 6.2 Mascots—Parallel Viewpoints

Existing Mascot Names	Possible Parallel Names
Apache	Germans, Ethiopians, Chinese
Chiefs	Popes, Premiers, Ministers
Chieftains	
Indians	Whites, Asians, Blacks, Latinos
Papooses	Infants
Red Raiders	White Raiders
Redskins	Whiteskins
Tomahawks	Guns

I encourage you to read more about the issue from the viewpoints of two Native Americans, Barbara Munson and Cornel Pewewardy. In the reference section are websites that will provide you with materials written by these educators. Caring and compassionate teachers are sensitive to issues of social justice. The mascot issue is a complex one and can provide students with the opportunity to examine how prejudicial attitudes and discriminatory actions are intimately connected. It is also critical for students to examine how prejudice and discrimination can be found in social institutions such as schools. ✸

Case Study

PREJUDICE LEVEL FIVE—EXTERMINATION: AMERICAN INDIAN EDUCATION

American Indians have experienced continual extermination not only of their culture but also their ways of life (McCarty 2002). The education of American Indians is an example of how U.S. policy of total **assimilation** almost destroyed their communities and cultures (Szasz 1977). Legally, the government had signed numerous treaties with various Native American communities, agreeing to provide services such as education. However, federal policies often were based on the belief that schools could be used to eliminate the values and beliefs of Native people and to replace their value systems with mainstream culture and the English language. These policies did not support the **self-determination,** or self-empowerment, of Native people. This change toward self-determination did not arise until the 1960s. For many decades, governmental officials worked toward civilizing communities such as the Nez Perce, Ponca, and Northern Cheyenne through the Bureau of Indian Affairs. However, in 1928 the Brookings Institution published the ***Meriam Report,*** which criticized the state of the Indian Bureau (Szasz 1977). Recommendations in the report suggested that schools should serve as centers for the community and include Indian culture.

The education of American Indians has been one of disappointment and destruction. The education of Indian youth has a dismal record. In 1964 only 60 percent of Native American children were enrolled in public schools (Szasz 1977). Indian Affairs policies have at times attempted the total annihilation of Indian culture: Many students were taken from their homes and put in boarding schools. Boarding schools were often not well funded, served poor-quality food, lacked quality teachers, and did not provide a caring community. Native students were not allowed to speak their home languages, whether in or out of school. After the *Meriam Report* was published, some schools included only classes in Indian art, history, and language to the exclusion of mainstream subjects like algebra, geometry, and European history. This made it difficult for students who wanted to develop a bicultural lifestyle (Szasz 1977). This shift also limited the economic and social opportunities of students. In culturally assimilated–oriented schools, students also had difficulty maintaining Native culture because the values of mainstream culture were in direct opposition to what their parents had taught (Szasz 1977). To some young Native youth who had been taught to be collaborative and reticent, the idea of individual success and the importance of aggressive competition placed them in cultural conflict. In addition, many of the schools advocated vocational education but not much else. For example, young girls were often taught cooking, sewing, and secretarial skills. It was believed the women would go back to the reservation and would not need additional skill development or education. The education of Native children has historically been one of conflict and the termination of home cultures.

In 1969 the **Kennedy Report** recommended that in issues of education, Native Americans should become active in designing and implementing schooling for their children. During this period many Native people testified against the paternalistic and colonial practices of the Indian Bureau. Why was it difficult for the Indian Bureau to accept the policy of self-determination? Szasz wrote:

"Self-determination has always been a difficult concept for the Indian Bureau to grasp, for in essence it implies that the Bureau itself is unnecessary" (1977, 196).

What has been the effect of Indian education or the lack of quality education for Native students? Historically, our nation's efforts have been to assimilate rather than to educate American Indian students, and there is little evidence to show success. In fact, scholars have found that Indian youth show the lowest levels of educational attainment (Astin 1977; Machamer and Gruber 1998). I also discovered that it was very difficult to find information about the achievement of the students in mainstream educational journals and publications. This points to the invisibility of Native students and their needs.

What did I find about the academic success of Indian students? Machamer and Gruber (1998) studied Chippaqua and Sioux students from Minnesota. The students reported that they were twice as likely as their Black peers and three times more likely than their White classmates to earn low grades such as Ds and Es. Forty-four percent of the Indian students sampled reported skipping school that month. This figure was higher than that of Blacks (38 percent skipped school) and White students (32 percent who skipped school). In addition, they found that Indian students who lived off the reservation were less likely to be successful in school or to feel connected to their families.

Because many of the members of the Navajo community were aware of the negative impact of schools on their children, the community created the Rough Rock Demonstration School in 1966 (McCarty 2002). The Rough Rock community wanted high-quality education that was relevant to and meaningful for their children. Parents, community people, and others also wanted to fight long-established policies of cultural extermination. The Rough Rock Demonstration School, Diné Bíólta, was the first community school established by American Indians. The school taught the Navajo language and used literature written by American Indians.

The school's curriculum evolved into a bilingual program. Initially the curriculum was patterned after the English development program, Kamehameha Early Education Program (KEEP), created in Hawaii. Later Rough Rock's program developed into a bilingual program called RRENLAP, Rough Rock English-Navajo Language Arts Program. It became a K–6 Navajo-English maintenance language program (McCarty 2002). As a bilingual program, there was evidence throughout the school of the bilingual nature of the curriculum. Not only did students write about holidays such as Halloween, but also there was a bulletin board showing the four sacred mountains of Dinétah, Navajoland (McCarty 2002, 151). In another classroom were samples of student writings in both Navajo and English describing Navajo dyes and rugs. Students not only explored stereotypes of Indians, but also examined historical events from the viewpoints of members in their community.

How effective has RRENLAP been? McCarty found that up to 60 percent of kindergartners speak Navajo fluently. This compared with another study of 3,300 other kindergartners of whom only approximately 30 percent spoke Navajo proficiently. However, language loss is still a grave concern in American Indian communities. The language taught in the school is a critical link to the Navajo culture. Language is a powerful force in the community because it shapes songs, prayers, greetings, blessings, stories, science, philosophy, geography, and history of the community. These components of culture were woven into the curriculum.

The academic achievement of children who participated in RRENLAP has been strong. Children who arrived at school speaking Navajo and were involved in early literacy education demonstrated the greatest gains on national standardized tests. McCarty found that children who learned to read in their first language, Navajo, learned how to read well in English also. Another important outcome is that described by Lomawaima and McCarty (2002):

> *The Native struggle for sovereignty and self-education is a powerful model for all U.S. citizens because public education in the United States was founded on the principle of local control . . . the lessons from Indigenous America . . . can illuminate and enrich the national debate surrounding educational issues that affect us all. American Indian education teaches us that nurturing "places of difference" within American society is a necessary component of a democracy* (280).

The Rough Rock community was able to stop assimilation and emphasized biculturalism. I encourage you to read McCarty's book, *A Place to Be Navajo,* so that you can better understand not only the successes of the Navajo but also their lengthy struggle against an educational system that was extremely detrimental to the community and their children.[4] ❀

How Prejudice Can Influence Teacher Confidence: Need for Self-Regulation of Bias

This chapter has described how prejudice can be hidden in individual and school practices. Most teachers do not consciously exclude or hurt students; however, many educators from all communities do not really examine what they think or believe.

---

[4]One of the purposes of this chapter is not to provide a complete educational history of different ethnic communities, but it is my hope that the examples I share will encourage you, the reader, to investigate and read more about schooling through various cultural filters.

My colleague Velma Sablan and I conducted a study on how confident teachers felt teaching African American students (1998). We used a questionnaire that was well designed and accepted in the field by Gibson and Dembo (1984). In this way we could examine more specifically how prejudicial attitudes may impact teacher attitudes.

The instrument we used looked at two different areas. The first area examined how teachers viewed their own personal teaching competence. Did they feel they were personally effective as a teacher? The second area examined whether teachers in general are competent. Did they believe that teachers can influence the learning of their students? Having two dimensions in the questionnaire helped us study how teachers felt generally about teaching and then explored how an individual teacher felt about her or his ability to reach students. Past research demonstrated that teachers with low levels of efficacy were more distrustful of students, tried to exert strong controls over students, and did not use a variety of instructional strategies. In comparison, high-efficacy teachers developed warm relationships with students, gave more positive feedback to students, and held high expectations for all students (Pang and Sablan 1998).

Teachers were asked to respond to 30 questions indicating one of the following: strongly agree, agree, uncertain, disagree, and strongly disagree. The only difference we made in the original questionnaire was to add the term *African American.* Read through a sample of the statements:

1. If an African American student masters a new math concept quickly, this might be because I knew the necessary steps in teaching the concept.
2. The hours in my class have little influence on African American students compared to the influence of their home environment.
3. If an African American student in my class becomes disruptive and noisy, I feel assured that I know some techniques to redirect him or her quickly.
4. If African American parents would do more with their children, I could do more.

We were concerned with how teachers looked at personal and general teaching efficacy as related to African American students. We also hypothesized that preservice and in-service teachers would show similar beliefs. Of the 100 pre- and 75 in-service teachers surveyed, 74 percent (129) were European American, 13 percent (24) were Latino, and the other 13 percent were made up of Asian Pacific Americans, African Americans, Native Americans, and several interracial individuals. Several of the questions we looked at were:

1. What perceptions do preservice and in-service teachers have regarding their African American students and African American communities?
2. What levels of personal and general teaching efficacy do preservice and in-service teachers hold as related to African American students?

The results were quite disturbing. We found that racial attitudes did affect teacher efficacy beliefs of preservice and in-service teachers in our sample. Preservice teachers were more positive about their ability to reach African American children than in-service educators. They indicated more ability to assess, redirect, teach, and adjust to the needs of African American students. Sablan and I believe that in-service teachers had been influenced over a period of time by others who had not been able to address the needs of African American students. Then as problems arose, new teachers used cultural conflict and lack of knowledge about African American students as scapegoats for academic failure.

One of the most troubling findings was that a large number of teachers, 65 per-cent, indicated that they did not believe, even with good teaching strategies, that they would be able to reach African American students. However, the subjects did believe that teachers are powerful forces in the lives of students.

Although the responses of teachers were mixed, our study seemed to show that generally teachers did not feel confident about their personal abilities to teach African American children and that school failure was not due to teacher failure. This can seriously impact the attitudes that teachers bring to the school and also to the classroom. Racial bias is sometimes difficult to detect; however, our study demonstrated that stereotypical views of Black families, low student interest, and lack of parental discipline are powerful perceptions and do impact teachers' belief systems.

Teachers need to develop self-regulation skills. In the self-regulation process individuals see how their values of equity and caring may not match their behaviors (Pang and Park, forthcoming). It is important for all of us to continually reflect upon our responses to students and others in light of equality. Preservice teachers were found to exhibit numerous biased views; however, until they used a set of carefully created questions, they were unaware of their prejudicial attitudes toward children from nonmajority ethnic groups. It is a struggle for many of us to eliminate our own prejudices. Most of us must engage in a vigilant process of growth in which we chal-lenge ourselves to see our shortcomings and to change our beliefs and actions.

Chapter Summary

Unfortunately, prejudice and discrimination are found throughout our schools. Bias can be found in the attitudes of students, teachers, parents, and administrators. It can also be found in our school policies, practices, curriculum, and many other components. Allport has provided a framework that we can use to examine how prejudice and discrimi-nation seep into what we do no matter how uninten-tional. His five levels of prejudice—antilocution, avoidance, discrimination, physical attack, and genocide—demonstrate that prejudice is a problem that all of us must struggle with and act to eliminate.

Schools must be places where students feel safe and accepted. Bias that is overtly shown through name-calling and other actions that are more obvi-ous is easier to combat and question. However, the practices and behaviors of people that are more covert or hidden are the most difficult to get rid of. Many people may say that we are all the same, but in reality they may favor some students over others in small ways, such as the tone of voice they use.

Prejudice and oppression are issues for individu-als to address; but institutions such as schools, so-cial service agencies, and businesses should also continue to review their actions and policies for bi-ases. As presented in this chapter, we often avoid discussion of racial and other issues by shaping the way we present them. For example, the presentation of Martin Luther King, Jr., as a national hero, may need to include the issue of institutional and na-tional racism. It is important for students in schools to look comprehensively at the issues that he fought.

His image can be presented from various points of view. Today, much that is taught about him has been shaped by mainstream society and our national mythology.

Identifying practices in school that exemplify Allport's five levels of prejudice can assist teachers in understanding that biased views still exist. All of us must work together to reevaluate our beliefs and attitudes about ethnic and cultural communities. In addition, there are issues in schools that are challenging to address, such as the one dealing with Native American mascots. However, it is critical for students to be encouraged to tackle complex issues and learn how to "unpack" the issues of social control, political capital, multiple ways of knowing, respect for others, and interdependence.

McCarty documented in her ethnography of the Rough Rock Demonstration School how Indian education, for the most part, was originally designed to eliminate Native American cultures and languages. The federal policies that guided Indian education were paternalistic and colonial in orientation. They advanced the beliefs of cultural assimilation and the termination of American Indian cultures. This has been a destructive social force in the lives of many. However, the Rough Rock Demonstration School is one example of self-determined educa-

tion, showing how local control can transform a school and community in its struggle for freedom, equity, and quality of life.

The only way that prejudice and discrimination can be eradicated is that all people in the school, from the custodians to food workers to students to principals to teachers, work together to address and find ways to reduce these destructive attitudes and actions. A study by Pang and Sablan demonstrated that both pre- and in-service teachers held negative feelings about their ability to reach African American students. These beliefs seemed to arise from a cultural deficit point of view. The cultural deficit model assumes that students from underrepresented groups lack the ability to achieve or have inadequate parenting, or both. In other words, there is something wrong with students' culture and/or families.

In comparison, Pang and Sablan (1998) encouraged teachers to move to a culturally relevant and caring model of teaching, in which relationships are the core of the learning process. In addition, teachers can integrate culture through a multipronged approach. Instructional strategies, curriculum, policies, materials, counseling strategies, the school calendar, and other areas in school must reflect the lives of students and be meaningful.

Chapter Review

Go to the Online Learning Center at **www.mhhe.com/pang2e** to review important content from the chapter, practice with key terms, take a chapter quiz, and find the Web links listed in this chapter.

Key Terms

antilocution, *177*
avoidance, *177*
discrimination, *177*
physical attack, *178*
genocide, *178-180*

institutional racism, *189*
national mythology, *189*
segregation, *192*
resegregation, *193*
assimilation, *201*

self-determination, *201*
Meriam Report, 201
Kennedy Report, 202

Reflection Activities

How Can I Limit Prejudice and Discrimination?

What are ways that you as a teacher, colleague, parent, or community person can work to eliminate social oppression in schools? Because schools are an institution of society, they harbor some of the same prejudices that individuals hold. In your journal, please answer questions 1 through 6.

1. To be caring advocates, I believe that all of us must deal with the hidden hurdles that exist in our minds. There are many things that you can do as a person and as a teacher to try to get rid of, or at least limit, prejudice and discrimination. Here are some suggestions.

   • Ask yourself what stereotypes or prejudices you have toward others. Where did you get these biases? Do you catch yourself thinking about others in stereotypical ways?

   • In the classroom or in the school hall, stop name-calling as soon as you hear it. Don't allow it to continue. Your inaction can be interpreted as acceptance of the name-calling.

   • After an ethnic joke has been told, talk about how people feel when they are ridiculed by others. Ask students why people like to put down others. What do they gain by that kind of behavior?

   • Do you ever refer to "those children" or "those people" when talking about students and culturally diverse communities? This can be a clue to your considering members of cultural groups as "others" or being in the "out-group."

2. Discuss the issue of prejudice with your students. The following questions may help create important sharing and reflection in your students.

   • Has anyone ever said anything to you that hurt you?

   • How did you feel?

   • Have you ever said anything mean to someone else?

   • How do you think they felt?

   • Have you ever wished you had said something to someone who shared an ethnic joke or made a racist, gender-biased, or classist comment?

Now that you have had time to reflect, what could you have said?

   • What does it feel like to be treated as an outsider or foreigner?

3. Videotape yourself in the classroom. Are you fair in how you interact with each child? How much time do you spend with each child? Do you tend to spend more time with some children than with others? Do you take more time to answer questions of some students?

4. Do you accept each child and her or his communities and characteristics without judgment? Do you celebrate the ethnic group, gender, or neighborhood of children whose identities are highly interconnected with the groups to help them keep a positive self-concept? A child of color's self-acceptance can be strongly reinforced in the classroom. Reinforcement is crucial in a society where prejudice and discrimination can threaten a child's self-image.

5. Do you use cooperative learning and integrate groups with children who represent various social classes, gender, and racial groups? Provide students with a common goal in a group where they have equal status. Personal interactions can help to break down prejudice (Byrnes 1988, 269).

6. Examples in this chapter show how prejudice and discrimination are part of the structure of schools. Looking at systemic changes in schools can help to promote equity and affirm diversity. I would like to share with you some of the questions Nieto has suggested that teachers think about (Nieto 1990):

   • If your school and/or classroom is not de-tracked, what can you do to avoid the negative effects of tracking in your classroom? (290)

   • Are there classrooms in your school (including special education, bilingual, and English as a Second Language) that are substantially separate from others? Develop a plan to work with some of the teachers in those classrooms. (290)

   • Encourage parents and other community members to participate in committees in which disciplinary policies are discussed. (295)

   • Find out how standardized tests are used and how other criteria may be better employed. (291)

Multicultural Education: Framework and Concepts

CHAPTER 7

What Is Caring–Centered Multicultural Education?

CHAPTER OVERVIEW

This chapter includes a more extensive discussion of the framework and principles of Caring-Centered Multicultural Education. In addition, the discussion explains why having a strong educational philosophy is a must for teachers. From research in the classroom, four teachers are identified, their strengths and weaknesses.

One of my favorite educators is Herbert Kohl. Kohl is real; he knows kids. Kohl has been teaching for numerous years and has inspired many of us. In his book *I Won't Learn from You,* Kohl tells the story of when he was a kid and followed an old man in the neighborhood. Kohl was fascinated with the tattered and proud man who bought rags every week. One day, Kohl asked the man, "What are you selling?" The man turned to him with a twinkle in his eye and said, "Hope; I am selling hope."

Since this event, Kohl calls himself a hopemonger. This book is about hope, too, a hope in teachers and in students. The trusting relationships of care among teachers and students can create the foundation for a strong democracy. This chapter describes how the integration of the ethic of care, sociocultural theory of learning, and education for democracy form the framework for an orientation called Caring-Centered Multicultural Education. In order to share my beliefs, this chapter is devoted to answering the questions, What is Caring-Centered Multicultural Education? What are the main principles of this framework?

Moving from Multicultures to Caring–Centered Multicultural Education

Have you ever held a belief about something and then found out you were mistaken? Many years ago, I thought Multicultural Education was about presenting cultural information and having cultural fairs in schools. Just like the children in the comic strip, below, I had a limited understanding of culture and cultural differences.

When I read this comic, I chuckled to myself. Don't children come up with the most creative ways of looking at life? In the lesson, the teacher carefully describes that Canada is a multicultural nation with people from many different ethnic groups.

© *Lynn Johnston Productions, Inc., Distributed by United Feature Syndicate, Inc.*

When she asks her students about how the groups were the same, April comes up with an important insight. They all have belly buttons. April sees a physical sameness. She and all her classmates check out April's hypothesis; they all find their belly buttons.

As the teacher in the comic explained, the concept of multiculturalism is a complex one. I find the same situation when I ask teachers about Multicultural Education. The following are examples of what they've said:

> "It's about sharing culture. We, as teachers, should get kids to appreciate each other's culture."

> "It's about prejudice."

> "It's about good teaching."

> "Multicultural Education focuses mainly on kids who aren't doing well, and in many cases the kids may be African American, Cambodian, Mexican American, or from low-income groups."

> "Isn't culture an important aspect of Multicultural Education?"

Teachers have many ideas about Multicultural Education because it is a complex field of study. How would you answer the questions "What is Multicultural Education?" "What do you think the goals of Multicultural Education should be?"

In my teaching, I find that Multicultural Education is one of the most misused and misunderstood terms in education. Many teachers come into class thinking it is cross-cultural sharing of foods and traditions; however, those aspects make up only a small part of Multicultural Education. Other educators believe Multicultural Education is primarily about eliminating prejudice in students and school personnel. Some believe Multicultural Education is about using culture as a vehicle for instruction. However, in this book, Multicultural Education is seen as a field in education. The field calls for total school reform, where the achievement of children from low-income and/or underrepresented ethnic communities is at the same level as that of their majority middle-class peers.[1]

What Are Some Misconceptions about Multicultural Education?

As I explained previously, I find that people hold a variety of misconceptions about the field of Multicultural Education. Teachers may not have had opportunities to take a class or read materials about the discipline. A few teachers feel that misconceptions have developed because the field itself lacks agreement or a collaborative definition (Sheets and Fong 2003). Some misconceptions show that people do not have a clear understanding of the goals and principles of Multicultural Education.

---

[1]Multicultural Education is an academic discipline that holds a range of views from total school reform to curriculum infusion to societal change. For more information about the views of others in the field, I suggest reading the following authors: Banks 1981; Banks 2003; Bennett 1995; Cajete 1994; Gay 1994; Gollnick and Chin 1990; Moll 1990; Nieto 1992; Pang 1994; Sleeter 1996; Sleeter and Grant 1987; Yeo 1997.

Other misconceptions demonstrate that individuals are reluctant to examine their personal and professional values and actions for bias (with regard to areas such as culture, language, ethnicity, class, gender, disability, sexual orientation, religion, and age). Also some individuals are unwilling to change because change takes effort. Oftentimes this change requires people to give up long-held beliefs and views.

Read Table 7.1 and reflect upon the many misconceptions some people hold about the field. Do you hold any of them?

People hold other misconceptions about the field. Those discussed previously are some of the more common myths that serve as barriers to understanding what

TABLE 7.1   Misconceptions

Misconceptions about Multicultural Education	Underlying Beliefs of Multicultural Education
Multicultural Education emphasizes separatism and causes divisiveness.	Multicultural Education builds upon national values of equity and diversity: Unity amidst diversity; *E pluribus Unum.*
Multicultural Education creates reverse discrimination.	One of the major goals of Multicultural Education is to eliminate racism and other forms of social oppression found in schools.
Multicultural Education seeks to replace U.S. culture with the cultures of ethnic groups.	People from many communities, including African Americans, Asian Pacific Americans, Latinos, and Native Americans, are a part of, have contributed to, and continue to contribute to the development and success of this nation.
Multicultural Education is only for schools with high numbers of ethnic minority students or schools with racial tension.	Multicultural Education is a field in education that is dedicated to equal opportunity for all students. Even groups who appear to be monocultural are diverse in regards to class, gender, and language.
Multicultural Education seeks to replace current school curriculum with Afrocentric curriculum that opposes the dominant society.	Multicultural Education seeks total school reform so that all aspects of schools reflect our national diversity. Schools will be effective for all students. Curriculum includes lived experiences of students from underrepresented groups.
Multicultural Education encourages lower standards for students from underrepresented groups.	Multicultural Education seeks to eliminate the achievement gap between majority students and those from underrepresented communities by creating more effective schools. Standards will be raised in the process. Equity and excellence are interwoven.
Multicultural Education is about food fairs, ethnic costumes, and cultural traditions.	Multicultural Education is a field in education that calls for total school reform and is built on the integration of caring, culture, and a socially just community.

Multicultural Education is really about. The next section discusses one of the lasting myths about many students from underrepresented communities that can lead to low teacher expectations.

Cultural Deficit, Cultural Difference, and Cultural Congruence Perspectives

One of the most damaging beliefs that many teachers, parents, and others hold is a **cultural deficit** orientation about students of color or young people from lower-economic families. People with this perspective view students from underrepresented groups as coming from inferior communities. When students of color do not do well on standardized tests or in mainstream classrooms, some teachers label the culture of students' families as being disadvantaged. The blame for student failure is placed on children and/or their families and cultures. Some teachers blame students because they come to school speaking another language like Spanish or Cantonese. Other teachers complain that the culture children bring to school does not value education; it is as if school personnel held little responsibility for low grades and low standardized tests scores of students of color or students from lower-income communities.

In contrast, other educators accept the cultural difference viewpoint. They believe that students may come from ethnic communities that have knowledge and values that differ from mainstream society. Some students who bring diverse worldviews may experience conflict with school culture. For instance, when Hmong refugees came to the United States from Laos during the Vietnam War, many had a preliterate tradition. Most did not have any formal schooling. Consequently, when young Hmong students went to school, they did not know what to expect nor did they know what was expected of them, and there were many cultural clashes. Hmong young people were expected to know how to sew, grow crops, and take care of their families. They did not know about school bells or homework. Parents were reticent to participate in school programs because they did not understand their purposes. Also parents believed they did not have the professional training needed to help their children. They respected teachers and relied on them to do the best for their children. This did not mean that Hmong parents were ignorant. Rather, they brought different skills to this country. For example, Hmong families brought a strong sense of community. In fact, Hmong children are taught collective responsibility; the needs of the family are more important than the needs of individual members.

King (1994) believes that the cultural difference theory still calls for the resocialization of students of color, especially African American youth, to mainstream culture because school personnel have not changed their value orientation. The knowledge and processes currently used still emulate mainstream society. King carefully explains that because mainstream society (including social institutions like schools) has continually oppressed African Americans, schools must be transformed from organizations of oppression to institutions of liberation. The entire system of education should be reorganized so that it challenges the status quo and calls for emancipation of the minds of all students. The inclusion of African American cultural knowledge would give all students a sense of presence of the African American community.

In collaboration with King, Au and Kawakami (1994) agree that schools should strive to be **culturally congruent,** also known as **culturally responsive;** however, their view is less political in orientation. Although they do not believe that schools must imitate the home setting of students, they do feel that schools must integrate knowledge and practices from students' home cultures. Au and Kawakami (1994) give the example of using communication styles in the classroom that may be more familiar to students. Their research has focused on young people in Hawaii. Many Hawaiian students were quiet and did not participate in discussions. However, when the teachers saw the children in other contexts, they were playful, laughing, and spontaneous. Why weren't they talking in class?

Au and Mason (1981) realized that there was more than one reason that students were not naturally participating. Because the researchers believed that learning occurred in socially constructed activities, as Vygotsky posed, they looked at how the social context impacted the reading process and researched the Hawaiian cultural practice called *talk story* (Au 1980). As part of the reading comprehension instruction, one of the teachers used a more culturally congruent practice that allowed for spontaneous responses. This teacher did not use the mainstream practice of calling on each student as a way of being fair. Au and Mason realized that student responses were more on task and logical when the teacher used the talk story format of discussion. Why did this happen? When students worked collaboratively, they built on each other's responses. The social and cultural context of learning encouraged them to work together. In this instance the social interaction practice that the teacher used built on what students already were comfortable with and encouraged them to participate more fully. It is critical for teachers to have knowledge of students' culture, and I believe Vygotsky's sociocultural theory of learning explains how culture impacts human development. The next section explains why it is important for teachers to know theories like Vygotsky's and to adopt their own educational framework.

> ᔕ *One of the most damaging beliefs that many teachers, parents, and others hold is a cultural deficit orientation about a student, any student.*

Adopting an Educational Framework: Why Is It Important?

Have you ever wondered why you are asked to study theory? You aren't the only one who may question why theory is taught in education classes.

Here are some typical comments that I have heard from preservice and practicing teachers:

"I don't have time to read about theory. It doesn't tell me what to do in the classroom."

"Get real. I teach 185 middle-school students. Don't waste my time with that stuff."

"I need ideas and activities for the classroom! Forget the theory. It doesn't help!"

You might want to reconsider throwing out theory and research. Have you chosen a belief system to guide your life? Many people have chosen a philosophy, religious dogma, or set of ethical principles to help direct their actions. These belief systems provide direction and rationale for people's actions. When individuals hold philosophies, they use them to guide them in making difficult decisions.

I encourage you to adopt an educational framework based on your beliefs and research. In today's schools, many forces continually push and pull at teachers. There are district, state, and national standards. There are subject area standards for social studies, mathematics, reading, language arts, science, physical education, character education, history, and literacy. There are district, state, and national standardized tests. There are accreditation requirements. Voucher issues are being studied. Small school forces are trying to be heard. Forces from the right and left of the political spectrum are petitioning school boards for change. Teacher unions are pushing for changes in the curriculum, and administrators are pushing for more accountability. How will teachers know which position to take on issues? It is sometimes overwhelming to make decisions about the many issues teachers face. How are teachers going to be able to sort through these important concerns? As a first grade teacher, I had made a moral commitment to do my best to teach Rosemary and her classmates and to develop their skills as a community of learners in the classroom. These values acted as a rudder that directed me to look at my own prejudices and to encourage compassion between students. Teachers need to have a system of beliefs that they have consciously decided on before they can address the issues that face them. That is where theory and an educational framework come in. If teachers have not chosen a strong framework, they will be more easily blown off the path. They may never reach their selected destination because they did not have a strong rudder to keep them on course.

What do you value as a teacher? What do you think are the most important goals in schooling? A strong framework is built upon the answers you give to these questions and assists you in choosing a philosophy. I believe in a Caring-Centered Multicultural Education framework because it integrates the beliefs of caring, culture, and community. The three themes form an integrated whole that focuses upon the importance of caring and trusting relationships, affirming and building on student culture, and creating a respectful and just community. For me, the caring-centered foundation acts as a rudder so that no matter how powerful the winds are, the framework keeps me on course. The next several sections extend the discussion about Caring-Centered Multicultural Education.

Caring–Centered Multicultural Education: Equity in Education

As the preceding section discusses, teachers must examine their misconceptions about students from underrepresented groups because Multicultural Education is far more than an acknowledgment of cultures and cultural differences. Sometimes teachers struggle with "how to teach multiculturally" and feel that there are few practical models in the field to follow (Sheets and Fong 2003). However, this is one of the strengths of Caring-Centered Multicultural Education. The framework integrates the theories, research, and practice that arise from the classroom. The philosophy celebrates the

A learning community

importance of education and the development of citizens who care for others and work collaboratively to fight for the creation of a compassionate and equitable society. This chapter extends the discussion of the framework from Chapter 1. How does Caring-Centered Multicultural Education differ from a general view of the field?

A caring-centered approach to Multicultural Education is built on the importance of developing trusting relationships and understanding the sociocultural context of learning. It is a relationship-centered and culture-centered framework in education. One of the key principles of the field is its holistic perspective. Teaching is seen not only within the development of the whole person, but also as a comprehensive process. Teaching is an art; it is not made up of many isolated skills. Rather, teaching is a complex combination of skills, knowledge, and beliefs that work in sync to create an environment that encourages maximum growth in the student and the teacher. The underlying premise is that conditions of caring, community, and culture in classrooms produce higher levels of achievement that lead to greater social efficacy. This more effective learning community empowers and prepares all students to work toward social, political, and economic justice.

Why Care Theory?

The caring-centered philosophical framework builds on the work of Carl Rogers and Jerome Freiberg (1994). They believed that the development of strong, caring relationships was key to a foundation for humanistic schools. Elements that they identified were teacher empathy, positive school climate, and trusting relationships; they believed that these characteristics fostered effective learning environments where students developed high self-esteem, confidence, and commitment to personal growth. In addition, other scholars have presented caring as a fundamental human capacity that translates into a coherent pattern of interpersonal behaviors rather than a romantic notion or sentimentality (Chaskin and Rauner 1995; Gilligan 1982; Ianni 1996; Noddings 1984, 1992). Care represents an educational orientation that stresses the creation of trusting relationships as the foundation for building an effective academic and social climate for schooling (Chaskin and Rauner 1995; Eaker-Rich and Van Galen 1996; Erickson 1993).

One of the most important contributors to care theory is Nel Noddings (1984, 1992). Noddings believes education is based on a moral purpose and should produce individuals who are ethical (Noddings 1992). She writes, "We should educate all our children not only for competence but also for caring. Our aim should be to encourage the growth of competent, caring, loving, and lovable people" (Noddings 1992, xiv). When teachers operate from the ethic of care, they consciously make a moral commitment to care for and teach students and to develop reciprocal relationships with them. These teachers create schools that are centers of care.

In these schools, students, teachers, and parents form a community where relationships are at the heart of school, and where the curriculum and policies focus on compassion, respect, and community building. Students are also encouraged to care for ideas, plants, nonhuman animals, distant others, and the self. In this way the care theory is a holistic orientation toward education with themes of care woven throughout the curriculum. Care theory is not only about teaching knowledge; the perspective also focuses on the whole student within an empowering and compassionate environment. Teachers consider the development of the whole person, whether in a math class, English class, or government class.

Noddings sees the care theory as an alternative approach in education. She raises the critical questions, "If we were to start from scratch and founded schools on care, what would they look like?" and "What kind of schools do you want for your children?" Noddings reminds us that probably schools would be very different if we could build them from the beginning. The way that we might structure our schools would, in part, depend on our definition of caring.

One of the most powerful discussions that I have found about caring was written by Noblit, Rogers, and McCadden (1995). They defined caring as a belief that may not be visible in an educational environment; however, it is integral to the structure and relationships built in schools and classrooms. They wrote:

> Morally and culturally, caring is a belief about how we should view and interact with others. In this way, caring is essential to education and may guide the ways we instruct and discipline students, set policy, and organize the school day . . . Caring in our schools lies hidden beneath the technical and instrumental ways of viewing culture and schooling . . . [Although] more technical aspects of teaching dominate our thinking . . . Caring gives priority to relationships" (Noblit, Rogers, and McCadden 1995, 680–81).

When teachers care for students, they want to know about their experiences and backgrounds. The next section moves to a discussion of Vygotsky's sociocultural theory of learning and how culture plays a powerful role in learning.

Sociocultural Theory of Cognitive Development

> ✍ "*Caring in our schools lies hidden beneath the technical and instrumental ways of viewing culture and schooling . . . [Although] more technical aspects of teaching dominate our thinking . . . Caring gives priority to relationships.*"
> —NOBLIT, ROGERS, AND MCCADDEN, 1995, 680–81.

Vygotsky saw learning embedded in sociocultural activity (Moll 1990; Cole 1996). How do we learn? We learn within social and cultural contexts as we interact with other people, ideas, and objects in our lives. He saw speech as key to our intellectual growth. Have you watched a baby coo or babble? The baby is developing her language as she interacts with her environment (Elliott, Kratochwill, Littlefield, Cook, and Travers 2000).

Michael Cole, who has studied Vygotsky's work extensively, discusses why language is one of the most important tools we use in learning. He explains that we use cultural "tools" like language and cultural expectations to mold, shape, and filter what we think. Cole believes that tools such as language, ideas, customs, behaviors, and practices act as cultural negotiators for us and shape our learning.

Learning is also historical. Many people have come before us and our cultural knowledge is built upon what they did in their lives and taught us (Cole 1996). Culture is accumulated over time and handed down from generation to generation over many years, parent to child. Because people change, culture is also changing and continually being reconstructed.

Through the many sociocultural interactions we have, we learn. Sometimes our learning comes from inner reflection and other times it comes from working with people or ideas or objects. Some teachers create powerful communities of learners, where individuals work together, giving those who participate more opportunities to learn from each other. The discussions and nonverbal communications that pass between people convey ideas and concepts. In addition, there is a social process that may be formal, casual, or spontaneous; this social context also impacts learning. When we bring different cultural experiences and viewpoints to the discussion, we can enhance our own learning and the growth of others. Cole (1996) suggests that cross-cultural teaching is like a bridge: "I would choose a bridging program in which traffic on the bridge moved in both directions . . . the bridge is a medium for two way exchange . . ." (Cole 1998, 3). We live in a diverse society and the diversity of our students can enrich our schools. When there is reciprocal sharing of perspectives, information, ideas, and practices, learning will be expanded.

Let me give an example. When a fourth-generation Japanese American 10th grader shared her family tree project, the other students learned about how the young girl's grandmother had been placed in a concentration camp in Idaho. Her peers were surprised to learn that the U.S. government took their own citizens who were of Japanese ancestry away from their homes to desolate camps in desert areas in such states as Idaho, Wyoming, and California. The student's grandmother had never been to Japan and was born in the state of Washington. Classmates of the young girl had the opportunity to learn in a personal way how history involves people they know. The granddaughter provided a bridge for other students to better understand the experience of the Japanese American community. This discussion added to the social-cultural knowledge of the classroom. In addition, sharing was beneficial to the Japanese American student, because the class asked her grandmother to talk to them. She learned more about what her grandmother went through as a result of her grandmother's presentation to her classmates.

Vygotsky's sociocultural theory of development recommends that teachers utilize cultural knowledge, carefully developed social interactions, and activities to heighten learning. Research by Cole, Moll, Au, Gonzalez, Brice Heath, Moses, and many others demonstrate that students can learn more effectively using a comprehensive orientation toward curriculum and instruction that simultaneously uses cultural knowledge, cues, social interaction patterns, and cultural models from the lives of students. Later, in Chapter 10, I describe three excellent programs utilizing culturally relevant teaching. They are the Algebra Project, Funds of Knowledge, and Organic Reading and Writing. All three programs use a holistic approach. They have a powerful value orientation upon which the curricula are built.

It is also not possible to use culturally relevant teaching without addressing the issue of institutional oppression. As King (1994) reminds us, some children come from cultural communities that face continual and historical social oppression. Oppressive practices are also cultural tools that people utilize in their lives. As this book has presented, prejudice, personal and institutional, hampers our ability to reach all students. Stereotypical cultural knowledge that we hold about others must be purged from our minds, but it may take numerous sessions of self-reflection and continual interactions with people who appear to be different from us to assist us in realizing the fallacies of our beliefs and to find common ground with others. In this way, those who assist us in better understanding our own misconceptions are extending our zone of proximal development. Vygotsky theorized that the zone of learning can be increased when teachers use effective strategies and materials to guide student learning beyond what a person could learn on their own. Chapter 10 discusses this phenomenon more fully.

Education for Democracy

Another important set of beliefs is education for democracy (Dewey 1916, 1938; Noddings 1995; Freire 1970; Gay 1994). The Caring-Centered Multicultural Education framework emphasizes the importance of developing individuals who will actively challenge inequities in order to create a socially just society. Education for democracy is student centered and it facilitates higher-order-thinking analysis skills in students so that they will examine racial inequities, class struggles, and gender discrimination (Dewey 1916; Freire 1970; Darder 1991; Banks 1995; Gibson 1999).

Schools should be places of activity where people work on common problems and establish rules collaboratively (Noddings 1995). Education for democracy focuses on teaching students how to analyze power relationships and build collaborative communities; it also encourages social communication skills. The result is that schools become places where students are actively involved in the process of democracy.

> Dewey did not look at democracy merely as a system of government in which everyone votes and majority prevails. For Dewey, democracy was a mode of associated living, and decisions were made by a shared process of inquiry . . . Democracy . . . is not a state; it is more a process, and its rules must be under continual scrutiny, revision, and creation (Noddings 1995, 35).

At the base of education for democracy is the value of social justice.

One of our country's strongest values is justice. Social justice as a part of education for democracy works in tandem with the ethic of caring because both orientations hold the values of mutual respect and community at the center. What is social justice? It can be viewed in many ways; however, I see it as a value in which individuals look to the common good. This common good is defined by discussions people have with each other and through reflection on the needs of our members from different groups (Bellah, Madsen, Sullivan, Swidler, and Tipton 1985). It is not easy to define common good. What is common? Toward what good are we striving? A discussion of this would be a book itself. However, for this framework, social justice refers to the values of fairness and equality. Bellah and his colleagues found in their interviews of U.S. Americans across the country that justice is often seen "as a matter of equal opportunities for every individual to pursue . . . Equal opportunities are guaranteed by fair laws and political procedures . . . applied in the same way to everyone" (Bellah et al. 1985, 26). Coupled with this view is the importance of equity. Gordon (1999) calls for schools to provide for both equal access and equity, which he says refers to addressing specific needs of students from nonmajority communities in order for them to reach the same levels of achievement as other students.

Our national value of social justice has given rise to the call for civil rights, which has led to the call for equal education of all students. Therefore, social justice directs us as a society to do all we can to effectively teach students. Unfortunately, research has shown that students from underrepresented groups do not have the same opportunities or outcomes in our schools (Banks 1995; Bennett 1995; Cajete 1994; Gay 1996; Irvine 1990; Moll 1990; Oakes 1985; Ovando and Collier 2000; Pang and Cheng 1998). This issue led to the development of the field of Multicultural Education (Banks 1995). Because teachers who care are concerned when their students aren't successful, they work tirelessly to restructure schools. In fact, many teachers believe that the extensive work they do with students is part of their social activism. At the heart of the caring-centered framework is caring within a social justice context. As James Banks (1981, 1995) has indicated, Multicultural Education as a field in education refers to a call for total school reform. The Caring-Centered Multicultural Education framework describes the philosophical base for the reform and paradigm change.

Take a Stand

EDUCATIONAL PHILOSOPHY AND THEORIES

Many teachers do not think that educational theories or philosophies are important. However, others believe it is imperative to choose a strong philosophical orientation that will direct and guide them through the political changes that often pressure teachers. Teachers should consider the following questions:

- Is it important to thoughtfully choose an educational philosophy or theory to guide one's teaching? Why or why not?
- If you consider it vital, which theories and/or philosophical orientation exemplify your beliefs?

Teachers reflecting on the linkages between social justice and school reform

Caring–Centered Multicultural Education: A Definition

Now that you have read about the ethic of caring, education for democracy, and cultural theories of learning, how would you define Caring-Centered Multicultural Education? Building on the previous discussions, I offer the following definition:

> **Multicultural Education** is a field in education that calls for total school reform and is based on the belief that education is an intellectual and ethical endeavor. The field seeks to develop happy, creative, ethical, and fulfilled persons who work toward a more compassionate and just society. Students are also encouraged to develop vital decision-making and intercultural communication skills. Multicultural Education, as part of a life-giving process of growth and joy, focuses on teaching the whole student with the goal of academic excellence and developing the potential of each student by integrating three critical belief systems: the care theory, education for democracy, and the sociocultural context of human growth and development.

What does this mean in the life of a student? Let me ask you: Who was your favorite teacher? What did the teacher do? How did the teacher treat you?

When I ask these questions of teachers in my classes, they say:

"She was a teacher who believed in me even when I didn't believe in myself."

"He understood my fears and helped me to see that I could do the math problems and that it wasn't my X chromosomes that held me back."

"She knew there was a lot of racism in the school from all the kids, Black, Asian, Latino, White. She wouldn't let other teachers shove it under the rug, but she also wouldn't let us use it as an excuse not to be the best we could be. She pushed us hard to do our work."

"I came from a poor part of town. I thought my teacher wouldn't like me because of that, but instead he wanted me to write about my life, like the problems I was having paying the rent and finding a job after school. I knew he cared."

These comments show that their favorite teachers believed in them and showed they cared. There was a shared relationship of trust between teachers and their students. Teachers expected them to do their work and supported them. Their favorite teachers accepted them for whoever they were and valued the contributions each student brought to the classroom. When students strongly identified with a culture or a language other than English, teachers saw these elements as enriching and celebrated them. Through an atmosphere of respect, caring, and community, teachers and students developed bonds of trust, and they also shared values of fairness and equality. Students and teachers knew that people were prejudiced, and they dealt with discrimination and biased attitudes as part of their writing assignments and class discussions. Life was part of the learning process. These teachers considered the needs of the whole student.

What else can teachers do to create strong relationships with students? They can develop bonds of connection and communication. Teachers may listen carefully to their students, and may also see themselves as members of the same community. For example, teachers may buy their groceries at the local supermarket. They may also go to the neighborhood church. Sometimes teachers attend local community festivals. They may also hold parenting classes in Spanish or Vietnamese. Educators who develop lasting bonds get to know parents and view parents as critical partners. Both parents and teachers may run a Saturday school where students may be part of math, science, or literacy clubs.

I believe what sets exceptional teachers apart from others is that these **star teachers** (Martin Haberman's (1995) term for exceptional urban teachers) understand their students. They know that their most effective teaching will occur when they build relationships of trust with their students and keep trying until they find instructional strategies that work so that their students achieve academic excellence. Both teachers and students are responsible that learning occurs; learning is a reciprocal responsibility. Teachers never give up on their students or themselves (Haberman 1995) and students also believe in and have faith in their teachers.

The teachers just described have made a moral commitment to care. I imagine the following self-talk:

"I'm going to make a difference in the lives of my students."

"I believe in every child, no matter what their color is or how much money their families have."

"I know there are many inequities in school and society, but those obstacles will not keep me from finding ways to reach my students."

Teachers who make that important difference in schools have made a conscious choice to provide the most effective and motivating learning environment they possibly can.

> Ⓢ A star teacher makes a moral commitment to care for each student.

This commitment is not an easy choice. Jonathan Kozol, in his book *Savage Inequalities* writes about the terrible conditions some students and teachers endure in schools. These schools are primarily found in inner cities. The bathrooms don't work, the ceilings are falling down, and it is so cold in the winter that students and teachers can see their own breath. Educators fought to make changes in schools so that children had textbooks; they painted the classroom walls, and they prevented drug dealers from hanging around schools. They were star teachers.

Star teachers not only care for students, but they are aware of the life experiences of their students, including cultural background, language needs, economic hardships, personal struggles, and community issues. These teachers see inequities in schools and society that hamper the education of students; however, these inequities are not used as excuses for not learning. Rather, teachers work to rid their classrooms and schools of the ugliness brought about by racism, sexism, classism, and homophobia. They listen to their students and integrate the students' own lives—knowledge, experience, and culture—into the curriculum. They also respect their students and believe they can learn; teachers present students with challenges and hold high expectations in the learning process. Students are given opportunities to learn and, in this way, they understand that learning is a reciprocal responsibility.

Teachers know that students can learn and hold high expectations for them. Students are not enabled; rather, they are supported and held accountable for their own learning (Pidgeon 1998). Learning is a two-way responsibility. Teachers must care enough to provide effective, interesting, and well-developed learning experiences, and reciprocally students must study and work hard in order to become successful in their learning. Teachers know that they cannot take away the struggle that comes when learning is difficult; however, star teachers assist their students as they work through these hard times. They do not give up on their students. These teachers offer support by using strategies such as offering extra tutoring times after school or providing additional study materials.

Star teachers find ways to reach students so that they are successful in school. For example, a teacher may demonstrate a chemical process using three different modes of learning to ensure that students who do not do well with a self-inquiry method will understand the operation: First, the teacher uses a large colorful poster that explains the chemical process; second, the teacher shows students on computers a three-dimensional visualization of the molecules for those students who need spatial pictures; and third, the teacher conducts the experiment and explains the process as she demonstrates it. Then students conduct the experiment themselves. Some students are able to extrapolate the scientific principles of an experiment using the scientific method and with minimal direction. Other students may need different organizers in order to understand what is occurring. When teachers provide numerous ways to view the chemical process through drawings, computer-generated models, and teacher demonstrations/explanations, students can develop a clearer understanding of the chemical principles being taught.

This book is founded on a model that centers on the care theory, education for democracy with a strong social justice core, and the sociocultural context of human development and learning. As Figure 7.1 shows, all three elements are key building blocks. The ethic of caring, which forms the base for Caring-Centered Multicultural Education, is interwoven with education for democracy and the sociocultural context of human development and learning to form the foundation for the framework.

Caring-Centered Multicultural Education is based upon three important beliefs:

- Many of us care about children.
- Every child possesses an innate desire to learn.
- Education should reflect a life-giving pedagogy. (Rivera and Poplin 1995)

Schooling is not only a life-giving process of growth, but it builds upon children's innate wonder of the world. They are excited learners who achieve and find joy in learning. Like the chick in the next comic, schooling breaks out of a rigid and monocultural shell and becomes a positive life force in which teachers and students care for each other and work toward a just and caring society.

In the context of this book, the chick also represents the transformation of a child when she or he learns. When a child learns, she is not a passive being but becomes an empowered being who thinks, questions, and creates in a democracy. The chick can also symbolize us as teachers. We become transformed when we make a paradigm shift from a teacher-centered, monocultural classroom toward a student- and caring-centered orientation about teaching. We understand that teaching

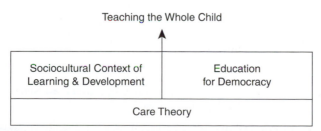

Figure 7.1   *Framework for Caring-Centered Multicultural Education*

FRANK & ERNEST reprinted by permission of Newspaper Enterprise Association, Inc.

is about breathing life into our classrooms, and learning is an exciting process of personal and communal growth. This process may not be an easy one. As Merry Merryfield explains in the next section, there are many challenges when a teacher finds herself teaching students whose cultural values are extremely different from U.S. mainstream culture.

Teacher Voices about Cultural Mediation: Merry Merryfield, Talks about Working with Somali Students

In the next section Merry Merryfield shares information about working with Somali refugees in Ohio. She is a professor at Ohio State University and lives in Columbus, Ohio, where many immigrants are from Somalia. She became a cultural mediator. Merryfield builds bridges of communication between teachers and their students from Somali. She provides a context and understanding of all three levels of culture: surface elements, interactional patterns, and underlying beliefs and values.

The experiences of many Somali students may differ from those of other refugees because many Somali children have had little formal experience in schools. A great number of people also arrived in the United States without formal documents because many families fled from their homes with few material possessions. This posed various problems in registering students for school. They did come with **cultural capital** or knowledge of their own country and culture; however, the frame of reference of Somali students was extremely different from that of their teachers. Their differing worldviews resulted in **cultural conflict,** mistrust, and the creation of misconceptions about each other. The next section provides information on cultural clashes that Somali refugee students may encounter in schools. You may find the information helpful in understanding how one group of people's worldview can differ from that of another community.

Cultural Clash Somali Refugee Students Face in American Schools: Questions and Answers with Merry Merryfield

Valerie Ooka Pang (VOP): Why is it so difficult for Somali parents to register their children for school?

Merry Merryfield (MM): Somali experiences often clash with American expectations. Many Somalis have lived in refugee camps for many years and do not have documents like birth certificates or records of inoculations. Birthdates were not important for most of these people when they lived in Somalia and what records existed probably were destroyed in the war. Yet those dates have to be written on countless forms that school districts require. Their lack of forms may raise suspicions. Most use January 1 for birthdates or just pull a date out of the air. They do know the year that their children were born. However, because of the trauma youngsters have been through, the children may look younger than they are, so school officials may be skeptical about the information that parents provide.

Somalis also interpret family and family members in a different way from what American schools expect. When Somalis talk about their families, they mean brothers, sisters, grandparents, uncles, aunts, first, second, even third cousins, and possibly children from more than one wife (Muslims can have up to four wives). A great uncle's grandchild is a family member. U.S. school officials may see Somalis as purposefully deceptive when they claim a boy or girl as a family member who in U.S. terms is a distant relative. In Somalia, it is the norm for families to send a child to live with a relative in another town or even country if that family member is better off or has readier access to good schools. People accept this obligation as part of their caring about their family. When these children are brought into an American school, such caring behavior may be looked upon as illegal.

VOP: Since many Somali refugees come here without formal schooling, what problems might that pose to teachers?

MM: Somalis often don't fit the norms of other immigrants teachers are used to working with. They lack the documentation. They don't have school records to show. Many school officials and teachers have had no experience with people who are illiterate in their first language.

Let me give you an example of how complex some of the problems are for young people. Think of a 14-year-old Somali boy who lost his father and three other relatives in the war. He literally grew up in a refugee camp in Kenya and every day his mother and six siblings had to work at simply surviving. He had never seen a school or even written his name when he arrived in the United States. When enrolled in school, he is placed in the ninth grade and given an hour or two a day of ESL work with a teacher who is unqualified as the demand for ESL teachers has outstripped the supply. The rest of his day he sits in social studies, science, math classes with 30 to 35 other students. Here we have a young man who does not know what the appropriate behaviors are in a classroom, cannot communicate with the teacher or his peers, and cannot read in any language. He has never read a book and does not understand the mechanisms of a written language. He has never had homework. He has not been in settings where he is expected to sit quietly for long periods of time. In order for this young man to be successful in school, he will need to learn much more than conversational English. And he is expected to pass high-stakes tests in math, science, social studies, and English within three years.

VOP: Since many Somalis are Muslims, immigrants, and Black, has prejudice increased since the events of September 11, 2001?

Since 9-11 I do see more prejudice toward Somalis, especially girls and women who can readily be identified as Muslim because of their dress. Before 9-11 the Somalis were often seen as just another immigrant group entering the schools along with Latinos, Asians, and others. Then after 9-11 people became more aware they are Muslim, and there were rumors that money Somalis were making here was being sent to fund terrorism. I know of teachers who have taken out their rage about 9-11 by verbally attacking Somalis. An elementary teacher told two little Somali girls in front of their class, *"You are the enemy."*

VOP: What cultural clashes do Somali girls have in American schools because they are Muslim?

MM: Most Somali girls are taught not to look directly at or be in direct contact with males, yet male teachers without knowledge of these norms often interpret their behavior as slow, inattentive, or resisting. Recently a principal shook hands with all students, including some Somalis, who had won awards in a local school. Yet many Somali girls would never shake a man's hand. In this school the principal understood Somali norms and was prepared for the girls' not taking his hand.

Somali girls must cover their bodies, and many families have their daughters cover their hair as puberty arrives. Yet some physical education teachers have been known to lower their grades when they break the dress codes which require them to wear shorts.

Most Somali girls don't date or participate in activities with boys after school. They may even leave school to get married. They also have arranged marriages, which are difficult for Americans to understand.

VOP: What conflicts do males have with women teachers in U.S. schools?

MM: Somali boys are used to men in roles of authority, and they may feel uncomfortable with female teachers.

VOP: There are reports that Somalis and African Americans may have conflicts. What are sources of those conflicts?

MM: Sometimes Americans of all backgrounds do not recognize the power of cultural, linguistic, and experiential distinctions. Just because they have African ancestry does not mean African Americans necessarily understand or empathize with Somalis. African Americans can have the same stereotypes and misinformation about Somalis as any other American since American schools in general do a poor job of teaching about Africans in the K–12 curriculum. Racism certainly affects Somalis as well as other people of color in the United States.

VOP: What are some of the most serious problems in schools?

MM: The most serious problems, however, stem from language. Most Somali students enter American classrooms with no previous school experience and without literacy in their own language. Yet they are expected to become competent in English and even take statewide high-stakes proficiency tests within a few years. Since many Somali students fail these exams due to limited English proficiency, many schools perceive Somalis as a liability, damaging their reputations and endangering their academic status. Amazingly, some Somalis overcome all these hardships and succeed, complete high school and go on to college.

VOP: Any closing suggestions for teachers of Somali students?

MM: Find out about Somali-led organizations in your community and refugee organizations that provide them services. In Columbus, materials developed by the city to help employers be sensitive to the needs of Somali employees have been also quite useful to teachers. Get your district to hold workshops with Somalis who are knowledgeable about issues in the schools and the needs of the Somali community. Read about Islam and its influence on students' behavior and needs. Read books by Somali authors as many are published in English. Network with teachers in Columbus, Ohio, and Minneapolis, Minnesota, two centers of Somali resettlement, who are experienced in working with Somali students.

This question and answer segment presented an example of how people who come from another country may bring to the United States a different worldview. In order to provide equal educational opportunities to all students, teachers must consider how culture shapes the way students, parents, and teachers interpret the world. A caring teacher is committed to equity in education and is someone who can make connections with students from other cultures. A cultural mediator acts as a bridge from the home culture to the school culture. In this process, the students learn new cultural practices from their teachers, while the teacher also is learning from her students. The teacher does not force students into cultural assimilation, but rather encourages biculturalism. She knows that new students benefit from a strong grounding within their home culture, and at the same time must learn new behaviors and beliefs of their new country in order to become successful. This teacher also understands that students may feel a tremendous loss of culture and a strong pressure from peers and school personnel to conform and fit into the mainstream.

To create an affirming classroom where culturally diverse students continue to be grounded in their home culture and are empowered to participate in mainstream society is challenging. However, teachers who hold both values of caring and social justice are dedicated to do so. A more complex discussion of equity and care in schools is presented in the next section.

Social Justice and Care Theory: Can We Have One without the Other?

In the past 10 years, there has been a much-heated debate about Multicultural Education, most of which has been political. The conservative camp claims that Multicultural Education is divisive and un-American, while liberals claim that Multicultural Education can ensure equality in our schools. Unfortunately, the discussion often has been diverted from the needs of our students and into the realm of political debate. This clouds the field's most important goal of all students' achieving academic excellence. Our main focus must be to close the achievement gap between children from low-income and/or culturally diverse communities and their majority peers.

Caring and social justice in a democracy are intimately connected. When we care, we act. Our laws, policies, politics, and methods for achieving social justice flow directly from what we care about and are committed to in society. Bell Hooks reminds us, "The civil rights movement was such a wonderful movement for social justice because the heart of it was love—loving everyone." (Hooks 2000, 36). Caring is more fundamental than justice, fairness, and equity. When we care about another person, we find ways to treat that person justly, fairly, and equitably. But the reverse is not always the case; one can value justice, fairness, and equity without truly caring or doing things to make life better for others.

Let's look at laws and schooling. Laws do not explain how to accomplish directives in education. For example, using Supreme Court decisions like *Brown* v. *Board of Education* or *Lau* v. *Nichols* and civil rights legislation as the foundational principles for an educational field is misguided and leads the field to an educational dead end. Why? Congress and judges recognize that their job is to make and interpret laws rather than to teach educators how to bring compassion, equity, trust, and effective teaching methods to the classroom (Valle 1997).

Policies and the law are representative of our core values; they are merely the context and tools for expressing and manifesting our values and goals from which we work to show caring and to improve society. I have seen that policies and the law can, by themselves, have only a limited influence on learning. Laws and policies do not change the real core of schools; people do. Caring is that important link between fair laws and effective policies within education.

Caring is a powerful force behind true political and legal reform, both from the right and the left. The ethic of caring is the essential foundation for Multicultural Education and a central element of our commitment to students; this commitment motivates people to rid schools of prejudice and discrimination. Caring also inspires us at a personal level to incorporate in our daily outward actions culturally relevant practices that make schools more meaningful, effective, and equitable. Caring teachers are willing to tackle painful inequities in schools and take hard looks at their own beliefs because they have made an ethical commitment to our children to make schools more relevant and effective for all kids. Unfortunately, schools are too often a reflection of a society in which people are oppressed because of their race, class, gender, sexual orientation, language, and other differences.

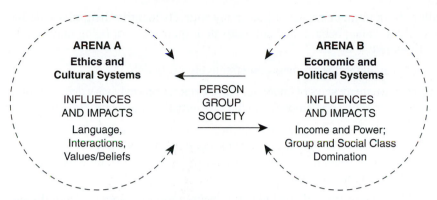

Figure 7.2   *Arenas of Multicultural Interaction and Impact*
Source: Valle, 1997

Valle (1997) has created a diagram that explains the two major arenas in society that should be considered: cultural and political. His first arena is made up of ethnic and cultural systems. His second arena, made up of economic and political systems, includes social class, income levels, social status, and political status. From one generation to the next, the values, language, attitudes, and beliefs of cultural groups are transmitted to their members. The interaction of both arenas, culture/ethnic systems and economic/political systems, impacts the way individuals and groups respond to each other. Figure 7.2 may help you to better understand that both dimensions are important in understanding how different social forces impact what people think, do, and value.

Both arenas A and B are essential components to Caring-Centered Multicultural Education framework. The principles of the philosophy are based on the integration of both.

Fundamental Beliefs of Caring–Centered Multicultural Education

I have discussed the importance of caring in depth. What does caring mean in the classroom and in school? The following are underlying beliefs about caring in teaching and learning:

- Relationships are reciprocal and built on trust.

- Trusting relationships form the basis and context for teaching and learning.

- Teachers and students feel an interconnection with each other. Each is concerned with the well-being of the other, and within this context a community of learners is created.

- Intellectual development is seen through diverse lenses and stimulated through diverse methods.

- Culture is an intimate aspect of how many students identify themselves, define themselves, value, behave, and are motivated; their sense of being may be culturally rooted.

- Culture is an asset that teachers can effectively build on.

- Students have many ways of knowing. These orientations may vary due to culture, diverse experiences, and emphasis on literary, artistic, or scientific traditions.

- Caring for others can lead to social justice. We want fairness for those we care for on a personal level. We still believe in social justice for those with whom we do not have a personal relationship, because we care for the humanity of the individual and larger community.

- Caring for others and self includes the examination of oppression and challenging practices that are inequitable.

- Caring students develop a capacity to feel, see, or view the world from someone else's perspective, which promotes problem-solving and academic skill development from a community orientation.

- The teacher feels like a part of the community and shares life experiences by participating in the community where she or he teaches.

- The teacher along with students creates a democratic classroom.

As a core element of Multicultural Education, caring is a part of a belief system that motivates and also acts as a compass that guides our way. In this analogy the compass directs us through politics, law, the economy, and our society toward a humane, democratic community. No matter whether one is a Marxist, conservative, critical pedagogist, feminist, constructivist, progressive, perennialist, multiculturalist, or one of many other professional orientations in the field of education, caring should always be a critical component for good teaching. A strong, healthy ability to care will motivate and guide teachers to be open and flexible so that they can be more effective, rather than being set in a particular political ideology or teaching method.

Table 7.2 presents beliefs and practices of four different types of teachers. All four teachers could be found in the same school. They do not represent *personality* types; rather, they exemplify different educational philosophies. As you read the table, do so with the thought in the back of your mind that the four teachers have *philosophical differences*. They may all have class rules, but their ultimate goals are not the same. The following is a summary of how the philosophies of the four teachers are extremely different.

- The assimilationist is a teacher who believes in the status quo of teaching the three Rs and social conformity. This teacher believes that the knowledge taught in schools is universal and not biased. There is no question that the knowledge chosen by the teacher and the school is the most appropriate for all students. This teacher's goal is to impart subject area content knowledge and ensure that students pass the standardized tests needed to exit the grade or graduate. Often the basics are taught

TABLE 7.2   Comparing Four Teachers

The Assimilationist, the Human Relations, the Social Action Multiculturalist, and the Caring-Centered Multiculturalist

Assimilationist Teacher	Human Relations Teacher	Sovial Action Multiculturalist Teacher	Caring-Centered Multiculturalist Teacher
Overall Societal Goal	Overall Societal Goal	Overall Societal Goal	Overall Societal Goal
Overall societal goal is to teach the basic knowledge and skills of reading, writing, mathematics, and technology, which students need in order to become responsible citizens and fit into the mainstream.	Overall societal goal is to teach the basic skills and knowledge of reading, writing, mathematics, and technology and to promote social harmony, unity, and tolerance so that students become responsible citizens in society.	Overall societal goal is for all peoples and cultures to experience equality and justice and therefore a lack of oppression. Goal of schooling is to prepare all students to become change agents in our society and in this process challenge inequities. One of the key concepts studied is the imbalance of power between members of various social groups such as the working class, communities of color, and women.	Overall societal goal is to value and build a multicultural society based on compassion, justice, and freedom. Goal of schooling is to develop compassionate and fulfilled individuals who achieve their full potential within a community of learners who work together to create a more just society. The individuals also develop critical intercultural communication skills for participation in a global community.
Assimilationist	Human Relations	Social Action	Caring-Centered
What Is Excellence?	What Is Excellence?	What Is Excellence?	What Is Excellence?
Excellence means that all students are to learn the canon of knowledge as set forth by a monocultural and Western tradition. The curriculum is subject centered and focuses on a liberal arts	Excellence means that all students are to learn the canon of knowledge as set forth by a monocultural and Western tradition. The curriculum is subject centered and focuses on a liberal arts	Excellence is interconnected with equity. Equity means freedom from bias and favoritism. Questions status quo measures of excellence. If students do not have equal access and outcomes in	Excellence and caring are integrally related. Caring forms the foundation for creating an atmosphere of excellence. Caring means an ethical commitment to the well-being and success of each student.

continued

TABLE 7.2 Comparing Four Teachers (Continued)

Assimilationist	Human Relations	Social Action	Caring-Centered
What Is Excellence?	What Is Excellence?	What Is Excellence?	What Is Excellence?
education. There is a body of knowledge that all students should master. The teacher is the authority in the classroom and directs the learning in the classroom. Students are taught to conform to the values of society. The classroom is teacher centered and teacher talk dominates classroom activities.	education. There is a body of knowledge that all students should master. The teacher is the authority in the classroom and directs the learning in the classroom. Students are taught to conform to the values of society. Limited school wide programs focus on diversity and racism. Posters may include, "Unity amidst diversity." The self-esteem and self-identification of students are seen as important.	schools, then excellence cannot occur. Schooling is seen through an equity/political and fairness lens. It is a rights-centered view of education. Emphasis is placed on educational equality, equal rights, and changing the social structure. Teacher discusses classroom relationships in terms of rights and responsibilities of citizens/children in the classroom of each other. It is the duty of students as members of a democracy and as citizens to be respectful to each other in the classroom. Posters in the room may include, "Dignity is not negotiable" and "You have the right to ask for help. You have the responsibility to assist."	Caring focuses on reciprocal relationships and the building of community. Schooling is seen through a caring/ethics lens. Emphasis is placed on building trusting relationships in the classroom between the teacher and students and each other within the context of cultural diversity. As part of relationship building, teachers and students care for each other and are responsible to each other. Students and teachers listen to each other without judgment and provide constructive assistance. Students celebrate each other and who they are. Teacher talks about the importance of civil and human rights within the context of caring and human interconnections. The teacher cares and so respects and supports the rights of others. Posters in the room may include, "Smiles are contagious" and "Pull together."

TABLE 7.2 Comparing Four Teachers (Continued)

Assimilationist	Human Relations	Social Action	Caring-Centered
Key Beliefs	Key Beliefs	Key Beliefs	Key Beliefs
Excellence is promoted by having high standards and a belief in meritocracy. Competition and high achievement are encouraged. The focus is the cognitive development of students. Questions students address may be as follows: How can students better prepare for their tests? How can students be encouraged to become more disciplined?	Cross-racial relationships are valued. Students are encouraged to work together cooperatively in groups to overcome personal social bias due to group membership. Questions students address may be as follows: How can we make our school a place where everyone feels accepted and belonging? How can we be peacemakers? How can we support each other?	Equity and social activism are promoted in part through actively practicing democracy in the classroom and school, helping students learn how to analyze inequalities in their own lives, training students to develop and use social action skills, and helping students learn to form coalitions to eliminate oppression. Questions students address may be as follows: Who makes the decision? Who has the power? How can the status quo be changed? Whose perspective is being taught?	Equity and excellence are key goals. High achievement of all students must occur for equity to exist. Caring is expressed in part through getting to know about students' lives both in school and outside of school, talking with children, listening to them, meeting their parents and families, developing trusting relationships with students, sharing power in the classroom, and building a community. Social justice is taught through the lens of caring. Respect is one of the key values in the classroom and lack of fairness can be one of the most negative influences in a school. Questions students address may be as follows: What does caring look like in a democracy? How can we develop empathy with others? What does caring look like in different cultures? How are caring and social justice related? How do caring and social justice relate to intercultural communication skills?

continued

TABLE 7.2 Comparing Four Teachers (Continued)

Assimilationist Curriculum	Human Relations Curriculum	Social Action Curriculum	Caring-Centered Curriculum
The curriculum is organized around traditional Western knowledge. Students are seen as sponges that soak up the knowledge teachers teach. Intellectual development involves a focus on basic subjects such as mathematics, science, English composition, literature, reading, and writing.	The curriculum is organized around traditional Western knowledge. Students are seen as sponges to draw in the knowledge teachers teach. Intellectual development focuses on basic subjects such as mathematics, science, English composition, literature, reading, and writing. Limited emphasis is placed on social bias and the societal walls that it creates. Includes schoolwide programs focusing on tolerance and respect for cultural diversity.	The curriculum is organized around current social issues involving oppressed and underrepresented groups, reflects the experiences and perspectives of many different cultural groups and voices, uses the context of students' life experiences to analyze oppression, and teaches critical thinking and social action skills. Social justice issues primarily center on bias due to racism, ethnocentrism, gender and cultural bias, classism, homophobia, language discrimination, and religion.	The curriculum incorporates a wide variety of content and the emphasis is consistent with an overarching theme of respect, honor, compassion, and justice for all people. The teacher naturally integrates students' life experiences and social issues impacting their lives into teaching. Culture is a key element of the curriculum. Teacher provides feedback for each child in content areas and, as a caring teacher, is sensitive to the need of some students for the teacher to approach the student when student is having problems so that the student can maintain peer group respect. The teacher scaffolds learning using peer, ethnicity, and neighborhood cultures in the curriculum.

Assimilationist Fundamental Direction for Curriculum	Human Relations Fundamental Direction for Curriculum	Social Action Fundamental Direction for Curriculum	Caring-Centered Fundamental Direction for Curriculum
Fundamentally believes that there is universal and permanent knowledge that should be imparted to	Fundamentally believes that there is universal and permanent knowledge that should be imparted to	Fundamentally believes that people will never be able to change until societal institutions change, so	Fundamentally believes that individuals and the society in which they live create a family of learners. Cultural

TABLE 7.2   Comparing Four Teachers (Continued)

Assimilationist	Human Relations	Social Action	Caring-Centered
Fundamental Direction for Curriculum	Fundamental Direction for Curriculum	Fundamental Direction for Curriculum	Fundamental Direction for Curriculum
students. The curriculum of schools focuses on transferring basic knowledge to children and the development of rational minds.	students. The curriculum of schools focuses on transferring basic knowledge to children and the development of rational minds. There is some focus on coalition building between racial groups to overcome social isolation.	directs limited educational resources toward equipping students to become citizens who actively work to challenge and change oppressive aspects of social structures so that they are more equal, democratic, and just. Much emphasis is placed on discussion of power relationships.	knowledge is naturally integrated into the curriculum; for example, social issues are taken from the lives of learners. Elimination of personal, institutional, and social prejudices.
Assimilationist	Human Relations	Social Action	Caring-Centered
Discipline	Discipline	Discipline	Discipline
Teachers and administrators handle discipline. Rules for behavior come from the teacher or school rather than students.	Although most discipline is handled by teachers and administrators, schools may have peer mediators available for students to talk with about altercations and other academic/social relationship issues.	Handles classroom discipline by involving students in democratic decision making. Teacher teaches responsibilities and duties of citizens and allows students to practice these skills in the classroom. For example, procedures for such things as when and how students leave the room for bathroom breaks are determined by majority vote.	Handles classroom discipline by assessing the unique needs of the students in the classroom. Teacher shares control of the classroom with students. Teacher is in control by not being controlling. Teacher teaches students how to care for themselves so that they do not need to be managed. She also believes in building democratic skills in students, but first works to develop in children an empathy for others and respect for themselves. Much discipline is handled one-on-one and not in

continued

TABLE 7.2 Comparing Four Teachers (Continued)

Assimilationist	Human Relations	Social Action	Caring-Centered
Discipline	Discipline	Discipline	Discipline
			front of the class because the teacher respects the emotional needs of students and does not embarrass or challenge students in front of others. Teacher is aware that discipline concerns may arise out of cultural conflicts and misunderstandings.

Assimilationist	Human Relations	Social Action	Caring-Centered
Staffing Patterns	Staffing Patterns	Staffing Patterns	Staffing Patterns
Staffing patterns reflect the majority population. Little emphasis is placed on diverse role models.	Staffing patterns reflect the majority population; however, there is a limited sensitivity to the need for cultural role models for all students.	Prefers to work in a school with diverse staff such as ethnic, gender, and persons with disabilities in traditional/ nontraditional roles.	Prefers to work in a school with diverse staff who represent various ethnic, gender, and disability groups, and a balance of intellectual diversity as well as cultural diversity on the faculty.

Assimilationist	Human Relations	Social Action	Caring-Centered
Instructional Strategies	Instructional Strategies	Instructional Strategies	Instructional Strategies
Most learning is in lecture style. Much of the homework is done individually. Standardized testing is extremely important because performance indicates knowledge learned and ability to think.	Most learning is in lecture style. Much of the homework is done individually. Standardized testing is extremely important because performance indicates knowledge learned and ability to think.	Uses cooperative learning for much of the classroom work and avoids testing and group procedures that would result in some students being seen as failures. Students are often involved in community service projects.	Uses a variety of learning and assessment techniques with sensitivity to the personal and academic needs of each of the students. This may include demonstration, roleplaying, field work, cooperative learning, and community service.

TABLE 7.2   Comparing Four Teachers (Continued)

Assimilationist	Human Relations	Social Action	Caring-Centered
Critical Obstacle	Critical Obstacle	Critical Obstacle	Critical Obstacle
Sees the biggest obstacle to student success as a lack of student discipline or lack of positive influences in child's background.	Sees the biggest obstacle to student success as the existence of stereotypes and individual prejudice.	Sees the biggest enemy to student success as institutional and social oppression.	Sees the biggest enemy to student success as the lack of an operationalized educational philosophy that integrates caring relationships, culturally relevant teaching, and truly democratic education that focuses on decision-making skill development and intercultural understandings.

using rote methods. The goal of this teacher is to impart accepted knowledge so that students fit into the existing social and political system. This often means that students must give up their primary languages and cultural values and take on mainstream culture in order to survive within the larger mainstream community.

- The human relations teacher is an assimilationist who does examine, to some degree, racism and other forms of social oppression. This teacher may also get students involved in functions like the International Festival. However, the teacher believes that the knowledge and skills presented are universal and she or he does not question chosen school knowledge.

- The social action teacher believes her goal is to teach students to critically think and to encourage them to become change agents. The teacher does not believe in social or intellectual conformity. Her primary concern is to facilitate students' thinking about issues of equity and civil rights; often discussions center upon legal ramifications. Schools are seen as institutions of cultural transmission where the status quo is supported. This teacher may consider the impact of culture on the learning process.

- The caring-centered teacher believes her goal is to teach students to critically think about social issues and to act; students learn these skills within a caring, culturally relevant teaching environment that emphasizes trusting relationships. This teacher focuses upon building a learning community that is built on democracy and intercultural understanding. This teacher is concerned about student empowerment. Social oppression is addressed by empowerment and working toward change. In addition, culture is seen as an asset and the teacher integrates the lived experiences of culturally diverse students into the curriculum.

The table has limited use in that it is difficult to explain various individual teacher behaviors without their social contexts.

I believe the first two teachers, the assimilationist and human relations educators, represent the status quo in education. The other teachers, the social action and caring-centered educators, both believe in Multicultural Education. They share some values. However, social action teachers usually have not integrated educational psychological theories of culture and learning in their philosophies. Please read through Table 7.2 and think about their diverse orientations.

Analyzing Critical Differences between Four Teachers

I chose four different types of teachers to show the differences between two teachers who have little knowledge of Multicultural Education and the issues of equity and culture and two teachers who have more knowledge of the field. Although I describe various characteristics of the four teachers, the most important element in each of these teachers is the philosophy he or she has chosen.

Here is a description of four female teachers; notice the differences.

The Assimilationist Teacher

The **assimilationist** teacher supports the *status quo* of schools. Her goal is social conformity and her teaching style is more directed and teacher centered. She has students sitting in rows facing the front of the classroom. There is student work on the bulletin boards. The teacher usually stands at the front of the room lecturing or directing the learning. As the authority of the classroom, she has a set schedule in her class and has certain periods for each subject that she teaches. Much of the curriculum she uses comes directly from her teacher manuals and textbook guides. Her viewpoints for the most part reflect a monocultural, Western tradition. There is a strong sense of teacher control in this classroom.

The teacher-centered orientation can also be seen in the words the teacher uses to call on her students. When students come to her class and she doesn't know how to pronounce names, she chooses substitutions (Perrone 1998). For example, a young man named Jésus is called Jessie. Another child whose name was Vito became Victor, and Yin Mui became Nancy (Perrone 1998, 13).

An example of the knowledge taught can be seen in her social studies curriculum. She follows her social studies textbook closely. It discusses the development of the United States from the East to the West. Much of the text focuses on the creation of the 13 colonies and the activities of the Pilgrims and other Anglo settlers to the East Coast from the colonist point of view. The majority of history is taught from a European American point of view; for example, the history of indigenous peoples is covered when they come into contact with Europeans. Little is mentioned about the indigenous people who lived in areas renamed as colonies. The students do not study other people who lived in other parts of North America, such as Mexico. Famous men such as George Washington, Thomas Jefferson, Benjamin Franklin, and Alexander Hamilton are highlighted. Limited reference is made to Harriet Tubman and Susan B. Anthony. For the most part, students read biographies on the founding fathers and present reports to their peers. A few female students ask her after class about including information about women, so the teacher asks them to research the topic. They do not follow through and little is said about women.

During a staff development session on cultural diversity in schools, the teacher feels defensive and responds with hostility to a conversation about the need for bilingual teachers. She quickly points out that it isn't her fault that children from underrepresented families are not learning as successfully as others. "I don't think people realize how many dysfunctional students come to school here. I can't be expected to solve all their problems," she says loudly from her chair in the back of the room. It is her belief that it is important for students from diverse communities to learn how to fit in and become American.

The school is located in a diverse neighborhood and composed of students whose ancestors were from Nigeria, Russia, Somalia, Poland, China, Ireland, Germany, Mexico, and Sweden. When someone asks the teacher about the importance of culture, she says, "I see students. I treat everyone the same." She believes she is color-blind. The teacher has a seating chart and students sit integrated in class. However, at lunch time, it is obvious that White students sit on one side of the cafeteria, while students from underrepresented groups sit on the other. Sometimes there are conflicts between different ethnic and cultural groups in the cafeteria, but like other school personnel, the teacher does nothing in her classes to address the underlying racial tensions. She is not concerned with building a sense of community, but with maintaining order and control. She believes that this orientation gives her more opportunities to teach reading, writing, and mathematics so that students will successfully fit into U.S. society.

The teacher believes she does the best she can, but complains daily about the high numbers of students, 35, in each of her middle-school classes. She doesn't feel she can do much to help each student and so she feels it is best to use direct instruction. She gives them seat work to complete individually and does not believe that cooperative learning is possible because of the large number of students; the noise level would become too loud.

During a faculty meeting, a colleague comments that he sees many students from culturally diverse groups taking classes in remedial English and math. He asks if this is academic tracking. This teacher replies, "No, it is just where the kids are. They need to work harder. They often don't do their homework. I don't know what else we can do." She also indicates that she feels picked on during diversity training sessions because she feels she is not racist nor does she harbor ill feelings toward students from other cultural groups. This teacher works very hard to reach her students; however, she is not open to self-reflection.

It will be difficult for this teacher to understand how her actions could impede the education of students if she does not examine critical underlying conflicts caused by the system, her own viewpoints, and cultural conflicts.

The Human Relations Teacher

The **human relations** teacher believes that it is important that all children treat each other with respect. She explains to her students that the United States is a society comprised of many different cultures that enrich our nation.

She is the faculty counselor to the human relations club at the high school. She is also a member of the Mini-Town staff, a special program on prejudice sponsored by the National Conference of Community and Justice. As a person who believes in equity, she feels it is very important to create cross-cultural bridges between different races and members of ethnic groups. She invites 60 high school student representatives to the Mini-Town four-day retreat to talk about racism, gender bias, classism, and homophobia. In addition, she encourages other student groups to sponsor cultural events during the school noon hour, like special food for Chinese New Year. She also supports their use of different languages to advertise events. The teacher/counselor provides much support to students to create other programs like peer mediation in which students help their peers talk about issues dealing with friends, family, and school problems. Some of the problems that arise deal with racism and usually these problems can be solved on an individual basis through one-on-one peer counseling.

As an English teacher, she includes the writings of many different U.S. authors like Amy Tan, Langston Hughes, Sandra Cisneros, and Maya Angelou. She brings in community people to help her students understand the cultural context of several of the writers, because most of her students are White. She encourages students to ask questions and to find similarities between different cultural life experiences. Through reading literature and having the opportunity to discuss cultural values, her students understand more clearly the implicit messages of the literature. This also encourages community building among students because many of the themes in literature are universal although they are discussed within various cultural contexts.

Because the teacher believes in diversity, she recommended and was able to get the faculty to agree to offer Mandarin as well as French, Spanish, and German as a foreign language. She supports the Multicultural Education Club, which sponsors the Martin Luther King, Jr., assembly for the school. Often students act out portions of one of Martin Luther King, Jr.'s speeches. In addition, she plans a Multicultural Week when students from different cultural groups share traditional dances, music, and speakers. She is also the advisor to the week-long Multicultural Fair in which student clubs choose a country, prepare food from that country, and sell the dishes to students during the lunch period. She believes that this activity helps to bring students together on a personal level and integrates cultural diversity. These activities have been highly supported by administrators and teachers in the school.

Like other educators in the school, this teacher believes that human relations activities are the key in creating equity in the school because the strategies focus on individual change and bring to the attention of students and other educators fun aspects of culture. Justice is seen as fair and balanced. Students are directed to care for others and clarify their values. However, she does not mention controversial social issues nor does she ask students to make decisions about them. The teacher does not look at the infrastructure of schools for issues such as academic tracking, the sink-or-swim English immersion policy for English learners, majority privilege as it relates to standardized assessment tools, or lack of input from parents of underrepresented groups. She maintains the status quo without working for structural school reform.

The Social Action Teacher

The **social action** teacher believes strongly in equality in school opportunities and outcomes. The lens through which she sees schooling is political. She believes in educational equality and sees institutional oppression as the most critical obstacle to student success. She tells students at the beginning of the year that they have "the right to be themselves." She teaches in a school where most of the students are Latino, African American, or Vietnamese. When asked if she has a strong commitment to social justice, she said, "Yes, I think social justice is so important that I have my students read biographies of Martin Luther King, Jr., during the month of January. I also have class meetings in which children learn how to work with each other. Once during the year, I also have the students who have earned the privilege come to my house for an afternoon party." When a controversial issue arises in class, she has the students convene for a community discussion session in which everyone in the room can contribute to resolving the problem.

All the walls in her classroom are filled with educational messages and the work of students. It is a classroom in which children are busily involved in many projects dealing with social issues. She encourages students to address such questions as, "Who has the power? Who makes the decisions? How can the status quo be changed? Whose perspective is being taught?"

Her students choose to learn about U.S. slavery by studying the lives of various abolitionists. They make a videotape presentation for parents and profile important figures like Harriet Tubman, Levi Cofin, John Brown, Frederick Douglass, and Sojourner Truth. Their video shows a courtroom where several people were on trial for helping Black slaves escape to the North during the 1850s. All members of the class participate in the role play.

Many students in her class are involved in the school's student government. Her students campaigned for one of their classmates who was elected president. As president of the student body, the young girl involves many of her classmates in various school projects. For example, they sold grocery store coupons to raise money for new playground equipment. The students learned much about the democratic process. The bulletin board displays this poster: "You have the right to ask for help. You also have the duty to assist." The social action teacher talks much about civil and human rights in her teaching. She not only wants her students to learn about civil rights history, but she also wants them to get involved in the school community to make it a better place for all students. In this way her students will know how democracy works in their city, state, and nation.

This teacher speaks up at faculty meetings regarding the need for the faculty to examine their practices, such as academic tracking. She leads a small group of teachers who continue to raise controversial issues dealing with equity and diversity.

The Caring-Centered Multicultural Teacher

The **caring-centered** multicultural teacher says this about why she teaches: "I want to make a difference with children. I live close by and am part of the neighborhood community. I know that kids can do well if they are given the chance. This is where I want to be." The teacher is student centered.

Her school classroom walls are filled with the work of her students. In addition, she has many posters that focus on the classroom as a family. The posters say such things as "Smiles are contagious," "Pull together," "Learning has no boundaries," "We are the future," and "Celebrate your heritage." She believes that caring and social justice form the foundation for her belief system.

She is a caring teacher who believes that when her students fail, she fails, and when her students succeed, she succeeds. At the beginning of the year, she spends time carefully observing each student and identifying specific skills they need; she can then guide her students to succeed.

She frequently calls parents on the phone, both to remind parents and students about their responsibilities and to congratulate students and their parents on excellent work. She understands that the success of students is dependent not only on her work, but also on the support of parents and the students themselves.

Her class climate is one of reciprocal caring and trust; she cares for her students and her students care for her and they also care for each other. It isn't easy to create a cross-cultural and equitable family atmosphere. She says, "It takes a lot of time at the beginning of the year. We have class meetings in which we choose the rules together. We talk about what it means to care for each other and what it means to be fair." She also has students sitting with their desks arranged to make small groups of four to six students. They often help each other or do group work. In many ways her orientation is similar to that of the social justice teacher. She models caring behavior all the time by attending and listening unconditionally to each child as he or she speaks and by making sure that all her students have a chance to talk in class. In addition, the teacher has students evaluate her three times a year. She uses her students' comments to help her reflect on her own practices and areas in which she should make changes. When she wasn't listening to her children, they told her and she became more attentive. Getting feedback from students works well because the lines of communication are open between teacher and students.

This teacher proactively works to address the achievement differences and disciplinary problems of students and understands that they may correlate with such factors as class, gender, and ethnicity. For example, in other classrooms, Black students are sent disproportionately more often to the office for discipline. This teacher prefers to work with parents and students first, before calling in the main office. One of her secrets is that she gives students several options and does not push young people into a corner where they must defy her in order to uphold their personal honor and pride. She understands cultural and personal dynamics. Because of her respect for students and understanding of peer values, the teacher always disciplines a student one-on-one and not in front of the entire class. Otherwise this again can be seen as a challenge, and students are sensitive to peer beliefs.

Because the teacher believes in providing all students access to higher-level courses, she created a club for students interested in math and science. Many young people attend and the teacher is especially sensitive to inviting women and students from some underrepresented groups who often do not take as many science and math courses as others. Through the activities in the club, the teacher built a social network of support for students who were interested in the sciences. More women and students of color are taking advanced classes because of this club. The members of the group provide each other with tutoring and advice throughout the year. Through the community, they develop vital intercultural communication skills.

In her social studies classroom, when she talks about communities in the 11th grade curriculum, she asks such questions as: "What does caring look like in our communities? What does caring look like in different cultures? Are caring and justice related? If so, how?" She gives examples of how her students' parents are volunteering in the school or at church.

One of the biggest differences between this teacher and others is her goal to guide students to become self-directed *and* community oriented. Classroom power is shared between students and teacher. The atmosphere in the classroom is one of mutual respect between students and between students and teacher. In this atmosphere the teacher considers the culture of students and works with them to create an understanding of caring based on trust. She knows that their self-esteem may be interwoven with their cultural identity. Her classroom allows students to express their ability to control their learning in their own unique ways, from putting on dramas to creating a song. Her management style is driven by the capacity to care for her students, which transcends race and ethnicity. This leads to collaborative and individual goals of academic achievement. In her classroom the students know that they are at the center of learning.

Because this teacher has developed important connections with the neighborhood, you can see her on Saturdays at the local library checking out books. Sometimes she is at the Latino bakery buying pan dulce, little breads, for her family's Sunday breakfast. This teacher is part of the community.

This teacher, like the social action educator, is an advocate for change. She believes that it is critical for schools to have a strong policy of caring and compassion in order to create a socially just learning environment. She also creates many opportunities for students to learn various points of view and intercultural communication skills by which students move away from an ethnocentric orientation toward an international point of reference.

This teacher knows the importance of understanding the cultures that students share and uses it as a bridge to support children in their learning. She knows that cultural values, language, behavioral codes, and motivational styles may differ in her students. This teacher has a holistic focus: she addresses social problems, focuses on issues of equity and culture, consciously strives to create a compassionate community of learn-

> ᔕ *Students know they are at the center of learning.*

ers, understands that schools are social institutions, and addresses individual needs. Her approach is especially important because many high school students "fall through the cracks" of our schools, often because of the sheer number of students that high school teachers are responsible for in a day.

Comparison of the Four Styles of Teaching

The first two teachers are more assimilationist in their orientation. Students are expected to take on the values and behaviors of the mainstream school culture. This is an accepted belief. Neither teacher incorporates the cultures of his or her students as a major aspect of their teaching. Assimilationists do not address the imbalance of power in the way schools are structured. If any cultural or equitable activities are presented in schools, they are added to the status quo. It is an additive approach to Multicultural Education. Social action and caring-centered teachers can be transformative in their orientation if teachers actively work to change the way schools are structured and alter the way their own classrooms are organized.

Although both the social action teacher and the caring-centered teacher are dedicated to changing society, the caring-centered multicultural teacher believes that caring is at the core of a democratic community. "We care and so we are fair." These teachers understand that consistency and fairness are the cornerstones of an effective classroom. This is evident in the way discipline, as well as rewards, is carried out in the caring classroom. The teacher is in tune with the need to reprimand students privately and may praise a student privately or publicly depending on what the student prefers. Student behavior may differ when a teacher privately talks with the student; it also shows respect for the student.

Social action and caring-centered teachers have similar value orientations, but they have different value priorities. The social justice teacher uses a political or legal filter as her core orientation. The social action teacher focuses on power relationships and the imbalance of power in U.S. society and how that impacts the employment, housing patterns, and other opportunities of various communities. Although the caring-centered teacher also is concerned about power relationships, this teacher is more likely to address issues of power by teaching students how to direct their own learning, bringing in student experiences, and encouraging the sharing of diverse cultural viewpoints. However, this teacher may not see culture as a critical component of the curriculum.

The caring teacher uses cultural lenses in the classroom and so brings cultural analogies and other cultural ways of knowing to the learning process. To give you a sample of how culture can be infused naturally into the teacher's instruction, let's take a first grade teacher's lesson about the concept of choral reading. Her first graders did not understand what she meant by the term, so she said to her students, "It's just like us singing together in the choir at church. That's why it's called choral reading. We read together as if we were in a chorus or choir." Many of her students are African American and they attend churches with large choirs. Using this example, the teacher was able to build on the cultural knowledge of her students. The caring-centered teacher chooses social issues that arise out of the lives of her students, therefore integrating the viewpoints and concerns of parents and students in the community. She knows that they hold "funds of knowledge" that are valuable and should be built upon in the curriculum.

Caring-centered teachers are extremely aware of how culture impacts the hidden or invisible aspects of the classroom (Hilliard 1974). For example, Hilliard (1974) sees the influence of culture on the way students and teachers make judgments, label, control space, pay attention, care, isolate, and respond to others. The classroom is a culturally rich environment in which intercultural communication skills are taught and modeled.

In order to better explain the basis for Caring-Centered Multicultural Education, the next section lists the core principles.

Important nonverbal communication skills

Principles of Multicultural Education from a Caring Perspective

Caring, education for democracy, and culture are key elements of Multicultural Education. The following principles help to summarize Multicultural Education from this perspective:

1. **Multicultural Education, as part of a life-giving pedagogy of human growth, is based on the belief that teachers and students form a family of learners.** People care for others, themselves, and the community as they work together and learn.

2. **The roots of a caring-centered multicultural framework rise from the integration of principles from human development, democratic education, and a sociocultural context of learning.**

3. **The choice to teach is an ethical one.** A moral commitment to care means that teachers are committed to finding ways to effectively teach all students and are especially sensitive to closing the achievement gap between majority children and students from underrepresented cultural groups. Teachers create situations and contexts in which all students are successful.

4. **Children are cultural beings; they are born, learn, speak, share, think, and create in complex linguistic and cultural settings.** Culture plays important roles in a person's development; it contributes to areas such as identity, motivation, gender roles, and learning modalities. Within this cultural and linguistic environment, teachers support the holistic developmental process, including intellectual, emotional, physical, and social growth.

5. **A caring relationship is reciprocal, based on trust, respect, and the honoring of each other among students and teacher.** This is expressed in the classroom through using the living experiences of students in the teaching-learning process. When people care, they share their lives and promote the interests of others along with their own.

6. **Parents and community members are members of a student's supportive social network.** Because learning occurs in a sociocultural context, the development of trusting relationships with significant others is critical to effective teaching.

7. **Because culture is a key component of learning, culturally relevant teaching is a core principle.** Teachers affirm the cultural identities of their students and parents as they skillfully integrate explicit and implicit cultural elements naturally into the classroom and school.

8. **Teachers and students examine and work to eliminate personal, social, and institutional oppression.** First, teachers understand the impact of prejudice and discrimination on the emotional and intellectual development of their students. Second, teachers understand that schools as social institutions reinforce, often unconsciously, social oppression brought about by racism, sexism, classism, and other harmful biases. Teachers and students engage in a continual process of examining personal prejudices and addressing discriminatory practices in schools.

9. **Teachers and students need a strong interdisciplinary knowledge base.** This base gives them the foundational background to make decisions about complex social problems in light of the common good. Therefore, it is imperative for teachers and students not only to have a background in reading and math skills, but also a strong content knowledge in the areas of science, social studies (this includes a wide range of areas such as history, government, civics, economics, and political science), the humanities, health, the arts, and physical education.

10. **Curriculum and instruction are founded on the belief that learning must flow from an attitude of caring and be participatory, hands-on, meaningful, cooperative, and reflective.** Students often are more motivated when the curriculum has real-life purposes. Teachers use interdisciplinary curriculum and strategies that recognize intuition, emotional and social intelligences, and the five physical senses.

11. **Caring teachers encourage and teach students to democratically take control of their own lives in the classroom while creating a classroom culture**

in which each student can achieve academic excellence. Teachers have definite expectations for students and encourage them to become self-directed, self-determined, collaborative, and compassionate people.

12. **Teachers believe and act on the premise that if students do not learn, then they did not teach.** Teachers who care continually seek ways to reach students and help them achieve academic excellence.

Chapter Summary

Caring-Centered Multicultural Education differs from other Multicultural Education frameworks because it directs a **paradigm shift** from a traditional basic skills orientation to a caring one, which sees schooling as a life-giving process of learning. Key values are empowerment, compassion, justice, equity, culture, and community. Other orientations are primarily founded upon democratic values. Although I agree that social justice is a key element of Multicultural Education, the commitment to care is most critical and must be interwoven with our democratic values. Caring for others leads to justice and fairness. Simply put, the care we feel for others moves us to develop views and appropriate approaches, such as value orientations and teaching methods that lead to fairness or social justice. Caring is an impetus for teachers to give students training in intercultural communication skills and sensitivity. In addition. caring leads teachers to provide students with classrooms that are student centered. Fairness does not necessarily lead to caring in a classroom.

Caring-Centered Multicultural Education encourages teachers to address students' individual needs within community and cultural contexts. The caring paradigm has six major shifts from other views of Multicultural Education:

1. The paradigm places caring for others/community and self at the foundation for social/economic justice and change.
2. The paradigm moves the focus from the teacher to the learner.
3. The paradigm explains how culture represents different realities—and ways of knowing.
4. The paradigm is founded on the interconnectedness of the learner and the teacher.
5. Learning and teaching are social processes.
6. Teachers and students are both responsible for learning.

A healthy commitment to care rather than a particular political ideology is a strong foundational belief for teachers in their quest to create effective learning environments. I believe that teachers who care will provide the kind of support that will result in the academic success of all children, especially children from underrepresented communities.

Caring-centered is not a style of teaching nor a specific personality type; rather it is a philosophical orientation that focuses on relationship building and the importance of the cultural context. This framework values students and parents and sees learning occurring within a social and cultural context. The section written by Merry Merryfield about Somali refugee students demonstrated how difficult it is for some students not only to learn the language, but also to discover the norms and expectations of U.S. American schools. A teacher who understands the power of culture becomes a cultural mediator. As you read in this section, some Somali women have more traditional duties in the home and family. Sometimes female teachers must explain to young Somali males about the authoritative role of educators in schools in this country. Bridging cultures that are quite unlike can be challenging and may take the skills of cultural mediators to bring about mutual understanding.

A teacher who has chosen the caring-centered philosophy has made an ethical commitment to her- or himself to create strong lines of communication with her or his students and to affirm the cultural background of students. An assimilationist teacher can be kind to her students, but when the teacher teaches only from a mainstream perspective and encourages students to shed important aspects of themselves such as cultural identity, language, and cultural beliefs in order to fit in or become more American, then students aren't valued. When students aren't valued, then their learning may be more limited because they may not become emotionally vested in the endeavor. When students aren't encouraged to challenge the status quo and address our social problems, they are not being prepared to contribute to our community. When teachers do not model collaboration or respect for different perspectives, then our national diversity isn't being honored.

Today, the dropout rates of many students from underrepresented groups are disturbing and signal a need for change. Perrone (1998) reports that from 35 percent to 55 percent of all African American, Latino, and Native Americans are dropping out of our high schools. This will have dramatic impact on our economic, social, and political national life. Perrone found that in "interviews with many of these young men and women, they speak of uncaring schools, of seeing little connection between the content of schools and their lives, of settings that are disrespectful of their families, or not having teachers to whom they can relate (1998, 35). The caring-centered framework seeks to address this disconnection between teachers and students and teachers and parents.

Chapter Review

Go to the Online Learning Center at **www.mhhe.com/pang2e** to review important content from the chapter, practice with key terms, take a chapter quiz, and find the Web links listed in this chapter.

Key Terms

cultural deficit, *214*
culturally congruent, *215*
culturally responsive, *215*
care theory, *217*
Sociocultural Theory of
Cognitive Development, *219*
Education for Democracy, *220*

Multicultural Education, *222*
star teachers, *223*
cultural capital, *226*
cultural conflict, *226*
assimilationist, *240*
human relations, *241*
social justice teacher, *243*

social action, *243*
caring-centered multicultural
teacher, *243*
caring-centered, *243*
paradigm shift, *249*

Reflection Activities

This chapter centers upon the Caring-Centered Multicultural Education framework. Here are questions for reflection.

1. Did you hold any misconceptions about Multicultural Education before you read this book? If so, describe those misconceptions carefully. Where did the misconceptions come from? If you have different beliefs now about Multicultural Education, what are they?

2. How are the social action and caring-centered teachers similar? Different? Describe in depth how they are similar and different. You may want to use a Venn diagram to help sort out the similarities and differences.

3. Which teacher are you most like: assimilationist, human relations, social action, or caring-centered? What are the differences between the four types of teachers? Why would you place yourself in that orientation? Many times teachers ask if they can choose more than one type of teacher; however, this choice often demonstrates that someone has not clearly identified the differences between the four types of teachers.

4. Which teacher would you choose to be like and why? What would you do differently, if anything, in your teaching after reading the first seven chapters in the book?

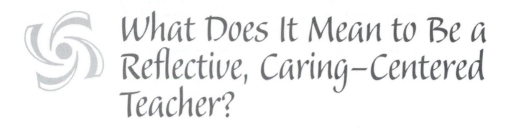

What Does It Mean to Be a Reflective, Caring–Centered Teacher?

CHAPTER MAIN IDEAS

CHAPTER OVERVIEW

This chapter is dedicated to teacher reflection. We all need to take time to think about what is our educational philosophy. This book is based on Caring-Centered Multicultural Education in which the three consistent themes are teaching the whole child, developing trust, and building communities of learners. Several controversial issues are raised.

Reflective Teaching: Important in Caring–Centered Multicultural Education

A growing body of research on teacher professionalism demonstrates that expert teachers engage in continuous inquiry involving consistent and sustained self-reflection about the effectiveness of their instruction (Pang and Park, forthcoming). The focus of this chapter is to present various issues for teachers to consider in their professional growth.

Reflective inquiry must involve reflection about ethical issues such as fairness and equitable treatment for all students. Self-reflection is rooted in Dewey's reflective teaching, a self-initiated, open-minded, and comprehensive process. Through self-reflection, expert teachers develop observational and analytical skills, resulting in action and/or behavioral changes (Dewey 1933; Zeichner and Liston 1987). Reflective teachers are those who base instructional decisions on carefully chosen theories and principles of human growth and learning. Reflective teachers also consider the evidence surrounding themselves—the day-to-day behavior of their students as they go about learning and growing.

As we build on these assumptions about reflection, it is critical to point out that reflective teaching as professional growth is not solely technical. Direct instruction through a mechanical model would be ineffective (Gore 1987), because self-reflection is needed in order for teachers to examine their beliefs and practices in light of their chosen goals, educational philosophy, and ethics (Irvine 2002; Zeichner and Liston 1987). Teachers must acquire the ability to examine how school practices and teaching strategies connect directly to or are in contrast to social attitudes about race, class, gender, and culture. They must come to realize how their actions may replicate or reinforce school practices that are inequitable (Sleeter 1992; Lee 1995; Valli 1997; Gay 2000; Moses and Cobb 2001; Pang 2001; Banks 2003; Nieto 2004). Therefore, one of the most important goals of the author of this book is to encourage teachers to be self-reflective intellectuals and thinkers who are grounded in educational theories and are dedicated to a reflective and democratic citizenry that questions and challenges hegemony (Gramsci 1971; Kincheloe and Steinberg 1993; Masucci and Renner 2000; Ross 2001). How does one engage in reflection? The next section is an introductory discussion of that process.

Reflective Thinking

Reflective thinking arises when there is some recognition of an impasse or a dilemma (Dewey 1933; Kolb 1984). Researchers have also identified many of these processes as part of thinking (Raths, Wasserman, Jonas, and Rothstein 1986; Beyer 1987). According to this viewpoint, reflection not only arises from cognition, but also includes the affective and creative aspects of life. Teachers must be able to appropriately question, analyze, and synthesize information along with their values. Within this process, questioning is an important condition for developing effective self-reflection because it raises consciousness that an impasse or dilemma exists (Hyman 1979). Through appropriate questioning, analysis, and synthesis, teachers gain the grounding to reflect upon their experiences and beliefs and to relate these reflections to their system of ethics. These skills will assist them in applying ethical criteria to their decisions regarding policy making, curriculum development, or examining relationships with students, parents, and colleagues. Valli (1997) explains the relationship between school practices and teacher questioning this way:

The quality of teacher reflection would be determined by the teachers' ability to apply ethical criteria to the goals and processes of schooling. Students would be encouraged to examine even the most simple teaching action in relation to broad social goals. Take teacher questioning, for example. In the United States, this topic is often taught simply as a technical skill without considering its moral aspects. Prospective teachers are taught how to ask different types of questions, probe for further knowledge, use questions to get students' attention, and select appropriate students for easier or harder questions. But teacher questioning has social and ethical implications. Programs that promote critical reflection would teach students not only questioning skills, but also the potential consequences of the use of questions (77).

Through these processes teachers gain the grounding to reflect on how their experiences and beliefs relate to their system of ethics (Noddings 1992).

Two of the most complex abilities that teachers and their students need are to make decisions and to develop solutions to social problems. Although this book is primarily about teachers and their instruction, decision-making skills are also a must for students. "If teachers provide a school life that is very rich in its opportunities for thinking, it is very probable that most children will reconstruct their own behavior . . . [W]here these opportunities are so much a part of the curriculum that they are present day after day and week after week, they begin to change their own behavior. They are not told to change it . . . Teachers are looking for change that is self-directed on the part of students" (Raths et al. 1986, xxv–xxvi).

The skills needed for decision making are key to the development of citizenship in a democracy. These skills are found in most states' standards relating to civics, citizenship, language arts, and U.S. history. They include lower-level skills such as knowing how to categorize information to the higher-order skill of examining the strength of an argument. The opportunities teachers provide their students to logically engage in inquiry include specific skills. Decision making or issues-centered education is built on skills development and the use of content area knowledge from diverse disciplines. The following are critical thinking skills identified by Barry Beyer (as cited by Leming 2003). Students need these skills to engage in a strong **decision-making process.** These skills taken alone can also enhance learning in many disciplines. Taken together these skills form a strong foundation for inquiry and are found in many state and federal standards:

Distinguishing between verifiable facts and value statements

Distinguishing relevant from irrelevant observations or reasons

Determining the factual accuracy of a statement

Determining the credibility of a source

Identifying ambiguous statements

Identifying unstated assumptions

Detecting bias

Identifying logical fallacies

Recognizing logical inconsistencies in a line of reasoning

Determining the overall strength of an argument or conclusion (Leming 2003, 136)

When teachers or students engage in decision making, they are not only examining various solutions and their consequences, but they are also weighing the various alternatives in light of their chosen values. Therefore, after students gather factual information and determine the credibility of the information, they also must reflect upon their own values and determine whether the chosen solution is in alignment with their ethics. The decision-making process has been summarized by Beyer (1998, 265) with the acronym **DECIDE:**

Define goal.

Enumerate alternatives.

Consider consequences.

Investigate effects.

Determine best alternative.

Execute.

Numerous issues arise in our lives. Some of these issues are complicated and difficult dilemmas to address. In order to examine the issues and to make appropriate decisions, teachers and students can benefit from using the skills they are taught through the decision-making process as identified by Beyer, above.

Friends on a trip to Washington, D.C.

Major Themes in the Caring-Centered Multicultural Education Framework

Chapter 1 provides an in-depth discussion of Caring-Centered Multicultural Education. In this chapter is a continued explanation of how the three theories in the framework build upon each other and hold common beliefs. One of the ways to view the three theories is to encapsulate their core ideas:

Care theory—caring.

Sociocultural theory of learning—culture.

Education for democracy—community.

The three theories are closely connected and therefore form a strong framework. First, the three theories are built upon the **integrity** of the individual. Teachers make ethical commitments to themselves and their students to do their best. They also see their interdependence with others and believe in compassion and social justice. Second, another common element is the importance of teaching the **whole student.** Teaching is about the development of the entire person. Teachers do not teach just mathematics or music; they consider the whole student in planning the curriculum and instructional strategies in teaching their subject area content. They are concerned with student emotional, social, physical, and academic growth, and to teach the whole child, teachers must understand the cultural backgrounds students bring to school. Teachers often have learned about students' goals and dreams and their fears, too. Third, the three theories focus on the importance of building trust and respect among teachers and students. **Trusting relationships** form the foundation for learning. When students and teachers develop reciprocal relationships of respect and compassion, they work collaboratively to learn and to build a community of learners. They are interested in learning about how each other lives and they seek out diverse perspectives. This leads to the fourth theme of **community.** When relationships are reciprocal and respectful, students and teachers learn from each other and create common, interdependent goals. They are members of a community that fosters equality, fairness, diversity, and personal growth. Teachers and students understand that they learn by interacting and sharing with each other in a compassionate and collaborative environment. In summary, the three theories hold the following common themes: (1) Have a strong sense of personal integrity, (2) educate the whole child, and (3) relationships of trust build a community of learners. (See Table 8.1.)

> ⑤ Caring-Centered Multicultural Education brings together caring, culture, and community.

Although it may be hard to see, the three theories—care theory, sociocultural theory of learning, and education for democracy—work together to create a new entity. These theories hold numerous ingredients that can transform the learning of a student. What is transformation? Have you ever baked a cake or made a tortilla? Let's take the cake, for example. After mixing all the ingredients together and baking the cake, it is

TABLE 8.1   Caring-Centered Framework

Connections

	Caring	Culture	Community
Common Elements	Care Theory	Sociocultural Theory of Learning	Education for Democracy
Personal Integrity	Values, interdependence, and reciprocal caring	Intellectual inquiry in collaboration with others	Ethics in schools and life
Teaching the Whole Child	Development of the whole child	Considers the whole child and her or his sociocultural context	Development of the whole person
Trusting Relationships/ Community	Trusting relationships, relationship-centered theory	Social and reciprocal interactions at base of learning	Build strong community through trusting relationships

eggs   flour   sugar   milk   chocolate

Separate Ingredients

not possible to see its individual ingredients. However, without the flour or eggs or sugar or milk or chocolate, the object would not be a cake. This is what happens in the process of transformation. There is a metamorphosis; something new is created!

cake

The Transformation: The Cake

Our Moral Commitment

Caring-centered teachers make the moral commitment to care for and teach students. It is a conscious commitment; teachers are committed to making a difference in the lives of students. Commitment also directs teachers to view education as a holistic process that is not only about teaching knowledge, but about teaching the whole student within an empowering and compassionate environment. Teachers consider the development of the whole person, whether they are teaching a math class, English class, or government class.

Teachers and students develop strong human bonds with each other. Teachers and students also care for the larger community and for various ideas. Unfortunately, caring and compassion within education are often seen as "touchy feely," holding little academic substance. Gilligan (1982) and Noddings (1984) have studied the importance of relationship building and the need for moral development. What happens when you care for another? You place the interests of another person next to your own; you look at a situation through someone else's eyes. Noddings (1984) believes there is also an emotional element to caring; one wants to do something to ease the other person's pain or assist them in reaching their dream.

Although some academics in universities often overlook this orientation, as a teacher, I felt this was the most important element of my classroom. I cared for the students. They cared for me and we were a family, a community of learners. Many students are most interested in being accepted and loved. This must occur before they are willing to trust teachers and pour their hearts into the learning process. I believe that caring is an integral aspect of the art of teaching. Many teachers are motivated by altruistic values of democracy and justice, and their personal interactions with students are what sustains the students, especially when they find learning difficult or frustrating.

> ⑤ *Teaching is not what we do; teaching is who we are.*

Caring-centered teachers also address difficult challenges. Individuals are directed by their own sense of justice to review their personal racial, social class, disability, and gender biases in social institutions such as schools. This can be extremely demanding because people may need to face aspects of themselves that are not flattering or positive. In addition, in order to care, we must also examine how we, as members of social institutions such as schools, may be participating in ways that limit the access of some children to the best education. For example, our daughter was in a school where Sally Ride, the first woman astronaut, was visiting. She wanted to have the opportunity to be part of a small group to speak to Ride because of her interest in NASA. Our daughter had attended two local space camps and had dreams of becoming an engineer for NASA. Only 10 students were allowed to meet Ride. Our daughter was not one of the children chosen. However, that wasn't what angered her. Our daughter was disturbed because only three young women were included in the group of 10. As I think back on this issue, I should have encouraged our daughter to speak to the principal about the issue of gender imbalance, especially since the students were meeting the first woman astronaut. Our daughter also felt disappointed that the school staff did not follow through on their convictions about gender equity in this opportunity. In some ways the choices made in this situation undermined some of the trust that the school tried to build. Also, by my not acting, my silence supported the status quo of gender bias. Sometimes it is not what we do that matters most; sometimes it is what we fail to do that is most powerful.

Caring teachers are **empowering** and not enabling. Caring teachers provide students with constructive and helpful suggestions. In this way, students are encouraged to mature, become more cooperative, and develop their talents and skills (Booth 1997). The teacher has high standards of excellence and encourages students to succeed on their own. They do not lower their expectations or do the work for their students. In Harlem at Central Park East Secondary School, students are continually assessed and encouraged to extend themselves (Meier 1995). Students must take on increasing responsibility for their learning, communicate effectively with their peers, and meet deadlines (Meier 1995). Students are encouraged and are mentored to be doers and thinkers.

On the other hand, enabling teachers may not push students to do their work or hold high expectations. Enabling teachers encourage dependency on the part of students by giving students the answer or providing too much help. Empowering and caring teachers understand the importance of providing a safe and positive environment that encourages students to learn on their own. This means that children might fail and learn from their mistakes. Caring teachers provide a learning environment that encourages children to do their best and to strive for excellence. Students know that these teachers support them as they struggle through difficult times.

> ⑤ Caring teachers are empowering and not enabling.

The Culture of Schools

Schools, like students, have a culture. The culture of schools is made up of accepted practices, rituals, norms, routines, and expectations (Sadker and Sadker 2003). Families who are members of mainstream middle-class society often accept and pass on to their children many aspects of schooling. For example, many youngsters have visited and used the public library and/or bookstore. Their parents may receive the local newspaper every day and have tradebooks in the home. Culturally relevant teachers understand that it may take time for students who have not grown up in a middle-class mainstream orientation to become familiar with these expectations. Students who have not grown up in mainstream environments will bring to school a different bank or different **funds of knowledge** (Moll 1990; McIntyre, Rosebery, and González 2001). They may arrive at school with diverse frames of reference. However, other students may arrive at school knowing many socially accepted practices. For instance, because she has attended Sunday school or preschool, a child may know that she is expected to raise her hand and be called on before she is allowed to speak in a classroom. This might be a hard rule for another child to learn if, at their home, children were expected to respond with quick wit. At school, students learn the cultural expectations of mainstream society, whether it deals with verbal interaction styles or knowledge of school practices. Cultural knowledge is always changing. For example, computers are becoming a common item for many students in today's school culture. Some parents see a computer as a necessary school supply. Today, the culture of schooling often requires students to have access to a computer at home to do their schoolwork because the culture of schools often represents middle-class mainstream culture. However, not all families are able to buy this expensive equipment.

There are other cultural school practices that students are often expected to know. Today, when students enter kindergarten, many teachers expect them to know how to turn the pages of a book, understand the sequence of a story, recite the alphabet, and even be able to read. Therefore, teachers often begin by teaching isolated skills like spelling and phonics. These skills are often taught in a decontextualized setting; that is, there is no context or reason for what they are learning. However, these types of skills do not assist students in developing meaning from their learning (McIntyre et al. 2001). Researchers have found that in urban schools little connection is often made between the materials students were reading and their everyday lives, so their skill development was being hampered by the teaching methods used (Lipman 1998; Delpit 1995). Because reading is about making sense of life, learning isolated skills can hamper students' abilities to understand without a meaningful context. For instance, I know some teachers in urban schools who have students read about farm work in lessons that teach comprehension skills. A story may be about a girl who milks a cow every morning and about how the cow chews her cud. If a student lived her whole life in the city and had never been to a farm, never fed hay to a dairy cow, and never milked a cow, it might be difficult for her to explain the sequence and vocabulary of the story. Teachers in this case are not only teaching comprehension skills, but also new social studies and science concepts. The student from the city is more likely to learn comprehension skills quicker when teachers use stories the students can relate to such as one about going on a trip downtown on the bus. Culturally relevant teachers build on what students know and develop reading skills in ways that relate skills being learned to students' local experiences. Then students do not have to learn both new reading skills and other cultural perspectives and information simultaneously. Teachers who are sensitive and responsive to cultures know that students from working-class families and communities of color bring rich cultural knowledge and social practices to school. Their backgrounds may be different, but they are not deficient (McIntyre et al. 2001).

Another good example of how a teacher builds on the richness that students bring to school was developed by Booth. Cleta Booth (1997) designed a unit on fibers, building on what students were interested in, and encouraged parents to contribute to the project, too. The unit was a collaborative effort between students and teacher that included historical information, discussion of farming, weaving from different cultures, and the arts. Through the learning process, one of her students wanted to share with the class the feel of wool, so his parents brought two sheep, Lucky and Lucy, to the school. Each child had the opportunity to feel the "warm but dirty, oily, smelly wool" (Booth 1997, 81). When the children saw one of the parents cut raw wool from the sheep, one youngster asked, "Does it hurt?" The parent answered that it was like getting a haircut. Later an artisan showed the class how to twist the wool into yarn and then weave it into fabric. Later another parent demonstrated how to use a knitting machine, and students discussed the concept of labor. Booth wrote that one of the most important aspects of the unit was that children became actively involved in directing their own learning and constructing meaning. Units such as this one provide students with the opportunity to be self-empowered learners and model the importance of collaboration and dialogue. These skills are critical in a democracy. The next section discusses conflicts within a social system that espouses equity, but may not always act in ways that support this value.

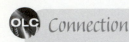

Connection

Please visit the text website **http://lchc.ucsd.edu** for Chapter 8 to link to the following sites: The Laboratory of Comparative Human Cognition is an organization that looks at the influence of culture on cognition and human development. Their work draws on the research of Vygotsky, Dewey, and Luria.

People have created cultures all around the world. 21st Century Schools is a good website for teachers to find teaching resources on topics such as diversity, population growth, immigration, and war. There is also a section developed by Merry Merryrfield, a professor at Ohio State University, of online modules that can be found at **http://www.coe.ohio-state.edu/ mmerryfield/global_resources/default.htm.**

The Paradox of Equity: Conflicts with Democratic Ideals

Caring for each other as precious human beings ties in with our nation's values of social justice, democracy, and moral courage (Hursh and Ross 2000). These values affirm the belief in human dignity and our commitment to care for each other. They also tie intimately to our commitment to freedom and equality. I believe that people struggle for justice, freedom, and equality because we care for others and hold human life sacred. Democratic education seeks to develop self-directed citizens for a pluralistic world (Dewey 1916).

One of our major objectives as a community must be to challenge an accepted system that has subordinated and continues to subordinate people based on race, class, and gender in schools (McLaren 1997). In other words, as educators, we must eliminate inequitable or damaging practices. Practices such as academic tracking, lack of a common core curriculum for all students, proportionately more African Americans suspended from school, lower levels of school funding in poor neighborhoods, and overcrowded classrooms in culturally diverse neighborhoods are examples of how we, as a nation, accept inequities in our schools (McLaren 1997; Kozol 1991; Oakes 1982). Deborah Meier, former principal of Central Park East, a high school in Harlem, spoke about this bias:

> When people think "those kids" need something special, the reply we offer at CPESS [Central Park East Secondary School] is, Just give them what you have always offered those who have the money to buy the best, which is mostly a matter of respect.
>
> I think we've created a framework at CPESS for creating such a respectful setting, day by day. We don't create all the conditions that affect our students' lives; we can't stop the world our students live in while we do our work . . . We have no guarantees to offer our kids, their families . . . beyond trying our best to make CPESS a place that at least temporarily makes life seem more interesting and worth the effort . . . This takes time and trust. Trust can't be mandated, but because students and families come to us by choice, at least some modest basis for mutual trust is built in . . . (Meier 1995, 49).

As Meier indicated, education for democracy will not be created without the underlying values of respect and interconnection. Schools do not seriously address the inequities of race, class, and gender bias. Why? Aronowitz (1997), a sociologist, believes that since the American **ideology of equal opportunity** is so pervasive in the majority culture, most people think that each individual has an equal chance to make it in society. In addition, the United States is an **open society** without distinct social class lines; therefore, each person, if she or he works hard enough and long enough, has unlimited opportunities in this country. An English teacher tells his class a story about this misconception. His father told him, "When I came to this country from Hong Kong, U.S. Americans told me the U.S. was the 'Land of Opportunity.' They were wrong. It is the land of struggle. And I found out that people don't treat you well. I had a good job as a cook at a large privately owned hotel, but then a corporation bought the hotel and laid me off. I was their best cook. I cooked French and U.S. American food, but then they hired new immigrants to cook at minimum wage and I was out of a job after 15 years."

The issue of social class is intricately tied to issues of race, ethnicity, culture, and other social groupings. As the Chinese immigrant related in his story, his struggles in the United States are primarily those of social class although he did understand there could also be covert racial bias operating. After being dismissed as a cook, he is now fighting to save a modest deli in an industrial area. He learned that it was not loyalty, length of service, or years of quality, but profit that was the underlying principle of business. The corporation put him out of a job, but also was treating the new cooks unfairly; at minimum wage, they were receiving much less for the work in comparison to others who cooked at other hotels.

Many U.S. citizens also believe that they live in a country ruled by consensus and where cultural assimilation is an accepted aspect of the U.S. culture (Aronowitz 1997; Darder 1991). In order to become a U.S. "American," it is necessary for immigrants or culturally different U.S. Americans in our country to conform to the dominant culture. Although people can air their differences of opinion, the beliefs and ways of the dominant group in society remain dominant and are reflected in the canon taught in U.S. schools. Aronowitz explains, "While Americans may differ with one another concerning economic and social policy and may form distinct political parties, on the whole they agree on the underlying free-market, capitalistic framework of social arrangements. Among other things, this agreement presupposes the historic success of assimilation of immigrant groups into a common ground of values and beliefs (Aronowitz 1997, 191).

What does Aronowitz mean? I believe that he is saying that there are conflicts between our value of equality and our economic system of capitalism. You may believe in political equality—that everyone should be treated justly before the law. However, think about how divided we are based on how much money we each have. How are you treated at a department store when you are dressed up? Now imagine yourself going to the store in shorts and a paint-stained T-shirt. Will you be treated differently? Unfortunately, you will probably be treated with more respect when you are dressed professionally than dressed casually. Furthermore, who will get more political power—someone who works as a food server or someone who is head of a software company? Most likely the person who is chairperson of a company knows others who have political power because they find themselves at similar meetings.

Take a Stand

EQUALITY AND EQUITY

In this chapter is a discussion of how we as a nation share national values such as equality and justice; however, many students from underrepresented groups are not succeeding in school. Because schooling is one of the major avenues for students of color and students from lower-income families to develop successful careers, some teachers believe that when students do not achieve, they are not receiving equal educational opportunities.

There is a difference between equality and equity. Equality refers to sameness, while equity in schools is directed toward addressing particular needs of students. In addition, as Edmund Gordon has written, "The requirement is not equality of input, but equity of outcome." In other words, are students from all groups successful in school? Two of the most important questions teachers should consider are as follows:

- What should teachers be providing their students—equality or equity? Why?
- How do these values tie in with the Caring-Centered Multicultural Education framework?

How can a person with little money and little political influence gain more political clout? The person can join a politically active organization, but it will be difficult as an individual to gain more influence. The system is set up to protect the status quo (Darder 1991). Those in power will continue to hold and increase their power base. Political and economic power are integrally tied. Financially powerful people usually have more access to political power. The conflict between the values of equality and justice and capitalism is one of the most difficult paradoxes for people to see and understand because democracy and capitalism are accepted aspects of the American way of life.

The paradox can also be seen in schools. Many people believe that we live in a nation built on the principles of equality and justice and that our schools reflect those values; yet the United States has a long history of underachievement among children of color when compared to their European American peers (Darder 1991). Schooling is the main institutional path children of color and children from low-income families have to climb from the lower rungs of society. However, schools are also products of that society. For example, parents from more affluent communities may have more clout within the school than do parents with little financial resources.

Because we are a nation that supports social justice, teachers must examine how schools are part of a larger system of privileges. As Peter McLaren (1997) has passionately reminded his readers, our goal is not just to include diverse voices from society and to develop a consensus viewpoint; the critical issue is for us to have a "noisy democracy" in which people are continually challenging, building, revising and creating a nation where democracy addresses the integral web of race, class, and gender. We live in a society where, as my colleague David Strom reminds me, our nation is becoming a democracy. Strom told me,

> We need a "noisy democracy" in which people are continually challenging, building, revising, and creating a nation where democracy addresses the integral web of diversity.

Teaching critical thinking skills

"As a nation we are more of a democracy today than in 1776, but we are still in the process of becoming a democratic nation" (Strom 1999).

In regard to schooling, many scholars have moved from the concept of equality to equity. Edmund Gordon explained the difference clearly. "**[E]quality** requires sameness, but **equity** requires that treatments be appropriate and sufficient to the characteristics and needs of those treated" (1999, xiv). Gordon later discussed the policy statement of the New York State Board of Regents on education, which stated, "Every child in New York State is entitled to the resources necessary to provide the sound, basic education which the state Constitution requires. The requirement is not equality of input, but equity of outcome" (Gordon 1991, 3). These statements celebrate the potential of all students and the importance of school faculty to be sensitive to their diverse needs. As this section demonstrates, educators need to reflect carefully on their values and beliefs. This process of reflection is critical for a caring-centered teacher who holds the values of citizenship and democracy. The following section will identify several complex issues that teachers may want to consider in their goal of creating an equitable learning environment. Utilize the critical skills that Barry Beyer suggests in addressing their complexities.

Connection

Please visit Chapter 8 of the text website to link to the following sites: **www.ncss.org,** National Council for the Social Studies website. One of the pages they offer is called Citizen Central with resources and lesson plans for teachers about citizenship: **http://www.citizenshipcentral.org/.** Another excellent resource is the Smithsonian Institution: **www.si.edu.** There are 16 museums in the organization and their museums hold many of our important cultural and governmental artifacts.

Hot Topics for "Cool" (Reflective) Educators

Hot Topic One: The Use of "Appropriate" Vocabulary

Words are powerful tools. We use words to challenge others, we use them to bring people together, and we use words to inspire. Most of us know Martin Luther King's "I Have a Dream" speech in which he said, on the steps of the Lincoln Memorial in 1963, "I have a dream that one day this nation will rise up and live out the true meaning of its creed: 'We hold these truths to be self-evident: that all men are created equal . . .' When we let freedom ring, when we let it ring from every village and every hamlet, from every state and every city, we will be able to speed up that day when all of God's children, black men and white men, Jews and Gentiles, Protestants and Catholics, will be able to join hands and sing in the words of the old Negro spiritual, 'Free at last! free at last! thank God Almighty, we are free at last!' Words we use can be important symbols of underlying values that direct and shape our lives.

One of the most problematic issues that we must continue to deal with is the terms used to identify people from nonmainstream ethnic communities. Recently, the term *people of color* has become popular in academic and journalistic writing. The label is used to identify people who are from groups such as African American, Asian American, Latino, Pacific Islander, Native Americans, and interracial folks. I often use this term but am concerned because, although it does not mean White folks, many European Americans are just as brown as others and so they do have a "color." The use of this term has been a recent adoption during the past 10 or so years. In fact, it is surprising that we use *people of color* because for many years in this country the term *colored people* was seen as extremely negative and demeaning.

Another term that is still used quite often is *minority*. It is true that nonmainstream ethnic people are numerical minorities when looking at the entire society. Approximately 69 percent are White U.S. Americans and 31 percent are folks from underrepresented groups. However, as shown in Chapter 1, the largest 25 districts in the country have majority student populations who come from nonmajority ethnic communities, so they are not numerical minorities; in fact, these students make up the majority of the students when taken all together.

The term *minority* also has negative connotations. Often, an undertone accompanies this word that seems to convey a sense of being disadvantaged, at-risk, deficient, or flawed. Therefore, I am more hesitant to use this term than others are.

Another term that is often used is *culturally diverse people.* This term identifies that nonmainstream ethnic people may hold a culture that is different from the general society. The term seems to say that White folks do not have a culture or that their culture is neutral or the standard. One of the major reasons why this term is problematic is that many European Americans have strong cultural ties. For example, many European Americans have a strong ethnic identification with the French, German, Italian, Russian, and/or Swedish community.

The phrase "people from underrepresented groups" is also used in literature. This phrase may be more accurate because many students who are from nonmajority ethnic communities, such as African Americans and Latinos, are not successful in schools and so are underrepresented in this way. Another way to view this is that nonmajority ethnic groups are often politically underrepresented also. For example, how many Latino presidents have we had in this country? None. How many senators from Latino backgrounds have represented various states in Congress? Few. Therefore, Latinos are often politically underrepresented in our national government.

Carol Lee's discussion of race and ethnicity in an issue of *Educational Researcher* (2003) clearly identified the difficulties in identifying terms that best describe people who have faced institutional racism and intergenerational poverty. Lee also grappled with dynamic issues of culture and ethnicity. She carefully explained how scholars often used the European American middle class as the point of reference in research. This practice places other groups, such as Latinos, African Americans, Native Americans, Asian Pacific Islander Americans, and European Americans who face continual poverty at the margins. The issue is one of authority and power. The use of a term such as *person of color* is an attempt to focus attention on the educational, developmental, and political needs of individuals who are not positioned at the center of society.

The most important issue that Lee presents is the need for educators and other service providers to talk about the challenges faced by African American, Latino/a, Native American, Asian Pacific Islander American, and European American people who must address continual poverty. She identifies four areas of concern:

a) [T]he range of normative psychosocial developmental tasks they face as human beings across their life spans;

b) [T]he additional threats with which they grapple due to racism, institutionalized assumptions of White and middle-class privilege, and inequitable access to institutional resources such as schools, health care services, employment, and housing;

c) [T]he range of diversity within ethnic groups; and

d) [T]he context-dependent nature of displays of competence (Lee 2003, 4).

In other words, Lee identified the need for educators and others to address the racism that is found in institutions and areas of life such as schools, universities, hospitals, businesses, banking, and housing. In addition, there is a range of diversity within groups although groups are often seen as a homogenous entity. However, an added complexity is that there are culturalethnic beliefs and behaviors that can be found within groups.

Lee (2003) indicated her frustration with the ability to identify the best term to use so that researchers will examine equity issues as they impact many people who are underserved or excluded from full participation in society. In much of the literature, *culturally diverse, people of color,* and *people from underrepresented groups* are the most common terms used to denote nonmajority ethnic individuals and groups. Throughout this text, I use several different terms to identify majority and nonmajority folks. Sometimes I use terms such as *European American* or *Asian American* so that the reader will recognize the populations I am referring to. These terms will probably change in the next 20 years.

What term or terms do you think we should use in schools? You may not arrive at a decision right away; however, this leads to the next issue of why we should use ethnic terms at all. The state of California is sometimes a trendsetter. For example, yogurt shops first became fashionable in California. Politically, certain issues also arise that sometimes spread to other states. The next section describes Proposition 54, *The Racial Privacy Initiative* and the issue of using ethnic labels.

Hot Topic Two: California's Proposition 54, *The Racial Privacy Initiative*

Some people may ask, Why do we use any ethnic label at all? Initially, I believe that people from nonmajority ethnic groups have been, and in some cases continue to be, excluded from participating in governmental affairs consciously or unconsciously. Although this section is not designed to be a review of U.S. history, I include two examples of how social categories have been used to exclude folks from being full members of society. During the early years of this country, a person who was African American or Native American was considered to be only two-thirds of a person. In addition, for many years, women were not permitted to vote. In fact, even Anglo women couldn't vote until 1920 when the Nineteenth Amendment was passed. Groups of people have been identified by their ethnic affiliation, characteristics, or gender and then excluded from participating in society.

In order to eliminate this type of exclusion, a movement led by Ward Connerly, a University of California regent, was launched to prevent the gathering of statistics by race, national origin, ethnicity, or color. Connerly and his followers introduced, for voters in the state of California, Proposition 54, otherwise known as the **Racial Privacy Initiative.** On the initiative's website (racialprivacy.com) is the statement, "We acknowledge our diversity, but we celebrate our unity. Instead of a nation of hyphenated-Americans, let us be one nation indivisible." Connerly and his group believed that it is discriminating to keep statistics based on the previously mentioned social categories. The initiative was designed to encourage a color-blind society. Connerly has been identified as a member of the African American community. The proposition would have prevented schools, governmental agencies, and contractors from keeping data regarding race, ethnicity, national origin, or color. Therefore, teachers would not be able to identify the academic achievement of students by race and the police could not accumulate information based on the ethnic background of the person. This initiative did not eliminate the keeping of statistics regarding gender.

Several organizations that supported this initiative were as follows: Coalitions for America, California Congress of Republicans, Association of Concerned

Taxpayers, and many individuals, such as Thomas Sowell, a sociologist, and Shelby Steele, a writer.

Certain federal regulations call for universities and schools to report various statistics by ethnic and/or racial groupings. For example, No Child Left Behind requires that reports be submitted that discuss the progress of various student groups. In these cases, what would the schools in California do? In order to address federal mandates, some statistics could be gathered by schools and other agencies; however, this information could not be used by the schools in other ways.

Numerous organizations that opposed this initiative included Anti-Defamation League, Japanese American Citizens League, NAACP, Organization for Chinese Americans, California Nurses Association, California Faculty Association, Mexican American Legal Defense and Education Fund, California Academy of Family Physicians, Native American Health Center, and California Teachers Association. These organizations were concerned about numerous inequities. They specifically identified three major issues. One was the increase in hate crimes toward groups such as Middle Eastern Americans. Second, police would not be allowed to keep statistics dealing with issues of racial profiling. Supporters of Proposition 54 indicated that the proposition was written in such a way as to keep law enforcement from profiling people based on race or ethnicity. Third, many students from nonmajority ethnic groups are not successful in schools. If gathering statistics on the achievement of students from various groups is prohibited, students can fall through the system.

One of the provisions of the initiative stated that some medical statistics could be kept for research purposes, but health care professionals were still concerned with the overall wording of the initiative. They believed that adult health issues would be impacted by the passage of Proposition 54. For example, cancers, health disease, sickle cell anemia, osteoporosis, and many other illnesses strike various ethnic groups in different ways. Researchers have found that people from certain groups are more prone to specific diseases. For example, African Americans and Latinos have a high incidence of diabetes or "the sugar." It is also important to keep statistics regarding the health of children. They often must deal with issues such as asthma, infant mortality, child abuse, and obesity. Health care professionals have been able to reduce rates of various childhood maladies by keeping statistics based on ethnic background and by conducting community-based informational campaigns. Without these statistics, health care prevention is hampered.

One possible consequence of Proposition 54's being passed was raised by Julian Bond, chairperson of the National Association for the Advancement of Color People (NAACP). Bond believed that the proposition would have made it unlawful for a person to sue another for discrimination based on race or ethnicity.

Many people may be able to understand why Connerly and his supporters wanted to move toward what he calls a color-blind society. Proposition 54 might have worked in an ideal social situation; however, in real life people are discriminated against continually due to their color, race, and/or ethnicity. Unfortunately, the statistics of hate crimes and low achievement of students from nonmajority ethnic groups identify a continual problem that must be addressed. People are treated as though there are different races. There is evidence that people with darker skin are arrested more often than other folks. Also in society, if people were discriminated against because of physical characteristics and this created more poverty in some communities than in others, the situation would have an impact on the ability of people to have access to health care. People discriminate against others based on perceived categories, and these social factors can lead to oppression in schools, medicine, employment, voting, and many other aspects of life. The question is, Would Proposition 54 lessen the discrimination in society or heighten it? What do you think? The most important issue is not race, but equity. Unfortunately, the initiative seemed misguided.

Regarding the outcome of the vote on the initiative, voters in California defeated the racial privacy proposition in the October 2003 election. Sixty-four percent of the voters voted against the initiative (*Los Angeles Times* 2003, A27).

Connection

To read more about issues surrounding the Racial Privacy initiative, go to the following website **www.adl.org** supported by the Anti-Defamation League website.

The next section raises the issue of how content area knowledge can add to institutional and social prejudice. An important aspect of being a teacher is to read materials in a broad range of disciplines. Although it is important to read educational books, it is also important to expand one's knowledge in areas such as biology, ecology, literature, mathematics, medicine, opera, and Mexican history. The next hot topic looks at how the concept of race has been presented in several content areas.

Hot Topic Three: The Influence of Content Area Knowledge: Race

The concept of race is a complex one that involves information from various disciplines, such as history, biology, evolution, genetics, and paleontology. One reason why I raise this particular topic is that teachers and students must be able to make decisions about extremely complex issues. There are few black and white answers and many grey ones to consider.

As a child I watched a television program called "To Tell the Truth." Three different contestants appeared on the program claiming to be the same person. The contestants would try to fool the panelists into thinking they were that individual. In my own education, sometimes I feel like a panelist on the show trying to decide the answer to Who is telling the truth? because I was not given a comprehensive knowledge of specific concepts such as race.

In my own education, most teachers and professors presented the issue of race as a biological fact. In fact, despite mounting evidence to the contrary, some colleagues continue to teach from that viewpoint. Africans are distinctly different from Asians. Asians are distinctly different from Europeans. Europeans are distinctly different from Native Americans—all because of their distinct and profound biological makeup. And it goes on and on.

How did people get the idea that Africans, Europeans, Native Americans, and Asians are different? The classification of animals and plants originated with the

Culturally diverse teachers

work of Carl Linnaeus. In 1735 Linnaeus identified humans as a species within the order Primate (Fredrickson 2002, 56), and he also wanted to further classify humans. Linnaeus created labels for four groups of humans, namely, Africans, Asians, Europeans, and American Indians. But there are serious problems with these categories. As biologists explain it, if we were really so different from each other—that is, if we were really different species—then we would not be able to mate and have children. However, we are all part of the biological category called *Homo sapiens.*

Fredrickson (2002) has provided evidence that the concept of race as we know it today did not exist for Greeks and Romans. The Greeks did not consider skin color. Rather, they made distinctions between those whom they considered civilized and those who were barbarians. The Romans had slaves who were considered inferior; however, the enslaved people came from many nationalities and were of many colors. Consideration of skin color is primarily a modern strategy. In Chapter 3 is a short discussion of how the modern concept of race was created by the work of Linnaeus (1758) and his protégé, Friedrich Blumenbach (1776), who were both naturalists during the 18th century. The views of Blumenbach were intimately tied to prejudicial beliefs based on outward physical appearances and his perceived view of personality differences. His work, called *On the Natural Varieties of Mankind* (1776) built upon the beliefs of Linnaeus, who identified such skin colors as black, red, yellow, and white with dispositions such as apathetic, angry, melancholy, and optimistic. Blumenbach moved from Linneaus's geographically oriented categorization to a hierarchical one (Fredrickson 2002). Blumenbach thought the people who lived near the Mount Caucasus were the most ideally beautiful. He also believed that human evolution had begun in that same area and he created the term *Caucasians.* His beliefs reflected those of other Europeans during the Enlightenment period. At that time many Europeans saw themselves as superior to other groups. Blumenbach became known as the father of physical anthropology and acknowledged that humans were members of the same species; however, he listed the following ideal types: Americans, Caucasians, Ethiopians, Mongolians, and Malays. People today still hold beliefs somewhat similar to Blumenbach, whose work is the source of how many categorize variations in humans. This belief system became part of European folk knowledge and contributed to White privilege (Johnson, Rush, and Feagin 2000).

The concept of racism also is of modern origin. Although oppressive practices are part of the history of many countries, Fredrickson (2002) found that the use of the word *racism* became popular in the 1930s to describe the theories of the Nazis and their persecution of the Jews (5). The rise of racism as a concept became synonymous with the maltreatment of people whose ethnocultural traits were seen as inborn, permanent, and irreversible. Fredrickson carefully explained, "Racism, therefore, is more than theorizing about human differences or thinking badly of a group over which one has no control. It either directly sustains or proposes to establish a racial order, a permanent group hierarchy that is believed to reflect the laws of nature or the decrees of God" (6). The difference between racism and xenophobia is about the intrinsic and unalterable inferiority of a group of people, not whether a group of people are strangers and not in-group members.

When people use externally visible physical characteristics as the markers in how they group people, these groups are referred to as phenotypes. One group may have members who are predominantly darker in skin, while others may be more fair in their coloration. Groups may have different body builds or hair textures or eye shapes. However, phenotypes have been used destructively. Phenotype has been used for hundred of years to *deny the humanity* of those who are seen as "others." Often one group may want to exterminate or may actually proceed to eradicate these others. For example, in the early days of the United States, people believed they could distinguish between free and enslaved people by the color of their skin and other physical attributes. There are numerous examples of how so-called phenotypically based racial membership has been used politically to segregate or exclude people, or to exterminate these others, such as the actions directed against Native Americans.

Returning to the question Who is telling the truth? I studied the work of geneticists, paleontologists, anthropologists, and biologists such as Gould, Olson, Ridley, Sykes, Rosenberg, and Ward. I did this so that I had a clearer understanding of the concepts and constructs of human evolution. I learned that the truth has become more unambiguous because of advances in scientific methods and gathering of new information about human origins.

Here were some of the questions that plagued me:

Where is the origin of humans?

What does it mean to be human?

What does it mean to be Asian or African?

As I get older, I realize how complex most issues are in education, and this necessitates that we, as teachers, have a strong background in many fields. Moreover, I believe that one of the more potent strategies that can help to dispel misconceptions and prejudice that are taught about us, the modern human, is to pull together clear and accurate knowledge about who we really are and how we arrived at the present day. This interest in expanding the field of education and in becoming a more complete educator has therefore led me to read and integrate the knowledge from many disciplines, such as history, anthropology, biology, cultural geography, genetics, and paleontology. Additionally, this new knowledge must be imparted to students so that they have more complete information about our essential underlying biological unity.

Scientific information has been used in the past (Gould 2002) to reinforce racist beliefs. The same tools of modern science can be used to break down long-held stereotypes and misconceptions that people hold about race. It is my hope that the emerging developments of modern science will be used to set the record straight, as well as to eliminate the racism that comes from using phenotypes to divide humankind into so-called races.

Myth 1: We are more different than alike.

Children are often told that we are more different than alike, as if this were a true statement. However, as Maya Angelou has said, "We are more alike than we are different." For example, in school, teachers can be heard saying, "We all have feelings and can be hurt." In other words, teachers may be telling their students that everyone has emotions that are universal. What teachers are reflecting in these beliefs is that we are all members of the human family that scientists call *Homo sapiens*.

As noted earlier, naturalists such as Linnaeus and Blumenbach desired to create more particular subspecie categories for humans. Linnaeus identified human categories as Africans, American Indians, Asians, and Europeans (Fredrickson 2002). Today people often use terms such as Africans, Asians, American Indians, Europeans, and Latinos. However, let's look at some of the newest information that has arisen out of genetics.

Although we all have the same set of genes, "there are differences in the DNA sequences of our genes" (Olson 2002, 17). There are variations in how the DNA sequences express themselves. Responses to physical environments and long isolation from each other over time do produce the secondary phenotypic differences such as physical characteristics, sensitivity to particular diseases, and geographical ancestry. However, does that mean that in reality every human has different DNA sequences? Or are we humans in the current modern era really different species, usually labeled black white, yellow, and brown peoples? The data suggest otherwise, namely, that we are biologically more similar than different.

As members of *Homo sapiens,* most humans have 23 pairs of chromosomes and the "same set of genes. But many of the genes come in slightly different versions" (Olson 2002, 17).[1] In each cell of our bodies, there is a six-foot string of DNA (deoxyribonucleic acid) (Olson 2002). Biologically we are all part of the same family, the human family. One of the most important research projects in modern science is the Human Genome Project (HGP) (O'Neill 2002). This project was a 13-year research program primarily focused on identifying the human genome sequence of three billion pairs of nucleotides (adenine, thymine, cytosine, and guanine, often referred to as A, T, C, and G) of which DNA is made up and also to distinguish the approximately 30,000 to 35,000 genes in the human DNA.[2] Our differences are actually quite superficial, although the isolation of some populations, their close intermarriage, and environmental differences have generated variations in how some genes express themselves. Yes, some groups are susceptible to different diseases, and yes, we do have pigmentation differences; however, to say that we are more different than alike is to perpetuate a myth. Underneath our skins, we are truly more alike than different.

Myth 2: Humans evolved from several regions on earth. This is often known as the multiregion hypothesis.

There seems to be some controversy regarding this myth. Scholars such as Thorne and Wolpoff (2003) argued that scientific evidence of multiregional evolution is compelling. However, many more scholars believe that modern humans evolved from eastern Africa. Various scholars (Gould 2002; Olson 2002; King and Motulsky 2002; Cann and Wilson 2003) have reported that there is little doubt that the origin of *Homo sapiens* comes from a small group of humans in Africa. Olson wrote about this belief: "Every single one of the 6 billion people on the planet today is descended from the small group of anatomically modern humans who once lived in eastern Africa" (Olson 2002, 3). "Everyone alive today is either an African or a descendant of Africans" (Olson 2002, 38). The evidence points to an origin in eastern Africa, where *Homo sapiens* lived in lush savannas in countries now known as Kenya and Tanzania. This is what Bryan Sykes, a genetics professor from Oxford University, wrote about the beginnings of humans:

> [W]e need only go back in time as far as Mitochondrial Eve. The genetics tell us very clearly that modern humans had their origins in Africa within the last hundred and fifty thousand years. At some point, about a hundred thousand years ago, modern

---

[1]Some persons may have more or less than the 23 pairs of chromosomes. For example, a person with Down syndrome has an extra chromosome 21. There are three copies rather than just two. This extra chromosome creates differences in physical appearance and intelligence and shortens the life span (Ridley 2000).

[2]There is controversy about the number of genes in the human body. Although many researchers believe there are 30,000 to 35,000, other scholars have estimated there may be more than 100,000 genes. See the article by Tom Hollon, "Human Genes: How Many?" *The Scientist* 15 no. 20: 1. The article can be found at www.the-scientist.com/yr2001/oct/hollon_p1_011015.html.

humans began to spread out of Africa to begin the eventual colonization of the rest of the world. Incredible as it may seem, we can tell from the genetic reconstructions that this settlement of the rest of the world involved only one of the thirteen African clans. It could not have been a massive movement of people (2001, 277).

How can scientists say that we descended from the same mother? In the late 1980s a group of scientists studied the mitochondria DNA of human cells (Sykes 2001). The mitochondria in our cells are passed down from our mothers through the egg cells. The Eve, whose mitochondria is found in all of us, most likely lived about 150,000 years ago in eastern Africa (Olson 2002). Other women lived at the same time as the "woman who produced all the mitochondrial DNA on the planet today." However, their mitochondria have gone extinct (Olson 2002, 26). Mitochondria are elements in cells that provide the energy needed to conduct various chemical reactions. The subsequent genetic and paleontological science that has been conducted from that point in time has consistently verified, that we modern humans are descendants from this Eve (Sykes 2001). It is important to note that Sykes brought up the importance of cultural orientation in naming the woman Eve. The use of *Eve* denotes a distinctly Judeo-Christian orientation, because it does not seem to be an African name. This is another indication of how science utilizes a powerful Western civilization orientation.

Myth 3: Race is an accurate biological construct and humans are members of five distinct categories.

Teachers need to review their understanding of the biological concept of race and how the belief in racial categories has resulted in misconceptions. Today's use of race is like a placeholder to indicate that "there are repeatable, regular, distinctions between groups . . . and races represent combinations of physical characteristics like color that would be noticeable in the field, coinciding with geographical correlations" (Newsome 2003). However, new scientific data have provided major findings about modern humans. In fact, Himla Soodyall, a geneticist from South Africa, said, "The data have the potential to abolish racism . . . Race is purely circumstantial. It establishes a social hierarchy that people can use to exploit others. But that hierarchy has no basis in biology" (as quoted in Olson 2002, 39).

If racial groups were real, how would they be defined? Would we look at the shape of our nose or texture of our hair? If skin color were one of the measures, how would skin color differences be quantified? Would there be a chart that indicated different skin tones and their corresponding racial categories? For example, how light is light or what is an olive skin tone? Today, people often use skin color and other physical characteristics to define a race. These categories often have connotations attached to them. However, few people may understand that there is much within group variance with regards to physical characteristics. Physical characteristics are adaptations from living in specific climates. As Jablonski and Chaplin (2002) have demonstrated, skin color patterns in the world are due to natural selection. In this process the body regulates the impact of ultraviolet radiation. "Throughout the world, human skin color has evolved to be dark enough to prevent sunlight from destroying the nutrient folate but light enough to foster the production of vitamin D"

(Jablonski and Chaplin 2002, 75). The earliest *Homo sapiens* evolved from Africa approximately 120,000 to 150,000 years ago, and their skin adapted to the conditions of ultraviolet radiation and the heat. Melanin acted as a natural sunscreen. Melanin "is a large organic molecule that . . . serves the dual purpose of physically and chemically filtering the harmful effects of UV radiation; it absorbs UV rays, causing them to lose energy, and it neutralizes harmful chemicals called free radicals that form in the skin after damage by UV radiation . . . Although most of the effects of UVB are harmful, the rays perform one indispensable function: initiating the formation of vitamin D in the skin" (Jablonski and Chaplin 2002, 75). As people moved to northern areas of the world, they lost their skin pigmentation. Therefore, skin color is an adaptation of the body to survive in various types of geographical environments and is not an indication of any level of intelligence or abilities.

At the same time, we teachers need to be aware of objections and seemingly real problems that have surfaced within the scientific research community. For example, although humans are genetically 99.9 percent the same, there are distinctive individual differences (Satel 2002). Researchers in medicine have found particular epidemiological tendencies in different populations. Here are several examples that Satel (2002) identified:

> [W]hen doctors transplant kidneys or bone marrow, they have more difficulty finding a tissue match for African Americans because there are more possible antigen (protein) combinations on their cell surfaces than on the cells of white patients; some of those antigens are very rare in the population at large. In treating pain, doctors often give low doses of narcotics to Asian patients, given their sensitivity to the effects of those drugs. Or consider the higher mortality rate from breast cancer among African-American women. While obstacles to timely diagnosis and treatment may partly account for this difference, it cannot tell the entire story, as African-American women have a 50 percent higher incidence of breast cancer before the age of 35, a greater likelihood of developing more aggressive tumors as well as the highest incidence of pre-menopausal cancer (75).

Satel contends we cannot have it two ways; in other words, we cannot say there is no such thing as race and then pour millions of dollars into research that targets specific racial groups. However, this difficulty can also be dispelled by the fact that no so-called racial group is actually genetically homogeneous. Many other factors such as oppressive socioeconomic circumstances (e.g., poverty) (Zigler and Syfco 2001) and other unhealthy situations in certain human groups labeled as races can account for the variations in the incidence of specific health conditions. Additionally, genetic studies of the so-called races have continually demonstrated that these groups have more individual variations within the group in which they are classified than between the different human groups that are labeled as races. Therefore, some scientists believe these categories are not separate authentic biological groupings (Romualdi et al. 2002). In addition, researchers found that many groups have similar attributes (Rosenberg, Pritchard, Weber, Cann, Kidd, Zhivotovsky, and Feldman 2002). In a genetic population study, Rosenberg, et al. (2002) looked at almost 400 markers in 1,056 people and found six genetic clusters that corresponded to five major geographical areas. However, the genetic differences found were small and reflected gradations rather than unique genotypes. This study, along with other research, supports the finding that most human genetic variation is due to differences among individuals *within* populations rather than to differences between populations (King and Motulsky 2002).

Summary

Issues do not arise in a vacuum. They evolve within complex cultural and social contexts. Because teachers and students must be able to make decisions about complicated issues dealing with ideals, values, and beliefs, they must gather relevant content area knowledge and examine divergent views. I hope that this section demonstrates that there are many complex issues that educators should consider. Science as a discipline has played several roles in modern racism; some scientific work has contributed to racism; other scientific information offers corrections to prejudicial ideas. In an important instance, much of the so-called scientific evidence about racial differences draws from the Middle Ages, a period in European history when the scientific classification of *Homo sapiens* was created (Fredrickson 2002). This was followed by early editions of now-distinguished journals in psychological measurement that sought publishable studies to demonstrate the inferiority of some racial groups. Much of the work of Jensen (1969), as well as *The Bell Curve* (1994), argues that some races are naturally inferior in intelligence to others by drawing on data from standardized test measures, the development of which is rooted in the separation of races by test scores. Intelligence tests do what they were designed to do, but they may not actually measure intelligence (Gould 1996).

The concept of race is complex and many scholars agree that race is a social and political construct that was developed by people to justify their behaviors of oppression, segregation, and extermination (Gould 1996; Fuchs 1997; Olson 2002; Hilliard 2002). Complex systems of oppression and privilege have been created to preserve the power of the dominant community (Johnson, Rush, and Feagin 2000). Researchers continue to provide new information about our human family. In a population study about human diversity, Romualdi and his colleagues (2002) found that it was difficult to accurately identify individuals with their continent of origin from a sample of about 6,000 individuals from around the world. This is what they wrote: "However, even when jointly considered, all of the markers we could use, including those of the Y chromosome, did not prove able to assign more than 70% of the individuals to their continent of origin. That is not what one would expect, if the human species were subdivided, and deep genetic discontinuities existed among continental groups" (607–8). They also stated that they thought that in the area of disease, the individual genotype was a better predictor of sensitivity to disease or drug response than was ethnic or geographic affiliation.

Other researchers do indicate higher incidence of diseases in specific populations. As Satel (2002) has reported, African Americans have a higher rate of heart disease than those who are today labeled White. In addition, specific medicines are more likely to make a difference in a Black patient's life than in a White individual. How should one think about these findings? There are biological differences between people. The question is, Are those small biological differences enough to define subspecies and create categories that can accurately classify an individual to a specific group? This does not mean researchers cannot look at disease in some folks as related to geographical ancestry. This information can be used as one of many indicators for prevention programs, treatment protocols, and research studies. This information must be used within the understanding that broad labels such as African American do not provide much information about the many subgroups that exist and the individual beliefs of people. For example, although Africa is a continent where genetic clustering can be found, that does not mean that all Africans have the same cultures, values, and histories.

Educators must have a broad knowledge base along with strong pedagogical understandings of teaching. As the "To Tell the Truth" program illustrated, people must search for and examine a comprehensive range of evidence because of the complexities of issues. Through this process teachers must question and challenge popular beliefs when they are based upon faulty information and biased social constructs. The next segment describes a teacher who has a broad grasp of issues and is a reflective educator. Linda Christiansen provides leadership in the area of equity, not only as a teacher but also as one of the editors of *Rethinking Schools,* a grassroots newspaper aimed at urban school reform.

Connection

Please visit the text website for Chapter 8 to link to the following sites:

- If you would like to read more about the Human Genome Project, I recommend the Human Genome Project Information website **www.ornl.gov/TechResources/Human_Genome/home.html.** Here you can find out information about the ethical issues, definition of terms, what the future plans are for the project, and many more aspects. It is an exceptional place to gather information.
- For hot topics for students, check out the website **http://www.justicelearning.org/** called *Justice Learning.* This website is a partnership of National Public Radio's Justice Talking and the New York Times Learning Network. The site provides materials on issues such as affirmative action, the death penalty, civil liberties in war, the drug war, gun control, and religion in schools.

Linda Christiansen: A Teacher Who Combines Caring and Social Justice

Caring-centered teachers build learning communities that address important social issues. They are committed to moving society toward more equitable solutions. They also teach their students how to question, evaluate, and make rational decisions. These teachers know that compassion and respect for others are at the core of social justice and a strong democratic community.

At a conference on Multicultural Education, I attended a speech given by an inspirational teacher, Linda Christiansen. She is a high school teacher from the Portland School District in Oregon. Linda helped me to better understand that in caring, teachers must tackle challenging social questions and review their own views and

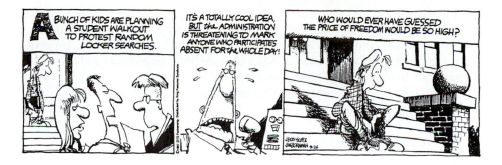

actions. Christiansen spoke from her heart about teaching English literature in a culturally diverse school with a majority of African American, Asian Pacific American, and Latino students. She believes that critical literacy does not center on language, but it is the teaching of basic skills and teaching about power relationships. Christiansen integrates the importance of both emotional and academic well-being. She provides students with an affirming and caring classroom where they learn to read, to write, to think deeply about social issues, to act upon their convictions, and to trust their own thinking. This is not an easy process for students. The comic strip, above, shows Jeremy, a high school student, weighing his beliefs and trying to decide what his actions should be. As Christiansen has explained, often students must make difficult decisions.

Christiansen carefully described how schools teach political values, even unconsciously. She said, Any piece of literature is political. It is part of the social blueprint of our nation. How I correct my students is political. Students must use tools of critical literacy to expose, toss back, and to remedy inequities. I want children to come away from my class knowing they can make changes in society (Christiansen 1997).

Christiansen asked the audience difficult questions, which I believe we all must ask ourselves. Although these questions are about language and literacy, they can be applied to other aspects of U.S. culture. Here is a sampling of them:

Whose language has power? Why?

Whose dialect has power? Why?

Whose voice carries more power? Why?

Who benefits from language power?

Who is hurt by language power?

How is language embedded in life? in culture? in power relationships?

When we are committed to caring for all students, we must not only look at our own biases but also at the social obstacles that are placed in front of many students of color, students from low-income families, and young women in our society.

Many people believe in social justice in theory or as an abstract thought, but they may not see or feel their human connections with others. I believe that, in part, this is why we have so many children of color not achieving in schools. We, as a nation, feel that nonachieving children, many of whom live in poverty or are from communities of color, are not our responsibility or that there is little we can do. Unfortunately, the result is that our nation has not addressed how our political and economic systems have impacted many young people.

Using Linda's model for questioning and returning back to the issue of race, here are some questions that arise:

Who created the social construct of race?

How is the social construct of race used?

Who benefits from the existence of the social construct of race?

Linda Christiansen is a leader in our national conversations on education. There are also examples of community groups who have provided guidance and direction in equal educational opportunities.

One of the critical issues in providing equal education is addressing language concerns. Language instruction has been heavily debated. The following section describes why language is a social justice issue and how bilingual education became part of the historical record and a component of many schools in our nation.

A Foundation for Bilingual Education: Latino and Chinese American Activism

Did you know that an important cornerstone in the foundation for bilingual education resulted from the activism of Chinese American and Latino parents? Although many people recognize the Chinese for the building of the railroads and know that many Latinos live in the Southwest, few may realize that members from these two communities have made important contributions to education. This section discusses several instances in which communities have fought for equality in education because of their strong moral commitment to young people.

In the 1960s after the large exodus of immigrants from Cuba, Cuban parents in Miami established private schools where Spanish was the primary language of instruction so that they could maintain the cultural and linguistic roots in their children (Ovando and Collier 1985). Bilingual classes were instituted due to the efforts of the Cuban community and "the first bilingual program was thus begun at Coral Way Elementary School in Miami" (Ovando and Collier 1985, 26). Other states followed this example. There are several reasons why Cuban Americans were able to implement bilingual instruction. As refugees, they were assisted by the Cuban Refugee Act, which provided special training and resources to new immigrants. Also, many Cubans who migrated were from middle- and upper-middle-class families; they had financial, educational, and social resources that were used to establish schools. Many teachers were part of the immigrant group and could teach in bilingual schools (Ovando and Collier 1985).

Another example of how the local community can impact education occurred in San Francisco in the 1970s. The Chinese American community struggled for many years with the San Francisco Unified School District in order to receive educational services for their children. As part of their moral commitment to education and students, members of the Chinese American community filed a class-action suit asking the district to hire bilingual teachers. The teachers would teach students academic content in their primary language so that the students could progress academically while they concurrently developed English language skills. Although it took over four years of litigation, the Supreme Court ruled in favor of the parents with the ground-breaking decision of *Lau* v. *Nichols* in 1974.

How did this momentous educational struggle begin? Kinney Lau and 12 other Cantonese-speaking students along with their parents filed a class-action suit on behalf of 1,800 children against Alan Nichols, the president of the San Francisco School Board. For many years Chinese American parents had been concerned because they did not feel their children were receiving adequate instruction because of their English language needs.

During the court hearing, the San Francisco Unified School District admitted that many children needed special instruction, but the district argued that it was not legally obligated to provide for those needs (Wang 1976). In *Lau* v. *Nichols,* the Supreme Court unanimously took the position that in order for children to participate equally in school, their education must be "meaningful" and "comprehensible"; because this was not the case, their civil rights had been violated. To address this problem, bicultural and bilingual programs were needed. The ruling became the backbone for bilingual education programs throughout the nation and supported the right of thousands of children who spoke languages other than English to equal access to education.

Other scholars contend that the right to an effective and appropriate education also comes from the Fourteenth Amendment, which calls for equal protection of each person under the law (Baca and Cervantes 1989). The importance of providing equal education to all was established in the 1954 Supreme Court decision of *Brown* v. *Board of Education of Topeka,* when segregation of Black and White schools was struck down as being "inherently unequal."

Since the decisions are legal ones, many discussions in the years following the rulings have debated how bilingual education programs should be implemented. The following is a discussion of one of the most effective models, a developmental bilingual education program.

Bilingual Education Programs

The term **bilingual education** refers to a variety of programs that differ in the use of different degrees of native languages and in the number of years students are participants (Ovando and Collier 1985; Moran and Hakuta 1995). Three of the more common programs are Transitional Bilingual Education (TBE), Maintenence Bilingual Education (MBE), and Two-Way Immersion.

In the TBE program the goal of teachers is to transition students from their home language to English as soon as possible. Although primary language is used to develop literacy skills that will transfer to English literacy once a certain level of English proficiency is reached, transition programs do not support the continued development of native language skills. In the MBE program, the goal is to support the development of social and academic language in the home/primary language as well as in English. Students become bilingual and biliterate. In a Two-Way Immersion program, students from the majority culture and youngsters from the ethnic community develop competencies in both languages. In this program, mainstream students learn a second language and ethnic students learn English while each community becomes bilingual and biliterate (Moran and Hakuta 1995). This is becoming a popular choice for mainstream students as they look toward learning more about others and developing their language capabilities.

What do many bilingual educators suggest? This is an extremely complicated issue. Research indicates that the longer students remain in transitional bilingual programs, the more likely they are to become proficient in English (Moran and Hakuta 1995). Why? When the content of the curriculum is taught in the first or home language of those who are learning English, students already know the social context, hidden meanings, abstract concepts, and nonverbal communications of the content. Their first language acts as a bridge in learning English because the vocabulary and concepts—especially in subjects like social studies—can be explained more easily and comprehensively in their first language. Because much of the language of mathematics is numbers, more English is utilized in this content area. One of the biggest problems that schools face in implementing solid bilingual programs is that students need approximately five to six years of instruction in both languages before they are truly able to perform at higher levels of academic competence. The bilingual education process takes time and cannot be accomplished in just one or two years. Another obstacle can come from school personnel who do not understand how linguistic bias in schools may be part of institutional racism that exists in society (Cummins 1989).

We are a multilingual and multicultural society. It is an advantage to be multilingual/bilingual and biliterate, whether it provides further employment opportunities, cognitive flexibility, or learning about a new worldview. Chapter 9 presents a comprehensive discussion of second-language acquisition and bilingual education programs.

Teaching is comprehensive. As Dewey suggested, teachers are teaching a way of life and not just the "facts of life." As such, caring-centered education focuses on the importance of teaching the whole student and integrating culture and language into the curriculum. The next portion presents how teaching the whole student can enhance the teacher's ability to reach each learner.

Teaching the Whole Student

People are complex beings, so it is critical for teachers to teach the whole student. Whether you are a secondary or an elementary teacher, you can consider teaching within the context of the whole person. High school teachers have told me that their job is to teach math, not students. I hold a contrasting viewpoint. I believe that students are not only beings who learn various subject area content, but they are affective beings who have emotions, values, dreams, and fears. Students do not learn in a vacuum.

They learn when they are motivated to learn. They learn when they eat a nutritional diet. They learn when they feel accepted and not ridiculed in class. They learn when parents and teachers support them. They also learn about society and what society thinks about economics, race, and gender from television, popular music, their friends, the history textbook, and what teachers say to them. A transformation occurs when classrooms become caring and culturally meaningful places where children succeed.

Can you visualize a classroom where Caring-Centered Multicultural Education forms the framework? It is a place where both teachers and students are excited to come every morning. It is a place where students make decisions about topics they can research. It is a place that values them and their cultural heritage. It is a school where people care for each other and work with others to achieve. They want each other to do well in school and support one another. The class becomes a family of learners. Since the pedagogy is student centered and encourages the development of an empowered, caring, and confident person who works well with others, cultural knowledge and diverse ways of thinking are encouraged and included in the classroom. Meaningful information can be used as an example to teach important skills, and also to provide children with a context with which they can understand and learn most efficiently. Children feel most comfortable in an environment where they know and understand the rules, expectations, behaviors, and values. Learning becomes a self-affirming action that is reinforced when teachers create classrooms where children appreciate cultural diversity, respect each other, and value the contributions each person makes to the community. Schooling then becomes a life-giving process of growth. One of the role models my children watched was Mr. Rogers on public television. He was concerned about the growth of the whole person. This is important whether the student is in 1st or 12th grade.

 ## Case Study

DASHELLE: EDUCATING THE WHOLE PERSON

This section gives an example of why it is important for teachers to view the whole student in the learning process. Peggy Orenstein (1994), in her book *Schoolgirls,* describes a student named Dashelle, an eighth grader. When she was a seventh grader, teachers labeled her as out of control and threatening. She almost failed seventh grade. One teacher told Orenstein that he hated Dashelle. In eighth grade she became the peacemaker. How did this change come about?

Orenstein asked Dashelle what made her change. This is what Dashelle said:

I was real bad . . . I thought, "F school," you know? I was like other kids. I thought it was nerdy or acting white or something to do good at school. I'd come to class and get kicked out and just sit in the office all day listening to everyone else's business . . .

She then explained that the night before school started in September, she had ironed her clothes and was ready when her little brother Demetrius said to her, "You know . . . I used to look up to you, but *you ain't gonna be nothin'.* You get in trouble at school, you go out every night . . . You still gonna do all that this year?" (Orenstein 1994, 229).

Dashelle told Orenstein that was her wakeup call. She said, "I know I'm not stupid. And all my little brothers and sisters, they probably look up to me like Demetrius. I thought, 'If I go down the bad path, then they might, too.' That would hurt me so much, to see them doing the wrong thing . . . If I do good, they'll see they can do it, too" (1994, 229).

At first the teachers did not believe she had really changed. But at the end of the year, Dashelle graduated from eighth grade with a special award from the school for her leadership and a grade-point average of 3.67. At the graduation Dashelle said, "Look, I made the honor roll in school . . . Everyone is so proud of me, but I'm proud of myself, too. Because I couldn't have done it without my brain, I couldn't have done it without me" (1994, 239).

Dashelle listened in social studies, science, English, and her other classes. But most of all she listened to her little brother, Demetrius. Although Dashelle learned more that year because she worked hard, her story showed how important it is to know the family and understand family relationships in African American communities. What motivated Dashelle was not the school, but the possibility of losing her brother's approval and seeing her siblings make the same mistake. Sibling relationships are extremely important in African American families (McAdoo 1988; Irvine 1991; Ford 1996). The intrinsic motivation of Dashelle's family was the key to her success in school. Dashelle also lived in a tough environment. Reggie Clark, an educational researcher, found that many high-achieving African American girls learn toughness and assertiveness from the neighborhoods in which they live. Some young women who are successful in school are able to transfer that resiliency they learned in the family and neighborhood to academic achievement (Clark 1983). Like Dashelle, many students feel the responsibility to be positive role models for their siblings. The case study of Dashelle helps to illustrate how important it is for us, as teachers, to know our students. ✳

As a first-grade teacher, I was often unaware of the choices that some of my African American students were making. Like Dashelle, the students had to deal with the negative perception that, if they did well in school, they were selling out and acting White (Fordham and Ogbu 1986). Oftentimes, African American students develop the strategy of dropping out of school or not working in school as a way to combat the frustration and anger they feel about a system that they see is trying to assimilate them and eliminate their culture. As a teacher, I did not understand the resilience it took for Becky, one of my students, to come to school day after day and be the best reader in the class. I remember many of the students of color teasing her about her excellent work, but she was always respectful and never boastful toward them. Becky was a loving and shy African American child, and although she was modest, Becky was able to handle those who tried to embarrass her by drawing on her personal strength and family support. Examples like Dashelle and Becky remind me that teachers teach children, not subject matter. One of the major principles of Caring-Centered Multicultural Education is teaching the whole person. It is an underlying belief that leads to the goals of this framework that incorporate the principles of caring, culture, and social justice.

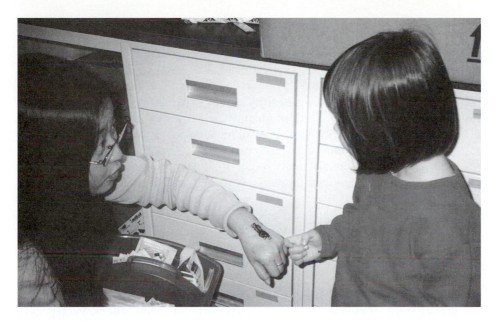

Caring about the whole student

What Are the Goals of Multicultural Education?

The goals of Multicultural Education deal primarily with children's learning the skills and knowledge they will need to develop into responsible citizens and people who can think, reason, and communicate. These are the goals that I believe are most important; you may have others that you consider critical. Add those to your journal.

1. **Each student will achieve academic excellence and have the opportunity to develop her or his interests and/or career aspirations.** This is one of the most important goals of Multicultural Education because so many of our students from nonmajority ethnic and low-income families have not found academic success in schools. In order for a person to develop personal satisfaction in life, she or he must be encouraged and supported to delve into her or his career interests. These interests may sustain her or him financially and help develop in her or him a sense of accomplishment.
2. **Each student will learn basic skills, be able to think critically, make decisions, learn how to care for herself or himself and others, and participate in making a more just society.** One of the crucial aspects of education is to think about and make decisions about complex social issues. Democracy is based on the ability of each citizen to do so.
3. **Each student will develop effective interpersonal and intercultural communication skills so that she or he can work with culturally diverse people in a**

respectful and caring manner. This may also mean that students learn a second language and become capable of functioning within many cultural contexts. Our world has become extremely complex and it is crucial that people from diverse communities, languages, and value orientations come together to solve social problems.

4. **Each student will develop a healthy and positive sense of self.** This includes ethnic/cultural identity, gender identity, and sexual orientation. Remember Abraham Maslow's (1970) hierarchy of human needs: physical, safety, belonging, self-esteem, intellectual achievement, and self-actualization. In order for students to become intellectually successful, they must feel accepted and loved by those around them and through this process children develop self-esteem. When individuals of all ages feel accepted and confident they are more likely to be motivated to think and learn new information.

5. **Each student will mature into an independent and rational thinker who has the ability to take responsibility for her or his own life and contribute to the community.** Each person must be able to take responsibility for her or his own development and well-being.

6. **Each student will develop moral and ethical judgment and will have a strong sense of personal integrity and compassion for others.** Each person needs to be an informed citizen who can make difficult decisions about controversial public issues based on a strong sense of morality. Many students struggle with balancing their own needs with the needs of others. This is part of the ethical process people go through in order to develop their own sense of virtue.

   In a democracy, citizens work toward the growth of the entire society through continued dialogue with each other, and this includes the right of those who dissent. It is also important for citizens to fight against the oppression of others, which includes racial discrimination, gender bias, and the exclusion of others based on social class. At times, one of the most challenging aspects of a democracy is to put the well-being of others before one's own. In addition, because our society is made up of many cultural groups, there are many perspectives regarding each issue.

7. **Each student will develop ways to build a strong equitable community based upon the values of caring, social justice, and respect.** Caring for others and building trust are important components of a socially just community. This is not easy to do in a society as diverse as that in the United States. Students and teachers will develop cross-cultural communication styles and strategies to build coalitions within the school and broader community.

8. **Teachers will create life-giving classrooms where culture is used to build meaningful learning environments and compassion and respect form the foundation for classroom interactions.** In order for most children to do well in school, classrooms must be places where they are affirmed rather than ridiculed. For example, my son came home unhappy from his first week of eighth grade. When I asked him what was the matter, he said, "I don't know

why I need to know this stuff. It doesn't have to do with anything." It was hard to explain how the Pythagorean theorem was going to help him right away in life.

The next week my son seemed even more disturbed. "I sure like your teacher," I said. He looked at me funny.

"What's wrong? The teacher seems like a caring person who knows her subject," I rattled on.

Although he did not want to talk about the teacher, he finally said, "Mom, the kids don't like being ridiculed in class. When you don't know the answer, the teacher makes fun of you in front of the entire class. It's really embarrassing. Yes, the teacher knows her stuff, but because she ridicules people, we don't learn anything."

Many times in life, I have been reminded by students about what really counts in schools. My son was trying to tell me that teaching means more than the content. Student-teacher relationships are a critical part of the learning environment. In my son's class, content coupled with compassion would have made a far more effective learning environment.

9. **Each school will be restructured around the principles of democracy and the belief that the United States is a nation of many cultures and ethnic communities.** Each school can utilize democratic values in how they structure school policies and what curriculum is chosen. Children, parents, and community can be contributing members of a school organization. In addition, because the United States is a pluralistic nation, the school calendar, policies, and other aspects can reflect our cultural diversity.

10. **Students, teachers, and parents will work together to eliminate racism, sexism, classism, homophobia, and other types of social oppression in schools and society.**

When I was a grade-school teacher, I found it was hard to see past the whirlwind of busy bodies and wonderful smiles. Now I realize that schools are powerful social systems in which relations based on race, class, gender, language, handicapping conditions, and sexual orientation continue to be reinforced. For example, many nonmajority ethnic students and young people from lower-income families were found in the lower reading and math groups. In addition, children called each other negative ethnic terms on the playground. Fortunately, teachers are finding ways to move away from tracking their children, and school personnel have focused on eliminating ethnic jokes or slurs.

In order to examine how well schools mirror our democratic values of equal status, freedom, and justice, I began to think about the following questions: How democratic am I? What values am I teaching in how I structure the activities or line up children or choose uniforms? How equitably are my students learning? Are some children involved in their learning more than others? Why? Do I value what the students already know? How do I include the community in our school activities and policies?

As John Dewey, the famous philosopher, reminded us, schools are small worlds where democracy can be learned and practiced every day. All of these listed goals are important and, as teachers, we attempt to pursue them simultaneously. Teaching is an art and not a technical skill and as such there are many things we must do automatically and almost intuitively. This is why I feel that it is critical that teachers have clear goals. We have so many decisions to make during the course of a day or week or month of teaching; without a thoughtful understanding of why we teach, we may get bogged down in the quagmire of paperwork and school chaos that have little to do with teaching.

How One School Sends Out Positive Messages

Multicultural Education is about students learning and succeeding in school. As you know, it takes a village to raise a child. No matter how effective you are as a teacher, it still takes parents, grandparents, siblings, cousins, friends, ministers, Girl Scout leaders, YMCA leaders, soccer coaches, and others to continually reinforce the lessons children need to learn. At Valencia Park Elementary in San Diego, teachers post affirmations for each year on the bulletin board, distribute the affirmations to both children and parents, and refer to them continuously throughout the year. Emily Jenkins developed the idea while working as a James Comer School resource teacher. These affirmations help to focus the attention of children, parents, and teachers on positive goals and are part of what Valencia Park Elementary does to "Teach the Whole Child."

Let's take a look at those affirmations:

September	My words of respect show that I care.
October	Only the best is good enough for me.
November	I am an important person in this world.
January	I can dream dreams and make those dreams come true.
February	Every new day is another opportunity to improve myself.
March	It may be difficult, but it is possible.
April	I care for and help each of my classmates.
May	It is never too late for me to improve.
June	I control the good that happens to me.
July	I can learn from others, and they can learn from me.

What new affirmations would you suggest for coming years? I know that students enjoy creating them too. This could be a whole school project where teachers and pupils suggest possible affirmations and a committee of students writes and chooses them for the new year.

Chapter Summary

Teacher reflection is the focus of the chapter. It is crucial for educators to think about and be thoughtful about what they value and do in schools. In the process of inquiry, teachers and students must make decisions about complex social concerns. Beyer's model of inquiry called DECIDE is provided in the beginning of the chapter.

One of the concepts covered in this chapter was how the Caring-Centered Multicultural Education framework integrates three important theories: care theory, sociocultural theory of learning, and education for democracy. The common themes they share are as follows:

1. Have a strong sense of personal integrity.
2. Educate the whole child.
3. Build a community of learners based on trust and respect.

These major themes are integrated throughout the philosophy. Effective teachers look at the holistic needs of children. Caring teachers know that students learn most effectively when they feel accepted for who they are. Teachers must have personal integrity in order to build a community of learners based on trust and respect. This foundation emphasizes the importance of caring for the whole child and reaffirms the moral commitment many teachers have to their students. Although many of my colleagues see Multicultural Education as a historical and political movement against oppression, I believe it is much more. We teach not only because we know that society has not always acted in a moral or humane way toward many groups of people, but more importantly because we want to be part of the life-giving process we call learning (Rivera and Poplin 1996).

Within this framework, reflective teaching is imperative. Educators are asked to reflect on their beliefs and practices. This chapter presented a list of skills, identified by Barry Beyer, that are needed for the decision-making process. These are critical for the examination of complex social issues. These skills should assist teachers by providing guidance about which facilities students should be able to readily engage in. The decision-making process of critical thinking is a difficult one because students must be able to identify and solve complex social issues. I encourage teachers to raise many questions in class so that students have the opportunity to think on their own, and develop critical thinking skills. Three hot topics about race were presented so that teachers would consider the implications in their own teaching and understandings.

Many folks have contributed to our schools and equal educational opportunity. Linda Christiansen, and members of the Latino and Chinese American community are excellent examples of leaders who have worked toward equity. Their stories are important ones because they show us that change is possible when people are committed to caring for others, which in turn manifests itself in a compassionate and socially just society.

Most importantly are the teachers and the strategies they have developed in their own schools to reinforce the importance of Caring-Centered Multicultural Education. The work of Emily Jackson and the affirmations that the school uses throughout the year reinforce the values of caring, excellence, and equity.

The primary focus of this chapter is to extend the discussion about Caring-Centered Multicultural Education and to provide examples of folks who have made a difference in our schools and others who have contributed to our knowledge base of understanding.

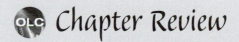

Chapter Review

Go to the Online Learning Center **www.mhhe.com/pang2e** to review important content from the chapter, practice with key terms, take a chapter quiz, and find the Web links listed in this chapter.

Key Terms

decision-making process, *253*
DECIDE, *254*
integrity, *255*
whole student, *255*
trusting relationships, *255*

community, *255*
empowering, *257*
funds of knowledge, *258*
ideology of equal
opportunity, *261*

open society, *261*
equality and equity, *263*
racial privacy initiative, *266*
bilingual education, *279*

Reflection Activities

1. What is Multicultural Education? As you think about the question, take a moment now and write in your journal what you think it is and continue to alter it as you read through this book. Keep track of the changes you make. At the end of the text, examine how your views may have evolved as you thought about issues brought up in this book. If you have difficulty writing, use the following sentence starter: I believe Multicultural Education is . . .

2. Table 8.2 summarizes the goals I propose for Caring-Centered Multicultural Education. After reading through Table 8.2, answer the following questions in your journal:

How would you prioritize the goals of Multicultural Education?

Are there other goals that you would include that I have not included?

What are they and why do you believe these goals should be added?

3. Table 8.3 provides a summary of how the culturally caring classroom looks in contrast with the status quo classroom. Circle the statements that you agree with in each column. Where do you find more of your circles? Think about what your

TABLE 8.2   Major Goals of Multicultural Education

1. Each student will achieve academic excellence and have the opportunity to develop her or his interests and/or career aspirations.
2. Each student will learn basic skills, be able to think critically, make decisions, learn how to care for herself or himself and others, and participate in making a more just society.
3. Each student will develop effective interpersonal and intercultural communication skills so that she or he can work with culturally diverse people in a respectful and caring manner.
4. Each student will develop a healthy and positive sense of self.
5. Each student will mature into an independent and rational thinker who has the ability to take responsibility for her or his own life and contribute to the community.
6. Each student will develop moral and ethical judgment and will have a strong sense of personal integrity and compassion for others.
7. Each student will develop ways to build a strong equitable community based upon the values of caring, social justice, and respect.
8. Teachers will create life-giving classrooms where culture is used to build meaningful learning environments and compassion and respect form the foundation for classroom interactions.
9. Each school will be restructured around the principles of democracy and the belief that the United States is a nation of many cultures and ethnic communities.
10. Students, teachers, and parents will work together to eliminate racism, sexism, classism, homophobia, and other types of social oppression in schools and society.

TABLE 8.3 The Caring and Culturally Meaningful Classroom

Culturally Caring Classroom	Status Quo
The United States is a color-conscious society. People are treated differently based on their color and race. Merit is a culturally defined concept.	The United States is a color-blind society. People are judged on their personal merit.
Schools are sociocultural institutions of society where racism, sexism, and classism have continued to impact the way children are treated and taught.	Schools have addressed the issue of equal opportunity of education through the implementation of bilingual education, multicultural education, and special education programs.
Equity is a key issue in Multicultural Education. Students must be encouraged to examine social issues for equity. They can take stands on public issues like welfare reform, affirmative action, bilingual education, and employment opportunities.	Diversity has been included in the policies, curriculum, and instructional strategies of schools. Diversity is the key component of multicultural education. For example, children from diverse communities work together in cooperative groups.
Culture is an important aspect of the learning, self-esteem, and communication process.	Good teachers can teach any children. Culture is not a critical aspect of teaching.
Children feel most comfortable with teachers who understand the values, history, behaviors, learning behaviors, expectations, and language they are most familiar with in life. Teachers naturally infuse information about children's lives, whether it deals with food, history, family outings, grandparents, neighborhood, or other real-life issues.	Teachers build trusting relationships with their students by caring and providing interesting classrooms.
Decreasing the achievement gap is one of the most important goal of Multicultural Education. Schools need to change in order to become effective with children who arrive at school with diverse views, ways of learning, and skills. Schools, not children, are at risk.	Children come to school from at-risk families and situations, and the source of failure comes from children and their families and culture.
Teachers are partners with parents and children in the learning process. Teachers encourage parents to be active in the classroom and to reinforce learning at home through working with and doing things with their children.	Teachers are the professionals who are best qualified to decide on what works with children.
Children are empowered to think and solve problems and challenge inequities. Teachers are facilitators in that process. Thinking is a critical aspect of their development as caring individuals and citizens of a democracy.	Children are to receive knowledge and learn information from their teachers who are experts.
Teachers who care believe they are called to advocate for their children and involve children in their empowerment.	Advocacy is not part of the job of teachers. Teachers are hired to teach children their basic skills so they can support themselves and be good citizens.

values are and how those values shape your viewpoints. If you had more circles under the "status quo" section, examine each statement under the "culturally caring" column and write some questions that you might ask your colleagues or professor during your next class. Can you begin to think about schools from the culturally caring perspective? What is holding you back from agreeing with some of the statements?

Write how you feel in your journal. If you are frustrated, write why. If you are confused, describe what it is that confuses you. If you agree with many of the culturally caring statements, write why you agree. Share these with a friend or colleague. The dialogue may help you to clarify your thoughts.

4. Get a copy of *Teaching for Thinking: Theory, Strategies, and Activities for the Classroom* by Louis E. Raths, Selma Wasserman, Arthur Jonas, and Arnold Rothstein. Read through the text and examine the activities for the development of various skills such as comparing, summarizing, observing, classifying, interpreting, criticizing, applying facts and principles to new situations, and decision making. Identify where you may be able to articulate more clearly in your instruction the teaching of one of the skills—maybe in math, science, social studies, or English. Many of the skills they teach are embedded in various standards in content areas such as social studies, language arts, and science.

5. Middle school and high school students should be encouraged to think about complex social issues that deal with class, ethnicity, and age. One issue that can be used to discuss democratic values and labor laws is identified by the *New York Times* in an article called "Farm Work by Chil-

dren Tests Labor Laws" by Steven Greenhouse (August 7, 2000). There is an accompanying lesson plan developed by educators at the New York Times Learning Network. You can access it at **www.nytimes.com/learning/teachers/lessons/20000807monday_print.html.**

This lesson explores the issue of young teenagers working on farms to help financially sustain their families. The article documents the work of many 14-year-olds. These young people work around pesticides and have no access to toilets or running water. They may work as long as 12 hours a day and may be paid as little as $2.50 an hour. One reason why so many young people are working is that farmers face a grave labor shortage. Read through the article and lesson plan.

The lesson tackles many important national standards. These standards help to identify the skills that students should be learning along with understanding the complexity of social issues. For example, the lesson addresses the following social studies standards: Students should "understand demographic shifts and the influences on recent immigration patterns; Understand how different groups attempted to achieve their goals." In addition, several language arts standards are addressed in this lesson: "Plays a variety of roles in group discussions; Asks questions to seek elaboration and clarification of ideas; Listens in order to understand a speaker's topic, purpose, and perspective; Conveys a clear main point when speaking to others and stays on the topic being discussed; Presents simple prepared reports to the class."

You could ask your students to make a decision regarding what should be done about child farm workers? What should our state and national policies be in this issue?

PART FOUR

Creating a Caring and Culturally Meaningful Classroom

CHAPTER 9

How Do Students Learn a Second Language?

CHAPTER OVERVIEW

Teachers need to understand how students learn a second language because many students arrive at school with a first language other than English. Various theories can help teachers effectively reach English-language learners. This chapter will do the following:

- Describe the difference between conversational and academic language.
- Describe various English-as-a-second-language programs.
- Explain differences between bilingual education programs.
- Provide examples and successful strategies in writing, math, and science classrooms.

Learning Language

Do you remember learning language as a toddler? Probably not because it was long ago. But you may have watched your own children, siblings, nieces, nephews, and other toddlers learn language. Most often, babies learn language by observing and listening to members of their families speak and interact with each other. Communication includes verbal language and also a lot of nonverbal actions. For example, parents may smile to encourage the baby to listen and try to repeat the sounds they are making. How do babies communicate before they speak? Babies babble, coo, smile, frown, and cry. These are all important communicative strategies. In fact, Laura-Ann Petito and Siobhan Holowka from Dartmouth College found that in the brain of a baby, communication centers are some of the first neural structures to advance (Hotz 2002).

When a baby hears language, she or he must make sense of the sounds. Although the baby is probably not aware of these questions, she or he is seeking answers to questions such as the following:

What is the sound my father is making?

How can I make the same sound?

Is that the right sound?

The baby often practices making the same sounds that her or his parents make. The baby imitates the sounds she or he hears, but initially does not know what the sounds mean. When a baby learns how to put different sounds together into words, she or he is actually learning **phonology.** She or he is studying sounds of language. Some people call this level of language "baby talk," but in actuality babies are learning how to put vowels and consonants together when saying something such as "da da." A baby is also learning patterns of language through the 16,000 examples of what her or his parents and others around her or him say in the first several months of life (Hotz 2002).

People who speak different languages may learn different sounds. English speakers spend more time learning the sounds of consonants, while Spanish speakers focus on vowels (E. Garcia 2002). Parents often sing songs to their children to teach them various sounds and patterns of the language. Not every language has the same sounds or phonemes. I remember that my grandmother could not say my name, Valerie; in Japanese there are no sounds exactly like the English sound for *V* and *L* and so she called me Bararie, in which the *r*'s are rolled. As a child, I just accepted that this was how she heard my name.

As toddlers mature into four-year-olds, they begin to better understand underlying principles of language and the syllables of words. For example, Garcia described how children at this age easily figure out words that rhyme because they hold **metalinguistic awareness.** This means they are aware of underlying principles of language. At this age students have learned that some words have a common final segment and children have learned to replace the beginning consonant to create new words like *cat, mat,* and *sat.*

Another aspect of phonology has to do with pitch or tone. A parent who sees a baby reaching to touch a hot stove may say loudly and in an emphatic tone that denotes danger, "No!" The emphasis in tone the parent places on words also adds to meaning of words. Have you ever been in a classroom where the teacher whispers to her or his students to model more quiet talking?

In tonal languages such as Vietnamese, words may be spelled the same, but have different sounds. These words differ in their tones and therefore their meanings. There are six tones in Vietnamese (Tran 1998). For example, the word *ma* means ghost, while the word *má* refers to cheek. The words differ in tone and accent. Vietnamese who arrive in the United States and do not know English may have difficulty understanding that English is not a tonal language. They may be looking for phonological patterns that do not exist.

While babies are learning sounds of a language, they are also learning **vocabulary.** Much of what they initially learn includes names of people they interact with or names of objects such as food items. I know many youngsters not much older than one who ask for a "cookie" or "treat." A treat may have more than one meaning, too. It may mean a cookie, but it can also be candy or crackers. Much later children learn appropriate use of vocabulary within specific contexts. In addition, when they are able to pronounce the words and know how to use them in grammatically correct sentences, they are skilled in lexicon. Díaz-Rico and Weed defined **lexicon** this way:

> The *lexicon* is the sum total of the meanings stored, the association of these meanings with the correct context, the ability to pronounce the word correctly, the knowledge of how to use the word grammatically in a sentence, and the knowledge of which morphemes are appropriately connected with the word. This knowledge is acquired as the brain absorbs and interacts with meaning in context (2002, 63).

Now how do toddlers put words together into sentences? They learn grammar and word order. **Syntax** is a system of rules that govern how we correctly use words and word order. Toddlers learn how to create a complete sentence and convey a thought. For example, a child may say, "Ann and I is going to school tomorrow." She knows to place the subject first and then the verb in her sentence so that the word order is correct; however, the child needs to learn about the grammatical rules regarding the use of a verb that denotes a plural subject.

Let's look at how students build up their developing vocabulary. Can they begin to see that words have parts to them? This leads to morphology. **Morphology** is the study of the basic meaning units in language (Díaz-Rico and Weed 2002). Children begin to learn that words can be broken up into parts and those parts have different meanings. For example, children learn that the ending *er* added to a root of a word can mean "a person who does something." For example, a baker is someone who bakes and a runner is someone who runs.

One of the most difficult aspects of language to learn is context or **pragmatics.** How does a child know how to use language in a specific context? Would the child

Learning new vocabulary

use the same language at a baseball game with peers as he or she would at a formal dinner of adults in black-tie attire? Probably not. Context can be challenging for second-language learners because they need to understand the culture of the community in order to develop this skill. Let's take another example. Maybe a friend says, "I've got to go catch a bus." This statement does not mean that the friend is going to catch a bus with a fishing pole or rope; it means she has to hurry so that she isn't late when the bus arrives at her stop. A great deal of cultural knowledge is packed into this casual expression. Pragmatics is the complex understanding of context, which includes not only how language is used within specific situations, but also which sentences are most appropriate within the flow of a conversation and inferences made by word choices (Díaz-Rico and Weed 2002).

This has been a short description of some of the skills that babies and children need to develop in order to become fluent and participating members of society. The purpose of this chapter is not to present an exhaustive section on language learning, but to explain that it is important for teachers and other service providers to understand linguistics and language learning.

Learning language is an extremely complex skill. Babies and children build millions of networks in their brains relating to verbal language and gestures in order to communicate with others. I never realized how smart babies and children are.

Second-Language Acquisition Development

What happens when a child or adult begins to learn another language? Is it easy? To a few it is, but to others learning a second language well is a challenge.

Let's say you have a new student named Ana Maria in your seventh-grade social studies class. She migrated with her family from Colombia in Central America and speaks only Spanish. How do you think Ana Maria feels when she comes to school on the first day? She doesn't know anyone in the class. She has just been brought to the door by the principal and looks down at the floor. Ana Maria makes some eye contact with you and with a friendly face you motion her to come into the classroom. She slowly walks in and looks blankly at the other students. You smile and then she smiles. You ask Carrie to come to the front of the room and take Ana Maria to a desk next to her.

Ana Maria seems to be watching everything. She also seems to be listening and trying to figure out what is being said. She may be thinking the following:

What is going on? I can't understand anything.

Who will help me?

Will someone make fun of me? What will they say?

Oh, no. I need to go to the bathroom. How can I tell the teacher?

Much of what Ana Maria does is to observe the nonverbal actions of you and her peers. Do the students smile at her? Do the students smile at you, the teacher? Do you smile and joke with your students? Ana Maria follows what the other students do. Carrie takes out a blue book, so Ana Maria does the same.

Ana Maria also is listening very carefully. She is trying to make sense of the sounds she is hearing. In second-language acquisition theory, this is called the **pre-production stage.** In this stage, Ana is silent or quiet because she is paying close attention to the sounds she hears because she knows they represent words. Ana may be anxious because she is unsure of herself. She is listening for patterns of sounds and learning new words.

As Ana Maria becomes more sure of herself and understands some of the conversation she hears around her, she is able to respond with a single word such as *yes, teacher,* or *no.* This is considered the **early production stage** in which a person begins to use language in a limited way. She might say, "Don't know," or "What?" Ana Maria is also able to participate in classroom routines. For example, she can recite parts of the Pledge of Allegiance with her peers. In this stage of language development, Ana Maria is becoming familiar with English and is feeling more confident.

In time Ana Maria finds her self in the **speech emergence stage** in which she is able to respond to questions more naturally. She can create simple sentences and often they are grammatically correct. Ana may say to the teacher, "I don't understand" or "I am confused."

Finally, in the **intermediate fluency stage,** Ana Maria is able to participate comfortably in a conversation with others. She can self-correct some of her syntax errors. She is able to speak smoothly and is confident in expressing herself in school and with her friends. Ana Maria understands much of the vocabulary that she hears, because people use it in her neighborhood.

Table 10.1 is a summary of stages of second-language development in the Natural Approach. It helps to identify the level at which an English language learner (ELL) is performing.

As Ana Maria learns English, she can also be influenced by outside forces. Ana Maria is sometimes hurt by her classmates, teachers, and others as she tries to communicate in English. Her self-esteem suffers once in a while when a peer laughs at her responses or her accent. As Ana progressed through the stages of language

TABLE 10.1   Stages of Second-Language Development

• **Preproduction—Silent stage**

Individuals are listening to the sounds and ways people put words together. They listen for patterns. This is also known as the silent period because the language learner has a much larger receptive vocabulary than speaking vocabulary.

• **Early production**

Individuals learn to answer some questions that can be replied to with a yes or no answer. They may be able to produce short sentences such as "How much?"

• **Speech emergence**

Individuals convey basic ideas and create short sentences. They are becoming more comfortable speaking to others and can correct some of their errors in sentence structure.

• **Intermediate fluency**

Individuals can convey more complex ideas although they are still having trouble creating correct complete sentences. They are speaking more naturally and confidently.

---

development two forces acted to slow her learning of English. They were anxiety and worry. Ana Maria did not want to be humiliated in class. She worried about being excluded and laughed at because of her pronunciation and grammar. English learners such as Ana Maria must deal not only with learning a language, but also with the affective component of communication. When Ana Maria makes mistakes when she speaks in class and her classmates laugh, this situation can impact her self-esteem. Stephen Krashen (1981, 1982, 1993), a researcher in language acquisition, calls this **Affective Filter Hypothesis.** Some of the problems that English learners have identified are poor attitudes in teachers and peers. For example, some elementary school second-language students reported that they spent much time watching movies, coloring, and drawing. In this atmosphere they weren't learning much language, and the students knew that the teacher was not really committed to teaching them. In other classrooms teachers were not pleasant to English learners and they were commonly called "stupid." As a result young people spent much time in the bathroom, which made teachers even more unhappy with their behavior. The affective filter, as Krashen has noted, can have a major influence on language learning, whether the student speaks Navaho, French, Mandarin, Yup'ik, or Hawaiian. When students feel threatened or defensive, language learning will be limited.

Much of what language is about is what makes sense and is meaningful. However, English language learners (ELL) face a difficult process because second-language learning entails the integration of linguistic components such as social context, cultural language and nonverbal cues, everyday conversation skills, and abstract formal language (the type of language we use to write research papers or give high-level speeches). When they enter U.S. schools English learners are exposed to many new things. This doesn't include the content being taught in subjects such as history, geography, art, and health education. A student may feel as if he or she is being thrown into the deep end of a large swimming pool without a sponge board or lifevest!

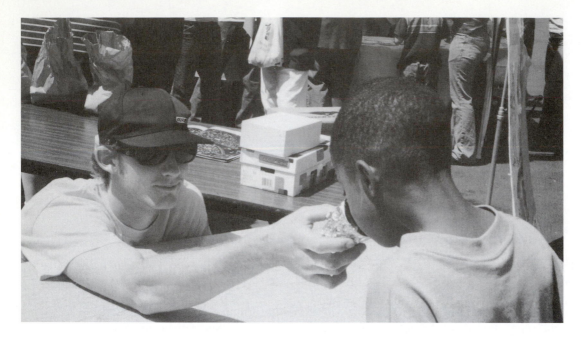

Experiential learning

Second–Language Acquisition Theories

What do the experts say about how a student learns a second language? There are several theories about second language acquisition. First, B. F. Skinner, the behaviorist, believed that language is learned by constant reinforcement and drill. This theory views our minds as being empty vessels into which teachers pour important information. Others, such as Noam Chomsky believed that people have innate abilities to create sentences and understand linguistic rules (Díaz-Rico and Weed 2002). Stephen Krashen, a linguist who built on Chomsky's theories, developed the **Monitor model,** which includes the Affective Filter Hypothesis that I described earlier (Díaz-Rico and Weed 2002). The Krashen model is a complex one. In a speech to educators, Krashen explained how we learn language:

> In my opinion, we all acquire language the same way. The reason this is an outrageous thing to say [is], because we live in an age of individual differences. . . There are individual variations and we see it in the research . . . [N]evertheless there are some things we all do the same [such as] . . . Digestion. We all digest food the same. No significant individual variation. First you put food in our mouth, then chew it up, and then it goes down into your stomach. That's how it is done everywhere (Krashen 1993).

Krashen makes it clear that there are two different avenues for people who learn a second language. Krashen believes that students can either acquire or learn language. To Krashen, acquisition is the process that students naturally or involuntarily understand and use language in their conversations on the playground or at lunch. Learning language refers to the formal aspects of language. It is about learning rules, grammar, spelling, and vocabulary through formal teaching (Díaz-Rico and Weed 2002). Krashen has labeled the difference between the two avenues of language learning as the **Acquisition-Learning Hypothesis.** Do you think you would learn a language best by being in a formal class that teaches grammar and spelling? If I gave you a list of verbs to conjugate, would it be best for you to be in a situation where you are motivated to learn something? Suppose you needed to know how to use the subway to get to a concert of your favorite musical group. You need to know vocabulary relating to the subway, such as *ticket,* and how to ask which way to go. In which situation would you more likely remember the new language? Oftentimes context is a critical aspect of language learning. The next section discusses how language acquisition is different from language learning.

Krashen Teaches a Lesson in Language Learning: Nervous Educators

I attended a speech where Stephen Krashen, a professor, explained to educators about the importance of acquisition rather than learning (Krashen 1993). Krashen, an extremely skilled teacher, began teaching a language lesson. The audience of deans and professors of education became very quiet because just like students in a classroom, some began to get anxious. Would he call on them to answer? What if they made an error in front of all their colleagues and bosses?

Krashen began teaching in German. No one knew what he was talking about. There was a lot of nervous laughter. He spoke for about 1 minute, but it seemed like 10 minutes.

Then he said in English, "Is this a good lesson so far?" Everyone laughed because of course no one understood a word.

In English Krashen then said, "What if I repeated it? Would that help?" Everyone laughed again because of course that wouldn't help at all. Yet teachers do this all over the country with English learners in their classes. They repeat the same phrases or questions to their Russian, Spanish, Farsi, or Vietnamese speakers and wonder why the kids shake their heads or look down.

Krashen continued speaking in German.

Then Krashen stopped and said in English, "What if I wrote the words on the board? Would that help?" Everyone laughed because they still wouldn't know what the lesson was about.

Krashen then said in English, "What if I talked louder?" Of course, the professors laughed again because some realized that they knew this was a common mistake teachers made.

Then Krashen held up his hand and said a word in German and pointed to his head. He then repeated the German word again as he pointed to his forehead. The audience began repeating after Krashen. Then Krashen drew a face on a piece of paper and again pointed to the forehead.

Next, when the audience pronounced the word correctly, he answered, "Yes," in German and nodded his head and smiled. Then the audience repeated the German word for *yes.* An audible sigh of relief could be heard in the room. Krashen smiled.

He proceeded to teach six features on the face by pointing to his own face and drawing on a piece of paper. Why could we understand what he was saying? It was **comprehensible input.** He used gestures and drawings to explain the German words he taught. This is what Krashen (1981, 1982) calls the **Natural Approach.** Students first understand what is being taught; then they learn how to pronounce the language. With this approach, there is a low level of anxiety and instruction is active and rich. This approach builds on what students know and affirms them as learners. The low-anxiety atmosphere is also a component of the caring-centered approach. Teachers create classrooms of care and affirm students so that they are then encouraged to learn. There are commonalities between the caring-centered philosophy to Multicultural Education and Krashen's approach. Teachers who care are committed to academic excellence, and together with students they create a meaningful curriculum (Noddings 1984).

Krashen also emphasized a caring and respectful classroom atmosphere in which the content is understandable. Krashen further explained: "We acquire language in one way—when we understand messages. Comprehensible input." He also explained that language acquisition rather than learning should be effortless. When the input that children receive is comprehensible, they acquire the language involuntarily. He later explained that language classes can be helpful to explain aspects that students must learn, such as grammar but that language isn't first taught by pointing out mistakes. Children acquire literacy when anxiety is low.

Following is another quote from Krashen (1993) that I believe is important for all of us to remember:

> If the child believes the language class is a place where his weaknesses will be revealed, he may understand the input, but it won't penetrate. It won't reach the parts of the brain where Chomsky says there is the language acquisition device. Our job is to get input into the language device.

In summary, Krashen's (1981, 1982) framework is made up of five hypotheses. The following provides a limited discussion of each hypothesis:

1. **Acquisition-Learning Hypothesis**—Two processes can occur when students learn a second language. They can acquire a language in a natural way when the context and language are meaningful. Messages are given within a context that is important. The second process is language learning through a formal avenue in which aspects such as grammar and rules of language are the focus. In this process, the learner may not be taught with content that is meaningful and relevant to him or her and so language learning can be more of a struggle.

2. **Monitor Hypothesis**—The English learner who acquires language develops fluency in the use of language, although a learner who learns it formally is more apt to develop a monitoring system based upon formal aspects such as grammar and language rules. This monitoring is most appropriate in writing and public

speaking rather than in every day conversation because a teacher does not want to inhibit the natural fluency of a second-language speaker.

3. **Natural Order Hypothesis**—The language learner looks for patterns in language usage. There are developmental aspects of language. Language is learned in a natural sequence.

4. **Affective Filter Hypothesis**—This refers to the negative impact of anxiety on language learning. Krashen suggests that language should be learned within a low-anxiety atmosphere.

5. **Input Hypothesis**—Input should be comprehensible and meaningful. When a learner understands what is conveyed, he or she is able to develop language skills.

Some researchers disagree with segments of Krashen's framework; however, many aspects of his scholarship can be seen in methods used today. His work has aided teachers to better understand how to reach second-language learners and has encouraged educators to move away from the memorization and drill approach of the past.

Take a Stand

LANGUAGE COURSES

Language issues are extremely important in today's world. The United States is a multilingual society. In addition, our economic, social, and political well-being are tied to folks around the world. However, our country seems to be slow in rising to these conditions. For example, although China has the largest population in the world, few high schools offer Mandarin. Other folks believe there is a greater need for additional language courses such as Spanish literature, rather than a course in Mandarin because many more students arrive at school with Spanish as their first language.

- Since most high schools have limited resources, which language courses should be offered at the local high schools? Why?

Case Study

FREE READING AND PERSONAL INTEREST: A GREAT PARTNERSHIP

A more challenging aspect of second-language acquisition relates to how a teacher can help students learn all they need to succeed in school. Krashen suggests that students should read as much as possible the books that they are interested in and enjoy. Through reading, students develop vocabulary, learn how to spell, become exposed to language patterns, learn patterns of sentence structure and grammatical rules, and much more. You may already take students to the library. Perhaps you could organize a field trip to the local library so that students can get their own library cards; the library may then become a place where they enjoy going to visit. When students choose their topics and books, they may be more willing to persevere when they encounter words they do not know.

🌀 *"Free reading is comprehensible input with a low affective filter."*
—STEPHEN KRASHEN 1993

Several years ago I applied Krashen's beliefs about free reading as a means to nurture motivation and engage children in a program called "My Personal Teacher." The participants were 40 third graders from an inner-city school. Over the course of a semester, preservice teachers from my education classes developed trusting relationships with the children, many of whom were English learners. Because the children were third graders, the college tutors were not intimidated by them. The tutors went to the school *to hear the children read to them;* they were the children's personal audience. The children chose the books they wanted to read to their tutors, and they were extremely proud of their reading. Sometimes a college tutor brought a book and, if there was time, read a story to the young student.

The second to the last session was a field trip to the local bookstore. A small grant from an Annenberg foundation enabled each child to pick two paperbacks to keep for her or his home library.

One of the most surprising aspects of the bookstore trip was the care the children took in choosing their books. They wanted to look at every text. They were excited about reading. The whole bookstore buzzed with voices reading. The only rule I gave the college tutors was that the books had to be something the children chose themselves and were interested in reading.

One young Vietnamese, Christina, was having the most difficult time making her choices. She turned down every suggestion from her college tutor. The tutor got frustrated because time was running out and the bus would soon arrive to return them to the school.

Finally, Christina found a picture book about a garden and a large nonfiction book on German shepherds. The nonfiction text was difficult and probably on the sixth-grade reading level, and the language was much denser than that in a picture book. The book had beautiful color photos of various dogs; however, the print was small. Her college tutor asked me if it was okay for her to pick the German shepherd book. After talking to her, I agreed with Christina.

During the next and final session, the college tutors and children celebrated their time together. We had cake and the children read their new books to their tutors. They were very excited about reading. Even Christina was able to read several pages of her difficult book on German shepherds. Her vocabulary increased by her reading words in context, such as Germany, bloodlines, and "bares his teeth." Much of the language was at a middle-school level. Although English was her second language, as Krashen explained, when a student is motivated, she will look up words, ask for help, and figure out words as she reads, even when the text is difficult. Christina was learning what is known as content area knowledge and academic-level English. This was an example of the Natural Approach.

Much later, when I saw the children's third-grade teachers at a restaurant, they were excited to tell me that the children had read the books to their own family members, too. The students continued to enjoy going to the library and they felt a special joy in owning their own books. Reading is an important aspect of language development. The next section discusses the language development of a child who was not only from a bilingual family but was also deaf. Not all children can hear, and language for a deaf child is just as important to develop. Language is not

> ↩ *Reading is fundamental for students of all ages!*

only a means for communication, but it also engages the intellect in cognitive growth. What languages do deaf children learn? What happens if the child's parents speak Spanish at home, but he or she lives in a predominantly English world? Is this child disabled? I asked a dear colleague, Kathee Christiansen, who is a deaf education specialist, to share with me a story of one of her students, Moises. ❋

Teacher Voices about Language Development: Moises and His Many Successes

Kathee Christiansen

A child born deaf in the United States faces the challenge of acquiring at least two languages. His most natural, visually salient language will, in most cases, be American Sign Language (ASL), a visual spatial language with its own unique syntax, semantics, and use. English, the language used for academic and social purposes by the majority of Americans, will be for the deaf child a second language, one that is difficult to acquire without the ability to hear. Deaf children, generally, are part of a larger group of individuals who learn to read, write, and understand English as a second language (ESL). These children are not "disabled" educationally when given the opportunity to acquire a visually salient first language, ASL, which can be used as a foundation for English as a second language. Bilingual ASL-English programs are becoming popular as an educational option for deaf children in the United States.

The majority of deaf children have some residual hearing. At an early age, many begin to associate what they see, along with what little they hear, to make sense of the environment. It is not uncommon to see young deaf children make mouth movements and incidental voicings as they imitate what they see in their immediate surroundings (e.g., they see Mom move her mouth, make some gestures, make some sounds, and magically all of the family members appear at the dinner table). Deaf children may wonder how that has happened and may try to manage the environment by trying to copy these behaviors.

A growing number of deaf children living in the United States come from families who speak a language other than English. These children may, for example, come from a family in which only Spanish is spoken and cultural celebrations center around Mexican events. A child may begin some incidental association of sounds, mouth movements, gestures, and printed words with the daily routines. This bank of cultural and communicative information may present confusion and conflict when the child enters a public school program where English and ASL are the dominant languages. Assessment may be difficult due to communication differences, teacher expectations may be affected by cultural mismatch, and the child may be a victim of a middle-class American system biased toward English and ASL. Further, parents who do not understand the academic language and the culture of the school may feel alienated. An example of this situation is found in the case of Moises.

Who Is Moises?

Moises was born in Guadalajara, Mexico. During his first year of life, he was diagnosed with meningitis and, as a result, lost most of his hearing. His father Jesus, a day laborer, and his mother Lupe had no resources to provide for expensive therapy services, so Moises was not given early intervention of any kind. When he reached school age, his parents found that no programs would admit their son, who, at this point, communicated only through a gesture system that had developed within his family. He had no formal spoken or signed language. After a neighbor told the parents about public school programs in the United States for children who were deaf, they began to dream about moving to California. By this time Jesus and Lupe had a family of four children, including nine-year-old Moises and his three hearing siblings. At great risk, the family arranged to travel to the United States. The importance of education for all of their children, including Moises, was paramount.

Jesus found a job in construction and eventually enrolled all of his children in public schools. Moises, then a bright, handsome, nine-year-old, was placed in a class for mentally retarded children. The rationale for this placement was his inability to speak English or Spanish. After several months, his teacher noticed that Moises was solving complex puzzles, learning to associate time on the clock with classroom activities, helping the other children, and trying to vocalize messages to adults. Moises was reassessed and given a hearing test. A profound loss was detected and Moises was referred to the deaf and hard-of-hearing program in his local school district. Meanwhile, his parents had gained green cards and, through an interpreter, they explained Moises's medical history and confirmed the fact that he had been functioning as a deaf child for most of his life.

Accurate assessment and educational placement were steps in the right direction; however, Moises was now an active 10-year-old boy who had never experienced the rigors of a structured class for learners who were deaf. His delay in language affected his performance in an age-appropriate class, and his large size and gifted mind made placement with younger children impossible. His parents found that managing his behavior at home was more difficult as he became older. Communication at home was frustrating, and Moises was growing up without understanding what was expected of him.

Fortunately, one of the teachers of the deaf knew about a clinic for deaf children at a nearby university. She arranged for Moises and his family to visit the clinic. A Spanish-speaking graduate student interpreted the initial session. The assessment team concluded that Moises and his family would benefit from learning American Sign Language together with the help of a trilingual (Spanish, English, ASL) clinician. Arrangements were made for the family to attend the clinic weekly. In addition, a trilingual clinician made weekly visits to their home to reinforce ASL communication and to provide suggestions to reduce their level of frustration. Eventually, Moises began to see himself as a family member with responsibilities and privileges.

The university team worked closely with the public school teacher, sharing communication goals and progress reports. When possible, the clinic reinforced classroom literacy activities. Gradually, Moises's acquisition of ASL led to emerging literacy in English at school. At home, the family spoke Spanish with ASL emerging as their second language. Cultural events could be explained to Moises in ASL, and, in turn, Moises was able to share with his family elements of the deaf culture that he was learning at school.

The plight of Moises and his family is not unusual. Closer collaboration among professionals in education is necessary. Personnel with expertise in deafness should

An educator teaching American sign language

be involved in communication assessments in order to detect possible hearing loss and ensure unbiased assessment. Parents can reinforce communication at home with their deaf children by learning and using ASL. To facilitate collaboration among deaf and hearing children and teachers, American Sign Language programs can be included in general education. When hearing children are given the opportunity to learn ASL and communicate with their deaf peers, both hearing and deaf learners can benefit, linguistically and culturally.

As you can see, Moises learned three languages: ASL, Spanish, and English. This did not include the communication system he had learned in his family. This young man was extremely capable, but it took teachers who understood the complex challenges this young man faced to find him the most effective school. Some districts do offer deaf education classes and/or schools; however, they may not have faculty members who are also bilingual educators.

The Challenge: Moving from Conversational English to Academic English

Have you ever talked with a student who learned English and could carry on a good conversation? Didn't he seem ready to take on anything in school? I often mistook conversational skills for academic language skill development. It takes a

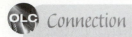 Connection

Visit the text OLC for Chapter 9 to link to the following site.

The Laurent Clerc National Deaf Education Center is located at Gallaudet University and includes information on deafness, family literacy, and assistive devices. Some of the most important links provide the reader with information on programs such as the Model Secondary School for the Deaf in Washington, D.C. Gallaudet University has regional centers throughout the nation that offer technical assistance in professional and educational needs of deaf and hard-of-hearing individuals. Their website is at **http://clerccenter.gallaudet.edu**

child approximately two years to develop conversational language. However, as Jim Cummins, a linguist, has written, there is a great difference in language levels between conversational English and the academic English needed in content areas (2000).

Cummins (1996, 2000) developed a theory that centers upon two concepts, CALP (cognitive academic language proficiency) and BICS (basic interpersonal communication skills). I have placed the acronyms first because they are better known in literature than the entire term. BICS is what we use in everyday conversation—the informal language people use that includes gestures, tone of voice, and social context. CALP, in contrast, is academic English: higher-level scholarly language. It takes students from five to seven years to develop CALP. The language of business, schools, and politics is often more complex than everyday conversational English. In addition, disciplines such as social studies, mathematics, literature, and physics contain high-level abstract concepts that contribute to academic English and challenge English learners. The comic on page 307 shows a grammatical challenge in learning English and how complicated the interpretations of the social situation can be.

Academic English is a broad category that includes many language skills. It is the ability to use English on an abstract level such as in writing. Several skills that have been identified in academic English are listed by Fillmore and Snow (2000):

Summarize texts, using linguistic cues to interpret and infer the writer's intentions and messages;

Analyze texts, assessing the writer's use of language for rhetorical and aesthetic purposes and to express perspective and mood;

Extract meaning from texts and relate it to other ideas and information;

Evaluate evidence and arguments presented in texts and critique the logic of arguments made in them;

Use grammatical devices for combining sentences into concise and more effective new ones, and use various devices to combine sentences into coherent and cohesive texts (Fillmore and Snow 2000, 21).

FRAZZ reprinted by permission of United Feature Syndicate, Inc.

The preceding are all high-level language abilities. These skills often are not only difficult for English language learners (ELL), but also challenging for many native speakers and must be taught in school (Fillmore and Snow 2000). Students need to be taught academic English in order to demonstrate the skills listed because the skills involve complicated and sophisticated use of the language.

One of the most difficult second-language skills is academic writing. English language learners come to school with languages that have different structures and with different language experiences (Fillmore and Snow 2000). Some languages teach a linear manner of expression and their writings reflect that orientation. However, other languages may support a more descriptive way of expressing ideas, so individuals may not understand the manner in which writing is expected. For example, a student's first language may not support the use of topic sentences, and a second-language learner may not have "broad knowledge of words, phraseology, grammar, and pragmatic conventions for expression, understanding, and interpretation" (Fillmore and Snow 2000, 20).

Educators can learn from the research of second-language experts. For example, Scarcella (2000) has identified common grammatical errors that she finds in writings of Asian English learners. A consistent error deals with verb form: Asian students find it difficult to understand the difference in time reference. Here are two illustrations she provided:

> I always *remembered* when my friend died.

> I *study* English since 1986 (Scarcella 2000, 2).

Another common error is the incorrect use or lack of prepositions. Because some Asian languages do not use prepositions in the same way as they are used in English, students may find them difficult to use.

> The nucleus is *on* the cell.

> He discriminate me (Scarcella 2002, 2).

Students also make errors because of their not knowing English vocabulary; when verbal statements are made, they may not understand the concepts being conveyed. The following is an example of a student who misinterpreted a title of a book because he or she didn't understand the vocabulary: "The book I read for my book report was Catch Her in the Right." (Scarcella 2002, 3).

When educators understand that students make consistent errors based upon the structure of their home languages, teachers are more able to assist learners in understanding the mistakes they make and how to eliminate them.

Researchers such as Garcia (2002) and Scarcella (1999) believe that academic English and basic conversational skills are not separate language skills. In fact, they consider the two to be highly linked and work collaboratively in communication. In addition, they view academic English more narrowly than Cummins in that this level of language competence means that students will be able to do the following: analyze, compare, contrast, classify, hypothesize, persuade, evaluate, predict, generalize, infer, and communicate (Garcia 2002). These are the higher-level thinking skills. Cummins has acknowledged the continuum between BICS and CALP and that there is overlap between the skill areas (2000).

Teaching in Content Areas: Sheltered English, SDAIE, and CALLA

As most teachers have found, it is easier to teach everyday English or BICS than academic English or CALP. This leads us to the question, How do I teach in content areas? Suppose English learners in your 10th-grade writing class can speak fluently, but are having trouble following a sequence of directions that you verbally give. This might be due to your use of specific terms in the discipline such as metaphor and irony. Also perhaps your students have not learned these concepts in Spanish, so your students are not already familiar with these terms.

When I was a young teacher, I often heard bilingual educators say, "I use the sheltered method." I didn't know what that meant. I could visualize a house, but that still didn't make much sense to me. Now I realize that *sheltered* meant "supportive." **Sheltered English** or the **SDAIE** approach to teaching is a method that teaches both subject area content and language skills.

How do you pronounce *SDAIE?* It sounds like *su* in *supper* and *die,* as in "not living." It means **specially designed academic instruction in English.** For some reason this was a difficult term for me to remember. I could say, "su-die," but couldn't remember what it meant. To me it was like learning a second language—the acronym had no meaning for me; it was not comprehensible input.

SDAIE and other content-centered approaches to instruction are based on the beliefs that second language is best learned when the material has meaning for students (Crandall 1994). Language skills are taught while students focus on academic content from basic disciplines such as geography, mathematics, science, and social studies. There are three major goals in these classrooms. First, English-language learners need to be taught the same subject area content as their native speaker peers are learning. Second, English-language learners also need to continue to work on developing their English language skills and becoming mature in their use of academic content in their writing and verbal communication. Third, students must learn the behaviors that are expected in the classroom, such as responding appropriately when a teacher calls on them. Crandall (1994, 1) suggests that the following conditions must be present for effective sheltered learning to occur:

1. Learning focuses on "meaning rather than on form."
2. Language is at or a little above the expertise of learners.
3. Creation of a stress-free classroom.
4. Creation of many opportunities to use language in ways that are relevant and understandable to learners.

In addition to these components, the SDAIE model is most effective when teachers bring to the classroom positive beliefs about the ability of their English language learners (Díaz-Rico and Weed 2002). Some of the skills that SDAIE teachers use are as follows:

- Link new concepts to ones already learned.
- Utilize many visuals (pictures, maps, graphs, charts, diagrams, photos) or demonstrations (role-playing, gestures, dramatizations, dance, singing) in teaching.
- Break the lesson into small chunks.
- Use student experiences in lessons to build concepts.
- Speak clearly and simply.
- Ask students if they understand.
- Use many visual organizers (e.g., concept mapping, data retrieval charts).

Another content-based approach, for those students who are intermediate or advanced English learners, is the **cognitive academic language learning approach, or CALLA** (Chamot and O'Mally 1994; Chamot 1995). This approach focuses on higher-level thinking skills. Students are involved in inquiry, questioning, and many hands-on activities. They provide sample lessons for teachers in disciplines such as science, math, language arts, social studies and literature and composition. In addition, English-language learners develop metacognitive strategies. These strategies are skills that students can use in various subject areas such as vocabulary strategies for new or confusing words, finding the key ideas in the text, and figuring out what information is most important to remember (Díaz-Rico and Weed 2002). Although some researchers believe CALLA and SDAIE are to be used only when students are at the intermediate fluency and advanced levels of English-language development, Chamot and O'Malley (1994) believe it is important to use content-based CALLA approaches even with early language learners because these strategies can make content concepts more understandable.

The following is an example of a student in a social studies class studying the issues brought up by the September 11, 2001, terrorist attack on the United States. The class is focusing on the issues of terrorism for the week. Students have tackled such questions as, What is terrorism? Who is a terrorist? Why do terrorists commit acts of violence against innocent people? What civil liberties, if any, are we willing to give up for greater security? Students wrote definitions for terms such as *terrorism,* providing important characteristics of the word. They consulted the Internet for information about other countries that were dealing with terrorism. They used atlases to find the locations of various countries on the globe. In addition, students were asked to write an essay describing their feelings about the day.

Rosa, a native Spanish-speaking, high school student wrote:

> I have mixed feelings about this day. I feel depress when I think about all the people that die that day.

Rosa's two sentences contained errors that she had made consistently in her papers during the week. The teacher noted that the student did not understand the proper use of the past tense. The word *depress* should have been *depressed* and the term *die* should have been *died.* The teacher gave this student a lesson about rules regarding the past tense verb form. In addition Rosa needed to think about the use of pronouns in her writing. Because the word *that* in the second sentence referred back to the word *people,* Rosa needed to think about using the pronoun *who.* Although Rosa was able to write about a more abstract concept such as "Call to Duty" because she was extremely interested in the work of firefighters, she was not aware of grammatical mistakes in her writing. The teacher noted that her errors were consistent and suggested that Rosa read her written work aloud, because that might help her hear some of the mistakes she was making. In social studies lessons, the teacher was able to teach about various issues related to September 11th and also focus on English-language skills. Language was a vehicle for Rosa to learn about her world and to understand the complexities in it.

How Long Does It Take Students to Acquire English?

The length of time it takes for an English language learner to become proficient varies depending on many factors, such as the extent of instruction the student has had in her or his first language, whether the student was schooled previously in a home country, the social and economic status of the family, the amount of English heard in the family and neighborhood, and the age of individual (G. Garcia 2000). Thomas and Collier (1997) found that students who were in bilingual programs and doing well in their native language (L1) performed at the 50th percentile in English (L2-second language) after approximately four to seven years of schooling. However, in the same study the researchers found that it may take 7 to 10 years for students who have had little instruction in their native language (L1), if most of their years of schooling are in English (L2).

What accounts for this difference in achievement? Gilbert Garcia (2000) explained that when students have been schooled in their first language, they acquire important language skills, such as syntax, vocabulary, discourse, and pragmatics—

features of language that students can use to learn English. That is why Thomas and Collier suggest that each English language learner be enrolled in a bilingual program for at least the first several years of school.

Another element that influences the ability of students to acquire English is the attitude of teachers. Castañeda and Ríos (2002) found that teachers resisted learning about second language and culture. In fact, some teachers were hostile to language-acquisition staff development. Here is a comment of one of the teachers Castañeda and Ríos had in their classes:

> I don't like it [diversity], really, because it seems to pose more problems than we previously had. We all wish for students who speak our language, are part of American culture and don't require special provisions (It makes our job easier.) (2002, 10).

They recommended that teachers be guided through much self-reflection about their own values and biases. It is imperative that teachers have knowledge of the power of culture and language in learning; otherwise, they may not be able to provide nurturing and effective instruction. Learning English may take longer in classrooms where students face negative attitudes about their home languages or schools where they are isolated and marginalized and therefore not learning much content or language.

Now let's move to another difficult challenge, teaching English learners how to write. Remember that Krashen has cautioned teachers not to be too critical in marking up the papers of their students. This may discourage students to a point where they do not want to learn English language skills. However, Evangelina Bustamante Jones learned from her college students what type of criticism they wanted from her. These young people, who were in their late teens and early 20s, were attempting to pass the college writing exit exam and sought feedback from their college professors. Here is her story.

Teacher Voices about Bilingual Education: Teaching Writing to Spanish Bilingual College Students

Evangelina Bustamante Jones

Some years ago, I taught developmental writing classes at a university extension campus located on the border of California and Mexico. The Mexican-born students had immigrated to this border area as young children or adolescents, while the Mexican American students were born to immigrant parents. All of them spoke and wrote Spanish, and had, at the least, an average English vocabulary, but English academic writing was an impossible barrier to all of them. As a bilingual Mexican American, I recognized that much of my students' writing problems stemmed from using linguistic features such as rhetorical style, sentence syntax, verb forms, and prepositions from the Spanish language when speaking or writing English. Thus, writing "errors" had logical and systematic bases; they were neither careless nor random mistakes, although they might appear so to someone who had no knowledge of Spanish. Regardless of the reasons for their poor writing, my students had to pass the gatekeeper writing exam by the end of the semester or they would lose the privilege of continued attendance at the university, and thus their college career.

I vividly remember the morning I skimmed through a stack of English essays on my desk and suddenly realized how fruitless my attempts to teach writing skills to university-level bilingual students had been. Adhering to widely held beliefs of writing instructors, my approach was to carefully examine the kinds of errors they consistently made, and focus on just a few at a time so as not to overwhelm them with too much "red ink" bleeding all over their essays. These students had already experienced years of frustration with writing; they feared it, loathed it, avoided it. Mike Rose, in his book *Lives on the Boundary: A Moving Account of the Struggles and Achievements of America's Educational Underclass* (1989), described a Latina student in his writing class at UCLA who could have been one of my students. Immigrated at an early age from a poor section of Tijuana, Laura and her working-class parents were now U.S. citizens. Though bright, she had trouble with writing, and with going to writing class:

I get in there, and everything seems okay. But as soon as we start writing, I freeze up. I'm a crummy writer, I know it. I know I'm going to make a lot of mistakes and look stupid. I panic. I stop coming (Rose 1989, 1).

My students were like Laura. I saw how they might remain at the margins, perhaps forever, if I didn't do something drastic, and soon. Teaching writing by dribs and drabs was like bailing out a seriously leaking rowboat with a teaspoon—time was running out for my students, and we had little to show for our efforts.

I decided to level with them by marking everything—all at once—rather than in small pieces as I had been doing. I hoped that since they had come to class for six weeks, they now trusted me enough to accept my feedback, painful as it might be. Before handing back their papers, I asked them not to freak out when they saw all the marks. I apologized in advance for any hurt this might cause, and assured them they were intelligent and potentially strong writers. I said that the content of their papers was strong, but the form and syntax needed a lot of work.

I passed their essays back. The room was absolutely silent for several minutes. Nobody spoke. I began to hear the rustling of pages, which told me that the students were looking at each and every mark and comment. Finally, Carmen, usually bubbly and animated, raised her hand; a profoundly sad look on her face gave way to an angry one as she said, "Mrs. Jones, all these years—since high school, teachers tell me, 'You are a poor writer.' Well, I already knew that. But nobody ever showed me *what* I was doing that made my writing so bad. I could never figure it out. Like a mystery. You are the first teacher that showed me *what* I am doing—everything. I'm doing a lot of things wrong. Now I can change. Thank you."

The rest of the class agreed with Carmen. Facing all their writing issues at once was a shock, yet they understood why I made extensive comments on their papers. Our work together in class had convinced them that they could trust me. They knew I marked up their papers to help them recognize the huge task before them, not to humiliate. Now they had a roadmap. The students came up with the idea of using this "keystone" paper to check every new essay against it for the kinds of errors they were likely to make so I didn't have to mark up their papers so extensively after that class session. Because they took control of their work, they developed a sense of self-efficacy as they addressed their writing. And all but two students passed the writing exam that semester.

My story illustrates the power that trust, honesty, and care wield in the relationships between students and teachers. I recognize, however, that my knowledge of bilingual writing issues gave me the ability to help students understand the linguistic differences between Spanish and English well enough to write at a native English-speaker level. It is of utmost importance that teachers who work with second language learners have specific knowledge about particular features of the native languages their students speak, not only to recognize why certain "errors" are made, but to give students explicit guidance on how to express themselves using correct English structure and usage.

Two small examples will illustrate this point: a Spanish speaker who thinks of the verb *bajar*—to descend, or to get off—when composing in English, can result in sentences like these: "I got off of the car" or "I got off the car" because in Spanish one says, "Me bajé del auto," in which the appropriate use of the verb *bajar* for this particular meaning includes the preposition "off." However, in English, we say "I got *out* of the car," not off of it. A teacher who recognizes that words don't always translate perfectly from one language to another can understand how the wrong preposition comes to be used, and can inform the writer about this particular detail. The writer becomes conscious of it and then self-corrects.

Other languages pose even more challenges because something that exists in English but may not be found in the student's primary language. This difference can be very difficult for students to understand. The Vietnamese language does not use singular or plural forms of nouns because the meaning is established through the context of the sentence. Thus a native speaker of Vietnamese might use mostly singular forms of nouns because these seem to parallel the pure form of nouns in Vietnamese. Seeing such a pattern in a student's writing, teachers can help them recognize the need to clarify meaning by using correct forms of words. Imagine how much more complex writing can be for ELLs when they attempt to compose in English using features from their primary language that are at the stylistic and rhetorical pattern level, rather than at the word level. The stylistic and rhetorical patterns affect the academic genres students must use in school, especially after the middle grades.

I cannot emphasize too much how important it is for teachers to undertake a sincere study of their students' home languages. With even a modest level of linguistic knowledge, we can diagnose and then give feedback that is more precise and more constructive than the teachers who did nothing but say to Carmen, my student, "You are a poor writer."

Suggestions from Professor Jones

From reading through Professor Jones's story, you can tell how important it is also to be honest with older students who want to know how to write more correctly. Of course, it was extremely crucial that Professor Jones had developed trusting and caring relationships with her students. They knew she really believed in them and was there to help them.

After the students saw the errors she had marked on their papers, they were extremely motivated to learn because they felt cheated by their previous education. It is important not to pass your students on to the next level without teaching them the English skills they will need. Professor Jones created a sheet that listed the common errors that the students were making in her class. In addition, she provided excellent correct examples from which her students could draw. In this way, Professor Jones not only pointed out their writing errors, but also gave them guidelines to follow in correcting their work.

As Jones explained to her students, many of their errors were errors in **transfer:** Students were transferring features of one language to another, a practice known as **crosslinguistic** influence. Here is an example. A common English rule is to add an *s* to a noun to express a number more than one; hence, the word *cookie* becomes *cookies* or *friend* becomes *friends.* But suppose you went to study in Vietnam. In all of your essays, the teacher would cross out the *s* in your plural words. You couldn't understand why because in English this was common practice. However, in Vietnamese *ban* means *friend* and several friends would be *vài ban* because *vài* is a plural marker for several (Davies 1996). Suppose you wrote the word *bans* for friends. In this case, you were demonstrating the phenomenon of crosslinguistic influence. You took a rule that works in English and applied it to Vietnamese. It wasn't correct, but it made sense to you! Many errors English learners make are not errors, but rules or practices from the first language. Just like many of the students in Professor Jones's class, you were making regular and logical mistakes. When a teacher can explain the difference between the two languages within a context that you already understand, you will be able to learn new language skills.

Bilingual Education: Do We Need It?

It was important for you to understand how language is learned and taught before discussing this issue. This section of the book provides a discussion of various programs in bilingual education.

Researchers such as Hakuta, Krashen, Fillmore, and Cummins believe that when children get a strong foundation in their home language, they can learn English more efficiently and quickly. When instruction is initially provided in their native language (e.g., Spanish), then children can build on what they already know. They know Spanish—the sounds, the rhythm of the language, sentence structure, vocabulary, pragmatics, and many other aspects of language—and can build their language skills. If schools have bilingual education programs that focus on maintaining Spanish, then children will have the time to learn the same subject area content their peers are also receiving in regular classrooms. When students' knowledge of Spanish is strong, then when teachers teach English as a second language, the skills in English are more understandable.

Remember Professor Jones's story. Students may already understand what a noun and verb are. Therefore, when those skills are taught in English, the teacher doesn't have to translate vocabulary and language concepts, too. Because Professor Jones's Spanish-speaking students already understood the rules of Spanish, she used their knowledge to teach the syntax and context of English.

Krashen uses the example of two children who speak Spanish. Suppose both have a good background in math and one has been in a bilingual classroom for three years. The second child is in a regular classroom. Their language resources are still in the early stages of developing CALP or academic language. Who is going to do better? The first student will understand more math and English because these subjects are more comprehensible. His teachers are able to build on his knowledge of

Spanish to teach English. The other child will not understand either because he does not have much background information about Spanish or English. As Krashen explains, "First language literacy transfers across languages." Other researchers have echoed what Krashen said. Why then is there so much resistance to bilingual education? James Crawford (1998) found that people believed several fallacies:

Bilingual education is far more costly than English-language instruction.

Research is inconclusive on the benefits of bilingual education.

The best way to learn a language is through "total immersion."

Go online and read the article by Crawford (www.cal.org/resources/digest/crawford01.html). Crawford refutes each of these fallacies and discusses many more. Let's examine the three fallacies listed.

Is bilingual education far more costly than English-language instruction? A study commissioned by the California legislature found that bilingual and English-only approaches cost about the same each year per pupil. In many English as a second language (ESL) classrooms, additional teachers had to be hired for these pull-out programs. This is quite expensive, so hiring bilingual teachers does not necessarily cost more. Research by scholars such as Collier, Fillmore, Hakuta, Ramirez, Krashen, Tomas, Garcia, Cummins, and Snow have shown that students who have been in well-designed and -implemented bilingual education generally do better than their second-language peers who have not had any bilingual instruction. These gains are found not only in elementary school, but also later in secondary school.

One of the major reasons is that when students are initially placed in submersion situations, they are neither learning English nor the grade-level content. The culture of the students is not being affirmed. Students' knowledge is not being built on because limited communication occurs between teachers and students. In the early grades, English as a second language students may do quite well, but when the students are placed in regular classrooms with little language support, they tend to fall behind native English speakers. This usually happens in the fourth grade, when instruction becomes more text-driven and the content areas are taught in more formal ways. If children have not been exposed to the academic language of the content areas in earlier grades, and they have not learned them through primary language instruction, they may have more difficulties in junior and senior high school.

Bilingual Education: What Is It?

This is not an easy question to answer. The term *bilingual education* has many connotations and means different things in various schools and districts. However, generally **bilingual education** refers to a student's receiving instruction in both his or her native language and English.

The goal of bilingual education is biliteracy. For example, bilingual education differs from pull-out ESL programs (teaching English as a second language) in which a child may get 20 minutes of English language skill instruction a day. There has been opposition to bilingual education. One example is Proposition 227 that was passed in

California in 1998. This proposition banned bilingual education unless parents requested that their children be placed in bilingual programs. Proponents of this law believed that students should learn English in school. Proponents also believed that parents should teach their children a native language at home and that teachers should be using research-based sheltered methods and not bilingual programs.

There are several types of language programs. The first two are those that provide little support for native language and progress to programs in which both native and second languages are nurtured and therefore would not be considered bilingual education programs.

Submersion is one type of language program. In this program, a student who does not speak English is placed in an all-English-speaking classroom and expected to learn English while she or he learns the grade-level content. The program is **subtractive** in that teachers ignore the first language of their students. The goal is learning English and these classrooms, for the most part, have an assimilationist orientation. Assimilation in this context means that the child is expected to learn the culture, language, behaviors, and so forth, of the majority group, while the culture and language of her or his group is placed in the background, becomes secondary, or is forgotten altogether in the learning process.

Suppose you were a 13-year-old adolescent from a country where there was civil strife, and your family has refugee status. You find yourself in a classroom where no one looks like you, no one speaks your native language, and you don't know what is going on. Your parents didn't want to leave their home country, but knew that their family would have been killed, so they reluctantly left and came to the United States. You are happy to be out of danger, but now you face a new type of uncertainty: How do you survive in another country, especially when you can't speak the language?

You end up in a middle school where you feel isolated. You are quiet and try not to do anything that would bring unwanted attention. As you become more accustomed to the school, you begin to pick up words and then phrases in English, but you are behind in your schoolwork. The teachers are extremely kind; however, few teachers or students ask about your background. You wish for the day when you don't seem so different. Your desire to be considered an American grows every day.

Many teachers would argue that this is best for students. They believe that it is important for English language learners to learn English as fast as possible so that they will be able to cope with and participate in their new country. I believe that teachers can help students to preserve their native language and culture while learning English and mainstream culture. It could be to our advantage as a society to have students who speak Arabic or Russian. We, as a nation, will need students who grow to be adults who can build relationships with global partners, people who understand and are comfortable in various cultural settings.

English as a second language (ESL) programs are in districts across the country. There are also programs that have ESL components and do not include bilingual education. Many of these programs are pull-out classes (also called withdraw classes) (Baker 1993, 2001). This means that students leave their main classroom and work with a specialist for 20 to 30 minutes a day or several times a week. The focus is only on English skills such as vocabulary, spelling, grammar, and conversational skills. Unfortunately, students have difficulty learning the material covered while they are "pulled out" because the curriculum of the ESL teacher usually does not include the missed content (Díaz-Rico and Weed 2002).

These programs have limited success for a variety of reasons. Here are several reasons for their nominal achievement. First, the student does not have continual support; rather, instruction is only for a very short period of time several times a week. The child does not have the opportunity to practice skills consistently. Second, many of these programs do not use the cultural knowledge of students because the main goal is to assimilate students. There is little understanding of affirming the culture and language that students bring to school. Because the teacher is not bilingual, students do not have the chance to continue to develop literacy in their native language and then transfer those skills to their second language. Little bridging may occur, so more complex concepts are difficult to teach. It is costly to hire resource teachers in addition to regular teachers. Students also may feel the stigma of being pulled out because their peers may see their going to another classroom as a sign of weakness, need for remediation, or being disabled (Baker 1993, 2001). I once tutored a young man in the classroom who was trilingual and English was his third language. He felt unintelligent because of lower language skills. However, because of his fear of leaving the classroom, the teacher asked me to work with him in his classroom. He thought that the other kids would think he was going to "special ed," if we went out of the room. For a year, we sat in the back corner, working on complex vocabulary and abstract concepts that he did not understand in his social studies and science texts. This approach worked effectively because I could observe for the hour what the teacher was covering and then help him with his seatwork.

In contrast to ESL instructional programs that do not foster content area instruction, sheltered instruction such as CALLA or SDAIE provide both language skill and content development. (For a further description, see the previous section titled "Teaching in Content Areas: Sheltered English, SDAIE, and CALLA"). There is little use of the primary language in ESL classrooms where these approaches are implemented (Díaz-Rico and Weed 2002).

Another program is **transitional bilingual education (early exit).** As Baker has carefully explained, in transitional bilingual education (TBE), the primary goal is to assimilate the child into English. He uses the pool analogy: The student is taught the free stroke and backstroke before being asked to swim in the larger pool; in other words, the student does have some English-language skills. Early exit refers to situations in which students have instruction for a maximum of two years, during which the first language is used part of the time and English, the other portion. Unfortunately, the curriculum may center on basic interpersonal communication skills (BICS) and not cognitive academic language proficienty (CALP) because two years is not long enough to develop complex cognition in English (Díaz-Rico and Weed 2002). The main goal is assimilation and learning English.

In the **transitional bilingual education (late exit)** program, the student is kept in the bilingual program until the sixth grade and may be receiving 40 percent of instruction in the home language (Baker 1993, 2001). Students in these programs can speak and read in both languages. Cultural relevancy is an important aspect of this approach. The teacher is a cultural mediator and usually has some ties to the native language community. However, some implementations of this approach are seen as weak because the focus is assimilation (Baker 1993, 2001), like that in the submersion models of English-language development. However, late transitional programs do afford students more opportunity to retain their primary language.

In **maintenance or developmental bilingual education (MBE)** programs, two languages, cultures, and viewpoints are maintained and developed. Bilingualism is seen as an important benefit and skill. The goal of MBE is to develop a student who is fully proficient in both languages (Baker 1993, 2001).

The goal of **immersion bilingual education (two-way immersion)** programs is to teach students to be skilled and to function well in two languages. *Language brings power and self-identification.* Both English learners and native speakers of English are members of the program. Bilingualism and biliteracy are major goals of this program (Baker 1993, 2001). In these programs, both cultures and languages of students are affirmed and utilized in instruction. Most dual-language programs feature Spanish and English, although Chinese or Japanese and English can be found where there are large numbers of Asian speakers.

Baker has identified four characteristics of two-way bilingual programs (1993, 164):

1. A language other than English is utilized for about 50 percent of the instruction.
2. In each instructional period, only one language is used.
3. The numbers of non-English and English-speaking students are approximately the same so that there is a language balance in the classroom.
4. Both English learners and native English speakers are participants in all lessons.

One of the goals of the program is student integration. In order to encourage the cross-mixing of students, students who are native Spanish speakers may help their English-speaking peers with their homework in Spanish, while English speakers assist Spanish-speaking students with their English seatwork. It is critical that our students have the opportunity to develop not only English but also other languages. Language brings power, control in one's community, and self-identity. For a more intensive discussion of the various types of bilingual and ESL programs available in schools, I highly recommend that you go to Jill Mora's website on bilingual education (http://coe.sdsu.edu/people/jmora). She is another important bilingual educator who provides important practical suggestions on her website.

Another Important Language Issue: Ebonics or Black English Vernacular

Because this chapter is about language, it is critical for teachers to understand that Ebonics or Black English vernacular is a language in its own right. Perry and Delpit (1998) provide evidence in their book *The Real Ebonics Debate* that Ebonics is "a legitimate, rule-based, systematic language, and that this language" is "the primary language of many African-American children" (3). Others believe it is a dialect of English. Dialect differences may refer to pronunciation and vocabulary and also include syntax or the word order and way that words are used (Rickford 1998; Garcia 2002).

Take a Stand

WHICH APPROACH IS BEST FOR A BILINGUAL STUDENT?

English Submersion	Maintenance Developmental Bilingual Education
Many immigrants have done well with this approach because they learned English quickly and became Americanized so that they fit in well with others. New immigrants need English in order to survive economically and socially.	Immigrants and other bilingual individuals can act as important linguistic and cultural mediators in our global society because they are bilingual and bicultural. This is especially important in the area of economics.
Bilingual education programs are extremely costly because specially trained teachers must be found for many language groups. It can be difficult and expensive to hire bilingual teachers who can speak Lao, Cambodian, Vietnamese, Spanish, and Somali.	Bilingual education programs do not cost more than English as second language pull-out programs. Schools have hired many ESL teachers to address the needs of English learners. ESL teachers do not cost any more than bilingual teachers.
It is not advisable to have children segregated into classrooms only for Spanish-speaking, Cantonese-speaking, or other non-English groups. We should encourage integration.	Many developmental programs are dual immersion so that students who are native language speakers are also learning a second language.
There are Latino parents who want their children in English-only classrooms and feel that without this approach their children will not learn English. Some children who have participated in bilingual programs have not learned either English or Spanish well.	Latino parents have requested bilingual education programs for their children because they and other elders want to be able to continue to communicate with their children. Language is an important vehicle in the preservation and the teaching of cultural values.
In English-only classrooms, test scores for second-grade Latino students in California rose on the STAR assessments from 1998 to 2001.	The most difficult time for English learners is after fourth grade when students are expected to use academic language and engage in higher-order thinking skills and concepts. Hakuta's research demonstrated that districts that banned bilingual education did not see their school test scores rise for English-language learners. (www.stanford.edu/~hakuta/SAT9/silence%20from% 20Oceansidehtmm)

Is Ebonics a real language? Should it be respected? The Linguistic Society of America (E. Garcia 2002) passed a resolution recognizing **Ebonics** as a "systematic and rule-governed" language and affirmed that it should not be described as "lazy," "slang," or "defective."

I highly recommend *The Real Ebonics Debate* because it comprehensively looks at the Ebonics controversy. Like bilingual education specialists, Perry and

Delpit (1998) believe that some educators do not value African Americans, and so they do not want to accept Ebonics because it would legitimize a community that has had second-class status throughout the history of the United States.

The Oakland School District School Board passed a resolution in 1996 to participate in the Standard English Proficiency Program (SEP) that used Ebonics as a link in teaching literacy in the only all-Black school district in California. As Hoover (1998) explained, "Its [Ebonics] emphasis is on teaching students Standard English speaking skills, on teaching the teachers about the Ebonics speakers' language and culture, and on teaching reading through 'Superliteracy,' which endorses phonics" and other critical components (73). Through this program students' cultures and language are affirmed and seen as bridges to learning standard English (Secret 1998). African and African American cultures are used to teach literacy skills because cultural background is seen as the foundation for learning. Secret also explained that Ebonics is not taught because the children already know the language; rather, she uses literature written in Ebonics by authors like Maya Angelou, Toni Morrison, and Alice Walker because of the beauty and cultural images found in their literature. These writers use the style and rhetorical characteristics of Black language and culture (Meier 2002).

Since the SEP program has been implemented, Secret has found parents to be more willing to come to school and not feel embarrassed when they speak Ebonics. Another teacher also has found that African American students are seeking out literature at the library written by Africans or African Americans (Meier 2002). In SEP, standard English is taught because teachers believe that all students need to be proficient in its use in order to survive in mainstream society. Students learn standard English and integrate aspects of Ebonics such as cultural images, culturally based analogies, rhythm, proverbs, and vocabulary in their own writings (Meier 1998).

Ebonics speakers, even young children, know that there are different language codes that people use in various aspects of their lives, so use is another important aspect of language (Delpit 2002). When high school students are asked to speak in standard English, they know what teachers are referring to; however, young people may still be learning about language codes. Delpit shared a story of a young student who said to her teacher, "Teacher, how come you talking like a White person? You talkin' just like my momma talk when she get on the phone!" (2002, 154). The young girl knew by the words chosen, tone, and style that the teacher was using a different dialect. She knew social acceptance differed based on language used. In addition, she may also be learning about how she identifies with the language she uses. One of the important aspects about language is that it can be an integral aspect of a student's cultural/ethnic identity, whether a student speaks Ebonics, Spanish, or Polish.

> ↻ "Human relationships are at the heart of schooling . . . devaluation of identity played out in the interactions between educators and students convinces many students that academic effort is futile."
> —JIM CUMMINS, 1996, 1, 3.

Teachers working in the community

The Integration of Spanish and Latino Culture into Math and Science Education

Research on strategies for English learners is growing. The following case describes the work of Rochelle Gutierrez (2002) who observed several successful high school mathematics teachers who worked with English dominant Latina/o students. These students did not attend bilingual education classes. The teachers supported bilingual education for their students, but were not bilingual themselves. The teachers that Gutierrez studied understood that access and retention of Latina/o students in mathematics class needed to be addressed, although many Latina/o students find themselves on the margins. Some of the insights can also be adapted by teachers of other content areas and by educators who have students with home languages other than English in their classroom. I found her work to be of special interest because unlike elementary grade subjects, math content is more abstract and often more challenging to teach. As Gutierrez explained, she has seen many math teachers who believe that mathematics is a "culture free" content area.

The High School Math Classroom: Recommendations

Gutierrez clearly explained that language, culture, and ethnic identity are intimately tied for many students. For example, if Spanish is used at home, the language represents family, home, and national cultures, along with a sense of community with others whose ancestors may have come from diverse countries such as Puerto Rico, Mexico, Cuba, and Guatemala. Spanish as a language can be an anchor for many students, although their levels of proficiency will vary. Gutierrez found in math classes that although students might be fluent in conversational Spanish, they might not have an academic background in the language. Many students were not familiar with high-level mathematical concepts and vocabulary in Spanish. Therefore, some students who come with a home language of Spanish need to study math in both languages in order to become bilingual (Gutierrez 2003). In the same classrooms, there were also second- and third-generation Latina/os who did not speak Spanish, although some of their teachers believed they were English-deficient (Gutierrez 2003). Their view resulted from stereotypes that teachers believed and associated with ethnicity.

Second, students come to school with much knowledge and experiences. It is important for teachers to build on the prior resources, information, and language that students already hold. Inclusion of cultural knowledge of students honors them and their families. Gutierrez carefully explained that learning for bilingual students is complex. They must grasp new mathematical concepts while learning new English vocabulary. In some situations, when students are encouraged to use Spanish, peers also help them to develop more academic Spanish language. The process can include three levels of learning: math academic concepts, Spanish vocabulary, and English vocabulary.

Third, mathematics has its own language and when students are told to plot a series of points or calculate differentials, they must understand the vocabulary and constructs. It is critical for educators to teach the language of mathematics and, as one of the teachers that Gutierrez studied explained, children need to understand both the forest and the trees (2003). The forest represented the "big picture" and math concepts that students learned. The trees were the details or particular examples of a concept. Mathematicians expect people to express themselves in the language of mathematics. One way to do this is to provide several ways to explain the same situation; this might include the use of visuals, role-playing, stories, and charts. Another strategy that teachers can use is to encourage students to use the language with each other in small-group discussions.

How effective is group work? Do you like working in a group? Many research studies indicate that students who work as partners or in small groups learn more effectively (Garrison and Mora 1999; Gutierrez 2003; Fullilove and Treiseman 1990). Researchers believe that some students act as cultural mediators or interpreters and help in solving problems by explaining the content in several ways. Sometimes, in small groups, individual students are more likely to make the content their own. They take charge or ownership of the material. In fact, one of the teachers whom Gutierrez interviewed explained how a student used Spanish in a small group to help two peers. James Shulman is an affirming Anglo teacher who did not believe

Latina/o students were deficient. He did not speak Spanish himself; however, he believed in his students and their cultures in the learning process. He practiced **additive bilingualism,** an approach in which students were encouraged to use both their native language and English in the learning process. This is what Mr. Shulman said:

> You know, I'm not sure to what extent [Spanish language] plays a role. I mean I think it does and it doesn't, . . . so yesterday, it was interesting. Manuel was working with two weak students, who were entirely lost and asking him questions. It was fairly hard in places, so he was asking me a few questions and some other kids, and then he was talking to Hesael in Spanish about the problems. I don't know that I've seen him that much in here talking Spanish, I could be wrong. But hearing it, I've seen other kids talk Spanish more. He speaks English quite well and he feels comfortable and maybe some other kids feel less comfortable, but they were really animated. And my comment to Hesael afterwards was, "Well, that was really neat to see you guys really into that." So it seemed like it was more real or more vital [to them] in doing it. It was like they were really at a much greater level . . . They probably did feel a little more comfortable, but they were, it seemed, more animated, so it was very neat (Gutierrez, 2002, 1067).

Fourth, Gutierrez found that effective teachers got to know students by observing and interacting informally with young people. In that way teachers developed strategies that addressed their individual and group needs. Caring and personal reciprocal relationships provide the foundation for a community of learners to thrive. The teachers held the belief that all students should have opportunity to participate in high-level quality mathematics education. They also believed in liberatory education and believed that teaching is a political act.

The following are points that Gutierrez found in her study of mono-English math teachers of Latina/o students:

1. Teachers believed in their students and saw teaching as a political act in providing education that liberated students rather than oppressed them.
2. Teachers wanted students to make mathematics their own and nurtured them in developing high-level problem-solving skills. This in turn gave students access to upper-division math and many were then able to take courses such as calculus.
3. Teachers created a learning community by encouraging group work and getting to know students informally. Teachers honored and affirmed the cultural and linguistic background of their students by observing their needs and developing caring, reciprocal relationships with them.
4. Teachers taught students the language of the content area and, in this case, the language was mathematics. The educators believed that in order for young people to participate in building their own understandings of the mathematical concepts being taught, they needed to know the language of mathematics.
5. When students did not understand the mathematical concepts fully, students were encouraged to use Spanish to help their peers more completely grasp the constructs. They not only learned the concepts more fully, but their mentors also took control and made the content their own.
6. Teachers realized that there are many ways of knowing.

Gutierrez found that monolingual English-speaking teachers could incorporate strategies that are often recommended to bilingual educators. These methods were also effective with English-dominant Latina/o students, monolingual English students, and bilingual (Spanish/English) youth. As you can see, the strategies could be helpful to a range of students.

 ## Case Study

A BILINGUAL/BICULTURAL EXAMPLE IN AN ELEMENTARY SCIENCE CLASSROOM

This case study discusses an example of a teacher building on student cultural knowledge in science education. Like math teachers, science teachers also have shown the importance of building on what students know. Okhee Lee (2003), a science educator, described how a Latina teacher used the experiences of her students in a lesson on Celsius and Fahrenheit to create connections between science concepts and what students had observed at home. The following is what the teacher explained to her elementary-grade students about the two systems:

> One example is taking temperature. I know now that I have to talk about the different measurements that you can get with the thermometer. Many students know that 38° means a fever, but some of them know it as around 100°. They don't use terms like Celsius or Fahrenheit. They bring in these different experiences that we need to recognize. Another example is all of the foods we cook at home. Cooking is important in feeding a family, and they relate to that well. Hispanics do a lot of cooking our homes. All the foods we cook at home require a lot of boiling, and they see the evaporation. So when they have lessons that involve boiling and evaporating, they have something to build on to learn science. When we do the activity on boiling, we talk about boiling frijoles [beans] and arroz [rice], things they relate to. When we measure the temperature of boiling water, we do it in both Celsius and Fahrenheit. Then they realize there are two systems of measuring the temperature. It is like speaking two languages, like bilingual (Lee 2003, 475).

This teacher not only affirmed what the kids knew and so the use of rice and beans was not stereotyped, but also affirmed bilingualism in their science lesson. ✳

When you, as the teacher, know your students well, you will be able to assess their educational needs. Within this process, you may create math problems that teach the constructs, but employ examples from the lives of students. When you do this, students know you are listening and tailoring their lessons to their needs and cultural experiences. You can see from this discussion that the strategies arose from the teachers' belief systems; their philosophy guided their choice of teaching methods. They cared and respected their students and believed that all students, including Latina/s, could learn advanced levels of mathematics. The teachers understood that schools do not always provide the best education for students from underrepresented groups, and they were committed to equity. They created classrooms built upon caring, culture, and community. They fought racism by providing quality education in which students succeeded.

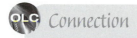

Connection

Please visit Chapter 9 of the text website to link to the following sites:

An excellent language website **www.crede.ucsc.edu** for teachers is the Center for Research on Education, Diversity and Excellence at the University of California, Santa Cruz. This center offers a wide range of information on language development and educational strategies. The faculty offer excellent short summaries of research. For example, Practitioner Brief #1 published in October 2000 is called "Family Visits Benefit Teachers and Families—and Students Most of All." This is an excellent piece about how to establish powerful school-home partnerships with parents from culturally or linguistically diverse families.

Another excellent website is the Center for Applied Linguistics. They also provide important information for teachers, administrators, and other service providers. For example, you can get a copy of their report called *Reading and Adult English Language Learner* at **www.cal.org/ncle/DIGESTS/Read.htm**

Chapter Summary

Effective language instruction is critical for many of our students who come to school with a home language other than English ('Aha Pūnana Leo 2002). Languages can vary from Somali, Russian, Spanish, Korean, Polish, or Farsi. In addition, students may come to class speaking Ebonics, Navaho, Cantonese, "Spanglish," or Pidgin English (mixture of primarily Hawaiian, Japanese, and Chinese phrases and vocabulary). In order for teachers to create a learning environment in which they can build on the language skills and experiences of their students, they need to know basic information about various languages and cultures in their classrooms. Teachers must also be careful not to identify students who are learning a second language as needing special education services. This also includes students who speak Ebonics.

There is a developmental process in which people acquire a second language. This process includes preproduction, early production, speech emergence, and intermediate fluency. It is important for teachers to understand that a student may have excellent command of conversational English or BICS (basic interpersonal communication skills) and not have mastered CALP (cognitive academic language proficiency). In order for students to do well in school, they must acquire CALP because these are the skills needed for abstract critical thinking and writing. These skills include categorizing, comparing, analyzing, evaluating, and synthesizing. Language learning is extremely complicated, and to provide an effective and successful education for your second-language learners, it is important to provide not only relevant curriculum, but also to make accurate assessments of student learning.

Krashen presented a framework to assist teachers in understanding ways to reach English language learners:

- Acquisition-Learning Hypothesis—Acquiring language occurs when language is meaningful. Learning refers to the more structural aspects of language such as grammar and rules.
- Monitor Hypothesis—Fluency develops when the learner can monitor her or his grammar and language use in writing and public speaking.
- Natural Order Hypothesis—The learner looks for patterns in language. Language is learned in a natural sequence.

- Affective Filter Hypothesis—Effective language acquisition occurs when students have low anxiety.
- Input Hypothesis—Input should be comprehensible and meaningful. When a learner understands what is conveyed, she or he is able to develop language skills.

The following are strategies and beliefs that can guide teachers in teaching English language learners:

1. **Get to know your students and build on their experiences.** You can make connections between what they know and what you are teaching. Students have many experiences and they may surprise you with what they have learned. Many are refugees and can describe to their peers firsthand experiences of their families from all over the world, whether from El Salvador, Somalia, Cambodia, or Kosovo.

2. **Plan your curriculum so that the themes, issues, and concepts are key content to the subject areas you teach.** It is critical for your students to learn the subject matter of the disciplines. They need the information for their own personal growth and to understand the world they live in.

3. **Create meaningful and relevant curriculum activities.** Most students, no matter what their languages or cultures are, learn from hands-on, engaging classroom activities. Although lecture may be the preferred mode of delivery for many educators, this may be more difficult for students to understand because of its reliance on language. In addition, all students need to be taught how to direct their own learning.

4. **New concepts are presented within a context that students can understand.** That is why visuals, photos, maps, role-playing, simulations, films, Internet sites, and other material can help students anchor the ideas, metaphors, similes, and symbolism being taught.

5. **Look for consistent errors.** Many students who are learning English make the same mistakes consistently. These errors may be based on rules that they have transferred from their first language to English.

6. **Affirming home languages and cultures must be at the philosophical core of instruction.** Students must be taught in an atmosphere that supports and respects the importance of a multilingual and multicultural society and world. Instruction should not be aimed at replacing a home language with English, but to teach a balanced viewpoint.

7. **Both primary and secondary languages can be used in complex problem solving.** One of the goals of schools is to educate students for lifelong learning.

8. **Bilingualism is good for the brain.** Learning languages and dialects stimulates the brain and encourages further cognitive development. Bilingualism encourages divergent thinking and understandings about the world.

9. **Students are *developing* language skills and are not limited in English proficiency.** A teacher reminded her colleagues that we might want to see our students as developing rather than "limited" or "deficient." She felt this was an important attitude to hold as a teacher with high student expectations and respect for other languages.

Chapter Review

Go to the Online Learning Center at **www.mhhe.com/pang2e** to review important content from the chapter, practice with key terms, take a chapter quiz, and find the Web links listed in this chapter.

Key Terms

phonology, *293*
metalinguistic awareness, *293*
vocabulary *294*
lexicon, *294*
syntax, *294*
morphology, *294*
pragmatics, *294*
preproduction stage, *296*
early production stage, *296*
speech emergence stage, *296*
intermediate fluency stage, *296*
Affective filter hypothesis,
297, 301

monitor model, *298*
Acquisition-learning hypothesis,
299, 300
comprehensible input, *300*
Natural Approach, *300*
Natural Order Hypothesis, *301*
Input Hypothesis, *301*
sheltered English instruction, *308*
SDAIE, *308*
CALLA, cognitive academic
language learning approach, *309*
transfer, *314*
crosslinguistic, *314*

bilingual education, *315*
submersion, *316*
subtractive, *316*
ESL, English as a second
language, *316*
transitional bilingual
education, *317*
Maintenance or developmental
bilingual education (MBE), *318*
immersion bilingual education
(two-way immersion), *318*
additive bilingualism, *323*
Ebonics, *319*

Reflection Activities

1. Understanding language acquisition is important to teaching. In this chapter, find the definitions for the following terms:

   Syntax

   Phonology

   Morphology

   Pragmatics

2. Have you ever thought about how difficult it would be for a student who does not understand English to come into your classroom? Observe one of your students who is an English language learner and see what problems she or he has in one day. Then develop a plan to address those needs. Remember the importance of what Stephen Krashen said about comprehensible input and the affective filter. How can you integrate his theories into how you work with your student? Can you develop strategies that help to minimize the embarrassment and stress that an English learner feels? How can you also make the content you are teaching more meaningful and relevant to your student?

   You may want to utilize some of the ideas found in the nine principles in the summary of the chapter.

3. How would you create a lesson plan for a 3rd- or 10th-grade student who was learning English as a second language in a content area such as social studies? Choose an issue or concept. Now determine the vocabulary your student will need to learn in order to understand the lesson. What visuals or hands-on materials will you use to teach the lesson? Are there posters you can use or a role-playing situation that you can integrate into the activities to help assist your students in understanding the objectives of the lesson?

4. Read through the piece about the child who is deaf. List all of the skills the young man would need to learn in order to use ASL. Go to the library or online and begin to read materials available about deaf education and bilingual deaf education. Be sure to look at the work of Kathee Christensen, Olga Welch, and Barbara Gerner de Garcia in your review.

5. If you have English learners in your classroom, every lesson you teach should have an

English-language development component integrated into it. Other children will also benefit from your careful consideration of your English learners. For example, if the vocabulary is extremely difficult to understand and teach, maybe having photos of concepts would provide more meaning.

This may help all students, even those who speak English as their first language, but who don't quite understand the concepts or vocabulary. Take a lesson that you have already taught or were going to teach and see if you could enrich it by using some of the ideas in this chapter.

CHAPTER 10

What Is Culturally Relevant Teaching?

CHAPTER OVERVIEW

Culture is often ignored in schools; however this chapter discusses how cultural context and content are vital elements of teaching and learning. Examples are given showing how culture shapes cognition. Vygotsky's zone of proximal development can guide teachers in assisting students in extending their learning. Several important programs founded on a deep respect for ethnic communities are described. These programs exemplify the principles of culturally relevant teaching, equal education, and caring communities. Finally key elements that can be integrated into a culturally relevant curriculum and how they can be used in scaffolding learning are explained.

ne evening in a teacher education class, I introduced the term *culturally relevant teaching*. During the break, James, a teacher of color, came up to me and said with much emotion, "*Those* kids won't work. They are never ready for class.

They don't even have a pencil and I teach an English class. All they want to be are boxers and they aren't interested in what I have to say. Nothing I use seems to get through. Now, why do you think anything about culture is going to make any difference? I don't believe you."

James looked at me with frustration in his eyes and raising his hands in the air in desperation. You could see he cared or he wouldn't have brought up the issue. But he conveyed his unhappiness about the Chicano students in his class not being interested in school. As a teacher he felt that he was failing his students. I suggested that he consider integrating culturally relevant teaching. Of course, his first question was "What is culturally relevant teaching?" Let me share with you my views about this approach, and at the end of the chapter I will let you know what this teacher did. Previous chapters have discussed how culture is an integral aspect of life. This chapter presents how culture can provide important links between the everyday experiences and knowledge of students to school knowledge, concepts, and skills.

Why Is Culture Often Ignored in Schools?

Ethnic culture is often seen as a marginal aspect of schools. Many educators do not believe that it impacts learning. A friend of mine who is an effective principal told me that his school won an award from the district for improved test scores. He told me that his large elementary school was divided into three small schools that shared the same campus. Class size had been reduced, and the curriculum was clearly articulated between the primary school and the intermediate school. However, when I asked my friend if they considered culture in the curriculum, there was a long pause and then he said, "No, we don't do much with culture." As a person from a non-mainstream ethnic group, I thought he would have a cultural thread woven throughout the school, especially since he learned English as the language of school and at home he spoke Spanish.

Ethnic culture was not a major concern. The principal explained that he believed that students who spoke Spanish, Vietnamese, Russian, Somali, and Lao would quickly adapt to the expectations of the school and in doing so would make the cultural shift to English and mainstream ways. He wasn't really concerned about how the assimilation process might affect student self-image or relationships with non-English-speaking parents. To him, academic achievement, as measured by standardized tests, was most important. He believed that it was critical to improve student scores. It never occurred to him what students might be giving up in the process of replacing home culture with school culture. However, teachers in the school felt that students would need to give up aspects of their cultures if they wanted to do well in school. The educators did not understand how the assimilation process could negatively impact student self-identity or cause students to give up home languages, behaviors, and community affiliations. When I asked the principal about Multicultural Education, he said that his staff didn't think it was relevant to the education of his students, and they didn't believe in holding international potlucks. Most of the faculty did not think that parents were interested in participating in the school.

A common misconception about Multicultural Education is that it is mainly the presentation of cultural fairs. The principal and his staff didn't realize that Multicultural Education is about school reform; this includes curriculum, teaching practices, and materials that are relevant and meaningful to students. Multicultural Education is a paradigm shift from a teacher-centered to a student-centered orientation. Many of the teachers at this school believed that the curriculum and methods of instruction were culturally neutral. They did not examine the fact that many aspects of their school taught a strong mainstream culture and that some students had to accept new cultural assumptions, beliefs, and values in order to do well in school. In the process of assimilation, students gave up vital aspects of culture such as their home language. For example, some students did not keep up their home-language skills because they felt it was more important to develop their writing skills in English.

Cultural Context and Everyday Learning

Although it is easier to list various components of culture, it is often more difficult to describe the domains or the cultural context of learning. Many activities we are engaged in occur within the cultural context. Barbara Rogoff, who studied everyday thinking, wrote:

> Central to everyday contexts in which cognitive activity occurs is interaction with other people and use of socially provided tools and schemas for solving problems. Cognitive activity is socially defined, interpreted, and supported . . . For example, people seldom commit a list of shopping items to memory in preparation for a trip to the grocery store. Rather, they make use of aids such as written lists of items, they ask other people to remind them of what to purchase, or they use the grocer's arrangement of items to jog their memory as they peruse the aisles for the needed items" (Rogoff 1984, 4).

In this example, using Vygotsky's theory, Rogoff explained how the shopper operates within a sociocultural historical context in which there are specific tools and practices. Maybe the shopper is using the tools of a shopping list and a calculator to decide if he or she can afford the items. In addition, practices that are familiar help the person solve the problem; how grocery items are arranged on the shelves and various words/phrases found in the supermarket may aid one's memory. As a child, the shopper may have been taught how to shop for groceries within a cultural context, using tools and skills of that culture. Through social interactions with others such as clerks, parents, and friends, the child learned to use various tools in the supermarket.

Globe: A cultural learning tool

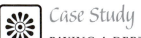 Case Study

PAYING A DEBT AND LITERACY DEVELOPMENT

Children learn a great deal of context-specific knowledge before coming to school. Their everyday thinking has been shaped by the specific goals of the community. Daily functions must be accomplished and children respond to those family and community needs. Young people may be charged with doing the dishes, taking out the garbage, or sweeping the floor. Within those contexts are specific symbols, practices, skills, and tools that are used to teach how to function and address the goals of family and community members.

For example, Scribner and Cole studied literacy of the Vai people in West Africa (Scribner and Cole 1981). The researchers wanted to understand the role of literacy, the use of knowledge and written language, within their specific cultural context. They found that different cognitive skills were developed from literacy used in the schools and literacy in everyday life. Many Vai who were literate had letter-writing skills because in their lives, letters were written to secure payment for a debt (Scribner 1984). Thus, people used the written language to reach a specific goal. Prior knowledge of the literate Vai was within the context of letter writing. They did not show any exceptional skill in repeating a story or remembering a list of words. However, Scribner observed that students who learned the Vai indigenous script did so more effectively by utilizing a system of learning a chain of three words at a time. Several chains would then be learned and put together. This informal observation led to Scribner and Cole's understanding of how literacy skills are shaped by the everyday needs and activities of a community or cultural group. Before this study, they had believed that literacy was a set of fixed universals. After this study, they theorized that literacy represented a variety of skills and differed within various cultural contexts.

The previous example shows how children may have certain literacy skills because they have been reinforced throughout their lives, but they may not have other skills. Children in families from the Vai community could learn strings of words quickly and efficiently because this was a commonly used method in their society. However, the Vai did not do well at repeating a story told to them or in learning a list of unrelated words. For the people in this community, work, literacy, and the written word were primarily seen in relationship to writing business letters. The purpose of their learning was clear. Context was an important aspect of shaping the way they learned. ❈

Case Study

ECONOMIC SURVIVAL AND MATH SKILL DEVELOPMENT

Another example of how culture impacts cognition comes from the work of Geoffery Saxe. As an educational psychologist, Saxe studied the way children who never went to school developed mathematical skills (1988a, 1988b). The children were 10- to 12-year-old candy vendors on the streets of Brazil. Because of the high inflation rate in the country, the value of money was continually changing. The children had to mentally convert money all the time in order to sell their candy on the streets. Saxe found that these children, who would be considered by U.S. standards illiterate and unschooled, were able to compute complex math problems more accurately than students who were formally educated.

The children who worked in the streets and sold candy regrouped large bills and added 500 + 500 and 200 + 200 + 100 in sets. The children did not use pencil and paper to compute these problems correctly. During Saxe's study, Brazil's inflation rate was 250 percent; children had to be able to manipulate large numbers when selling their candy, adjusting for continual changes in the inflation rate. Saxe's study found that children developed complex mathematical problem-solving strategies based on the currency system. The children had a specific goal; their goal was to sell candy and make money. The cultural context created a goal. As Scribner has pointed out, some skills are school oriented and other skills address the functions needed in a specific community. Although all learning is not culturally familiar, teachers need to understand that some children have learned much within a cultural context that may differ from majority culture. Teachers may be able to better reach children when using the culturally familiar content and contexts that act as bridges to school knowledge and skills. �֍

Cultural Context: A Vital Element of Teaching

Understanding cultural context can be challenging. Here are some questions you might ask yourself to begin delving into cultural context: How do you like to learn? Do you prefer working in a group where you can brainstorm with your peers, or do you like the independence of working by yourself? As a child, did you hope that your parents knew how well you were doing in school, or did you prefer that they didn't know what your grades were? Do you prefer to be verbally expressive and role-play situations as part of the performance assessment, or do you prefer to choose from multiple-choice answers? Do you need to see the relevance of what you are learning? Do you prefer a lecture when you are learning something new, or do you like watching someone demonstrate a new skill?

All of these questions give rise to different sets of social situations in learning. Many students from all communities prefer to work in small groups rather than independently. Many students from African American, Asian Pacific American, Latino, and European communities feel more supported by a sense of community. However, some individuals from these communities prefer working alone because they are task oriented, and when a group of learners get together, the process takes longer and can frustrate them. Even though there may be trends in a group, not everyone responds to the same cues because people are individuals.

To understand the concept of sociocultural context, teachers can begin to identify various elements in action. Susan Philips's book, *The **Invisible Culture,*** gives excellent examples. Philips conducted an ethnographic study of the Warm Springs community in Oregon. She clearly describes how the cultural context of the classroom is the major component of the learning process. She talks about accepted and expected behaviors of people in the community.

Philips discovered that there were many underlying patterns of behavior. In some ways, one could say that the students created an underlying rhythm in the classroom. Philips found the Native American students to be more reserved and less responsive in their verbal interactions with the teacher than students from the majority culture. Students conveyed their feelings through gestures, facial movements, or expressions with their eyes. The students were also oriented toward their peers and not the teacher, so teachers who are not part of the community had difficulty understanding this style of interaction. Because students were also more apt to look at their peers rather than the teacher when the teacher was speaking, it appeared as if they were not listening. If a teacher used a fixed gaze as a management technique, it might be seen as extremely hostile. Young people preferred team games rather than games like Jeopardy or Trivial Pursuit. Students were also more likely to take turns collaboratively. This behavior contrasts to that of mainstream students who try to take control of classroom conversations by calling out to get the attention of the teacher. Some young people rejected school because it represented mainstream society, a society that has oppressed Native peoples for many years; they did not want to sell out to the oppressor.

These elements demonstrate how the social context includes not only accepted behaviors, but also interactional patterns, value orientations, historical understandings, and nonverbal communication styles. Teachers may become frustrated with students who do not actively participate in class discussions or who do not seem to be attending to them while they are talking. Teachers are not the focus of learning in Warm Springs classrooms; the students as a community are at the center.

What can teachers do to address the context issue? For example, some Native American students may reject school because schooling may seem like an assimilationist tool teaching them to be more White. Historically, ethnic communities have come into conflict with and often feel the pressure to assimilate into majority culture. Hap Gilliland (1986), a Native American teacher, suggests that educators should be open to conversations about the conflicts Native American students may have with mainstream society. In addition, integrating social science lessons about events like the Trail of Tears, The Long Walk, Baker Massacre, Sand Creek, and Wounded Knee can create opportunities for communal discussions (Gilliland 1986) that include the study of controversial issues such as treaties, land management, and cultural assimilation. Teachers also can make comparisons with other events in history, such as the overthrow of Queen Liliuokalani, the Japanese American internment, the Sleeping Lagoon case, the Zoot Suit riots, and the March on Washington. Through the presentation of these events, teachers can introduce issues-centered discussions that focus on governmental policies and their impact on nonmainstream ethnic communities. To provide a balanced view of the struggles of people from underrepresented groups, it is also imperative for teachers to present information about how communities empowered themselves and challenged oppressive social structures. The self-determination movement as a theme can be incorporated into the curriculum. Instead of feeling like pawns, many Native people have gained control over medical, educational, and business programs, as well as restored tribal government to their communities (Olson and Wilson 1984). For example, Native people fought for the passage of the Indian Self-Determination and Education Assistance Act in 1975 (Olson and Wilson 1984). With this act, the power of tribal governments was strengthened and the law established the ability of tribal governments to set their own goals and priorities for social service funds and financial resources targeted for education. Teachers can assist Native American students in understanding that, in order to make changes in a society, they must have the skills to do so. Students must be able to read, write, and compute, and more importantly they must also understand the system they are a part of as members of this country (Delpit 1995). Using role models like Malcolm X, Helen Keller, Scott Momaday, and César Chavez, teachers can discuss the anger, frustration, and disillusionment of others and present how these individuals developed political knowledge and skills that were needed to effectively change national policies and practices.

The **cultural context** is extremely important to the learning process. This includes not only the behaviors and ways of communicating that students bring to school, but it also refers to the value orientation of teachers. For example, knowledge is seen as objective. Also, the teacher is visually at the center of instruction and regulates classroom talk (Philips 1993). However, the cultural community context of students may come into conflict with the teacher's context. For example, as was discussed previously, some students from culturally diverse communities come to school with the concern that they do not want to do well because this would be considered "acting White" (Gilliland 1986; Delpit 1995; Fordham and Ogbu 1986). They would be giving in to an oppressive White society and accepting assimilation. This belief may result in behaviors that are seen as obstinate and uncooperative. Teachers must consider and address the issue because context is as much a part of the learning process as instructional content. Even though lessons may contain cultural content from a student's home (e.g., bringing in ethnic newspapers) in order to fully utilize culturally relevant teaching, teachers need a comprehensive understanding of student communities to appreciate the fuller meaning of issues reported in the newspapers.

Listening and observing students can provide teachers with knowledge of interactional patterns, expectations, frustrations, and underlying values. This information can assist teachers in knowing how to motivate, affirm, present concepts and issues, and appropriately respond. In the case of students from a culture like the Warm Springs nation, the teacher would need to take a student-centered approach in which there is more emphasis on communal activities. Otherwise, young people might withdraw completely from what was going on in the classroom. Philips found that students completed group tasks but an identifiable leader was not chosen. Instead, they quickly divided responsibilities and the work was done. She found cultural context to be a powerful component of the learning process because the expectations of Warm Springs students directly conflicted with mainstream practices. Does culture influence teaching in other communities? The next section takes us to Jerry Lipska's classroom in Alaska.

 *Case Study*

AN EXAMPLE OF THE POWER OF CULTURAL CONTEXT: A YUP'IK CLASSROOM

One of the Native communities in Alaska is the Yup'ik. Jerry Lipska (1996) researched how experienced Yup'ik teachers used culturally relevant pedagogy that affirmed student ethnic identity. Overall, Lipska reported a rhythm and flow of learning in the classroom. He watched a lesson focusing on the beaver round-up festival, which signals the end of the winter. In the discussion about how to trap and skin beavers, the male students in this fifth-grade classroom spoke in animated tones and quickly explained how to stretch the beaver pelt. The teacher reinforced their responses with a short, "Right." He used the term *aqsatuyaaq* (young beaver) in his lesson. At first, the teacher gave directions, using art materials, about how to make the beaver blanket.

Then he allowed the students to make their blankets on the floor or at their own desks. The teacher made his own beaver blanket at his desk. Some students went to the teacher's desk to watch the teacher. Students talked to each other as they worked. When several students came into the room from another activity, the teacher did not stop to tell them what to do. Rather, other students explained the activity to them. In this way the teacher was a collaborator in the classroom, not the center. The teacher asked those students surrounding his desk what they might write on the blanket when they were finished making them.

To outside observers, the lesson seemed to lack substance; however, to the Yup'ik teacher it was a carefully built lesson that integrated the themes of survival, sustenance, respect, care, and patience. The teacher not only taught how a beaver is trapped, dried, and its pelt stretched, but he also taught students how they were expected to behave during this process (Lipska 1996). ❋

Responding to the cultural context in a classroom is challenging, especially when there are 20 different cultures represented. I don't think it is possible to create one environment that is culturally congruent to all students all the time. However, it is possible for teachers to create an affirming environment that values the cultures that students bring to school and integrate information about specific cultures naturally throughout the curriculum.

If you are interested in reading about other scholars who have specific programs or knowledge of what works for students from underrepresented groups, I recommend that you get to know the work of educators such as Kathryn Au, Lisa Delpit, Donna Deyle, Bob Moses, Susan Philips, and Karen Swisher. I have included a list of further readings in the Teacher Resource section. These educators began their work focusing on a question or issue that interested them and then became educational detectives. Their work can assist you in better understanding what to be sensitive to and what to look for and expect in your classrooms.

Culturally Relevant Teaching: A Definition

Culture is a broad concept. It encompasses everything that is made by people. Caring teachers see culture as assets to be built on in the learning process. The following is a working definition of **culturally relevant teaching:**

> Culturally relevant teaching is an approach to instruction that responds to the sociocultural context and seeks to integrate the cultural content of the learner in shaping an effective learning environment. Cultural content includes aspects such as experiences, knowledge, events, values, role models, perspectives, and issues that arise from the community. Cultural context refers to the behaviors, interactional patterns, historical experiences, and underlying expectations and values of students. Culturally literate teachers develop an insider perspective of a cultural community. They understand that cultural elements operate simultaneously and respond in congruence with their students. Culturally knowledgeable teachers are keen observers, understand the importance of context, and can read nonverbal communication cues such as facial expressions or the hand gestures of students.

> ⟲ *Culturally literate teachers develop an insider perspective of a cultural. . . .*

Good teachers integrate culturally relevant teaching because they understand how it makes their teaching more effective (King 2001; Ladson-Billings 1994). For example, researchers like Jackie Jordan Irvine (1990, 2002) and Janice Hale-Benson (1982) have studied African American students. They found that many came to school with behaviors that contrasted with those expected in schools. Therefore, they advised teachers to observe their young people to determine whether they came with a strong cultural orientation. If so, then teachers might provide students who are expressive and higher in energy with opportunities to make presentations as a vehicle for displaying their competence rather than always being required to perform on written examinations. Researchers like Park (1997) and Litton (1999) found that Filipino American, Korean American, Vietnamese American, and Chinese American students had a learning style preference for visual learning in comparison to their European American peers. With these populations, teachers may need to utilize more three-dimensional models, graphic organizers, photographs, concept mapping, charts, and writing on the board while teaching to convey their ideas. Because many Latinos and Asian American students are immigrants who came to the United States with different cultural understandings, Cheng (1998a) recommends that teachers provide students with opportunities to practice colloquial patterns and interactional behaviors using scripted role plays. In addition, Fung (1998) suggests that teachers present interdisciplinary units on immigration. These units would integrate cultural content from all major subject areas such as mathematics, science, history, and music. For example, educators may have

Culturally relevant teachers

students compare and contrast different types of musical instruments that were brought to the United States as part of the immigration process. Students could also be directed to study the multiple reasons for migration. All of these recommendations demonstrate the importance of adjusting teacher practices in the classroom to meet the needs of culturally diverse students.

Why do cultural elements work? Cultural elements can assist us in our teaching because they provide us ways to enhance the learning process. The next section discusses how teachers can use Vygotsky's theory of the zone of proximal development, which is a theory of how to increase the zone of learning in a person.

Zone of Proximal Development

Many teachers wonder, How can theory help me in the classroom? or What does it have to do with what I do in the classroom? Vygotsky was a researcher who developed a theory of learning. His theory of development does not look at an individual in isolation; rather, he believed that intellectual growth must be viewed as a process of meaningful interpersonal interactions (Goldstein 1999). Children develop through their social interactions (Tharp and Gallimore 1988). As part of his sociocultural framework for cognitive development, Vygotsky constructed the concept of the zone of proximal development. Vygotsky saw the role of a teacher as someone who could assist students in learning more than they could on their own (Tharp and Gallimore 1988). Can you think of teachers who did this by the questions they asked or the materials they gave you to read? The **zone of proximal development** is the extended range of a child's learning, from the actual developmental level to the potential level achieved through the guidance of an adult or collaboration with a more knowledgeable peer (Tharp and Gallimore 1988). Vygotsky was not referring to the teaching of specific, isolated skills or knowledge; he was opposed to drill-and-kill instruction (Moll 1990). Rather, he believed that teachers should provide a well-developed set of social interactions and meaningful content. As the child learns

Take a Stand

CULTURALLY RELEVANT TEACHING

Building on what students know and bring to the classroom can energize and support learning. Researchers such as Luis Moll, Carol Lee, Bob Moses, and Sylvia Ashton-Warner have utilized cultural models, values, and knowledge in the curriculum. However, some teachers have not had the opportunity to get to know the cultural backgrounds of their students so that the student's lived experiences can be integrated into the instruction and curriculum of the classroom.

A question that teachers may want to consider is:

- What role can culturally relevant teaching take in your classroom?
- In addition, if a teacher believes that culturally relevant pedagogy is valuable, how can a teacher build a culturally relevant curriculum? Where does the teacher begin in this process?

skills from interactions with the teacher or others in the first phase, he or she moves into the second phase of the zone of proximal development by guiding the use of the skills on her or his own. In the third phase, the child internalizes the skill or capability; in the fourth phase, the student may have forgotten a skill and may ask the teacher for help and the process repeats itself: (1) Performance is assisted by more capable others; (2) performance is assisted by self; (3) performance becomes internalized or "fossilized"; and (4) assistance is requested and the process begins again (Tharp and Gallimore 1988). Wertsch (1985) believed that mental processes arise out of sociocultural ways of knowing and knowledge systems through social interactions in the zone of proximal development. In this process the teacher is a guide, facilitator, and evaluator (Goldstein 1999).

Because learning is socially mediated and Vygotsky integrated affect and cognition, Goldstein (1999) believed that Vygotsky saw interpersonal relationships as being fundamental to the zone of proximal development. She also thought many teachers responded to students out of an ethical ideal of caring; they consciously choose to care. In socially mediated learning, Goldstein expanded on Noddings's use of the metaphor of the student as an apprentice: The teacher observes the student and then responds in ways that will engage the student.

Utilizing Vygotsky's theory, Goodman and Goodman (1990) believed that teachers should act as initiators. They shared an example about how a teacher, along with his eighth-grade students, designed a unit on evolution. The teacher's objective was to assist students so that they more fully understood the issues of creationism and evolution. She also wanted to sharpen their reading comprehension and social studies skills in the process. As an initiator, the teacher assisted students by selecting materials for the unit, provided time for student discussions, and encouraged students to choose pieces of literature that would deepen their understandings of the issues. However, the teacher did not control the learning process. Students independently defined terms such as *evolution* and *creationism* and also picked a biography about Charles Darwin. Students used the filter of examining the role of science while reading the biographical novel. This instructional unit demonstrated that both process and content were important aspects of learning. Not only did students become more competent readers, but they also built on what they already knew and investigated various aspects of the issues. Their understanding of the conflict and difference in value orientations between creationism and evolution deepened while they learned reading and social studies skills, such as reading for meaning, reading for evidence, and grasping the difference between fact and opinion. Students learned specific skills within a large context. Their zone of proximal development increased because the teacher helped them develop their thinking processes and challenged them to reflect beyond the acquisition of knowledge by encouraging them to examine complex issues. Learning expanded because the concepts and knowledge that students gained arose from a meaningful context.

In this process, learning occurred on two planes. First, learning was a socially constructed phenomenon in which students learned by interacting with the ideas and with other people. Second, students grew because they reflected on those experiences. They developed a metacognitive understanding of their own thinking. Through this process, the skills became automatic and internalized. When people share with each other their perspectives, information, ideas, and practices, the understandings and comprehension of students can be expanded. Students can learn on their own, but greater growth can be achieved when they are assisted by teachers or peers. The role of the teacher as an active participant in the learning process is to assist students in providing modeling, feedback, coaching, instructing, questioning, and cognitive structuring (Tharp and Gallimore 1988).

The zone of proximal development can be greatly increased when teachers have clear goals, provide assisted performance opportunities, and evaluate the progress of students with the aim of guiding them to become independent learners and problem solvers (Moll 1990). Learning is placed within a meaningful sociocultural context; interactions are key elements of the process. In contrast, much of the teaching found in schools lacks interaction and often relies heavily on rote learning. However, using this theory of cognitive development, teachers not only facilitate further cognitive growth in students, but interactions also guide students to develop skills that they regulate and utilize themselves. What are some of the cultural tools that teachers can use? Cultural models provide ways of thinking. The next segment presents cultural tools such as analogies, metaphors, similes, and proverbs.

Cultural Tools: Analogies, Proverbs, Similes, and Metaphors

Have you ever attended an interesting lecture about a theory of teaching? As you were listening, did you find yourself thinking, "That's a great idea, but how would I use this method with Maria or Brian?" The speaker should provide practical examples so the listener can more fully understand the theory. Cultural examples and comparisons can assist people in developing new understandings of how things work in another context. In the following comic strip, the mother explains how long it will take them to get to their destination by using the analogy of time as related to a television program. The mother linked the children's knowledge of television with their trip in the car.

As a teacher you might be looking for images or explanations that make sense within your classroom. Cultural anthropologists, linguists, educators, and psychologists such as Holland and Quinn (1987) believe that examples are important elements of cultural models. **Cultural models** are composed of shared cultural

knowledge, folk theories, and folk wisdom. Those shared values can be found in proverbs, myths, metaphors, and stories of a group. They represent fundamental themes and values in a culture.

Cultures differ from society to society. In order to understand how cultures differ, it is important for teachers to understand the meaning system of a group (Holland and Quinn 1987, 3). Metaphors, similes, analogies, and proverbs are elements of that cultural meaning system. The meaning system includes not only cultural knowledge but also socially acceptable goals and motivations.

Cultural models are cognitive schemas that are shared by a group of people (D'Andrade 1987, 112). These schemas can act as tools of conformity by which people learn what is desired, but these schemas can also act as bridges that teachers can use to deepen student understandings of new concepts and ideas. Using cultural tools such as metaphors and analogies from the lives of students, teachers may be able to tap into existing networks of cultural knowledge, ways to solve problems, and value orientations. I believe that we as teachers consciously need to use cultural analogies, metaphors, similes, and sayings in our teaching. Cultural models are important resources that many teachers do not utilize in their instruction to more effectively teach new content. Cultural tools can assist children to make connections, reason, and develop mental models about their world. Teachers can learn cultural models by studying the cultural knowledge, linguistic patterns, cultural behaviors, discourse patterns, and cultural assumptions of students' communities.

Cultural models can make learning more meaningful because they tap what children already know about the world and act as important scaffolding. This process adds to children's cognitive mapping of images and conceptual understandings of the world. Relationships become clearer to students because they may see new connections between what is being taught and what they already understand. This section of the text is written to help teachers to better understand how they can use analogies, similes, metaphors, and proverbs in their teaching to make cultural connections and provide clearer meaning of new concepts, ideas, and information. It is best to use a comprehensive cultural context when using metaphors, similes, and other examples. They were developed by a society to explain or problem solve. They represent how people reason (Quinn and Holland 1987).

Here are definitions showing the differences between analogies, similes, metaphors, and proverbs:

Analogies provide an inference about how identified objects or concepts are similar. Culturally familiar analogies can provide a bridge from one cultural context to another (Au 1990; Baker 1998; Collins and Gentner 1987; Moll 1990). Analogies present mental models of how the world works using what an individual already knows (Collins and Gentner 1987). By using existing information, people can develop new understandings about relationships and comparisons through analogical mappings (Collins and Gentner 1987).

Metaphors are words or phrases that imply a comparison; they suggest a new comparison for an object or concept. Cultural metaphors are comparisons that link one cultural context to another.

Similes show a comparison between two distinct things using the words *like* or *as*. **Proverbs** are common sayings that usually provide a belief about life.

Because young people learn more effectively when the materials and instructional activities make sense and are related to what they already know (Smith 1979; Moll 1990), it is important for teachers to introduce culturally familiar analogies, metaphors, similes, examples, proverbs, and sayings to make connections with them. In fact, D'Andrade (1987) found that by using concrete examples in a reasoning task, the performance of students improved. The heart of learning, according to Tobin (1991), is to **negotiate meaning**—that is, compare what is known to new experiences and to resolve inconsistency between what is known and what is new knowledge. Using these cultural elements can help students access their schema more quickly and aid in creating deeper understandings.

In order for teachers to tap into the cultural understandings of their students, they will need to know and have shared life experiences with their students. Cultures vary in how the language and orientation of a group has shaped cultural images, whether about anger, marriage, proverbs, or other aspects of life (Holland and Quinn 1987).

Many phrases and images come from our physical world and are culturally bound. They not only bring to the mind various images from the shared cultural experience, but the images reinforce cultural values and reasoning. For example, here are some common U.S. proverbs that express ways in which a person looks at or solves a problem (White 1987):

Every cloud has a silver lining.

The grass is always greener on the other side.

Don't make a mountain out of a mole hill.

Where there is a will there is a way.

God helps those who help themselves.

Rome wasn't built in a day.

The squeaky wheel gets the grease.

You can't have your cake and eat it too.

There's no use crying over spilt milk.

These proverbs are culturally based viewpoints. Some of the sayings have strong pictorial images, using concepts such as cake, milk, and grass; these images are common in U.S. culture. Proverbs are helpful to people because they appeal to a person's reasoning and are based on accepted cultural values (White 1987). The sayings represent cultural folk wisdom used to help people deal with everyday life experiences. Several of these proverbs advise people to work hard and to keep persevering. The wisdom of the other proverbs says to be patient or not to worry about things in the past.

We also use many similes and metaphors in our lives. The following is a small sampling:

Similes

> run like the wind
> strong as a bear
> cold as ice
> flies like an eagle
> sweet as a rose

Metaphors

> Time is money.
> Love is blind.
> Honesty is the best policy.
> Life is a journey.

Similes, metaphors, and proverbs give glimpses into how people within a culture use symbols in various images as part of the value and belief system. There are many people who grow roses or who enjoy them. The eagle and bear come

Experiential learning

from the history of the United States. Bears and eagles were part of the frontier environment, and their images are often used to present the idea of strength and courage.

> ⑤ *Cultural models can make learning more mean-ingful because they tap what children already know about the world and act as important scaffolding.*

People learn many different cultural models when they are young. Following are similes, metaphors, and proverbs from other cultures and countries. Do they call to mind different examples than ones you are familiar with? Are the symbols used unfamiliar to you? Why do you think this occurs?

China: Similes (Cheng 1998b)

as red as fire
as black as lacquer
as smooth as a mirror
as soft as cotton

China: Proverbs

If you lose one sheep, it is not too late to mend the fence. (Don't worry about one problem because it is possible to make sure that it doesn't happen again.)

A piece of rotten wood cannot be carved. (A person with a rotten heart cannot be changed.)

A piece of jade needs to be polished to look beautiful. (One must struggle in life in order to acquire wisdom.)

You can draw the picture of a tiger, but you cannot draw his bones. (You can know a person's face, but you cannot know what's in her or his heart.)

Mexico: Similes (Mora 1998)

Son muy cuates. (They are such good friends as to be like twins.)

Te queda como anillo al dedo. (It fits you like a ring on a finger.)

Es más feo que pegarle a Dios. (It's uglier an act than hitting God.)

Echar la casa por la ventana. (A party or a gift that is so great that it's like throwing the house out the window.)

Mexico: Proverbs

Dime con quien andas, y te diré quien eres. (Tell me whom you go around with, and I'll tell you who you are. Or you are known by the company you keep.)

Aunque la mona se vista de seda, mona se queda. (Although the monkey dresses up in silk, she is still a monkey. You can't make a silk purse out of a sow's ear.)

No hay mal que dure cien años, ni enfermo que lo aguante. (There is no illness that lasts 100 years, nor a sick man that could last through them; or "This too shall pass.")

Al nopal lo van a ver sólo cuando tiene tunas. (No one goes to the cactus plant until it has prickly pears; in other words, no one cares about you until you're rich and famous.)

Additional Proverbs from Mexico (Park 1998)

Cada cabeza es un mundo. (Each head is a world: Everyone has a world of experience within his or her mind and memory that bespeaks a separate reality.)

La experiencia es madre de ciencia. (Experience is the mother of skill, or one learns from experience. Similar to English metaphor: Necessity is the mother of invention.)

Camarron que duerme, se lo lleva el corriente. (Animals are used in an Aesop's tale: The shrimp who sleeps will be carried away by the current, or he who snoozes loses.)

Puerto Rico: (Park Proverbs 1998)

No sea una mosquita muerta. (Don't be a dead fly, which means either don't be a tattletale or don't be socially isolated.)

Vietnam: Similes (Tran 1998)

fresh as a flower
fast like lightning
black like ink (like a very dark night)
pretty as a fairy
aggressive and mean like a tiger
ugly like a ghost

Vietnam: Proverbs

You want a fairy and an elephant. (You can't have your cake and eat it too.)
Don't open your shirt for people to see your back. (Don't say bad things about someone in your own family.)

The metaphors, similes, and proverbs listed are examples of cultural images and beliefs found in the lives of people in various cultural contexts. For example, the tiger is a symbol found in various Asian images and sayings. My colleague from Taiwan shared the proverb "You can draw the picture of a tiger, but you cannot draw his bones." This saying refers to the importance of knowing what is in a person's heart, not just her or his physical appearance. My colleague from Vietnam also shared an image of the tiger. In her simile, she noted that a person might be as "aggressive and mean as a tiger." Tigers are important in the Chinese and Vietnamese cultures. They represent strength, intelligence, and courage. Some characteristics of the tiger can be compared to the image of the brown bear in the United States, where it symbolizes courage and natural strength.

Regarding one of the proverbs from Vietnam, a similar idea can be found in U.S. culture. In the United States, some people are said to "want their cake and eat it, too." Cake is a pleasurable and important food for some people, so they want to have and eat it, too. In Vietnam, this idea is expressed as people wanting both the elephant and the fairy. The elephant represents supreme power and the fairy represents beauty. People often want to be both powerful and attractive. However, it isn't always possible to have both at the same time.

In the section of proverbs and metaphors from Mexico, the images of the cactus and monkey are used. Both objects are part of the folk culture of Mexico. People in Taiwan use jade, cotton, and lacquer in their cultural images. The proverbs from Mexico, Latin America, Vietnam, and Taiwan show how personal integrity is an important aspect of the cultural folk wisdom of many societies. People are encouraged to develop strong character by working hard and gaining wisdom from experience.

In the United States, African Americans use proverbs not only in everyday communication, but also in the lyrics of songs (Smitherman 1977). Geneva Smitherman has written an excellent book about Black vernacular called *Talkin and Testifyin*. She discusses how proverbs can be found in the titles of songs such as Aretha Franklin's "Still Water Runs Deep" and Undisputed Truth's "Smiling Faces Sometimes Tell Lies" (Smitherman 1977, 95). Proverbs are also important components used in childrearing in the African American community and represent African cultural-linguistic patterns that were adapted in the New World. Smitherman shared some common proverbs:

If I'm lying, I'm flying. (Proving truth: I must not be lying; if I were, I'd be flying.)
A hard head make a soft behind. (Being stubborn, refusing to listen can make you pay a stiff price.)
Pretty is as pretty does. (You are known by your actions.)
What goes around comes around. (You reap what you sow.) (Smitherman 1977, 245–46.)

In exploring these images, you can learn more about the shared life experiences of people from other cultures. These aspects of culture can be used to more fully understand student frames of reference.

Cultural Models: Movies in Our Minds

The previous section describes how numerous cultural elements are used together to create a holistic curriculum. This section describes a particular technique that teachers can use. I am always looking for better ways to explain concepts or ideas to students and believe that cultural models have been overlooked in education. In fact, the Funds of Knowledge, Algebra Project, and Organic Reading and Writing programs use many cultural models throughout their curricula. These programs are discussed in the second half of this chapter.

Cultural models are excellent tools that teachers can use from the lives of their students. Gee (1996), a sociolinguist, sees cultural models as videotapes or movies that are stored in a person's mind and represent what a person experiences in life or believes life should be. These cultural models contain a sequence or broad understanding of an aspect of life. Often, cultural models include both context and content. These tools include aspects of life such as stories, sayings, patterns of behavior, procedures or policies, and conceptual understandings. Here is an example from a first-grade classroom: The teacher is standing at the front of the class by the chalkboard. The children are sitting on a large rug. They have their reading textbooks open to a story they were introduced to the day before.

Teacher: What are some of the ways we read?

Rayleen: Echo reading.

Teacher: That's when we repeat after someone else.

Teacher: What's another type of reading?

Scott: Silent reading.

Teacher: How do we read silently?

Maria: We read quietly.

Teacher: Our lips are sealed and our eyes are reading. Your lips are closed. Your eyes are moving. This is silent reading.

Teacher: What's another type of reading?

Paul: Choral reading.

Teacher: Clarise, do you remember what choral reading is? That's when we do what?

Clarise: (She looks up at the teacher and doesn't answer.)

Teacher: Let's give her some wait time.

Clarise: I don't know.

Teacher: You do know. Just like when we sing together in the choir at church, we read together. That's why it is called choral reading.

In this way, Miss Gray utilized a series of understandings. First, students knew that the people sing together as one voice. Second, they knew that people in a choir sing the same song. Third, students knew that they were to follow her lead in order for everyone to read in coordination with each other. This is an example of a cultural model. It includes a specific context, a group setting. In addition, there are particular behaviors associated with the example.

The next story is a short excerpt from a discussion in a high school English class. What cultural models does the reading evoke?

Teacher: Why did Lorraine Hansberry name her play *A Raisin in the Sun*?

Linda: I think it comes from a poem by Langston Hughes called "Harlem," in which he wrote about dreams being deferred and drying up like raisins in the sun. She is referring to how African Americans have been poorly treated.

Teacher: Why do you think Hansberry picked the image of a raisin?

Akio: Because it is the only part of Hughes's poem that could be both a negative and a positive. It could be negative in that it is rotting and drying up in the sun or it could be sweeter because as a raisin it might be more powerful.

Teacher: What is the main message of the play?

Linda: When society kills your dream, it breaks you. Walter found what was important to him. It was his family and so no matter what happened in life, his family would always be there for him and he would be there for them. His dream was to be someone, to be successful. His epiphany was that he didn't need to own a liquor store. His dream turned from owning a business to being a real part of the family.

Matt: Walter didn't want to be subservient any more. He was festering. He knew that people didn't treat him equally. Walter felt he had a dead end job. But even through all of that, he was proud of himself and didn't need the dream. He had grown past it.

Students understood the analogy of the raisin dried by the sun and presented underlying values that the raisin may symbolize.

Do you recall the story in Chapter 1 about my friend's experiences at his grandmother's 80th birthday party? The short movie in his mind included not only appropriate behavior and underlying values about family roles, but also the meaning of cultural symbols such as peaches and cranes. My friend's cultural model about his grandmother's birthday included the importance of family role models such as his aunt and her authority to teach him appropriate behavior in this social context.

As I think about how cultural models can be used in the classroom, let me share with you something that happened in a first-grade class. Most of the children were African American. I remember going over test-taking skills and the importance of reading each word carefully. As you know, a cultural model of test-taking includes certain instructions about how to mark the correct answers. Tests also include vocabulary; some words are more familiar to some students than to others. One of the vocabulary words on this particular test was the term *brush*. That seemed simple to me. The students were supposed to look at the picture of a hair brush on the left and then to circle the correctly spelled word on the right side of the box. Many of my students missed this item. I wasn't sure why.

One of the best readers in the class was Eugene. He was able to read on a second-grade level, so I couldn't understand why he missed what I thought was an easy vocabulary word. Looking back at the situation, I remember that almost everything in those days was on ditto paper, so many of the pictures were somewhat smeared, and everything printed came out in the same bluish color.

I asked Eugene if he would help me. He smiled.

I showed him the dittoed paper and pointed to the picture of the hair brush. He looked at it and his eyes went blank.

"Eugene, do you know what this is a picture of?" He shook his head no.

I was flabbergasted. Thinking that he was teasing, I looked at him again and asked in a puzzled voice, "You really don't know what this is?"

Eugene was beginning to look worried. His forehead wrinkled.

"I'm not sure."

I could see from his nonverbal reaction that he was not pulling my leg and so I said, "It's a hair brush."

Immediately Eugene said, "Oh, that's right. But I don't use one. I use a pick in my hair."

Cultural models took on a clearer notion to me. I could better understand how people have different understandings and contexts that they use to interpret their experiences. Eugene used a pick to style his hair, while I used a brush. We had developed two different cultural models of taking care of our hair. This particular example showed me how home cultural knowledge can conflict with the cultural knowledge of schools.

However, cultural knowledge can be used by teachers as examples of subject area principles being taught. The next section provides examples from the playground and shows how they can be used in a physics classroom.

Math and the Comics: Connecting Abstract Mathematical Formulas with the Playground

Teachers in math and science often have difficulty understanding the importance of culture in learning. They see math and science as value-free and culture-free. As I discussed in Chapter 8, knowledge is culture bound. Scientists discover new information within a cultural context. The interpretations of one scientist may differ from those of another because of cultural background (Gould 1996). The issue of race and its conceptual core is a good example of how views of scientists may vary.

Oftentimes teachers see culture only as ethnic culture. As this book has indicated, culture is much broader. Students have taken in elements of many cultures, whether they arise from ethnic communities, neighborhoods, national identity, interests, subject areas, or other aspects of life. An important insight is that culture can be used to make teaching more meaningful. I like the comic on page 351 because it shows how math can be tied to our daily experiences.

Many children enjoy a playground. Jason, the boy in the comic strip, has fun trying out all the toys at a playground. As he enjoys each piece on the playground, he sees how math equations describe what is happening to him. This comic is an excellent way to show students that math can be used to describe aspects of life. A physics teacher can make connections between various math formulas and experiences on the playground.

For example, the first panel of the comic shows Jason going down the slide, and the formula given is for acceleration. In another panel, Jason is swinging and thinking about how to figure out how long it takes for him to make one complete swing from start to start. Another picture shows the young person on a merry-go-round type of ride, and he is thinking about the formula for centrifugal force. The fourth picture shows Jason riding on a horse attached to a large wire spiral. The formula he thinks about can tell him the distance he travels back and forth. The last panel shows Jason on the monkey bars. Jason thinks about the gravitational force on his body as

he hangs from the bars. Math is the language of science and the symbols in the comic are good examples of how one needs to understand the artifacts, shared knowledge, strategies, and situations. Unless you studied the culture of math and physics, you probably would not understand the concepts that were explained by the formulas in the comics. As in any classroom, when students do not understand the language, symbols, and accepted practices of schools, they, like those of us who had trouble translating this comic, may find themselves unable to comprehend what teachers are trying to teach.

Signifying and Deepening Literary Understanding

Carol Lee's scholarship has provided another important example of how cultural knowledge can be used to teach new skills and principles. Her research is based on the theories of Vygotsky. In her work, Lee developed a culturally based cognitive apprenticeship model with African American high school seniors that integrated both cultural content and strategies. This framework is called **Cultural Modeling** (Lee 2000). Using the Cultural Modeling philosophy, Lee worked with students so that they were able to use elements of **signifying,** a form of social discourse in the community, as a framework for teaching literary skills. "To signify within the African American community means to speak with innuendo and double meanings, to play rhetorically on the meaning and sounds of words, and to be quick and often witty in one's response" (Lee 2000, 197). Lee studied the impact of students' prior knowledge of signifying in their reading and interpretation of fiction. Could elements of signifying be used as a scaffold in the literary interpretation?

Teachers in the control group used lecture and recitation as their primary model of instruction in their discussion of Western European texts and also dominated the instructional periods. In contrast, teachers in the experimental group structured lessons so that students were responsible for analysis and discussion of African American fiction. The teacher also accessed the prior knowledge of students of signifying and the social context of the community. For example, students in the experimental group examined dialogues of signifying and built scaffolding for discussion of more complex materials. Students were able to identify strategies in signifying such as irony, point of view, symbolism, metaphors, and satire.

Students from both the control and experimental groups wrote essays answering questions that ranged from literal to complicated inferences. Lee (1995) found that the experimental group significantly gained in achievement from pre- to post-test measures. Lee believed that the achievement could be explained in the cultural strategies students learn in the community. This is what she wrote:

> The instructional intervention provided conditions under which students extrapolated from their understandings of signifying dialogues those strategies that they intuitively used to make the interpretations. The students did not state the strategies as generalizations. Rather, the explanations they offered were specific to the examples they were analyzing . . . A series of classroom discussions of this order helped produce a list of general strategies for signifying that a passage demands interpretation beyond a literal level . . . Making expert heuristics explicit, modeling both their generation and their use, and coaching and scaffolding students into the strategic use of these heuristics are at the heart of cognitive apprenticeship (620–21).

Making strategies in signifying explicit assisted students in understanding literature from other cultural orientations. Students analyzed African American literature and identified elements such as symbols and irony in pieces. These literary components were more easily discovered in reading mainstream authors because students had already developed a deep understanding of the concepts. Lee found that the modeling, scaffolding, coaching, and self-monitoring strategies that were taught utilizing culturally meaningful prior knowledge were critical in teaching readers problem-solving techniques and heuristics that could be applied to various literary genres such as poetry, short stories, rap, and European literature. Lee found that students could apply their new skills of analysis to other settings. She relied on the students' own knowledge of their culture and used it to create cross-cultural cognitive bridges. The next section also demonstrates the importance of getting to know the cultures of students and building a comprehensive curriculum on the intellectual resources of children.

Culturally Relevant Programs

Three important culturally relevant programs have arisen out of a deep respect for ethnic communities and an ethical commitment to equal education. Each program is an example of Caring-Centered Multicultural Education. Their curricula are culturally relevant, but more importantly, the faculty in each one have developed strong partnerships with parents in the community. These programs have arisen out of a dedication to the community and the goal of contributing to the self-empowerment of the young people.

Funds of Knowledge: Teaching within a Holistic Orientation

Teaching the whole person means to know the whole person, including her or his cultural background. Luis Moll, an educational researcher, sees culture not as a static concept but as a dynamic one. Moll believes that culture is really about "how people live culturally" (Moll 2000, 256). He and his colleagues wanted to better understand the cultural resources students brought to the classroom. Therefore, their **Funds of Knowledge** project was founded on the belief that students come to school with a rich bank of information. Caring teachers want to know about their students and view teaching as an opportunity to be part of caring encounters (Goldstein 1999). Teachers who are cued into the sociocultural background of students know that scaffolding is an important cognitive strategy. In order to build on what students know, teachers must learn examples, analogies, metaphors, similes, and stories from the formal and informal economics and social networks of the family. However, some teachers view students from blue-collar families as not living information-wealthy lives.

Luis Moll and his colleagues demonstrated that a holistic orientation toward learning is more effective than teaching skills in isolation. When the curriculum and context of learning arise from the lives of students, the knowledge and culture of students become valuable school resources, and students can build on what they know. With his colleagues, James Greenberg and C. Vélez-Ibáñez, Moll studied the cultural knowledge of family relationships and social networks of 35 Mexican families in a working-class community of Tucson, Arizona (Moll and Greenberg 1990). Their average yearly family income was $14,500. The cultural riches of the family were called "funds of knowledge." What did the researchers mean by funds of knowledge? Every family and community hold information about relationships and activities in everyday life. For example, funds of knowledge include information about how families use their money, how families prepare nourishing meals, ethnic traditions, and how to solve household problems. Every family has a large bank of knowledge that contains skills on how to survive. For example, Moll, Vélez-Ibáñez, and Greenberg (1988) discovered that families knew about different kinds of soils, veterinary medicine, ranch economy, carpentry, masonry, herbal medicines, and midwifery. They also had knowledge about society and could find out about school programs, enroll in local community college classes, and other community services. Researchers interviewed family members, forged trusting relationships, and built partnerships.

In the process of getting to know parents and children, Moll (2000) carefully explained that, although teachers need to know about the knowledge resources in the family, educators also must examine the way children construct their own meaning. Children have social worlds in which they have brought together what they have learned. Therefore, Moll and his colleagues also wanted to know each child because the child is the most important element in understanding child development.

How have teachers used Moll's model of cultural learning in the classroom? Researchers worked with a sixth-grade bilingual teacher who was in her fourth year of teaching. All her children were Mexican American and spoke Spanish. Her goal was to integrate more writing activities into her curriculum. The teacher decided to introduce a unit on construction because many of the parents had experience in building, and this unit could become a bridge between home and school knowledge. The teacher was particularly sensitive to the parents because she felt they did not feel welcome at school. She wanted to do something to encourage the parents to become partners in the classroom so that they would become more involved in their children's learning.

This is the process through which she took her students:

1. The class brainstormed and suggested possible topics they could research at the library.
2. Students researched the history of dwellings and how to build different kinds of structures. In fact, they used their mathematics skills to figure out how many bricks would be needed in one of the projects.
3. Students built a model of a building and wrote a short essay explaining their research and how they built their model. In fact, one of her students compared the analogy of building a house to the human body. He wrote, "Without steel rods, you couldn't maintain a house upright. It would fall to the ground like a puppet without strings to sustain it. A house without a frame would fall the same way. Nevertheless, the frame (*esqueleto,* skeleton) of a house is not constituted by bones like ours, but by reinforced steel" (Moll and Greenberg 1990, 338).
4. The teacher then invited parents, who held funds of knowledge, to school. Because their parents lacked formal schooling, the students were surprised that she would invite them as experts to share their knowledge.
5. About 20 parents (carpenters, masons, draftspersons, and others) brought their intellectual knowledge about construction to the learning process of the classroom. Students wrote detailed essays about the parent visits.
6. Students wanted to extend the unit on construction by creating a community of many buildings. They researched extensively what made up a town. For example, they learned about how to obtain water and electricity. In addition, students had to look into the development of streets, services, parks, schools, and other public service agencies. Writing became a meaningful way to present their research.
7. At the end of the year, the teacher developed a career unit based on the work and the questions students raised during the construction unit. She guided their work with the question, "What do you see in your future?" (Moll and Greenberg 1990, 344). Students created posters showing different professions. They invited a variety of people, including university professors, to talk about their work and what steps they would need to take in order to get a job in that career.

The unit centered upon a fund of knowledge found within the children's families. The knowledge that community people shared with the students helped them to identify topics, increase their understanding of construction, and motivate them to write about what they learned. They interviewed many members of their families, engaged in much library research, and were taught important writing skills in the process. Their skills in spelling, grammar, and conceptualization improved.

The sixth graders read and wrote in both English and Spanish. Their skills of expression and analysis increased because they engaged in a series of writing assignments around a culturally meaningful topic. The activities were not isolated or unrelated. The teacher also instituted peer-editing groups and taught students how to critique each other's work so that their recommendations would help peers write more clearly. Students were engaging in the third phase of the zone of proximal development, internalization/fossilization. This approach encouraged a more holistic orientation to teaching, connecting the everyday life of students with the classroom.

Skills were not taught in isolation; they were taught within a comprehensive community-based curriculum.

For example, a teacher interviewed a parent who was an expert in medicinal plants (Gonzalez 1995). The teacher then developed a language arts unit around these plants. Students wrote about various regional plants and their health benefits. In another example, Amanti (1995) found during her home visits that several of the families of her students knew about horses and how to care for them. On many ranches in Mexico, horses have contributed to cattle ranching. She developed a unit on the evolution of horses, explored animal behavior, presented information on saddles, created horse math, and used literature and movies that focused on horses (Amanti 1995). The teacher even borrowed a video that an uncle of one of the students had filmed of his own horses. The students made true-to-size graphs of different breeds of horses and investigated their various characteristics. Students were experts on the topic and they had more control in the study of the unit because the curriculum reflected their local cultural knowledge. Some of the students also visited relatives in Mexico who owned ranches. Many of the children had natural and cultural ties to this topic. In addition, family members came to the classroom to discuss their work with horses.

This program affirms and values the knowledge of students. Relationships between students, teachers, and community people become strengthened and reciprocal. Ties of trust are built and maintained. Students are engaged in motivating instructional units that focus on higher-level thinking skills rather than recitation or drill because they are sources of information and have more control of their own learning.

The work of these researchers is extremely exciting because it guides teachers in developing anthropological and cross-cultural skills that assist them in creating motivating and effective learning contexts for students. In addition, this program centers on building trusting and reciprocal relationships with parents. Although it is not possible to go to every student's home, it is possible to learn about a community through interacting with students and parents from the neighborhood.

One of the strengths of the Funds of Knowledge approach is that it addresses the issue of school power. Many of the leading multicultural educators focus a great deal of attention on what Lisa Delpit (1995) calls the culture of power. The **culture of power** refers to the beliefs, behaviors, standards, and expectations for success in U.S. society. Delpit believes that children in schools are asked, in both small and large ways, to give up their culture. Sometimes children give up small things, such as what they eat at lunch; sometimes the cultural elements are much larger, such as speaking Cambodian or Spanish at school. Because the Funds of Knowledge teachers build instructional units that arise out of the living experience of their students and because they ask parents to become active instructional partners within the classroom, the program naturally addresses this hierarchical power issue. At the same time, stronger support networks of care develop between teachers and families.

Many multiculturalists believe that the ultimate goal of schooling is to develop social action skills in students and teachers so that they become active in changing society. I agree with these educators that social action is the ultimate goal of schooling; however, I think that it is also important for teachers to consider how to restructure

Students make learning choices

schools so that all students are academically successful. Another excellent program that teachers can learn from is the Algebra Project.

The Algebra Project: "If We Can, We Should Do It"

The **Algebra Project** is another example of how a culturally relevant curriculum can have profound results. Bob Moses, the founder of this program, is a civil rights activist who believes that all students should have equal access to education. When Moses found that African American students were either failing algebra or not taking it, he worked with other parents to develop a curriculum that used concrete student experiences in teaching mathematical skills. Like Funds of Knowledge, the Algebra Project was holistic approach to learning.

The math skills that students learned were part of a larger community project based on the values of equal access to schooling and the importance of preparing young people for college. Math was taught not only within the social context of students and their cultural knowledge such as the subway, but it was part of a larger community movement. This project included not only culturally familiar knowledge, but also the social networks and motivation of the African American community. These are powerful social forces for students because they convey the message that math skills are not just isolated skills, but are expected to be acquired by their African American elders.

Bob Moses was concerned that African American students did not have the same access as other youth to higher-level math classes. Instead, most African American students were funneled into lower-level math courses. Algebra was a gatekeeper course for many students from underrepresented groups who wanted to go to college (Silver 1997). Students had to pass algebra to be admitted to college. Although some districts have mandated that all students have access to algebra, this across-the-board change can have a negative impact on student success if students do not have proper preparation (Silver 1997). In addition, Moses wanted African American students to have the option of taking advanced math classes in junior and senior high school. Bob Moses was already committed to equality. He and his colleagues developed the transition curriculum to teach concepts in the middle school that prepared students for high school algebra. Then in seventh and eighth grades, students took algebra, which prepared them to take geometry and other higher-level courses in high school.

In order to reach African American students, Moses and his colleagues felt that it was critical for young people to see the relevancy of algebra (Moses, Kamii, Swap, and Howard 1989). Two questions that he asked parents and students to think about were What is algebra for? and Why do we want children to study it? With Moses's direction, parents and students realized that young people needed math skills not only to get into college, but also to become full members of society and develop their career dreams. Members of the community became more actively involved in schools and aware of the importance of math skills. Moses built a strong community of people who were interested in school reform. These parents continuously participate and monitor the progress of local sites of the Algebra Project and work with local school district teachers and administrators.

Algebra had to be more than separate and unrelated theories and formulas. Moses developed a transition curriculum using the experiences of students. For example, students knew how to use the subway. Their knowledge of the subway and the map of travel was used to guide them to raise questions about math concepts such as the number line, positive and negative integers, and measuring distance.

In another activity, sixth graders made lemonade. This unit on lemonade concentrate centered on the importance of ratio and how the concentration of the lemonade was related to proportions. Another example of an innovative unit taught ratios using African drums. Students explored the concept of proportions and ratios in making the drums. This particular unit utilized a variety of learning activities from visual, aural, and kinesthetic learning.

The curriculum is built on the following five-step process:

1. Students participate in a physical experience.
2. Students draw a picture or model of the experience.
3. Students discuss and write about what happened in their own words.
4. Students discuss and write about the experience in formal language.
5. Students build and use symbols to express the experience.

Using the Algebra Project curriculum, teachers guide students from concrete and meaningful knowledge to abstract concepts and theories in mathematics. Moses found that many students with whom he worked did not understand how mathematical symbols and operational signs were put together to create an idea or thought. The abstract symbols had no real meaning to some students. This project used cultural knowledge from various subgroups. The African drum unit applied ethnic knowledge to math instruction, while the units on lemonade and the subway used local and personal cultural knowledge. In all cases, the shared lives of the children were taken into consideration and affirmed the student role in constructing knowledge and learning academic skills. The results of the program were impressive. The original group of students advanced either to the college preparatory mathematics series of courses or into honors algebra or geometry (Moses, Kamii, Swap, and Howard 1989). The students were proud of their accomplishments, and the parents and community became more involved in schools. The next section describes a culturally oriented literacy program.

Organic Reading and Writing: Teacher

Culturally relevant teaching, student choice, and student life experiences are at the core of another educational program, **Organic Reading and Writing.** It is another holistic-oriented approach in which learning is seen within a community context. Skills are not taught in isolation; children learn to read within the context of their desire to communicate to others. This program is described by Sylvia Ashton-Warner (1963) in her book *Teacher.* Although this is an old book, the method she uses has been utilized in various formats by many teachers through the years. Ashton-Warner described a method that she used to teach reading and writing in New Zealand, which used the vocabulary that the students suggested. Many of her students were from the Maori community. She began by having her students identify one-word sentences. These words had great emotional value to students: for example, "Mummy," "Daddy," "ghost," "kiss," "love," "touch," "truck," and "haka" (Maori war dance). Ashton-Warner described the best first words or key vocabulary as being the following:

> First words must have an intense meaning.
> First words must be already part of the dynamic life.
> First books must be made of the stuff of the child himself,
> whatever and wherever the child (Ashton-Warner 1963, 32).

Ashton-Warner found that her students could understand the importance of words quickly because the words they picked had strong meanings to them. The strong emotions of key vocabulary urged students to write complex sentences and express themselves. The stories that students wrote described life in their society. Sometimes this had to do with violence or conflict in the family or community.

One of the examples a student wrote was:

> "When I went to sleep.
> I dreamt about the war.
> The Chinese never won.
> The Maoris won" (Ashton-Warner 1963, 97).

The books they wrote were full of the drama of living and not like *Dick and Jane* books in which the everyday life of the characters was superficial and unreal to the students. Jane was never scared and Dick never fell and hurt himself (Ashton-Warner 1963). Reading and writing rose out of the lives of each student and what they were afraid of and happy about.

With this method, a Maori child not only learned how to read and write, but also saw that reading and writing could mean something personal and often spontaneous to them (Ashton-Warner 1963). Writing was a way to communicate with others. Reading was also a source of great individual joy. This affirmed to the students who they were and also what they could do.

Common Themes in the Three Holistic Educational Programs

Reflecting on the four holistic educational projects—Cultural Modeling, Funds of Knowledge, the Algebra Project, and Organic Reading and Writing—can you list common elements? Write your comments in your journal.

These projects provide teachers with strategies and understandings that can enrich their teaching. The following are some of the shared characteristics of the four programs:

1. Teachers learned about their students. In each project, the educators became familiar with the culture and lives of their students within a comprehensive context. Their understanding of culture was not superficial or piece by piece.
2. The living experiences of students were integrated into the curriculum and acted as bridges to learning writing, mathematics, reading, and other academic skills and knowledge.
3. Communities of learners were developed in which students became active and engaged partners and participants in the learning process.
4. Parents and other community people were invited to become partners with teachers and school personnel. Some parents acted as experts and taught along with the teachers.
5. Trusting and reciprocal, caring relationships were developed among students, teachers, parents, and community people, and they all became active members in the community of learners.
6. Teachers created learning activities that engaged students because the activities were meaningful, relevant, and hands-on. Students understood the purpose of the units and made choices in their own learning.
7. Focus was on learning and student academic success. Students were not asked to give up their culture in school and thus did not become more culturally assimilated.

These programs are excellent ways to incorporate cross-cultural knowledge and skills within much of the district, state, and federal standards that teachers must follow.

The research of Moll, Greenberg, Moses, Gonzalez, Amanti, Gee, Lee, and Ashton-Warner demonstrates a great need for teachers to understand and use culture more effectively in our teaching. Children come to school with different ways of living and valuing. The cultural models that teachers use can serve as bridges in the learning process from home to school. In the process, students can see the relevance of schooling and learn the culture of power at the same time. All students should be encouraged to reach beyond their home culture, whether that culture is an underrepresented community or the majority culture (Gee 1996). Students then are given the opportunity to see how others interpret the world. This is a challenging goal, especially for teachers unfamiliar with underrepresented ethnic, neighborhood, or family cultures. Educators should routinely provide students with opportunities that teach new perspectives and cultural models.

Teachers who value their students learn about and integrate cultural elements naturally into their teaching. This creates a more caring and comfortable environment and also builds a more effective learning atmosphere. As Gee wrote, "Just as many women have sought to replace our cultural models of gender roles with new ways of thinking, interacting, and speaking, so humans at their best are always open to rethinking, to imagining newer and better, more just and more beautiful words and worlds. That is why good teaching is ultimately a moral act" (Gee 1996, 89).

Key Beliefs about Culture and the Learning Process

Culturally relevant teaching is based on the interconnections of learning and culture. Culturally relevant teaching stresses the importance of looking not only for cultural bridges, but also for cultural models of knowledge. It also considers the importance of social context in the learning process. As Moll wrote, culture is about "how students live culturally." Students do not learn information in a vacuum; students learn within a specific milieu. This context is a combination of many elements, such as the relationships and roles between individuals, the underlying assumptions and beliefs people hold, the meaning of nonverbal behaviors, and cultural models of information. Much of this information is embedded in what happens in the classroom. Teachers may not have time to think about how schools have specific cultural elements that all students are expected to know. Why is culture important in the learning process? The following presents six reasons why culture should be considered in the classroom:

1. Real-life experiences give relevancy to learning.
2. Using culture permits students to use their prior knowledge.
3. Using cultural models and analogies can serve as bridges to new concepts.
4. Children have learned at home through family and cultural practice and cultural context.
5. Culture provides the structure through which experiences are interpreted, patterns are seen, behavior is expected, and values and motivation are learned.

6. When children believe that teachers listen to them and value who they are and what they bring to school, trusting relationships are built that form an important educational, emotional, and motivational foundation for learning.

Key Curriculum Elements in Culturally Relevant Teaching

It is important that teachers integrate cultural elements naturally throughout the curriculum. Teachers can *link* together several elements in the same unit or lesson that will provide a more holistic approach to cultural integration. When teachers do not plan how to integrate both process and content into their lessons, elements of student culture may be included in a disconnected way; like the image of throwing spaghetti at the wall, some of it will stick, but most of it will fall. Teachers might read a story about a famous person of color or serve tacos in the cafeteria, but there is no overall structured plan.

One of the best ways to integrate culture in a significant way is to use an issues-centered approach. Students and teachers choose public issues or problems and investigate significant questions surrounding them in order to make thoughtful decisions (Ochoa-Becker 1996). Students gather evidence, engage in reflective analysis, raise questions, and clarify their values before making a choice or decision. In this way, students have the opportunity to share comparative viewpoints and information and to examine various alternatives and their consequences. Students may investigate individual and societal issues such as free speech, school censorship, dress codes, admissions policies, immigration policies, academic tracking, and employment bias.

After teachers identify the key issues, problems, or themes, they can build their curriculum units by incorporating and naturally integrating the following seven major cultural elements:

1. Personal experiences from children's/students' lives.
2. Role models.
3. Culturally grounded stories, songs, and photos (ways of expressing community values, beliefs).
4. Language and linguistic expressions (analogies, metaphors, images, proverbs, sayings, symbols, dialect forms, and phrases from home languages).
5. Multiple perspectives on the issue/theme/problem.
6. Formal subject content from traditional areas such as history, literature, art, and music.
7. Community issues.

Each component is valuable; however, because the knowledge and experiences that students bring to school are extremely important, I have placed them first on the list. Some elements can be identified readily, while others are more difficult and will take time to gather. It is best not to use one element in isolation but to use several together in order to provide a broader understanding of a community's cultural values and beliefs. Students do not learn well when given isolated information; they are more apt to retain knowledge when they recognize contexts, connections, and patterns. The goal of the culturally relevant curriculum is to provide multiple ways to teach information and skills by using culture so that students understand the connection of the content to real life, see reasons for their study, and are successful academically. When culture is incorporated into the classroom in numerous ways, it becomes more of an integral aspect of the curriculum rather than an added or marginal component.

All of these elements are interconnected. For example, let's discuss a poem written by Langston Hughes that is often included in high school English classes. The poem is titled, "Harlem," but it is also often known as "Dream Deferred" (Hughes 1987, 268).

The poem begins with a powerful question, "What happens to a dream deferred?" Then Hughes describes numerous images such as a raisin withdrawing in the heat of the sun and a raw sore that oozes over. In just over 50 words, he takes the reader through powerful images of frustration and desperation. Finally, Hughes asks how a person whose dream has been extinguished would feel. He sees that individual slumping down from a heavy burden, but also feeling the anger boiling over inside, ready to explode.

This poem has many connections to the seven noted aspects of curriculum integration. First, Hughes raised the issues of racism and rage. Then he used a variety of images from his own life experiences. He described a dream that had been shattered. His use of strong images described a sore that smelled like rotten meat, but crusted over a deep scar. Hughes called our attention to issues of freedom, social justice, and community. He cared about others, so his writings emphasized the importance of standing up against prejudice and discrimination. He believed in justice and also held the moral commitment to speak out against oppression. In this short poem, Hughes used images such as the heavy load and exploding to evoke strong historical contexts and emotional understandings that are based on the experiences of African Americans.

Five elements of the curriculum integration model are included in this one poem. Hughes uses these numerous characteristics to reinforce and deepen the understanding of his cultural viewpoint. Teachers who integrate these many elements will strengthen their curriculum.

Chapter Summary

Mainstream culture is not neutral and may be different from the cultures of students. Works by Cole and Scribner and Saxe demonstrated that adults and children develop cognitive tools and strategies that differ depending on their cultural needs. Culturally relevant teaching offers educators an effective way to develop, create, and utilize linkages from the lives of their students. Sometimes you can see the "ah ha" in students' eyes when they gain an insight from the example, story, picture, or comment that you use in your teaching. At such times, you as their teacher are serving as a cultural mediator by providing important links. I believe that this is an exciting aspect of teaching. When you learn about the lives and cultural background of your students, you can naturally bring in stories about what they know, value, and experience.

Using culturally familiar examples, metaphors, symbols, and analogies integrates cultural elements into the curriculum. Scholars such as Lee see that ethnic cultures are assets to be used in scaffolding. She utilized student knowledge of an African American discourse style of signifying in teaching high school students literary devices in her English class. Other programs, such as Funds of Knowledge, the Algebra Project, and Organic Reading demonstrate how committed teachers, who care for their students and are committed to equal educational opportunities, have created curricula that incorporate more of culture than a holiday or food. These programs integrate the beliefs, dreams, values, and expertise of their students and the parents. They bring the community into the classroom and the students became the center of the curriculum.

Five approaches are presented in this chapter. Teachers may use interdisciplinary themes, a comparative orientation, and an issues-centered approach. In addition, they may restructure their curriculum and teach by example. The approaches can include key curriculum elements such as the personal experiences of students, community role models, key events, culturally grounded stories/songs/photos, language, linguistic expressions, analogies, multiple perspectives, and traditional content of formal subject areas.

The knowledge that you gain from your students is unlimited. They will bring to the classroom a richness that reflects the diversity of our nation. The cultural models that you learn from your students not only enhance your ability to reach students, but also strengthen your teaching. These models will bring to your teaching exciting new examples that make learning relevant and meaningful. In addition, it is fun to see students' eyes light up because you remember what they told you or shared with the class, and that you are able to link this information in the lesson. Such teaching not only affirms students, but also motivates and enhances their understanding of the skill or knowledge that you are teaching.

Culturally relevant teaching is like the fertilizer in the garden: It enriches learning. Students benefit from the scaffolding that you naturally integrate throughout the curriculum. The knowledge that you convey to your students seems more relevant to their lives and they also see themselves as valued members of the learning community.

Remember James, the teacher mentioned at the beginning of this chapter who was very skeptical of culturally relevant teaching? On the last day of our college methods course he said to me, "I didn't think it would work. I really didn't think it would."

James threw up his hands and said, "But I was surprised. *These* big, huge kids who were boxers began coming to class prepared. They brought pencils and notebooks. They were sitting in their seats. They were ready to listen."

Of course, I was anxious to find out what James was doing that was reaching his students, so I asked, "So what did you do?"

"I designed an issues-centered unit based on the questions, 'Was Pancho Villa a hero or was he a villain as portrayed by others?' I brought in passages about Pancho Villa. They researched his life and then wrote about different aspects" (Allen 1999).

"In addition," James said, "because I was teaching English skills, I was able to include various morphology skills. For example, I explained that *-er* can be added to a verb to indicate a person who does the action: box to boxer, play to player, and lead to leader. In Spanish, *-er* has a corresponding morphology, *-dor*. Therefore, when using the following examples, the students were better able to make that code switch: *correr* becomes *corredor, ensenar* becomes *ensenador,* and *jugar* becomes *jugador.*"

James paused. "I can't believe the students actually come to school now ready to learn. The students are Chicano and, though I didn't believe you, I was desperate so I decided to try the culture thing. I guess culture can make a difference. I didn't believe you and I'm Mexican myself, but it worked for me." James smiled widely.

James is primarily bringing in content. However, by choosing topics that interest the students and that have roots in Mexican culture, he is causing the cultural context of the curriculum to shift. James plans to consider other cultural aspects such as social interaction patterns, too. He sees how culturally relevant teaching can be used to reach his students.

⊙ Chapter Review

Go to the Online Learning Center at **www.mhhe.com/pang2e** to review important content from the chapter, practice with key terms, take a chapter quiz, and find the Web links listed in this chapter.

Key Terms

Invisible Culture, *334*
cultural context, *336*
Culturally relevant teaching, *337*
zone of proximal
development, *339*
cultural models, *341, 347*

analogies, *342*
metaphors, *342*
similes, *343*
proverbs, *343*
negotiate meaning, *343*
Cultural Modeling, *351*

signifying, *351*
Funds of Knowledge, *352, 353*
Culture of power, *355*
Algebra Project, *356*
Organic Reading and
Writing, *358*

Reflection Activities

1. Integrating culture into the classroom curriculum is important. How can you learn about your students' living experiences? Do you have the opportunity to develop an ethnographic study like that in the Funds of Knowledge, or is it possible for you to use strategies from the Algebra Project to teach new skills? Develop a plan to learn about your students and their lives. Write what you learn and develop in your journal. Keep a log of your reflections. As time goes by, you will see that if you are persistent, you will become more efficient and natural in integrating the lives of students into the curriculum.

2. Using what you have learned about your students' lives, develop a curriculum that incorporates cultural knowledge into your teaching. Use state and district standards and guidelines to assist you in identifying the skills and knowledge students need, but utilize other materials to teach those skills. Keep a culturally relevant teaching file and build on it. You will find materials from many places. For example,

if there is an article from the local ethnic or community newspaper about an issue that the students are discussing, cut it out and use it in your teaching.

3. To find more about teacher-assisted performance, read Tharp and Gallimore's book, *Rousing Minds to Life*. The text provides many examples of how teachers learned to use culture and Vygotsky's theories in their teaching. The authors discuss in depth their work at the Kamehameha Elementary Education Program (KEEP) in Hawaii. By utilizing the knowledge of their students and the cultural patterns of student interactions, teachers became more responsive to young people. As a result, the focus of the learning moved from teacher centered to student centered and teachers built on the students' contributions. Teachers can learn how to observe and listen to their students more fully. Educators who are most responsive are able to involve their students so that they take more control of their own learning.

4. The Algebra Project and the Funds of Knowledge programs have arisen out of the importance of community and engaging the community in a partnership. One of the goals of the founders of these programs was to provide equal educational opportunities. In the Algebra Project, Bob Moses found algebra to be a gatekeeper in the educational advancement of many African American students. Luis Moll, in the Funds of Knowledge program, was extremely concerned that Spanish-speaking students were not developing comprehensive literacy skills in a culturally affirming environment that would enhance learning. What strategies did they use that worked in the communities they collaborated with? How can you utilize some of the strategies they employed in your classroom?

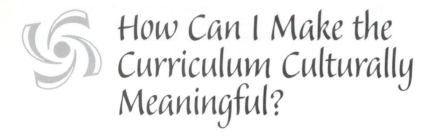

CHAPTER 11

How Can I Make the Curriculum Culturally Meaningful?

- *Culturally Relevant Education: Important Considerations*
- *Using an Issues-Centered Approach to Teaching Science: Research Findings*
- *Integrating the Three Important Aspects of Education: Caring, Justice, and Intercultural Communication*

CHAPTER OVERVIEW

This chapter is aimed at providing numerous examples to help teachers in developing curriculum that integrates culture and social justice into subject areas such as math, reading, literature, social studies, science, and history. Through culturally relevant teaching, teachers make critical connections with their students by integrating cultural knowledge that students bring to school and expand students' understandings of topics and issues by introducing them to other cultural viewpoints.

How can you integrate cultural curriculum elements into your teaching? Culturally relevant teaching points to the importance of making connections with the learner. For example: Does the learner understand the purpose of the learning? Does the learner understand where this knowledge will fit in his or her life? Does the student, as a member of the global community, understand the implication of the information? Why is this knowledge important? Teachers often have the same concerns about culturally relevant teaching. They don't see the relevance of culture in schools. For example, in history classes we teach about the purpose of a democracy, the important people who have shaped the policies of our country, and important events in our nation's record. However, a seventh grader said to his teacher, "Why do we have to learn about this stuff? It's boring and it's past. It doesn't mean anything to me." If teaching isn't meaningful, then students are less likely to learn.

This chapter presents ways teachers have incorporated various components of culture into their curricula to help make learning more relevant and meaningful. The curriculum can become a vehicle for affirming the cultural heritage of many underrepresented students while teaching the cultural contributions and values of nonmainstream ethnic communities to majority youth.

Culturally Relevant Education: Important Considerations

Research on the impact of culture has become an essential aspect of good teaching. Educators such as Geneva Gay, James Banks, Jacqueline Jordan Irvine, Kathryn Au, Don Nakanishi, Karen Swisher, Joyce King, Lisa Delpit, Asa Hilliard III, Luis Moll, Gloria Ladson-Billings, Pat Larke, Estella Matriano, Sonia Nieto, Michele Foster, Valerie Ooka Pang, and Janice Hale-Benson have created a knowledge base of information that is extremely helpful to teachers of culturally diverse students. They believe that educators must be *culturally responsive and relevant* teachers. I have listed many scholars who can help you to better understand the needs of children from diverse groups. Consider a trip to the library to review their works. It can be an exciting journey of new insights and effective strategies.

Insights from Gilbert and Gay (1985) explain why culture impacts the learning of low-income African American students in different ways than it impacts mainstream youth:

> The means appropriate for teaching poor urban black students differ from those appropriate for teaching other students because teaching and learning are sociocultural processes that take place within given social systems. When different social systems interact, the normative rules of procedure often conflict. This is the case when the school culture comes up against the urban black culture. Many of the instructional procedures used by schools stem from a set of cultural values, orientations, and perceptions that differ radically from poor black students (Gilbert and Gay 1985, 134).

Who are culturally responsive or culturally relevant teachers? These terms refer to educators whose manner and ways of teaching are meaningful to the children they teach. Jacqueline Jordan Irvine and James Fraser (1998) outline ways some African American teachers are culturally responsive to African American students. They suggest that teachers provide a high cultural context in their teaching. They do not suggest using isolated, fragmented parts of culture. The list provides a quick overview of how teachers can utilize culture so that their teaching becomes more comprehensible and relevant to students. Teachers should:

1. Use rhythmic language and a call and response style of communication.
2. Be highly emotional and animated in their teaching.
3. Use creative analogies.
4. Engage in nonverbal gestures and other body movement.
5. Use aphorisms naturally in class.
6. Encourage spontaneous and lively discussions.

7. Integrate students' everyday personal and historical experiences into the curriculum to link past knowledge with new concepts.
8. Develop strong interpersonal relationships with students using slang, jokes, or cultural phrases.
9. Teach with authority, demanding respect and success from their students.

Teachers who understand various components of hidden and explicit culture are more likely to make connections with students. They often use all of these components naturally as part of the cultural wisdom they have acquired and developed in their teaching.

As discussed in Chapter 2, many teachers tend to integrate isolated aspects of culture into their instruction. For example, teachers may believe that integrating particular events from African American or Iroquois history into the curriculum is enough. Other teachers may believe culturally relevant teaching implies the reading of multicultural children's books. Individually these are cultural components, but when they are included in the curriculum without a context, the elements cannot provide a comprehensive worldview of a group. It is like reading one page out of a book; you don't really know what the entire book is about. I believe that culturally relevant and responsive teaching is a holistic way of integrating culture into the daily curriculum that is also natural and comprehensive. Let me give you an example of a teacher who uses cultural elements in her classroom.

I have had the opportunity to observe and talk with Sarah Gray, a teacher in San Diego. Like many other teachers, she is a warm, caring person who knows her content well. Unlike many teachers, she also understands the importance of culture in the classroom.

I observed Ms. Gray teaching basic skills such as reading, writing, math, social studies, and science. During many language arts lessons, Ms. Gray writes the vocabulary on the board and explains to her students the meaning of the words before they read them in their textbooks. She models lesson activities on the board, providing students with examples before asking them to do their seat work. She continually encourages her students, letting them know how successful they will be and how intelligent they are.

Her class is primarily African American, but there are also a Latina, three Filipino American males, a Caucasian female, and a Caucasian male in the class of 21 students.

Part of her success as a teacher is Ms. Gray's ability to use culture in her classroom; there's almost a rhythm of teaching that occurs between Ms. Gray and her students. Geneva Gay would describe Ms. Gray and her children as being expressive in their behavior. The teacher is demonstrative in communicating with children. During a lesson, she may use many different facial expressions and clasp her hands in her lap and say, "Oooooh," in a tone so that a child knows that she doesn't approve. Her stiff stance coupled with a displeased tone is almost like she is saying, "Don't go there!" Her inflections and nonverbal behavior get the attention of her students right away and they know what she expects of them.

Ms. Gray is extremely animated. She often emphasizes important words. Sometimes she elongates a word and almost sings it—for example, not *comfortable,* but "*c-o-m-m-f-o-r-r-t-a-b-b-l-e.*" In this way, her students know that it is an important vocabulary word or the right answer.

From watching Ms. Gray, I learned how she naturally integrates culture into elements such as classroom climate, classroom curriculum, classroom motivational style, and classroom management. One of the most prevalent ways that culture has been included in schools is through what James Banks coined as an **additive approach** to multicultural curriculum. This refers to the way teachers present isolated pieces of information about groups, such as a holiday celebration about Martin Luther King, Jr., or the inclusion of a unit on indigenous peoples of New York. Unfortunately, because of the spotty, isolated, and superficial presentation of information about people from underrepresented ethnic and cultural groups, students may not have a deep understanding of the cultural richness of the United States. Because the main focus of the school curriculum from kindergarten through 12th grade is primarily Western and European, many students do not really understand the impact of other cultures on our society.

This focus hurts students from underrepresented groups because it does not affirm the belief that they are full, participating members of society. In addition, students may not learn about the important contributions individuals from their communities have made. Students from majority communities also are hampered by this misconception. They are not given the opportunity to learn new ideas and ways of looking at life from other cultural communities. In addition, majority students may not perceive how society is structured to keep the status quo and how this

Is this Ms. Gray?

impacts social relationships for everyone. This can lead to a lack of dialogue (Delpit 1995). Delpit suggests that to have serious communication between members of various communities, those in power must take more responsibility in opening dialogue. The discussions also should arise from open hearts and minds.

Collegial Dialogue

James Banks (1995) suggests that teachers consider **integrating** or **restructuring** their curriculum rather than making simple additions of holidays or foods. In order to build on his recommendation, I recommend the following approaches:

1. Include themes or threads in your curriculum that focus on language, culture, interdependence, community building, civil rights, power, and compassion.
2. Use a comparative orientation of study that presents diverse perspectives on the issue, theme, event, or concept.
3. Employ an issues-centered orientation.
4. Restructure existing units by using a culture/caring/social justice filter.
5. Teach by example.

Integrating units into the existing curriculum is easier for teachers to accomplish at first than restructuring a total curriculum. Instead of adding only a name of a nonmajority ethnic student here and there or other nominal inclusions, use themes and the comparative approach to teaching. By adding a theme such as equity, interdependence, power, diversity, oppression, caring in a democratic society, multiculturalism, racial identity, bilingualism, gender roles, self-determination, Harlem Renaissance, Civil Rights Movement, or immigration, teachers can introduce knowledge from many groups. Take the Zoot Suit riots, for example. The instructor can encourage several students to bring in various Mexican American viewpoints from the time period, and other youths may find information about the perspectives of African Americans, White Americans, or Asian Americans who lived in Los Angeles during the 1940s. In this way, students not only learn the importance of using a comparative view as a skill, but also they gain a comprehensive understanding of the case.

The Zoot Suit riots could also be presented as an issue. Teachers can ask students to formulate open-ended questions to study. For example, students may suggest, "What role did race play in the Zoot Suit riots? What impact did the riots have on Mexican American and police relationships?" In the next section, I will present a more comprehensive discussion of this approach.

Teachers have courses and units already developed; however, they may want to restructure them using a culture/caring/social justice filter. This filter may assist them in their own learning. For example, let's say Sally teaches a course in American (U.S.) government. She had, in the past, started with discussion of the Magna Carta and other documents from Europe. One of her students mentioned that he had read an article that talked about Benjamin Franklin's study of the Iroquois League of Nation's governmental structure. This organization was created to solve conflicts between groups and to promote peace (Olson and Wilson 1984). Each of the Indian nations elected delegates to a local council and then other delegates were chosen for the Grand Council of the League (Weatherford 1988). Sally discovered that the Iroquois Chief Canassatego proposed the federal model in 1744 (Weatherford 1988). After considerable research, Sally realized that she needed to include knowledge not only about the Iroquois Confederation, but also about the diversity of political organizations found in the early days of this land (Olson and Wilson 1984). For Great Plains Indians such as the Comanches and Cheyennes, representatives from small groups of hunters came to a larger community council (Olson and Wilson 1984). In many Native American tribes, governing was egalitarian, and tribal heads of families made decisions. A few tribes in California did not have a central leader, whereas those in the Northeast had powerful chiefs. Sally restructured her class to include a comparative and cross-cultural view of governmental structures. In some ways, Sally is teaching by example. She told her students about her own growth and research and engaged them in a discussion of her findings.

The fifth approach to curriculum development, teaching by example, is one of the most powerful. When teachers treat students with respect, students are more likely to treat others in the same way. When teachers are fair to students, students have daily examples of what behaviors and attitudes are desired. When teachers are open-minded and investigate topics that arise in class, students can learn how to critically examine and search for new information. When teachers are interested in learning about student cultures, they demonstrate their belief in cultural diversity. In the curriculum, teachers can model the importance of looking at issues through a culture/caring/social justice lens. For example, an educator can choose to present Helen Keller as a person to study during a unit on the socialist movement in the United States during the early 20th century. In the discussion of her work, the teacher explains that he read *The Lies My Teacher Told Me* (Loewen 1995) and this book sparked his research on Keller. Although many people know that Keller had several physical disabilities, they do not know that she was committed to socialism (Loewen 1995). Keller fought for equality, especially economic equality. Keller discovered that many cases of blindness were found in low-income families because many had less access to health care or were involved in industrial accidents (Loewen 1995). History books do not provide a complete picture of Keller, and she would be disappointed to find that they focus on her early life and not on her political activism. The authors of these textbooks have filtered her life and in doing so have silenced her work. Teachers have limited resources and may not be able to develop the curriculum that centers upon the learner to the extent that the Funds of Knowledge project was able to create, but through their actions they can show respect, interest, and understanding of other ways of life.

The following sections describe how curriculum and instruction can be enriched through the use of the seven cultural curriculum elements described in Chapter 10. The seven components are as follows: personal experiences of students; role models; culturally grounded stories, songs, and photos; language and linguistic expressions; multiple perspectives; traditional content; and community issues. Although I believe it is best to take an issues-centered approach, it is not always possible to do so. In cases where teachers would like to incorporate diverse concepts, ideas, information or perspectives, I suggest using a combination of several elements. One or two elements by themselves provide only a limited view. Try to utilize as many as possible of the seven cultural elements described in this chapter, because together they provide a more comprehensive context of a cultural community. As you read through the examples, think about how you can build on these ideas in your own classroom.

Personal Experiences of Students

Infusing the **personal experiences** of students is a great way to motivate people to listen and to build curriculum bridges. As shared in Chapter 10, one of the best examples of integrating the knowledge of students into the curriculum is demonstrated in the Funds of Knowledge project. This can include children's hobbies, talents, roles at home, favorite books, chores, and information they learn from their families. I have found the strategy of integrating experiences and comments of students to be very effective at all levels. In my college classes, the more I know about students, the easier it is for me naturally to tie in concepts and principles I am trying to teach. For example, when Tammy talked about her father's working with many individuals in an employment office, I asked her to comment on the need for bilingual employees. Tammy then told the class that being fluent in Spanish or Vietnamese is an asset in many stores because when customers come in and need assistance, the clerk can make them feel at ease and answer their questions.

In another example, a third-grade teacher naturally incorporated the comments and experiences of one of her youngsters. A student mentioned that she had just gone on a vacation. The teacher then responded, "That is wonderful that you went to Paris, France. What was it like?"

The little girl looked at the teacher and smiled. She said, "It was lots of fun. My mom drove us there to visit my aunt."

The teacher appeared to be a little perplexed. She then said, "Did you go to Paris in France?"

The little girl said in an unsure and quiet voice, "Yes, I went to Peris."

"Is it in California?" asked the teacher.

"Yes, it is," she said proudly.

Then the teacher finally realized that the little girl meant Peris, California.

The teacher reminded the students about homonyms: "Remember how some words sound the same but are spelled differently?"

She pulled down a map of California and showed the children where Peris, California, was located. The teacher then pulled down a world map and pointed to Paris, France.

The teacher naturally built on the comments of her student. She did not embarrass the student because of the misunderstanding that they had. In a caring way, the teacher carefully taught an impromptu lesson about homonyms and geography. It was one of those important teachable moments.

Role Models

Role models are an important aspect of life. Many of us have role models who serve as inspirations for how we can strive to live our lives. These models often show us how they have struggled against great obstacles while fighting for social justice or equality in society. They also provide insights into an understanding of others and oneself. An excellent activity that I have seen used in middle and high school is the **bioboard** (biography board). This is an instructional approach developed by Ron Torretto, a social studies and arts teacher at Grossmont High School in San Diego (Torretto 1999).

Ron Torretto has used the bioboard in music, biology, art, language arts, and social studies because it is an adaptable interdisciplinary project. In history, students may choose to study someone like Chief Joseph or research an issue like the exclusion of Chinese immigrants due to the Geary Act of 1882. Art students may profile a particular musician like Mozart or present a genre of music such as jazz or the blues. In biology, students have studied important scientists like Rosalind Franklin, who helped to identify the structure of DNA. They not only provided a biography of Franklin, but also included a diagram explaining DNA. Mr. Torretto encourages students to develop bioboards about people who are important to them. The student's job is to describe clearly the importance of this role model to whoever reads the board.

Students share their bioboards with each other. Mr. Torretto has each board laminated and another student develops 10 questions based on the information provided on the board. Later, other students are asked to choose a board and check its number. Then they go to the file and pick out a sheet with the student-created questions and answer them. The students can find all the answers on the bioboard. Thus, students are involved in teaching each other. In the following text are two examples of student work.

The bioboard can also be used to address the background information of a social issue. Our daughter's high school teacher, Mr. Ron Torretto, asked students to choose someone whom they wanted to research and who meant something to them. Our daughter had many ideas. She talked with me several times about whom she might choose. Finally, I asked her whom she chose. She said, with a twinkle in her eye, "Mom, you'll just have to wait and see."

Of course, I was very curious. We had talked about many famous U.S. Americans such as Eleanor Roosevelt, Martin Luther King, Jr., and Albert Einstein. When she finished making her project, she brought it for me to see. My daughter had chosen Sadako Sasaki. I didn't know who this was, but I remembered reading a children's book called *A Thousand Cranes.*

Our daughter wanted to find out about the young girl who dedicated her short life to world peace. She had remembered the children's book and wanted to find out more about the real Sadako. In fact, the children's book didn't give Sadako's last name, but my daughter discovered that her name was Sadako Sasaki.

Sadako was known by some people as the Anne Frank of Hiroshima. Sadako wanted to be remembered as a peace maker. When Sadako was only two years old, the United States dropped the first atom bomb on Hiroshima, where she was living. Because her home was so close to where the center of the bomb exploded, she was hurt by the radiation that fell.

Her mother, her brother, and she got in a neighbor's boat and tried to get away from the explosion. Unfortunately, many radioactive particles were left in the air after the atom bomb exploded, and fell from the sky on everyone outside.

Sadako grew up like many other children in Japan. She studied, was healthy, and played with her friends. In fact, Sadako was called "monkey" because she was an agile and fast runner. About 10 years after being showered by the radioactive rain, she developed a lump in her throat. Her parents thought she had a sore throat. She found out later that she had the atom bomb disease, leukemia, and was very sick.

Sadako was in the hospital for many months and hoped to get back to normal life. In fact, she started a project of making a thousand origami cranes, because cranes represented long life in Japanese culture. Some people believe that making a thousand cranes will bring a person good luck. Unfortunately, Sadako did not get better and she later died of leukemia.

In Hiroshima is the Children's Monument, which is dedicated to peace and to the memory of children like Sadako. It is also named the Statue of Sadako.

Several questions that my daughter addressed were as follows:

Who was Sadako?

What happened to Sadako?

What did Sadako do to champion world peace?

What impact did Sadako have on world peace?

A larger question that this bioboard includes is:

Why did the United States drop two atomic bombs on the civilian population in Japan?

Here is our daughter's bioboard that she let me share (Figure 11.1).

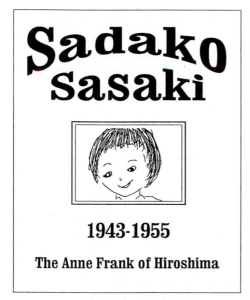
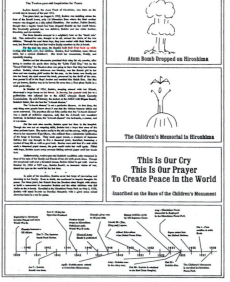

Figure 11.1 *Bioboard*

Her project focuses on Sadako's role in promoting peace. The bioboard includes a short biography and picture of Sadako, a drawing of the sculpture of Sadako in the Peace Park in Hiroshima, and a time line of her life in the context of other world events.

Culturally Grounded Stories and Songs

Culturally grounded stories may come in the form of myths, legends, and folktales. These stories, often handed down from generation to generation, are not necessarily what the general society calls formal literature. An example is a story that a grandmother tells her family about her leaving Mexico to work in the United States, or a story of the origin of a community such as the Haida, a Native American community in the Pacific Northwest.

I hesitate to suggest using a legend, myth, or folktale because although these represent important cultural stories, teachers may use them out of context. Teachers may not understand the underlying values that the story is trying to convey and so the deep cultural meanings are lost. Students may remember the story line, but not much about the belief system of a community.

I once heard a member of the Yakima nation from the state of Washington tell a group of educators that people from the majority group may refer to American Indian stories as legends or myths, which is a misconception. The consultant told us that what others may refer to as legends or myths are actually stories of today because they suggest how people should conduct their lives. She was expressing her cultural viewpoint. She helped me understand that culturally grounded stories are important in people's lives today and why presenting multiple perspectives is vital in education.

Consider the following true story that has become part of a community's cultural legacy. One holiday season a brick was thrown through the window of a Jewish home that had a menorah in the window. Several other Jewish homes were also vandalized. Members of this small rural town were very upset. They wanted the vandals to stop; however, they didn't know who was at fault. After much sharing in the community, they thought of a unique solution. Members of the town decided that they would all put menorahs in their windows; then the vandals wouldn't single out any particular family. This strategy worked. The destruction stopped because everyone worked together. The town's story is used across the United States today to help students understand that it takes the moral courage of everyone in the community to stop discrimination.

Teachers and parents often read children's books to their young people. There are many excellent ones such as Jamake Highwater's *Moonsong Lullaby,* Sherry Garland's *The Lotus Seed,* Lucille Clifton's *Everett Anderson's 1 2 3,* Allen Say's *Grandfather's Journey,* Francisco Jiménez's *The Circuit,* Faith Ringgold's *Dinner at Aunt Connie's House,* Gary Soto's *Baseball in April,* Gary Paulsen's *Nightjohn,* Patricia Polacco's *Pink and Say,* Debra Frasier's *On the Day You Were Born,* and Gary Spinelli's *Stargirl.* These books depict various aspects of the lives of culturally diverse families in the past and present. However, I am concerned when teachers read picture books depicting a favorite folktale to young children who have no background in the culture presented in the book. For example, if teachers use the original version of the *Five Chinese Brothers* by Claire Bishop, students may learn stereotypical images of the Chinese. This book was published in 1938 and the drawings of the Chinese brothers are extremely stereotypical. I am disturbed by the depiction of the Chinese brothers with large teeth, small or no eyes, and everyone looking almost exactly alike. This book does not represent Chinese Americans or Chinese from China. It is an outsider viewpoint of another group's beliefs, their physical appearance, and story. The important message that the brothers cared for each other and that they each had a unique talent is lost in the negative depiction of the brothers and the others in the book.

Teachers must carefully review the materials they choose to use in the classroom. It is not possible to learn about Multicultural Education one day and then the next day present "cultural" information. Like many aspects of teaching, choosing materials that are sensitive to and reflect a general perspective of the group is a skill that requires much knowledge. Cultural information and views have specific contexts, historical backgrounds, and a long tradition of values.

Well-known stories can also be used to teach a concept. The next comic strip shows a grandfather playing ball with his grandchildren. The young granddaughter accidentally hits him in the head with a baseball, and the grandfather falls down. The story of David and Goliath is often taught to explain how someone who does not have the same strength as another can also be effective. The comic is another example of that principle.

Songs also can reflect the deep values of a cultural community. A belief in civil rights is an important value held by many African Americans. Their commitment to social justice can be seen in poetry, stories, folktales, musical styles, and songs. If a teacher is presenting a unit on the 1960s and the contributions of the Civil Rights Movement, she could teach the following song to her students. Some students may already know it; others will have the opportunity to learn a new song. It may even peak the interest of those who have little chance to sing.

A song that has strong civil rights messages is "Lift Ev'ry Voice and Sing" by two teachers who were also brothers, James Weldon Johnson and J. Rosamond Johnson. The song is about fighting for freedom without losing hope. Many African Americans are extremely spiritual and believe in God; this belief is strongly reflected

in the piece. This song is often called the Black National Anthem (Johnson 1993). It represents an anthem or hymn that African Americans sing about participating fully in society. Here are the lyrics to the song:

Lift ev'ry voice and sing
Till earth and heaven ring,
Ring with the harmonies of Liberty;
Let our rejoicing rise
High as the listening skies,
Let it resound loud as the rolling sea.
Sing a song full of the faith that the dark past has taught us,
Sing a song full of the hope that the present has brought us,
Facing the rising sun of our new day begun
Let us march on till victory is won.
Stony the road we trod,
Bitter the chastening rod,
Felt in the days when hope unborn had died;
Yet with a steady beat,
Have not our weary feet
Come to the place for which our fathers sighed?
We have come over a way that with tears has been watered,
We have come, treading our path through the blood of the slaughtered,
Out from the gloomy past,
Till now we stand at last
Where the white gleam of our bright star is cast.
God of our weary years,
God of our silent tears,
Thou who has brought us thus far on the way:
Thou who has by Thy might
Led us into the light,
Keep us forever in the path, we pray.
Lest our feet stray from the places, Our God, where we met Thee,
Lest, our hearts drunk with the wine of the world, we forget Thee;
Shadowed beneath Thy hand,
May we forever stand.
True to our GOD,
True to our native land.

This song not only provides a cultural story of the values of many African Americans; it also gives another perspective on the oppression African Americans have encountered and still face today. The song is direct in talking about the slaughtering of people, but also about how people rose above the terrible oppression with great faith in God.

   Discussion of issues from U.S. history should include multiple perspectives because when teachers present a more comprehensive view of our nation, students gain a deeper understanding of our ongoing struggles.

Since a comparative viewpoint provides students with a more comprehensive view of an event, issue, or concept, I also suggest that, in teaching the African American National Anthem, you consider using the lesson given in Carl Grant and Christine Sleeter's book, *Turning on Learning,* called "Our National Anthems." They have included an excellent lesson on how students can be guided to look at the issue of national anthems and review different ones (Grant and Sleeter 1998, 217–21). They suggest the following national anthems: "The Star-Spangled Banner," "*Himno Nacional*" (Mexican national anthem), "Lift Ev'ry Voice and Sing" (Black National Anthem), and "Bread and Roses" (women's anthem).

Language and Cultural Expressions

In some ways language provides teachers with the most important vehicle for culturally relevant teaching. Much of culture is transmitted through language. An excellent use of languages can be found throughout the community. When I was using the bus system in Seattle, Washington, I picked up a brochure called "Riding the Bus." The brochure covered topics such as how to identify the correct bus, what to do when boarding the bus, rules for riding the bus, and fare information. The leaflet was small enough to fit in my coat pocket. When I unfolded it, I was happily surprised. The brochure was translated into nine languages: English, Korean, Vietnamese, Cambodian, Chinese, Spanish, Russian, Laotian, and Ukranian. Not only did the brochure provide information to people from various language groups, but it also indirectly conveyed the idea that Seattle is a multilingual city where diverse languages are valued.

As Vygotsky has written, language is one of our most important cultural tools. Through language we engage with others and with ideas. Today, more and more people, young and old, are learning new languages. In Chapter 9, many concepts in second-language acquisition were discussed. Bilingual education specialists emphasize the need for children to learn literacy skills in their home language so that those skills and vocabulary will be learned more easily and quickly in English.

Language includes cultural expressions such as metaphors, similes, analogies, images, proverbs, sayings, symbols, and phrases that can be easily included in a teacher's lesson. As I discussed in Chapter 10, these types of **cultural expressions** convey not only important cultural images but also connotations and values. It is important that teachers listen to the phrases and terms children use with each other and the language that parents use with their children. Language is often tied to ethnic and self-identity. One of my African American students often said to me, "Have a blessed day." I was warmed by her kindness and felt a special closeness to her because she shared an important family and religious blessing sent to another. I later thanked her and wished her "a blessed day" too. Teachers can incorporate affirming cultural phrases into their teaching if they understand the meaning and context in which these expressions can be appropriately used.

My mother used to tell us "*gambare,*" which means to "grin and bear it." If my teacher had said something like that when I hit my knee, I would understand that I am to be tough and not complain. She would not be referring to my physical strength, but to my character. So much is understood in that one word. In this way, my teacher would also be affirming who I was as a Japanese American and know that the word communicated much to me.

Many examples of cultural phrases and expressions appear in the Spanish song, "De Colores." This song about spring includes a linguistic interpretation of the sound of the rooster, hen, and baby chicks. For example, the hen says, "Cara, cara, cara." The rooster says, "Quiri quiri quiri quiri quiri." The chick says, "Pío, pío, pío, pi." Students can compare the sounds of the animals in various languages found in the classroom.

"De Colores" is a fun song that reminds many people of their childhood. My friend told me that her mother used to sing this song to her when she was a toddler. Then she began to sing it to me and I could hear the happiness in her voice. The song reflected the warmth my friend felt when she and her mother sang the song together, which ties in with the theme of caring and family. "De Colores" is often sung at Latino community affairs because it signifies the importance of unity. Like the many colors of the flowers, we as diverse people make up a beautiful rainbow. We make up a wonderful family, the human family.

De Colores

Spanish Translation by Cynthia D. Park
De colores
De colores se visten los campos en la primavera
De colores
De colores son los pajarillos que vienen de afuera
De colores
De colores es el arco iris que vemos lucir

Y por eso los grandes amores
De muchos colores
Me gustan a mi,
Y por eso los grandes amores
De muchos colores
Me gustan a mi

Canta el gallo
Canta el gallo con el quiri quiri quiri quiri quiri
La gallina
La gallina con el cara cara cara cara cara
Los pollitos
Los pollitos con el pío pío pío pío pi

Y por eso los grandes amores
De muchos colores
Me gustan a mi
Y por eso los grandes amores
De muchos colores
Me gustan a mi.

All the Colors

English Translation by Cynthia D. Park
All the colors
In springtime the countryside dresses itself in all the colors of the rainbow
All the colors
The birds which return each spring from faraway are marked by all the colors
All the colors
All the colors make up the rainbow which we see shining (across the blue sky)
For these reasons it pleases me that the greatest loves (of the world) are made up
of all the colors of the rainbow.
Sings the rooster
Sings the rooster with his kiri kiri kiri kiri kiri
(Also) the hen
The hen with her cara cara cara cara cara
And the baby chicks
And the baby chicks with their pío pío pío pío pi
For these reasons it pleases me (greatly) that the greatest loves (of the world) are
made up of all the colors (of the rainbow).

Another example of the use of language is having students translate traditional literature, such as Shakespeare's *Julius Caesar,* into everyday English and place the
story in modern terms using their own experiences to frame the plot (Lipman 1998).
In doing this, students feel more ownership in the learning process and have a deeper
understanding of how language takes on many forms. In her research on restructured
schools, Lipman (1998) also discovered that when teachers make changes in the curriculum so that it has more meaning to students, there is a lighter climate in the
school. One of the teachers she studied said, "You can feel a cheerfulness. It's almost like a song" (Lipman 1998, 256).

Students can also be shown that the work of writers such as Shakespeare can be
found in use in general society. Politicians, teachers, writers, and others may use
phrases from Shakespeare such as "To be or not to be, that is the question." The following comic demonstrates several often-used expressions that were taken from the
works of the European writer Shakespeare and are now part of the mainstream culture.

Another excellent example of the power of language is the connotations of
words. For example, when teachers cover various topics in social studies or English,
they may want to consider the differences in the way students may respond to terms
like *slavery* and the *Holocaust.* These terms can represent complex issues with
strong implied meanings. A Jewish student whose family members had personal experiences with the Holocaust may have a powerful emotional response to the word
and to discussions of the issue. The student may also have a more comprehensive
understanding of the topic. This can also be said for the issue of slavery. Some members of families have handed down stories about how the institution of slavery had
a devastating impact on their family lives. These descriptions also contain values and
beliefs that shape the way some students view the issue today. Teachers can tap into
the rich resources of their students in understanding how phrases, terms, and stories

of family members have molded their viewpoints on various aspects of history and understandings of social issues. Teachers may ask students what emotions words evoke. For instance, to some students, the word *slavery* may be almost a neutral term, a term from a textbook; however, to another student, the word may evoke strong personal feelings. Students can discuss how the connotations surrounding words may arise from the shared experiences and history of a community.

Multiple Perspectives

One of the most effective ways to facilitate learning is to present **multiple perspectives** on an issue, event, concept, or idea. Multiple perspectives offer students more than one way to understand what is being taught, which is especially important when there is a complex issue to consider.

In the world of diversity in which we live it is important for people to hear various viewpoints in resolving issues, whether they are based on city or country, employee or employer, student or teacher, older person or younger, Buddhist or Muslim, mathematician or biologist, or the many other things that we traditionally consider in Multicultural Education. Of course this doesn't mean that we always agree with each other, but as my father used to say, "Life is not supposed to be simple." In a high school conference I attended, students saw diversity in a broad way. They identified themselves as members of various social groupings, such as a jock, Christian, heavy metal, Latin dancer, lesbian, vegan, gay, Jewish, athlete, surfer, born in East Los Angeles, and short. Sharing multiple perspectives encourages

Sharing multiple viewpoints

dialogue and the possibility of finding common ground. Most important aspects of life need dialogue. When people examine diverse viewpoints, they come to a deeper understanding of their own positions and a respect for those who have opposing views (Nelson, Palonsky, and Carlson 2002).

Let's take the issue of immigration, for example. My class watched the movie *El Norte,* or "The North." The movie was about the journey of a sister and brother from Guatemala who sought safety and work in the United States. The two came to the United States without their parents because their father had been murdered by the military and their mother had been taken away and the children did not know where she was. The movie provided information about the struggles of immigrants from Guatemala. Before the teachers viewed the movie, they held many misconceptions. For example, most of the teachers thought that since Mexicans and Guatemalans looked similar, they were from the same place.

After viewing the movie, the students shared the following misconceptions:

- "I didn't realize there was so much turmoil going on in Central America."

- "I did not know there was prejudice against the Guatemalans from Mexicans."

- "I didn't realize that when people come here they leave behind important aspects of their lives such as family, respect, and cultural connections."

- "I didn't know that people are escaping persecution."

In comparison, the teachers also watched *Becoming American,* a film about a Hmong refugee family from Laos. The family first lived in a camp in Thailand and finally, after living there for several years, were allowed into the United States. They could not bring everyone in their family and they cried because their extended family couldn't come with them.

Some teachers in the class made the following comments:

- "I didn't realize the United States used the Hmong as fighters for us."

- "There is such a rift now between the parents and kids because the kids assimilate much easier than their parents."

- "I didn't realize how much people give up to come here. Even though they were tortured and killed, the people love their country so much they really don't want to leave it. Leaving must be so difficult."

The teachers examined the similarities and differences of the experiences of each family. Both families missed their countries. Both families had to learn English and found it hard to find jobs. In each situation they were refugees fleeing from persecution. The Guatemalans fled from a country that had an oppressive government. The Hmong family fled because they had been allies with the United States during the Vietnam War; while the Communists were in power, the Hmong were seen as the enemy. However, because the Asian family came from a preliterate tradition, they had little knowledge of written communication or schooling. In contrast, the brother and sister from Central America had gone to school and learned English quickly. The process of assimilation for the Guatemalan family seemed to proceed more rapidly.

The two films gave two perspectives on the issues of immigration and persecution. Both families shared common problems and struggles, but they also displayed different ways of dealing with those struggles. The two different views enable the teachers to look at the issues in greater depth.

Formal or Traditional Subject Content

This section describes the **traditional subject content** already found in schools. The curriculum in schools already includes subjects such as history, literature, philosophy, psychology, government, sociology, music, dramatic arts, and visual arts. Is it possible to integrate culture into the traditional content being taught? In Chapter 3, I described how the European viewpoint of naturalists Linnaeus and Blumenbach influenced their scholarship and the creation of racial categories. Many people believe these categories are based on biological data; however, as you have read, most scientists see race as a social and political construct and not biological truth.

Two areas in which cultural information is more often integrated are social studies and literature (Civil Rights Project 2002). The following describes how some teachers have rethought their curriculum roots in social studies. Most history textbooks primarily focus on the growth of the 13 colonies; history is seen as a movement from the East to the West in the United States. Many books mention Ellis Island in New York, where immigrants were housed before they were allowed into the United States. The stay of most detainees was approximately several hours. However, some groups have different immigration detention experiences. Angel Island in the San Francisco Bay near Alcatraz marks the beginning of the history of many Asian immigrants, because this was their point of entry. Many were held there for many days and months before being allowed into the United States. The experience of many Chinese American families begins on the West Coast and moves eastward. Unfortunately, most students in schools have never heard of the Angel Island Immigration Station. Information about this immigration center as an important historical place should be included in the formal curriculum along with information about Ellis Island.

Most of the 175,000 Chinese immigrants who came to the United States from 1910 through 1940 passed through Angel Island. Another 150,000 Japanese immigrants also were held there. The site is now a state park where people can visit the old barracks and offices. (See the photos of the barracks and the old sentry tower on page 384.)

The Chinese made many major contributions to the development of the United States, although they were not welcomed (Lai, Lim, and Yung 1991). They were "instrumental in building the transcontinental railroads, reclaiming swamplands in

Angel Island Detention Center and Sentry Tower

California's Sacramento-San Joaquin River delta area, developing the shrimp and abalone fisheries, the opulent Napa-Sonoma vineyards, new strains of fruit, and providing labor for California's growing agricultural and light industries" (Lai, Lum, Yung 1991, 10). Because of a long history of animosity felt toward Chinese immigrants, the Chinese Exclusion Act of 1882 was passed. This law was the first legislation that barred a particular ethnic group from entering the United States. Immigration officials treated many Chinese individuals unfairly and these individuals often complained to Chinese diplomats. The Angel Island Immigration Station was an abysmal place where Chinese Americans were held like prisoners. They left sad and bitter poems etched in the walls of the two-story wood detention center. Originally, Chinese immigrants were detained on the wharf in San Francisco; then in 1910 the immigration station was moved to Angel Island. This situation was extremely difficult because Chinese immigrants were kept apart from their families and witnesses who were needed to testify for them.

Other immigrants who were also held at Angel Island included Australians, New Zealanders, Mexicans, Canadians, Russians, Koreans, Filipinos, and Japanese. Europeans were separated from the others. Wives and husbands were kept apart until they were admitted in the United States. People were kept for days, weeks, months, and even years at the island, depending how long it took their witnesses to testify on their behalf. They were kept in wooden barracks that were extremely crowded and under guard 24 hours a day and seven days a week. A good source of more information about Angel Island is The Angel Island Immigration Station Foundation that can be accessed at http://www.aiisf.org/.

Some educators have made a conscious effort to utilize history texts that provide a comprehensive view of our history. For example, much of our history does entail a movement from the south. States such as California, New Mexico, Arizona, and Texas have roots in Mexican history. The history of many families does not entail a move from east to west, but rather from south to north or west to east. My family immigrated to the United States almost a hundred years ago from Japan. My grandfather settled in Hawaii and became a citizen there, and my own father moved to Seattle, Washington. My family history moves from the Hawaiian Islands to the mainland. My neighbor's family is originally from St. Thomas in the Caribbean Islands. He was raised in New York City and now lives in California. Although the East Coast may be the beginning of our formal governmental institutions, citizens have taken many routes of settlement because we are a nation of many peoples.

In fact, indigenous people are the original inhabitants of what we now know as the United States. Native Americans from the Pacific Northwest do not view history with the same perspective as that presented in our students' textbooks. Many communities believe that their people have arisen from the land and animals that first inhabited the area. These viewpoints should be included because they represent the beliefs of the earliest people. Traditional subject areas such as history can include comparative perspectives to demonstrate the diverse nature of our nation.

History as a formal content area has begun to accept the contributions of various scholars who present different understandings of diverse groups. The works of researchers like John Hope Franklin, Ronald Takaki, Wilbur Jacobs, and Lee Francis have enriched our knowledge of U.S. history. There are still teachers who see history of underrepresented groups as ethnic history, but many other educators understand that the events, contributions, and people of ethnic groups are integral to U.S. history and therefore pertain to all of us. These latter educators are careful to integrate the history of underrepresented communities naturally into the curriculum because their experiences are part of U.S. history.

Another aspect that can be included in the formal curriculum is the integration of information about the history and cultures in Africa. African American families have strong roots in various African cultures and countries. For example, teachers need knowledge of one of the most powerful trading civilizations in Western Africa between 1300 and 1600 A.D., the Songhoy culture. Our history has roots in Songhoy (spelled by some as "Songhay") civilization. Many people were enslaved through the early trans-Sahara Arab slave trade before the existence of the classical West African empires of Ghana, Mali, and Songhoy. The people also came later in the "Middle Passage" from Benin to Haiti after 1591 and the destruction of the Songhoy Empire. Hassimi Maiga, a professor at Isfra-University of Bamako, Mali, has written a resource called *Notes on Classical Songhoy Education and Socialization.* The book is a good introduction for teachers and others who want to begin to explore the values, history, and customs of the Songhoy culture from West Africa.

The Songhoy civilization was an advanced culture in which peace and prosperity flourished for hundreds of years. At this time Europe was in the Dark Ages. Songhoy art was dominated by beautiful objects made of gold. Today, one of the legacies of Songhoy culture is the strong focus on family and kinship. Women play a major role in the family "Thus, in Songhoy-senni (Songhoy language) it is said: 'Hugu mana ti kala way': ('A household only lasts because of women')" (Maiga 2002, 13). The culture has also integrated many aspects of Islamic religious and Arabic cultural practices. One of the most important issues raised in the monograph by Maiga is that few schools teach African languages; this troubles him because it is difficult to pass on cultural knowledge and a Songhoy worldview without students knowing African languages.

Literature is another area in which cultural content can be easily integrated into the curriculum. In recent years, the curriculum may include literature by writers such as Lawson Inada, Sandra Cisneros, John Okada, Toni Morrison, Gary Soto, Alan Lau, Scott Momaday, Garrett Hongo, James Baldwin, Joy Harjo, and Richard Rodriguez. The inclusion of the work of these gifted artists provides another window into the diversity of our nation by providing different points of reference. These authors may not write about well-known cities such as Boston or New York City, but rather a small town in central California called Marysville or Fresno. These authors also present different values. They may challenge blind patriotism and use different heroes and images. Their heroes might question the status quo. Their written language may arise from a home language other than English and may not adhere to mainstream conventions of grammar and form, but these writers represent U.S. America too.

> ৩ Individuals must move away from an ethnocentric orientation and the belief that there are absolute ways of responding.

Community Issues-Centered Curriculum

Integrating community issues into the curriculum can vitalize learning. These issues are part of who students are, what they see as important, and what students stand for as members of communities. The communities may represent a nation-state like the United States or various subgroups that are defined by ethnicity, sexual orientation, hobbies, region, religion, or political interests. In Caring-Centered Multicultural Education, students are encouraged to think and to critically analyze complex social issues. The most effective approach to higher-order thinking and the integration of subject-matter content is an **issues-centered curriculum** (Nelson 1996). Jack Nelson provides insights into why this approach benefits all areas in schooling:

> Throughout human existence and across cultures and regions, issues have been at the core of the human quest for knowledge. Issues provide motivation, challenge ideas, inform scholars and students, and set criteria for judging progress in civilization. They represent the cauldron within which myth, theory, fact, value, and perspectives mix with multiple realities (Nelson 1996, 22).

Nelson also reminds us that solutions are usually not simple, easy, or quick. Research conducted by the Civil Rights Project at Harvard University (2002) found that high school students in Louisville, Kentucky, and Cambridge, Massachusetts, reported that one of the major benefits of an integrated school is the opportunity to learn about issues more comprehensively because they have the chance to understand various viewpoints (Kurlaender and Hun 2000).

Teachers in my classes share with each other a variety of issues-centered units. The units are guided by strategic questions (Hyman 1979; Singleton 1989). These questions are used to focus the students' attention on a general public issue and to encourage critical thinking. Various types of questions focus on different aspects of study such as ethics, definitions, explanations, and the finding of facts (Singleton 1989). In each of these units, students make decisions about an issue or take a stand. The following are some of ideas that teachers have shared. The prompts may spark some interest in you and your students.

Take a Stand

PUBLIC ISSUES

One of the most important curriculum components of Caring-Centered Multicultural Education is the inclusion of public issues. Not only do students learn various points of views, but they also develop vital higher-order thinking skills. In a democracy people make decisions that impact others. In this chapter various issues have been raised that can be discussed in the classroom, such as immigration policies, high-stakes testing, and violence in schools. Take time to consider what the critical issues are in your local area. Here are several questions to consider:

- What is the most important issue that students face today?
- What evidence can you share to support your stand?
- What should students, staff, and faculty do to address this issue?

Middle through High School

Issue: **Immigration**

Focal Unit Questions: What criteria should the United States use in deciding who should be allowed to immigrate to this country? What responsibilities do we as a country have to new immigrants? To refugees?

Grade Level: 9–12

Subject Areas: Social Studies, Civics, U.S. History, U.S. Literature

Issue: **High-Stakes Testing: Scholastic Aptitude Test (SAT)**

Focal Unit Questions: Are SAT scores a true predictor of how successful a student will be in college? Why or why not? What measures should be used to measure the academic competence of students?

Subject Areas: Statistics, Social Studies, Sociology

Issue: **Gender Equity in Sports**

Focal Unit Questions: What proportion of the sports budget should women and men sports receive? Should the funding be the same for women and men? Why or why not? Should the funding depend on the cost of the sport? Should it depend on revenue the sport brings to the school? Why or why not?

Grade Level: 5–12

Subject Areas: Social Studies, U.S. History, Sociology, Government, Civics, Women's Studies

Issue: **Women and Equity**

Focal Unit Questions: What are the major contributions of women in the area of science? How have the contributions of women been taught in the schools? Why? How should teachers address this issue?

Grade Level: 5–12

Subject Areas: Social Studies, American Literature, U.S. History, Sociology, Sciences, Government, Civics, Women's Studies

Issue: **Violence in Schools**

Focal Unit Questions: Why does school violence exist? What can we do to prevent it?

Grade Level: 4–12

Subject Areas: Social Studies, Sociology, Government, Civics

Issue: **Ethnic Segregation in the Cafeteria**

Focal Unit Questions: Where do students choose to sit in the cafeteria? What are the seating patterns? Do the seating arrangements students choose show an integrated community? Why or why not?

Grade Level: 4–12

Subject Areas: Social Studies, U.S. History, Sociology, Government, Civics

Issue: **Ethnic Music**

Focal Unit Questions: What impact does rap music have on young people and their ideas about women, issues of culture/ethnicity, and aggressive behavior?

Grade Level: 6–12
Subject Areas: Music, Sociology, Social Studies

Issue: **Affirmative Action**
Focal Unit Questions: What is the purpose of affirmative action? Should our country continue to support affirmative programs? Why or why not?
Grade Level: 10–12
Subject Areas: Social Studies, U.S. History, Sociology, Government, Civics

Primary and Elementary Level

Issue: **Social Activism**
Focal Unit Questions: Can children take leadership roles in social change? Why or why not? What leadership roles have children played in civil rights? What contributions did Ruby Bridges make to our lives?
Grade Level: 1–3

Issue: **Name-Calling**
Focal Unit Questions: Is name-calling a problem in the school? What evidence demonstrates your viewpoint? What is our responsibility when we hear people call others names? What should we do? Why? What should the school's policy be toward name-calling? Why?
Grade Level: K–12

Issue: **Heroes**
Focal Unit Questions: Who is your hero? What qualities do you think a hero should have?
Grade Level: K–3

Issues-centered curriculum provides an excellent way to comprehensively study complex social issues. A real-life example of a person's impact on a social issue is illustrated by the story of Rosa Parks.

Let me share with you the conversation of a group of student teachers and how they came to study the life of Rosa Parks. (Although Rosa Parks is a national hero, the students in your classroom may pick a local hero. To adults and children in this school, she is a national hero with strong local ties.)

Issue One: Teaching about Social Protest: Rosa Parks

A group of student teachers were asked what issue they wanted to develop for an issues-centered assignment. The student teachers first brainstormed; someone suggested pollution; another suggested homelessness. One student teacher recommended the idea of Rosa Parks and social protest. The last suggestion brought a chain reaction. Here is a little of that conversation:

Lucy suggested, "We are going to be teaching at the Rosa Parks Elementary School. I think we should know something about her. That's a great idea."

Rosa Parks: "I sat down for justice."

"I only have a little understanding of what she did. I think it is important that we teach our students who she is. It will give all of us more of a sense of identity and purpose," Bob said enthusiastically.

"Hey, that's a wonderful idea because she visited the school last year and the kids were very excited to meet her," Laura remarked. "She is a great role model of social justice and has so much courage."

After their discussion, the student teachers decided to develop a unit, initially for their own understanding. The focal unit question was, What should we teach the students about Rosa Parks?

The subquestions that they compiled were as follows:

Who is Rosa Parks and why is she important in U.S. history?

What did she do, and why do her actions exemplify an important social issue?

What is social protest?

What was the Montgomery bus boycott? What would be different now if it had not happened?

What is the NAACP and why is it important?

Why were Jim Crow laws enacted and who was responsible?

Why was there segregation in society?

What values did people have in order for segregation to exist?

What role did Rosa Parks play in the Civil Rights Movement?

Should Rosa Parks have defied the law? Why or why not?

Why did she refuse to get up from her seat?

What does she mean to the children at Rosa Parks Elementary School?

Why should we teach students about Rosa Parks and her role in the Civil Rights Movement?

Should students today continue to fight for equality and social justice? Why?

Because there were 30 student teachers, they divided themselves into six groups and decided what information and questions each group would address in order for them to gather a comprehensive understanding of the life of Rosa Parks and civil rights issues. Here is a list of the group assignments:

Groups 1, 2, and 3: Develop a Web page that answers the following questions:

Group 1: What was Rosa Parks's life like before the bus boycott?

Group 2: Why was Rosa Parks arrested? What was the Montgomery bus boycott?

Group 3: What did Rosa Parks do after she was arrested? What impact did she have on the national Civil Rights Movement?

Group 4: Create a teacher newspaper called "Civil Rights for Children Newsletter."

Group 5: Produce a video called "The Bus Ride: What Happened on December 5, 1955."

Group 6: Simulate a talk show interviewing Rosa Parks, the bus driver, police officer, and passenger.

The student teachers also developed lessons covering important historical information about segregation and the Civil Rights Movement, presented information on the National Association for the Advancement of Colored People, and reviewed the change of U.S. policies from segregation toward integration and equality. In addition, the unit included the following vocabulary words and their definitions: segregation, integration, racism, oppression, stereotypes, prejudice, discrimination, civil rights, Jim Crow laws, equality, boycott, and NAACP.

This information gave the student teachers background into the courage, actions, and beliefs of Rosa Parks, as well as the social and historical setting in which she acted. As a result, they no longer viewed her as a distant image; to them she became a real person who had great courage.

In their own study, the student teachers discovered that Ms. Parks demonstrated how one person can make an important stand against racism. As part of an organized movement against segregation, Rosa Parks was a highly respected member of the community. She was the secretary of the National Association for the Advancement of Colored People (NAACP) in Montgomery, Alabama. She kept track of instances when African Americans were discriminated against. There had been several other arrests of

African Americans who refused to move from their seats on the bus, but the leadership of the community was looking for a person who was well known and respected.

On December 1, 1955, Rosa Parks boarded the bus, paid the fare, and sat down (Parks 1992). She sat in the section labeled "colored." However, when the front of the bus was filled, the bus driver told her that she must give up her seat to a White man who had just entered the bus. Rosa Parks refused to move and the bus driver had her arrested. The police fingerprinted Rosa Parks and put her in jail.

Because many of the riders on the bus were African American, leaders in the African American community believed that a boycott of the buses would be a successful way to protest inequality. The following message was written all over the city:

Don't ride the bus to work, school, or any place on Monday, December 5, 1955.

This was the beginning of the Montgomery bus boycott. Leaders like E. D. Nixon had already planned for a boycott, but were waiting for the right situation. The leadership decided it was the time to mobilize the boycott. In protest of the arrest of Rosa Parks and segregation on buses, African Americans and others did not ride the bus for 381 days (Parks 1992). Martin Luther King, Jr., helped to lead the protest. On November 13, 1956, the Supreme Court outlawed segregation on Montgomery buses. However, most African Americans still would not ride the buses until the Supreme Court order became an official document and was sent to Montgomery.

How did the community deal with having no public transportation? People carpooled, took taxis, and walked all over the city during the long boycott. Taxis charged the same fare as buses. In addition, Rosa Parks worked with the Montgomery Improvement Association through which the community bought cars to use to take people to their jobs. As a dispatcher, Parks sent these cars to various individuals who called. Some White people also helped by giving rides to African Americans. Many people, Black and White, were threatened during the boycott.

The most critical question that the teachers had to debate was, Why was there segregation? This question led to an intense discussion about racism. Racism is a difficult issue to address in schools. Many teachers feel uncomfortable talking about it and are unsure about what to say about it. However, students need the opportunity to think through and discuss racism because it has been and still is a critical problem in our nation and world. It is easier to glide over this as the core issue and talk about social inequalities.

One activity in the unit was a decision-making lesson in which the student teachers had to answer the question, Should Rosa Parks have defied the law? This was an important activity because each teacher was asked to take a stand. The decision was a difficult one because the teachers believed that we should obey the laws, but they struggled with what they should do if they believed the law was wrong. Social protest is an important perennial issue for us as citizens. We are members of a democratic republic and have laws that we must follow, but sometimes we may disagree with those laws. It is important for students to consider what their responsibilities are to challenge unjust laws and actions of society.

The student teachers gained a clearer and more comprehensive understanding of the role Rosa Parks played and continues to play in making the United States a more just society. In addition, the student teachers researched other aspects of the Civil Rights Movement. For example, several teachers examined the work of

Thurgood Marshall and the *Brown* vs. *Topeka Board of Education* Supreme Court decision ending segregation in schools.

When the student teachers taught a unit on Rosa Parks, they were able to introduce the activities using the video of Rosa Parks that was made when she visited the school. Students and master teachers who had had the opportunity to meet Rosa Parks excitedly talked about meeting her and hearing her speak. It was a great way to excite the students and affirm their identity as a school community. History came alive for students because they saw that history is not only about the past but also about today.

In their discussions, students saw Rosa Parks as a caring person who is also a critical civil rights leader. Students took stands regarding the issue of when or how citizens, along with an organized group, can defy a law that they believe is unjust. In addition, student teachers and their children contributed to the school website after studying about Rosa Parks and her courageous actions. They also created a large photo mural of civil rights leaders, both national and local.* This unit was an opportunity for students to see that Rosa Parks was part of a larger movement to make a difference in society. It took the courage of many people, primarily African American, to make our nation address its values of freedom, democracy, and equality.

Issue Two: Literacy and Humanity: Teaching about Malcolm X

Integrating content that interests students can be a powerful learning tool. A familiar figure for many students from underrepresented groups is Malcolm X. I asked Michael, a friend of mine, why he chooses to incorporate the life of Malcolm X into his curriculum and classroom.

> I have a picture of Malcolm X and Martin Luther King, Jr., on my wall. Malcolm X and Martin are in a picture together and they are pointing at the temple of their minds and what I use that as is they're pointing to their minds as thinkers. No matter what went on in their life personally, they stood for their beliefs . . . and were willing to die for them. And I gear more towards Malcolm because of his experience with losing his parents and being street-wise and then converting into religion, then rising to become international and not just national . . . I use Malcolm's life as a parable.

Michael continued to explain what students can learn from the life of Malcolm X.

> He is a hero to many African American males, especially those who are struggling in life. Malcolm is also a role model with Mexican American males . . . because what they've been through, what their ancestors have been through . . .

When asked to talk about what issues of life Malcolm brings to students, Michael said,

> We have to realize we're all human. We make mistakes. We have to reach down. And this is what Malcolm X did. He reached down to people [African Americans

*Many thanks to Joshua Anthony, Lucy Torres, Leslie Fisher, Heather Hawkins, Elizabeth Sparks, Dawn Silhavy, Roseanne Hodges, Bob Ford, Sandy Smith, Rob Gibbs, Dennis Panganiban, Patrice Duggan, Vikki Viarmontes, Linda Villareal, Donna Miller, Sara Camm, Jennifer Bytheway, Suzanne Ellet, Lisa Castro, Annie Bretado, Melissa Ontingco, Laura Mansell, Julia Mulvey, Serena Mulvey, Shauna Howard, and Julie Walsh for sharing their issues-centered units on Rosa Parks.

and others who have been marginalized by society]. Martin did this, too. But Martin had the degree that Caucasians respected. Malcolm got his from in jail when it was nighttime, he was up reading the dictionary, learning the words of the slave master and those same words he used them against them and used them to protect himself when they tried to attack him . . . He studied so much that it caused him to have to wear glasses because he strained his eyes reading so much at night.

Malcolm knew that truth is knowledge and those without knowledge are the ones who are left behind or they're left with the left overs . . . I tell my students that they're a slave to the system if they don't have the knowledge in order to combat ignorance.

Michael shared his insider viewpoint and beliefs about Malcolm X. Michael gave me a richer understanding of Malcolm X's life and how, as an African American male, he was moved by Malcolm X's work and dedication to the community. Malcolm X is my friend's role model and his life represents the struggle that he and his family go through every day. He gathers strength and a clearer understanding of his own role as a teacher from reflecting on Malcolm X's life, because Malcolm cared passionately about people, especially those whom society had abandoned.

After I interviewed Michael, another colleague recommended Theresa Perry's book, *Teaching Malcolm X.* Perry has edited an excellent text in which various authors present effective ways to examine and utilize the life and values of Malcolm X in a classroom that is based on democratic reflective thinking and dedicated to a compassionate and just society. I encourage you to read this book because she clearly explains the following important beliefs of Malcolm X:

Reading and writing affirms one's humanity (Perry 1996, 9).
Reading and writing is an act of resistance (Perry 1996, 9).
Reading and writing is a political and communal act (Perry 1996, 9).
Literacy is freedom (Perry 1996, 18).

Malcolm X: The Interconnections of Literacy and Civil Rights

As I began to study the life of Malcolm X, I was struck with his passionate love of reading and learning. He became a voracious reader. As a child, he had been an excellent student and was well liked by his peers. He was someone who also believed in the equal rights and freedom of every citizen and was willing to speak out and ultimately to die for his beliefs. In studying Malcolm X, students understand not only the work of an individual, but also how he exemplified and challenged members of the community to become active in their own learning and in the restructuring of a better society.

Because students must be able to interpret, analyze, synthesize, and evaluate information, they must be taught how to examine complicated issues and problems. Many teachers are unsure how an issues-centered curriculum differs from a thematic approach. Table 11.1 demonstrates the difference between a theme and an issues approach to curriculum. Students gain a broader understanding of Malcolm X's contributions and roles in our lives today by using an issued-centered orientation. In addition, students can learn of the social context of the time. In one of my classes, several teachers, Suzanne Negoro, John Allen, and Lisa Hernandez, raised the following questions while developing a unit on Malcolm X:

TABLE 11.1   Comparing a Theme Approach to an Issues-Centered Approach

Using the Life of Malcolm X

Theme Topics on the Life of Malcolm X	Focal Questions of an Issues-Centered Curriculum on Malcolm X
Malcolm X	Why was civil rights important to Malcolm X? What role did Malcolm X play in the Civil Rights Movement and U.S. history? Why did Malcolm X believe racism had to be addressed before Black Americans could achieve civil rights in the United States? What if Malcolm X had not lived?
Civil rights	How does Malcolm X exemplify some of the key issues of the Civil Rights Movement? What impact does literacy have on civil rights participation? Why is literacy important to civil rights?
Freedom	Why did Malcolm X believe education was freedom? How can reading and writing impact community and political roles? What role does education play in a democratic nation?
Malcolm X: His life and work	Why are many people unaware of the work and life of Malcolm X? Should students study his life? Why or why not?
Literacy and self-affirmation	Why did Malcolm X believe that literacy was a key aspect of what it means to be human? How can literacy be used to affirm a person's humanity?

1. How might your personal values bias your teaching of Malcolm X? How can you best present the material in a fair and responsible way?
2. What are ways to teach both the strengths and weaknesses of Malcolm X's life?
3. How can you teach about racism and systems of privilege in a way that will not alienate students who come from privileged status groups?
4. What values of the African American community does Malcolm X represent?

They used these questions to guide them as they developed the unit.

My preferred model of inquiry and decision making in issues-centered education comes from the work of Byron Massialas and C. Benjamin Cox (1966), Shirley Engle and Anna Ochoa (1988), and Oliver and Shaver (1966). See Table 11.2 for an adaptation of their models which guide students through the identification, research, decision making, and action of an issue. It shows one way that the life and work of Malcolm X can be taught in an issues-centered classroom. The questions posed are suggestions only and your students may create much more insightful ones. The more involved students become in shaping the study of an issue, the more effective the unit/lesson will be.

TABLE 11.2   An Issues-Centered Approach to Malcolm X

Orientation In this phase, students begin to think and learn about Malcolm X.	Teacher brings in a poster of Malcolm X. Teacher poses questions (examples): **Focal Question:** • Should teachers cover the life of Malcolm X? Why or why not? **Subquestions:** • What were the social issues that Malcolm X passionately addressed in his life? Are those issues still prevalent today? • Why did Malcolm X believe that education was freedom? • Do you think Malcolm X's actions hindered or advanced the progress of civil rights? Why? What role did Malcolm X play in the Civil Rights Movement? • What impact does his race have on how people perceive Malcolm X? Teacher has students read the *Autobiography of Malcolm X* (high school/adult level) by Alex Haley or *By Any Means Necessary: Malcolm X* (middle school level) by Walter Dean Myers. Students begin to explore and clarify aspects of Malcolm X's life. They have posed the following questions: • Who was Malcolm X? • What do you know about his life? • What were his goals? Were any of them like yours? • Why are there many misconceptions about him? • Who killed him and why? • What does the *X* stand for and why doesn't he have a last name? • Was he racist?
Identification In this phase, students identify key issues that are important to study and research. They also identify facts and concepts and define terms.	Students collaboratively make a time line of Malcolm X's life. They may also find other materials to read about Malcolm X. In addition, the class lists key issues that would provide important new understandings and knowledge. Students may also write statements about what they learned while discussing Malcolm X. • Through literacy people could more effectively fight social oppression. • Freedom of the mind was more important than freedom of the body. • People must work for and be committed to community and the struggle for equality. • Malcolm Little fought for the rights of all people, especially people such as African Americans, who had not been treated equally.
Evidence and Multiple Perspectives In this phase, students seek evidence and describe multiple views and perspectives of the issue.	Students identify different perspectives about Malcolm X. Some people think he was an important leader in the Civil Rights Movement. Others believe he was a hoodlum and was destructive because he defied the law. They can organize the information they have found. Students can identify various communities and individuals and how they differ in their views of Malcolm X.

TABLE 11.2   An Issues-Centered Approach to Malcolm X

	Students examine competing values and clarify their own beliefs. Students review original questions from the orientation phase to see if they have gathered sufficient information to answer those questions.
Values and Beliefs In this phase, students identify their own values and beliefs in relation to the person, event, or issue being studied.	Students identify their own values. Students identify the values of others. For example: • "I thought Malcolm X believed in violence. I can see that he didn't want violence. He believed in community, but also wanted to challenge the system. I agree, but I don't have the courage he had." • "Malcolm X was too angry and couldn't see part of his anger. Although I felt bad about what happened to him, I think he shouldn't have been as aggressive. That ties in so much with the stereotypes about African American men." • "I never thought that education gave me freedom in my mind. I thought it was just something I had to do." • "Malcolm X was about reading and doing. He was awesome. He is my role model now. I think I will try to do better in school because I can be somebody." • "I believe teachers are afraid to talk about him because they don't know what might happen. Maybe kids will get too aggressive." • "Malcolm knew it took courage to speak out. People should stand up to change things, not sit back and just complain about how things are not fair."
Solutions/Perspectives and Their Consequences In this phase, students deal with values and ethical conflicts and differences. Students look at various perspectives or ideas about resolving a problem. In addition, they identify consequences for each one.	Teacher again asks: Should we teach about Malcolm X in schools today? Why or why not? What if Malcolm X had not lived or he had not become nationally and internationally known? How would the Civil Rights Movement have been different? Students share their views about the impact of Malcolm X on today's youth and society. Teacher asks about consequences of each student position/decision. Possible student discussions: • "If we don't talk about Malcolm X, we may be losing an important person in our civil rights history. He challenges people to do something about unfairness in society." • "If we talk about him, people might get mad at each other. He brings up stuff from the past. What happened to Blacks in the past is over. It is only adding salt to the wound." • "If we don't talk about him, then we are discounting the contribution of a person from the Black community. There is already so much rage about being left out of society or not being treated fairly."

continued
397

TABLE 11.2   **An Issues-Centered Approach to Malcolm X (Continued)**

Take a Stand and Justify a Decision	Students replies:
In this phase, students provide their argument about why they have decided on their position.	• "I still believe teachers do not want to teach about Malcolm X because they don't want to talk about racism." • "Teachers don't really understand Malcolm X. They think he was about violence, but he was really about education because he thought education gave people freedom, freedom of the mind, and that is what was most important." • "Malcolm X was too violent. He broke laws. Is that right? We must all follow the law or else there would be chaos. He might have gone about getting equality in other ways, more like Martin Luther King, Jr., using nonviolence." • "Malcolm X stood for all people no matter what their race. He stood for equality and justice. That goes above any one color."
Action	• Students may write a letter to the history department in the school asking that more time be spent on the life of Malcolm X. • Students may give the book to their friends to read and discuss it with them. • Students may decide to volunteer in an after-school program helping younger students with their homework because they see how important education, and literacy in particular, is to kids.
In this phase, students develop a plan for action.	

Issue Three: Creating a Unit on Citizenship and Civil Rights Leadership

The previous section presented two units on civil rights leaders, Rosa Parks and Malcolm X, who were extraordinary examples of individuals who were willing to challenge the status quo. Movement forward in civilization is dependent on citizenry who are willing to struggle to protect the rights of all people to life, liberty, equality, and the pursuit of happiness. Instead of having separate units as presented in the previous sections, you may want to combine the study of the two individuals as well as add other role models. You may want to find out more about other important leaders such as César Chavez, Mitsue Endo, Black Elk, Minoru Yasui, Eleanor Roosevelt, Gordon Hirabayashi, Lillian Smith, Philip Vera Cruz, Patsy Mink, Dolores Huerta, and John Brown. As community leaders, they dedicated their lives to social justice. They could be included in a unit on social protest and civil rights.

The health of our democracy is dependent on the ability of all citizens, irrespective of their cultural or ethnic background, to work collaboratively toward justice. Many schools often state that their goal is to nurture students who will mature into empowered, responsible citizens, but what do they mean by empowerment? Issues-centered education gives students the opportunity to develop essential higher-order thinking and important decision-making skills. In fact, state social studies standards such as those of Texas indicate the importance of citizenship. Here are two standards for grade eight Texas schools:

Citizenship. The student understands the importance of the expression of different points of view in a democratic society. The student is expected to: A) identify different points of view of political parties and interest groups on important and historical and contemporary issues; B) describe the importance of free speech and press in a democratic society; and C) summarize a historical event in which compromise resulted in a peaceful solution" (State of Texas 1998, 53–54).

Culture. The student understands the major reform movements of the 19th century. The student is expected to: A) describe the historical development of the abolitionist movement; and B) evaluate the impact of reform movements including public education, temperance, women's rights, prison reform, and care of the disabled" (State of Texas 1998, 54).

Both of these standards could be addressed with a unit on social protest and civil rights. The questions that could be covered include: What are the most pressing civil rights issues that we should address today? Who are some of the leaders in those issues? What motivated people to speak out and protest the status quo?

The following are short biographies of several leaders whose work you may want your students to investigate.

Patsy Takemoto Mink—Representative Mink was the first Japanese American woman to become a licensed lawyer in Hawaii. Originally she had dreams of becoming a physician, but was not admitted into medical school in 1948, so she later switched to law school. She was also the first woman of color elected to Congress in 1964. Mink was co-author of Title IX, the civil rights legislation passed in 1972 that provided equal educational opportunities to women and girls. She also was an advocate for environmental protection. She, along with 32 other members of Congress, sued the Environmental Protection Agency under the Freedom of Information Act when the organization would not give her information about effects of nuclear testing in the Aleutian Islands. The case is known as *Mink* v. *Environmental Protection Agency*. Her case, which was heard by a federal appeals court, became a landmark case that gave the public more access to information from governmental agencies.

Dolores Huerta—Dolores C. Huerta, cofounder of the United Farm Workers of America, worked side-by-side with César Chavez. She was a grassroots organizer whose leadership resulted in voter registration drives and better social services for farmworkers. Originally she was an elementary-grade teacher, but she left teaching because of her grave frustrations with the poor living conditions of students. Her students often arrived at school extremely hungry and without health care. Later she became a powerful lobbyist in Sacramento, California, for the rights of farmworkers. She was one of the leaders of the nonviolent "Delano Grape Strike" in 1965 and a negotiator for the United Farm Workers Organizing Committee. In 1966, the Schenley Wine Company relented and engaged in collective bargaining with Huerta as the central negotiator. One of the most important issues Huerta lobbied for was to get growers to stop the use of pesticides such as DDT and Parathyon.

Key questions students might investigate while studying the lives of these important U.S. figures are:

Is the United States a just society? Explain your position.

Are there issues that we as U.S. Americans must address in order to make society more just? If so, what issues must we tackle? Whose responsibility is it to take on those changes?

Using the lives of Patsy Mink and Dolores Huerta, how would you define the responsibilities of citizens in a democracy?

Another question regarding the topic of women in civil rights might be: What contributions have women made in the area of civil rights? This question leads students to examine perennial issues and how these individuals impacted the way society conceived of, acted on, and responded to social justice concerns. As a result students will develop a more comprehensive understanding of the historical context of each person's life and how his or her actions contributed to a long legacy of civil rights in our country. Women whose lives can be examined and studied might include Rosa Parks, Elizabeth Cady Stanton, Lucretia Mott, Susan B. Anthony, Sarah and Angelina Grimke (abolitionists), Nelly Bly, Janice Mirakitani, Maya Angelou, Fannie Lou Baker, and Yoshiko Uchida.

> ৩ *The health of our democracy is dependent on the ability of all citizens, irrespective of their cultural or ethnic background, to work collaboratively toward justice.*

Issue Four: Fighting for the Neighborhood in the Mathematics Classroom: Carrying On the Tradition of Malcolm X and Carter Woodson

Teachers often ask me how they can integrate civil rights issues into their math instruction. Bill Tate (1995) has written an excellent article explaining how he collaborated with a teacher, Sandra Mason, who incorporated a social issue into her math class. She taught middle school math in a school that was primarily African American. Mason believed that the goal of schooling is to prepare students to solve issues that arise in their lives (Tate 1995). Mason had a three-phase teaching approach that integrated math with decision making, student experiences, and participation in a democracy.

Students began the unit by naming issues they believed were hurting their community. This gave students the opportunity to express their opinions about a variety of issues and to look at these issues from the viewpoints of others. Students suggested issues such as drugs, the AIDS epidemic, sickle-cell anemia, and building the city for the future (Tate 1995). In the first part of the process, they focused on one problem that the class would address as a community. The students decided to examine the proliferation of liquor stores in the neighborhood and problems that alcohol brought to the community. In the second phase, students researched the issue and decided on strategies to address the problem of too many liquor stores. In the third phase of the activity, students were actively involved in doing something about the liquor stores and the selling of alcohol too close to the school.

The students developed an action plan. They read through the local laws and regulations. In their research students found that there were financial benefits for liquor stores to be open for business in the neighborhood. As part of their mathematics, they developed a new incentive plan using percentages, decimals, and fractions (Tate 1995). Next, the young people gathered information about local city codes and measured the distance from the liquor stores to their school.

Then the students talked with a newspaper editor, who wrote an editorial about the liquor store issue. Students developed short presentations in which they used mathematics to discuss the issue and carefully describe their arguments. This led to a meeting with congressional representatives in the state capital. Members of the class also developed a plan to move the liquor stores and presented their proposal to the city council. Their plan included a tax savings benefit for those liquor stores that moved away from the school. Through the brave actions of the students and their teachers, the police gave over 200 citations to various liquor stores and two of the stores were even pushed to close. In addition, the city council passed a resolution that stated that liquor could not be drunk within 600 yards of the school.

Sandra Mason's educational beliefs grew out of a civil rights orientation and the work of Carter Woodson. She believed that it was critical for schools to address the realities of the lives of African American students. She felt that it was even more important for students to learn mathematics skills and concepts because many African American young people have not been successful in math. Tate summarized the accomplishments of the teacher: "Mason's pedagogical strategies represent efforts to 'center' her students in the process of acquiring knowledge for social change. Her success represents the power of returning to the root of African American tradition" (Tate 1995, 172).

 Connection

Issues-centered education is an excellent approach to teaching. The method provides students with the opportunity to examine opposing and diverse points of view about social issues. The approach also encourages students to identify various solutions and the consequences to each possible solution. It is important for students to have the option of examining information not only from textbooks and teachers, but other resources. Four organizations that publish information for educators on various social issues are Educators for Social Responsibility (**esrmetro.org**), Dollars and Sense (**dollarsandsense.org**), The Rouge Forum (**rougeforum.org**) and Rethinking Schools (**rethinkingschools.org**). Some of the issues they cover are voting patterns, wealth, the presidential election, and terrorism.

For example:

Educators for Social Responsibility have a special section called Teachable Moments and can be found at **teachablemoment.org.** On the Rouge Forum website I suggest that you read through Rich Gibson's thoughtful book available free online called *How Do I Keep My Ideals and Still Teach*? at **rougeforum.org.**

Using an Issues–Centered Approach to Teaching Science: Research Findings

What have researchers found about using an issues-centered, relevant, integrated approach to teaching? I have shared with you various studies focusing on language arts skills development, social studies, and mathematics. Jeffrey Weld (1999) looked at the research in teaching science. He found that teachers using the **science/technology/society (STS)** approach had improved academic achievement. The STS approach integrates contemporary issues facing students and society. Students problem-solve. For example, students in a high school ecology class may list topics they would like to research. Perhaps they decided to investigate the level of pollutants in a neighborhood creek. Students choose various roles. One person may go to the library to find background information about the creek, such as its history and any news stories about it. Another student may interview local ecologists who might have studied the creek and the wildlife. Others may develop a multimedia presentation at the conclusion of the unit so that all the information can be shared with the entire class (Weld 1999).

The STS approach has been extremely successful (Weld 1999). Young women find that science is fun and they perform as well as their male peers. In addition, the attitude of most students is significantly more positive. In one research study, Weld reported that girls and boys had similar success on the Iowa Tests of Basic Skills after being part of STS science classes. Results with students of color were also impressive. These students were more positive about science after STS classes, and they made more gains on the Iowa Tests of Basic Skills in comparison to underrepresented students in traditional classrooms. The context in which information is presented has a powerful role in the motivation, interest, and performance of students.

Integrating the Three Important Aspects of Education: Caring, Justice, and Intercultural Communications

This chapter brought together culture and curriculum in the discussion about culturally relevant teaching. Caring and justice are two values that continually appear throughout the chapter. Educators must focus on teaching students how to care for each other and for themselves within a society that holds values such as freedom, equality, and justice. Caring for others is a powerful foundation for social justice.

The most important goals that we want to teach our students are not only higher-order thinking abilities, but also the importance of linking caring for others and social justice. It is important for people to develop intercultural communication skills in order to work collaboratively with others and to understand

Engaged in active learning

diverse points of view. Individuals must move away from an ethnocentric orientation and the belief that there are absolute ways of responding. In fact, people may react differently to the same event. People need to know that their response is not a neutral one. A caring individual knows that everyone may not hold her or his viewpoint.

In addition, people from various communities may understand the concept of caring in different ways. For example, a fourth-generation Japanese American young woman told me that she thought it was important to tell people what she felt even if it wasn't what the other person wanted to hear. In the same conversation, an Asian Indian woman, who was born in India, disagreed with the first woman, saying that she thought a caring person would understand the cultural laws of the pan-Asian community and know that it wasn't appropriate to be that brash or outspoken because it could be interpreted as being critical. Because they had reciprocal trust, they were willing to continue talking in an attempt to find some common ground. This was not easy, but they were finally successful.

The following are questions for you to consider that have to do with the ethics of caring and social justice in a culturally diverse society:

What is caring to me?

How are caring and community interrelated?

What are the characteristics of a caring community?

What role do the values of caring play in my personal and professional life as a teacher?

How do different cultures operationalize caring?

What common ground can I find with those who seem to be from unfamiliar communities?

What linkages can I make with parents, students, and other teachers?

What can I do now to teach them how to be more caring?

How can I make the classroom more democratic and caring?

Answers to these questions will vary depending on your own personal relationships, membership in various community groups, and values. I encourage you to reflect on each question and find ways to ask your own students about them. We as teachers can assist in intellectual growth and personal development. This is an extremely challenging task, but we can do it. As Noddings writes, "The primary aim of every teacher must be to promote the growth of students as competent, caring, loving, and lovable people" (Noddings 1992, 154).

Chapter Summary

In this chapter I suggested ways to integrate cultural content into the curriculum. Using curriculum as a vehicle is often the most comfortable way for teachers to integrate culture into their classroom. Using an issues-centered approach is one of the most comprehensive methods of integrating culture into the curriculum. Teachers can guide their students to examine complex social problems from various cultural viewpoints. This approach focuses on higher-order thinking and decision-making skills.

When this approach is not possible, teachers can use the following seven components to integrate cultural content into their curriculum: students' personal experiences, role models, culturally grounded stories, songs, photos, language and linguistic expressions, multiple perspectives, formal subject content, and community issues.

In collaboration with cultural content is the sociocultural context of learning. As I have discussed in previous chapters, there is a cultural rhythm in many classrooms because teachers understand the culture of their students. However, as I mentioned previously, when teachers have children from 20 different cultures in their classroom, it is not possible to holistically respond to each culture because that requires insider knowledge. Yet teachers can provide other ways to integrate the home and cultural knowledge of students, which affirms who they are and provides a cognitive bridge to new information and skills. This can be done by naturally inserting examples from the lives of students when teaching about general concepts and topics. Caring

is a vital foundation for a culturally relevant teacher because teachers spend much time observing and listening carefully to their students. Your students are often the most important cultural resources in a school.

Have fun being creative. When you get to know your students, they often act as cultural mediators for other students. As a result, you learn much from them and develop intercultural communication skills. Teaching is always a two-way street. You present information to students and they respond and present new ideas to you.

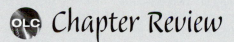

Chapter Review

Go to the Online Learning Center at **www.mhhe.com/pang2e** to review important content from the chapter, practice with key terms, take a chapter quiz, and find the Web links listed in this chapter.

Key Terms

additive approach, *369*
integrating, *370*
restructuring, *370*
personal experiences, *372*
role models, *372*

bioboard, *373*
culturally grounded stories
and songs, *375*
cultural expressions, *378*
multiple perspectives, *381*

traditional subject content, *383*
issues-centered curriculum, *387*
science/technology/
society (STS), *402*

Reflection Activities

1. Role models are an important aspect of teaching and living. Identify several of your own personal role models and why you chose them. Now list White people who are civil rights activists or antiracists. Many teachers talk about reducing prejudice and discrimination, and yet they offer few antiracist role models who are White. This has been the most difficult question

that I have asked teachers in class. They cannot list many names of White people who have worked hard to eliminate racism. When I ask for African American civil rights role models, immediately they mention Martin Luther King, Jr., or Harriet Tubman or Jesse Jackson. Can you list in your journal White civil rights role models that you know? Teachers have mentioned

Branch Rickey, manager for the Brooklyn Dodgers who first hired Jackie Robinson, and Morris Dees, who founded the Southern Poverty Law Center. John Brown was another role model, an important abolitionist, but someone few people know. Another is Eleanor Roosevelt. If you can't think of any White antiracist role models, maybe that would be a good research project for you to consider.

2. Teaching students how to care for themselves and others is an important educational goal. If schools are to be centers of caring as Noddings has suggested, what units or issues could you integrate into the curriculum? As she has recommended, the units may deal with personal health, health costs, the study of religions, relationship building, and moral development. Which issues would you present, knowing the needs of your students? Make a list and begin thinking of how you might develop those issues.

3. In your journal throughout the day, write down some of the thoughts and experiences that your students have shared with you and the class. As you plan for the next day's curriculum, design lessons in which you use some student experiences as examples of the concepts or skills that you are teaching. For example, suppose you are teaching the concept of place value. Listen to what the students tell you about how they spent their money or how they learned how to count money. Students may come up with several good examples of how place value is used every day. When they were little, they would count 10 pennies and put them in one pile. They would have many piles of pennies and then they would count by 10 and add them all up. It does take time to think of examples that students have shared; however, this is a good way to scaffold learning. Students also are affirmed and know that you have listened and value their contributions.

PART FIVE

Personal Professional Development

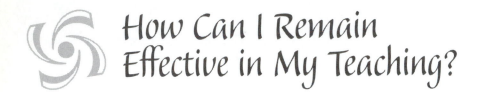

CHAPTER 12

How Can I Remain Effective in My Teaching?

CHAPTER OVERVIEW

I n this final chapter, the reader is asked to consider what meaningful teaching is and to consider the need for total school reform. Teachers can be active in interviewing students and examining all aspects of schooling for caring, culture, and equity.

Introduction: Caring and Controversial Issues: September 11

This is the last chapter, but it is not the final word. I hope this chapter gives you much more to think about as you continue your journey of teaching. The goal of this chapter is to present suggestions and questions that can help you continue your process of reflection. I present two models: One can assist you in assessing how meaningful your teaching is to students, and the other summarizes the six areas of reflection that I have covered in this text.

Caring-Centered Multicultural Education calls for *teaching that is meaningful and affirming* to students. When teachers care for their students, they reflect on what they say and do and how it impacts their students. Teachers continually think about the following key questions:

Are my students learning?

What am I doing to create a caring and affirming learning community?

How am I integrating the cultural context of students in my classroom every day?

In what areas can I improve my skills and knowledge? Whom can I ask to help me?

Am I a good role model for social justice and caring? How do I act toward students?

In the classroom, students must understand the connections to and relevance of what we do every day. This is a daunting task under easy circumstances but extremely challenging after the attacks of terrorism in our country.

Young people and adults in the United States and in other countries around the world were bewildered and shocked by the events of **September 11, 2001,** when four airplanes were used as weapons of terrorism. This was one of the most difficult days for students and their teachers in modern times. Having a caring and affirming classroom and school to attend was especially important during the immediate days after the horrific events.

We are impacted by the social and political context that we live in, and those who experienced the events of September 11 have now integrated into their knowledge base this new term. The expression "September 11" is synonymous with the *events* of September 11, 2001. This day was a powerful illustration of how interdependent we are all around the world. People in many countries felt empathy and concern for those in the World Trade Center and the Pentagon. Individuals who died that day were from many, many countries and not just the United States. The World Trade Center held various international companies, too.

During this period of time, schooling was not just a place where information was taught. The goal of many teachers was to provide a safe place for students and a haven where students could express their fears. Later young people became angry and frustrated. At first, many students came to school numb and later others came with a strong feeling of retaliation. For some, the values of compassion and respect were pushed to the margins because they had never before experienced anything that devastating. Many soon learned that terrorism is an act of aggression targeting civilians. Although folks in the United States had not had to deal with severe terrorism, they found out that acts of aggression directed toward people from many other countries such as Afghanistan, Ireland, Indonesia, Israel, Palestine, Chechnya, and the Philippines have occurred for years.

Learning can come from fun situations and from extremely difficult ones. The principles of Caring-Centered Multicultural Education were implemented by many educators during trying times such as the Gulf War and September 11. Would it have been meaningful and affirming to ignore the stress students were feeling? Teaching became more than imparting basic skills. Many teachers were compassionate listeners who encouraged their students not to abandon care for others while understanding a need to protect themselves. Through discussion students could perceive how complex the issue was and how people held many different perspectives. School faculty members acted as counselors; Alan Singer, a former high school teacher, is a good example of a caring teacher. He worked with students to create student clubs to support an empowered student body. Singer (2003) explained how important it was during the Gulf War to "put the students' decisions ahead of my own views. Sometimes, when students did not agree with my ideas, I had to backoff . . . [In another situation] I chose not to bring students to a local rally against racial violence because we heard there would be hostile counterdemonstrators." He had taught students how to discuss issues by laying respectful ground rules. The climate Singer created was one of caring and openness so that students felt that their perspective would be welcomed. He also believed in shared decision making. Because Singer knew that one of the most important healing strategies he could provide was to encourage students to take action, he thought of himself as a supportive mentor. Being a caring teacher is not always easy or simple; however, Singer, through his actions, demonstrated his compassion and respect for students.

Along with tending to the mental-health issues of students, teachers also addressed students' need for information about the issues surrounding September 11, 2001. One of Singer's colleagues, Michael Pezone, who teaches in New York City, is another faculty mentor to a student club that examined social issues (Singer 2003). His students integrated civics principles while using critical thinking skills about the serious issues of September 11. The students did not want a knee-jerk reaction. Pezone also knew how important it was for the students to gather information from a variety of sources in order to develop a comprehensive understanding of why the events took place. For example, his students examined some of the historical antecedents of September 11. They looked at countries that the United States had invaded and what our foreign policy has been toward them. Students also investigated the **USA Patriot Act** (Uniting and Strengthening America by Providing Appropriate Tools Required to Intercept and Obstruct Terrorism Act). This law was signed by President George W. Bush on October 26, 2001, about a month after the September 11 attacks. The law provided for more extensive security methods with the goal of thwarting terrorism and building homeland security. Students were surprised by the extensive nature of the law and how civil liberties of U.S. citizens and others were at risk. Pezone took much time to investigate the issues himself. Although it was a time-consuming process, he wanted his students to learn from and not just continue to be shocked by the sadness of the events.

Students identified three major concerns: the loss of civil liberties, the alarming increase in so-called patriotic acts in which expressions of free speech questioning actions of the Untied States were vilified, and the rise in hate crimes against, and profiling of, Arab Americans, Asian Americans, and Muslims. The students also took various actions. For example, after the destruction of September 11, 2001, the New York City Board of Education made it mandatory for all students to participate in the recitation of the "Pledge of Allegiance." Pezone's students were concerned that, although this might be a good response for some folks, it might not represent true patriotism for all citizens. Students contacted the New York Civil Liberties Union and discovered that by law student participation could not be required. Members in the club discussed with their peers the legality of the pledge and encouraged students to behave respectfully and professionally if they did not want to participate. The comic on page 411 centers around one of the key questions regarding civil liberties.

FRANK & ERNEST reprinted by permission of Newspaper Enterprise Association, Inc.

Students learned that the events of September 11 were related to many other beliefs and events in countries such as Afghanistan, Pakistan, Iran, Russia, India, Iraq, Israel, Palestine, Saudi Arabia, and Somalia. Soon after September 11, the United States began its offensive in Afghanistan. Students began studying the history and goals of groups such as the Taliban and the Northern Alliance. The complexities of world violence around the world became clearer to students in Pezone's classes. They recognized that issues of human rights, imperialism, terrorism, and capitalism are closely linked.

Being a caring-centered teacher is not always comfortable. Pezone was committed to the education of his students and believed that in a democracy caring extends to difficult times when teachers and students collaborate in asking tough questions.

 Connection

"Talking to Children about Terrorism and Armed Conflict" by Judith A. Myers-Walls is an excellent resource for teachers about helping children with the trauma of September 11. Visit Chapter 12 on the book's website (**www.mhhe.com/pang2e**) to access a copy.

The National Association of School Psychologists provides a website (**www.nasponline. org/NEAT/war_terrorism.html**) about dealing with traumatic events in schools. Although the lesson ideas they present do not focus on the events of September 11, they do provide important suggestions for teachers about dealing with violent events. Focus is on young children although there are ideas for middle and senior high school teachers. See website **http://www.nasponline.org/NEAT/teachmoment.html#admin.**

The American Library Association website provides information regarding how the Patriot Act can impact your library and business records. Go to **www.ala.org.** In the search box type Patriot Act and the Resolution of the organization regarding this act can be found.

Visit Chapter 12 of the book's website (**www.mhhe.com/pang2e**) to link to these sites.

Setting Goals and Knowing Where You Are Going

It is important that teachers set clear goals that will assist them in reaching each student. I encourage you to think about your classroom and school's goals and write them in your journal. One of the books that I have found most helpful in giving an overview of how to develop goals and ways educators can implement them was written by General John Stanford with Robin Simons. It is called *Victory in Our Schools*. Stanford was a much-loved superintendent for the Seattle Public Schools in the 1990s. Initially, few people believed that a retired general would be able to turn a school district around, because he wasn't a former teacher. Many skeptics did not realize that General Stanford had a positive vision of what a community could do for its children, and he had the skills to lead them. He was able to energize the city behind his vision and his vision became the city's vision. The children and students believed in him as well. Here is the oath that he wrote and shared with the city on the first day of school when students, parents, and teachers gathered at a large stadium:

Oath on Behalf of Children

- I, John Stanford, do solemnly affirm that I will love, cherish, and protect every child entrusted to my care.

- I affirm that I will endeavor to prepare all students to meet the highest standards of achievement, conduct, and citizenship possible, knowing that this will help to maintain the health of our city both now and in the future.

- I affirm that I will work cooperatively with parents and members of the community to produce a world-class, student-focused learning system for our precious children and students (Stanford, September 1997).

Stanford focused on creating clear goals and a plan to reach those goals based on his philosophy shared in the oath (Stanford and Simons 1999, 16). He stressed the importance of every element of the plan to directly support a goal. The goals must also be measurable so that we can tell if we have reached them. Each person who is involved in the process must be accountable for the success of the plan. In our schools, our goals must have timetables and people identified as responsible for them. A collaborative task force for the district identified the following five goals for Seattle schools:

1. Increase academic achievement.
2. Recruit, develop, and retain an effective diverse workforce.
3. Create and maintain a healthy, safe, and secure learning environment.
4. Seek stable and sufficient funding for schools.
5. Increase the ability of the district to respond to and meet the needs of diverse students and parents and to attract and retain more students.

From these broad goals, teachers in each school developed school plans with detailed strategies to put new practices into place. For example, the staff at one of the elementary schools, Sanislo, set the goal of increasing parent involvement because they felt that would fit into their goal of increasing academic achievement. The school faculty created and worked collaboratively with parents. One of the new practices was to ask parents to read to their children 20 minutes every night. The children brought in signed sheets from their parents. The school followed up with a Reading Thermometer so that everyone could see they were contributing to the school goal of 50,000 nights of reading. In addition, teachers developed weekly homework packets and included letters to parents describing how they could help their children complete their work. They established a family reading night once a year when families bring books to read along with sleeping bags and stay overnight at the school. It is fun to see parents and children spread on blankets and tumbling mats in their pajamas. Another innovative activity is the family fitness night. Families come to school and join in many different physical activities, such as jumping rope, rollerblading, or juggling. To increase literacy, books on tape are also available in the school library for parents or students to check out with cassette tape recorders.

Superintendent Stanford was an excellent leader, not only because of his skills in setting goals and developing plans, but also because he had a deep commitment to children that came from his soul. He was a bright light in a dark storm, showing people that in addition to using technical skills, they also had to believe in the children—believe that they could make a difference. Stanford was a role model of both leadership and love; one did not come without the other. One of his sayings was, "Loving and leading means creating victories every day."

When Stanford talked about love in the schools, he also meant that teachers and principals needed to be cared for, too. In order for teachers to be successful, they also needed to be loved. Stanford gave an example of a caring principal in his book (Stanford and Simons 1999). He talked about the leadership of Eric Benson at Nathan Hale High School. Benson showed his love for his staff through the many little things he did every day. He fought for the resources they requested. Benson found resources to provide his faculty with the planning time they needed. In addition, he often celebrated and congratulated his teachers. For example, he remembered their birthdays and put notes of thanks in their mailboxes. He honored their success, whether it was with specific students, earning advanced degrees, or engaging in volunteer work. Benson had yearly teacher appreciation dinners and thanked teachers with dinner certificates, hotel getaways, and other gifts from local businesses. Within this context, teachers and students grew in environments that were meaningful and that honored them.

Meaningful Teaching

What is meaningful teaching? It is teaching that oftentimes comes out of and incorporates the lived experiences of students. **Meaningful teaching** is instruction that is relevant, interesting, and purposeful to *all students.* When we respect and are committed to our students, we want to listen to and know about them. This shows how we care. Looking at life from other perspectives enriches our knowledge of the world, especially in a classroom where children may speak 10 different languages and come from many communities. Creating a community of learners who come from diverse backgrounds is a difficult but exciting aspect of being a teacher.

An excellent way to design relevant programs for students is to ask them their opinions about the needs of the community and to use that information to create relevant curriculum. In Philadelphia, the University of Pennsylvania organized the West Philadelphia Improvement Corps (WPIC) after interviewing several teachers and approximately 100 students about what could be done to improve their schools and neighborhoods. From their responses, WPIC designed and implemented a plan that included landscaping, removal of graffiti, and other neighborhood beautification projects (Nothdurft 1989). WPIC was a coalition of the University of Pennsylvania, local corporations, community agencies, and schools, and the project rose out of the beliefs of the students; therefore, the young people could see how school and the real world were linked. They also saw that their efforts did make a difference. Through this program, students learned geometry and carpentry by being involved in rehabilitating row houses; they learned biological principles by running a greenhouse and learned economic principles by being responsible for a school store. Dropout rates decreased and the academic achievement of students increased. Several of the WPIC schools have become community centers with outside funding. This program demonstrated that connecting learning in schools to real life is a key element.

Another aspect of relevancy in the classroom deals with culture. Evangelina Bustamante Jones (1998) believes that teachers must act as cultural mediators. Teachers should explain to children and help them understand the differences in values and social contexts. Thus, teachers can honor both the world of the child and the majority society. As cultural mediators, teachers can affirm both the home and school cultures. Teachers must have the ability to take school information and skills and make connections to the lives of their children.

In order to be cultural mediators, teachers must have time to reflect on the five areas found in Table 12.1. These areas highlight key aspects that contribute to meaningful teaching practices: collegial discussions, personal reflection on values and beliefs, meaningful content knowledge development, meaningful practice, and purposeful accountability. Teachers must reflect on all components of the meaningful teaching model. The five components work collaboratively and integrally as if to create a large tapestry. If any area is missing, a hole will appear in the fabric. Each component contains a series of recommendations, but they are not separate lists. The suggestions represent attitudes, knowledge, and skills that teachers need to consider when creating a caring, culturally affirming, and effective classroom. Table 12.1 explains each of the five areas.

Collegial Discussions

One of the most exciting aspects of teaching is to find others who are willing to share and learn together in a safe, nonthreatening environment of encouragement. Changes in schools can occur when teachers have open lines of communication with each other. **Collegial discussions** serve as a support system, but they also help teachers to grow and develop their teaching gifts and their understanding of the school system. Oftentimes teachers are busy trying to survive on their own; having

TABLE 12.1 Meaningful Teaching

Collegial Discussions	Personal Reflection of Values and Beliefs	Meaningful Content Knowledge Development	Meaningful Practice	Purposeful Accountability
• Create/clarify the mission, integrating values of caring, justice, culture, and effective teaching. • Discuss the institutional issues of equity, such as tracking, discipline policies, and monocultural curriculum. Design ways to address them. • Discuss the impact of culture (language, cultural conflict, cultural relevancy). • Discuss prejudicial attitudes (such as racism, sexism, classism, homophobia) found in the students and teachers. Find ways to eliminate them.	• Review one's personal biases. • Look at one's own competing values. • Reflect on personal behavior. • Reflect on contrasting viewpoints. • Review teaching goals. • Review one's expectations of students. • Reflect on one's understanding of race, class, ethnic, and gender issues and how they impact one's teaching. • Reflect on one's growth as a teacher.	• Learn about the history of underrepresented groups. • Learn about the history of women. • Review current immigration issues and immigration history. • Learn about language acquisition processes, bilingual education, and multicultural education. • Reflect on how the economic status of various groups impacts their social status. • Learn about the cultures of students in the class. • Strengthen your knowledge of liberal arts and science, math, and technology. • Learn about caring in various cultural contexts. • Find out what issues are impacting students' lives.	• Tie instruction to the student's world. • Use relevant content. • Build caring relationships with students. • Use cultural experiences, such as cultural analogies, stories, history, literature, and shared life experiences. • Use purposeful decision-making and problem-solving activities. • Model the concepts one teaches. • Assist students in finding common ground with each other through cooperative group work and dialogue. • Create an issues-centered curriculum based on students' lives.	• Seek evidence demonstrating student learning for all groups of students. • Seek evidence that changes are being implemented to create a caring and equitable school. • Keep a journal of progress of students, strategies that work and do not work, and insights. • Review the articulation of skills and knowledge one teaches. • Listen carefully to your students—they often provide important feedback. • Build a professional portfolio focusing on teaching effectiveness.

a support group helps to breathe life into the profession. Discussions may focus on the following questions:

What is our mission?

What kind of classroom am I trying to create?

What do caring and social justice mean on the classroom level?

What works best with children?

How can I best understand institutional barriers that may be biased?

How can I change those institutional barriers?

What can I do with my colleagues to change those institutional barriers?

What richness do my students and their parents bring to the classroom?

Let me give you an example of how powerful dialogue can be. In a high school, several students went to an English teacher. This teacher was one of the informal leaders in the school, but the students did not know that. They saw him as a caring and listening adult at the school.

Here is a sample of their conversation:

Cindy: Mr. Johnson, we wanted to talk with you about something that bothers us here. We knew you would listen. We don't know if there is anything we can do. (*She begins to look down at the floor. Her friend interjects.*)

Araceli: Mr. Johnson, some of the kids aren't eating lunch. They won't get in *those* lines. (*Her voice is emphatic and frustrated.*)

Cindy: Yes, it's humiliating. It isn't right.

Mr. Johnson: Can you explain why kids aren't eating? What lines are you talking about?

Cindy: We feel ashamed of getting free lunch. Didn't you know there are separate lunch lines for kids on free or reduced lunch? (*Mr. Johnson shook his head no.*)

Araceli: Mr. Johnson, we aren't the only students not eating. There are so many kids who just won't get in those lines. They feel the other kids are looking at them. We are in high school. This is different from elementary school. Don't the teachers care about how we feel?

Cindy: I graduate this year and I am counting the days. I can't wait to get out of here because the school doesn't care about us. (*The lunch bell rings. It is time to return to classes.*)

Mr. Johnson: I didn't know this was happening. I usually eat lunch in the teachers' room so I don't see what the students are doing at lunch. Let me look into this. I don't want you to miss your lunch. Thanks for letting me know. I will let you know if something can be done. In the meantime, let's work out something so you two will eat your lunch.

The students hurried to class. Mr. Johnson was left in his portable classroom watching his fifth period students come into class. His face was serious. Mr. Johnson was extremely troubled after talking with Cindy and Araceli.

Because Mr. Johnson was the head of the English department of the high school, he felt it was best to raise the issue first with teachers on his team. He wondered if other teachers were aware of this problem.

When he shared the lunch line issue with members of his team, he found that few teachers knew that this was happening. They looked at Mr. Johnson with blank stares.

Mrs. Wong said, "I didn't know this was happening to students. Why wasn't something done right away?"

Mr. Rodriguez agreed. "I don't think most teachers know about it."

After some discussion, they asked a small group of teachers and students led by Mr. Johnson to see the principal. A coalition of teachers and students working together became an empowered group. This coalition not only helped teachers become more sensitive to the needs of their students, but it taught students how to develop their own voice and become active in social change.

The principal was aware of the problem and knew that some students were not eating their lunch. He said, "We just don't know what to do. This has been a continual problem over the years. In the beginning we had few students who qualified for the reduced or free lunch, but now there are many more. So to accommodate them, we put in two lines only for free and reduced lunch students. It is a cafeteria management issue." After some discussion, the principal agreed to bring up the issue at the monthly school faculty meeting. Few teachers knew of the practice.

Mr. Johnson became very frustrated. He felt that the school had numerous oppressive practices and this was one of them. The issue of social class had become an important one because the high school, although located in an upper-middle-class neighborhood, also bordered a lower-income community. This practice showed that the school was insensitive to class issues.

Apparently, having separate lunch lines was a district practice because the cafeteria division had mandated this practice. After numerous meetings with district administrators, high school administrators, and teachers, the small group of faculty and students led by Mr. Johnson finally convinced district administrators to provide students with individual lunch numbers. Students told clerks their number when paying for lunches. Although this was not a perfect solution, it did eliminate separate lines for free/reduced lunch participants and other students. For the school of 2,000 high school students, this was a major change.

Schools are extremely hierarchical systems. Cindy and Araceli learned to take a stand about an issue that was important to them. The students realized that their high school was not as democratic as they had thought, and they had to challenge the school structure. The food issue became an opportunity to put into practice the citizenship skills the students were learning in history. It reminded teachers and students that together they were more powerful to make changes than they were working separately or ignoring problems.

The next comic explains that everyone wants to be treated with respect. In the lunchroom issue, some students felt that they had been forgotten. They were upset about missing lunch, but the students were most upset about not being treated with dignity.

High school students may have adult-size bodies, but like many younger students, they continue to need nurturing, care, and guidance. Lack of food and understanding impacted the learning of some of the students at this high school. The lunch line was much more than just one issue; it was symptomatic of the isolation and frustration some students felt because of class differences. Because the school did not address class issues, some students did not have a sense of belonging to the school community.

Personal Reflection of Values and Beliefs

The second area for reflection is values and beliefs. This book is primarily aimed at personal change. All of us must examine our views, beliefs, and values about race, ethnicity, class, gender, religion, sexual orientation, neighborhood, physical appearance, and many other social aspects of life. Most of us operate from a complex belief system. Many of our values are not clearly understood until we are challenged to look at them or until we have taken the time to clarify them. One's behavior often indicates one's values and others may comment on what they see in us. Although we might not agree with what others see in us, we can begin to examine our behaviors and values with the goal of becoming more effective and caring teachers.

As the lunchroom example demonstrated, we must also examine how schools as institutions, through their practices and policies, teach and support certain values. For example, the issue of the lunch line indicated that the management needs of the district cafeteria personnel at that high school were more important than the feelings of the students. The students knew this. The school was part of a large bureaucratic system and making changes in that system was difficult. However, as teachers responsible for the education of every student, we must work tirelessly to make those institutional and personal changes.

We are part of a community. We do not have all the answers and never will, but if we work with students and parents, we will be able to accomplish more together. For example, teachers have found that they may ask male students more often than

© *Lynn Johnston Productions, Inc. Distributed by United Feature Syndicate, Inc.*

female students to take on leadership positions. Reflect on your unconscious and conscious beliefs. Reading pieces by educators such as Herbert Kohl has challenged me to reflect on my own personal behaviors and how my actions may reinforce institutional values that are clearly wrong. In his book *Basic Skills,* Kohl (1982) gave an eye-opening story about Christine, a bright high school student who was labeled as handicapped by her teacher in fourth grade. One day, $5 was stolen from a student in her class. The teacher demanded to search every student's desk or pocketbook. Christine resisted, saying that if the teacher searched her purse, she would search the teacher's. Christine knew she did not have $5 and that it was more likely that the teacher had $5. Christine said that whoever had the money would be the thief. She was sent to the psychologist and reassigned to a special education class. Not only was the labeling of Christine as handicapped disturbing, but the teacher's actions toward her were unloving and undemocratic (Kohl 1982). Searching every student's desk and purse was not a way to build a sense of trust or community. However, Kohl believes that both students and teachers suffer from school systems that are demoralizing and depressing. Christine showed that she believed in herself by taking a stand, and later in her schooling she became president of her high school.

Meaningful Content Knowledge

Lee Shulman, a former professor at Stanford University, has specifically focused on the importance of the teacher's knowledge. This can be knowledge of teaching methods, but also knowledge of core subject areas. For example, in Chapter 8, I presented biological and evolutionary information about race to assist readers who have little background on that issue. Teachers need a strong liberal arts, math, science, and technological background. In many universities, elementary teachers earn a degree in liberal studies in order to develop a strong, comprehensive content background. Some teachers also seek historical and cultural knowledge, because the United States is a nation of many peoples and educators must be able to present knowledge of our diverse communities.

Teachers must have a comprehensive understanding of U.S. history and the contributions of both majority and underrepresented communities. For example, teachers must have knowledge not only of the original 13 colonies and their beginnings, but also of Native American nations that aided the colonists and were the original inhabitants of the area. I was going to use the term *settlers,* but this would not be accurate because many Native American peoples believe they are ancestors of the earth and arose from the land. Few Native Americans see themselves as settlers, which has a connotation of people moving into an area and making changes. Many Native peoples came from and lived in balance with their natural environments.

The following story shows how a high school U.S. history teacher took a dry passage in the student history book and made it more meaningful. She was covering the Articles of Confederation in her class discussions. Most students had little knowledge that the Articles of Confederation were the first Constitution of the United States (Bailey and Kennedy 1994). The teacher told the students that they were connected to the 1780s. That didn't seem possible to the high school students. What would they have in common with "those old folks" who had white hair and died many years ago? She explained that one of the first laws that the new Congress of the Confederation passed was the Land Ordinance of 1785 (Bailey and Kennedy 1994, 167). The students were still skeptical.

The teacher said, "How do you think schools are paid for? Do you pay for your education?"

One student answered, "We pay taxes. And the school gets its money from our taxes."

"Yes," said the teacher, her eyes smiling. She still had a historical secret to share with them.

"But in those days remember the second Continental Congress did not have the power to collect taxes from states. What could they do to support public education?"

"Students would have to pay for their own education," said a young woman in the middle of the second row.

"Then it would be a private school and not a public school," interjected a young man with a diamond earring in his left ear.

The teacher said, "Let me ask again, Who would pay for your education? It costs lots of money to build a school and to pay teachers. What should be done?"

She paused and then continued, "To ensure that public education would really take hold in new areas of the Union, the Congress passed the Land Ordinance of 1785. In this law, every 16th section of each township sold in the Old Northwest would go to fund schools. A township was a piece of land six miles by six miles. It was divided into 36 pieces of land and sold. Money from the other 35 parcels of land would be used to pay the large debt from the Revolutionary War. Over 200 years ago, the founders of our nation believed in education and they set aside the funds for schools." "The second Continental Congress made a critical decision for you! They believed in you and education."

Some of the students smiled, while others just looked surprised. The teacher was wise enough to engage them in thinking about their own schooling and history. She used a bridge from their lives to their textbook in order for students to make history more meaningful. She knew the information and how to effectively convey it to students.

Meaningful Practice

Most children like to learn, but sometimes they may not seem too interested in school. This attitude may come about when students do not believe the teacher is interested in them or if they do not understand the purpose of the activity. Students may also rebel or act bored when they see little purpose to the information they are learning. Oftentimes teachers methodically write the daily learning objectives on the board, but these can become muddled by lack of connection to the real world of children. Caring teachers are extremely sensitive to being relevant. Meaningful practice encourages teachers to find ways to connect content with what students know and how it will impact their lives.

Lisa Delpit (1995) gives the example of how Martha Demientieff, a Native Alaskan teacher of Athabaskan students, gives a meaningful context to her writing assignments. She explains that there is a difference between writing in "Our

Heritage Language" of her students and writing in "Standard English." She carefully describes the nuances and ways English is used in their heritage, more informal, language. The teacher explains to them that it is almost like being at a picnic enjoying oneself. Then she takes the same message written in formal English and compares the two styles. She explains to students that academic writing is like eating at a formal dinner. Demientieff has her students dress up in formal attire and set tables with tablecloths, china, and silverware. In this way the students understand that academic writing uses formal English. At this meal the students speak formally. The students follow the meal with writing that is academic. The students are involved in a series of writing activities that provide important contexts for writing. Demientieff teaches standard linguistic forms within powerful cultural contexts (Delpit 1995). She also exemplifies the use of **pedagogical content knowledge** (Shulman 1987). This approach links subject area content with pedagogy, teaching methods.

Now let's take the issue of the lunch line that was discussed in the previous section and develop meaningful practice like Martha Demientieff did. Teachers could have asked their students to write letters to the principal of the high school and superintendent of the district expressing their views. By doing this, students would not only learn how to write business letters, but they would also practice using their formal English skills and sharpen their skills of writing a strong persuasive argument.

Both examples demonstrate the power of meaningful practice.

Purposeful Accountability

Teachers must continue to look at their effectiveness. Standards can help us focus on and identify important knowledge and skills that we need to teach. They represent a general core curriculum and often do not address local and personal knowledge that students may have. Standards are primarily knowledge and skills that educators believe students need in order to participate in the general society.

If we want to close the achievement gap between underrepresented children and majority students, we must be able to assess accurately the competence of our students. I think standards are important; however, I feel that much of the movement toward them represents what students will need from a majority view of knowledge. Teachers must also understand that standards can be used to culturally assimilate our students without their making that choice. Teachers must find a balance between accountability as measured by standardized tests and support of the cultural identity and background that students bring to school. Much of what we teach is Western in orientation, so we as teachers must understand how schools can be tools of assimilation.

Don't misunderstand me. I do believe that all students need to learn how to use the computer, read, write, and compute. They need a basic body of knowledge in order to survive in society. However, I also believe that students need skills to seek multiple perspectives on an issue, respect and listen to other people's views, and place themselves in the "shoes" of someone else to gain a more comprehensive understanding of the world. Teachers face the challenge of having a balanced classroom that respects the culture of students while they also learn the skills and knowledge of the general society. Much of what we teach, how we teach, and what we reinforce is rooted in the majority culture. Yes, students will need to know what is expected of them in order to succeed in society, but it is possible to weave into the curriculum the cultural aspects of students. As the work of Luis Moll has shown, it is possible to teach the writing and communication skills that students need by using the cultural and personal experiences of youth as the vehicle for learning.

In addition, I would like to share a caution about scripted teachers' guides. Today much of the curriculum is carefully prescribed and sometimes the teacher has few opportunities to bring local or cultural knowledge into a lesson. However, good teachers are continually bringing in examples from the lives of their students. They are careful observers of their children and they utilize the living knowledge of youth in their curriculum. Tharp and Gallimore's work (1988) reminds us that if the lesson is so scripted by a teacher's guide, when children bring up new ways of thinking about the topic being covered, the teacher may not feel she or he can respond to the child's comments or build on them because they are not part of the lesson presented in the guide. Relying on a teacher's guide limits the teacher's ability to be responsive and—in the context of this book—culturally responsive to the students.

Many of us know that standardized and mandated testing will not fix our schools. The Spring 1999 issue of the journal *Rethinking Schools* is devoted to testing. In the issue, Bob Peterson and Monty Neill (1999) carefully suggest alternatives to standardized testing. These alternatives move away from the belief that one correct answer is what schooling is about. Instead, they suggest using student portfolios, cautiously implementing multiple performance exams, exhibiting more student work, organizing parent-teacher conferences, and employing trained school quality review teams. A combination of these strategies is probably the most effective.

Teachers must be accountable, and to do this they must develop means of assessing the learning of their students. The following section describes some aspects of authentic assessment.

Authentic Assessment   Linda Darling-Hammond, Jacqueline Ancess, and Beverly Falk (1995) studied schools that used "authentic" assessment. What do they mean by authentic? In this type of assessment students are engaged in real-life activities (Darling-Hammond, Ancess, and Falk 1995). They pointed out that assessment is a process that does not end with a product such as a student exhibition. Rather those products are catalysts for further reflection and discussion among teachers, students, and parents. They write,

> It is the action around assessment—the discussions, meetings, revisions, arguments, and opportunities to continually create new directions for teaching, learning, curriculum, and assessment—that ultimately have consequence. The "things" of assessment are essentially useful as dynamic supports for reflection and action, rather than as static products with value in and of themselves (Darling-Hammond, Ancess, and Falk 1995, 18).

The purpose of assessment is for students and teachers to collaboratively work with each other to learn and build critical thinking skills. Thus, students have the opportunity to engage in real-life and meaningful activities that also affirm cultural diversity.

Excellent teachers have always given substantial and meaningful feedback to their students, and they have a finger on the pulse of the classroom. They know which students are doing well and which students are having difficulty. They know when it is appropriate to intercede and make suggestions to students or when it is best to encourage them to struggle with the material with limited guidance in order to teach important problem-solving and decision-making skills.

Teachers often keep journals or logs of their own impressions, shortcomings, successes, and funny stories that happen in class. These journals are valuable tools for self-reflection and collaborative discussions.

Meaningful teaching focuses the classroom on the lives of students. Students share wise perceptions. Write them down in your journal and think about them later if you don't have time to respond to students immediately. Many times young people are insightful and can provide important reasons why an activity or assignment is not successful.

Meaningful teaching must be supported by a framework that emphasizes community, culture, and social justice.

A caring teacher provides meaningful teaching

Important Principles for Educators

A group of scholars* led by James A. Banks worked for more than four years and identified 12 essential principles of education. These principles integrate the values of equity and excellence in schooling. They are divided into five areas: teacher learning; student learning; intergroup relations; school governance, organization, and equity; and assessment. This list comes from the document they wrote called ***Diversity Within Unity*** (2001, 3). Many of these principles overlap with those in Caring-Centered Multicultural Education.

Teacher Learning

Principle 1: Professional development programs should help teachers understand the complex characteristics of ethnic groups within the U.S. society and the ways in which race, ethnicity, language, and social class interact to influence student behavior.

Student Learning

Principle 2: Schools should ensure that all students have equitable opportunities to learn and to meet high standards.

Principle 3: The curriculum should help students understand that knowledge is socially constructed and reflects researchers' personal experiences as well as the social, political, and economic contexts in which they live and work.

Principle 4: Schools should provide all students with opportunities to participate in extra- and cocurricular activities that develop knowledge, skills, and attitudes that increase academic achievement and foster positive interracial relationships.

Intergroup Relations

Principle 5: Schools should create or make salient superordinate cross-cutting group memberships in order to improve intergroup relations.

Principle 6: Students should learn about stereotyping and other related biases that have negative effects on racial and ethnic relations.

Principle 7: Students should learn about the values shared by virtually all cultural groups (e.g., justice, equality, freedom, peace, compassion, and charity).

Principle 8: Teachers should help students acquire the social skills needed to interact effectively with students from other racial, ethnic, cultural, and language groups.

Principle 9: Schools should provide opportunities for students from different racial, ethnic cultural, and language groups to interact socially under conditions designed to reduce fear and anxiety.

---

*It is important to list all the authors of the document *Diversity Within Unity*. They are as follows: James A. Banks, Peter Cookson, Geneva Gay, Willis D. Hawley, Jacqueline Jordan Irvine, Sonia Nieto, Janet Ward Schofield, and Walter G. Stephan.

School Governance, Organization, and Equity

Principle 10: A school's organizational strategies should ensure that decision making is widely shared and that members of the school community learn collaborative skills and dispositions in order to create a caring environment for students.

Principle 11: Leaders should develop strategies that ensure that all public schools, regardless of their locations, are funded equitably.

Assessment

Principle 12: Teachers should use multiple culturally sensitive techniques to assess complex cognitive and social skills.

This monograph is aimed at providing professional development for teachers in a world that is multicultural and multilingual. Teacher growth and reflection are key aspects of providing effective schooling for all students. In addition, the teacher can guide students in critical analysis and reflection of issues dealing with many kinds of social oppression. The document *Diversity Within Unity* also presents an extensive checklist for schools to use to evaluate the status of their schools. For example:

> 3.0 Does the curriculum in your school help students to understand that knowledge is socially constructed and reflects the personal experiences and the social, political, and economic contexts in which they live and work? (Banks et al. 2001, 15).

> 3.2 Does the curriculum help students understand the ways in which the unique experiences of peoples or groups cause them to view the same historical and social events differently? (Banks et al. 2001, 15).

These are important questions that every educator should reflect on and consider in his or her own teaching. Your answers to these queries may provide directions for change in your school. It is vital to review all aspects of the school because equity must be a theme that can be found throughout the institution in order for equal educational opportunities to exist for all students. *Diversity Within Unity* is primarily a document that can be used to set policy. Another important aspect of schooling is the perception of students. How do they feel about the messages they receive about their ability to go to college or the importance of diverse perspectives? The next section describes research undertaken by faculty of The Civil Rights Project at Harvard University in which students were asked about the insights they received in school about issues of equity.

 *Connection*

Diversity Within Unity: Essential Principles for Teaching and Learning is an excellent piece. Every teacher and administrator should read it. Visit Chapter 12 of the book website (**www.mhhe.com/pang2e**) to link to this important document.

How Do High School Students Feel about Issues of Diversity and Equity?

A critical element of schools is the students. Although students are not always asked about their feelings concerning various issues, faculty from The Civil Rights Project at Harvard University partnered with members of the National School Boards Association's Council to create the Diversity Assessment Questionnaire (DAQ) (Kurlaender and Hun 2000). The questionnaire, made up of 70 items, can be administered in the classroom. The survey is designed to examine four areas: student learning and peer interaction, citizenship and democratic principles, future educational aspirations and goals, and perceptions of support by the school. Surveying the students is a valuable reality check for teachers, administrators, and parents. This is another way to ensure that the views of students are being heard and used to create an effective learning environment.

One of the major issues examined dealt with the impact of school-level desegregation. The first study was conducted in Louisville, Kentucky (Kurlaender and Hun 2000). When schools in Jefferson County (metropolitan Louisville) were ordered by the court to desegregate in 1975, initially, there was great opposition to desegregation. Although the court did not make it mandatory after 1980, the school board continued to desegregate. DAQ was given out to a total of 1,164 10th, 11th, and 12th graders in 2000. For the purpose of statistical analysis, students were placed into three groups: 26.13 percent African American, 62.36 percent White, and 11.51 percent Other (this category included students who identified themselves as Latino/Hispanic, Native American, Asian, and other). Would the experiences of students show positive or negative gains in attitudes about diversity?

Question 19 focused on peer interactions. Here is how the item was phrased: How comfortable are you working with students from different racial and ethnic backgrounds in group projects? The percentage of White students who indicated *very comfortable* was 61.8 percent, and if you add 30.8 percent White youth who responded with *comfortable,* then a total of 92.6 percent indicated being comfortable working with diverse students. Similarly, 61.3 percent of African Americans were *very comfortable* and *35.3* percent were comfortable, for a total of 96.6 percent. These extremely positive responses indicate the success of desegregation in Louisville.

It is also important that the issues of equity and diversity are included in the curriculum. Therefore, researchers looked at how often students believed that experiences of various cultures were included in English and social studies classes. Students were asked to choose one of four possible responses (frequently, sometimes, rarely, never). In English classes, only 19.2 percent of African American and 19.5 percent of White students reported that teachers frequently presented experiences of different cultures. However, 45 percent of the African American sample and 46.5 percent of the White students reported that their social studies classes included information about various racial and ethnic groups.

More positive results were found in Cambridge, Massachusetts (The Civil Rights Project 2002). A total of 379 high school seniors were surveyed using the same DAQ questionnaire in 2001. Of these students 18 percent were African American, 4 percent were Asian, 10 percent were Latino, 30 percent were White, 14 percent were "other", and 14 percent were not identified. This was a more diverse population than the sample in Louisville. Researchers were unsure how students would respond to the questionnaire because they resided near Boston where there had been serious race resistance to desegregation. However, the Cambridge sample demonstrated extremely positive responses to the question about how comfortable they were working with students from diverse racial and ethnic backgrounds. All the groups indicated that at least 90 percent reported being *comfortable* and *very comfortable* with folks from different cultural groups (African American—90 percent; Asian—94 percent; Latino—92 percent; White—99 percent; Other—96 percent; Multiracial—95 percent).

The study also found many more students who indicated that in their social studies or history classes racial issues were discussed frequently (70 percent of African Americans, 80 percent of Latinos, and 87 percent of the White sample). Although the question was not exactly the same as the one posed to the Louisville students, their responses do indicate that issues of diversity and culture are being integrated into these subject areas.

The DAQ can be used by students, parents, or educators to better understand the impact of desegregation on student attitudes and beliefs. Here is a sample of several of the questions:

> During classroom discussions in your social studies or history class, how often are racial issues discussed and explored?
>
> To what extent do you believe that these discussions have changed your understanding of different points of view?
>
> How do you believe your school experiences will affect your ability to work with members of other races and ethnic groups? (The Civil Rights Project 2002, 3, 4, 7).

The studies conducted by The Civil Rights Project using the DAQ demonstrated that school-level desegregation can design contexts in which students from many cultural groups can benefit from working with diverse people. The experiences provide students with opportunities to hear various perspectives and in so doing to gather a more comprehensive understanding of complex social issues.

Six Fundamental Components for Implementation

This book has focused on presenting six components of Caring-Centered Multicultural Education. As part of the process of growth, teachers should consider each one carefully. They represent four intimately tied areas of schooling: philosophical orientation, professional development, curriculum and instruction, and school policies and structure. Because professional development and philosophy are keys to teacher belief and practice, much discussion has centered on the framework. This framework arises from care theory, education for democracy-progressive education, and the sociocultural context of learning. Culture is also an integral aspect of learning, and this book emphasizes culturally relevant teaching. However, the inclusion of critical

Students sharing diverse perspectives

professional development and subsequent curriculum changes will not occur if we do not look at our school policies and structure. The philosophical orientation for a caring, socially just, and collaborative community must be incorporated in the way our school system is designed and policies are set. The six components are as follows:

1. Understand how caring can be implemented into schools.
2. Review and eliminate prejudice and discrimination.
3. Understand the impact of culture on teaching and learning.
4. Utilize culturally relevant teaching.
5. Blend and integrate caring and social justice into the curriculum, instruction, policies, and practices of schools.
6. Design and implement classroom and school change.

These six fundamental components are parts of a large whole; they fit together like a puzzle. When one segment is missing, the puzzle is not complete. First, it is critical for educators to hold a moral commitment to care and to create trusting relationships with their students. This dimension is foundational. Then, building on care theory, teachers must actively work to eliminate prejudice and discrimination. Oppressive attitudes and actions undermine the building of a compassionate and just community. The third and fourth components emphasize the impact of cultures and

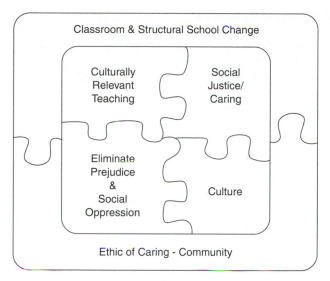

Figure 12.1 *Components of Caring-Centered Multicultural Education*

the cultural context on the learning process. It is imperative that teachers know how to design and implement culturally relevant teaching. The fifth element focuses on the blending and integration of caring and social justice. Both must be present in order to foster relationships that are compassionate and just. These five components integrate caring, social justice, and culture into teaching. Finally, the sixth element centers around the importance of implementing structural changes in schools so that they become centers of care that affirm culture, and they become communities where social justice and democratic practices are found throughout the curriculum, school practices, and policies. Figure 12.1 provides a visual of the integration of the six components of Caring-Centered Multicultural Education.

The process of change takes time, and Table 12.2 summarizes the areas in the framework. What beliefs would you add to those listed? Write them in your journal as you read through the table.

The following reviews the six components.

Component One: Implementing Caring into Schools

Like the basis for this book, the ethic of caring is an important foundation for teachers to use in shaping and building their classroom. Caring is more than hugs and caring is not enabling. Rather, caring involves developing trusting reciprocal relationships that assist students in becoming self-empowered and directed learners. In addition, caring means addressing the individual needs of students while simultaneously keeping your fingers on the pulse of the entire classroom family. As the teacher, you work with students and parents to create a compassionate and collaborative learning family. This support network encourages learning and also a sense of personal and group efficacy (Kohl 1982).

TABLE 12.2 Caring-Centered Multicultural Education

Six Components for Implementation

	Component 1: Understand the Ethic of Caring	Component 2: Review and Eliminate Prejudice and Discrimination, Individual and Institutional	Component 3: Understand the Impact of Cultures	Component 4: Utilize Culturally Relevant Teaching	Component 5: Blend and Integrate Caring and Social Justice into Teaching and the School Culture	Component 6: Design and Implement Classroom and Structural School Change
Selected Beliefs	The goal of schooling is a happy, ful-filled person who is a criti-cal thinker and works to make society a caring and socially just community.	Prejudice and discrimination work against the building of a caring and just society.	Children are complex beings who live, think, learn, speak, write, share, and identify with a complex combination of linguistic and cultural communities.	Students become independent learners by actively engaging in hands-on, meaningful, and cooperative learning that is relevant to their lives. Teachers build on what students know, what they are interested in, and what they can do.	Caring forms the foundation for a just society; caring and social justice are intimately connected.	Teachers examine practices and policies using the lenses of caring, social justice, democracy, and culture.
	An ethical commitment to care serves as the founda-tion for teach-ing and trusting rela-tionships.	Educators, students, and parents examine all aspects of schooling for biases that act as barriers to equal educational access and success.	Learning is shaped by sociocultural interactions and contexts. Children are	Teachers are cultural mediators who believe in a holistic orientation in which cognitive development is linked to social, emotional, and ethical development.	Caring teachers work in collaboration with students and parents to create the most effective, meaningful, and successful educational environment.	Students join their teachers in designing and implementing mechanisms and practices for democratic and caring classrooms and schools.

TABLE 12.2 Caring-Centered Multicultural Education (Continued)

Six Components for Implementation

Caring relationships are built on trust, respect, and reciprocal responsibility.	The United States and most other countries are color-class-gender-conscious and not color-class-gender-blind societies.	Children are taught about caring within a cultural context, which varies from group to group and also differs because of family interpretations.	Teachers believe learning occurs within and through social interactions and within the individual student.	Students, parents, and teachers develop a caring theme/curriculum within the context of a democratic, culturally diverse, and just society to be integrated throughout all subject areas.	Students and teachers develop caring projects that may result in programs like peacemakers, peer mediators, or peer tutors.
Learning should be a life-giving process of joy and self-fulfillment.	There are various types of prejudice: personal, institutional, cultural, and social. All must be addressed and eliminated.	Teachers prepare students to function in the general society and cultural communities while affirming their bicultural/multicultural and linguistic identities.	Educators teach the basic skills and critical thinking skills that will enable children to address and solve social issues; students become contributing and responsible people.	Students create avenues in which they can raise and discuss issues in a compassionate forum; students will take actions to address these issues.	Community members and parents participate in caring school projects such as career day (taking students to work), reading to students, tutoring, and other activities.

Strong and trusting relationships form the elements for personal growth, development, and change. James S. House, a professor of sociology at the University of Michigan, talked about his research and why he feels trusting and supportive relationships are so important in people's lives.

> There is a sense, whether you take it from religion or psychology, that people have a need for meaning, coherence, understanding of the world. People need a sense that their life, their existence, has some purpose . . . that sense of meaning and purpose is defined . . . most strongly, by the relationships they have with other people—with spouses; with other family, parents, children; with friends, with people they associate with at work or in voluntary organizations (Ornish 1998, 240).

When the lives of young people are integrated with school, the environment can be a place of meaning, respect, and trust. Unfortunately, school also can be a place of isolation where learning is abstract and not related to life (Kohl 1982; Goodman and Goodman 1990). A caring-centered teacher understands the importance of developing a community in which students feel a sense of belonging and acceptance. Within this context, the teacher sees education as being alive. She inspires students. Students learn not only basic skills such as reading, writing, math, and technology; they also learn critical thinking skills, value clarification strategies, and collaboration. The classroom becomes a place of intellectual stimulation and challenges where students are taught how to wrestle with social issues such as responsibilities versus rights of citizenship, individualism versus community, minority versus majority needs, and protection of civil rights through the integrated lens of caring, compassion, and justice. Focusing on the whole person is important, but with Caring-Centered Multicultural Education also comes a holistic view of growth (Moll 1990) that includes not only cognitive gain but also social, emotional, and ethical development.

Component Two: Review and Eliminate Prejudice and Discrimination

Prejudice and discrimination hurt. They hurt both the victim and perpetrator because they create a wall between people that makes it difficult to create trusting relationships and to work toward building strong communities in which the education of individuals and the whole group are addressed. In addition, prejudice and discrimination can result in poor policies and ineffective practices. For example we all lose when thousands of students drop out of school. We lose their potential and abilities.

This book addresses what individual, district, and building-level educators can do to make their schools more meaningful and therefore more academically successful. However, we as a collective, a society, contribute to an almost impossible situation in our schools by ignoring issues of unemployment, housing, and living

Take a Stand

ESSENTIAL PRINCIPLES OF EDUCATION

James Banks and a team of prestigious educators believed that one of the most vital responsibilities of teachers is to integrate the values of equity and excellence throughout schools. In their work they identified 12 essential principles of education. These principles focused on teacher learning, student learning, intergroup relations, school governance, and assessment. The principles are listed on pages 424–425. Here are several possible questions that teachers should consider:

- How would you rank the 12 principles? Why? What criteria would you use to rank them? Are there other principles that you would add?
- Another way to look at the document that Banks and his colleagues developed is to answer the following:
- Which five of the 12 essential principles identified by James Banks and his team are the most important and why?

Students building trusting relationships

conditions. The largest 10 districts in the United States are made up of students from underrepresented groups. These students may be from low-income families or members of African American, Asian Pacific American, or Latino communities. Jean Anyon's book *Ghetto Schooling* clearly demonstrates that unless underlying issues of racial isolation and poverty are effectively addressed, restructuring schools or bringing in new teaching methods will have minimal impact (Anyon 1997). The members of inner-city families must have improvements in their living conditions and access to educational and political opportunities; otherwise, the anger and frustrations of their day-to-day struggles will limit what teachers can do. Anyon believes that our personal biases have impacted our willingness to act.

People do not understand their connection to others in the community. For example, she cites the continual cutting of taxes for schools and points to the cost of society's inability to keep high school students in school; every year we are losing $50 billion in lifetime earnings from dropouts (Anyon 1997, 182). Her work is echoed by Pedro Noguera's research (2003) described in *City Schools and the American Dream.*

As members of a caring community, it is critical that all of us—students, teachers, administrators, parents, and community people—examine ourselves and our institutions for bias. This is a difficult process, but it must be accomplished in order to address the inequities that can be found in schools. For example, "Why do schools in the same state have chemistry labs where specialized experiments can be conducted, while schools five minutes away have no lab at all?" Jonathan Kozol (1991) not only asked questions like these, but courageously found answers to them. Kozol discovered that schools in Camden, a depressed city of New Jersey where most of the students were Latino and Black, had only about $4,000 a year to spend on each pupil, while the neighboring high-income community of Princeton spent over $8,000 per student. Kozol often found that the poorest schools represented segregated situations. Unfortunately, through his national study of schools, Kozol discovered that many students from underrepresented groups did not have the same opportunities to learn as others. The schools often lacked safe and comfortable physical spaces, complete copies of textbooks, adequate science equipment, working computers, and well-paid teachers.

Discrimination is often unconscious, but whether conscious or unconscious, it hurts all parties. In some states there have been attempts to fund schools equally. Thus, schools built in higher-income neighborhoods do not benefit from higher property taxes of the area in comparison to schools built in lower-income areas. The result is that students who attend schools in inner cities will have the same resources as those who live in more prestigious areas. However, there are other ways that schools can raise money. For example, parent and booster clubs can raise large sums of money that pay for various services such as teacher assistants, technology instruction, physical education programs, and other programs (Smith 1999). Therefore, schools in wealthier neighborhoods can provide benefits that schools in low-income communities cannot (Smith 1999). Students can benefit from this increase of money into a school, but the issue of equality of funding and services arises.

The *Los Angeles Times* conducted an analysis of almost $7 million that was donated to the Los Angeles Unified School District. The district had a $200 per student maximum rule that schools can raise to supplement their budget. However, the analysis demonstrated that some schools raised more money than was allowed. These schools were found in more affluent areas of the district (Smith 1999). The district also had rules regarding how the funds could be spent. Additional funding could be used to support teaching aides, but not to fund a teacher. Schools have resorted to raising money because California ranks as one of the lowest of all 50 states in per pupil funding. This has led to problems such as large classes, lack of physical education instruction, and inadequate personnel needed for attendance tracking.

The issue of raising outside money for schools does not directly deal with prejudice, but it does raise the concern of equality of programs and discrimination that can occur because of the disparity among schools. The *Los Angeles Times* reports that many donations are not recorded, so the difference in school funding cannot be fully known (Smith 1999). Table 12.3 is part of a chart from the *Los Angeles Times* that indicates how the funding varies among schools. Twenty-six schools recorded funds of more than $100 per student and 22 were from more affluent neighborhoods in the west side of Los Angeles or the San Fernando Valley (Smith 1999, A17).

Discrimination can occur on many different levels. We must be aware of the ways our institutions can reinforce or support social oppression so that we can work to prevent it. Schools, in their need to provide effective education to students, can integrate practices that are unequal. When a school can raise more than $200 per student, it can provide additional services that poorer schools will not be able to offer. Most people think about outward signs of prejudice like name-calling, but more complicated issues such as this one also impact our students and our ability to provide equal educational opportunities to all.

We must also look at our personal biases. Teachers and students may treat each other in ways that are hurtful and discriminatory. Teachers can use a variety of strategies that will increase the students' awareness and skills in dealing with prejudice and discrimination. The following strategies can assist teachers in addressing this issue:

1. Students establish clear expectations for classroom behavior and discuss the values of community, respect, dignity, and honor.
2. Teachers can provide positive antiracist role models from various ethnic groups.
3. Students are encouraged to review and clarify their values and behaviors.
4. Students reflect on their own actions and how they impact others.
5. Students are encouraged to place themselves in the shoes of another.

In order to address the pervasive nature of social oppression, students must examine not only their own personal biases, but also the injustices found in our institutions and organizations.

Component Three: Understand the Impact of Culture on Teaching and Learning

Culture is a critical aspect of how children and adults identify themselves, interpret the world, and what they value. Culture is also an asset that teachers can build on. For many teachers, culture is hard to identify because they are born into a family culture and it surrounds them. Like the air we breathe, culture is there but almost invisible because it is so ingrained in the way we think and act. Culture is a natural aspect of one's life.

TABLE 12.3 Uneven Distribution

Private Contributions to Schools

School	Community	Budget	Per Student
Van Nuys Medical Magnet	Van Nuys	$ 56,855	$244
Westwood Elementary	Westwood	$163,443	$235
Coeur d'Alene Elementary	Venice	$ 59,598	$222
Pacific Palisades Elementary	Pacific Palisades	$100,007	$215
Serrania Elementary	Woodland Hills	$120,750	$194
Community School	Pico-Robertson	$ 63,991	$178
Wonderland Elementary	Hollywood Hills	$ 42,451	$175
Wilmington Park Elementary	Wilmington	$198,343	$172
Canyon Elementary	Pacific Palisades	$ 54,790	$170
Grant Communication Science Magnet	Van Nuys	$ 59,000	$156
Multnomah Environmental Science Magnet	Los Angeles	$ 18,359	$150

Adapted from Lynn Meersman's chart in Doug Smith's article, "Funding and Fairness Clash in Public Schools," *Los Angeles Times* (February 16, 1999), A17.

- What are the connections between caring and social justice? What does caring mean in a democracy?
- How can caring, social justice, democracy, and cultural relevancy be integrated into the curriculum and instruction?
- How can caring enhance our understanding of justice? How are caring and social action integrally linked?
- How does student maturation impact their understanding of caring and social justice?
- What are the issues of caring and social justice that children are concerned about in their own lives?
- How can those issues be addressed in the school curriculum?
- What knowledge and skills will students need in order to become more caring change agents?
- What projects can be instituted in the classroom where children actively work toward making society a more just and democratic community?
- What impact does culture have on the learning process?
- How does culture shape the values, beliefs, expectations, and actions of a person?
- What is culturally relevant teaching and how does it relate to content and strategies?
- Why is culturally relevant teaching important?
- How does a culturally relevant educator think and act differently from other teachers?
- How can I integrate culturally relevant teaching into my classroom?
- What role can students have in creating a culturally relevant and academically successful classroom?
- What is culture? How do I define culture?
- What impact does culture have in my life, in my students' lives, and in other people's lives?
- Why is culture important in how people live, learn, and identify themselves?

Asa Hilliard is an educator who has given great insight into how culture impacts learning. He has contributed much to my understanding. In one of my favorite excerpts from Hilliard's writings, he identifies major teacher competencies and attitudes that he believes are essential for an effective teacher of diverse students. Think about his insights and how they may impact your teaching.

- "Teaching is always a cross-cultural encounter" (Hilliard 1974, 44). Each student brings to the classroom a different cultural context, and the teacher also brings her own cultural dynamics.

- "The personality, values, and social background of the teacher are critical cultural inputs" (Hilliard 1974, 45). You are a cultural being and your very personal ways have a profound impact on students.

- "All teaching is culture bound" (Hilliard 1974, 44). Everything we do, everything we say, everything we present—these are all aspects of our personal culture. When children do not see themselves represented in schools, they do not feel valued or honored.

- "The classroom is not a benign context but a potent matrix" (Hilliard 1974, 44). The teacher affirms or rejects students in the way she or he labels, rewards, controls time and space, selects, presents, requests, and in an infinite number of actions that occur in class.

One of the ways that we can develop intercultural sensitivity is to understand the views of others. When teachers have difficulty understanding different cultural orientations, I encourage them to watch a movie that is told from another cultural perspective. For example, I suggest viewing one of the following movies that show people in the United States and other countries. I also suggest while they watch a movie they should be careful not to stereotype people from other cultures. Sometimes a character may be a unique individual and not someone who represents many others from the community.

Shall We Dance?—This film from Japan shows the Japanese nonverbal communication styles of several protagonists. In addition, it presents some values dealing with female-male relationships, work ethic, and family roles. Although much is missing in the subtitles, see it with someone who speaks Japanese and ask for a fuller explanation of the characters and values they represent.

Smoke Signals—This is a film about two young men from the Coeur d'Alene community in Idaho. The two men exemplify the differences and similarities of Native Americans from this part of the Northwest. One character represents the views of the warrior while the other protagonist seems to signify the storyteller. The cultural conflict between the majority and the Coeur d'Alene community values is easily seen in this movie. The humor is delightful.

Mi Familia—This film provides insights into a Mexican American family that deals with the problems of life. The movie displays the warmth of the characters and the struggles they work through, not only as family members, but as members of an underrepresented group that must deal continually with cultural assimilation. It shows a rich tapestry of family life.

Malcolm X—This film is based on the autobiography of Malcolm Little and was produced and directed by Spike Lee. It presents to the viewer the type of continual oppression that African Americans have had to deal with in society as individuals and as members of a physically identifiable group. *Malcolm X* provides the audience with a deeper understanding of the cultural values, religious roots, and belief in freedom of many African Americans.

Rabbit Proof Fence—This film tells the story of three young girls who escape from an internment camp for Black indigenous youth in Australia. This true story is based on the lives of Molly Pilkington and her two relatives, Gracie and Daisy. The children were not allowed to speak their native language; the purpose of the camp was total cultural assimilation. Their escape home takes them over 1,000 miles by foot in the desert.

Whale Rider. Outstanding film about a Maori girl from New Zealand and her struggles against gender bias in a culture that is patriarchal. The relationships are rich and unsettling at times. Demonstrates the cultural conflict that arises when women desire a more active role in a traditional cultural community. This story centers around a 12-year-old youngster whose strong mind and love of culture provide the basis for an important role model for young people today.

Bend It Like Beckham. This is another excellent film about the cultural conflicts a young woman in a South Indian family who lives in England must cope with. Her parents want her to become a traditional Indian woman, however this young person has dreams of becoming a professional women's soccer player. Also the story provides some discussion of cross-cultural misunderstandings and the influence of racism on personal goals.

Culture is a powerful force in our lives. Because schooling in our country is a common cultural experience, we may not understand that school practices and policies teach many cultural values. For example, much research has shown that teacher talk dominates about 95 percent of the conversation in the classroom. Teachers not only talk more often than children, but they talk most of the time. In some way, this reinforces the belief that children are to be seen and not heard. Although teachers in some schools are encouraging students to be responsible for their own learning and to choose the activities they become involved in, for the most part, this is the exception in schools. If you were to visit many high schools across the country, you would probably see most students sitting in rows of about five or six students, facing the front of the classroom. Students often face the teacher, which makes the assumption that the teacher is the giver of knowledge. Few people question this arrangement and what the physical layout of the classroom says about how learning occurs. Many schools are based on a teacher-centered paradigm to learning.

The most powerful reason why culture is ignored in schools is that most teachers cannot see the elements of culture in their own lives. Teachers may not understand that culture is always operating. Some cannot identify aspects of their culture. They don't see themselves as cultural beings. Many teachers believe they are individuals, not cultural beings. This is similar to the idea that when a person comes from the majority, he or she is culturally neutral.

Component Four: Utilize Culturally Relevant Teaching

Much of what is taught and how it is taught arises from mainstream culture. For example, why is Mark Twain or Robert Frost read more than Langston Hughes in many junior and high school English classes? Many times these choices are cultural rather than academic. The choice and construction of knowledge and skills is, in great part, a reflection of cultural values. Much of what is taught in schools comes from a Western tradition. However, I found in my own teaching that many students from underrepresented groups identified with and had stronger personal connections to the life of Malcolm X rather than to John F. Kennedy. Both figures are important to U.S. history. Although each role model made critical contributions to the Civil Rights Movement, students from many communities prefer reading about Malcolm X. Many students of color that I know identify with and feel a sense of community with Malcolm X. They have an understanding of the struggles that he suffered as a person of color. He is an important role model who came from a community like theirs and taught himself not only the importance of intellectual development, but also how to fight racism.

Culturally relevant teaching represents meaningful content, and also refers to a holistic way of teaching. Teachers know that their students learn within a sociocultural context. Goodman and Goodman (1990) recommend that teachers watch and talk with their students and find out what they are interested in, what they know, and what they can do. The goal of a teacher is to guide students into being independent learners. They also believe that the values and beliefs that students bring from their lives play an important role in how they interpret and understand school materials. Goodman and Goodman (1990) believe that teachers must be mediators in the learning process. They are not to control the learning context, but they are to assist students in their learning. They shared a lesson about Black fourth-grade students' reading Langston Hughes's poem, "Mother to Son" (Goodman and Goodman 1990, 237). Students led the class discussion of the poem. The teacher was not sure what Hughes meant in the poem by the term *crystal stair.* The teacher explained that she thought it meant that the mother was trying to raise herself out of difficult conditions, because Langston Hughes often wrote about social oppression. Students shared another viewpoint. They believed that the image referred to the mother climbing up the struggles of life, the "crystal stair," to heaven.

In this context, the teacher made a choice of the poem and acted as an initiator for the lesson. However, learning was reciprocal between students and teacher; they learned from each other. The teacher was a mediator in the learning. The poem she chose had definite connections to the lives of her students, and she encouraged and respected their viewpoints.

Important sociocultural factors are linked to school success and failure. Robert Rueda, a professor at the University of Southern California, has identified important aspects about culture in learning:

- Culture is dynamic.
- Understand one's own sociocultural frame of reference and social position and how these elements impact one's teaching.
- Thinking and learning are social processes, not individual processes.
- Learning requires active participation, not passive processing.
- Utilize multiple strategies for effective instruction based on actual and concrete contact with cultures other than one's own.
- Mediate multiple frames of reference, including the ability to facilitate cross-cultural dialogue and conflict mediation.
- School failure is a product of the interaction of several factors—including the environment, the student, and the teacher—not just the student (Rueda 1993).

With society's overemphasis on standards and national textbooks, teachers must look for ways to bring into the curriculum the lived experiences of various cultural groups to make learning real and authentic. Teachers often feel they must follow the curriculum as set up in their teachers' guides; however, when the materials have little in common with students, meaningful learning may not occur. I have seen teachers so intent on following the scripted guides of textbooks that they do not feel they have time to incorporate additional cultural examples into their lessons. Students may flounder because they do not have a clear understanding of the content or context of traditional materials.

Component Five: Blend and Integrate Caring and Social Justice into Teaching and School Policies and Practices

Caring and social justice are intimately connected in a culturally pluralistic and democratic society such as the United States. Caring can enhance our understanding of justice because the ethic of caring emphasizes trust and respect of others. The word *caring* rather than *care* was chosen because *caring* is a word of action and not just a value orientation. When we care for others, we act. This is how caring and social action are inseparably linked. We care for others, we treat others with fairness and respect, and we continually act with care and fairness in our everyday and professional lives to build a strong community. Caring is at the core of social justice and community. Within a school context, teachers must be especially aware of the need to integrate culture in order to make schooling more meaningful and relevant to children who are not successful. Caring and social justice values point to the great importance of equal educational opportunity and achievement outcomes for all students.

Providing equity is not easy to accomplish. In one of my graduate classes, Stefan, a chemistry teacher in a school that is primarily African American, shared his frustrations with having an average of 35 students per period and trying to care for each one of them. He has almost 200 students a day and it takes much emotional and physical energy to even say "hi" to each student as they come into the room.

One of the issues he continually wrestles with is homework. Many of the students work or take care of siblings after school. He knows that students also goof off. In order to develop strong study skills in his students, he must continually remind, prod, and demand that they do their homework. He cares deeply for his students, but his frustration increases when he realizes that he has only so much time. There is not enough time to call the parents of 15 to 20 students every day to follow up on their homework. It took several years for him to understand that caring means he must not only proactively care for students, but also teach students and parents how to create a more supportive environment that encourages study and homework skills. He as the teacher cannot do it all alone. Students and parents must be responsible for their own actions, too. Now he understands that he can be the catalyst in creating a caring community that focuses on academic excellence.

Component Six: Design and Implement Classroom and School Change

When implementing the six components, teachers must look not only at how they can change their classrooms, but also at how schools can be restructured in order to implement a commitment to caring and social justice. Do practices, policies, or beliefs act as obstacles because of unconscious prejudice or ignorance of other cultural values? Some of the obstacles to structural change may occur because of lack of communication between members of different communities.

I believe that we need total school reform. For example, all schools should not be larger than about 300 students, and a class should not have any more than 20 students. Individual educators and groups of teachers can make needed structural and pedagogical changes in schools. One way to enrich classroom curricula is by naturally infusing culture into them as the Algebra Project did in Cambridge, Massachusetts, and Funds of Knowledge accomplished in Tucson, Arizona. You, as an individual teacher, may not be able to reform all aspects of your school or need to; however you can improve what you are doing to reach students more effectively. One of your long-term professional goals may be to work with the teachers, administrators, and parents in your school to plan for and institute total school reform.

Sometimes it is easier to make structural changes in your own classroom, rather than tackling total school reform. For example, Paul Skilton Sylvester (1994), a third-grade teacher in the large district of Philadelphia, changed the social structures in his room rather than simply replicating current practices. Sylvester and his students created a classroom economy that they named "Sweet Cakes Town." He wanted to teach students real-world skills and to demonstrate that they could control their own lives. Sylvester (1994) believed in a critical pedagogy approach that emphasized students' learning knowledge and skills within the context of self-empowerment, decision making, and continual questioning.

Sylvester was a caring teacher whose commitment toward his students manifested itself in creating a learning context that exposed social and economic inequalities and assisted students in developing skills that would serve them to overcome discrimination in society. Sweet Cakes Town was a real neighborhood. Students had jobs and earned money for the neighborhood and the teacher paid them for being good students, which included their social behavior and academic performance. Each day, students rated their performance using the class guidelines for jobs they had accomplished. They added up their pay for the week on Fridays. From the funds they received, students were then able to take on roles in the neighborhood such as bankers, small business owners, clerks, and beauticians. Students not only used basic skills such as multiplication and division in order to calculate their profit and losses, but they also developed much deeper understandings of the obstacles in society such as lack of jobs, need for higher-level skills, and lack of public transportation (Sylvester 1994). Later, students realized that they needed governmental officers such as the mayor in order to run the city; thus, each citizen had to pay taxes. Sweet Cakes Town connected the learning of basic skills with real-life purposes. In addition, students saw why their participation was needed in order for social changes to occur.

Other educators provide ways for teachers and administrators to review schools for equity. Poston (1995) encourages educators to look at a school system like a healthy human body. This is what he wrote:

> The body is made up of many individual parts and components, with each part having an important task to perform . . . So it is within a healthy school system. Each system is made up of many components or operations with an interdependency . . . No one part can predominate over the others if the body is to benefit or succeed as a whole (Poston 1995, 153).

Of the various areas that must be addressed, one of the most vital areas is equity. This refers not only to equity of curriculum, course access, and allocation of resources, but also consistency within the curriculum that arises from stated district goals (Poston 1995). Unfortunately, achievement-level disparities exist between various cultural groups, especially those from lower- and higher-income communities (Frase 1995). These discrepancies call for an analysis of equity throughout the organization.

Change can also come about on a community level. Some schools today invite their local neighborhoods to become their partners, knowing that it does "take a village to raise a child." For example, the Chula Vista School District in California built a school next to a senior center and retirement home. Some seniors in California were opposed to their taxes being spent on schools; however, the district took a proactive stand. They invited representatives from the local senior citizen organizations to help create the direction and goals of the schools. The partnership has become a wonderful success. Elder Americans take an active role in volunteering and providing needed tutoring to children of all grade levels. Some of the volunteers often use their second language of Spanish and act as nurturing liaisons to many of the children whose home language is not English. They demonstrate their care for youngsters in the neighborhood. In addition, the children are learning what it means to be part of a caring neighborhood community. The children write letters to their senior friends, visit them, and often give holiday musical concerts and plays.

At a nearby high school, a dance was sponsored by the Associated Student Body (ASB). After they hired the band, ordered the food, and planned the decorations, the ASB decided to charge each couple $10 to attend. Unfortunately, many students could not afford the charge. Resentment among students began to fester. The principal was concerned about this issue of equal access to school functions, but did not know what to do. The faculty was apathetic because most of the teachers did not think it was an important issue.

A group of students cared about their community and wrote a letter to the school newspaper suggesting that one first-period class be devoted to discussing this issue and developing possible suggestions. Initially, the faculty felt forced by students to allow this discussion; however, by engaging faculty in this process, they took some ownership of the equal-access issue. Student facilitators, trained by school counselors, were used in some classrooms where faculty felt incapable of leading a discussion of the topic. The issue was not resolved immediately, but it was also discussed in various club meetings, such as the human relations and the community service clubs. In addition, the ASB made the issue one of its priorities for the year. They made a policy limiting the price of general school dances.

Change does occur. Often it is a struggle, but when students, parents, and teachers work with each other to make a more just and caring environment, structural changes can occur.

Chapter Summary

Learning and teaching can be empowering processes. For continuous growth, each of us must be continually involved in reevaluation of our teaching and our students' learning. To do this, I suggest that teachers carefully monitor the progress of their students, looking for patterns of success and failure. Are there students who are always failing? Are you able to integrate culture in one part of the curriculum more effectively than in others? Whose parents have you developed partnerships with? One teacher shared with her peers that she wanted a way to invite parents to come to an informal and fun event at school. The teacher developed a newsletter, but many parents did not read English well. She was able to have some newsletters translated into Spanish and Lao; however, she thought that the best way to reach parents was to talk to them in person. Thus,

she created a monthly "lunch bunch celebration." The teacher now invites parents of various students to come to school for pizza. Approximately six young students and their parents share lunch and the teacher talks about the accomplishments of the students at the celebration. Everyone has the opportunity to invite his or her parents. This has been a big success in the school. Teachers are looking for ways to build a sense of caring with their students and parents. This example affirms the importance of home life and the coordination of parents with teachers.

One of the best ways to ensure that equal education is being provided to all students is to examine all aspects of a school. The document *Diversity Within Unity* has an excellent checklist that can help you investigate where the strengths and weaknesses are in the school. In addition, the work of The Civil Rights Project demonstrated that students should be included in a comprehensive review of a school. The study of schools in Louisville and Cambridge found that desegregation can positively influence the beliefs of young people. Along with these strategies, I believe educators should review six essential components of schooling because they provide vital themes that should be found throughout schools.

The six fundamental components of Caring-Centered Multicultural Education provide important suggestions regarding what teachers must know in order to create an affirming, caring, and culturally relevant learning environment. These components represent an integration of different aspects of education: philosophy, pedagogy, school policies, and professional development.

Each of the components is important in creating a community of learners that is based on social justice and compassion. In addition, it is important for educators to examine their teaching to see that it is meaningful. Teachers can make their teaching more relevant and connected to the lives of their students by talking with each other and examining personal biases. Teachers can learn how to reach culturally diverse students by increasing their knowledge of the literature and history of various groups. These areas may be labeled as Chicano literature or Lakota literature, for example, but they are also part of American (U.S.) literature. Practice must also be expanded to include models, styles, and strategies that not only build on a caring orientation, but also provide cultural contexts that may be more familiar to students than those presently used in schools. Finally, teachers must continually consider their effectiveness. In considering accountability, educators must keep the goal of academic achievement at the top of their list.

The suggestions shared in this chapter are designed to assist you in thinking carefully about how to make schools a place of life and joy. *Caring is exciting and hard work.*

⊙ Chapter Review

Go to the Online Learning Center at **www.mhhe.com/pang2e** to review important content from the chapter, practice with key terms, take a chapter quiz, and find the Web links listed in this chapter.

Key Terms

September 11, 2001 *409*
USA Patriot Act, *410*
meaningful teaching, *413*
collegial discussions, *414*
personal reflection, *418*

meaningful content knowledge, *419*
meaningful practice, *420*
pedagogical content knowledge, *421*

purposeful accountability, *421*
authentic assessment, *422*
Diversity Within Unity, 424

Reflection Activities

1. Read through Table 12.1. Use it as a guide and write about specific actions that you might take to address the suggestions posed.
   Make a list of changes that you can implement in your classroom now and in the future. Come up with ideas for each of the five areas described as elements of meaningful teaching.

2. Because you are at the conclusion of the text, what are some issues you would like to further investigate? Take time to ponder them and then write

some ideas. Use Google or other search engines to help you start seeking new information. You also might want to go to the nearest public library or large university library. You may find books and journals in your search. Can you compose some open-ended questions that begin with *what, how,* or *why*? Try to use broad questions at first so that you have the opportunity to examine the issue that concerns you. As you explore and read a variety of materials, you will then narrow the issue or topic.

3. If you are interested in equity within the entire school and district, think about how resources are used in the school or district. Do all schools have the same financial resources? Human resources? Why are they the same? Are there district policies that help to ensure equity? What new policies can be implemented?

One of the important issues is the issue of human resources. Are the best teachers used in gifted programs or in other classrooms? In a district review, a team of folks will perform an audit. In this audit they may look for equity in program development and implementation. Here are possible questions that a team may use to guide their review process:

What is the achievement of students from a variety of cultural groups?

Do certain groups of students continually find themselves at the lower end of achievement?

Are students from specific groups suspended more often than others?

Do students from identified groups drop out more than others?

Do students from all groups have access to the same curriculum?

Do all schools offer the same high level of classes?

What are the library resources available to students? Is there parity across schools?

Do all schools have the same amount of funds for professional development?

In order to more systematically assess the status of your school or district, download the document from the Center of Multicultural Education at the University of Washington and examine in depth various areas for equity and culture. The link to the document can be found in Chapter 12 of the book website (www.mhhe.com/pang2e). http://www.educ.washington.edu/coetestwebsite/pdf/DiversityUnity.pdf.

4. Investigate the work of The Civil Rights Project at Harvard University. Go to their website at www.law.harvard.edu/civilrights/. Review various documents that are available on the website. Figure out what are the most pressing issues at your school or in your classroom. Develop short-term and long-term strategies for your school. Are other folks interested in issues of equity? It is helpful to bring together folks who really care about a common issue and begin to create a community for change.

 # Epilogue

Dear Reader,

I saw a program on Fred Rogers, the creator of *Mister Roger's Neighborhood*. I was moved by what he said. Mister Rogers was talking about children, but I believe what he said refers to people of all ages. Mister Rogers believes that every child wants to be valued. He tries to send across as much love as he can to his young viewers. Later that day, I also received an e-mail message about the comments of Leon Botstein, president of Bard College. On *CBS News Sunday Morning* on April 11, 1999, this is what he said:

> [U.S.] American institutions of higher education don't need managerial skills; they need leadership that comes of a love of learning and a love of the subject and the love of the act of scholarship-teaching.

Botstein shares important thoughts about education in general, and I want to add, "We need educators who care for others and their communities, too."

Like Mr. Rogers said, I believe we all want to be valued. I wrote this book in hope that I might provide some new understandings about children, cultural differences, and institutional structures. My goal was to suggest ways to increase joy, excitement, growth, compassion, and collaboration in the educational process.

In my own life, the field of Multicultural Education has brought new people, new knowledge, new skills, and wisdom into my development as a person and as a teacher. I have much more to think about, learn, and implement in my own teaching.

As I thought about the teachers who have inspired me, I realized that they were teachers who cared. They quietly listened to me without interrupting and sometimes they disagreed with me. They encouraged me to clarify my ideas and generously shared their insights with me. They brought new people and their work into my life. They let me bear my disappointments. They taught me how to forgive myself and others and helped me struggle through difficult times. They celebrated all students. Through their actions and words, they taught me how to care.

The purpose of this book was to share with you how the underlying values of caring and social justice can support the building of an effective school. When we care, we realize we have vital responsibilities. We want to know more about our students. This includes knowing about their cultures because they are important aspects of our students' identities. When we care, we have the courage and strength to review our own biases and how our actions may contribute to the continuation of institutional oppression in schools. We address inequities. Although these are difficult tasks, our caring for others sustains us in our quest for equitable education.

The characteristics of a successful student and a successful teacher are similar. Just like the comic in Chapter 7 on page 226 of a chick that comes out of an egg, Caring-Centered Multicultural Education presents a new paradigm. In the new framework, schools are places that are student centered and culture centered. Students become self-empowered learners who are dedicated to building a trusting and respectful community. Both teachers and students are people who believe in themselves and create compassionate relationships. Please read through the following chart to see the characteristics of a successful student and successful teacher:

What would you add to the profiles that I may have forgotten? What did I include that you may not have considered?

Characteristics of a Successful Student and Successful Teacher in a Caring-Centered Multicultural School

Successful Student	Successful Teacher
• Believes in self and teacher.	• Believes in each child/student and self.
• Self-directed learner.	• Self-directed learner.
• Happy, fulfilled person.	• Happy, fulfilled person.
• Caring toward others and self.	• Caring toward others and self.
• Empowered, contributes to the community.	• Empowered, contributes to the community.
• Cooperative, community oriented; makes connections with peers and others.	• Cooperative, community oriented; makes connections with parents, students, colleagues, and others.
• Supportive of classmates, friends, family, and teacher.	• Supportive of colleagues, students, parents, family, and others.
• Open minded, flexible.	• Open minded, flexible.
• Moves from ethnocentrism to incultural understanding.	• Moves from ethnocentrism to other cultural frames of reference.
• Knows when to keep on task and when to provide assistance to classmates.	• Knows when to step in to assist students and when to step back and encourage students to direct their own learning.
• Affirms the worth of self and classmates (includes culture, gender, language, social class, religion, etc.).	• Affirms each child's/student's worth (includes culture, gender, language, social class, religion, etc.).
• Listens without criticism; accepts others' ideas; gives helpful feedback.	• Listens without criticism; accepts others' ideas; gives constructive suggestions.
• Reflects on own learning.	• Reflects on own teaching and learning.
• Is comfortable and can function within a variety of cultural contexts (culture, race, language, religion, etc.).	• Is comfortable and can function within a variety of cultural contexts (culture, race, language, religion, etc.).
• Has high expectations for self and teacher.	• Has high expectations for self and all students.

continued

**Characteristics of a Successful Student and Successful Teacher
in a Caring-Centered Multicultural School (Continued)**

Successful Student	Successful Teacher
• Enjoys and is enthusiastic about learning.	• Uses a variety of instructional approaches to teach information and skills, monitor student progress, and provide feedback.
• Understands and works toward identified learning objectives.	• Has clear learning objectives and conveys them to students.
• Sees connection between school learning and real life.	• Conveys connection and meaning between school knowledge and skills and lives of students.
• Shares cultural background with others.	• Integrates the cultural background of children naturally into all aspects of the classroom, from bulletin boards to teaching basic skills.
• Develops a "voice" and speaks out on public issues; works to make society and the community a more just and compassionate place.	• Encourages students to develop their own value orientation and "voice"; supports students in learning to make their own decisions and to become active in directing their own education; speaks out on public issues and works to make society a more just and compassionate place.
• Desires to be part of and works toward a strong collaborative community in the classroom and school.	• Has goal of creating a learning community in the classroom and school that is collaborative and affirming for all participants—students, parents, community people, and administrators.
• Disciplined and successful learner.	• Disciplined and successful learner.

The author wishes to thank Maria Marshall for her input to this chart.

We live in a chaotic and quickly moving time. Many folks are not connected to a community, whether a school, religious community, or family. However, there is still a strong call by individuals for communal caring. They seek acceptance and belonging. Caring-Centered Multicultural Education is founded upon the belief that we are all equal and worthy people. As teachers and students, whether one is 6 or 86 years old, we can encourage each other and build a caring community. The successful teacher and successful student mirror each other.

Every student who comes to your classroom *believes in you* and your ability to teach them. Even a student who says skeptical things to you is hoping that you will see her or his abilities and help her or him to develop and learn. As educators, we know that teaching is more than just conveying information; we must come to

know the whole person. We can understand our students' dreams and hopes, guide them through their weaknesses, and enhance their strengths. When students care for others, they contribute to the creation of a community and build stronger human bonds with others. In the process, their own self-worth increases. Some of our students will find a cure for a cancer. Some of our students will become great teachers and teach other students how to be peacemakers. Some of our students will provide important services to others as plumbers, librarians, and mail carriers. We have one of the most exciting and important careers that impacts all avenues of society.

Caring-Centered Multicultural Education is founded upon the belief that schooling should be an exciting and joyous part of life. Learning is really about being alive (Sark 1992). Life and learning cannot be separated.

Caring and sharing are keys to effective teaching. Remember the first grader named Eugene who used a pick instead of a brush to fix his hair? Eugene could have said to me about my lack of knowledge, "Mrs. Pang, why don't you know about a pik? What's wrong with you?" Instead, he patiently explained to me what a pik was. He did not think less of me; rather, he respected and cared for me enough to share his knowledge without criticism. That is one of the main insights I hope this book brings to you.

Students bring a wealth of knowledge to school. Their knowledge of the world and the knowledge that is taught in schools may represent different perspectives on life. Neither is better than the other—their perspectives and knowledge base are just different. In order to survive in this society, students will need general societal knowledge and skills to get a job and earn a living. However, students can live a bi-cultural or multicultural life in which they are able to code switch according to the cultural context in which they find themselves. I have learned so much from students like Eugene. They have enriched my life and helped me become a more effective teacher.

When you are surrounded by people who say it isn't possible to reach all students, find others you can talk to who know teaching isn't always easy, but who are committed to making a difference. Build up your professional libraries. Read the works of dedicated educators such as Geneva Gay, Jackie Jordan Irvine, Vivian Gussin Paley, Ed Gordon, Alfie Kohn, Frank Smith, Robert Rueda, Nel Noddings, James Banks, Jack Nelson, Christine Bennett, Patricia Larke, Gregory Cajete, Pedro Noguera, Luis Moll, Lisa Delpit, Christine Sleeter, Carl Grant, Joyce King, Pauline Lipman, Jessica Gordon Nembhard, A. Lin Goodwin, and Jean Anyon. They say, "Yes, all children have great potential and yes, all teachers can be effective" and they provide ideas on how to reach even the most distant and disenfranchised students.

When we are really teaching and working effectively with students, we are also sharing life with others. When students are learning, they are living the fullness of life. Their minds and sense of selves are growing. Learning is meaningful to them. I know students who can't wait to get to school because it is a place of success and belonging. I believe that this occurs most frequently within the context of trusting, respectful, and caring relationships. Students and teachers form a family, a community of learners who care about each other, care for themselves, and care for ideas. However, caring teaching is not always easy. General John Stanford wrote:

> Loving and leading doesn't mean going easy on people no matter what they do; it means coaching people to do their best, it means pushing them farther than they want to go, it means letting them know when you think they can do more. Love and leading can mean giving tough love. We often assume, when people disappoint us, that they can do no better. But that's rarely true . . . Often, their problem is really our problem; the person isn't performing because we weren't clear in our directions . . . America, our children are waiting and we must not disappoint them. Let's all love them and lead them (Stanford and Simons 1999, 206, 213).

Enjoy all the precious moments that your students share with you. Learning can be very joyous and exciting. Schools can become places of care (Noddings 1992). Learning is not only about ideas; it is about community and building a trusting and just place to live.

I hope that you never forget: *You* and your *students* are precious gifts of life. As Robert Fulghum has written, "No matter how old you are—when you go out into the world, it is best to hold hands and stick together."

Take care,

Val

Caring for Kids (Young and Older)

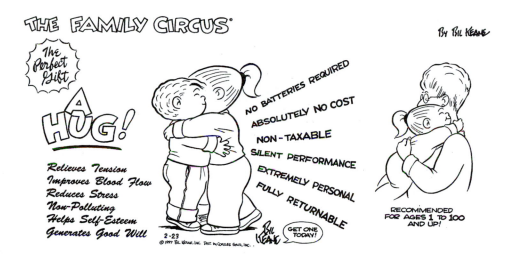

Sing out loud.
Be silly.
Giggle.
Use caring words.
Listen to their dreams.
Smile widely.
Tell them great stories of kind deeds.
Smile with your heart.
Jump rope.
Laugh lots.
Dream of happy kids.
Build trust.
Cherish culture.
Foster curiosity.
Ask questions.
Encourage them to think and question.
Praise, praise, and praise some more.
Laugh, laugh, and laugh some more.
Celebrate each learner.

© 1998 Valerie Ooka Pang

 Appendix

Population Information

TABLE A.1   U.S. Population Growth, 1960–2000

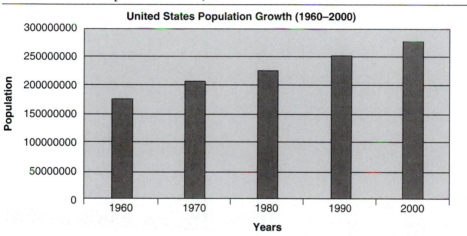

TABLE A.2   U.S. Population, 1960–2000

U.S. Population 1960–2000	1960	1970	1980	1990	2000
Total	179,323,175	203,302,031	226,545,805	248,709,873	281,421,906
Change		23,978,856	23,243,774	22,164,068	32,712,033
Percent change (%)		13.4	11.4	9.8	13.2

Source: Census 2000, Social Science Data Analysis Network (SSDAN).

TABLE A.3   U.S. Multiracial Composition: 2000 Census

Selected Number of Racial Groups	Number	U.S. Total Population	Percent of Total Multiracial Population
Two Races	6,368,075	2.26	93.30
Three Races	410,285	0.15	6.01
Four Races	38,408	0.01	0.56
Five Races	8,637	0.00	0.13

Source: Census 2000, Social Science Data Analysis Network (SSDAN). http://www.censussope.org.

✿ Teacher Resources

Teacher Resources: Children's Literature, Reference Materials, and Videos

Part 1: Annotated Bibliography of Children's Literature for a Culturally Diverse and Caring Society

I recommend that you read the books prior to using them in the classroom. Each group of students reacts differently to books. Some of the books may have strong language or other aspects that you may need to explain to your students before they can understand the story. Reviewing them in advance ensures that the books are appropriate for your students and relate to your instructional objectives.

This list represents only a limited selection of new and old favorites.

Picture Books

Abells, Chana Byers. 1983. *The children we remember.* New York: Greenwillow Books. A powerful book of actual photographs telling the story of the Holocaust. Although the book has only about 170 words, much is conveyed. There is great sadness and hope presented in the text. The book is not for young children. It should not be presented without background information being shared first. (Grades 4–12, Jewish community, Holocaust, genocide, anti-Semitism)

Alarcón, Francisco X. 1998. *From the bellybutton of the moon and other summer poems.* San Francisco, Calif.: Children's Book Press. This is an excellent bilingual Spanish and English poetry book. Can be used in both bilingual and monolingual classsrroms. (K–3, humor, bilingualism, cultural diversity)

Bradby, Marie. 1995. *More than anything else.* New York: Orchard Books. Booker wants to learn how to read more than anything else. He finds someone who can share the secret of reading with him. (K–3, literacy, Booker T. Washington, courage)

Bunting, Eve. 1988. *How many days to America.* New York: Clarion Books. A story of a family who leaves their home to find freedom in the United States. Their journey was difficult but they find freedom on Thanksgiving. (K–3, immigration, refugees, political asylum, hope)

———. 1989. *The Wednesday surprise.* New York: Clarion. Anna has a secret. She is teaching someone she loves how to read. Who is it? Why will her father be surprised? Excellent story about the importance of literacy and the abilities of a young girl. (K–3, families, literacy, grandparents)

———. 1994. *A day's work.* New York: Clarion. This is another wonderfully written picture book by the award-winning author. When Francisco goes with his *abuelo* (grandfather) to find work, he learns more than how to garden. Francisco learns the importance of telling the truth. (K–5, Latino families, honesty, truth)

———. 1995. *Smoky night.* San Diego, Calif.: Harcourt Brace & Company. A story about how a community came together during a night of rioting to find a neighbor's cat. (Grades 3–6, cross-cultural understanding, compassion, community building)

———. 1998. *So far from the sea.* New York: Clarion Books. This story is about Laura, a seven-year-old, who goes with her family to visit her grandfather's grave at the Manzanar Internment Camp in California. (Grades 3–6, Japanese Americans, family, Japanese American internment)

T-1

Cannon, Janell. 1993. *Stellaluna.* San Diego, Calif.: Harcourt Brace & Company. Stellaluna, a fruit bat, loses her mother when an owl attacks them. Stellaluna is too young to fly and lands head first into a nest with three baby birds. She learns how to eat and fly like a bird. But one day Stellaluna finds her mother. She also learns how to eat and fly like a bat. Stellaluna shares her new knowledge with her bird friends. They all find out that they are similar and different. However, what was most important was that they were friends. (K–3, friendship, cross-cultural differences)

Cha, Dia. 1996. *Dia's story cloth.* New York: Lee and Low Books. This book uses a story cloth to tell the story of a Hmong family who must leave their homes in Laos because of the civil strife there. The family later comes to the United States. Pictures of story cloths are used in the book. (Grades 1–5, Hmong families, refugee, civil strife, Southeast Asia, courage)

Clifton, Lucille. 1983. *Everett Anderson's goodbye.* New York: Holt. Everett Anderson's father dies and Everett goes through the five stages of grief: denial, anger, bargaining, depression, and acceptance. It is a beautiful story of a child who struggles with losing a parent. (K–3, death, love, the loss of a loved one)

Coerr, Eleanor. 1993. *Sadako.* New York: G. P. Putnam's Sons. Beautifully written story about Sadako Sasaki who contracted leukemia from the fallout of the atom bomb that was dropped on Hiroshima during World War II. Sadako becomes a symbol of peace and, through her creation of a thousand origami cranes, becomes an inspiration for many children and adults across the world. (K–5, peace)

Coles, Robert. 1995. *The story of Ruby Bridges.* New York: Scholastic Books. An important book for every person who believes in equality and social justice. This is a true story of Ruby Bridges, a first grader, who integrated an all-White elementary school in Louisiana. A remarkable book about a special young person. (K–5, civil rights, African American families, forgiveness, inner strength)

de Paola, Tomie. 1989. *The art lesson.* New York: G. P. Putnam's Sons. A young boy delivers an important message to his teachers about individuality and art. (K–3, individuality, negotiation, nonconformity, following one's bliss)

Deedy, Carmen Agra. 2000. *The yellow star: The legend of King Christian X of Denmark.* Atlanta, GA: Peachtree. It is a story of the Danish King Christian who defied the Nazis and saved many Jewish Danes. (K–5, Anti-Semitism, courage, interdependence, leadership)

Dorros, Arthur. 1991. *Abuela.* New York: Dutton Children's Books. The story is about a granddaughter who goes on a bus with her grandmother and explores the sights of New York City. Story also integrates some Spanish. (K–3, family, imagination, travel, Latinos)

Durrell, Ann, and Marilyn Sachs, eds. 1990. *The big book of peace.* New York: Dutton Children's Books. A wonderful collection of stories and illustrations about peace from exceptional children's authors like Steven Kellogg, Yoshiko Uchida, Maurice Sendak, and Diane and Leo Dillon. (Grades 3–8, peace, community building, respect, compassion)

Feeney, Stephanie. 1980. *A is for aloha.* Honolulu, Hawaii: University of Hawaii press. This is one of my personal favorites about Asian Pacific American children. It is a culturally based book without relying on the usual Asian stereotypical images. The photos of the children are beautiful. (K–3, Asian Pacific Americans, the alphabet, community, family, culture, personal growth)

Garland, Sherry. 1993. *The lotus seed.* San Diego, Calif.: Harcourt Brace & Company. One of the best picture books for young people about Asian Pacific Americans. This book tells the story of a grandmother from Vietnam who had to leave because of the Vietnam War. What does she take with her on the treacherous journey to the United States? The grandmother takes in her heart the image of the young emperor and the values that carried her through the struggles of life. Exceptional illustrations. (K–5, Vietnamese American families, inner courage, cultural values)

Golenbock, Peter. 1990. *Teammates.* San Diego: Voyager Books. A great story about the courage of Jackie Robinson and Pee Wee Reese, both members of the Brooklyn Dodgers Baseball team. The story emphasizes the importance of all of us fighting prejudice. (K–4, racism, teamwork, Jackie Robinson, Pee Wee Reese, Branch Rickey, social justice, inner courage)

Hamanaka, Sheila. 1990. *The journey: Japanese Americans, racism, and renewal.* New York:

Orchard Books. An exceptional book about the Japanese American historical experience. Hamanaka created a huge five-panel mural to tell this important story. (Grades 4–8, Japanese American historical experience, racism, courage, cultural conflict, social justice)

———. 1995. *On the wings of peace: In memory of Hiroshima and Nagasaki.* New York: Houghton Mifflin Company. Another excellent selection of poetry, stories, and illustrations to present information about the atomic destruction of Hiroshima and Nagasaki during World War II. The book celebrates peace and encourages all of us to become actively involved in eliminating prejudice, discrimination, and destruction. (Grades 5–12, peace, prejudice, war, discrimination, respect, community building)

Hazen, Barbara Shook. 1989. *The knight who was afraid of the dark.* New York: Dial Books for Young Readers. A humorous book about a knight named Sir Fred. This knight was terribly afraid of the dark. His love, Lady Wendylyn, was not afraid of the dark, but she was scared of bugs. The book is a funny take off of the Dark Ages. It can be used to discuss gender role bias. Although some teachers find the stereotypes of romance and bugs to be present, most educators utilize it as a springboard for discussion. (Grades 3–5, gender roles, fears)

hooks, bell. 1999. Happy to be nappy. New York: Hyperion Books for Children. A fun book about hair and its many styles and textures. The book celebrates "nappy" hair. This book has been controversial in some schools because of the negative stereotypes that some individuals associate with the term *nappy.* Read this book in advance before presenting it to your students. (K–3, self-image, physical self-concept, cultural differences, cultural conflicts)

Isadora, Rachel. 1976. *Max.* New York: Collier Books. Max is a youngster who loves baseball and ballet. He can do many things and likes himself, too. (K–3, positive self-concept, gender bias)

———. 2002. *Bring on that beat.* New York: G. P. Putnam's Sons. A picture book about jazz that uses rhyme to celebrate this musical form and highlights one of its greatest artists, Duke Ellington. The pictures also are a celebration of this musical genre. (K–5, jazz, Black and White artistry, cultural contributions)

Knight, Margy Burns. 1993. *Who belongs here? An American story.* Gardiner, Maine: Tilbury House. Nary, a young boy from Cambodia, knows of the horror of Pol Pot and civil strife in his home country. His family leaves Cambodia for a refugee camp in Thailand. Later they move to the United States where they find not only an abundance of food and freedom, but also prejudice. The book also presents definitions of words such as *refugee,* information regarding the immigration of various groups, discussion of Pol Pot, and features knowledge about the leadership of Dolores Huerta and the United Farm Workers. (Grades 3–6, immigration, civil rights, Dolores Huerta, the United Farm Workers, social justice)

Lawrence, Jacob. 1993. *The great migration.* New York: HarpterCollins Children's Books. A powerful picture book for upper elementary and middle school students. The text of the book is from a poem written by Walter Dean Myers about the movement of African Americans out of the South to the North that began around the 1910s. It chronicles an important story of African Americans struggling to create a better life for their families. (Grades 4–8, African American history, racism, industrial labor, courage)

Miller, William. 1997. *Richard Wright and the library card.* New York: Lee & Low Books. The story tells the time in Richard Wright's life when he uses the library. Although there was much prejudice against African Americans, Richard found a way to check out books. The books became a way for him to learn about how many others, Black and White, were like him and longed for freedom. (K–3, literacy, prejudice, racism, learning, friendship)

Munsch, Robert. 1980. *The paper bag princess.* Toronto, Canada: Annick Press Ltd. Princess Elizabeth learns how to rely on her own intelligence and courage to outwit a fierce dragon. (Grades 3–5, courage, wit, gender bias)

Palatini, Margie. 1995. *Piggie pie!* New York: Clarion Books. This is a fun read-aloud story for grades preschool through third grade. The story is about Gritch the Witch who is looking for her dinner. In this funny book, Gritch the Witch looks far and wide to find eight plump piggies for her piggie pie. The pigs use teamwork to stump the grouchy and hungry witch. Be sure to screen this one in advance because of language. (K–3, team-work, humor)

Pearson, Emily. 2002. *Ordinary Mary's extraordinary deed.* Layton, Utah: Gibbs Smith. A fun book about how anyone can send warmth to others. The story reminds children to help others and their good deeds may multiply to many more good acts for others. There is a math chart that shows how one good deed can become billions. (K–3, community, personal courage, care)

Polacco, Patricia. 1991. *Applemando's dreams.* New York: Philomel Books. This is an inspiring story about young people who have colorful and alive dreams, until several adults in their hometown throw water on their dreams. However, find out how the youngsters used their dreams to find their way when they became lost. (Grades 3–5, courage, dreams, community, caring, belief in oneself)

———. 1992. *Chicken Sunday.* New York: Philomel Books. Grandma longs for a new hat, but without money, Stewart, Winston, and Patricia didn't know what they could do to buy it for her. Three youngsters learn that by doing something for others, their actions can snowball into more wonderful friendships. (K–5, teamwork, compassion, community building, caring for others)

———. 1998. *Thank you, Mr. Falker.* New York: Philomel Books. Trish feels stupid because she can't read. She works hard at learning how to read, but it doesn't seem to matter because the page just looks like a bunch of squiggles. Other kids laughed at her. She began to believe she was stupid, until Mr. Falker, her teacher, found a way to help her unlock the door to her reading disability. (Grades 3–6, caring, learning disabilities, teacher belief, self-efficacy, courage, autobiographical story)

Prelutsky, Jack. 1991. *For laughing out loud: Poems to tickle your funnybone.* New York: Alfred A. Knopf. A fun book of poems about animals, food, people and rattlesnake stew. Read the poems to your students. You will lighten up their day. (Grades 3–6, family, humor, community building, fun)

Rathman, Peggy. 1995. *Officer Buckle and Gloria.* New York: G. P. Putnam's Sons. Officer Buckle gives speeches all over Napville about safety. However, when Gloria, the police dog, becomes a partner, his speeches come alive. Kids really listen because they like Gloria's funny expressions. Officer Buckle and Gloria find out that they are an important team. (K–3, teamwork, humor)

Ringgold, Faith. 1991. *Tar beach.* New York: Crown Publishers. Cassie and her family spend many wonderful nights on the roof of their apartment building. Cassie teaches her brother how to fly over the various landmarks in the city. She tells him about her dreams and how she hopes for a more just world. Ringgold weaves in the African American historical value of flying. (K–3, family, caring, and social justice)

———. 1992. *Aunt Harriet's underground railroad in the sky.* New York: Crown Publishers. Harriet Tubman, one of the most famous conductors on the underground railroad, takes Cassie on a journey along the underground railroad to find her brother. (Grades 2–5, underground railroad, courage, racism, slavery, Harriet Tubman)

———. 1993. *Dinner at Aunt Connie's house.* New York: Hyperion Books for Children. Aunt Connie invites Melody to dinner and she learns about 12 accomplished African American women. (Grades 1–5, African American heroes, community, family)

———. 1995. *My dream of Martin Luther King.* New York: Crown Publishers. A picture book biography of the work and dream of Martin Luther King, Jr. The illustrations are extremely powerful and display King's passion for social justice. (Grades 2–5, Martin Luther King, Jr., civil rights, courage, social justice, racism)

Rosa-Casanova, Sylvia. 1997. *Mama Provi and the pot of rice.* New York: Atheneum. Mama Provi is the kind of grandmother many people would love to have. She makes delicious *arroz con pollo,* chicken with rice. As Mama Provi climbs the seven floors to her granddaughter's apartment, she shares her *arroz con pollo* with the neighbors and they share their yummy food with her, too. (K–3, Puerto Rican community, family, sharing, grandmothers, caring, kindness)

Ross, Dave. 1980. *A book of hugs.* New York: Thomas Y. Crowell. A fun book about hugs. Read the book and find out how many kinds of hugs there are in the world. For example, there are fish hugs, piggyback hugs, knee hugs, and sandwich hugs. (K–2, caring, family, friends)

Say, Allen. 1993. *Grandfather's journey.* New York: Houghton Mifflin. A Japanese American young person describes his grandfather's journey to the United States. His grandfather loved both countries, his home land of Japan and his new home in the United States.

Spinelli, Eileen. 1991. *Somebody loves you, Mr. Hatch.* New York: Simon and Schuster. Mr. Hatch goes to work every day, eats a cheese and mustard sandwich every day, and pretty much keeps to himself. One day he receives a mysterious Valentine. It is a box full of chocolates from a secret admirer. When Mr. Hatch finds out that the box was given to him by mistake, he feels very sad. However, his neighbors rally around him and he finds out that others do love him. (K–5, caring, community)

Tsuchiya, Yukio. 1988. *Faithful elephants: A true story of animals, people and war.* New York: Houghton Mifflin Company. A moving story about the elephants at the Ueno Zoo during World War II. The text helps students understand the tragedy that war brings animals and people. Although this is a picture book, it is not for young children. (Grades 5–12, war, fear, sadness of war, peace, sensitivity to animals)

Uchida, Yoshiko. 1993. *The bracelet.* New York: Philomel Books. Emi is a seven-year-old who lived in San Francisco. Although Emi and her family were U.S. citizens, during World War II they were taken from their home and moved to internment camps because they were of Japanese ancestry. Emi received a bracelet from her friend Laurie. The bracelet symbolized friendship and their mutual love for each other. (Grades 3–6, war, fear, Japanese American internment, courage, caring, frienship)

Williams, Vera B. 1982. *A chair for my mother.* New York: Greenwillow Books. A young girl, her mother, and grandmother save for a wonderful new stuffed chair after a fire destroys everything in their apartment. (K–3, caring, family, saving)

Novels

Anzaladúa, Gloria. 1987. *Borderlands/La frontera: The new mestiza.* San Francisco, Calif.: Aunt Lute Book Company. Powerful text of prose and poetry about the life of Anzaladúa, who grew up on the Mexico-Texas border. She focuses on her bilingual, bicultural experiences and the conflicts she faced as a person who straddled both communities. (Adult readers, self- and ethnic identity, oppression, biculturalism, courage, family)

Bauer, Joan. 2000. *Hope was here.* New York: Scholastic. A great novel for upper-elementary readers about Hope a 16-year-old waitress who is left by her mom with her aunt Addie. Hope created a new sandwich called Keep Hoping. Her real name is Tulip, but she chooses the name Hope to remind her that in life there is always hope. Hope moves to Mulhoney, Wisconsin, with her aunt and works at the Welcome Stairways café. G. T. Stoop, Hope's boss, runs for mayor when he finds out that a local corporation seems to be buying political influence. (Grades 4–8, social class, self-determination, community action, election, and voting)

Boyle, T. Coraghessan. 1995. *The tortilla curtain.* New York: Viking Press. An excellent novel about two liberals who live in California and whose lives become intertwined with a Mexican immigrant couple. The premise of the novel revolves around the couple's values of equity and how difficult it may be to integrate those values in their everyday lives. The couple finds it challenging to understand their social privilege in a world where they feel little connections with others who may be from another community. (Adult readers, elitism, racism, classism)

Delgado, Richard. 1995. *The Rodrigo chronicles.* New York: New York University Press. Delgado, a professor of law, is the consummate storyteller. This is one of my all-time favorite novels. Delgado weaves an engrossing story of how different races challenge each other in life. Delgado has created Rodrigo, an "everyperson," who listens, searches, asks, and tackles complex questions of equality and justice in hopes of making a better nation for all. (Adult readers, racism, democracy, and equity)

Elison, Ralph. 1947. *The invisible man.* New York: Random House, Inc. One of the most powerful books written about the experiences of an African American male who is confronted with the racism of society. The novel is full of important symbolism about the impact of materialism, sex, and racism on the development of African

Americans. (High school–adult, African American communities, cultural assimilation, racism, materialism, social oppression, social justice)

Fox, Paula. 1991. *Monkey Island.* New York: Doubleday Dell Books for Young Readers. Clay Garrity, an 11-year-old, finds himself homeless in New York City. Where has his mother gone? What will he do? The weather is bitter cold. The story is about a young boy living on the streets and the two men who share their wooden crate in the park with him. (Grades 5–8, homelessness, family, personal growth, foster care, social services)

Houston, Jeanne Wakatsuki, and James D. Houston. 2002. *Farewell to Manzanar: A true story of Japanese American experience during WWII.* Boston: Houghton Mifflin. The story of a young female whose family must leave their home and live in an internment camp in California because they are Japanese American. (Grades 8–12, coming of age, institutional racism, ethnic identity, and cultural assimilation)

Myers, Walter Dean. 1988. *Fallen angels.* New York: Scholastic Inc. Richie Perry, a young man from Harlem, enlists in the army. He goes to Southeast Asia and has a difficult year during the Vietnam War. (High school–adult, Vietnam War, violence, personal growth, adult language)

———. 1993. *Malcolm X: By any means necessary.* New York: Scholastic Inc. This is a biography of Malcolm Little, who later took the name Malcolm X. An important story for many students to read. Shows the phases that Malcolm goes through in his life and how he transforms himself into an international leader for social justice. (Grades 6–10, Malcolm X, literacy, courage, leadership, social justice)

Okada, John. 1981. *No-no boy.* Seattle, Wash.: University of Washington Press. Story of a Japanese American who was released from prison because he would not sign a loyalty oath. The book also describes the inner conflicts of Japanese Americans in the cultural assimilation process. (High school–adults, Japanese American internment, loyalty oath, cultural conflicts, cultural assimilation, family issues, community conflicts)

Paulsen, Gary. 1993. *Nightjohn.* New York: Delacorte Books. This novel describes the violence and inhumanity that slaves were subjected to through the voice of a young girl named Sarny. The youngster learns how to read from John, another slave, who is persecuted for his knowledge. To John, reading and living were the same. (Grades 6–12, slavery, literacy, courage)

Ryan, Pam Muñoz. 1998. *Riding freedom.* New York: Scholastic. Who is One-eyed Charley? Well, he's the best stagecoach driver in New England. This novel of historical fiction is about how Charlotte Parkhurst becomes Charley, gifted horse trainer. Charlotte was an orphan who later moved to California and became the first woman to vote in Santa Cruz County. (Grades 3–5, woman role model, California history, New England history, community, courage)

Soto, Gary. 1990. *Baseball in April and other stories.* San Diego, Calif.: Harcourt Brace & Company. This is a collection of 11 short stories about growing up in Fresno, California. The stories are about the fears and dreams of young people. (Grades 4–6, Latino youth, family, growing up)

———. 2003. *The afterlife.* San Diego, Calif.: Harcourt Inc. This is a haunting story about Chuy, a high school student, who is stabbed. As a spirit he visits people he loves and misses. (Grades 5–9, family, Latino community, selected Spanish vocabulary included)

Spinelli, Jerry. 1990. *Maniac Magee.* New York: HarperCollins. Jeffrey Magee became an orphan at three years old when his mother and father were in a trolley accident. Magee was left to live with his feuding aunt and uncle. Later Magee found himself without any home. Humor is woven throughout the story about Magee's life and his activities as a hero. A book with heart. (Grades 3–6, homelessness, racism, caring, family)

Tademy, Lalita. 2001. *Cane River.* New York: Warner Books. A riveting story about four generations of women who fight to keep their families whole in the South during and after the Civil War. Tademy based this novel on her own family geneology. The women in this book are strong role models of family, inner courage, and freedom. This book describes the familial and cultural connections of many Black and White families in the South. (High school–adult, Creole culture, Louisiana plantations, African Americans, emancipation, cultural connections, interracial families)

Uchida, Yoshiko. 1985. *Journey to Topaz: A story of the Japanese American evacuation.* This novel is about the life of Yuki Sakane from Oakland, who is taken with her family to the desert when 120,000 Japanese Americans were uprooted from their homes during World War II. Yuki first was taken to Tanforan Racetrack and then to Topaz, a concentration camp in northern California. (Grades 4–8, Japanese Americans, racism, internment, courage)

Young, Russell. 2000. *Dragonsong: A fable for the new millennium.* Auburn, Calif.: Shen's Books. A wonderful modern folktale about a dragon from China who travels the world and receives gifts from dragons of other cultures. Illustrations are especially beautiful. (Grades 1–4, dragons, China, England, Mexico, Central Africa, courage, hope)

Materials for Older Readers

Freedman, Russell. 1994. *Kids at work: Lewis Hine and the crusade against child labor.* New York: Scholastic. Excellent resource material for older students that describes the dedication of Lewis Hine, a school teacher in New York City, who worked to get child labor laws passed. As a photographer, Hine told a powerful story of the abuse of children who worked in factories, canneries, fields, and coal mines. (Grades 5–12, child labor, child labor laws, labor reform)

Part 2: Teacher Resources

Albom, Mitch. 1997. *Tuesdays with Morrie.* New York: Doubleday. One of the most insightful books about the wisdom that a teacher imparted to a student. Mitch Albom goes back to visit his sociology professor, Morrie Schwartz, and learns not only about death, but about love and life. Morrie shares with Mitch his philosophy about teaching and living. Morrie says that the most important values in life are love, compassion, responsibility, and community.

Ansary, Tamim. 2002. *West of Kabul, East of New York: An Afghan American story.* New York: Picador. This is an excellent nonfiction autobiography of a man who moved to the United States as a teenager from Afghanistan. His mother was from the United States and his father was native to Afghanistan. After the September 11, 2001, terrorist attack, he wrote an e-mail message that was distributed to many people. He explained as an Afghan American how the horrific events impacted him. He also explained why the situation in Afghanistan is so difficult for the people there. Ansary clearly explained that Osama bin Laden and the Taliban are not from his native country of Afghanistan. An important book for all teachers to read.

Asian American Resource Workshop. 1991. *The Asian American comic book.* Boston, Mass.: Asian American Resource Workshop. This is a comic book for use with high school students, centering on the following issues: the impact of the internment on a Japanese American family, students dealing with cross-generational and cross-cultural conflicts, a refugee young person encountering racism and cultural differences, and the strength of a woman working to address labor problems in a factory.

Banks, James A., and Cherry A. Banks. 2004. *Handbook of research on multicultural education.* San Francisco: Jossey-Bass. This second edition is an outstanding collection of articles on Multicultural Education from the leaders in education. Banks and Banks have developed an important text for anyone studying Multicultural Education and teacher education. There are 49 chapters in this major resource.

Beyer, Barry K. 1987. *Practical strategies for the teaching of thinking.* Boston, Mass.: Allyn and Bacon. Excellent book for teachers providing various models and activities to teach higher-order thinking. Well-organized text with strategies that can be used in many different subject areas.

Bigelow, William, and Norman Diamond. 1988. *The power in our hands: A curriculum on the history of work and workers in the United States.* New York: Monthly Review Press. Excellent collection of 16 lessons that present valuable information about the history of workers in the United States. The activities are engaging and encourage students to look at their own values and make important decisions regarding labor issues.

Caduto, Michael J., and Joseph Bruchac. 1989. *Keepers of the earth: Native American stories and environment activities for children.* Golden, Colo.:

Fulcrum Publishers. Excellent educational resource for elementary-grade teachers about various Native American nations. The stories present information and activities about Native American values regarding the environment, focusing on themes such as creation, fire, the seasons, plants, and animals.

Comer, James, and Alvin Poussaint. 1992. *Raising Black children.* New York: Penguin Books.Comer and Poussaint are two psychiatrists who have written an excellent question-and-answer format text for teachers, parents, and community people. Their book begins with discussion of the development of infants and continues to answer questions about the teenage years. The authors provide excellent responses to difficult questions about racism, curriculum in the schools, sex education, and many other aspects of growing up. For example, the answers to these questions will assist both teachers and parents:

My son's teacher says he is hyperactive and should be put on drugs. Do Black children tend to be more hyperactive or is this a racial stereotype on the part of the school? What should I do? (181). Some of the children in my first-grade class call each other names when they are angry—"black nigger," "black pig," and so on. How should I handle this? (212)

Crawford, Susan Hoy. 1996. *Beyond dolls and guns: 101 ways to help children avoid gender bias.* Portsmouth, N.H.: Heinemann. A good reference for teachers on ways to fight and avoid gender bias. The author provides 101 ideas for educators to think about and to utilize in their teaching. She also includes various resources in the book, including a list of job titles that can be changed. For example, Crawford suggests we change titles such as chairman to chairperson or convener, and weatherman to forecaster or meteorologist.

Fadiman, Anne. 1997. *The spirit catches you and you fall down.* New York: The Noonday Press. This is an important book for anyone who would like to understand how cultural differences can have a devastating impact on the care of children. The clash of cultural values and language differences created serious problems for a Hmong family in Fresno. An excellent resource for educators who may not understand how culture can create serious conflicts among people who in reality have the same goals of living a happy and healthy life.

Fedullo, Mick. 1992. *Light of the feather: Pathways through contemporary Indian America.* New York: William Morrow. Mick Fedullo is a White teacher who learns about the struggles and triumphs of Indian communities. Fedullo is able to move beyond the cultural divide and learns about the richness of the Crow and Pima communities.

Fredrickson, George M. 2002. *Racism: A short history.* Princeton, N.J.: Princeton University Press. An important resource book for readers who are interested in learning about the evolution of racism. Fredrickson's work brings together anti-Semitism, European expansion, and slave trade from Africa and examines the similarities and differences between these movements in the development of Western racism.

Gay, Geneva. 2000. *Culturally relevant teaching: Theory, research, and practice.* New York: Teachers College Press. An excellent resource for teachers, written by one of the leaders in Multicultural Education. Gay is an outstanding scholar who understands the need for the integration of culture throughout the curriculum.

Gould, Stephen Jay. 1996. *The mismeasure of man.* New York: W. W. Norton and Company. Gould was a well-known paleontologist who was an expert in human evolution. This book refutes the finding of biological determinism in general and more specifically the claims made in the book, *The Bell Curve.* Using scientific evidence, Gould challenges the belief that people can be placed in biological categories, such as race, that reflect natural inherited economic and social differences.

Irons, Peter. 2002. *Jim Crow's children: The broken promise of the Brown decision.* New York: Viking Press. Irons is a lawyer and political science professor who has worked to further the movement of civil rights. Although the Supreme Court decision of *Brown* v. *Board of Education* mandated the end of segregation in schools, today many schools find themselves involved in a pattern of resegregation. He also discusses the social benefits of integration.

Kidder, Tracy. 2003. *Mountains beyond mountains: The quest of Dr. Paul Farmer, a man who would cure the world.* New York: Random House.

Kidder, a Pulitzer Prize winner, has written an informative book about Dr. Paul Farmer who is a specialist in infectious diseases. His work in Haiti and other countries throughout the world, demonstrate how one person can provide hope and health care to thousands of others. An inspiring read.

Kohn, Alfie. 1999. *The schools our children deserve: Moving beyond traditional classrooms and "tougher standards."* Boston: Houghton Mifflin. Kohn is an important educator who has written extensively about how standardized tests are turning our students and schools into places of regurgitation and memorization. Schools obsessed with testing are pushing critical thinking out of the classroom. Students are being short-changed by an approach that does not include analysis, synthesis, and decision making; rather, the curriculum often reflects a top-down authoritarian atmosphere in schools. Grades and getting high grades on standardized test become the goals of students, rather than critical thinking or the solving of social problems.

Ladson-Billings, Gloria. 2003. *Critical race theory perspectives on social studies.* Greenwich, CT: Information Age. An edited volume that discusses the need for social studies education to consider issues of race and racism in the curriculum. One of the best chapter is written by Geneva Gay who reviewed social studies textbooks for teachers and found that the issue of racism is, for the most part, absent. Thoughtful collection.

Lee, Enid, Deobrah Menkart, and Margo Okazawa-Rey. 2002. *Beyond heroes and holidays: A practical guide to K–12 anti-racist, multicultural education, and staff development.* Washington, D.C.: Teaching for Change.

Levine, David, Robert Lowe, Bob Peterson, and Rita Tenorio. 1995. *Rethinking schools: An agenda for change.* New York: The New Press. Excellent text with a variety of readings from educators such as Henry Louis Gates, Jr., Louise Derman-Sparks, Bill Bigelow, Linda Christensen, and Lisa Delpit. The articles challenge teachers to consider carefully the underlying messages that present practices in schools convey about equity issues, whether they deal with class, race, or other aspects of society. Important reading for all teachers.

Loomans, Diane, and Karen Kolberg. 1993. *The laughing classroom: Everyone's guide to teaching with humor and play.* Tiburon, Calif.: H. J. Kramer, Inc. A fun book that presents excellent ideas about how to teach with laughter and humor.

Maiga, Hassimi Oumarou. 2002. *Notes on classical Songhoy education and socialization: The world of women and child rearing practices in West Africa.* Atlanta, Ga.: Murehm Books. An introductory monograph about the Songhoy civilization and its impact on life today in West Africa. For other materials by Maiga, you can contact him at songhoy@yahoo.com.

McIntosh, Peggy. 1992. Unpacking the invisible knapsack: White privilege. *Creation Spirituality.* January/February: 33–35, 53. This is an excellent article about privileges that European Americans hold but are often unaware of. The article talks about the unearned power that members of the majority have in society. To McIntosh it is clear that racism is an institutional issue. When we are silent or deny the existence of the advantages given because of racial group membership, she believes the pattern of dominance continues and is reinforced.

Noguera, Pedro. 2003. *City schools and the American dream: Reclaiming the promise of public education.* New York: Teachers College Press. An excellent book about the many issues and obstacles facing many parents and students of urban communities. Although many educators believe extensive testing and the increase in standards will make the difference in schools, Noguera's work indicates that achievement issues are social issues that involve financial instability, lack of school reform, and lack of substance for schools.

Olson, Steve. 2002. *Mapping human history: Genes, race, and our common origins.* Boston, Mass.: Houghton Mifflin. This book provides easy-to-read scientific explanation about extremely complex issues about human evolution. A must book for any teacher who is interested in the latest genetic and biological information about evolution.

Perry, Theresa. 1996. *Teaching Malcolm X.* New York: Routledge. An outstanding collection of readings for teachers by teachers that explain how they have presented the life and ideas of Malcolm Little. The chapters share information from educators from the elementary grades to college level. The perceptions and insights are extremely valuable for anyone who is considering developing and teaching a unit on Malcolm X.

Pilkington, Doris. 2002. *Rabbit-proof fence.* New York: Miramax Books. This is a powerful story of three young interracial Aboriginal and European girls who escaped from a camp in Southern Australia where they had been sent to learn the cultural ways of White society. The children were not allowed to speak native languages, practice cultural customs, or maintain cultural values. These three young girls escaped from the camp with the determination to return home over 1,500 miles away through a harsh desert. The story is one of courage, determination, and cultural identity so strong that the three children were willing to risk death. Similar to the experiences of Native Americans and the governmental policy of cultural genocide, this story provides teachers with the knowledge of prejudice and discrimination as global issues and not found only within our national boundaries.

Root, Maria P., and Matt Kelley. 2003. Multiracial child resource book: Living complex identities. Seattle, Wash.: Mavin Foundation. This is an excellent resource for teachers, social workers, counselors, psychologists, and other social service individuals who are interested in understanding how ethnic and racial identity influences the ideas and values of folks from various communities. The photos alone are worth the price of the book. See the wonderful diversity of our country and read the stories that folks share. Information also found at www.mavinfoundation.org.

Shaver, James P., and William Strong. 1982. *Facing value decisions: Rationale-building for teachers.* New York: Teachers College Press. Excellent book that describes how teachers can utilize an issues-centered approach to teaching. The authors provide various lessons for teachers that cover values such as democracy, human dignity, pluralism, conflict, cohesion, the Chicano Maverick, and civil disobedience. One of the most important aspects of teaching is to assist students in developing skills so that they can effectively deal with conflicts, issues, and decision making.

Stavley, Louise. 1989. *The Education of a WASP.* Madison: University of Wisconsin Press. This is an excellent look at the issue of society having different rules for different groups of people. Stavley found through her own experiences in the 1960s that even though, as a nation, we espouse the values of justice and fair play, in reality African Americans were being discriminated against in schools, on the job, and in the media. She realized that much of our views of other groups has been transmitted by television, movies, the newspapers, and magazines. Let me ask, If you have had little contact with others from another group, how do you learn about who they are and what they believe in? Usually it is through the media. Reading this book can give you a deeper understanding of the system of rewards and punishments in society and that it is based upon factors such as skin color, gender, social economic class, and sexual orientation.

Sykes, Bryan. 2001. *The seven daughters of Eve.* New York: W. W. Norton and Company. A critical reference for every teacher in all content areas. Skyes is a professor of genetics and traces the DNA of Europeans today to seven women from the past. Through the stories of the seven women, the author explains the migration patterns of people and the impact of the environment on their lives. He explains that women and not men pass on the mitochondrial DNA found in our cells. The author also presents evidence that supports the "Out of Africa" theory about human evolution.

Tatum, Beverly D. 1997. *Why are all the Black kids sitting together in the cafeteria?* New York: Basic Books. Beverly Tatum has written one of the easiest-to-read texts on racial identification formation. She carefully includes theoretical frameworks of Erik Erickson, Janet Helms, and William Cross. Much of the literature on racial identification is hard to understand, but Tatum has written a book that you will learn from and enjoy. As an African American professional, she shares her real-life experiences. This mother of two youngsters gives a special view of how she helps her own children deal with racism and racial identity.

Walling, Donovan. R. 1996. *Open lives, safe schools.* Bloomington, Ind.: Phi Delta Kappa Educational Foundation. An important resource for teachers about homophobia and how to address the needs of lesbian, gay, and bisexual students in schools. The edited text provides important approaches that can be included in schools, from minimal levels of change such as replacing the terms *mother* or *father* to *parent* or *parents* in letters home, to changing school policies that include antiharassment of students based on sexual orientation.

Wise, Time. Membership Has Its Privileges: Thoughts on Acknowledging and Challenging Whiteness. He provides a thought-provoking article on being part of the majority culture. The website for this essay is http://www.zmag.org/sustainers/content/2000-06/22wise.htm.

Part 3: Videos for Teachers and Students

ABC News. Annenberg Foundation/CPB. 1994. *Calculating change.* New York: National Urban League, Inc. Video for teachers to look at how parents and educators have created successful programs in science and math education. Discussion of Bob Moses's *The Algebra Project.* (Distributed through the Annenberg/CPB Math and Science Collection, P.O. Box 2345, S. Burlington, VT, 05407-2345)

Family Communications. 1995. *The different and the same video series.* Pittsburgh, Pa.: Family Communications. Series of videos to use with grades K–2 about prejudice and discrimination. There is also a teachers' manual and training video. This comes from the producers of *Mr. Rogers' Neighborhood.* (Distributed by GPM, P.O. Box 80669, Lincoln, Nebr., 68501-0669)

Filipino American National Historical Society. 1994. *Filipino Americans: Discovering their past for the future.* Seattle, Wash.: Filipino National Historical Society. Presents the history of Filipino Americans from 1587 to the early 1990s. Excellent resource. (Distributed by Wehman Video, 2366 Eastlake Avenue East, Suite 312, Seattle, WA, 98102)

Kroopnick, Stephen, and Stu Schreiberg. 1998. *Underground railroad.* New York: The History Channel. Excellent video about the history of the underground railroad. The film highlights the courage and actions of people such as Frederick Douglass, Harriet Tubman, and William Lloyd Garrison. (Distributed by New Video Group, 126 Fifth Avenue, New York, NY, 10011)

McCray, Judith. 1995. *Mississippi, America.* Carbondale, Ill.: WSIU Carbondale and the Department of Radio-Television at Southern Illinois University at Carbondale. Excellent documentary chronicling the struggle for the right to vote in Mississippi during the summer of 1964. The work of many civil rights activists resulted in the passage of the Voting Rights Act of 1965. (Distributed by Warner Home Video, 4000 Warner Boulevard, Burbank, CA, 91522)

Miramax Films. 2002. *Rabbit-Proof Fence.* Excellent film about the impact of the Australian government's policy of cultural assimilation on Black Aboriginal youth. A true story about the determination and courage of three young girls in holding onto their cultural identity and homes. (Distributed by Miramax Films, Burbank, California)

New Market Films. 2003. *Whale rider.* Outstanding film about a Maori girl from New Zealand and her struggles against gender bias in a culture that is patriarchal. The relationships are rich and unsettling at time. Demonstrates the cultural conflict that arises when women desire a more active role in a traditional cultural community. This story centers around a 12-year-old youngster whose strong mind and love of culture provide an important role model for young people today.

Searchlight Pictures. 2003. *Bend it like Beckham.* This is another excellent film about the cultural conflicts a young woman in a South Indian family who lives in England must cope with. Her parents want her to become a traditional Indian women, however this young person has dreams of becoming a professional women's soccer player. Also some discussion of cross-cultural misunderstandings and differences.

Glossary

Analogies Mental models of how the world works using what an individual already knows (Collins and Gentner 1987).

Anti-Semitism Prejudice and/or discrimination against Jews (Anti-Defamation League).

Assimilation A process that seeks to eliminate ethnic and linguistic practices and cultures and replace them with the host culture and language.

Assimilationist Person who believes in assimilation.

Authentic assessment An approach to assessment whereby students demonstrate an interdisciplinary understanding and analysis of knowledge. For example, students devise a solution to a problem or create a blueprint for a new school playground.

Bilingual Education Various forms of educational programs in which both English and a home language are used in instruction.

Bilingualism Able to speak and write in two languages.

Binomial classification system Carolus Linnaeus developed a system to classify plants and animals.

Black vernacular Also referred to as Black English or Ebonics.

Blame the victim Shift the fault of a problem to a victim or targeted party.

Brown* v. *Board of Education Linda Brown was an eight-year-old child in Topeka, Kansas, who was told to attend a school several miles from her home although she lived five blocks from a neighborhood school. Her parents filed a lawsuit. Thurgood Marshall was a lawyer on the team for the Brown family. The Supreme Court ruled in 1954 that "separate, but equal" schools were inherently unequal. This led to federally mandated desegregation.

Care theory Theory primarily developed by Nel Noddings that maintains that trusting, reciprocal relationships are at the core.

Classism Prejudice and/or discrimination based on perceived or actual income level.

Comprehensible input Auditory language that is understandable and meaningful and by which the information is presented at a somewhat higher learning level than the learner's performance level.

Constructivism An educational approach that builds on the belief that individuals construct their own meaning; teachers are encouraged to use student knowledge and experiences in the learning process.

Critical Theory Critical theory directs scholars to look at the structure of schools and/or other social institutions to see who benefits from its organization and policies.

Cultural capital Knowledge of society and ability to use this knowledge to gain entry.

Cultural mediator Person who can navigate between two cultures, bridging one culture to another.

Culturally responsive education "Using the cultural knowledge, prior experiences, frames of reference, and performance styles of ethnically diverse students to make learning encounters more relevant to and effective for them. It teaches *to* and *through* the strengths of these students. It is *culturally validating* and *affirming*" (Gay 2000, 29).

Culture A complex system that includes three levels: surface components (such as dress, artifacts, history, food, art work, etc.), interactional patterns (greeting practices, expected classroom behaviors, etc.), and values and beliefs (philosophy, religious beliefs, etc.).

Deficit theory   A belief that students from under-represented groups come with cultures and languages that place them at risk of failing in school; intellectual inferiority is often part of the belief linking cultural differences with cultural deficiency.

Discrimination   The act that "comes about only when we deny to individuals or groups of people equality of treatment which they may wish" (Allport 1954, 50).

Ethnic prejudice   "An antipathy based upon a faulty and inflexible generalization. It may be felt or expressed. It may be directed toward a group as a whole, or toward an individual because he is a member of that group" (Allport 1954, 10).

Ethnicity   Ethnicity is seen as a group category that deals with culture, ancestry (Omi and Winant 1994; Valle 1997), and sense of oneness (Kleg 1993).

Ethnocentrism   One's own culture shapes his or her view of the world and other cultures.

Gatekeeper   A practice or person that keeps individuals in specific groups from opportunities available to others.

Hegemony   The dominant culture, the ruling culture and society, and its ability to ensure the status quo of advantage through the use of institutions such as education and governmental structures.

High-stakes testing   Isolated tests used to decide life-affecting decisions of student tracking, placement, admissions, and so on.

Higher-order critical thinking skills   In contrast to recall and memorization skills, these skills call for analysis, synthesis, evaluation, and decision making.

Homo sapiens   Genus and species name given to humans in the binomial classification typology that means "wise man."

Homophobia   Irrational fear of gays, lesbians, and bisexuals.

Human Genome Project   A genetic research project identifying the three billion base pairs of nucleotides in human DNA and identifying approximately 30,000 to 35,000 genes.

Institutional racism   A system of legalized practices designed to keep the dominant group in power (McIntosh 1992).

Intercultural sensitivity   Cross-cultural understandings and skills used to communicate with people from other cultures

Kinship   Strong bonds of trust and the creation of a strong community.

Lau* v. *Nichols   Cantonese-speaking parents filed a class-action suit against the San Francisco School District on behalf of Chinese-speaking children. Lau is Kinney Lau, who was a first grader. Alan Nichols was the superintendent. The Supreme Court ruled in 1974 that students who spoke a language other than English were denied an equal education. This decision led to the inclusion of Bilingual Education programs.

Meritocracy   Belief that those who hold higher-status careers or position do so because they merit them because of intellectual superiority and high work ethic; they have earned their status and opportunities.

Metaphors   Words or phrases that imply a comparison; they suggest a new comparison for an object or concept. Cultural metaphors are comparisons that link one cultural context to another.

Minority group   Members of ethnic groups that had less status or were members of underrepresented communities were referred to as minorities. Today many students who are members of underrepresented groups make up a numerical majority of the 25 largest school districts in the United States; therefore, the term is not used in this book.

Natural approach   A method used to assist the learner in acquiring language that emphasizes the importance of context in teaching.

No Child Left Behind (NCLB)   Federal legislation passed in 2001 and signed by George W. Bush, reauthorizing the Elementary and Secondary Education Act of 1992.

Phonology   Patterns of sounds that are used in speech. Can also include pitch and emphasis placed on syllables or words.

Public Law 94-142   Originally known as the Education of All Handicapped Children Act of 1975, this law was renamed the Individuals with Disabilities Education Act. There has been a change to encourage mainstreaming or the inclusion of students in the regular classroom.

Pragmatics   Study of how individuals use language within a social context; this includes the behaviors expected, formality of the situation, and subject content.

Prejudice   "A feeling, favorable or unfavorable, toward a person or thing, prior to, or not based on, actual experience" (Allport 1954, 7).

Proverbs   Common sayings usually providing a belief about life.

Race   An extremely complicated social and political concept used to categorize people based on physical differences; it has no foundation in the biological sciences.

Racism   Various types of racism include personal, cultural, and institutional. It is prejudice and resulting discrimination based upon perceived racial differences. Racism is the belief that one's race is superior and that others are inferior. It also defines a system of privileges and penalties based on the belief in the dominance of some over others.

Scaffolding   Arises out of the constructivist orientation and refers to the support or scaffold teachers use to build student knowledge. Teachers may use examples from student experiences, photos of objects students are familiar with, targeted questions, and inspiration or encouragement.

Scapegoating   Shifting the blame of a problem to a victim.

Sexism   Prejudice based on gender that often limits opportunities; some scholars now refer to sexism as gender bias.

Similes   A comparison between two distinct things using the words *like* or *as*.

Social capital   Resources that come from one's social network, such as jobs, educational opportunities, investments, loans, and access to organizations.

Stereotype   Overgeneralized image of a person; an untrue fixed picture that has a value judgment attached to it.

Subjective culture   "The learned and shared patterns of beliefs, behaviors, and values of groups of interacting people" (Milton Bennett 1998, 3).

Title IX of the Education Amendment   Legislation passed in 1972 that stated that women and men could not be discriminated against in "any educational program or activity receiving federal aid."

Total physical response   A method in which the learner listens carefully to language and the student learns language by watching the teacher modeling the action.

Tracking   Refers to the sorting of students by achievement levels.

White privilege   A system of unearned assets and benefits used consciously or unconsciously by people who are members of the majority that results in social control.

References

Allport, Gordon. W. 1954. *The nature of prejudice.* Reading, Mass.: Addison-Wesley.

Collins, Allan, and Dedre Gentner. 1987. How people construct mental models. In *Cultural models in language and thought.* Edited by Dorothy Holland and Naomi Quinn, eds., New York: Cambridge University Press.

Gay, Geneva. 2000. *Culturally responsive teaching: Theory, research, and practice.* New York: Teachers College Press.

Kleg, Milton. 1993. *Hate, prejudice, and racism.* Albany, N.Y.: State University of New York Press.

McIntosh, Peggy. 1992. Unpacking the invisible knapsack: White privilege. *Creation Spirituality* (January/February): 33–35, 53.

References

CHAPTER 1

Allport, Gordon W. 1954. *The nature of prejudice.* Reading, Mass.: Addison-Wesley.

Banks, James A. 2002. *An introduction to Multicultural Education.* 3rd ed. Boston: Allyn and Bacon.

Bennett, Christine. 1995. *Comprehensive multicultural education: Theory and practice.* Needham Heights, Mass.: Allyn and Bacon.

Blassingame, John. 1979. *The slave community: Plantation life in the Antebellum South.* New York: Oxford University Press.

Boston Public Schools. 2002. Facts and figures, Boston Public Schools enrollment. http://boston.k12.ma.us/bps/enrollment.asp.

Brennan, Robert T., Jimmy Kim, Melodie Wenz-Gross, and Gary N. Siperstein. 2001. The relative equitability of high-stakes testing versus teacher-assigned grades: An analysis of the Massachusetts Comprehensive Assessment System (MCAS). *Harvard Educational Review* 71, no. 2:173–216.

Cole, Michael. 1996. *Cultural psychology: A once and future discipline.* Cambridge, Mass: Belknap Press of Harvard University.

Cornelius, Carol. 1999. *Iroquois corn: In a culture-based curriculum.* Albany, N.Y.: SUNY Press.

Cremin, Lawrence A. 1988. *American education: The metropolitan experience 1876–1980.* New York: Harper and Row.

Darder, Antonia. 1991. *Culture and power in the classroom: A critical foundation for bicultural education.* New York: Bergin & Garvey.

Delpit, Lisa. 1995. *Other people's children.* New York: New Press.

Dewey, John. 1916. *Democracy and education.* New York: The Free Press.

Gay, Geneva. 2000. Culturally responsive teaching: Theory, research, and practice. New York: Teachers College Press.

Grant, Carl A., and Christine Sleeter. 1998. *Turning on learning.* Englewood Cliffs, N.J.: Prentice Hall.

Gutstein, E., P. Lipman, P. Hernandez, and R. de los Reyes. 1997. Culturally relevant mathematics teachers in Mexican American context. *Journal for Research in Mathematics Education* 28, no. 6:709–37.

Hilliard, Asa. 2002. Beneficial educational research: Assumptions, paradigms, definitions. Presidential Invited Address. American Educational Research Association, New Orleans, La.

Irvine, Jacqueline Jordan. 2002. *In search of wholeness: African American teachers and their culturally specific classroom practices.* New York: Palgrave.

King, Joyce. 1994. The purpose of schooling for African American children: Including cultural knowledge. In *Teaching diverse populations: Formulating a knowledge base,* edited by Etta R. Hollins, Joyce E. King, and Warren C. Hayman. Albany, N.Y.: SUNY Press, 25–66.

Kohn, Alfie. 1999. *The schools our children deserve: Moving beyond traditional classrooms and "tougher standards."* New York: Houghton Mifflin.

Ladson-Billings, Gloria. 1994. *The dreamkeepers: Successful teachers of African American children.* San Francisco, Calif.: Jossey-Bass.

———. 1995. Toward a theory of culturally relevant pedagogy. *American Educational Research Journal* 33 no. 3:465–92.

Larke, Patricia and Norvella P. Carter. 2002. *Examining practices in multicultural education.* College Station, Tex: JOY Publishing.

Leguizamo, John. 2002. John Leguizamo: Actor and comedian. In *The right words at the right time,* edited by Marlo Thomas. New York: Atria Books, 191–94.

Lipman, Pauline. 1998. *Race, class, and power in school restructuring.* Albany, N.Y.; SUNY Press.

Los Angeles Times. 2002. "Value of standardized tests," 31 May, B 14.

Mathison, Sandra. 1997. Assessment in social studies: Moving toward authenticity. In *The social studies curriculum,* edited by E. Wayne Ross. Albany, N.Y.: SUNY Press, 213–24.

Matriano, Estela. 2000. The impact of global changes on teacher education: Challenges, opportunities and a vision for a culture of peace. *International Journal of Curriculum and Instruction* 2, no. 1:85–93.

McAllister, Gretchen and Jacqueline Jordan Irvine. 2002. The role of empathy in teaching culturally diverse students: A qualitative study of teachers' beliefs. *Journal of Teacher Education* 53, no. 5:433–43.

McIntyre, Ellen, Ann Rosebery, and Norma González. 2001. *Classroom diversity.* Portsmouth, N.H.: Heinemann.

Merryfield, Merry. 2001. Moving the center of global education: From imperial world views that divide the world to double consciousness, contrapuntal pedagogy, hybridity, and cross-cultural competence. In *Critical issues in social studies research for the 21st century,* edited by William B. Stanley. Greenwich, Conn.: Information Age Publishing, 179–207.

Moll, Luis. 1990. *Vygotsky and education: Instructional implications and applications of sociohistorical psychology.* New York: Cambridge University Press.

Murdock, Steve. 2002. Demographic changes and educational implications in the urban South. Presentation at the 2002 National Invitational Conference for Educational Research in the Urban South. Texas A&M University, College Station, Texas, December 6–8.

National Center for Education Statistics. 2001. *Mini-Digest of Educational Statistics.* U.S. Department of Education, Office of Education Research and Improvement NCES 2002-026, 13.

Nisbett, Richard E. 2003. *Geography of thought: How Asians and Westerners think differently.* New York: Free Press.

Noddings, Nel. 1984. *Caring: A feminine approach to ethics and moral development.* Berkeley, Calif.: University of California Press.

———. 1992. *The challenge to care in schools: An alternative approach to education.* N.Y.: Teachers College Press.

———. 2002a. *Educating moral people: A caring alternative to character education.* New York: Teachers College Press.

———. 2002b. *Starting at home: Caring and social policy.* Berkeley, Calif.: University of California Press.

Nussbaum, Martha C. 1997. *Cultivating humanity: A classical defense of reform in liberal education.* Cambridge, Mass.: Harvard University Press.

Palmer, Parker. 1998. *The courage to teach: Exploring the inner landscape of a teacher's life.* San Francisco, Calif.: Jossey-Bass.

Sadker, David Miller, and Myra Pollack Sadker. 2003. *Teachers, schools, and society.* Boston, Mass.: McGraw-Hill Publishers.

Schaeffer, Bob. 2003. SAT gender and racial gaps increase misuse of test results will hurt college diversity, excellence; state score trends undermine claims of exit exam promoters. August 26. www.fairtest.org/pr/SATscorerelease03.html.

Singer, Alan. 2003. Student clubs: A model for political organizing. *Rethinking Schools.* Summer. www.rethinking schools.org/wor/readings/cllub174.shtml.

Social Science Data Analysis Network. 2002. 2000 Census. www.censusscope.org.

Starratt, Robert. 1994. *Building an ethical school: A practical response to the moral crisis in schools.* New York: Falmer Press.

Takaki, Ronald. 1989. *Strangers from a different shore: A history of Asian Americans.* Boston, Mass.: Little, Brown and Company.

Tanner, Laurel N. 1997. *Dewey's laboratory school: Lessons for today.* New York: Teachers College Press.

Thompson, Audrey. 1998. Not the color purple: Black feminist lessons for educational caring, *Harvard Educational Review* 68, no. 4:522–24.

Villegas, Ana María. 2002. *Educating culturally responsive teachers: A coherent approach.* Albany, N.Y.: SUNY Press.

———, and Tamara, Lucas. 2002. *Educating culturally responsive teachers.* Albany, N.Y.: SUNY Press.

Vygotsky, Lev. 1978. *Mind in society.* Cambridge, Mass.: Harvard University Press.

Walker, Vanessa Siddle. 1996. *Their highest potential: An African American school community in the segregated South.* Chapel Hill, N.C.: University of North Carolina Press.

Wink, Joan, and LeAnn G. Putney. 2002. *A vision of Vygotsky.* Boston: Allyn and Bacon.

CHAPTER 2

Bennett, Milton J. 1998. Intercultural communication: A current perspective. In *Basic concepts of intercultural communication,* edited by Milton J. Bennet. Yarmouth, Maine: Intercultural Press, 1–34.

Brislin, Richard. 1993. *Understanding culture's influence on behavior.* New York: Harcourt Brace College Publishers.

Bruner, Jerome. 1990. *Acts of meaning.* Cambridge, Mass.: Harvard University Press.

Bustamante-Jones, Evangelina. 1998. *Mexican American teachers as cultural mediators: Literacy and literacy contexts through bicultural strengths.* Claremont Graduate University and San Diego State University.

Cajete, Gregory. 1993. *Look to the mountain.* Skyland, N.C.: Kivaki Press.

Christiansen, Linda. 1997. Reading, writing, and outrage. Keynote address, National Association of Multicultural Education. October, Albuquerque, N. Mex.

Cleary, Linda Miller, and Thomas D. Peacock. 1997. *Collected wisdom: American Indian Education,* Boston, Mass.: Allyn and Bacon.

Cole, Michael. 1996. *Cultural psychology: A once and future discipline.* Cambridge, Mass: Belknap Press of Harvard University.

Cornelius, Carol. 1999. *Iroquois corn: In a culture-based curriculum.* Albany, N.Y.: SUNY Press.

Cushner, Kenneth, Averil McClelland, and Philip Safford. 2003. *Human diversity in education.* 4th ed. Boston, Mass.: McGraw-Hill.

Gibson, Rich. 2000. Outfoxing the destruction of wisdom. *Theory and Research in Social Education* 29: 2, at www.pipeline.com/~rgibson/Outfoxing.htm.

Gould, Stephen Jay. 1996. *The mismeasure of man.* New York: W.W. Norton.

Heath, Shirley Brice. 1983. *Way with words: Language, life, and work in communities and classrooms.* New York: Cambridge University Press.

Hong, Peter Y. 2002. The kosher kitchen is a hit at Caltech. *Los Angeles Times,* 10 August, B16.

Kochman, Thomas. 1981. *Black and White styles in conflict.* Chicago: University of Chicago Press.

Lipman, Pauline. 1998. *Race, class, and power in school restructuring.* Albany, N.Y.: SUNY Press.

Loewen, James. 1995. *Lies my teacher told me.* New York: Simon and Schuster.

Martuza, Victor. 1977. *Applying norm-referenced and criterion-referenced measurement in education.* Boston, Mass.: Allyn and Bacon.

McNamee, Gillian. 1990. Learning in an inner-city setting: A longitudinal study of community change. In *Vygotsky and education: Instructional implications and applications of sociohistorical psychology,* edited by Luis Moll. New York: Cambridge University Press.

Minami, M., and C. Ovando. 1995. Language issues in multicultural contexts. In *Handbook of research on multicultural education,* edited by J. A. Banks and C. M. Banks. New York: Macmillan.

Moran, C. E., and K. Hakuta. 1995. Bilingual education: Broadening research perspectives. In *Handbook of research on multicultural education,* edited by J. A. Banks and C. M. Banks. New York: Macmillan.

Mydans, Carl. 1997. Flyer on Carl Mydans exhibition. The Studio Gallery of Old Town, 2501 San Diego Avenue, San Diego, Calif. 92110, October.

Ovando, Carlos, and Virginia Collier. 1985. *Bilingual and ESL classrooms.* New York: McGraw-Hill Book Company.

Pipher, Mary. 2002. *The middle of everywhere: The world's refugees come to our town.* New York: Harcourt, Inc.

Quinn, Daniel. 1992. *Ishmael.* New York: Bantam/Turner Books.

Ragin, Charles C., and Jeremy Hein. 1993. The comparative study of ethnicity: Methodological and conceptual issues. In *Race and ethnicity in research methods,* edited by John Stanfield and Rutledge M. Dennis. Newbury Park, Calif.: Sage Publications, 254–72.

Sherman, Howard, and James L. Wood. 1989. *Sociology: Traditional and radical perspectives.* New York: Harper and Row.

Smith, James F. 1999. The lowly tortilla gets a boost. *Los Angeles Times,* 4 August, A1, A6.

Soto, Hiram. 2002. Two thumbs up?: Blackbuster video is seeking rave reviews from its Latino customers. *San Diego Union-Tribune,* 13 November, C1, C3.

Valle, Ramón. 1997. *Ethnic diversity and multiculturalism: Crisis or challenge.* New York: American Heritage Custom Publishing.

———. 2001. Ethics, ethnicity, and dementia: A culture-fair approach to bioethical advocacy in dementing illness. *Georgia Law Review* 35:465–515.

———, and Lee Brason. 2002. Research priorities in the evolving demographic landscape of Alzheimer disease and associated dementias. *Alzheimer Disease and Associated Disorders.*

CHAPTER 3

Allport, Gordon W. 1954. *The nature of prejudice.* Reading, Mass.: Addison-Wesley.

Bennett, Christine. 1995. *Comprehensive multicultural education: Theory and practice.* Needham Heights, Mass.: Allyn and Bacon.

Brennan, Robert T., Jimmy Kim, Meoldie Wenz-Gross, and Gary N. Siperstein. 2001. The relative equitability of high-stakes testing versus teacher-assigned grades: An anlysis of the Massachusetts Comprehensive Assessment System (MCAS). *Harvard Educational Review* 71, no. 2: 173–216.

Center on Hunger and Poverty. 2002. National facts and figures on hunger and food insecurity in the U.S. http//:www.centeronhunger.orgfsifacts.html.

Delpit, Lisa. 1995. *Other people's children.* N.Y.: New Press.

Ehrenreich, Barbara. 2001. *Nickel and dimed: On (not) getting by in America.* New York: A Metropolitan/Owl Book.

Fredrickson, George M. 2002. *Racism: A short history.* Princeton, N.J.: Princeton University Press.

Gordon, Milton. 1964. *Assimilation into American life: The role of race, religion, and national origin.* New York: Oxford University Press.

Gould, Stephen Jay. 1996. *The mismeasure of man.* 2nd ed. New York: W.W. Norton and Company.

Henderson, Vallane L., and Carol S. Dweck. 1990. Motivation achievement. In *At the threshold: The developing adolescent,* edited by Feldman and Elliott. Cambridge, Mass.: Harvard University Press.

Hernstein, Richard J., and Charles Murray. 1994. *The bell curve: The reshaping of American life by difference in intelligence.* New York: Free Press.

Hilliard, Asa. 2002. *Beneficial educational research: Assumptions, paradigms, and definitions.* Presidential Invited Address Distinguished Lecturer, American Educational Research Association, Annual Meeting, New Orleans, April 4.

Jackson, Maggie. 1997. Slow progress seen for minority women. *San Diego Union-Tribune,* 23 October, C-2.

King, Joyce. 1994. The purpose of schooling for African American children: Including cultural knowledge. In *Teaching diverse populations: Formulating a knowledge base,* edited by Etta R. Hollins, Joyce E. King, and Warren C. Hayman. Albany, N.Y.: SUNY Press, pp. 25–66.

Kleg, Milton. 1993. *Hate, prejudice, and racism.* Albany, N.Y.: State University of New York Press.

Kohn, Alfie. 1999. *The schools our children diverse: Moving beyond traditional classrooms and "tougher standards."* New York: Houghton Mifflin.

Kozol, Jonathan. 1991. *Savage inequalities: Children in America's schools.* N.Y.: Harper Perennial.

Lipman, Pauline. 1997. *Race, class, and power in school restructuring.* Albany, N.Y.: SUNY Press.

Litsky, Frank. 2003. Bush administration says Title IX should stay as it is. *NY Times,* 12 July, www.nytimes.com/2003/07/12/sports/12TITL.html?th=&pagewanted=print&position=7/12/2003.

McIntosh, Peggy. 1992. Unpacking the invisible knapsack: White privilege. *Creation Spirituality.* January/February: 33–35, 53.

Nieto, Sonia. 1992. *Affirming diversity: The sociopolitical context of multicultural education.* New York: Longman.

Noddings, Nel. 2002. *Educating moral people: A caring alternative to character education.* New York: Teachers College Press.

Nord, Mark, Nader Kabbani, Laura Tiehen, Margaret Andrews, Gary Bickel, and Steven Carlson. 2002. *Household food security in the United States.* Washington, D.C.: Economic Research Service, U.S. Department of Agriculture. http://www.ers.usda.gov/publications/fanrr21/.

Nussbaum, Martha. 1997. *Cultivating humanity.* Cambridge, Mass.: Harvard University Press.

Olson, Steve. 2002. *Mapping human history: Genes, race, and our common origins.* Boston, Mass.: Houghton Mifflin.

Omi, Michael, and Howard Winant. 1994. *Racial formation in the United States: From the 1960's to the 1990's.* 2nd ed. New York: Routledge.

Pang, Valerie Ooka. 1995. Asian Pacific American students: A diverse and complex population. In *Handbook of research on multicultural education,* edited by James A. Banks and Cherry McGee Banks. New York: Macmillan.

———, and Velma A. Sablan. 1998. Teacher efficacy: How do teachers feel about their abilities to teach African American students? In *Being responsive to cultural differences how teachers learn,* edited by Mary Dilworth. Thousand Oaks, Calif.: Corwin Press.

Ridley, Matt. 1999. *Genome: The autobiography of a species in 23 chapters.* New York: Perennial.

Riley, Richard and Norma Cantú. 1997. *Title IX: 25 years of progress.* U. S. Department of Education and Office for Civil Rights. http://www.ed.gov/pubs/TitleIX/title.html.

Sadker, Myra Pollack, and David Miller Sadker. 2000. *Teachers, schools, and society.* 5th ed. Boston, Mass.: McGraw-Hill.

Schniedewind, Nancy and Ellen Davidson. 1998. *Open minds to Equality.* Boston, MA: Allyn and Bacon.

Sherman, Howard J., and James L. Wood. 1989. *Sociology: Traditional and radical perspectives.* New York: Harper and Row.

Siegfried, Donna Rae. 2001. *Biology for dummies.* New York: Hungry Minds.

Stephan, Walter. 1999. *Reducing prejudice and stereotyping in schools.* New York: Teachers College Press.

Suggs, Welch. June 21, 2002. Title IX at 30. *Chronicle of Higher Education.* http://chronicle.com/free/f48/i41/41a03801.htm.

Sullivan, Tim. 2002. "Wrestling with gripes on Title IX? Get a Grip." *San Diego Union-Tribune,* 5 July, C1, C6.

Swim, J., Kathryn Aikin, Wayne Hall, and Barbara Hunter. 1995. Sexism and racism: Old-fashioned and modern prejudices. *Journal of Personality and Social Psychology* 68 no. 2:199–214.

Tyack, David and Elisabeth Hansot. 1990. *Learning together: A history of coeducation in American schools.* New York: Russell Sage Foundation.

U.S. Department of Education. 1994. *NAIA and NCAA Annual reports, Fall Enrollment in Colleges and Universities Surveys and Integrated Postsecondary Education Data System surveys.* National Center for Education Statistics, August.

Valle, Ramón. 1997. *Ethnic diversity and intercultural understanding.* New York: American Heritage Custom Publishing.

Valle, Ramón. 1998. *Caregiving across cultures: Working with dementing illness and ethnically diverse populations.* Washington, D.C.: Taylor and Francis.

West, Cornel. 1993. *Race matters.* Boston, Mass.: Beacon Press.

Ziegler, Mark. 2003. Title IX panel to air dissent. *San Diego Union-Tribune,* 30 January, D1, D3.

CHAPTER 4

Allport, Gordon W. 1954. *The nature of prejudice.* Reading, Mass.: Addison-Wesley.

Bennett, Milton J. 1993. Towards ethnorelativism: A developmental model of intercultural sensitivity. In *Education for intercultural experience,* edited by R. Michael Paige. 21–71. Yarmouth, Maine: Intercultural Press.

———. 1998. *Basic concepts of intercultural communication: Selected readings.* Yarmouth, Maine: Intercultural Press.

Brislin, Richard. 1993. *Understanding culture's influence on behavior.* New York: Harcourt Brace College Publishers.

Clark, Christine, and James O'Donnell. 1999. *Becoming and unbecoming White: Owning and disowning a racial identity.* Westport, Conn.: Bergin & Garvey.

Cross, Jr., William E. 1991. *Shades of black: Diversity in African-American identity.* Philadelphia, Pa.: Temple University Press.

Daniels, Roger, and Harry Kitano. 1970. *American racism: Exploration of the nature of prejudice.* Englewood Cliffs, N.J.: Prentice Hall, Inc.

Gordon, Edmund W. 1999. *Education and justice: A view from the back of the bus.* New York: Teachers College Press.

Helms, Janet (Ed.). 1990. *Black and White racial identity: Theory, research and practice.* Westport, Conn.: Greenwood Press.

Hilliard, Asa. 2002. *Beneficial educational research: Assumptions, paradigms, and definitions.* Presidential Invited Address Distinguished Lecturer, American Educational Research Association, Annual Meeting, New Orleans, April 4.

Johnson, Lauri. 2002. "My eyes have been opened": White teachers and racial awareness. *Journal of Teacher Education* 53, no. 2:153–67.

Knowlton, Clark. 1972. The New Mexican land war. In *Pain and promise: The Chicano today,* edited by Edward Simmen. New York: New American Library.

Loewen, James. 1995. *Lies my teacher told me.* New York: Simon and Schuster.

Manglitz, Elaine. 2003. Challenging White privilege in adult education: A critical review of the literature. *Adult Education Quarterly* 53, no. 2:119–134.

McIntosh, Peggy. 1992. Unpacking the invisible knapsack: White privilege. *Creation Spirituality* (January/February): 33–35, 53.

McLaren, Peter. 1997. Decentering Whiteness: In search of a revolutionary multiculturalism. *Multicultural Education* 5 no. 1:4–11.

Nelson, Jack, and Valerie O. Pang. In press. Race and ethnicity in social studies education: How racism and prejudice are perpetuated in the field. In *The social studies curriculum: Purposes, problems, and possibilities.* 2nd ed., edited by Wayne Ross. Albany, N.Y.: SUNY Press.

Oakes, Jeannie. 1985. *Keeping track: How schools structure inequality.* New Haven, Conn.: Yale University Press.

Omi, Michael, and Howard Winant. 1994. *Racial formation in the United States: From the 1960's to the 1990's.* 2nd ed. New York: Routledge.

Paley, Vivian Gussin. 1979. *White teacher.* Cambridge, Mass.: Harvard University Press.

Pang, Valerie, and Jesus Nieto. 1995. *The emotional responses of European American teachers to issues of prejudice and discrimination.* Unpublished manuscript.

Ryan, William. 1976. *Blaming the victim.* Rev. ed. New York: Vintage Books.

Sadker, Myra Pollack, and David Miller Sadker. 2000. *Teachers, schools, and society.* Boston, Mass.: McGraw-Hill.

Scheurich, James Joseph. 2002. *Anti-racist scholarship: An advocacy.* Albany, N.Y.: SUNY Press.

Sleeter, Christine. 1994. White racism. *Multicultural Education* 1, no. 4:5–8, 39.

Takaki, Ronald. 1993. *A different mirror : A history of multicultural America.* Boston: Little, Brown and Company.

Tatum, Beverly Daniel. 1992. African-American identity, academic achievement, and missing history. *Social Education* 56, no. 6:331–34.

———. 1992. Talking about race, learning about racism: The application of racial identity development theory. *Harvard Educational Review* 62, no. 1:1–24.

———. 1997. Why are all the black kids sitting together in the cafeteria? New York: Basic Books.

Valle, Ramón. 1997. *Ethnic diversity and multiculturalism: Crisis or challenge.* New York: American Heritage Custom Publishing.

Valli, Linda. 1995. The dilemma of race: Learning to be color blind and color conscious. *Journal of Teacher Education* 46, no. 3:120–29.

Wise, Tim. 2000. Membership has its privileges: Thoughts on acknowledging and challenging Whiteness. *Znet,* June 22. http://www.zmag.org/sustainers/content/2000-06/22wise.htm.

Zinn, Howard. 1980. *A people's history of the United States.* New York: Harper and Row.

———. 1990. *Declarations of independence.* New York: HarperCollins.

CHAPTER 5

Allport, Gordon W. 1954. *The nature of prejudice.* Reading, Mass.: Addison-Wesley.

Byrnes, Deborah. 1988. Children and prejudice. *Social Education* 52, no. 4:267–71.

Comer, James, and Alvin Poussaint. 1979. Foreward. In Paley's *White teacher,* Cambridge, Mass.: Harvard University Press.

Derman-Sparks, L., C. Higa, and B. Sparks. 1980. Children, race and racism: How race awareness develops. *Interracial Bulletin for Children* 11, nos. 3 and 4:3–9.

Derman-Sparks, Louise, and the ABC Task Force. 1989. *Anti-bias curriculum: Tools for empowering young children.* Washington, D.C.: NAEYC.

Gevelinger, Sister Mary Ellen, and Laurel Zimmerman. 1997. How Catholic schools are creating a safe climate for gay and lesbian students. *Educational Leadership* 55, no. 2:66–68.

Goodman, Mary Ellen. 1964. *Race awareness in young children,* New York: Collier Books.

Hatecrime.org. 2002. Coretta Scott King links gay rights and African-American civil rights. www.hatecrim.org/subpages/coretta.html.

Kohl, Herbert. 1993. The myth of "Rosa Parks the Tired": Teaching about Rosa Parks and the Montgomery bus boycott. *Multicultural Education* 1:6–10.

Lantieri, Linda and Janet Patti. 1996. *Waging peace in our schools.* Boston, MA: Beacon Press.

Mathison, Carla. 1998. The invisible minority: Preparing teachers to meet the needs of gay and lesbian students. *Journal of Teacher Education* 49, no. 2:151–55.

Nakagawa, Mako. 1992 (July). Private interview.

Pang, Valerie Ooka. 1988. Ethnic prejudice: Still alive and hurtful. *Harvard Educational Review* 58, no. 3:374–79.

Perrone, Vito. 1998. *Teacher with a heart: Reflections on Leonard Covello.* New York: Teachers College Press.

Pohan, Cathy, and Teresa E. Aguilar. 1998. *Facing homophobia: Preservice teachers grapple with their fears, misconceptions, and religious beliefs.* Paper presented at the 1998 annual meeting of the American Educational Research Association (April). San Diego, Calif.

Prince, Tony. 1996. The power of openness and inclusion in countering homophobia in schools. In *Open lives: Safe schools,* edited by Donovan R. Walling, Bloomington, Ind.: Phi Delta Kappa Educational Foundation.

Reis, Beth, Mona Mendoza, and Frieda Takamura. 2000. "If these were racial slurs, teachers would be stopping them" . . . three activists object. *Safe Schools Coalition.* www.safeschoolcoalition.org.

Scheurich, James Joseph. 2002. *Anti-racist scholarship: An advocacy.* Albany, N.Y.: SUNY Press.

Sleeter, Christine E., and Carl A. Grant. 1987. An analysis of multicultural education in the U.S.A. *Harvard Educational Review* 57:421–44.

Teaching Tolerance. 1992. Celebrate values (an interview with Robert Coles) 1, no. 1:18–22 (Spring).

Teaching Tolerance. 1999. *Starting Small: Teaching tolerance in preschool and the early grades.* Montgomery, Ala.: Southern Poverty Law Center.

Teaching Tolerance. *Responding to hate at school: A guide for teachers, counselors and administrators.* Montgomery, Ala.: Southern Poverty Law Center.

CHAPTER 6

1992. Celebrate values: An interview with Robert Coles. *Teaching Tolerance* (1): 18–22.

1996, January. The wage gap. *The National Times* 5: 4.

Allport, G. 1954. *The nature of prejudice.* New York: Doubleday Anchor Books.

Astin, Alexander W. 1977. *Four critical years.* San Francisco: Jossey-Bass.

Bennett, Jr., Lerone. 1984. *Before the Mayflower: A history of Black America.* New York: Penguin Books.

Boyle, T. C. 1995. *The tortilla curtain.* New York: Viking Press.

Brown, Tom. 1992. Joel Barker: New thoughts on paradigms. *Industry Week* (May 8):12–19.

Byrnes, Deborah. 1988. Children and prejudice. *Social Education* 52, no. 4:267–71.

Delgado, R. 1995. *The Rodrigo chronicles.* New York: New York University Press.

Derman-Sparks, L., C. Higa, and B. Sparks. 1980. Children, race, and racism: How race awareness develops. *Interracial Bulletin for Children* 11, nos. 3 and 4: 3–9.

Espinosa, Paul. 1986. *The Lemon Grove Incident.* KPBS Television, film.

Frankenberg, Erica, Chungmei Lee and Gary Orfield. 2003. *A multiracial society with segregated schools: Are we losing the dream?* The Civil Rights Project, Harvard University Press, http://www.civilrightsproject.harvard.edu/research/reseg03/AreWeLosingtheDream.pdf.

Franklin, John Hope and Alfred A. Moss, Jr. 1994. *From slavery to freedom: A history of African Americans.* New York: McGraw-Hill.

Franklin, John Hope and Alfred A. Moss, Jr. 1988. *From slavery to freedom: A history of Negro Americans.* New York: Knopf.

Frelick, Bill. 1985. Teaching about genocide as a contemporary problem. *Social Education* 49: 510–15.

Fulwood, S. 1995. Farrakhan calls men shunning march "fools." *Los Angeles Times* (October 15): A-1, A-14.

Gibson, Sherry, and M. H. Dembo. 1984. Teacher efficacy: A construct validation. *Journal of Educational Psychology* 76, no. 4: 569–82.

Goodman, M. E. 1964. *Race awareness in young children.* New York: Collier Books.

Helms, Janet, ed. 1990. *Black and White racial identity: Theory, research and practice.* Westport, Conn.: Greenwood Press.

Irons, Peter. 2002. *Jim Crow's children.* New York: Viking Press.

Kohl, Herbert. 1993. The myth of "Rosa Parks the Tired": Teaching about Rosa Parks and the Montgomery bus boycott. *Multicultural Education* 1: 6–10.

Kozol, Jonathan. 1991. *Savage inequalities: Children in America's schools.* New York: Crown Publishers.

Loewen, James W. 1995. *The lies my teacher told me.* New York: Touchstone Books.

Lomawaima, Tsianina, and Tersa L. McCarty. 2002. When tribal sovereignty challenges democracy: American Indian Education and the democratic ideal. *American Educational Research Journal* 39: 272–305.

Machamer, Ann Marie, and Enid Gruber. 1998. Secondary school, family, and educational risk: Comparing American Indian adolescents and their peers. *The Journal of Educational Research* 91: 357–69.

Mathison, Carla. 1998. The invisible minority: Preparing teachers to meet the needs of gay and lesbian youth. *Journal of Teacher Education* 49: 151–55.

McCarty, Teresa L. 2002. *A place to be Navajo: Rough Rock and the struggle for self-determination in indigenous schooling.* Mahwa, N.J.: Lawrence Erlbaum Associates.

Munson, Barbara. Nondated. *Common themes and questions about the use of "Indian" logos.* http://www.iwchildren.org/barb.htm.

Nakawaga, Mako. 1992. Private discussions (July).

Nieto, Sonia. 1990. *Affirming diversity: The sociopolitical context of multicultural education.* New York: Longman.

Noddings, N. 1984. *Caring: A feminine approach to ethics and moral education.* Berkeley, Calif.: University of California Press.

Oakes, Jeannie. 1985. *Keeping track: How schools structure inequality.* New Haven, Conn.: Yale University Press.

Pang, Valerie Ooka. 1988. Ethnic prejudice: Still alive and hurtful. *Harvard Educational Review* 58, no. 3: 374–79.

———. 1994. Asian Pacific American students: A diverse and complex population. In *Handbook of research on multicultural education,* edited by A. B. James and Cherry M. Banks. New York: Macmillan Publishing.

———, and Cynthia D. Park. Forthcoming. Examination of the self-regulation mechanism: Prejudice reduction in pre-service teachers. *Action in Teacher Education.*

———, and Velma A. Sablan. 1998. Teacher efficacy: How do teachers feel about their abilities to teach African American students? In *Being responsive to cultural differences how teachers learn,* edited by Mary Dilworth. Thousand Oaks, Calif.: Corwin Press.

Pewewardy, Cornel. Nondated. Why educator's can't ignore Indian mascots. http://www.aics.org/mcascot/cornel.html.

Ryan, William. 1971. *Blaming the victim.* New York: Vintage Books.

San Miguel, Guadalupe. 2001. *Brown, not White: School integration and the Chicano movement in Houston.* College Station: Texas A&M University Press.

Sleeter, Christine. 1994. White racism. *Multicultural Education* 1, no. 4: 5–8, 39.

Starratt. Robert. 1994. *Building an ethical school: A practical response to the moral crisis in schools.* New York: Taylor and Francis.

Swim, J., Kathryn Ikin, Wayne Hall, and Barbara Hunter. 1995. Sexism and racism: Old-fashioned and modern prejudices. *Journal of Personality and Social Psychology* 68, no. 2: 199–214.

Szasz, Margaret Connell. 1977. *Education and the American Indian: The road to self-determination since 1928.* Albuquerque, New Mex.: University of New Mexico Press.

Tatum, Beverly Daniel. 1992. Talking about race, learning about racism: The application of racial identity development theory. *Harvard Educational Review* 62, no. 1: 1–24.

Valli, Linda. 1995. The dilemma of race: Learning to be color blind and color conscious. *Journal of Teacher Education* 46, no. 3: 120–29.

Washington, James B. 1991. *A testament of hope: The essential writings and speeches of Martin Luther King, Jr.* San Francisco: Harper San Francisco, 21.

West, C. 1993. *Race matters.* Boston, Mass.: Beacon Press.

Wood, George H. 1993. *Schools that work.* New York: Dutton/Plume.

Zinn, Howard. 1980. *A people's history of the United States.* New York: Harper and Row.

CHAPTER 7

Au, Kathryn H. 1980. Participation structures in a reading lesson with Hawaiian children: Analysis of a culturally appropriate instructional event. *Anthropology and Education Quarterly* 11, no. 2: 91–115.

———, and Alice J. Kawakami. 1994. Cultural congruence in instruction. In *Teaching diverse populations: Formulating a knowledge base,* edited by Etta R. Hollins, Joyce E. King, and Warren C. Haymans. Albany, N.Y.: SUNY Press.

———, and J. M. Mason. 1981. Social organizational factors in learning to read: The balance of rights hypothesis. *Reading Research Quarterly* 17, no. 1: 115–52.

Banks, James A. 1981. *Multicultural education: Theory and practice.* Boston, Mass.: Allyn and Bacon.

———. 1995. Multicultural education: Historical development, dimensions, and practice. In *Handbook of research on multicultural education,* edited by James A. Banks and Cherry McGee Banks. New York: Macmillan.

———. 2003. *Teaching strategies for ethnic studies.* 7th ed. Boston, Mass: Allyn and Bacon.

Bellah, Robert N., Richard Madsen, William Sullivan, and Stephen M. Tipton. 1985. *Habits of the heart: Individualism and commitment in American life.* New York: Harper and Row.

Bennett, Christine. 1995. *Comprehensive multicultural education: Theory and practice.* 3rd ed. Boston, Mass.: Allyn and Bacon.

Cajete, Gregory. 1994. *Look to the mountain.* Skyland, N.C.: Kivaki Press.

Chaskin, R., and Diana M. Rauner. 1995. Youth and caring. *Phi Delta Kappan* 70, no. 9: 667–74.

Cole, Michael. 1996. *Cultural psychology: A once and future discipline.* Cambridge, Mass.: Belknap Press of Harvard University.

———. 1998. Can cultural psychology help us think about diversity? Presentation delivered at the American Educational Research Association Meetings, San Diego, Calif., April 13–18.

Darder, Antonia. 1991. *Culture and power in the classroom.* New York: Bergin and Garvey.

Dewey, John. 1916. *Democracy and education.* New York: Macmillan.

———. 1938. *Experience and education.* New York: Collier Books.

Eaker-Rich, D., and Jan Van Galen. 1996. *Caring in an unjust world: Negotiating borders and barriers in schools.* Albany, N.Y.: SUNY Press.

Elliot, Stephen N., Thomas R. Kratochwill, Joan Littlefield Cook, and John F. Travers. 2000. *Educational psychology: Effective teaching, effective learning.* 3rd ed. Boston, Mass.: McGraw-Hill.

Erickson, Frederick. 1993. Transformation and school success: The politics and culture of educational achievement. In *Minority education: Anthropological perspectives,* edited by Evelyn Jacob and Cathie Jordan. Norwood, N.J.: Ablex Publishing Corporation.

Fordham, Signithia, and John Ogbu. 1986. Black students' school success: Coping with the "burden of acting White." *Urban Review* 18, no. 3, 176–206.

Freire, Paulo. 1970. *Pedagogy of the oppressed.* New York: Seabury Press.

Gay, Geneva. 1994. *At the essence of learning: Multicultural education.* West Lafayette, Ind.: Kappa Delta Pi.

Gibson, Rich. 1999. Paulo Freire and pedagogy for social justice. *Theory and Research in Social Education* 27, no. 2: 129–59.

Gilligan, Carol. 1982. *In a different voice: Psychological theory and women's development.* Cambridge, MA: Harvard University Press.

Gollnick, Donna M. and Philip C. Chinn. 1990. *Multicultural education in a pluralistic society,* third edition. Columbus, Ohio: Merrill.

Gordon, Edmund. 1999. *Education and justice: A view from the back of the bus.* New York: Teachers College Press.

Haberman, Martin. 1995. *Star teachers of children of poverty.* West Lafayette, Ind.: Kappa Delta Pi.

Hilliard, Asa. 1974. Restructuring teacher education for multicultural imperatives. In *Multicultural education through competency-based teacher education,* edited by William A. Hunter. Washington, D.C.: American Association of Colleges for Teacher Education.

hook, bell. 2000. How do we build a community of love? *Shambhala Sun* 8, no. 3: 32–40.

Ianni, F. 1996. The caring community as a context for joining youth needs and program services. *Journal of Negro Education* 65, no. 1: 71–91.

Irvine, Jacqueline Jordan. 1990. *Black students and school failure: Politics, practices, and prescriptions.* Westport, Conn.: Greenwood Press.

King, Joyce. 1994. The purpose of schooling for African American children; Including cultural knowledge. In *Teaching diverse populations: Formulating a knowledge base,* edited by Etta R. Hollins, Joyce E. King, and Warren C. Hayman. Albany, N.Y.; SUNY Press, 25–66.

Kohl, Herbert. 1994. *I won't learn from you.* New York: New Press.

Kohn, Alfie. 1991. Caring kids: The role of the schools. *Phi Delta Kappan* 72, no. 7: 496–506.

Kozol, Jonathan. 1991. *Savage inequalities: Children in America's schools.* New York: Harper Perennial.

Moll, Luis. 1990. *Vygotsky and education: Instructional implications and applications of sociohistorical psychology.* New York: Cambridge University Press.

Nieto, Sonia. 1992. *Affirming diversity: The sociopolitical context of multicultural education.* New York: Longman.

Noblit, G., Dwight Rogers, and B. McCadden. 1995. In the meantime. The possibilities of caring. *Phi Delta Kappan* 76, no. 9: 680–85.

Noddings, Nel. 1984. *Caring: A feminine approach to ethics and moral development.* Berkeley, Calif.: University of California Press.

———. 1992. *The challenge to care in schools: An alternative approach to education.* New York: Teachers College Press.

———. 1995. *Philosophy of education.* Boulder, Colo.: Westview Press.

Oakes, Jeannie. 1985. *Keeping track how schools structure inequality.* New Haven, Conn.: Yale University Press.

Ovando, Carlos, and Virginia Collier. 1985. *Bilingual and ESL classrooms: Teaching in multicultural contexts.* Boston, Mass.: McGraw-Hill.

———. 1998. *Bilingual and ESL classrooms: Teaching in multicultural contexts.* 2nd ed. Boston, Mass.: McGraw-Hill.

Pang, Valerie Ooka. 1994. Why do we need this class?: Multicultural Education. *Phi Delta Kappan* 76, no. 4: 289–92.

———, and Li-rong Lilly Cheng. 1998. *Struggling to be heard: The unmet needs of Asian Pacific American children.* Albany, N.Y.: SUNY Press.

———, and John Rivera. 1998. The ethic of caring: The foundation of multicultural education. Unpublished manuscript.

Perrone, Vito. 1998. *Teacher with a heart: Reflections on Leonard Covello and the community.* New York: Teachers College Press.

Pidgeon, Judith. 1998. Private communication. November 30, San Diego, Calif.

Rivera, John, and Mary Poplin. 1995. Multicultural, critical, feminine, and constructive pedagogies seen through the lives of youth: A call for the revisioning of these and beyond: Toward a pedagogy for the next century. In *Multicultural education, critical pedagogy, and the politics of difference,* edited by Christine E. Sleeter. Albany, N.Y.: SUNY Press.

Rogers, Carl R., and H. Jerome Freiberg. 1994. *Freedom to learn for the 80's.* 3rd ed. New York: Merrill.

Sheets, Rosa Hernández, and Adrienne Fong. 2003. Linking teacher behaviors to cultural knowledge. *The Educational Forum* 67: 372–79.

Sleeter, Christine. 1995. *Multicultural education as social activism.* Albany, N.Y.: SUNY Press.

———, and Carl Grant. 1987. An analysis of multicultural education in the United States. *Harvard Educational Review* 57: 421–44.

Tharp, Ronald, and Ronald Gallimore. 1988. *Rousing minds to life: Teaching, learning, and schooling in social context.* New York: Cambridge University Press.

Valle, Ramón. 1997. *Ethnic diversity and multiculturalism: Crisis or challenge.* New York: American Heritage Custom Publishing.

———. 1998. Personal interview. San Diego, Calif., January 15.

CHAPTER 8

Aronowitz, Stanley. 1997. Between nationality and class. *Harvard Educational Review* 67, no. 2: 188–207.

Baca, Leonard, and Hermes T. Cervantes. 1989. *The bilingual special education interface.* Columbus, Ohio: Merrill Publishing Company.

Banks, James A. 1996. The historical reconstruction of knowledge about race: Implications for transformative teaching. In *Multicultural education, transformative knowledge, and action,* edited by James A. Banks. New York: Teachers College Press.

———. 2003. *Teaching strategies for ethnic studies.* 7th ed. Boston: Allyn and Bacon.

————. 1996a. The African American roots of multicultural education. In *Multicultural education, transformative knowledge, and action,* edited by James A. Banks. New York: Teachers College Press.

Beyer, Barry. 1987. *Practical strategies for teaching of thinking.* Boston, Mass.: Allyn and Bacon.

————. 1998. Improving student thinking. *The Clearing House* 71, no. 5: 262–67.

Booth, Cleta. 1997. The fiber project: One teacher's adventure toward emergent curriculum. *Young Children* 52, no. 4: 79–85.

Bruner, Jerome. 1990. *Acts of meaning.* Cambridge, Mass.: Harvard University Press.

Cann, Rebecca. L., and Allan C. Wilson. 2003. The recent African genesis of humans. *Scientific American* 13, no. 2: 54–61.

Christiansen, Linda. 1997. Reading, writing, and outrage. Keynote address. National Association for Multicultural Education (November), Albuquerque, New Mexico.

Clark, Reggie. 1983. *Family life and school: Why poor Black children succeed and fail.* Chicago, Ill.: University of Chicago Press.

Cummins, Jim. 1989. *Empowering minority students.* Los Angeles, Calif.: California Association for Bilingual Education.

Darder, Antonia. 1991. *Culture and power in the classroom.* New York: Bergin and Garvey.

Delpit, Lisa. 1995. *Other people's children.* New York: New Press.

Dewey, John. 1916. *Democracy and education.* New York: Macmillan.

————. 1933. How we think: A restatement of the relation of reflective thinking to the educative process. Lexington, Mass.: Heath.

Ford, Donna. 1996. *Reversing underachievement among gifted Black students.* New York: Teachers College Press.

Fordham, Signithia, and John Ogbu. 1986. Black students' school success: Coping with the "burden of acting white". *Urban Review* 18 no. 3: 176–206.

Fredrickson, George M. 2002. *Racism: A short history.* Princeton, N.J.: Princeton University Press.

Fuchs, Lawrence H. 1997. What we should count and why. *Society* 34, no. 6: 24–27.

Gay, Geneva. 1994. *At the essence of learning: Multicultural education.* West Lafayette, Ind.: Kappa Delta Pi.

————. 2000. Culturally responsive teaching: Theory, research, and practice. New York: Teachers College Press.

Gilligan, Carol. 1982. *In a different voice: Psychological theory and women's development.* Cambridge, Mass.: Harvard University Press.

Gollnick, Donna, and Phil Chinn. 1986. *Multicultural education.* 2nd ed. Columbus, Ohio: Charles E. Merrill.

Gordon, Edmund W. 1991. *A new compact for learning.* Albany, N.Y.: New York State Education Department.

————. 1999. *Education and justice: A view from the back of the bus.* New York: Teachers College Press.

Gore, Jennifer. 1987. Reflecting on reflective teaching. *Journal of Teacher Education* 38, no. 2: 33–39.

Gould, Stephen Jay. 1996. *The mismeasure of man.* New York: W. W. Norton & Company.

————. 2002. *I have landed: The end of a beginning in natural history.* New York: Harmony Books.

Gramsci, A. 1971. *Selections from the prison notebooks.* New York: International.

Heath, Shirley Brice. 1983. *Ways with words: Language, life, and work in communities and classrooms.* New York: Cambridge University Press.

Hillard, Asa. 2002. Beneficial educational research: Assumptions, paradigms, definitions. Presidential Invited Address. American Educational Research Association, New Orleans, La.

Hursh, D. W. and E. W. Ross. 2000. *Democratic social education. Social studies for social change.* New York: Falmer.

Hyman, Ronald. 1979. *Strategic questioning.* Englewood Cliffs, NJ: Prentice-Hall.

Irvine, Jacqueline Jordan. 1991. *Black students and school failure.* New York: Praeger.

————. 2002. In search of wholeness: African American teachers and their culturally specific classroom practices. New York: Palgrave.

Jablonski, Nina G., and George Chaplin. 2002. Skin deep. *Scientific American* 287, no. 4: 74–81.

Johnson, Jacqueline, Sharon Rush, and Joe Feagin. 2000. Reducing inequalities: Doing anti-racism: Toward an egalitarian American society. *Contemporary Sociology* 29, no. 2: 95–110.

Kincheloe, J., and S. Steinberg. 1993. A tentative description of post-formal thinking: The critical confrontation with cognitive theory. *Harvard Educational Review* 63: 296–320.

King, Mary-Claire, and Arno G. Motulsky. 2002. Human genetics: Mapping human history. *Science* 298, no. 5602: 2342–43.

Kochman, Thomas. 1981. *Black and white styles in conflict.* Chicago: University of Chicago Press.

Kozol, Jonathan. 1991. *Savage inequalities: Children in America's schools.* New York: Crown Publishers.

LA Times. 2003. The recall election: Results. 9 October, A27.

Lee, Carol D. 2003. Why we need to rethink race and ethnicity in educational research. *Educational Researcher* 32, no. 5: 3–5.

Leming, James. 2003. Ignorant activists: Social change, "higher order thinking skills," and the failure of social studies. In *Where did social studies go wrong?* edited by James Leming, Lucien Ellington, and Kathleen Porter. Washington, D. C.: Thomas B. Fordham Foundation. http://www.edexcellence.net/socialstudies/Contrarians/ContrariansChap7.pdf.

Lipman, Pauline. 1998. *Race, class, and power in school restructuring.* Albany, N.Y.: SUNY Press.

Maslow, Abraham. 1970. *Motivation and personality.* 2nd ed. New York: Harper and Row.

Masucci, M., and A. Renner. 2000. Reading the lives of others: The Winnston Homes Library Project: A cultural studies analysis of critical service learning for education. *High School Journal* 84, no. 1: 36–48.

McAdoo, H. P. 1988. *Black families.* 2nd ed. Newbury Park, Calif.: Sage.

McIntyre, Ellen, Ann Rosebery, and Norma González. 2001. *Classroom diversity.* Portsmouth, N.H.: Heinemann.

McLaren, Peter, ed. 1997. *Revolutionary multiculturalism.* Boulder, Colo.: Westview Press.

Meier, Deborah. 1995. *The power of their ideas.* Boston, Mass.: Beacon Press.

Moll, Luis. 1990. *Vygotsky and education: Instructional implications and applications of sociohistorical psychology.* New York: Cambridge University Press.

———, and James B. Greenberg. 1990. Creating zones of possibilities: Combining social contexts for instruction. In *Vygotsky and education: Instructional implications and applications of sociohistorical psychology,* edited by Luis Moll. New York: Cambridge University Press.

Moran, C., and Kenji Hakuta. 1995. Bilingual education: Broadening research perspectives. In *Handbook of research on multicultural education,* edited by James A. Banks and Cherry McGee Banks. New York: Macmillan.

Moses, Robert P., and Charles E. Cobb. 2001. Radical equations: Civil rights from Mississippi to the algebra project. Boston: Beacon Press.

Newsome, J. 2003. Private interview. September 8. San Diego, Calif.

Nieto, Sonia. 2004. *Affirming diversity: The sociopolitical context of Multicultural Education.* Boston, Mass: Pearson.

Noddings, Nel. 1984. *Caring: A feminine approach to ethics and moral education.* Berkeley, Calif.: University of California Press.

———. 1992. *The challenge to care in schools.* New York: Teachers College Press.

Oakes, Jeannie. 1982. *Keeping track: How schools structure inequality.* New Haven, Conn.: Yale University Press.

Olson, Steve. 2002. *Mapping human history: Genes, race, and our common origins.* Boston, Mass: Houghton Mifflin.

O'Neill, Lucinda M. 2002. An interview with Francis Collins, M.D., Ph.D., director of the human genome project. *The Exceptional Parent* 32, no. 10: 28–30.

Orenstein, Peggy. 1994. *Schoolgirls: Young women, self-esteem, and the confidence gap.* New York: Doubleday Anchor Books.

Ovando, Carlos, and Virginia Collier. 1985. *Bilingual and ESL classrooms.* New York: McGraw-Hill.

Pang, Valerie Ooka. 2001. *Multicultural education: A caring-centered, reflective approach,* first edition. Boston, MA: McGraw-Hill.

Raths, Louis E., Selma Wasserman, Arthur Joans, and Arnold Rothstein. 1986. Teaching for thinking: Theory, strategies, and activities for the classroom. New York: Teachers College Press.

Ridley, Matt. 2000. *Genome: The autobiography of a species in 23 chapters.* New York: Perennial Publishers.

Rivera, Juan, and Mary Poplin. 1996. Multicultural, critical, feminine and constructive pedagogies seen through the lives of youth: A call for the revisioning of these and beyond: Toward a pedagogy for the next century. In *Multicultural education, critical pedagogy, and the politics of difference,* edited by Christine Sleeter and Peter McLaren. New York: State University of New York Press.

Rosenberg, Noah A., Jonathan K. Pritchard, James L. Weber, Howard M. Cann, Kenneth K. Kidd, Lev A. Zhivotovsky, and Marcus W. Feldman. 2002. Genetic structure of human populations. *Science* 298, no. 5602: 2381–85.

Ross, E. W. 2001. *Social studies.* Albany, N.Y.: SUNY Press.

Romualdi, Chiara, David Balding, Ivane Nasidze, Gregory Risch, Myles Robichaux, Stephen T. Sherry, Mark Stoneking, Mark Batzer, and Guido Barbujani. 2002. Patterns of human diversity, within and among continents, inferred from biallelic DNA polymorphisms. *Genome Research* 12, no. 4: 6002–612.

Sadker, David and Myra Sadker. 2003. *Teachers, schools, and society.* Boston, MA: McGraw-Hill.

Satel, Sally. 2002. Medicine's race problem. In *The best American science writing 2002,* edited by Matt Ridley. New York: Harper Collins, 72–82.

Silberman, Charles. 1970. *Crisis in the classroom.* New York: Random House.

Sleeter, Christine E. 1992. Keepers of the American dream: A study of staff development and multicultural education. Washington, D.C.: Falmer.

———, and Carl Grant. 1988. *Making choices for multicultural education.* Columbus, Ohio: Charles E. Merrill.

Strom, David. 1999. Personal communications. January 7. San Diego, California.

Suzuki, Bob. 1984. Curriculum transformation for multicultural education. *Education and Urban Society* 16: 294–322.

Sykes, Bryan. 2001. The seven daughters of eve: The science that reveals our genetic ancestry. New York: W. W. Norton and Company.

Tharp, Rolland, and Ronald Gallimore. 1988. *Rousing minds to life: Teaching, learning, and schooling in social context.* New York: Cambridge University Press.

Thorne, Alan G., and Milford H. Wolpoff. 2003. The multiregional evolution of humans. *Scientific American* 13, no. 2: 46–53.

Valli, Linda. 1997. Listening to other voices: A description of teacher reflection in the United States. *Peabody Journal of Education* 72 no. 1: 67–88.

Walker, Vanessa Siddle. 1996. *Their highest potential: An African American school community in the segregated*

South. Chapel Hill, N.C.: University of North Carolina Press.

Wang, L. 1976. *Lau v. Nichols:* History of a struggle for equal and quality education. In *Counterpoint,* edited by Emma Gee. Los Angeles, Calif.: Regents of the University of California and the UCLA Asian American Studies Center.

Ward, Carol. 2003. The evolution of human origins. *American Anthropologist* 105, no. 1: 77–88.

Zeichner, Ken, and Dan Liston. 1987. Teaching student teachers to reflect. *Harvard Educational Review* 57, no. 1: 23–48.

Zigler, Edward, and Sally J. Syfco. 2001. Extended childhood intervention prepares children for school and beyond. *Journal of the American Medical Association* 285, no. 18: 2378–80.

CHAPTER 9

'Aha Pūnana Leo. 2002. *'Aha Pūnana Leo.* http://www.ahapunanaleo.org.

Baker, Colin. 1993. *Foundation of bilingual education and bilingualism.* Buffalo, N.Y.: Multilingual Matters.

Baker, Colin, 2001. *Foundation of bilingual education and bilingualism,* third edition. Buffalo, N.Y.: Multilingual Matters.

Castañeda, Lillian Vega, and Francisco Ríos. 2002. Teachers as students: Resistance to diversity. In *Examining practices in multicultural education,* edited by P. Larke and N. Carter. College Station, Tex.: JOY Publishing.

Chamot, Ana Uhl. 1995. Implementing the cognitive academic language learning approach: *CALLA* in Arlington, Virginia. *The Bilingual Research Journal* 19, no. 374 (Summer/Fall): 379–94.

———, and J. M. O'Malley. 1994. *The CALLA handbook: Implementing the cognitive academic language learning approach.* Reading, Mass.: Addison-Wesley.

Crandall, Joann. 1994. Content-centered language learning. *ERIC Digest* (January): 1–5. www.cal.org/resources/digest/cranda01.html.

Crawford, James. 1998. Ten common fallacies about bilingual education. *ERIC Digest* (November). www.cal.org/resources/digest/crawford01.html.

Cummins, Jim. 1996. *Negotiating identities: Education for empowerment in a diverse society.* Sacramento, Calif.: California Association for Bilingual Education.

———. 2000. Language, power, and pedagogy: Bilingual children in the crossfire. Multilingual Matters Ltd.

Davies, Sally. 1996. *Vietnamese: A rough guide phrasebook.* London: Lexus.

Delpit, Lisa. 2002. Language diversity and learning. In *Beyond Heroes and holidays: A practical guide to K–12 anti-racist, multicultural education and staff development,* edited by Enid Lee, Deborah Menkart, and Margo Okazawa-Rey: 154–65. Washington, D.C: Teaching for Change.

Díaz-Rico, Lynne T., and Kathryn Z. Weed. 2002. *The cross-cultural, language, and academic development handbook.* 2nd ed. Boston, Mass.: Allyn and Bacon.

Fillmore, Lilly Wong, and Catherine Snow. 2000. *What teachers need to know about language.* U.S. Department of Education: Office of Educational Research and Improvement. ED-99-CO-0008, http://www.cal.org/ericcll/teachers/teachers.pdf. www.cal.org/resources/teachers/teachers.pdf.

Fullilove, Robert E., and Philip Uri Treisman. 1990. Mathematics achievement among African American undergraduates at the University of California, Berkeley: An evaluation of the mathematics workshop program. *Journal of Negro Education* 59, no. 3: 463–78.

Garcia, Eugene. 2002. *Student cultural diversity: Understanding and meeting the challenge.* 3rd ed. Boston, Mass.: Houghton Mifflin Company.

Garcia, Gilbert N. 2000. Lessons from research: What is the length of time it takes limited English proficient students to acquire English and succeed in an all-English classroom? *Issues and Brief: National Clearinghouse for Bilingual Education* 5: 1–15.

Garrison, Leslie, and Jill Kerper Mora. 1999. Adapting mathematics instruction for English-language learners: The language-concept connection. In *Changing the faces of mathematics: Perspectives on Latinos,* edited by L. Ortiz-Franco, N. Hernandez, and Y. De La Cruz. Reston, Va.: National Council of Teachers of Mathematics: 35–48.

Gutierrez, Rochelle. 2002. Beyond essentialism: The complexity of language in teaching mathematics to Latina/o students. *American Educational Research Journal* 39, no. 4, 1047–88.

Hoover, Mary Rhodes. 1998. Ebonics: Myths and realities. In *The real Ebonics debate: Power, language, and the education of African-American children,* edited by Theresa Perry and Lisa Delpit. Boston, Mass.: Beacon Press, 71–76.

Hotz, Robert Lee. 2002. Baby's 'Goo-Goo' a building block of human speech. *Los Angeles Times,* 30 August, A16.

Krashen, Stephen. 1981. *Second language acquisition and second language learning.* Oxford: Pergamon.

———. 1982. *Principles and practice in second language acquisition.* Oxford: Pergamon.

———. 1993. Second Language Education: The Monitor Model. Speech at the Multicultural Education Infusion Center, February 23, San Diego.

———. 1996. *Under attack: The case against bilingual education.* Culver City, Calif.: Language Education Associates.

Lee, Okhee. 2003. Equity for linguistically and culturally diverse students in science education: A research agenda. *Teachers College Record* 105, no. 2: 465–89.

Meier, Terry. 1998. Kitchen poets and classroom books: Literature from children's roots. In *The real Ebonics debate: Power, language, and the education of African-American children,* edited by Theresa Perry and Lisa Delpit. Boston, Mass.: Beacon Press, 94–104.

Meier, Deborah. 2001. *In schools we trust: Creating communities of learning in an era of testing and standardization.* Boston, MA: Beacon Press.

Noddings, Nel. 1984. *Caring: A feminine approach to ethics and moral development.* Berkeley, CA: University of California Press.

Perry, Theresa and Lisa Delpit. 1998. *The real Ebonics debate.* Boston, Mass.: Beacon Press.

Rickford, John. 1998. Holding on to a language of our own: An interview with linguist John Rickford. In *The real Ebonics debate: Power, language, and the education of African-American children,* edited by Theresa Perry and Lisa Delpit. Boston, Mass.: Beacon Press, 59–70.

Rose, Mike. 1989. *Lives on the boundary: A moving account of the struggles and achievements of America's educational underclass.* New York: Penguin Books.

Scarcella, Robin. 1999. *Academic English: A conceptual framework.* Santa Barbara, Calif.: University of California Language Minority Institute.

———. 2000. *Effective writing instruction for English learners.* Conference on English Learners. Sacramento, Calif.

Secret, Carrie. 1998. Embracing Ebonics and teaching Standard English: An inteview with Oakland teacher Carrie Secret. In *The real Ebonics debate: Power, language, and the education of African-American children,* edited by Theresa Perry and Lisa Delpit. Boston, Mass.: Beacon Press, 79–88.

Thomas, Walter, and Virginia Collier. 1997. School effectiveness for language minority students. *NCBE Resource Collection Series,* Number 9, Washington, D.C.: National Clearinghouse for Bilingual Education.

Tran, MyLuong. 1998. Behind the smiles: The true heart of Southeast Asian American Children. In *Struggling to be heard: The unmet needs of Asian Pacific American children,* edited by Valerie Ooka Pang and Li-rong Lilly Cheng: 45–57. Albany, N.Y.: SUNY Press.

CHAPTER 10

Allen, J. 1999. Pancho Villa: An issues-centered lesson plan. Unpublished manuscript.

Amanti, Cathy. 1995. Teachers doing research: Beyond classroom walls. *Practicing Anthropology* 17, no. 3: 7–9.

Ashton-Warner, Sylvia. 1963. *Teacher.* New York: Bantam Books.

Au, Kathryn H. 1990. Changes in a teacher's view of interactive comprehension instruction. In *Vygotsky and education,* edited by L. Moll. New York: Cambridge University Press.

———, and Alice J. Kawakami. 1994. Cultural congruence in instruction. In *Teaching diverse populations,* edited by Etta R. Hollins, Joyce E. King, and Warren C. Hayman. Albany, N.Y.: SUNY Press.

———, and J. M. Mason. 1981. Social organizational factors in learning to read: The balance of rights hypothesis. *Reading Research Quarterly* 17, no. 1: 115–152.

Baker, Keith. 1998. Magic bullets, slate, and Stradivarius: Analogies, research, and policy making. *Phi Delta Kappan* (January) 79, no. 5: 402–5.

Banks, James A. 1995. Multicultural education: Historical development, dimensions, and practice. In *Handbook of research on multicultural education,* edited by James A. Banks and Cherry A. McGee Banks. N.Y.: Macmillan.

Cheng, Li-rong Lilly. 1998a. Language assessment and instructional strategies for limited English students. In *Struggling to be heard: The unmet needs of Asian Pacific American children,* edited by Valerie Ooka Pang and Li-rong Lilly Cheng. Albany, N.Y.: SUNY Press.

———. 1998b. Private communications.

Cole, Michael. 1996. Cultural psychology: A once and future discipline. Cambridge, Mass.: Belknap Press of Harvard University.

———. 1998. *Can cultural psychology help us think about diversity?* Presentation delivered at the American Educational Research Association Meetings, San Diego, Calif., April 13–18.

Collins, Allan, and Dedre Gentner. 1987. How people construct mental models. In *Cultural models in language and thought,* edited by Dorothy Holland and Naomi Quinn. New York: Cambridge University Press.

D'Andrade, Roy. 1987. Folk models of the mind. In *Cultural models in language and thought,* edited by Dorothy Holland and Naomi Quinn. New York: Cambridge University Press.

Delpit, Lisa. 1995. *Other people's children.* New York: New Press.

Elliott, Stephen N., Thomas R. Kratochwill, Joan Littlefield Cook, and John R. Travers. 2000. *Educational psychology: Effective teaching, effective learning.* Boston, Mass.: McGraw-Hill.

Fordham, Signithia, and John Ogbu. 1986. Black students' school success: Coping with the "Burden of acting White." *Urban Review* 18, no. 3: 176–206.

Fung, Grace. 1998. Meeting the instructional needs of Chinese American and Asian English language development and at-risk students. In *Struggling to be heard: The unmet needs of Asian Pacific American children,* edited by Valerie Ooka Pang and Li-rong Lilly Cheng. Albany, N.Y.: SUNY Press.

Gay, Geneva. 1995. Curriculum theory and multicultural education. In *Handbook of research on multicultural education,* edited by James A. Banks and Cherry McGee Banks. New York: Macmillan.

Gee, James. 1996. *Social linguistics and literacies.* Bristol, Pa.: Taylor and Francis.

Gilbert, Shirley, and Geneva Gay. 1985. Improving the success in school of poor black children. *Phi Delta Kappan* 66: 133–37.

Gilliland, Hap. 1986. Discipline and the Indian student. In *Teaching the Indian child,* edited by Jon Reyhner. Billings, Mont.: Eastern Montana College.

Goldstein, Lisa S. 1999. The relational zone: The role of caring relationships in the co-construction of mind. *American Educational Research Journal* 36, no. 3: 647–73.

Gonzalez, Norma. 1995. The funds of knowledge for teaching project. *Practicing Anthropology* 17, no. 3: 3–6.

Goodman, Yetta, and Kenneth Goodman. 1990. Vygotsky in a whole-language perspective. In *Vygotsky and education,* edited by Luis Moll. New York: Cambridge University Press.

Hale-Benson, Janice E. 1982. *Black children their roots, culture, and learning styles.* Baltimore, Md.: Johns Hopkins University Press.

Irvine, Jacqueline Jordan. 1990. *Black students and school failure.* New York: Greenwood Press.

———. 2002. *In search of wholeness: African American teachers and their culturally specific classroom practices.* New York: Palgrave.

———, and James Fraser. 1998. "Warm demanders": Do national certification standards leave room for the culturally responsive pedagogy of African-American teachers? *Education Week,* May 13: 56, 42.

Hanesbery, Lorraine. 1994. *A raisin in the sun: The unfilmed original screenplay.* New York: Signet Publishers.

Holland, Dorothy, and Naomi Quinn. 1987. *Cultural models in language and thought.* New York: Cambridge University Press.

Hughes, Langston. 1987. *Selected poems of Langston Hughes.* New York: Vintage Press.

King, Joyce E. 1994. The purpose of schooling for African American children: Including cultural knowledge. In *Teaching diverse populations,* edited by Etta R. Hollins, Joyce E. King, and Warren C. Hayman. Albany, N.Y.: SUNY Press.

———. 2001. Facing the new millennium: A transformative research and action agenda in Black education. Report of the AERA Commission on Research in Black Education. Paper presented at the annual meeting of the American Educational Research Association, New Orleans, La.

Ladson-Billings, Gloria. 1994. *Dreamkeepers: Successful teachers of African American children.* San Francisco, Calif.: Jossey-Bass.

Lee, Carol D. 1995. "A culturally based cognitive apprenticeship: Teaching African American high school students skills in literary interpretation." *Reading Research Quarterly* 30, no. 4: 608–30.

———. 2000. Signifying in the zone of proximal development. In *Vygotskian perspectives on literacy research,* edited by Carol D. Lee and Peter Smagorinsky. Cambridge, United Kingdom: Cambridge University Press, 191–225.

Lipman, Pauline. 1998. *Race, class, and power in school restructuring.* Albany, N.Y.: SUNY Press.

Lipska, Jerry. 1996. Toward a culturally based pedagogy: A case study of one Yup'ik Eskimo teacher. In *Transforming curriculum for a culturally diverse society,* edited by Etta Hollins. Mahwah, N.J.: Lawrence Erlbaum Association Inc.

Litton, Edmundo F. 1999. Learning in America: The Filipino-American sociocultural perspective. In *Asian-American education: Prospects and challenges,* edited by Clara Park and Marilyn Mei-Ying Chi. Westport, Conn.: Bergin and Garvey.

Loewen, James W. 1995. *The lies my teacher told me.* New York: Simon and Schuster.

Moll, Luis. 1990. *Vygotsky and education: Instructional implications and applications of sociohistorical psychology.* New York: Cambridge University Press.

———. 2000. Inspired by Vygotsky: Ethnographic experiments in education. In *Vygotskian perspectives on literacy research,* edited by Carol D. Lee and Peter Smagorinsky. Cambridge, United Kingdom: Cambridge University Press, 256–68.

———, Cathy Amanti, D. Neff, and Norma Gonzalez. 1992. Funds of knowledge: Using a qualitative approach to connect homes and classrooms. *Theory into Practice* 31, no. 2: 132–41.

———, and James Greenberg. 1990. Creating zones of possibilities: Combining social contexts for instruction. In *Vygotsky and education,* edited by Luis Moll. New York: Cambridge University Press.

———, Luis, Javier Tapia, and K. Whitemore. 1993. Living knowledge: The social distribution of cultural resources. In *Distributed cognitions,* edited by G. Salomon. Cambridge, Mass.: Cambridge University Press.

———, Luis, C. Vélez-Ibáñez, and James Greenberg. 1988. *Project implementation plan. Community knowledge and classroom practice: Combining resources for literacy instruction.* Tucson, Ariz.: College of Education and Bureau of Applied Research in Anthropology.

Mora, Jill Kerper. 1998. Private communications.

Moses, Robert P., M. Kamii, S. M. Swap, and J. Howard. 1989. The algebra project: Organizing in the spirit of Ella. *Harvard Educational Review* 59, no. 4: 423–43.

Myers, Walter Dean. 1989. *The young landlords.* N.Y.: Puffin Books.

Noddings, Nel. 1992. *The challenge to care in schools: An alternative approach to education.* New York: Teachers College Press.

Ochoa-Becker, Anna. 1996. Building a rationale for issues-centered education. In *Handbook on teaching social issues,* edited by R. Evans and D. Saxe. Washington, D.C.: National Council for the Social Studies.

Olson, James S., and Raymond Wilson, 1984. *Native Americans in the twentieth century.* Provo, Utah: Brigham Young University Press.

Pang, Valerie Ooka, and Li-rong Lilly Cheng. 1998. *Struggling to be heard: The unmet needs of Asian Pacific American children.* Albany, N.Y.: SUNY Press.

Park, Clara. 1997. Learning style preferences of Asian American (Chinese, Filipino, Korean and Vietnamese) students in secondary schools. *Equity and Excellence in Education* 30, no. 2: 68–77.

Park, Cynthia D. 1998. Private communications.

Philips, Susan Urmston. 1993. *The invisible culture: Communication in classroom and community on the Warm Springs Indian Reservation* (reissued). Prospect Heights, Ill.: Waveland Press.

Quinn, Naomi, and Dorothy Holland. 1987. Culture and cognition. In *Cultural models in language and thought,* edited by Dorothy Holland and Naomi Quinn. New York: Cambridge University Press.

Rogoff, Barbara. 1984. Introduction. In *Everyday cognition: Its development in social context,* edited by Barbara Rogoff and Jean Lave. Cambridge, Mass.: Harvard University Press.

Saxe, Geoffery. 1988a. Candy selling and math learning. *Educational Researcher* 17, no. 6: 14–21.

———. 1988b. The mathematics of street vendors. *Child Development* 59: 1415–25.

Scribner, Sylvia. 1984. Studying working intelligence. In *Everyday cognition: Its development in social context,* edited by Barbara Rogoff and Jean Lave. Cambridge, Mass.: Harvard University Press.

———, and Michael Cole. 1981. *The psychology of literacy.* Cambridge, Mass.: Harvard University Press.

Silver, Edward A. 1997. "Algebra for All": A real-world problem for the mathematics education community to solve. *NCTM Xchange* 1, no. 2: 1–4.

Smith, Frank. 1979. *Reading without nonsense.* New York: Teachers College Press.

Smitherman, Geneva. 1977. *Talkin and testifyin.* Detroit, Mich.: Wayne State University Press.

Swisher, Karen, and Donna Deyhle. 1992. Adapting instruction to culture. In *Teaching American Indian students,* edited by Jon Reyhner. Norman, Okla.: University of Oklahoma Press.

Tharp, Ronald G., and Ronald Gallimore. 1988. *Rousing minds to life: Teaching, learning, and schooling in social context.* Cambridge, Mass.: Cambridge University Press.

Tobin, K. G. 1991. Constructivist perspective on teacher learning. Paper presented at the Eleventh Biennial Conference on Chemical Education. Atlanta, Ga.

Tran, MyLuong. 1998. Private communications, San Diego, Calif.

Weatherford, Jack. 1988. *Indian givers.* New York: Ballantine Books.

Wertsch, James V. 1985. *Vygotsky and the social formation of the mind.* Cambridge, Mass.: Harvard University Press.

White, Geoffrey M. 1987. Proverbs and cultural models: An American psychology of problem solving. In *Cultural models in language and thought,* edited by Dorothy Holland and Naomi Quinn. New York: Cambridge University Press.

CHAPTER 11

Amanti, Cathy. 1995. Teachers doing research: Beyond classroom walls. *Practicing Anthropology* 17, no. 3: 7–9.

Au, Katherine. 1992. Constructing the theme of a story. *Language Arts* 69: 106–11.

Banks, James. 1994. *Multiethnic education: Theory and practice.* Boston: Allyn and Bacon.

Bishop, Claire Huchet. 1938. *The five Chinese brothers.* New York: Coward-McCann.

Civil Rights Project. 2002. *The impact of racial and ethnic diversity on educational outcomes: Cambridge, MA school district.* The Civil Rights Project, Harvard University.

Clifton, Lucille. 1977. *Everett Anderson's 1 2 3.* New York: Holt, Rinehart and Winston.

Cole, Michael. 1996. Cultural psychology: A once and future discipline. Cambridge, Mass.: Belknap Press of Harvard University.

———. 1998. Can cultural psychology help us think about diversity? Presentation delivered at the American Educational Research Association Meetings, San Diego, Calif., April 13–18.

Cordova, Fred. 1998. The legacy: Creating a knowledge base on Filipino Americans. In *Struggling to be heard: The unmet needs of Asian Pacific American children,* edited by Valerie Ooka Pang and Li-rong Lilly Cheng. Albany, N.Y.: SUNY Press.

Delpit, Lisa. 1995. *Other people's children.* New York: New Press.

Engle, Shirley, and Anna Ochoa. 1988. *Education for democratic citizenship: Decision-making in the social studies.* New York: Teachers College Press.

Frasier, Debra. 1991. On the day you were born, New York: Harcourt, Inc.

Garland, Sherry. 1993. *The lotus seed.* San Diego: Harcourt Brace Jovanovich.

Gay, Geneva and Willie L. Baber. 1987. *Expressively Black: The cultural basis of ethnic identity.* New York: Praeger.

Gee, James. 1996. *Social linguistics and literacies.* Bristol, Pa.: Taylor and Francis.

Gonzalez, Norma. 1995. The funds of knowledge for teaching project. *Practicing Anthropology* 17, no. 3: 3–6.

Grant, Carl, and Christine Sleeter. 1998. *Turning on learning.* 2nd ed. Columbus, Ohio: Merrill.

Highwater, Jamake. 1981. *Moonsong lullaby.* New York: Lothrop, Lee and Shephard.

Hyman, R. T. 1979. *Strategic questioning.* Englewood Cliffs, N.J.: Prentice Hall.

Jiménez, Francisco. 1997. *The circuit: Stories from the life of a migrant child.* Albuquerque, N. Mex.: University of New Mexico Press.

Johnson, James Weldon. 1993. *Lift ev'ry voice and sing.* New York: Walker and Company.

Jordan, Jacqueline, and James Fraser. 1998. Warm demanders. *Education Week,* May 13. http://www.edweek.org/ew/1998/35irvine.h17.

Klutz. 1998. *The Klutz yo-yo book.* Palo Alto, Calif.: Klutz.

Kurlaender, Michal, and John T. Hun. 2000. *Is diversity a compelling educational interest? Evidence from metropolitan Louisville.* The Civil Rights Project, Harvard University. www.law.harvard.edu/civilrights/publications/louisville.html.

Lai, Him Mark, Genny Lim, and Judy Yung. 1991. *Island: Poetry and history of Chinese immigrants on Angel Is-*

land *1910–1940.* Seattle, Wash.: University of Washington Press.

Lipman, Pauline. 1998. Race, class and power in school restructuring. Albany, N.Y.: SUNY Press.

Loewen, James. 1995. *Lies my teacher told me.* New York: Simon and Schuster.

Maiga, Hassimi Oumarou. 2002. *Notes on classical Songhoy education and socialization: The world of women and child rearing practices in West Africa.* Atlanta, Ga.: Murehm Books.

Massialas, Byron G., and C. Benjamin Cox. 1966. *Inquiry in social studies.* New York: McGraw-Hill Books, Inc.

Moll, Luis, Cathy Amanti, D. Neff, and Norma Gonzalez. 1992. Funds of knowledge: Using a qualitative approach to connect homes and classrooms. *Theory into Practice* 31, no. 2: 132–41.

———, Javier Tapia, and K. Whitemore. 1993. Living knowledge: The social distribution of cultural resources. In *Distributed cognitions,* edited by G. Salomon. Cambridge, Mass.: Cambridge University Press.

Moses, Robert P., M. Kamii, S. M. Swap, and J. Howard. 1989. The algebra project: Organizing in the spirit of Ella. *Harvard Educational Review* 59, no. 4: 423–43.

Myers, Walter Dean. 1995. *The dragon takes a wife.* New York: Scholastic.

Nelson, Jack. 1996. The historical imperative for issues-centered education. In *Handbook on teaching social issues,* edited by Ronald W. Evans and David Saxe. Washington, D.C.: National Council for the Social Studies.

———, Stuart Palonsky, and Kenneth Carlson. 2003. *Critical issues in education: Dialogues and dialectics.* Boston, Mass.: McGraw-Hill.

Noddings, Nel. 1992. *The challenge to care in schools: An alternative approach to education.* New York: Teachers College Columbia University.

Oliver, Donald W., and James P. Shaver. 1966. *Teaching public issues in the high school.* Logan, Utah: Utah State University Press.

Olson, James Stuart and Raymond Wilson. 1984. *Native Americans in the twentieth century.* Provo, Utah: Brigham Young University Press.

Pang, Valerie Ooka, and Li-rong Lilly Cheng. 1998. *Struggling to be heard: The unmet needs of Asian Pacific American children.* Albany, N.Y.: SUNY Press.

Parks, Rosa. 1992. *Rosa Parks, my story.* With Jim Haskins. New York: Dial.

Paulsen, Gary. 1993. *Nightjohn.* New York: Delacorte Press.

Perry, Theresa. 1996. *Teaching Malcolm X.* New York: Routledge.

Philips, Susan. 1972. *The invisible culture: Communication in classroom and community on the Warms Spring Reservation.* New York: Longman.

Polacco, Patricia. 1994. *Pink and say.* New York: Philomel Books.

Ramirez, Manuel, and A. Castaneda. 1974. *Cultural democracy, bicognitive development, and education.* New York: Academic Press.

Ringgold, Faith. 1993. *Dinner at Aunt Connie's house.* New York: Hyperion Books for Children.

Say, Allen. 1993. *Grandfather's journey.* New York: Houghton Mifflin.

Singleton, Laurel R. 1989. *Public Issues Series.* Boulder, Colo.: Social Science Education Consortium.

Soto, Gary. 1990. *Baseball in April and other stories.* San Diego: Harcourt Brace Jovanovich.

Swisher, Karen Gayton. 1994. American Indian learning styles survey: An assessment of teachers' knowledge. *Journal of Educational Issues of Language Minority Students* 13: 59–77.

Tate, William F. 1995. Returning to the root: A culturally relevant approach to mathematics pedagogy. *Theory into Practice: Multicultural Education* 34, no. 3: 166–73.

Texas State Board of Education. 1998. Texas essential knowledge and skills for the social studies. http://www.tea. state.tx.us/rules/tac/ch113.html#s1131.

Torretto, Ronald. 1999. Private interview, March 25, 1999.

Weatherford, Jack. 1988. Indian givers. New York: Ballentine Books.

Weld, Jeffrey. 1999. Achieving equitable science education. *Phi Delta Kappan* 80, no. 10: 756–58.

CHAPTER 12

Anyon, Jean. 1997. *Ghetto schooling: A political economy of urban educational reform.* New York: Teachers College Press.

Bailey, Thomas A., and David M. Kennedy. 1994. *The American pageant.* Lexington, Mass.: D.C. Heath.

Banks, James A., Peter Cookson, Geneva Gay, Willis D. Hawley, Jacqueline Jordan Irvine, Sonia Nieto, Janet Ward Schofield, and Walter G. Stephan. 2001. *Diversity within unity: Essential principles of teaching and learning.* Seattle, Wash.: University of Washington Center for Multicultural Education.

Bustamante-Jones, E. 1998. *Mexican American teachers as cultural mediators: Literacy and literacy contexts through bicultural strengths.* Claremont, Calif.: Claremont Graduate University and San Diego State University.

The Civil Rights Project. 2002. *The impact of racial and ethnic diversity on educational outcomes: Cambridge, MA school district.* The Civil Rights Project, Harvard University. www.law.harvard.edu/civilrights.

Darling-Hammond, Linda, Jacqueline Ancess, and Beverly Falk. 1995. *Authentic assessment in action: Studies of schools and students at work.* New York: Teachers College Press.

Delpit, Lisa. 1995. *Other people's children.* New York: New Press.

Echevarria, Jana, and Anne Graves. 1998. *Sheltered content instruction: Teaching English language learners with diverse abilities.* Boston, Mass.: Allyn and Bacon.

Frase, Larry. 1995. *The curriculum management audit: Improving school quality.* Lancaster, Pa.: Technomic Publishing.

Goodman, Yetta M., and Kenneth S. Goodman. 1990. Vygotsky in a whole-language perspective. In *Vygotsky and education,* edited by Luis C. Moll. New York: Cambridge University Press.

Heller, Carol, and Joseph Jawkins. 1994. Teaching tolerance: Notes from the front line. *Teachers College Record* 95, no. 3: 337–68.

Hilliard, Asa. 1974. Restructuring teacher education for multicultural imperatives. In *Multicultural education through competency-based teacher education,* edited by William A. Hunter. Washington, D.C.: American Association of Colleges for Teacher Education.

Irvine, Jacqueline Jordan. 1990. *Black students and school failure.* New York: Greenwood Press.

Kohl, Herbert. 1982. *Basic skills.* Boston, Mass.: Little, Brown and Company.

Kozol, Jonathan. 1991. *Savage inequalities.* New York: Crown Publishers.

Kurlaender, Michal, and John T. Hun. 2000. *Is diversity a compelling educational interest? Evidence from metropolitan Louisville.* The Civil Rights Project, Harvard University. www.law.harvard.edu/civilrights/publications/louisville.html.

Moll, Luis. 1990. *Vygotsky and education: Instructional implications and applications of sociohistorical psychology.* New York: Cambridge University Press.

Noguera, Pedro. 2003. *City schools and the American dream.* New York: Teachers College Press.

Nothdurft, William E. 1989. *Schoolworks: Reinventing public schools to create the workforce of the future: Innovations in education and job training from Sweden, West Germany, France, Great Britain, and Philadelphia.* Washington, D.C.: Brookings Institution.

Ornish, Dean. 1998. *Love and survival.* New York: HarperCollins Publishers.

Peterson, Bob, and Monty Neill. 1999. Alternatives to standardized tests. *Rethinking Schools* 13, no. 3: 1, 4–5, 28.

Pilkington, Doris, and Noris Garimara. 2002. *Rabbit-proof fence.* (first published in Australia by University of Queensland Press in 1996). New York: Miramax Books.

Poston, William K. 1995. Standard three: The connectivity and equity standard. In *The curriculum management audit: Improving school quality,* edited by Larry Frase. Lancaster, Pa.: Technomic Publishing, 153–84.

Rodriguez, James L., Rafael M. Diaz, David Duran, and Linda Espinosa. 1995. The impact of bilingual preschool education on the language development of Spanish-speaking children. *Early Childhood Research Quarterly* 10: 475–90.

Rueda, Robert. 1993. Cognition and culture. Presentation in San Diego State University, June 1999. Why the testing craze won't fix our schools. *Rethinking Schools* 13, no. 3: 1–2.

Scribner, Sylvia. 1984. Studying working intelligence. In *Everyday cognition: Its development in social context,* edited by Barbara Rogoff and Jean Lave. Cambridge, Mass.: Harvard University Press.

Shulman, Lee. 1987. Knowledge and teaching: Foundations of the new reform. *Harvard Educational Review, 57,* 1–22.

Singer, Alan. 2003. Student clubs: A model for political organizing. *Rethinking Schools.* Summer. www.rethikingschools.org/war/readings/club174.shtml.

Smith, Doug. 1999. Funding and fairness class in public schools. *The Los Angeles Times,* 16 February, A1, A17.

Stanford, John, and Robin Simons. 1999. *Victory in our schools.* New York: Bantam Books.

Sylvester, Paul Skilton. 1994. Elementary school curricula and urban transformation. *Harvard Educational Review* 64, no. 3: 309–31.

Tharp, Roland, and Ronald Gallimore. 1988. *Rousing minds to life: Teaching, learning, and schooling in social context.* New York: Cambridge University Press.

Tran, MyLuong. 1998. Behind the smiles: The true heart of Southeast Asian children. In *Struggling to be heard: The unmet needs of Asian Pacific American children,* edited by Valerie Ooka Pang and Lilly Li-Rong Cheng. Albany, N.Y.: SUNY Press, pp. 45–47.

EPILOGUE

Fulghum, Robert. 1988. *All I Really Need to Know I Learned in Kindergarten.* New York: Ivy Books, 6.

Noddings, Nel. 1992. *The Challenge to Care: An Alternative Approach to Education.* New York: Teachers College Press.

Sark. 1992. *Inspiration Sandwich.* Berkeley, Calif.: Celestial Arts.

Stanford, John, and Robin Simons. 1999. *Victory in Our Schools.* New York: Bantam Books, 206–13.

 Credits

Chapter 1

Jerry Scott & Jim Borgman (page 11)
Zits Partnership. Reprinted with special Permission of King Features Syndicate.

Jerry Scott & Jim Borgman (p. 29)
Zits Partnership. Reprinted with special Permission of King Features Syndicate.

Chapter 2

Bill Keane (page 41)
Bil Keane, Inc. Reprinted with special Permission of King Features Syndicate.

Greg Evans (page 42)
LUANN Reprinted by permission of United Feature Syndicate, Inc.

Lalo Alcaraz (page 49)
LA CUCARACHA © 2003 Lalo Alcaraz. Dist. By UNIVERSAL PRESS SYNDICATE. Reprinted with permission. All rights reserved.

Michael Ramirez (page 56)
Michael Ramirez, Copley News Service. Reprinted by permission.

Jerry Scott & Jim Borgman (page 74)
Zits Partnership. Reprinted with special Permission of King Features Syndicate.

Chapter 3

Armstrong (page 81)
JUMP START Reprinted by permission of United Feature Syndicate, Inc.

Armstrong (page 86)
JUMP START Reprinted by permission of United Feature Syndicate, Inc.

Kathryn Lemreux (page 100)
Bil Keane, Inc. Reprinted with special Permission of King Features Syndicate.

Greg Howard (page 108).
Reprinted with special permission of King Features Syndicate.

Chapter 4

Drawing of The White House (page 132). Reprinted with permission of the author.

Armstrong (page 133)
JUMP START Reprinted by permission of United Feature Syndicate, Inc.

Chapter 5

Baby Blues (page 150)
Baby Blues Partnership. Reprinted with special permission of King Features Syndicate.

Bil Keane (page 154)
Bil Keane, Inc. Reprinted with special Permission of King Features Syndicate.

Lynn Johnston (page 171)
© Lynn Johnston Productions, Inc., Distributed by United Feature Syndicate, Inc.

Chapter 6

Tony Auth (page 179)
AUTH © 1999 The Philadelphia Inquirer. Reprinted with permission of UNIVERSAL PRESS SYNDICATE. All rights reserved.

Chapter 7

Lynn Johnston (page 211)
© Lynn Johnston Productions, Inc., Distributed by United Feature Syndicate, Inc.

Bob Thaves (page 226)
FRANK & ERNEST Reprinted by permission of Newspaper Enterprise Association, Inc.

Chapter 8
Jerry Scott & Jim Borgman (page 277)
Zits Partnership. Reprinted with special Permission of King Features Syndicate.

Chapter 9
Jef Mallett (p. 307)
FRAZZ Reprinted by permission of United Feature Syndicate, Inc.

Chapter 10
Baby Blues Partnership (p. 341)
Reprinted with special permission of King Features Syndicate.

Bill Amend (p. 351)
FOXTROT © 2000 Bill Amend. Reprinted with permission of UNIVERSAL PRESS SYNDICATE. All rights reserved.

Chapter 11
John Allen (page 376)
John Allen, Copley News Service. Reprinted by permission.

Sadako Sasaki (page 374)
Reprinted with permission of the author.

Chapter 12
Bob Thaves (page 411)
FRANK & ERNEST Reprinted by permission of Newspaper Enterprise Association, Inc.

Lynn Johnston (page 418)
© Lynn Johnston Productions, Inc., Distributed by United Feature Syndicate, Inc.

Epilogue
Jennifer M. Pang (page 449)
By permission of Jennifer M. Pang.

Bil Keane (page 452)
Bil Keane, Inc. Reprinted with special Permission of King Features Syndicate.

Index